CU00536425

THE 2ND CITY OF LONDON REGIMENT (ROYAL FUSILIERS) IN THE GREAT WAR (1914-19)

THE COLOURS OF THE REGIMENT.

THE 2ND CITY OF LONDON REGIMENT (ROYAL FUSILIERS) IN THE GREAT WAR (1914–19)

▾ ▾ ▾

BY MAJOR W. E. GREY

Published from

THE HEADQUARTERS OF THE REGIMENT

9, *Tufton Street, Westminster, London, S.W.* 1

1929

TO

THE 1,345

OFFICERS, WARRANT OFFICERS, NON-COMMISSIONED

OFFICERS AND MEN OF THE REGIMENT

WHO GAVE THEIR LIVES

COLONEL SIR CHARLES CHEERS WAKEFIELD, BART., C.B.E., LL.D.

FOREWORD

By Colonel Sir CHARLES CHEERS WAKEFIELD, Bart., C.B.E., LL.D.
Honorary Colonel, 2nd City of London Regiment (Royal Fusiliers)

THE story of a Regiment is always of interest not only to past and present officers, non-commissioned officers, and men, but to students of our national history. A record such as this throws a strong light upon particular parts of the great field of historic happenings. It stirs us by its reminder of the part played by men, who until their country called them, lived their lives in surroundings familiar to us. Thus, the heroism and sacrifices associated with the great place-names of the war—such as Ypres, the Somme, Gallipoli, Cambrai, and Bullecourt—take on a new and poignant significance when linked up with the history of a Regiment known to us.

The history of the 2nd City of London Regiment is an example of this. It gains added value and interest from the fact that the origins of the Regiment have been elucidated as far as possible. In an introductory chapter the story of the militia and volunteer movement is outlined. Thus, the splendid war record of the Regiment and its present efficiency under Lieut.-Colonel P. R. Whalley, D.S.O., are both seen to be in accordance with fine traditions of patriotic service, and the City of London takes pride in its gallant sons.

In contributing this brief foreword to a story which I know will be read with deep interest by all friends of the Regiment, I wish to pay tribute to Major W. E. Grey, its compiler. Major Grey has devoted much time and thought to the completion of his task, and as a complete record of the heroic service freely given by the Regiment in the Great War, the book will be treasured by all who possess it.

PREFACE

AT the time when this book was begun three years ago there was little to prevent the work of the 2nd City of London Regiment in the Great War from falling gradually into unmerited oblivion. Previous attempts to compile the Regiment's war record had failed; important documents, worthy of careful preservation in the Regiment's archives, had disappeared; personal diaries and memoranda, some of which undoubtedly still existed, were increasingly hard to come by; and men's memories of scenes and experiences of those crowded years, forming an invaluable supplement to written records, were daily becoming less vivid and well defined and must ultimately fade away. All these facts clearly indicated the need for some comprehensive scheme, if any record of this important period of the Regiment's history was to be preserved for future generations of 2nd Londoners; and, moreover, as every month that passed added to the difficulties of elucidating the facts and elaborating the details of the Regiment's share in the campaign, the matter brooked no further delay. The advantages of presenting a record of this kind in the form of a connected story are obvious; and so, in the absence of a more competent historian, the present writer, without any special qualifications for the task, and, as the reader may think, with unjustifiable optimism, decided to make an attempt on these lines himself.

The writer began this book with little hope of its eventual publication; his aim was to compile an accurate and connected story of the Regiment's four battalions during the war for preservation in manuscript form as the complement of the war diaries; and it was only as the work proceeded and the manuscript was submitted to many of those concerned in the events recorded that the book received official recognition, its scope was widened, and the idea of publication, should the opportunity ever occur, took definite shape.

The writer hopes that the foregoing will explain, though it may not excuse, his presumption in thus trespassing on the preserve of the historian. He is only too conscious of the book's many shortcomings and regretfully realizes that the perfect regimental history has yet to be written; nevertheless, he feels that if he has succeeded in portraying, even in general terms, the parts taken by the various battalions of the 2nd City of London Regiment in the Great War, and in thus preserving an accurate and reasonably concise record for the future, so that their successors may take courage from their deeds and profit by their mistakes, the work that has occupied nearly all his scanty leisure for three years will not have been altogether in vain.

The absence from Headquarters, either through loss or destruction, of many of the wartime records of the various battalions and the comparative failure of attempts to induce past members of the Regiment to come forward, at so late an hour, with diaries, letters, or even anecdotes, have added materially to the difficulties. The lack of personal information is inevitably reflected in the loss of that vitality which such information contrives to impart to a narrative of this kind; and the lack of records has involved a protracted search in the archives of the Historical Section (Military Branch) of the Committee of Imperial Defence and elsewhere, which, though productive of much information of great value, has not enabled the writer to give all the details he could wish, as, for instance, a complete nominal role of the recipients of honours and decorations, nor, in some battles, reliable figures of the Regiment's casualties and awards. Indeed, two things alone encouraged and justified the writer in persevering with his self-appointed task: the first of these was a story of the 2/2nd Londons from January 1917 to July 1918, written by Lieutenant A. V. Hyde, M.C., and the second a very complete series of documents—orders, messages, reports, maps, etc.—dealing with the 1/2nd Londons, methodically kept by Captain J. P. Kellett, D.S.O., M.C. Lieutenant Hyde's work formed part of a projected history of the whole Regiment which that officer had begun soon after the end of the war and had been prevented by pressure of business from finishing. Subordinating his own feelings to the good of the Regiment, he placed his manuscript unreservedly at the disposal of the present writer, who wishes to acknowledge the great help he has derived from this source.

That the opportunity of publishing this book has occurred so soon— or, indeed, has occurred at all—is due solely to the generosity of Colonel Sir Charles Wakefield, Bart., C.B.E., LL.D., who has shouldered the entire cost himself. Sir Charles Wakefield's generosity and public spirit are by-words, and it is no new thing for him to give practical proof of his interest in his Regiment; but his superlatively generous action on this occasion, enabling a seemingly impracticable scheme to be converted into a reality, has placed all 2nd Londoners, past, present, and to come, deeply in his debt. The opportunity is here gladly taken of acknowledging, albeit quite inadequately, his large and generous share in bringing this scheme to fruition. The writer wishes to express his own thanks to Sir Charles Wakefield for his sympathy and help, and for the keen personal interest he has taken in the work.

The writer's thanks are also due to Colonel J. Attenborough, C.M.G., T.D., Colonel H. M. Pryce-Jones, D.S.O., M.V.O., M.C., Lieut.-Colonel E. L. Marler, T.D., and Captain J. P. Kellett, D.S.O., M.C., Royal Fusiliers, for constant encouragement and advice; to these and a number of other officers for kindly reading parts of the manuscript and offering valuable criticism; to Captain F. Clive Grimwade, author of *The War History of the 4th Battalion The London Regiment (Royal Fusiliers) 1914-1919*, and to the 4th City of London Regiment, for permission to base the outline of this story on their own, and for permission to make use of a number of their maps; to Major J. Q. Henriques, T.D., author of *The War History of the 1st Battalion Queen's Westminster Rifles 1914-1918*, and to the Queen's Westminster Rifles, for similar help with regard to maps. The use of these maps has saved the writer much time and labour; he is deeply indebted to these officers and their respective Regiments for thus putting their work at his disposal, and he finds it difficult to write appre-

Preface

ciatively enough of the generous and helpful spirit that prompted their kind actions. The maps from the Queen's Westminster Rifles' book have been used in their original state or very slightly amended, those from the 4th Londons' book have been redrawn by the draughtsman of the Queen's Westminster Rifles' maps, Mr. H. Burge, the excellence of whose work speaks for itself. The remainder are from tracings made from official maps by the writer and drawn by Mr. Burge. The accuracy of all maps has been checked by Major A. F. Becke, of the Historical Section (Military Branch) of the Committee of Imperial Defence, who has also very kindly given his expert advice upon their form.

Invaluable suggestions and help, and invariable courtesy, have been received from Mr. E. A. Dixon and the staff of the Historical Section (Military Branch) of the Committee of Imperial Defence, who have proved themselves a never-failing source of information, and from Mr. Alan Collingridge, Mr. Herbert Pratt and Mr. J. J. Hedley Willis, of Messrs. W. H. and L. Collingridge, Ltd., under whose helpful guidance the difficulties of printing and publishing have been successfully surmounted.

Above all, the writer's thanks are due to his wife, not only for her practical help in the arduous tasks of typing manuscript and reading proofs, but especially for her constant sympathy and forbearance throughout these three years. Without her loyal support this book could not have been written.

W. E. G.

CONTENTS

Contents

Contents

Contents

LIST OF ILLUSTRATIONS

List of Illustrations

LIST OF MAPS

xxi

List of Maps

IN THE TEXT

Nos. 4, 5, 6, 7, 9, 11, 14, 17, 19, 20, and text map No. 3 are the property of Major J. Q. Henriques and the Queen's Westminster Rifles, by whose permission they are reproduced in this book. Nos. 3, 8, 10, 12, and 16 have been drawn from maps belonging to the 4th City of London Regiment, and the remainder from tracings made by the writer from official maps.

ADDENDA AND CORRIGENDA

Page 20 Line 21   *For* ' D. Williams '
                                read ' T. D. Williams.'

" 86 " 24   *For* ' Lieut. R. Carfax Bailey '
                                read ' Lieut. R. Carfax Bayley.'

" 87 " 20   *For* ' Lieut. R. Carfax Bailey '
                                read ' Lieut. R. Carfax Bayley.'

" 109 " 12   *After* ' a stay of ten days was made '
                                insert ' At Halloy the Battalion was joined by Rev. G. K. Allen, who was to serve with it as chaplain for upwards of fifteen months until the end of August 1917.'

" 159 " 19   *For* ' Lieut. H. J. Snell '
                                read ' Lieut. H. W. J. Snell.'

" 204 " 25   *For* ' Lieut. H. J. Snell '
                                read ' Lieut. H. W. J. Snell.'

" 330 " 5   *For* ' 2nd Lieut. A. F. Sterckx '
                                read ' Lieut. A. F. Sterckx.'

" 357 " 23   *For* ' Marrières '
                                read ' Maricourt.'

" 397 " 17   *For* ' Pte. East '
                                read ' Pte. E. C. Easto.'

" 416 " 17   *For* ' October '
                                read ' November.'

INTRODUCTION

VOLUNTEER organizations for the defence of this country against the invader have undoubtedly existed from a remote period in its history; but it is not until the middle of the eighteenth century that we find anything at all comparable with the system of national defence as we know it to-day. The origin of these early volunteer forces is shrouded in the mists of antiquity, and of their growth and development little can be learnt before the reign of Henry VIII., when the activities of certain voluntary military societies in various parts of the country can be definitely traced. Although during the two succeeding centuries these societies increased in number, it is the year 1758 that really marks the creation of an organized volunteer force on a large scale in England. In the previous year, the Militia, a force compulsory in character that had existed from even earlier times than the Volunteers, had been reconstructed, and under the provisions of a new Militia Act each parish had to furnish, *pro rata* with its population, a number of militiamen. The men were chosen by lot, and a practice grew up whereby compulsory militiamen who were themselves unwilling to serve procured volunteers to take their places in the ranks. These substitutes were readily accepted by the authorities; and thus a Militia composed largely of volunteers was created. The formation of volunteer corps entirely unconnected with the Militia was the next step, and by 1778 a large number of such corps had come into being. Abuse of the volunteers for political purposes led to their disbandment in 1783; but on the outbreak of the Napoleonic Wars at the end of the eighteenth century the force was raised once more. The constant menace of a French invasion of this country at that time gave to the volunteer movement an impetus that was only checked by the general peace of 1814, when the force then in existence, with the exception of the Honourable Artillery Company and the Yeomanry, was disbanded.

A period of close upon half a century elapsed before the warlike attitude of France called for further measures of national defence; and, although our alliance with that country during the Crimean War allayed the fear of invasion for a time, the French danger was revived in 1857. At this period the war in China and the Indian Mutiny were imposing a severe strain upon the small British Regular Army, and the garrisons at home were quite inadequate to deal with any threatened invasion. Moreover, these constantly recurring scares had a very unsettling effect on British trade, and any one of them might easily have produced a serious commercial panic. For these reasons it was decided to create a permanent Volunteer Force; and on 12th May 1859, when the crisis was at its height, the necessary authorization was issued by the War Office in a letter to the Lords-Lieutenant of the Counties. The action taken by the War Office was universally approved, and, as a result, volunteer corps, composed of good citizens who desired to protect their country from invasion, came into existence everywhere, and in the course of a few months a force of 119,000 was created.

The history of the 2nd City of London Regiment (Royal Fusiliers), which was first raised at this time, up to the outbreak of the Great War has much in common with the histories of other Volunteer and Territorial battalions in London, though details of birth and development are, in its case, singularly lacking. The only authoritative work that mentions its early existence is *Regimental Records of the 7th or Royal Regiment of Fusiliers,* by Lieut.-Col. Percy Groves, and this only carries us to the end of the South African War. Since that period, except in a short article in *H.M. Territorial Army,* by Mr. Walter Richards, and in pamphlets of a semi-official nature, the deeds of the Regiment have not been chronicled. Although, at this distant date, it is not possible to discover much that will throw further light on its early days, it is as well that the opportunity should be taken of setting down such facts as are known for the benefit of present and future 2nd Londoners.

It is not until 1860 that definite traces of the Corps are to be found, although it is probable that it had had a previous incarnation at the time of the Napoleonic Wars. Indeed, some volunteers from Westminster took part in the great Review of Volunteers held in Hyde Park by King George III. on 26th October 1803, and there is mention of ' Westminster Fusiliers ' in the early part of the nineteenth century. It is not possible to connect these ' Westminster Fusiliers ' with the Volunteer battalion of Royal Fusiliers that later had its headquarters at Westminster, and it seems more than likely that they were the forerunners of the 5th (Militia) Battalion Royal Fusiliers of the present day.

In the summer of 1860 the first move was made towards the formation of the 2nd Londons by the issue of the following notice to the public :

ROYAL NATIONAL RIFLES

Patrons:

LIEUT.-GEN. SIR DE LACY EVANS, G.C.B., M.P.,
SIR JOHN VILLIERS SHELLEY, BART, M.P.

This Brigade for the Defence of the Metropolis is formed of Artisans and other respectable persons whom it is proposed to supply with the Uniform by establishing a Benevolent Fund from subscriptions of the Patriotic Public. Subscription List of two shillings and upwards.

(*Sd.*) JOHN R. L. WALMISLEY,
5, VICTORIA STREET,   *Vice-President.*
WESTMINSTER ABBEY.

'The first pecuniary response to this appeal,' records Lieut.-Col. P. Groves, 'appears to have been forthcoming on 6th August of the same year, but although a large number of meetings were held in the interval, it was not until the following December that steps were taken formally to enrol the Corps.' The formal acceptance of its services on behalf of Her Majesty Queen Victoria was announced in January 1861, Sir John Villiers Shelley, Bart., M.P. for Westminster, being appointed to the command. The Corps was designated the 46th Middlesex Volunteer Rifle Corps, and had its head-quarters first at 5, Victoria Street, removing thence in June 1861 to 31, Great Smith Street, Westminster, a substantial two-storeyed house, with, behind it, a shed that was used as a store and lecture room. The Corps consisted of eight companies, four of which were recruited from the City of London, and the other four, known as the 'Westminster Companies,' mainly from Westminster and Pimlico. From this fact came its unofficial title of the 'London and Westminster Rifle Volunteers'—a name by which the Corps was known for a number of years. In this early connexion with the City of London may be traced the reason why, at a later date, the Corps was chosen to become one of the Volunteer battalions of the Royal Fusiliers— the City of London Regiment.

An old statute of George III. at first governed the enlistment of the men. Its main provisions being found inapplicable to the altered conditions, this statute was superseded in 1863 by another (Volunteer Act, 1863). This held good, with various modifications, until the introduction of the Territorial and Reserve Force Act in 1907; and throughout these forty-eight years of the Volunteer Force's existence the terms of service and the training liabilities underwent no material change of principle.

The initial step in the formation of a corps was the convocation of a general meeting of officers and men; thereat rules were drawn up for the administration of the corps' property, which was then vested in the commanding officer. These rules were submitted to the Queen and, having received her approval, became legal. The terms of service gave the commanding officer power to dismiss a man from the corps, and, on the other hand, permitted each volunteer, unless on active service at the time, to terminate his engagement at fourteen days' notice; but it became the practice for the men to enlist for a period of three, four, or five years' service, and if, by exercising their statutory right, they resigned before the expiration of this period, to refund part of the cost of the uniform issued to them.

In the early days of the Volunteer Force, the cost of uniform and equipment, and all expenses incidental to his service, had to be borne by the volunteer himself; but the Government, having decided to maintain the force as part of the regular defensive system of the country, soon took over the duty of equipping it and later, when it was realized that the system of public and private subscriptions operated unfairly against certain units, particularly as subscriptions steadily declined, provided a capitation grant for its maintenance.

The uniform of the newly-formed 46th Middlesex was a drab-grey with green facings. The belt and other accoutrements were black, and the head-dress was a black shako with a green tuft. Officers' tunics were laced with silver. No change of importance was made in the pattern of the uniform until 1876, when the colour was changed to scarlet with blue facings, belts and accoutrements being changed at the same time to white buff. The shako, now blue with a red and white tuft, continued to be worn until 1878, when the ordinary infantry pattern helmet was adopted. In addition to this new full dress, the officers adopted a frogged undress uniform, with which was worn a 'cheese-cutter' cap.[1] Though seemingly of small importance beyond the expense involved, this was really a revolutionary change, in effect marking the conversion of the unit from a rifle to a line battalion, and, no doubt, contributing in some measure to the next, and important, change in the unit's status that occurred in 1883.

The original establishment of the 46th Middlesex was not long maintained, and on 2nd November 1864 its eight companies were reduced in number to six. No special reason for this reduction can be traced, and it must therefore be attributed to lack of recruits. Close upon fifteen years were to elapse before the larger establishment was restored.

Lieut.-Col. Sir John Shelley commanded the 46th Middlesex until his

---

[1] So called from its straight peak.

THE 46TH MIDDLESEX VOLUNTEER RIFLE CORPS, 1861-1875.
From the original water-colour drawing by R. Simkin.

death, which occurred in January 1866. Major Lord Stratheden and Campbell then assumed temporary command until 19th February 1873, when Lieut.-Col. F. Burlton Bennett, who had formerly served in the Regular Army, was appointed. On 11th November 1874 Lieut.-Col. Bennett resigned; and the battalion once again came under Lord Stratheden and Campbell, who was promoted to the rank of Lieutenant-Colonel on 9th May 1875. At about this period the appointment of Honorary Colonel was sanctioned for units of the Volunteer Force; and in 1876 Lieut.-Col. Lord Stratheden and Campbell left the 46th Middlesex to become the Honorary Colonel of the 40th Middlesex. He was succeeded in command by Major R. W. Routledge, who was promoted Lieutenant-Colonel on the 13th September of that year. It was not until 1877 that the 46th Middlesex had an Honorary Colonel of its own, Lieut.-Col. Sir Charles Russell, V.C., who had served in the Grenadier Guards and had won distinction in the Crimean War, being appointed to this rank on 2nd July—an appointment that he held until his death on 14th April 1883.

In 1878 the establishment of the 46th Middlesex was again raised to one of eight companies. This was a preliminary step in a general reorganization of all units of the Middlesex Volunteer Rifle Corps that took full effect two years later. Certain administrative units were then consolidated into the Corps; others were disbanded; and the whole Corps was then renumbered. This renumbering applied alike to all Middlesex units, with the exception of the 1st and 2nd; and the 46th now became the 23rd Middlesex.

The 23rd Middlesex retained this title barely three years, there occurring in July 1883 the important change referred to above that was to have a considerable effect on the future of the unit. At about this period the British Regular Army was reorganized, and the 'Cardwell System' of short service was introduced. A simultaneous step in the reorganization was the linking of the Militia and Volunteers to the Regular Army. As an outcome of this part of the scheme, three battalions of Militia and three of Volunteers[1] were attached to the Royal Fusiliers (City of London Regiment); and of the three Volunteer battalions selected one was the 23rd Middlesex. This now became the 2nd Volunteer Battalion Royal Fusiliers, and adopted the uniform of the old 7th Foot.[2] This association with the Royal Fusiliers has

---

[1] A fourth Volunteer battalion was added in 1903, when the Tower Hamlet Rifle Volunteers were converted into the 4th Volunteer Battalion, Royal Fusiliers.

[2] Scarlet with blue facings, and racoon-skin cap. For a time, the old pattern helmet, with the Middlesex badge, continued to be worn by the 2nd Volunteer Battalion, Royal Fusiliers, Royal Fusilier grenades being worn as collar-badges of the tunic; but as stocks were exhausted, the helmet was replaced by the Fusilier cap, to

been continued to the present day; and the 2nd City of London Regiment, which still bears the title of 'Royal Fusiliers,' is very proud of its connexion with this distinguished regiment.

Shortly before this important phase of the Regiment's history, Sir Charles Russell had died; and in his stead General (afterwards Field-Marshal) Lord Wolseley, to whose genius for organization the British Army owes so much, was appointed Honorary Colonel in May 1883. Throughout his tenure of this appointment, Lord Wolseley, who aimed at a high standard of efficiency, was the inspecting officer of his Regiment almost every year, and, to quote Mr. Walter Richards, his 'remarks on the occasion of the Annual Inspection of the Regiment came to be looked for as not improbably shadowing the military views of the Government at the time.'

In 1893, after a period of seventeen years in command, Lieut.-Col. Routledge resigned. Of Lieut.-Col. Routledge Mr. Walter Richards records: 'He was one of the most enthusiastic Volunteer officers of that period; he had no less than seven sons serving under him as officers in the Regiment!' He was succeeded by Lieut.-Col. Albert L. Keller on the 16th December. Lieut.-Col. Keller was granted the honorary rank of Colonel in February 1896 and was awarded the Volunteer Decoration in the following month.

---

which the white hackle, on the right side, was added after the South African War, in recognition of the distinguished part played by the various Fusilier Regiments in that campaign. In addition to full dress, the officers had a frogged undress uniform and a cap with a silver-laced peak, and they also adopted the Mess dress of the Royal Fusiliers. The latter had innumerable small buttons down the front, and, save for the removal of these, the simplification of the braid ornament, and the substitution of a roll-collar for the stand-up collar of the original, it remains much the same to-day. A glengarry cap, with Royal Fusilier grenade, was at first worn with Mess dress, but was succeeded by a blue cap of ordinary service-dress pattern. For field training, full dress, with black leggings, was worn by all ranks. For such occasions, the shoulder-belt and pouch, sword-belt, and slings, of the officers, were of buff, pipe-clayed. For reviews and levees and for ceremonial occasions of a like nature, the officers required an even more elaborate dress, 'overalls,' with two half-inch silver stripes 'laid on,' with a crimson stripe between them, and special accoutrements, made of red leather, heavily stitched with silver, being the chief items. To distinguish them from the Regulars, the Volunteer officers wore silver lace on their uniforms instead of gold, a distinction that was abandoned on the introduction of the Territorial Force.

The uniform was later simplified by the introduction for all ranks of a red 'serge,' with blue facings, to be used instead of the full-dress tunic for field training. Later, again, this gave place to a blue 'serge' and finally to khaki service dress. The frogged undress uniform of the officers was replaced by the blue patrol jacket, which, just prior to the Great War, was cut like the khaki service-dress jacket, and was worn with a white shirt and collar, and a black tie.

THE 2ND VOLUNTEER BATTALION, THE ROYAL FUSILIERS, 1883.
From the original water-colour drawing by R. Simkin.

In these times of peace, one year in the life of the 2nd Volunteer Battalion Royal Fusiliers was much like another, field-days, camp, and the usual social events, following one another with almost monotonous regularity. Apart, therefore, from the changes of command and the alterations of its name, the chief events in its life inevitably took the form of reviews by distinguished persons, or functions of a similar nature. The most important of these were the following:

1864, 28*th May*—Queen Victoria's Birthday Review, at which 22,000 London Volunteers were present.
1866, 23*rd June*—Review by H.R.H. The Duke of Cambridge.
1881, 9*th July*—Review by H.M. The Queen at Windsor.
1889, 7*th Aug.*—Review by the Emperor of Germany.
1891, 11*th July*—Review by the Emperor of Germany at Wimbledon.

These reviews were varied by more ambitious ceremonies for special occasions, as on 7th March 1863, when 18,000 Metropolitan Volunteers assembled in Hyde Park on the occasion of the entry of Princess Alexandra of Denmark into London, and on 1st July 1876, when H.R.H. The Prince of Wales inspected Regulars, Militia, and Volunteers. A more practical test of efficiency was a concentration march which the Brigade of Guards and the Volunteers of the Home District made on 2nd February 1895. The Queen's Jubilee in 1887 was celebrated on 2nd July by a march-past before Her Majesty at Buckingham Palace, the troops moving along the Mall to the Palace and then away to the Embankment, and on 9th July by a review at Aldershot, at which the Queen was present. In the Diamond Jubilee celebrations of 1897 the Battalion lined the route along the Mall on the occasion of H.M. The Queen's progress through London.

Route-marches formed an integral part of the Battalion's training, and until 1910, when a different policy was adopted by the authorities and this form of training no longer actively encouraged, a large number took place each year. The Easter holidays were peculiarly suitable for more ambitious schemes of this nature, and were generally devoted to a long march under billeting conditions. In like manner encouragement was given to individual companies to make marches during week-ends in the summer months. Another form of training that bulked largely in programmes of work at this period was close-order drill. Until the South African War close-order drill was considered to be of the utmost importance as being the foundation of successful tactics, and units were trained to move in the field as formed bodies and to fire in volleys. The lessons of the South African War caused a revolution in tactical training; and, as a direct result, drill in the Volunteers and Territorial Force, where the limitation of time is such an important factor in training, ceased to hold such an important place as formerly. Nevertheless the drill of the Battalion remained of a very high standard; and the 2nd Volunteer Battalion Royal Fusiliers earned a high reputation for its steadiness and precision on ceremonial occasions.

At this period of its existence, the Battalion had a very efficient Ambulance Section; and for fourteen years in succession from 1893 the West London Infantry Volunteer Brigade Challenge Cup for ambulance work was won by the Battalion's team, under Col.-Sergt. T. Barnes. The cup then became the Battalion's property, and is to-day a proud possession of the Officers' Mess. The Volunteer Medical Association's Shield was also won by the same team on no less than eight occasions.

The South African War, which broke out in 1899, gave the Volunteers an opportunity of proving their worth—an opportunity of which they were not slow to avail themselves. It was soon evident that the Regular Army was insufficient in numbers for the task imposed upon it; and the Volunteers were asked to supply men for active service. The 2nd Volunteer Battalion Royal Fusiliers was one of the first Volunteer battalions to respond to this call. A 'Service Company' was formed from the 1st, 2nd, and 3rd Volunteer Battalions Royal Fusiliers, and was sent to the front under Major W. S. Freidberger (2nd Volunteer Battalion Royal Fusiliers). It joined the 2nd Battalion Royal Fusiliers, under Lieut.-Col. C. G. Donald, on 7th May 1900, at Fourteen Streams. Although it arrived too late to take part in any of the great battles that were fought in the early part of the war, this company served with the Regular battalion throughout the 'guerilla' warfare that followed the capture of the capitals of the Boer Republics and the defeat of their main forces.

The campaign consisted largely of stiff marching, varied frequently by skirmishes with the enemy; and an extract from the War Diary will suffice to show its strenuous nature : 'Between 1st May and 17th June (1900) the Battalion has marched 374 miles and proceeded by rail 43 miles. The time occupied in actual marching was 30 days, giving an average of 12½ miles a day.' On 1st July the Battalion went to Pretoria and took part in the operations south-east of that town, being later employed in the Eastern Transvaal under General Ian Hamilton. Subsequently the Battalion was transferred to the Delagoa Bay Railway, and in August and September saw some stiff fighting, while holding a 'sangared' ridge above Elands River Station. In January 1901 it took part in the operations against De Wet, and later garrisoned a 'blockhouse' line. In May 1902 it joined the Namaqua-land Field Force; and on the 31st of this month its active service was brought to an end by the signing of the Peace Treaty.

A second composite company was sent out in 1901 and joined the 2nd Battalion Royal Fusiliers on the 22nd July. This was followed by a third company, under the command of Lieut. R. W. Ironside (2nd Volunteer Battalion Royal Fusiliers) on 1st April 1902.

In addition to the men who joined these service companies, many from the 2nd Volunteer Battalion Royal Fusiliers served with the City Imperial Volunteers, of which 'G' Company was formed of men from the three Royal Fusilier Volunteer battalions. Capt. E. L. Marler was selected for the command of this company. Capt. Marler was at the time in command of 'D' Company of the 2nd Volunteer Battalion Royal Fusiliers—the best shooting company in the battalion—, and he owed his selection partly to this fact; for Colonel Mackinnon, commanding the City Imperial Volunteers, needed especially marksmen and marchers. Unfortunately Capt. Marler was taken seriously ill and was obliged to hand over the coveted honour to Capt. A. A. Howell, of the 3rd Volunteer Battalion Royal Fusiliers. The City Imperial Volunteers were in action at Jacobsdaal before the first Service Company reached South Africa, but returned to England on 27th October 1900, as soon as the general situation had improved as the result of the defeat of the main Boer forces. Altogether a total of 4 officers (Major W. S. Freidberger, Lieuts. R. W. Ironside, R. A. Ironside, and H. E. Stevens) and more than 150 men saw active service in South Africa; and of this total 9 were killed or died on service. As a result of the Battalion's efforts in the war, it was granted the Battle Honour 'South Africa, 1900-02.'

In the meanwhile, the present Headquarters of the Regiment at 9, Tufton Street, Westminster, were built in 1899 by means of subscriptions from officers and men and well-disposed sympathizers. The serving officers subscribed £1,000; and, backed by them, Colonel Keller borrowed £4,000 from the Government. The patriotic action of these subscribers is beyond all praise; for, although the building is not now adequate for the needs of a modern battalion, it represented, with its floor-space of one hundred feet by fifty, and its Officers' and Sergeants' Messes,[1] its Canteen, and Miniature Range, a considerable improvement on the house that had hitherto served

---

[1] Up to this time the officers, when they dined together, had been obliged to go to one of the West-End hotels, Limmer's (long since departed) being the most favoured.

the purpose. It is interesting to note that the new Headquarters were first used, shortly before their completion, for the medical inspection of the men of the South African Service Company.

The next few years passed uneventfully. It is noteworthy that, at about this time, Mr. H. O. Arnold-Forster, a former Secretary of State for War, served in the Battalion as an officer, and that Capt. C. T. Shipley, Royal Fusiliers, subsequently Br.-General, was for a time its adjutant. On 16th December 1906, Lieut.-Col. P. Carlebach succeeded to the command, and Colonel A. L. Keller was appointed to the Honorary Colonelcy now vacant by reason of the resignation of Lord Wolseley. Of Colonel Keller, Lieut.-Col. P. Groves, writing in 1903, says: 'He has always been a zealous and keen soldier and, since taking over the command, a most competent C.O., being held in high esteem and keeping thoroughly in touch with and possessing the entire confidence of the men.'

As a result of the South African War, the British Army underwent another period of reorganization, culminating in the reforms introduced by the late Lord Haldane. Foremost of these was the reorganization of the Volunteers and their conversion into the Territorial Force—or Army, as it is known to-day. The Volunteer units in the London area were formed into battalions of a newly-constituted 'London Regiment'; and the 1st, 2nd, 3rd, and 4th Volunteer Battalions Royal Fusiliers, which by reason of being Royal Fusiliers were already connected with the City of London, became the 1st, 2nd, 3rd, and 4th (City of London) Battalions, The London Regiment. These battalions, however, were allowed to retain the title of Royal Fusiliers and to wear the same uniform.

Among the privileges now granted to units of the Territorial Force was that of carrying Colours, the necessary qualification for this honour being a strength equal to, or exceeding, three-quarters of establishment. The 2nd London Regiment was not able to qualify at once; but Lieut.-Col. Carlebach and his officers worked energetically to this end. The requisite number of men was at last recruited; and the Battalion was able to take its place with the other units of the London Regiment at the ceremony of Presentation that took place on 19th June 1909. Colour parties from each battalion went to Windsor for the purpose; and on the East Terrace of Windsor Castle the Colours were confided to their keeping by H.M. King Edward VII. in person. The ceremony was an imposing one; and the Colour parties in full-dress uniform, with the beautiful old building as a background, made a magnificent spectacle. The Colours of the 2nd Londons were brought back to Finsbury Square, where the Battalion was paraded to receive them;

LIEUTENANT-COLONEL
SIR CHARLES RUSSELL, V.C.

COLONEL R. W. ROUTLEDGE.

COLONEL A. L. KELLER, V.D.

COLONEL P. CARLEBACH, C.M.G., T.D.

and at the conclusion of the ceremonial the Battalion marched through the City to its Headquarters, with Colours uncased.[1]

This 'Colours' recruiting campaign—for such it may be called—had one interesting and important development. The home area of the Battalion, Westminster, Pimlico, and North Lambeth, had been skimmed clean of good recruits, and Lieut.-Col. Carlebach, casting about for some new sources of recruiting to tap, conceived the idea of establishing an outlying company in a district not largely touched by other Territorial units. The area of Willesden and Kilburn was selected; the necessary permission was obtained; and 'C' Company was duly established there in 1909. The company's first headquarters consisted of two rooms in a house in the Kingsgate Road, Kilburn, close to the school of that name, whose yard proved invaluable for drill. After several moves nearer Kilburn, the company finally settled down at the Red Lion Hotel in High Street, Kilburn, where it was still established on the outbreak of the Great War.

From the point of view of recruiting, this company was an immediate success. Little difficulty was experienced in filling up the ranks, and thereafter the company was, more often than not, over strength. In addition to a full complement of infantrymen, the Battalion's cyclist section, a keen and efficient body of about 20 men, was raised and maintained by 'C' Company's Headquarters. All training, save the annual musketry course on the open range, was conducted under the guidance of the company officers and non-commissioned officers; and an important feature of the training was a number of week-end tactical exercises, of a simple character, for which the company rarely paraded less than 95 strong. On the social side, the company was equally successful; and its concert party and mouth-organ band were both popular institutions in the Battalion.

For the execution of this successful venture credit is due to Capt. C. J. Goodwin, who was in command of 'C' Company during the whole period of its independence. This officer was ably assisted at various times by Lieuts. R. I. Marians, S. Walrock, W. Attenborough, R. C. Hoyle, and O. Emmanuel, and by Col.-Sergt. Bayliss and his successor, Col.-Sergt. R. W. Whitehead. These non-commissioned officers, together with Sergt. Robinson, who was in charge of the cyclists, Sergts. S. Taylor, and E.

---

[1] The Colours of the Regiment are similar to those carried by the Regular battalions of the Royal Fusiliers. The main points of difference will be found on the Regimental Colour, where in the centre, in place of the United Rose within the Garter, the Territorials have the Arms of the City of London, and in each of the four corners, in place of the White Horse of Hanover, they have the United Rose within the Garter.

England, all did splendid work and contributed in no small measure to the marked success of this experiment.

On 16th December 1910 Lieut.-Col. E. L. Marler, who had joined in May 1894, and who was destined subsequently to take the 1/2nd Londons overseas, succeeded Lieut.-Col. Carlebach in the command of the Battalion. The Honorary Colonelcy had been vacant since the death of Col. A. L. Keller in August 1907, and Lieut.-Col. Carlebach was now promoted to fill the vacancy. Two events that varied the routine of these years must be chronicled: the Coronation of King George V. on the 22nd June 1911, and a review of all Territorial troops in the London District by H.M. The King on the 5th July 1913. For the former, the 2nd Londons supplied a representative detachment, under Capt. R. Heumann; and at the latter, which was held in Hyde Park, the whole Battalion was present.[1]

And so we are brought to the eve of those four momentous years wherein the 2nd Londons won for themselves a fame that shall endure for evermore. In the mud of Flanders, on the downs of Artois and Picardy, amid the marshes of the Oise, in the massive fortifications of the Hindenburg Line, the rugged gorges of Gallipoli, the Egyptian deserts, they fought and marched, endured unspeakable hardships and heavy losses, with a devotion to duty that is worthy of the highest traditions of our race. Their successors may well feel proud of the name, earned on the battle-fields of the Great War:

'THE SECOND TO NONDONS.'

[1] This review was the last occasion on which full dress was worn by the Regiment; and it is interesting to note that, for reasons of economy, dress caps were worn by the men in place of the racoon-skin caps. Officers, Band, and Drums, however, wore the proper head-dress.

THE OFFICERS, I/2ND LONDONS, 1914.

BACK ROW: 2nd Lieut. E. J. Harington, Lieut. E. E. H. Bate, 2nd Lieut. H. B. T. Wakelam, Lieuts. L. H. R. Inglis, R. E. F. Sneath, 2nd Lieut. W. E. Grey, Lieut. P. J. A. Handyside, 2nd Lieut. J. P. Kellett.

MIDDLE ROW: Capts. C. H. Taylor, C. J. Goodwin, Lieut. F. J. T. Moon, 2nd Lieuts. A. T. Taylor, F. L. Rolleston, F. C. Edwards, A. G. L. Jepson, C. Gordon, E. T. Cooper, Capt. and Q.M. J. H. Warrener, Lieut. H. W. Everitt.

FRONT ROW: Capts. R. I. Marians, G. A. Stacey, J. McHoul, R.A.M.C., J. H. S. Westley, Yorkshire Regt., Major E. J. Hogan, Lieut.-Col. E. L. Marler, T.D., Major J. Attenborough, Capts. E. O. Davies, M. F. Scott, R. Heumann, L. Beck.

CHAPTER I
MOBILIZATION AND THE RAILWAY LINE

THE events leading up to the outbreak of the Great War are likely to be remembered for many years to come with exceptional clearness; for such was the magnitude of the catastrophe that then overtook the civilization of Europe, and so widespread were its effects that not a single individual in any of the belligerent countries—whether victorious or defeated —can have remained entirely unaffected by it. None but the briefest reference to these momentous events is therefore necessary in this book. The conflagration that had flared up in South-Eastern Europe in July 1914 spread rapidly; and first one great nation and then another became involved, until a mighty conflict was inevitable. At first, Great Britain stood aside; but a policy of neutrality was rendered impossible by Germany's attitude in the negotiations that preceded the war and by her violation of Belgium. On 3rd August, therefore, an ultimatum was sent; and, as no reply was received, the formal declaration of war followed. Thus before the expiration of the 4th August Great Britain found herself engaged in the greatest war of history; and the mobilization of her armed forces was ordered forthwith.

On Sunday morning, 2nd August 1914, the 2nd (City of London) Battalion The London Regiment (Royal Fusiliers)[1] left Waterloo Station, in company with other units of the 1st London Division (Major-General W. Fry, C.B., C.V.O.) for its fortnight's training in camp. It had been arranged for this year's annual training of the Division to take place in the neighbourhood of Wareham in Dorset, and, as this country had not at the time declared its intention as to the war, the arrangements were not cancelled. For reasons that will be hereafter explained the Territorial Force was intended to play an important part in the mobilization and embarkation of the British Expeditionary Force in the event of war; and the Government felt that a cancellation of Territorial camps might be construed abroad as an order almost as menacing as that for general mobilization. By thus deciding to delay the cancellation of Territorial camps, in its natural desire not to precipitate war, the Government risked delaying the dispatch of the Expeditionary Force.

The various Territorial units accordingly set out as originally ordered.

[1] Hereafter the abbreviated title of ' 2nd Londons ' will always be used.

B

The atmosphere was charged with excitement. Although the routine orders for the move were executed without flurry, there were tense feelings underlying this apparent calm; and everyone wondered what would be the outcome of the next few hours.

Camp was reached shortly after noon; and no sooner had the Battalion marched in than orders were received for its immediate return to London, the Government having at laſt decided, in view of the increasingly serious position of affairs, to take the now inevitable ſtep. No rations were available, the Navy having commandeered the meat intended for the Division; and so the Battalion, perforce forgoing its food, entrained at once for its journey back to town.

The Battalion arrived in London at about 10 p.m.; and the men slept at Headquarters and in neighbouring buildings, making the beſt of the very limited accommodation. The Commanding Officer, Lieut.-Col. E. L. Marler, who had been warned some days earlier to hold himself in readiness for mobilization, had very wisely provided rations for six hundred, and had had them ſtored at Headquarters. These, with bread that was haſtily obtained from local sources, proved quite sufficient for the needs of the Battalion. Next morning mobilization, or 'embodiment' as it is officially called when applied to the Territorial Force, was begun in Dean's Yard, in the shadow of Weſtminſter Abbey; and this usually peaceful spot resounded to the clamour that is inseparable from a military concentration. Field dressings and identity discs were issued; deficiencies in clothing and equipment were made good; and separation allowance and next-of-kin rolls were prepared. With smoothness and dispatch the novel task of mobilization was completed.

From its creation in 1908, the Territorial Force was never intended to be other than a framework for the expansion of the Nation's forces in time of war, and its peace-time training was only sufficient to provide the nucleus of a second-line army for that eventuality. Although Lord Haldane, bearing its limitations in mind, provided in his scheme for a period of six months' training at home for the Territorial Force before its employment on active service, the authorities were rightly alive to its potentialities in the event of an attempted invasion of this country, when no such probationary period could be granted to it; and in the years before the war units such as the 2nd Londons were encouraged frequently to practise defensive schemes on various parts of the coaſt. In the early part of 1914 this hitherto somewhat nebulous policy regarding the immediate employment of the Territorial Force on the outbreak of war was abandoned; certain units were definitely detailed for special duties in connexion with the possible dispatch of an expeditionary force to a deſtination abroad; and full plans and inſtructions for their action on mobilization were drawn up.

The 1ſt London Infantry Brigade, consiſting of the four Territorial battalions of the Royal Fusiliers, was one of the formations selected for these special duties, and it was given the highly important task of guarding the main line of the London and South-Weſtern Railway between London and Southampton, the branch line from Southampton to Salisbury as far north as Amesbury, the area around Southampton Docks, and the main line of the London, Brighton, and South Coaſt Railway from London to Newhaven. As Southampton was the port selected for the embarkation of all troops, and Newhaven of all ſtores and supplies, these lines became among the moſt vital in the country; for any interference with the syſtem here muſt inevitably have delayed the dispatch of the troops. The Brigade undoubtedly owed its selection for this important duty to the fact that it was a homogeneous unit, of which the component battalions had trained together for a considerable number of years. The section allotted to the 2nd Londons, known as 'X' Section, included the area of Southampton Docks and the line thence via Eaſtleigh and the Andover Junction to Amesbury, along which were to pass during the next few weeks the troops that had concentrated on Salisbury Plain.

Picking up at the ſtation food for two days, and also blankets and other ſtores that had come up from Woolwich by water, the 2nd Londons left Waterloo Station during the morning of the 3rd Auguſt. Before the dawn of the 4th the railway was under ſtrict surveillance, and the Battalion was at its war ſtation some eighteen hours before Great Britain declared war—a minor manifeſtation of that triumph of efficiency, the mobilization of the British armed forces.

For adminiſtrative and disciplinary purposes the Battalion was temporarily organized into four double companies, and, on arrival on the line, was diſtributed as follows:

> Battalion Headquarters: Lieut.-Col. E. L. Marler, T.D., in command; Capt. J. H. S. Weſtley, Yorkshire Regt., Adjutant; Lieut. L. H. R. Inglis, Machine-Gun Officer; and Rev. W. G. Bell, Chaplain, at Romsey.
> 'C' Company (Capt. C. J. Goodwin) and 'H' Company (Lieut. Thurſton, Calcutta Volunteer Rifles attached, 2nd Lieut. H. Everitt), under Major J. Attenborough—Headquarters at Southampton.
> 'A' Company (Capt. G. A. Stacey, Lieut. P. J. A. Handyside), and 'F' Company (Capt. R. I. Marians, 2nd Lieut. E. E. H. Bate), under Capt. G. A. Stacey—Headquarters at Redbridge.

3

'D' Company (Capt. R. Heumann, Lieut. R. E. F. Sneath) and 'E' Company (Capt. M. F. Scott), under Capt. M. F. Scott—Headquarters at Fullerton.
'B' Company (Capt. C. L. V. Marno) and 'G' Company (Capt. E. O. Davies), under Capt. E. O. Davies—Headquarters at Andover Junction.

Brigade Headquarters (Br.-General The Earl of Lucan, Major R. F. Legge, Leinster Regt., Brigade Major, and Capt. Cornelius Wheeler, 3rd Londons, Staff Captain) were established at Waterloo Station. Of the remaining units of the Brigade, the 4th Londons were in charge of the line from Waterloo to Basingstoke, and the 3rd Londons from Basingstoke to Eastleigh; and the 1st Londons were on the London, Brighton, and South Coast Railway from London to Newhaven.

The men soon settled down to their new duties, rapidly accommodating themselves to their strange environment, as is the way of all Londoners. They were mostly accommodated in the station buildings, and soon contrived to make themselves tolerably comfortable in these unusual billets. Their new duties were arduous but not without interest. 'X' Section was divided into sub-sections, to each of which was allotted a company. A detailed plan of the line had been prepared by the London and South-Western Railway before the war, and thereon were carefully scheduled all bridges, tunnels, and level-crossings. The protection of these vulnerable points as well as the active patrolling of the whole length of track within its sub-section were the tasks of each company; and, as the companies were much under strength, their proper fulfilment required that the men should be continually on duty, with but short intervals for rest and refreshment. The company in the Southampton area had the additional duty of finding piquets for all roads leading into the town; and every motor-car entering the town was stopped and scrutinized. The part of 'X' Section that gave the Battalion most anxiety was that south of Fullerton Junction, where the railway line crosses the River Test, the track being carried on wooden piles that could easily be set on fire. The line then passed through a deep cutting, with steep banks, covered with gorse and ferns; and its security at this point could only be ensured by vigilant and constant patrolling.

Despite the hard work, the duties had their enjoyable side. Most men retain in later life some of their juvenile affection for railways and railway trains, and the opportunity now presented to them of studying a great railway system at close quarters was unsurpassed. Moreover, there was always the interest of watching the transportation of the Expeditionary Force on the first stage of its journey, a splendid example of efficient staff-work and railway organization.

4

The German secret service syſtem may have been excellent, but no attempt was made by it to prevent or to hinder the embarkation of the Expeditionary Force. There were, of course, inevitable ' alarums and excursions.' Occasional shots were fired at night by sentries at unsubſtantial shadows; and sometimes raids were made by patrols on cows peacefully sleeping in fields near the line. Any civilian whose occupation or duty brought him near the line at night carried his life in his hands; and at leaſt one splendid express locomotive had a bullet through its massive bulk. Such incidents are the natural corollary of ſtrained nerves. Nevertheless, no spy materialized; and there were no enemy casualties. One incident, however, deserves special mention; this was the capture of the SS. *Hanna Larsen,* a German vessel lying in Southampton Water. The vessel had recently arrived at Northam Wharf from Archangel with a cargo of timber; and Capt. Goodwin, in charge of the seƈtion about Northam, where the railway line runs close to the quay, had his suspicions aroused. He made an immediate raid on the vessel with a party of 'C' Company, and took possession of it until the arrival of the Cuſtoms officials, to whom it was handed over. The crew, who had left in an attempt to get back to Germany, did not succeed in this design, and on their return to Northam were arreſted by the police, and were interned for the reſt of the war.

Meanwhile, at Headquarters in Tufton Street the work of recruiting the Battalion to full ſtrength and of equipping the recruits proceeded apace throughout the month of Auguſt. Immediately after war was declared, telegrams had been sent to all non-commissioned officers and men who had been granted leave from camp, ordering them to report at once. All these came in, and, in addition, large numbers of recruits. The men who volunteered for service were of all classes; solicitors, poets, and gentlemen of leisure, joined up with the artisans of Weſtminſter. Many young men came from the 1ſt Royal Fusiliers Cadet Battalion, in which Colonel Carlebach, T.D., then the Honorary Colonel of the Regiment, took a keen and energetic intereſt; and their training in the Cadet unit proved of ineſtimable value. Owing to the limited accommodation at 9, Tufton Street, the recruits were housed in St. John's Inſtitute next door and in the building now occupied by the National Library for the Blind, both of which had been requisitioned for the purpose.

The Second-in-command, Major E. J. Hogan, together with the Quartermaſter, Capt. J. H. Warrener, and Capt. A. G. Houlder, had been left in London to complete the details of mobilization and to enliſt and train recruits. The last-named officer was busy requisitioning and mobilizing from civilian sources the necessary transport which the War Office was not then in a position to supply. Later, Capts. C. H. Taylor and L. Beck, both from the Territorial Force Reserve, and Lieut. F. J. T. Moon—an officer who had been seconded from the Regiment while on business in China and who, at the outbreak of war, was spending a holiday in England —returned to the active list and were attached to the staff at Headquarters. At the same time, several gentlemen who, with previous service in the Officers' Training Corps or elsewhere, had been accepted for commissions in the Regiment reported for duty pending gazette. All these officers were actively engaged in training the recruits, being assisted therein by R.S.M. W. Francis and Sergt.-Instructor Gavin, of the permanent staff, and by Sergt. W. J. Robinson and Corpl. F. Jones, of 'C' Company, all of whom did useful work in this connexion. All recruits were given elementary training in Dean's Yard and, as soon as they were partially trained, were sent to the Battalion Headquarters at Romsey, where their training was continued under the supervision of the Adjutant.

By the middle of August the greater part of the Expeditionary Force had been dispatched to France; but the 2nd Londons still remained at their war station, the only change in their dispositions being the transference, four days before the end of the month, of 'D' and 'E' Companies to the Great Western Railway, from Basingstoke to Reading (with headquarters at Mortimer), and a consequent reorganization on the London and South-Western Railway about Fullerton. On the night of 31st August/1st September, however, the 2nd Londons were ordered to withdraw from the railway line and return to London. The move was promptly carried out, and before noon on the 1st September the Battalion had arrived at its Headquarters in Tufton Street. The other units of the 1st London Brigade were also withdrawn; and two days later the duties of the whole Brigade on the railway were taken over by the 3rd London Infantry Brigade. As the Drill Hall in Tufton Street was far too small to accommodate the Battalion with its swollen ranks, the 2nd Londons bivouacked in Vincent Square and in the Royal Horticultural Hall. Speculation and rumour concerning the future employment of the Battalion were soon cut short by definite information that the whole Brigade was to be dispatched immediately for garrison duty in Malta. As the existing engagement of Territorial soldiers did not include service out of England, volunteers were called for; and a splendid response was given at once by all ranks. The Battalion was inspected on 3rd September by the G.O.C., Major-General W. Fry, who conveyed an assurance from

Lord Kitchener that the Brigade would only be kept in Malta until such time as it was fully trained for active service—an assurance that was very welcome, the prospect of doing garrison duty in Malta for the rest of the war not being one that appealed to the 2nd Londons at this period.

Immediate preparations were made for departure. Although no general leave could be given, as many men as possible were allowed to go home each night. Recruits poured in, and were rapidly equipped and made ready to move with the Battalion. Many came from the Army and Navy Stores and from Harrods Stores, and the equivalent of half a company from Messrs. John Barker and Co., while many former members of the Battalion rejoined. These additions brought the Battalion up to strength, and likewise made good the wastage that resulted from the medical examination for foreign service.

As soon as the 2nd Londons were ordered abroad, the formation of a second-line unit was at once decided upon, with the original intention of keeping the first-line battalion supplied with reinforcements. Later, however, when the scope of the Territorial Force was extended, third-line and fourth-line units were formed, the second-line thus being released for active service. The command of this new unit was given temporarily to Capt. A. G. Houlder, of the 1/2nd Londons, Capt. C. L. V. Marno being appointed Adjutant. Capt. L. Beck, therefore, took over 'H' Company from Capt. Houlder, who had nominally been commanding it, though the appointment of Transport Officer had also been combined in his person. Capt. C. H. Taylor took over 'B' Company from Capt. Marno, and Lieut. F. J. T. Moon became Transport Officer. The Chaplain, Rev. W. G. Bell, much to his sorrow, was also unable to go with the Battalion, because he could not obtain his release from the parish of which he was at the time vicar. It was some consolation to him that the Colours of the Regiment were left in his keeping; and on the 3rd December 1914 they were duly installed in his church, Christchurch, Streatham Hill. Here they remained in sanctuary until after the Armistice, when they were taken to Flanders to share in the final triumph of the Battalion.

Amid scenes of indescribable enthusiasm, which few who witnessed them will ever forget, the Battalion left Vincent Square late at night on the 3rd September and marched to Waterloo Station. It reached Southampton in the early morning of the 4th September and later in the day embarked on the British India H.T. *Nevasa,* together with the Brigade Staff and two companies of the 3rd London Regiment.

The following officers proceeded overseas with the Battalion:

7

Lieut.-Col. E. L. Marler, T.D., in command.
Major E. J. Hogan, second-in-command.
Major J. Attenborough.
Capt. J. H. S. Westley, Yorkshire Regiment, Adjutant.
Capt. G. A. Stacey, commanding 'A' Company.
Capt. M. F. Scott, commanding 'E' Company.
Capt. E. O. Davies, commanding 'G' Company.
Capt. C. J. Goodwin, commanding 'C' Company.
Capt. R. I. Marians, commanding 'F' Company.
Capt. R. Heumann, commanding 'D' Company.
Capt. C. H. Taylor, commanding 'B' Company.
Capt. L. Beck, commanding 'H' Company.
Lieut. L. H. R. Inglis, Machine-Gun Officer.
Lieut. R. E. F. Sneath.
Lieut. P. J. A. Handyside.
Lieut. F. J. T. Moon, Transport Officer.
Lieut. E. E. H. Bate.
Lieut. H. W. Everitt.
2nd Lieut. A. T. Taylor.
2nd Lieut. E. T. Cooper.
2nd Lieut. J. P. Kellett.
2nd Lieut. F. L. Rolleston.
2nd Lieut. C. Gordon.
2nd Lieut. E. J. Harington.
2nd Lieut. A. G. L. Jepson.
2nd Lieut. P. C. Taylor.
2nd Lieut. W. E. Grey.
2nd Lieut. F. C. Edwards.
2nd Lieut. H. B. T. Wakelam.
2nd Lieut. W. S. C. Stephens.
Capt. J. H. Warrener, Quartermaster.
Capt. J. McHoul, R.A.M.C., Medical Officer.

The remainder of the Brigade, in company with two Territorial battalions of the Middlesex Regiment,[1] embarked on the H.T.'s *Galician, Galeka,* and *Gloucester Castle,* all of the Union Castle Line, and the first-line transport of all battalions was loaded on a smaller vessel, the H.T. *Kelvingrove.* At five o'clock in the afternoon, one month after the declaration of war, the convoy, carrying the first Territorial brigade to leave this country, steamed down Southampton Water on its voyage eastwards.

[1] These battalions were bound for Gibraltar to relieve the Regular infantry of the garrison of that Fortress.

CHAPTER II

1/2ND LONDONS IN MALTA—FORMATION OF THE 2/2ND LONDONS

I

THE voyage proved uneventful. Except for some rough weather in the Channel and in the Bay of Biscay, the sea was calm; and everyone enjoyed the trip along the coast of Spain and later along the coast of Africa in the Mediterranean. The passage to Malta was too short to allow the men to become weary of the monotony of the ship's routine and the discomfort of their somewhat confined quarters. There was, moreover, plenty of incidents in the voyage to interest them: the glimpse of Cape Trafalgar, the sudden dash of the escorting warship to gain a closer view of some suspicious-looking stranger, the call at Gibraltar (though no one was allowed to land), the exotic appearance of the African shore; every detail of the voyage was a new experience to a great majority of the Battalion. Progress as far as Gibraltar was slow; for the convoy, escorted by H.M.S. *Amphitrite* (Capt. Aplin), was obliged to keep close together, and the speed had to be reduced to that of the slowest ship, the H.T. *Kelvingrove*. After the convoy had passed Gibraltar, the escort left it; and each ship made for Malta at her fastest pace, the *Nevasa* outstripping the others and reaching the islands first.

Shortly before dawn on 13th September the *Nevasa* was off the harbour of Valletta. As the ship lay to, awaiting the hour at which the boom protecting the entrance was raised—for no shipping was allowed to enter the harbour during the hours of darkness—, the first view of the island in the half-light of the breaking day, vouchsafed to those who had risen early enough, was not impressive. From the sea, the island appears to be nothing but a barren rock; for no vegetation can be seen owing to the existence of innumerable walls built along the rocky hillsides to prevent the thin layer of soil from being washed away. Few houses were visible, and these, closely shuttered, merely accentuated the deserted appearance of the island. On the other hand, Valletta, as the ship drew nearer, presented a far different appearance in the broadening light of day. The white houses, nestling in the cliffs round the harbour, the grey bastions of the fortifications, the gaily-coloured awnings that protected every window, the riot of colour

9

on the quays, the blue sky above, and the blue Mediterranean beneath, all tinged with the glory of the rising sun, made a wonderful picture.

At 6 a.m., on the raising of the boom, the ship steamed into the harbour, and after receiving a great ovation from some French warships came alongside her berth. Owing to the fact that the sun-helmets intended for issue for the troops had been packed at the bottom of the ship's hold, from which they could only be extracted with difficulty, the Battalion did not disembark until the morning of the 14th, when it relieved the 2nd Battalion Middlesex Regiment in Valletta, Battalion Headquarters and the left half-battalion going to Floriana Barracks, just outside the gates of the town, and the right half-battalion, with the transport, machine-gun, and signal, sections, under Major E. J. Hogan, to Fort Manoel, on an island in the Marsamuscetto Creek. The news that the Battalion was to remain in the neighbourhood of Valletta was received with much pleasure by all ranks, not only because of the attractions of the principal town, but because a long march in service dress in the heat of the day would be avoided. The 1/1st Londons went to St. Andrews Barracks, the 1/3rd Londons to Imtafa, and the 1/4th Londons to a camp at Ghain Tuffieha on the west coast of the island. To these battalions was allotted the duty of guarding the perimeter of the island, while the 1/2nd Londons acted as an inlying battalion for the defence of the town and port of Valletta.

On the day after the arrival of the 1st London Brigade, the Regular infantry of the Malta garrison left for the front; and the Brigade thus became at once responsible for the defence of the Fortress, a vital link in the Empire's chain of communication. For the first few weeks the duties of the 1/2nd Londons were arduous, because a large number of guards had to be found for the various vulnerable points around the town. The work was monotonous; and the great heat made it very trying until khaki 'drill' suits were issued. In compensation, however, the Battalion had the honour of finding the Main Guard over H.E. The Governor's Palace in the centre of Valletta. This was a 'public duty;' and the guard mounted with due ceremony amidst crowds of interested spectators. Lieut. R. E. F. Sneath was the first Territorial officer to be in command of this guard. The walls of the officers' quarters in the Guard Room were decorated with the crests of the regiments that had done this duty in the past; and to their number the Battalion, as the first Territorial battalion to do this duty, added its own.[1]

---

[1] The crest of the Regiment was likewise put up in the courtyard of Floriana Barracks, on the walls of which previous occupants had commemorated in this manner their stay in the barracks.

The Main Guard remained one of the duties of the Battalion during the whole period of its stay on the island, even after the majority of the other guards were withdrawn—an event that occurred some weeks later when another failure in the enemy's espionage system rendered the retention of such guards unnecessary.

When the guards were withdrawn, the training of the Battalion began in earnest; and considerable progress towards efficiency was made. One of the chief difficulties with which the Battalion had to contend was the unsuitable nature of the ground for training purposes; for the native custom to which allusion has been made of building walls along the hillsides to confine the precious and highly cultivated soil, had the effect of converting the latter into terraces over which manœuvres were both slow and difficult. Fortunately for the 1/2nd Londons, however, there was, not far from Valletta, a large flat area that had been converted into the semblance of a sports ground. This ground, known as the Marsa, and containing the only racecourse on the island, provided ample space for the manœuvres of several companies at the same time; and for this purpose the Battalion made full use of it.

The exacting musketry course of the Regular Army was later carried out on the Pembroke Ranges, close to the St. Andrews Barracks, some miles from Valletta, two companies at a time being attached for this purpose to the 1/1st Londons, who were stationed there. Sergt. Hicks, Royal Marine Light Infantry, was attached to the Battalion as Musketry Instructor, and to his keenness its progress in this important branch was largely due. The field training of the machine-gun section and its firing were also carried out at St. Andrews Barracks, the section being stationed here for the last six weeks of the Battalion's stay in the island. The more advanced training of the transport section was taken in hand, and the section went to Musta Fort for special instruction in Army Service Corps duties. Throughout this training period, all ranks worked hard and conscientiously with the result that the Battalion rapidly began to take shape as a useful and well-disciplined unit.

Malta proved a very pleasant spot for a short tour of duty, despite the climatic vagaries usual at this time of year. When the 1/2nd Londons landed in the middle of September, the hot season was drawing to a close; nevertheless the temperature was high enough to cause some discomfort, especially as a week or two elapsed before 'drill' clothing could be issued to the men. In the beginning of October came the scirocco, a warm south-westerly wind originating in the Sahara. This wind is extremely enervating in its effects, and was as trying to the troops as the great heat of the previous month had been. The wet season set in at the end of October, and November was marked by some very heavy storms; but with December came the beginning of the most pleasant season in the island's year. The temperature was mild, and the weather more settled. Vegetation sprang up everywhere in an amazing fashion; and the island soon presented an appearance very different from the drab uniformity of three months earlier.

The chief impressions that Malta left with members of the Battalion were the number of priests, the number and sanctity of the goats, and the fact that all streets appeared to be named 'Stick no Bills.' The *Strada Reale*, the '*Regent Street*' of Valletta, the *dghaisa* men, and the Marsa, will also remain in memory. On the Marsa's hard, unfriendly surface, football matches, both rugby and association, were played against the other battalions and against the crews of the battleships in the harbour. In addition to football, swimming was the chief recreation of the men; and full advantage was taken of the magnificent harbours with their deep water. The officers *tried* to play polo, frequented the Union Club, and attended the Opera. *Carrozza* races down the *Strada Reale* provided amusement in the early days; and a game called 'Popes'—far too irreverent for the rules to be detailed here—helped to while away many a journey to St. Andrews or Imtafa. On the whole, the Battalion had a very happy time in Malta—a fact that it better appreciated a few months later when it was in France. The following lines, written by Lieut. E. T. Cooper, after the Battalion had reached France, echoed the sentiments of all those who little realized at the time how well off they were in Malta's isle.

MARSMASCETTO[1]

Lapping by the Lazaretto,
    Far away in Malta's Isle,
Flows the creek of Marsmascetto,
    Languid as a lady's smile.

Swarthy 'dghaisa' men are plying,
    Lazily with dripping oars,
Little ferry boats are flying,
    In between the rocky shores.

Now amidst a world of worries,
    Death and I play hide and seek,
But the water never hurries,
    Down the Marsmacetto creek.

---

[1] Reprinted by courtesy of Major E. T. Cooper and Messrs. Burns and Oates, Ltd., from *Soliloquies of a Subaltern*.

On the 30th September Lieut.-Col. Marler had met with a severe accident from the effects of which he never really recovered, and on the 5th December, at the termination of his period of command, he was obliged regretfully to leave the Battalion and return to England. He was accompanied by Major Hogan, who went to take up his duties with the newly-formed third-line unit. Major J. Attenborough assumed command of the Battalion, with Capt. G. A. Stacey as the second-in-command. Capt. M. F. Scott, handing over ' E ' Company to Lieut. L. H. R. Inglis, took command of ' A ' Company vice Capt. Stacey. Among other changes in the Battalion's organization that were made at this time the most noteworthy was the appointment of Lieut. A. T. Taylor as Transport Officer, an appointment that he was to hold with great advantage to the Battalion until the end of the war.

On 22nd December a warning order was issued that the Brigade would leave the island at an early date; and on 24th December the Brigade was reviewed by H.E. The Governor, General Sir Leslie Rundle, G.C.B., G.C.V.O., K.C.M.G., D.S.O., who issued the following Fortress Order on the same day:

> The Commander-in-Chief, after having inspected the units of Lord Lucan's Brigade this morning, desires to place on record his great satisfaction at the evident progress made by them to become efficient soldiers of the King. H.E., who fully appreciates the patriotic sentiments which have caused such a magnificent body of men to respond to the call of the Empire in this hour of national danger, has had much pleasure in telegraphing to Lord Kitchener reporting the high state of efficiency which the Brigade has reached. Such a result, which must have been apparent to everyone who saw them on parade this morning, could only have been obtained by the whole-hearted devotion to their country's cause, of every officer, N.C.O. and man, and the Commander-in-Chief wishes to congratulate the Earl of Lucan and the whole of his Brigade on achieving such highly satisfactory results.

Christmas Day was celebrated none the less heartily for the knowledge that at last the Battalion was to take its share in the fighting. Although the Battalion was split up, two companies and the machine-gun section being still at St. Andrews Barracks, the festivities were a great success; and the first Christmas of the war passed happily.

II

As related in the previous chapter, the decision to raise a second-line battalion, with the primary object of providing reinforcements for the service battalion, was made within a few hours of the 1/2nd Londons being ordered overseas. On Capts. A. G. Houlder and C. L. V. Marno, who, on the departure of the 1/2nd Londons overseas, had been left in England, fell the task of forming this new unit; and these officers were assisted by Sergt.-Instructor Gavin, of the permanent staff, and by a number of non-commissioned officers and men of the 1/2nd Londons who had been found unfit, on medical grounds, to accompany that battalion abroad.

Recruiting for the new battalion, which was at first known as the 2nd (1st Reserve) Battalion The London Regiment, but later as the 2/2nd Londons,[1] began at once and proceeded with amazing rapidity. A large number of men who were too late to be admitted into the ranks of the 1/2nd Londons formed the nucleus; and the daily influx of recruits was such that in an incredibly short space of time the Battalion was almost at full strength.[2] The type of recruit obtained was extremely good, and a very large percentage of the non-commissioned officers and men of this Battalion subsequently obtained commissions. Of these, the following were gazetted to the 2nd London Regiment: S. H. Stevens, who afterwards commanded the 1/2nd Londons for some months, C. F. H. Attneave, W. F. Hopkins, S. K. G. Foster, H. G. Guildford, H. Inwards, W. F. White, and J. H. J. Dickens.

The newly-formed battalion was at first commanded by Capt. A. G. Houlder, who was promoted Major, while Capt. C. L. V. Marno acted as adjutant; but in the course of a fortnight, Colonel P. Carlebach, T.D., at that time the Honorary Colonel of the Regiment, returned to the active list, and was appointed to the command. At the same time, Lieut. J. D. Rees, a seconded officer of the 1/2nd Londons, was restored to the establishment, granted the temporary rank of Captain, and appointed adjutant in place of Capt. Marno, from whom he took over the duties, the latter officer being placed in charge of the Depot at Tufton Street. Several officers who had had previous service either in the Regiment, such as Major W. Whitaker Thompson and Capt. M. C. V. Hurst, or in some other unit of the Volunteers or Territorial Force, rejoined, or were at once granted com-

---

[1] Hence was derived a favourite nickname of 'The Two and Twopennies.'
[2] Two companies were recruited from the Westminster Training College.

missions; and these formed a useful cadre for the task of raising and training a battalion *ab initio*.

As soon as sufficient men were available—and this was almost at once—, training was begun in Vincent Square; but the available accommodation at Tufton Street proving totally inadequate for the growing numbers, the Headquarters of the Battalion was moved at an early date to Epsom Downs. Here the Battalion was billeted in the stables and jockeys' quarters at Tattenham Corner, and in the buildings of the station nearly adjoining them. For the use of the stables the Battalion was indebted to Mr. F. A. Houlder, a brother of Major Houlder, and to Mr. Dorling, of Epsom, through whose agency they were put at its disposal. The South-Eastern and Chatham Railway allowed the Battalion the use of the station buildings, and in addition to this accommodation later provided a number of old railway coaches. These were run alongside the platforms; and the compartments formed excellent temporary billets for one or two men. The Regiment owes a considerable debt of gratitude to Mr. F. Houlder and Mr. Dorling, and to the railway company for their efforts on its behalf, but especially to Mr. Houlder, who proved a good friend not only of this battalion, but also of the 3/2nd Londons and the 4/2nd Londons during their sojourns at Epsom at a later period of the war.

With as little delay as possible training was begun afresh at Epsom, and was continued energetically, though under great practical difficulties. The magnificent downs provided, of course, excellent ground for elementary training and offered ample facilities for more advanced tactical exercises; but the lack of stores of all kinds, including arms and equipment, was a very serious handicap. The lack of these essentials was common to all the newly-formed units, the supply not at first being equal to the demand, and it was only by a gradual process that deficiencies in equipment were made good, and 'wooden equivalents' exchanged for rifles.

The Battalion remained on Epsom Downs until 15th December, when it left to join the rest of the 2/1st London Infantry Brigade, which was now concentrating in the area of Maidstone and Tonbridge. The 2/2nd Londons were sent to Tonbridge, where they occupied comfortable billets in the town. On the 17th December, a warning order was received that the Brigade would proceed on foreign service at short notice. Immediately there was bustle and excitement; officers and men were medically examined and inoculated; and all necessary preparations were made for an early departure overseas. The Battalion was finally inspected by Major-General W. Fry, C.B., C.V.O., who, expressing himself well satisfied with its progress, informed the Battalion that it was being sent to Malta to relieve its first-line unit, and indicated that that would probably be only a step to yet more active service.

It was fortunately possible to grant forty-eight hours' leave to all ranks before departure—the last home leave for nineteen months—; and on 23rd December the Battalion entrained for Southampton and there embarked on the H.T. *Neuralia,* of the British India Steam Navigation Co.

The following officers proceeded overseas with the Battalion :

Colonel P. Carlebach, T.D., in command.
Major A. G. Houlder, second-in-command.
Capt. J. D. Rees, Adjutant.
Major W. Whitaker Thompson, commanding ' B ' Company.
Capt. M. C. V. Hurst, commanding ' A ' Company.
Capt. A. E. Rees, commanding ' E ' Company.
Capt. J. W. Ginsbury, commanding ' C ' Company.
Lieut. G. N. Hunter, commanding ' G ' Company.
Lieut. D. Dutfield, commanding ' D ' Company.
Lieut. O. Shimwell, commanding ' H ' Company.
Lieut. P. C. Burnett, commanding ' F ' Company.
Lieut. P. R. Faulkner.
2nd Lieut. B. Attenborough.
2nd Lieut. W. R. Rawle, Transport Officer.
2nd Lieut. E. D. Symes.
2nd Lieut. R. H. Wagner, Signalling Officer.
2nd Lieut. A. S. Rawle.
2nd Lieut. G. Dearmer.
2nd Lieut. S. Jones.
2nd Lieut. C. R. W. Attenborough.
2nd Lieut. H. S. Elton.
2nd Lieut. R. L. Cooper.
2nd Lieut. H. Shimwell.
Lieut. G. J. Bradley, Quartermaster.
Lieut. E. Coplans, R.A.M.C., Medical Officer.

The H.T. *Neuralia,* carrying, in addition to the 2/2nd Londons, the 2/3rd Londons less two companies, put to sea the same evening, and early next morning joined the convoy. The convoy consisted of two ships, the H.T. *Neuralia* and the H.T. *Avon*—the latter carrying the 2/4th Londons and two companies of the 2/3rd—, and was under the escort of H.M.S. *Eclipse.*

Christmas Eve was a miserable day; the sea became very rough; and in the afternoon rain fell heavily. Unfortunately, this bad weather continued on Christmas Day, and had a somewhat depressing effect on the time-

MALTA—
FLORIANA BARRACKS,
VALLETTA.

MALTA—

MAIN GATEWAY,
FORT MANOEL,
VALLETTA.

MALTA—

MAIN GUARD,
VALLETTA.

Taking in bullion.

honoured celebrations. The gloom was deepened by the fact that the Christmas puddings that a kindly City Corporation had provided for the men's delectation had been inadvertently loaded on the H.T. *Avon,* and could not, of course, be transhipped at sea. Despite these drawbacks, however, those of the Battalion who were well enough celebrated the day with as much good cheer as the circumstances permitted.

After Christmas the weather improved; and everyone enjoyed the voyage with its varied incidents. As at this time there was little danger in the Mediterranean from the action of enemy submarines, H.M.S. *Eclipse* did not accompany the transports beyond Gibraltar. The last part of the voyage was exceedingly pleasant; the weather was perfect—so warm indeed that the men were allowed to sleep on deck—; and the African coast to starboard, with its tropical vegetation and strange-looking towns and villages, was a source of never-failing interest. At dawn on the 31st December the island of Gozo (one of the Malta group) was sighted. A few hours later the H.T. *Neuralia* was off the port of Valletta, and about noon entered the Grand Harbour, receiving an enthusiastic welcome from the warships there lying at anchor.

CHAPTER III

THE 1/2ND LONDONS IN FRANCE—ARMENTIÈRES AND THE ACTION OF L'EPINETTE

I

ON 1st January 1915, the 1/2nd, 1/3rd, and 1/4th Londons were relieved by their corresponding second-line units and embarked at Valletta under sealed orders, the 1/1st Londons, alone of the Brigade, remaining behind to form a stiffening for the new troops. The 1/2nd Londons—28 officers and 891 other ranks—having left behind rifles, machine guns, and all heavy baggage, sailed next day in the H.T. *Neuralia*. The sealed orders, when opened at sea, were found to contain instructions for the vessel to proceed at once to Marseilles. This news came as a great disappointment to all ranks of the Battalion, who had naturally looked forward to a short leave in England before going to the front.

Throughout the voyage the sea was very rough; and the Gulf of Lions did not belie its evil reputation. The ship rolled unmercifully for three days; and everyone was glad when she entered the protection of Marseilles harbour early on the 5th January. The Battalion, whose arrival was apparently unexpected by the authorities, was for this reason unable to disembark at once, and remained in its comfortable quarters on board until the following day. The officers, however, were given leave to go ashore, and they availed themselves of the opportunity of seeing the town, which was at that time the base of our Indian troops.

On 6th January orders were received for the Battalion to move by train to the north of France to refit. Accordingly, it disembarked at 7 p.m. and marched to the railway station, where for the first time it was introduced to those famous French railway trucks, bearing the legend: *Hommes*—40, *Chevaux en long*—8, with which it was later to have a long and close acquaintance. The men, nothing daunted by the inhospitable appearance of these trucks, covered the sides with such remarks as 'Don't breathe on the windows,' 'Non-stop train for Berlin,' and the like, and speedily made themselves as comfortable as circumstances would permit. Rations for two days were issued; and shortly after 9 p.m. the train set out, in the leisurely manner of all troop trains, on its tedious journey across France. Through

Avignon, Lyons, and up the Rhône valley, the train passed slowly, enabling
the men to see, albeit uncomfortably, the beauties of the French countryside.
At Mâcon a *halte repas* was made—that is to say, a halt long enough in
theory to allow the men to cook their dinners, but in practice far too short.
Thereafter the journey became a triumphal progress. The people of every
village through which the train passed hailed the Battalion with fervour;
bands played; guards turned out; and the populace was always at hand to
regale the men with gifts of fruit, coffee, and food of every kind.

In the early hours of the 8th the train passed round the outskirts of Paris;
and not long afterwards signs of war appeared on either hand; lines of
trenches, shelled villages, broken bridges, marking the limits of the fighting
in the autumn of 1914, were to be seen; and trainloads of wounded
were frequently encountered—, reminders, if such were needed, of the
grim realities of the conflict that was being waged unceasingly day and
night.

In the cold, wet afternoon of this day, the train came to a final standstill
at Etaples, near Boulogne. Here, as at Marseilles, the arrival of the Battalion
was not expected. A camp should have been ready for it; instead, the
Battalion had to pitch its own camp in the gathering darkness of the winter
afternoon, being the first British troops to occupy an area that by the end
of the campaign was covered, acre after acre, by tents, huts, offices, stores,
and hospitals. In spite of these initial difficulties, the Battalion quickly made
itself at home in its new surroundings and settled down to refit. The
weather was bitterly cold, snow lying thickly on the ground; and the rapid
change from the mild climate of Malta to the severe and wintry conditions
of Northern France was at first very trying, and for some days militated
against the health and comfort of the troops.

New rifles, machine guns, and equipment of every kind, were issued.
Nineteen vehicles and fresh horses, to the number of fifty-nine, were obtained
from the depot at Abbeville. One of these horses at once became the mascot
of the transport section: she was a mare, known as 'The Rabbit,' old, but
with a willing heart, and she was to serve with the Battalion throughout the
war either in the Officers' Mess cart or as a spare horse. On demobilization
in 1919, owing to her age, the Transport Officer had her shot to prevent her
meeting a worse fate.

As soon as the Battalion was equipped, training among the sand-hills of
the coast was begun; and at the same time a reorganization into four double
companies, concordant with the practice of the Regular Army, was accomplished as follows:

19

BATTALION HEADQUARTERS:
Lieut.-Col. J. Attenborough, in command.
Major G. A. Stacey, second-in-command.
Capt. J. H. S. Westley, Yorkshire Regt., Adjutant.
Lieut. A. T. Taylor, Transport Officer.
Lieut. W. E. Grey, Machine-Gun Officer.
Capt. J. McHoul, R.A.M.C., Medical Officer.
Capt. J. H. Warrener, Quartermaster.

NEW 'A' COMPANY—(Old 'A' and 'B' Companies):
Capt. M. F. Scott, in command.
Capt. C. H. Taylor, second-in-command.

NEW 'B' COMPANY—(Old 'C' and 'D' Companies):
Capt. R. Heumann, in command.
Lieut. R. E. F. Sneath, second-in-command.

NEW 'C' COMPANY—(Old 'E' and 'F' Companies):
Capt. R. I. Marians, in command.
Lieut. L. H. R. Inglis, second-in-command.

NEW 'D' COMPANY—(Old 'G' and 'H' Companies):
Capt. E. O. Davies, in command.
Lieut. F. J. T. Moon, second-in-command.

The Company Sergeant-Majors were respectively A. J. Frakes, D. Williams, W. Drage, and G. Michaels.

The strength of the Battalion at this period was 28 officers, 884 non-commissioned officers and men, and one interpreter. The last-mentioned, Corpl. L. Boissevain, familiarly known as ' Boys,' had joined at Marseilles.

After a few days the 1/2nd Londons moved to Wisques, near St. Omer, and thence a few miles to Arques, where training was continued. It is worthy of note that, on arrival at St. Omer, the Battalion was met by a staff officer, the brother of a famous Cabinet Minister, and that he was so impressed or amused by the equitation of some of the gallant officers that he enquired whether he had met ' the 2nd London Regiment or a travelling circus.' At Wisques the Battalion was billeted in a convent, formerly of the Benedictine Order of Nuns, which had been unused for many years and which must have been one of the coldest places in the world, being built entirely of stone, and having no fireplaces. At Arques the greater part of the Battalion was billeted in a distillery, until this building was condemned as unfit for billeting purposes, when alternative, but not much more satisfactory, accommodation was found.

Here it will be as well to mention the episode of the Doctor's charger. The Medical Officer of the Battalion, Capt. McHoul, had been unfortunate enough, when horses were allotted to the officers, to be given one almost

20

white in colour; and solicitous subalterns were never tired of pointing out that the enemy marksmen could not fail to hit such a target. The 'Doc.,' taking these remarks to heart, decided to try what his science could do to remedy Nature's mistake; and so, one day, the white horse appeared as a horse of a deep violet hue. It subsequently transpired that the 'Doc.' had dyed it with permanganate of potash. But worse was to come—a few days later the Battalion was on parade, ready to move off, and Lieut.-Col. Attenborough was issuing his orders to his officers, who were gathered round him, when his attention was attracted by loud and continued whistling in a very shrill key, varied occasionally by chirping. The volume of sound increased until it seemed as though every man in the Battalion had become a bird-fancier. The Colonel glanced round, and the reason for this demonstration was at once plain to him. The 'Doc.' was riding on parade mounted on his horse, which was now the colour of a perfect Norwich canary. How this transformation had been effected it is not pretended to know—suffice it to say that the Doctor's 'canary coloured charger' was a source of joy to the Battalion for many months to come.

To quote Lieut. E. T. Cooper's lively verses once more : [1]

> Thereafter when he rode abroad
>   A ribald whisper flew,
> Whilst Tommies tittered, Captains roared
>   And urged a dry shampoo.
>
> The rumour was he murmured 'cheep'
>   Instead of saying 'whoa,'
> And gave it groundsel in a heap
>   To make the beggar grow.

While at Arques the Battalion lost its Quartermaster, Capt. Warrener being obliged by continual ill-health to go into hospital. His duties were taken over by Sergt.-Instructor A. G. Shackleton, Royal Fusiliers, who had been on the permanent staff of the Battalion before the war and who had, since leaving Malta, been acting as R.Q.M.S. Shackleton, more familiarly known as 'Old Shack,' was later confirmed in his appointment and received his commission. He served throughout the war with the Battalion, being one of the very small number to do so; he was subsequently promoted to the rank of Captain, and was awarded the O.B.E. for his invaluable services.

The Battalion now began a very strenuous course of training under the

[1] Reprinted, by courtesy of Major E. T. Cooper and Messrs. Burns and Oates, Ltd., from *Soliloquies of a Subaltern*.

immediate supervision of Br.-General R. S. Oxley, G.O.C., G.H.Q. Troops. Each day it left billets early in the morning and did not return until late in the afternoon, the intervening hours being spent in field-training, and more especially in the 'Open Warfare' attack. Occasionally the programme was varied by work on a reserve line of trenches, under construction in the neighbourhood of St. Omer. This work was under the supervision of the Royal Engineers, and gave the Battalion useful practice in the art of digging. The weather throughout this period was almost invariably bad, but fortunately did not affect the health of the troops to any great extent, and certainly did not succeed in damping their ardour.

At the conclusion of this training and after an inspection by the Inspector-General of the Territorial Force, Major-General Bethune, who complimented the troops on their soldierly appearance, news was received that the 1/2nd Londons were to proceed by route-march to join the 17th Infantry Brigade, 6th Division, at Chapelle d'Armentières. This information was enthusiastically received, all ranks realizing that they were now destined for the front line. On the 19th February the march from Arques began, and was accomplished in two days and a half. Hazebrouck was reached the first night, after a march of twelve miles; and in this interesting old town the Battalion was billeted in a building that had been an institute of some kind, either a workhouse or a hospital. It had no glass in the windows and no doors in the frames, and it was in a filthy condition.

On leaving Hazebrouck next morning, the Battalion marched past the Commander of the Second Army, General Sir Horace Smith-Dorrien, and proceeded to Bailleul (ten miles), where it was billeted in *Les Grapperies,* a large vineyard under glass. Next morning a bill for this accommodation was presented by the owner to Lieut.-Col. Attenborough, who, being not altogether unacquainted with the legal aspect of the matter, was wise enough to refuse it. The Battalion left Bailleul on the 21st February under the eyes of the III. Corps Commander, Lieut.-General Sir William Pulteney, and reached Armentières (seven miles and a half) shortly after noon on the same day, having completed the three days' march without a single man falling out of the ranks. The only casualty was one heavy draught horse, which, having broken a leg, had to be shot. The strength of the Battalion on marching in was 27 officers, 848 other ranks, and one interpreter.

II

At Armentières an unexpected pleasure awaited the 1/2nd Londons. They had known that the 17th Infantry Brigade included the 1st (Regular) Battalion Royal Fusiliers, and they now found that this battalion was willing and anxious to take charge of the Territorials who bore its title, and to help them over their initial difficulties. It is fitting to acknowledge the debt of gratitude that the 2nd Londons owe to this fine Regiment for its friendliness and loyalty towards its affiliated Territorial unit. The officers and non-commissioned officers extended a warm welcome to the 1/2nd Londons and took endless trouble to help them and to make them comfortable and at home in every respect. To their introduction to the realities of war under such helpful and experienced guides, there is no doubt that much of the subsequent success of the 1/2nd Londons is largely due.

No mention of the 1st Royal Fusiliers can be complete without a reference to their Commanding Officer, Lieut.-Col. R. W. Fowler-Butler. The exploits of this intrepid officer will not be forgotten by those who witnessed them, and undoubtedly they served to encourage the troops. Many are the stories told about Lieut.-Col. Fowler-Butler, especially by Lieut.-Col. Attenborough, who, being placed under his instruction, was frequently the involuntary participant in his intrepidity. He would invariably ride up to the front line on a bicycle in broad daylight, and, covered by a ground-sheet, he was in the habit of wandering about No Man's Land in daylight. On one occasion, when orders had been received that, in order to conserve ammunition, the machine guns were not to fire for a period of twenty-four hours, the crew of one of the 1/2nd Londons' guns, who had mounted the gun at dusk to see that all was in order, was exceedingly surprised to see the head of Colonel Fowler-Butler pop up in front of the muzzle of the gun, followed by the Colonel himself, hoping that he had caught the crew about to disobey the 'no-firing' order. The relations of the Battalion with this officer were invariably cordial, except on one point. The 1/2nd Londons were at that time armed with long rifles; and it was the desire of every man to possess himself of a short rifle at the earliest possible moment. Unfortunately this was done partly at the expense of the 1st Royal Fusiliers and led to trouble with Colonel Fowler-Butler, who found the rifles on the charge of his battalion disappearing at an alarming rate.

The infantry of the 6th Division at this period comprised the following units:

6TH DIVISION
Major-General J. L. Keir.

16TH INFANTRY BRIGADE—Br.-General C. Ingouville Williams.
1st East Kent Regiment (The Buffs).
1st Leicestershire Regiment.
1st Shropshire Light Infantry.
2nd York and Lancaster Regiment.
1/5th (T.F.) Loyal North Lancashire Regiment.

17TH INFANTRY BRIGADE—Br.-General G. M. Harper.
1st Royal Fusiliers.
1st North Staffordshire Regiment.
2nd Leinster Regiment.
3rd Rifle Brigade.
1/2nd London Regiment (Royal Fusiliers).

18TH INFANTRY BRIGADE—Br.-General W. N. Congreve, V.C.
1st West Yorkshire Regiment.
1st East Yorkshire Regiment.
2nd Durham Light Infantry.
2nd Sherwood Foresters.
1/16th London Regiment (Queen's Westminster Rifles).

The Headquarters of the Division were at Croix du Bac, west of Armentières; and the Headquarters of the 17th Brigade were established, east of the town, in the shell of a large house on the left of the Chapelle d'Armentières road, a hundred yards or so from the level-crossing over the main railway line to Lille.

The Brigadier-General Commanding the 17th Brigade, Br.-General (afterwards Lieut.-General Sir G. Montague) Harper, known to one and all in the B.E.F. as 'Uncle,' always had a warm corner in his heart for the Territorial battalion under his command, whom he called 'his little Londoners,' and he did everything in his power for their welfare and success.

The 1/2nd Londons were billeted in the front of the town, in the *Faubourg de Lille,* between the railway station and the asylum, Headquarters being established in the main road leading via Chapelle d'Armentières to Lille, and the companies being quartered in the *rue de la Cité* and in neighbouring streets, composed of modern artisan houses. The transport was billeted some way from the rest of the Battalion, part being accommodated in a yard on the main road out of the town to the west, and part in a large spinning-factory in the *rue de la Paix*. This spinning-factory contained an excellent farrier's shop, and provided good accommodation for men, horses, and vehicles; it also made an ideal Quartermaster's store, plenty of covered space being available for keeping dry the large quantity of miscellaneous stores carried by a battalion on active service. Lieut. Taylor himself, after changing his quarters several times, finally settled down in the *rue Sadi Carnot,* where he was joined by his ally, the Quarter-master.

The town of Armentières had been knocked about during the fighting of 1914 and was, at this time, frequently shelled. Nevertheless, the troops could live in comparative comfort and—a very important point—could regularly obtain proper rest, clean clothes, and hot baths. Despite the frequent shelling, many civilians, chiefly old men and womenfolk, were still living in the town; a number of *estaminets* and *brasseries* were still open; there was one *patisserie,* much frequented by officers, where typical French cakes and pastries could be obtained; and the enterprising agent of Messrs. Burberry's, Ltd., carried on a restricted business in the *Grande Place.* The buildings of the asylum, mentioned above, were invaluable, and were used for billets and engineers' stores, while the heating installation provided hot baths for all and sundry.

Two days after its arrival, the Battalion was inspected, outside its billets, by the G.O.C. 6th Division, Major-General (afterwards Lieut.-General Sir J. L.) Keir, who complimented it on its appearance and expressed his satis-faction at having it under his command.

Little time was lost in accustoming the Battalion to fire, and, as soon as it had settled down into its new quarters, it had to provide numerous working parties at night behind and in front of ' the line.'

Night at the front was a time of feverish activity. The friendly cloak of darkness was used by both sides to do the essential work of defence that could not be done under the eyes of the enemy. In the front line, trenches had to be dug or repaired, wire entanglements erected, patrols sent out, and the hundred and one things done to maintain a position precariously held. To newcomers to the battle-area, perhaps most remarkable of all was the activity on all roads and tracks behind the line. No sooner had darkness fallen than these roads seethed with humanity; battalions relieving, or being relieved; working parties, wiring parties, ration parties, going or returning; a strangely heterogeneous crowd, with seemingly little order, tramping along with hardly a word, save a muttered curse as someone tripped or stumbled. The confusion was made worse by strings of ration carts and waggons, which, in some parts, came surprisingly close to the front line. These rattled along the *pavé* or the rough tracks with a noise like thunder, advertising to all and sundry their existence and their route. Indeed, the enemy often sprayed the roads with streams of machine-gun bullets, or dropped a shell at intervals on some likely place of assembly. Yet casualties were surprisingly few; and it almost seemed as if Providence had ordained that the work, without which the troops of the front line could not have existed, should be allowed to go on with little or no serious interruption.

The officers of the Battalion were first taken into the trenches for instruction; and a day or two afterwards individual companies went in with their 'Regular' brethren to learn some of the details of trench warfare. Thereafter two companies were always in the line, 'A' and 'B' going in alternately on the right of the Brigade front with the 1st Royal Fusiliers or 3rd Rifle Brigade, whichever happened to be in the line, and 'C' and 'D' on the left, with the 2nd Leinsters or 1st North Staffords. There is a good story of 2nd Lieut. Edwards—better known as 'Bill'—, who, leading his platoon into the trenches on one occasion in these early days, remarked to a North Stafford non-commissioned officer: 'Any room here?' 'No, sir,' replied the Midlander, not recognizing 'Bill's' impeccable southern accent, 'they don't serve it out until five o'clock!'

Men's impressions of their first experience in the battle-line are apt to be confused, their sensations vague and indefinite; but many will recall the queer feeling engendered by sitting in a hole in the ground, between life and death, as it were, and watching the dawning of a glorious spring day over the Flanders fields. To a man, himself in such strange surroundings, it was yet more strange to see Nature pursuing her daily tasks as though peace reigned throughout the world, the rising sun gilding the roofs of distant Armentières and lighting up the lush green meadows, the trees —or such as had escaped the ravages of war—bursting into bud, the birds fluttering in the stark branches, while on every side were the grim and ugly evidences of war, and over all brooded an unnatural stillness broken only by the occasional crack of a sniper's bullet or the stutter of a machine gun.

Under the stress of war, too, memory plays curious tricks and allows details of greater events to slip away, leaving no trace behind, while things of lesser moment remain indelibly imprinted on the mind, and incidents like the following take on a significance out of all proportion, perhaps, to their actual importance.

It is dawn and down the Lille road comes a party of Regulars returning from the trenches, marching with that long, slow pace that the heavily-laden infantry always affected in France. The men are singing, not loudly, but, as they approach, the words can be distinguished: 'Here we are, here we are, here we are again.' Only those who have returned from the jaws of death, as these men had just done, can appreciate the depth of meaning that they gave to the simple words of this once popular song.

At this period the British line at Armentières ran some 3,000 yards east of the town. Leaving the Lys, on the north, at a point just south-west of Frélinghien, it passed in front of Houplines, and after crossing the Lille railway line and road, the latter at no great distance west of the hamlet of Wez Macquart, ran south-west to the vicinity of Bois Grenier. As was only too obvious to anyone going up the line at night, when the gun-flashes and Very lights illuminated the whole horizon, north, east, and south, it thus formed a salient of which the Countembu trenches between the Lille railway and the main road formed the apex.

This line represented roughly the low-water mark of the British efforts in the fighting of October 1914, before trench warfare supervened and put an end to all progress. The British, in their advance eastward in October, had gained a footing on the Pérenchies ridge, protecting the city of Lille on the west; but before the line became stabilized, the Germans took good care to drive their opponents off the ridge into the flat meadows at its foot and to acquire for themselves the observation and other advantages that the high ground conferred on its possessors.

Owing to the nature of the country, which is typical of Flanders, flat and low-lying, and to the proximity of the Lys, which constantly overflowed its banks, both British and Germans had been obliged to leave their trenches and to build breastworks. Yet even these defences, behind which it was possible to live more or less above ground, were wet; and the dug-outs, or rather shelters, which were on ground level, were very poor things, whose roofs of corrugated-iron and a layer of sand-bags, could hardly be counted upon to keep out the rain. It was during work on one of the support breastworks that the Battalion suffered its first casualty, Pte. Goldsby, of 'B' Company, being wounded. A few days later Pte. A. E. Kosman, of 'D' Company, who had previously served in the German 'Death's Head' Hussars, was killed. The first officer casualty occurred on the 5th March, when 2nd Lieut. C. Gordon was slightly wounded, and the second on the 7th March, when 2nd Lieut. P. C. Taylor was also wounded.

The Battalion had now been abroad for over six months, and no leave had as yet been granted to its members, many of whom had left home and

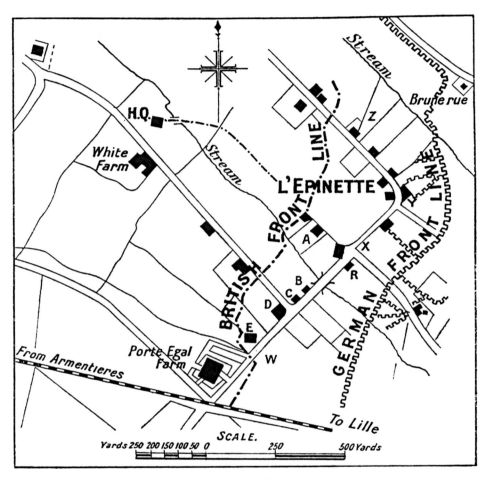

THE ACTION OF L'EPINETTE.

business in the early days of the war without having any opportunity of putting their affairs in order. Strong representations were accordingly made to the authorities, with the result that a few officers and men were granted

28

leave, in special circumstances, to visit England, a privilege that was later widely extended.

The failure of the Russian offensive of January 1915 had been followed by a serious disaster to our Allies in the Carpathians, brought about in part by the transfer of large German forces from the Western Front. The situation had become very critical; and General Joffre and the British Commander-in-Chief were agreed that an effort should be made to relieve the hard-pressed Russians, and, if possible, to break through the German line in France. The approach of spring and the accompanying improvement of the weather also indicated that the time was ripe for a resumption of offensive warfare. Plans for a joint offensive were prepared; but, almost at the last moment, the French for a variety of reasons found themselves unable to participate. Preparations were by now far advanced; and Sir John French, who, in the words of the *Official History of the War,* 'particularly wished to foster an offensive spirit in the Expeditionary Force after its trying and enervating experiences of a severe winter in the trenches,'[1] determined to proceed with the plan.

'The failure of the British,' to quote the *Official History of the War* once more, ' to accomplish anything in the " December Battle " in Flanders had undoubtedly impressed the French very unfavourably, and it is more than probable that they did not think that the Field-Marshal was in earnest. Until the Battle of Neuve Chapelle was fought there is small doubt but that they were of opinion that the B.E.F. might be helpful to hold the line and act defensively, but would be of little use to drive the Germans out of France.'[2]

For the British operations, the area of Neuve Chapelle, a few miles south of Armentières, had been selected, with the Aubers Ridge as the main objective; and on the 10th March 1915 the attack was launched. To engage the enemy's attention and to prevent him moving troops to the point attacked, operations of varying importance were undertaken all along the British line. One such fell to the lot of the 17th Brigade, and was the first 'show' in which the 1/2nd Londons took part. The 17th Brigade was holding, on a front of two battalions, the sector of the line known as the Porte Egal and Countembu trenches, from the Armentières-Lille road on the right to a point just left of the Houplines-l'Epinette road, the main railway line from

---

[1] *The Official History of the War,* Vol. III. Brig.-Gen. J. E. Edmonds, C.B., C.M.G., R.E., and Capt. G. C. Wynne.
[2] *Ibid.*

Armentières to Lille running roughly through the centre of the sector. On the left front, the hamlet of l'Epinette lay 300 yards ahead, and was incorporated in the German defence system. With the object of pinning the enemy to the ground on this front, the 17th Brigade was ordered to capture this village.

To carry out this task, it was decided to make the attempt on the village during the night of the 11th/12th March, in the hope of surprising the garrison during the hours of darkness and of cutting off its retreat. The operation was to be accomplished in two phases. The first phase was to be complete by 11.45 p.m., and included the rapid occupation and defence of the line W-X (see map), which, it was thought, could be done without encountering much opposition. The second phase was timed to start at midnight, and aimed at the capture of the main objective—the line X-Y-Z. The main attack was entrusted to the 1st North Staffords, whilst the preliminary capture of the line W-X, including the occupation of the houses E to R, was to be effected by the 2nd Leinsters, who were then to be responsible for covering the main operation and for protecting the right flank.

The 1/2nd Londons were detailed to assist the attacking battalions both in the preliminary work and in the attack itself, the following tasks being allotted to the companies:

'A' Company (Capt. Scott): 3 platoons, attached to the 2nd Leinsters, to support the right attack; 1 platoon to make gaps in the wire.

'C' Company (Capt. Marians): Attached to the 1st North Staffords to support the left (and main) attack.

'D' Company (Capt. Davies): 2 platoons to hold the breastworks in the old front line vacated by the attacking companies of the 2nd Leinsters; 2 platoons to supply working and carrying parties.

'B' Company (Capt. Heumann): In reserve in billets. This company was ordered to be ready to move at a moment's notice.

In order to ensure surprise, it was decided to dispense with a preliminary bombardment; but the guns were laid on their various targets, and the artillery arrangements, which were in the hands of Lieut.-Col. C. E. Lawrie, D.S.O., were completed. Fire support for the attack was to be provided by the machine guns of the attacking battalions and by the 18th Brigade. As a counter-attack was to be expected at dawn, the artillery was ordered to subject the enemy's probable assembly positions to a heavy bombardment at that hour.

On 10th March, the opening day of the Battle of Neuve Chapelle, a brisk fire-fight was opened by the 17th and 18th Brigades with the object of keeping the enemy's attention occupied on this front, apparently with satisfactory results. During the night, the area of the attack was reconnoitred by some of the officers concerned in the next night's operations; and this party, while out in No Man's Land, had an unpleasant experience. The Germans suddenly switched on one of the two powerful searchlights that they had in this area, and opened a murderous machine-gun fire. Fortunately their aim was bad and no serious casualties resulted.

On the night of the 11th/12th March the attack on l'Epinette was delivered. Two platoons of 'D' Company, having previously reported at the White Farm, duly relieved the attacking companies of the 2nd Leinsters in the trenches about the barrier on the White Farm road. The latter, together with 'A' Company of the 1/2nd Londons, advanced at zero hour and succeeded in occupying the line W-X without difficulty. The main attack was equally successful. The 1st North Staffords, supported by fire from the 18th Brigade and from the machine guns, attacked in two columns, closely followed by 'C' Company, and succeeded in bombing the enemy out of the village. The operations resulted in a gain of 300 yards on a front of half a mile. All details had been carefully worked out beforehand, and there was no confusion; but the village was so heavily wired that the attack was considerably held up, and, while the troops were getting through the wire, many of the garrison effected their escape; nevertheless, a number of prisoners of the 133rd Regiment and of the 22nd Pioneer Battalion were captured.

Consolidation of the position was hurriedly undertaken, only a few hours being available before dawn, when a counter-attack by the enemy was highly probable; and it was now that the 1/2nd Londons rendered invaluable service in digging in and wiring the new line. By an unfortunate misunderstanding, the tools for 'A' Company, which were being brought up by a party detailed specially for the purpose, did not arrive; and the company was obliged to dig in with their entrenching implements and with such picks and shovels as could be obtained from the troops holding the original line. Under the guidance of Major Sargent, of the 12th Field Company, R.E., who was in general charge of the work, the whole place was put in a sufficiently good state of defence to enable it to be held; and it says much for the men's devotion to duty and hard work that this was successfully accomplished in face of the various difficulties of time and circumstance.

Although the hostile rifle and machine-gun fire had been very heavy during the attack, there had been little shelling. Now, however, the enemy subjected the captured position to a very heavy bombardment, and, under the cover it afforded, he made three counter-attacks on the left. In accordance with the pre-arranged plan, the British artillery opened fire on the German lines, but did not prevent the launching of these counter-attacks, which were finally repulsed by rifle and machine-gun fire. At the conclusion of the operation, the 1/2nd Londons, with the exception of a sub-section of machine guns, established in the captured position, were withdrawn to the old front line, and before dawn on the next day had returned to their billets in Armentières.

On the evening of the 12th March 'A' Company was sent forward again, and took over the trenches in the old line, near the barrier on the White Farm road. No sooner was the company in position than a message was received from Lieut.-Col. V. de Falbé, commanding the 1st North Staffords, asking Capt. Scott to move up into the forward line to reinforce his battalion, which had suffered heavy loss in the attack and in the course of the succeeding day, and was finding it difficult to hold on without assistance. The move was duly carried out; and 'A' Company, taking over the right of the forward line, with the North Staffords on the left, held it throughout the next day. The casualties of the North Staffords were, indeed, so heavy that their own stretcher-bearers could not cope with them; and therefore, on Lieut.-Col. de Falbé's request, Capt. Scott detailed Ptes. W. J. Coleman and G. L. Willis to assist in tending and evacuating the wounded. These two men carried out their work with great devotion to duty; and Pte. C. Leeks and Dr. Cashman also rendered valuable service.

Throughout the day the enemy continued to keep up an accurate shell and rifle fire on the captured village and the old front line, thus making any improvement of the position very difficult. The men, too, suffered much from thirst, as the day advanced, there being a scarcity of water that was accentuated, in the case of 'A' Company, by the fact that one of the water jars, by mistake, contained rum. During the day, L/Corpl. A. Windybank performed a brave deed which won for him the D.C.M., and for the Battalion the first honour conferred on it in the Great War. Some men were lining a ditch twenty yards from 'A' Company's headquarters, when the sergeant in charge shouted that a man was hit and that the wound could not be staunched. To reach the man, it was necessary to cross a bullet-swept space, absolutely devoid of cover. Notwithstanding this, L/Corpl. Windybank at once rushed out, bullets striking the ground all round him. Fortune

32

ARMENTIÈRES, 1915—
THE TRENCHES.

ARMENTIÈRES —
FERME DE BUTERNE
CEMETERY, 1926.

HOUPLINES, 1915 —
THE TRENCHES.

favoured him; and he reached the man unscathed, and, being unable to get him back, he remained with him, practically in the open, for the rest of the day.

On the night of the 13th/14th 'B' Company (Capt. Heumann) relieved 'A' Company in the forward trenches, the latter going back to the old front line. 'B' Company was led by a guide from the 1st North Staffords straight up the road to l'Epinette and suffered heavy casualties from machine-gun fire, several non-commissioned officers being killed, notably Corpls. Weaver and Gardiner and L/Corpls. Webber and Few. The advanced trench, which by this time had been considerably knocked about by shell fire and by the inclement weather, wet and muddy, with no trench boards, with sides that persisted in falling in to obstruct the way and to increase the mud, with no shelter for the garrison, with no communication to the rear, and with scarcely any wire entanglements in front, was no very safe or delectable spot.

The enemy made several counter-attacks against l'Epinette on this night. All these took the form of bombing attacks up communication trenches, and were repulsed without great difficulty. As time progressed, however, the situation gradually became normal; and the Germans ceased bombarding the village and desisted from their attempts to turn out its garrison. The whole position was soon completely consolidated, and included in the British front-line system. The Battalion's casualties during these successful operations amounted to 9 other ranks killed and 16 wounded.

The rest of the month of March was passed in the routine of ordinary trench warfare. Casualties included Sergt. Thompson, who was killed, and C.S.M. G. Michaels and Sergt. Flintham, wounded. Officer reinforcements during the month were:

Lieut. J. E. Richardson, 2nd Lieut. H. C. Lightbody.

On Easter morning, the 4th April, the Germans made an organized effort to obtain a truce, which actually began while the 17th Brigade was standing to arms, and lasted about two hours. While it was still dark, the Germans could be heard talking excitedly in their trenches, which were not many yards away from our own. Later they began to sing and to shout remarks to the 1/2nd Londons and to the Leinsters, who were in the line at the time, and who returned the compliment with interest. There was now no firing, and when day dawned it was amusing to see the heads of Germans popping up and down like marionettes, behind their trenches, to the accompaniment of loud laughter. A German, standing on his fire step, juggled with three bottles; and, when this 'turn' was ended, another German—a very small man—walked out as far as his own wire, struck an attitude, and hurriedly scampered back. A third then stood up and boldly challenged our men to play a game of 'soccer' against them in No Man's Land, but was immediately howled down when he confessed that they could not provide the football.

Meanwhile the officers, being afraid of treachery, had kept their men in their trenches, and were making full use of the opportunity of locating, through their field-glasses, the exact positions of the enemy's sniping posts, the state of his entanglements, and surveying, undisturbed, the country behind his lines—an opportunity that seldom presented itself in this sniper-infested area. The truce ended by treachery, a man of the Leinsters being shot in the mouth. Angry warnings were shouted by the British, followed by a volley, aimed purposely high; and thereafter sniping continued throughout the day.

On 24th April, at the time when the Second Battle of Ypres was at its most critical stage, a demonstration was arranged on the front of the 17th Brigade, to prevent the enemy from moving troops from this sector to Ypres. Heavy artillery and rifle fire apparently secured the desired result; for the enemy's guns replied, and subsequently the German Intelligence reported that a heavy attack west of Lille had been checked.

The shortage of shells at this time began to make itself felt; and the Machine-Gun Officer received instructions to assist our artillery by harassing roads and by engaging the German field batteries, where possible, by indirect fire. Bombs, too, were scarce, those available being of the 'jam tin' variety and manufactured locally. These, when filled with old iron and some explosive, were considered as dangerous to friend as to foe; and 'Tickler's Artillery,' as the bombers were called, were never very popular in the trenches.

In addition to bombs, two other novel forms of armament were introduced to the 1/2nd Londons at this period. One of these was the trench mortar, which, needless to say, became the toy of the officer in whose charge it was placed, but was far otherwise regarded by everyone else. It was indeed more dangerous to friend than to foe; and great care had to be exercised in its use. This primitive weapon would only function twelve times; and the thirteenth bomb would explode it. Hence, before requesting an exhibition, an inspecting officer would never forget to ask 'How many bombs has the mortar fired?' Although the bomb on explosion made a goodly noise, the mortar had a low average for hitting anything in particular, and before long was superseded by a more useful type. The other innovation was the gas respirator, the introduction of which was rendered necessary by the enemy's use of gas in the Second Battle of Ypres. This respirator was a quaint affair into which the nose was fitted. A lump of cotton waste was held between the teeth, and the whole thing tied by tape under the nose and round the neck.

A large number of the many casualties suffered by the Battalion during its stay at Armentières was due to the enemy's snipers, who were very active in this area. It is recorded that on one occasion the Brigadier was looking through a periscope at some saps—a subject on which he held strong views —, when the periscope was hit by a German sniper, the force being sufficient to cause it to cut his eye. The Brigadier decided at once that the enemy had obtained the upper hand and ordered counter-sniping to be carried on with much more vigour than had hitherto been the case. Although the sniping of the Brigade was in reality quite efficient, it was felt that it would be politic to do something to meet the Brigadier's wishes. So, when he next inspected the sniping posts, he was the spectator of a series of demonstrations, involving a little by-play and a large number of empty cartridge cases, specially arranged for his benefit.

The officer casualties during April included 2nd Lieut. F. L. Rolleston, who was killed on the 21st while attending to the wire in front of his trench, and Capt. R. I. Marians, who was wounded. The latter was succeeded by Lieut. L. H. R. Inglis in the command of 'C' Company. Among the senior non-commissioned officers, Sergts. A. H. Soundy, E. J. Dawson, W. J. Thomson, and J. T. Alford—the smart and cheery machine-gun sergeant— were killed, and Sergts. L. F. Stone and Newlyn wounded.

The loss of 2nd Lieut. Rolleston was keenly felt throughout the Battalion. He was the first officer to be killed, and he was one of the youngest. His boyishness, his cheery nature and his enthusiasm in everything that he did, had endeared him to all ranks. Francis Lance Rolleston was the son of Sir Humphrey and Lady Rolleston, of Upper Brook Street, W. He was born in 1895 and was educated at Eton, where he served in the school Officers' Training Corps. He was gazetted to the 2nd Londons on the 29th August 1914, and served with the first-line battalion until his death. He was buried in Ferme de Buterne Cemetery.

The death of 2nd Lieut. Rolleston moved Lieut. Cooper to write the following beautiful lines:

THE COST[1]

Take back the honour and the fame,
 The victory we've won,
Take all the credit from my name,
 If this can be undone—
  Let him, my friend that used to be,
  Somehow be given back to me.

Don't mock me with the pride of it,
 The glory of his death,
I only know he sighed a bit—
 I felt him catch his breath.
  O God, if miracles can be,
  May he be given back to me!

Officer reinforcements during the month were:

Lieut. J. Devane, 2nd Lieuts. F. R. C. Hammond, H. C. B. Way, and J. W. Long.[2]

On the 29th April the 6th Division's front was reorganized; and the 1/2nd Londons relieved the 1st West Yorkshires in the Pont Ballot, or Houplines, trenches, to the left of the Houplines-l'Epinette road. This sector was much the same as that previously occupied, and calls for no special comment. The ration convoys now came up the road leading from Houplines church almost to the reserve line; and, as this road was under continuous small arms' fire at night, Lieut. Taylor and his transport had some remarkably unpleasant trips.

The month of May was passed in the usual routine of trench warfare; and little occurred to break the monotony. Armentières was heavily bombarded on the 6th; and on the 8th and 9th the 17th Brigade took part in a demonstration arranged to assist the operations of the First Army at Aubers. Trains were run into Armentières station, and were run out again half-an-hour or so later, while bodies of troops were marched through the town, to create the impression of a large concentration in the area. At the same time, heavy rifle and machine-gun fire was maintained along the front.

---

[1] Reprinted by courtesy of Major E. T. Cooper and Messrs. Burns and Oates, Ltd., from *Soliloquies of a Subaltern*.

[2] 2nd Lieut. Long was commissioned from the ranks of the Battalion, in which he had served for some years. He had reached the rank of Sergeant, and had been in command of a platoon since the beginning of 1915.

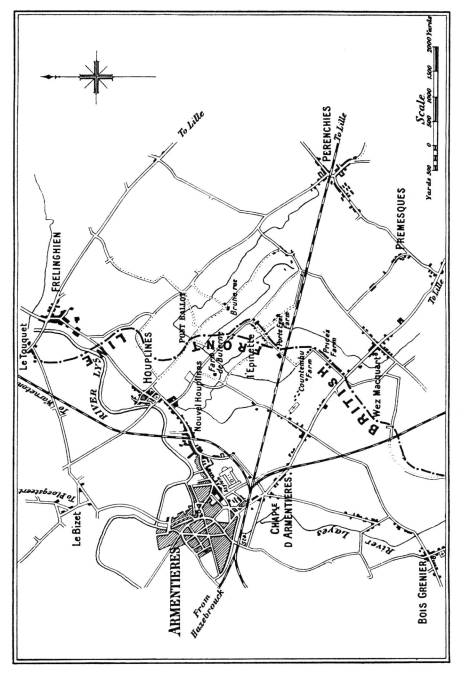

THE ARMENTIÈRES FRONT, FEBRUARY TO MAY 1915.

There is interest in the fact that the 1st Royal Fusiliers, when they relieved the Battalion on the 20th, were accompanied by personnel of the New Armies, sent for instruction; and there is a touch of pathos, as well as humour, in the recollection that R.Q.M.S. Macrow, of 'A' Company, broke two jars of rum, full of their precious contents, on two successive nights. Out of the line, the Battalion kept fit by training and by route-marches, and managed to find ample occupation and amusement for its leisure time. The 4th Division's 'Follies' and the 6th Division's 'Fancies,' in Armentières, gave excellent entertainments that were much appreciated. A Divisional Horse Show was arranged, and thereat Lieut.-Col. Attenborough's horse 'Tommy' obtained an 'honourable mention.'

During the whole of the Battalion's stay at Armentières there were frequent spy scares. Indeed, for some of these there were substantial reasons, as it is said that Armentières owed its comparative immunity from enemy bombardment to the number of spies it harboured. The *curé* of the church around which the Battalion was billeted was even suspected; and Lieut.-Col. Attenborough tells an amusing tale of a spy who, dressed almost correctly as a British staff officer, rode past his headquarters, and was smartly saluted by R.S.M. Francis.

During May officer casualties included Lieut. J. E. Richardson, who was killed on the 5th, and Capt. E. O. Davies and Lieut. E. E. H. Bate, who were wounded, and among senior non-commissioned officers, Sergt. W. J. Robinson and L/Sergt. H. Gant were wounded. The command of 'D' Company was taken over by Lieut. R. E. F. Sneath in succession to Capt. Davies. The Battalion also lost the services of R.S.M. W. Francis, who was obliged by illness to go into hospital. He was succeeded by C.S.M. A. J. Frakes, who was promoted Regimental Sergeant-Major. The following officers joined during the month:

2nd Lieuts. J. H. Clive and F. C. Langley.

Lieut. J. E. Richardson, who was born in 1893, was gazetted to the 2nd London Regiment from the University of London O.T.C. on the 29th August 1914, and joined the second-line unit on its formation. He was not sent overseas until the end of March, and, although he had been with the Battalion less than a month, he had endeared himself to all by his coolness, courage, and undoubted ability. He was buried at Ferme de Buterne Cemetery.

At the end of the month there were persistent rumours of an impending move, and on the 2nd June these took definite shape, the Battalion being relieved by the remnant of Princess Patricia's Canadian Light Infantry. On the next day the 6th Division left Armentières and marched to Bailleul, arriving the same night, the 1/2nd Londons being billeted in a concert hall. On the 4th the march was resumed; and the Division reached Poperinghe.

CHAPTER IV

THE 1/2ND LONDONS IN DEFENCE OF YPRES

I. First Impressions of the Salient

ON its arrival at Poperinghe, the 17th Brigade was billeted in the woods about the town. The accommodation was very bad; there were few buildings in the area, and these were, for the most part, derelict; and no tents were available. The change from the comparatively comfortable billets of Armentières came as something of a shock to the 1/2nd Londons; but the men, when once they had grasped the reality of the situation, set to work, with their usual initiative and cheerfulness, to make themselves as comfortable as circumstances would permit. At first, they considered themselves fortunate in having allotted to them four huts, three farm houses, and one or two ruined barns, while the Regular battalions had to be content with bivouacs under the hedges and trees, until they discovered that the peculiar smells, the stifling heat, the rats, and the lice, made these buildings uninhabitable. Indeed, not a man slept indoors for a single night; everyone preferred the hedges. The Headquarters office was a dirty little tumble-down cottage on the main Poperinghe-Ypres road. Its single room was invaded by goats and fowls in the daytime and was the hunting-ground of mosquitoes at night. So Battalion Headquarters took to the hedges likewise.

The Poperinghe-Ypres road was constantly filled with refugees who had lived for six months or more under shell fire until their own houses in Ypres or the neighbouring villages were wrecked, and who were now moving westward, they knew not whither. Most of them were walking, carrying what remained of their worldly possessions in bundles on their backs. It was a sad and touching sight; for here, driven from their homes, were old people and young children who, after experiencing many of the horrors of war, had now no place in which to take refuge in their misery.

Few will forget this long, straight road, which, lined on either side with poplars, ran through Vlamertinghe with its ruined church, past the old mill-house, afterwards a casualty clearing station, across the railway line, and past the stark walls of the prison, into the centre of Ypres. Until the 'Second Battle' in March 1915, Ypres itself, though by no means intact, had remained an inhabitable city in spite of the fighting that had raged so close

39

to its walls. The ancient Cloth Hall and Cathedral, which, standing close together, made a conspicuous target, had been heavily shelled. Although both these buildings had been gutted by fire, their stout old walls still stood. Apart from the damage done to these prominent and historic objects, Ypres had suffered surprisingly little; and many streets remained almost undamaged. This condition did not long continue; the bombardment that accompanied the opening of the Second Battle of Ypres hurled the old Flemish city into ruins; and little beyond the heaps of broken masonry and the husks of houses now remained to bear witness to its glorious memory.

As the result of the Second Battle of Ypres, the Salient had been much reduced in extent, and it was, at the time of which we write, extremely unsafe and unpleasant. Day after day it was the target of the enemy's guns, to which our own artillery, by reason of the shortage of shells, could make no adequate reply. Trenches were very poor; and of dug-outs there was almost none worthy of the name. The troops in the line or in close support had to exist in conditions incredibly bad, amid all the filthiness of war.

To this fearful spot the 1/2nd Londons were introduced, after a few days' rest and training, when the 17th Brigade relieved the 10th and 11th Brigades, of the 4th Division, in the Wieltje sector of the Salient. On 9th June the 1/2nd Londons moved up to the Yser Canal, a mile and a quarter north-east of Ypres, in brigade reserve, where they remained until the 25th, the men occupying small 'cubby-holes,' for the most part derelict and very unsafe, on the banks of the canal. The canal was a source of great joy; it was used by all ranks for bathing and boating, and by the Colonel on one occasion for fishing—until a shell dropped alongside his boat.

The trenches taken over by the Brigade in this sector were in a very bad state. The old trenches were constantly falling in; and new ones had to be revetted and provided with 'duckboards.' For the next twenty-one consecutive nights, therefore, every man in the 1/2nd Londons worked in the front line from 9 p.m. to 2 a.m.; and their work was much appreciated by the other battalions, judging by the letters of thanks received from the battalion commanders concerned. On at least two occasions during this period the men returned to their dug-outs on the banks of the Yser Canal, to find that the rain had loosened the earth round their billets, that the roofs had fallen in, and that their little holes in the ground had become nothing better than puddles. Still the men kept up their spirits in a remarkable way, and a tot of rum and the cheering rays of the rising sun soon dispelled any feelings of discouragement. The canal bank was shelled and bombed regularly every day, resulting in heavy casualties to the Battalion; and every night took its toll of men, no working party returning as strong as it went out. The work, too, was very tiring—this constant digging close to the enemy, with the long march back to the canal. It is on record that one man was so worn out on his return that he slept through a bombardment, during which he was wounded in the thigh by a shell splinter. Even this did not arouse him, and it was not until three hours later that the pain of his wound caused him to wake, when he went to the medical officer, and the piece of shrapnel was removed. Although troops holding the front line suffered inconvenience and discomfort, they escaped much of this arduous digging, and had, besides, the satisfaction of feeling that they were soldiers and not merely navvies. It is not too much to say, therefore, that the 1/2nd Londons awaited a tour of duty in the front line with mixed feelings, in which desire for a change was blended with the fatalism and 'wind-up' usual upon such occasions.

On the 26th the Battalion went back for a few days' rest to huts in a wood north-west of Vlamertinghe. The accommodation here was slightly better than in the previous rest billets, all the huts having roofs, and some of them doors. The presence in the neighbourhood of the Divisional concert party, 'The Fancies,' was much appreciated by all ranks.

During the month, the welcome news was received that the honour of C.M.G. had been conferred upon Lieut.-Col. J. Attenborough. This distinction was the first awarded to an officer of the Regiment in the Great War, and was a well-deserved recognition of Lieut.-Col. Attenborough's services to his country.

The Brigade relieved the 16th Brigade on the 3rd July in the Wieltje sector, the North Staffords being on the right of the Brigade front, the Leinsters in the centre, and the 1/2nd Londons on the left. Enemy snipers were active as usual, and on the 4th July 2nd Lieut. F. R. C. Hammond was seriously wounded, dying the next day in hospital. The 5th July was marked by very heavy shelling—so heavy, indeed, that the 8th Rifle Brigade, to the right of the Brigade front, were obliged to withdraw from their trenches. The enemy's bombers entered the vacated trenches and began to work along them; but the North Staffords, supported by fire from the other battalions of the Brigade, immediately counter-attacked and drove them out with considerable loss. Apart from this, little of interest occurred. Every night patrols went out into No Man's Land, but never came once in contact with the enemy, who preferred to snipe by day and use his machine-guns at night, and to shell regularly by day and night, rather than to meet our men in the dark. One company commander had taken a gramophone into the front trenches, and, starting it one afternoon, was disappointed to find that the Germans opposite were not appreciative of music. It took eight men five hours to repair the trench afterwards.

2nd Lieut. Frederick Robert Cyprian Hammond, who was the son of the Rev. and Mrs. F. J. Hammond, of All Saints Vicarage, near Rochester, Kent, was born in 1893. He was educated at the Cathedral School, Rochester, and St. Edward's School, Oxford, and prior to the war had adopted the stage as a profession. Soon after the outbreak of war he obtained a commission in the 2nd London Regiment, serving first with the 3/2nds and joining the first-line battalion in April 1915. He was buried at No. 10 Casualty Clearing Station, opposite the *estaminet,* 'In dem Boonvert,' two miles south-west of Poperinghe.

The Battalion was at this time comparatively short of men, its strength being, despite the arrival of drafts, only 25 officers and 618 other ranks. This shortage was caused not only by heavy casualties, but by reason of the fact that the men, being Territorials and thus in many cases skilled at a particular trade, were constantly taken for employment on administrative work at various headquarters. As a result, more work fell to the men when the Battalion was in the line, seeing that it then held the same extent of trenches as did the Regular battalions, which were, at this time, invariably 1,000 strong. The 1/2nd Londons, of course, were fully aware of this handicap against them; but such an excellent spirit prevailed among the men that they were, for this reason, the more determined not only to resist successfully any attacks by the enemy, but to work hard at the improvement of the defences, with the result that the stronger Regular battalions had nothing but praise for their zeal and devotion to duty.

The 1/2nd Londons went back into brigade reserve on the canal bank on the 12th July; and on the 19th the Brigade, less the 1/2nd Londons, was relieved and went back to rest billets. The 1/2nd Londons remained where they were, and dug regularly for the next sixteen nights under the command of the B.G.C. 18th Infantry Brigade. The Battalion had been detailed for a special task—that of digging three lines of trenches from Crump Farm to Sherwood Farm, in front of the main line, to link up the outposts. Every man in the Battalion was employed on this work, the whole operation being under the superintendence of Lieut. J. P. Kellett.

On the 22nd of the month, the Adjutant, Capt. J. H. S. Westley, received orders to join the 140th Infantry Brigade, of which he had been appointed Brigade Major. The Battalion regarded his departure with real regret and with some misgiving as to the future without the guidance and professional knowledge of a Regular soldier. Capt. Westley had worked whole-heartedly for the 2nd Londons, and under his care and direction during the early and difficult days of the War the Battalion had been brought to a high pitch of efficiency. Lieut. J. P. Kellett succeeded him as Adjutant. Officer reinforcements during the month were:

2nd Lieuts. H. R. Barton, L. W. Bindon, G. B. Henderson, and J. R. Garland.

Casualties during June and July included Sergt. W. H. Dixon, the second machine-gun sergeant to be killed, and Sergt. A. E. Willson, wounded.

On the 3rd August, the Battalion went back to rest again in the woods near Vlamertinghe, but this time to a different camp—one slightly better than the former, in that it had huts with doors, and could even boast the possession of a chair for the Colonel. This was duly signed for as camp stores.

II. The Actions of Hooge

It will now be as well to take a brief survey of the general situation on the British sector of the Western Front and to recapitulate the events that led to the next phase of the Battalion's activities.

After the Battle of Neuve Chapelle, which, in the words of the *Official History of the War*, ' was the first planned British offensive and is therefore an important landmark in trench warfare,'[1] negotiations between General Joffre and Sir John French for a joint offensive were resumed. 'The result of the Battle of Neuve Chapelle,' to quote the *Official History* once more, ' did not change the strategical situation on the Western Front; nevertheless certain definite and substantial advantages had been gained,' and not the least of these the raising of ' the prestige of the B.E.F. as an efficient instrument of war in the opinion of both friend and foe.'[2]

Preparations for a fresh offensive were put in hand; but in the meanwhile the British Army was called upon to fight the great defensive battle of ' Second Ypres ' at the end of April 1915. Despite the surprise effected by the use of gas by the enemy, Ypres still remained in our possession at the end of the battle, though the encircling German line had been drawn closer.

Early in May the projected British offensive was launched, and the battles of the Aubers Ridge and Festubert were fought. In its turn, this offensive drew to a close, with substantial gains to our troops but without

[1] *The Official History of the War*, Vol. III. Br.-Gen. J. Edmonds, C.B. C.M.G., R.E., and Capt. G. C. Wynne.
[2] *Ibid.*

any decisive effect on the course of the war. The next move was made by the enemy, who now delivered further attacks against the Ypres salient, the neighbourhood of Bellewaarde and the Menin road being the scenes of continual fighting. At the end of July, the Germans attacked the British position at Hooge, on the Menin road, with great determination. The 14th Division bore the brunt of the attack, in which the enemy for the first time employed the device—more terrifying than dangerous—of emitting liquid fire, and, yielding three lines of trenches and the mine crater at Hooge under the tremendous pressure, was forced to withdraw from the extremity of the spur along which runs the Menin road, back to the northern edge of Zouave and Sanctuary Woods. After losing Zouave Wood next day, the 14th Division succeeded by stubborn fighting in checking the enemy's advance, and even delivered some hastily organized counter-attacks. These counter-attacks were unsuccessful; and it became evident that only a deliberate and carefully planned attack could regain the lost ground, whose importance lay in the fact that it afforded the enemy observation over a wide expanse of country to the west. On 1st August orders were accordingly issued for the 6th Division to re-establish the line at Hooge; and during the next two days the Division was withdrawn from the sector it had hitherto been holding to prepare for the attack. The 16th and 18th Brigades were detailed to make the attack, with the 17th in divisional reserve.

In the midst of this excitement, the 1/2nd Londons, who were still near Vlamertinghe, celebrated Lieut.-Col. Attenborough's birthday on the 7th August, and held an impromptu concert in the wood at dusk.

At 3.30 a.m. on the 9th August the counter-attack was launched by the 16th Brigade astride the Menin road, with the 18th Brigade on its right. The attack was preceded by an intense bombardment of one hour, for which purpose most of the Divisional Artillery was concentrated in the wood wherein the 1/2nd Londons were billeted. The sound of very heavy machine-gun and rifle fire could be plainly heard, and indicated that the fighting was severe. The frequent rumours that reached the Battalion concerning the progress of the battle at last gave place to definite news of the 6th Division's success; all objectives had been gained, and, save for later adjustments, were all held.

The turn of the 17th Brigade came on the 10th, when it was ordered to take over and consolidate the recaptured line. From that day until the 24th the 1/2nd Londons, whose reputation for hard work was second to none, were employed in consolidating the position gained. Night after night the whole Battalion would be out, one company, perhaps, carrying materials, ammunition in boxes, mortar shells in bags, six-foot frames, coils of barbed wire, and the hundred and one things required in the front line, another digging out a blown-in trench or making a new one to link up the outposts, a third digging a new communication trench or improving an existing one, while the fourth would be out in front erecting more entanglements. Even the machine-gun section was employed on this work, its own particular task being to carry up the large quantities of lime required for burying the enemy dead, of whom there were large numbers, particularly in the neighbourhood of the crater. The identification of the bodies of British officers who had fallen in the earlier fighting in Sanctuary Wood fell to the lot of the Battalion; and much of this trying and difficult work in No Man's Land was done personally by Major Stacey and Capt. Sneath.

That long straight road leading eastward from Ypres, known to fame as the Menin road, will always live in memory—'the red, red road to Hooge'—and the crowds of men who nightly gathered at the Birr cross-roads, waiting for guides to lead them to the site of the work. Little less famous, or infamous, at least to the 1/2nd Londons, that awful communication trench, called Grafton Street, which, deep in mud and slime, was always crowded with battle-worn men returning from the fighting in front. But if Grafton Street was quite useless as an approach, the cross-country tracks were equally as bad—water-logged shell-holes and mud everywhere. As soon as a track was made, so surely was it blotted out by the enemy's guns and rendered useless and dangerous.

Throughout the twelve days during which the work of consolidation was going on the troops were subjected to heavy shelling by the enemy. The crater was the object of his special attention, and on the 14th he caught the Brigade staff there. No casualties resulted; but the staff, unable to escape or to communicate with the artillery, had an unhappy time. The position in the front line was by no means settled; and the British working parties were nightly interrupted and frequently drawn into fighting, by the enemy, who had established bombing posts within a few yards of our own trenches. There was a severe bomb fight, on the 14th, in the sector held by the Leinsters, north of the Menin road; and, on the 17th, the enemy delivered a bombing attack along the whole front, which was repulsed with considerable loss to himself.

The 1/2nd Londons' casualties during these operations were :

KILLED : 10 other ranks (including Sergt. W. G. Slater).
WOUNDED : 1 officer (Lieut. A. G. L. Jepson), and 22 other ranks (including Sergts. E. Cashman and L. Parkes).

The Germans did not succeed in regaining what they had lost; and on the 24th the 17th Brigade was able to hand over to the 3rd Division the Hooge line, duly consolidated and with the battle-field cleared. It was now possible for the working parties to be relieved; and the 1/2nd Londons, therefore, went back to the Hop Factory in Poperinghe for a rest. It should be noted that during a part of this period, owing to the illness of both Lieut.-Col. Attenborough and Major Stacey, the Battalion had been under the command of Major Scott.

The action of Hooge was eminently successful. The extremity of the Hooge Ridge and some ground north of the Menin road were captured; and the objects of the operation were thus completely attained. At the beginning of the operation, General Harper had sent a special message that: 'As the work in the Hooge district was of the utmost importance, he knew that all ranks of the 2nd London Regiment would do their allotted task in their usual methodical and cheery manner.' When the work was finished and the position successfully consolidated, the Brigadier expressed his appreciation as follows: 'The consolidation of the defensive line at Hooge has been far more arduous and no less responsible than that entailed in the original capture of the position. In this unselfish devotion to duty all ranks have maintained the highest traditions of the British Army'—an opinion that was confirmed by the C.R.E., who wrote: 'The 2nd Londons have done splendid work for the Royal Engineers.'

The awful experiences of the 1/2nd Londons at Hooge, and their devoted labours on this shell-torn ground, 'in the presence of death, in the stench of corruption, in the filthiness of war,' called forth the following lines from Sergt. G. E. Attwood, then serving in the Regiment:

'THE RED, RED ROAD TO HOOGE'[1]

'On parade, get your spade;
    Fall in, the shovel and pick brigade.'
There's a 'Carry fatigue' for half a league
    And work to do with a spade,
Through the dust and ruins of Ypres town,
    The 'seventeen inch' still battering down,
Spewing death with its fiery breath
    On the red, red road to Hooge.

Who is the one whose time has come,
    Who won't return when the work is done,

---

[1] Reprinted by the kind permission of the author.

Who'll leave his bones on the blood-stained stones
  Of the red, red road to Hooge?
Onward the Londons, never a stop,
  To the sand-bagged trench and over the top,
Over the top—if a packet you stop,
  On the red, red road to Hooge.

The burst and the roar of a hand-grenade
  Welcomes us on to the 'death parade'—
The pit of doom—the valley of gloom—
  The crater, out at Hooge.
Full many a soldier from the Rhine
  Must sleep to-night in a bed of lime;
'Tis a pitiless grave for a Brave—or Knave—
  Is the crater, out at Hooge.

Hark to the 'Stand-to' fusilade;
  Sling your rifle, bring your spade
And fade away ere break of day,
  Or a hole you'll fill at Hooge.
Call the roll . . . another name
  Is sent to swell the scroll of fame;
So we carve a cross, to mark the loss
  Of a chum who fell at Hooge.

Not a deed for the 'paper man' to write,
  No glorious charge in the dawning light,
The *Daily Mail* won't tell the tale
  Of that 'fatigue' at Hooge.
But our General knows, and his praise was won
  For the work the 2nd Londons had done
In the shot and shell at the gates of Hell,
  On the red, red road to Hooge.

III. THE DEFENCE OF THE BLUFF

General Sir Herbert Plumer, commanding the Second Army, inspected the Battalion on 1st September, and at the conclusion of his inspection thanked the Battalion for the way in which it had worked at Hooge, saying that the units to whom the task of consolidating the position had been allotted had suffered heavier casualties than those who had carried out the actual assault.

Three days later the Battalion moved into the la Brique trenches between the 14th and 49th Divisions, relieving the 1st King's Shropshire Light Infantry. The weather had been appallingly bad, and the trenches

47

were water-logged and in a terrible condition. The sides of the trenches and most of the dug-outs collapsed if a shell burst fifty yards away; and as soon as one part was strengthened another fell in. One trench, known as Cornhill, was a favourite target of the enemy's artillery, and consequently was in constant need of repair. These discouraging features did not deter the 1/2nd Londons from trying to improve the position, and, with the timely arrival of another draft, they were able, at the end of fourteen days, to hand over the trenches to the relieving unit in a much more satisfactory condition.

At the end of the month the Battalion did another tour of duty in the same trenches; during this period, which lasted until 2nd October, the only event serving to break the monotony of patrolling, sniping, and work on the defences, was a feint attack made with the object of assisting the operations of the V. Corps at Bellewaarde and Hooge. This was on the 24th September, and took the form of a discharge of smoke and gas, accompanied by heavy rifle fire and an artillery bombardment. It was very successful, and apparently caused the enemy considerable alarm.

Officer reinforcements during August and September included:

Capt. P. A. E. Wood, 2nd Lieuts. H. G. Guildford, J. Crosfield, M. Whittingham, W. Gray, and St. J. R. St. Ledger.

At the end of September the Battle of Loos had been fought by the British Army, in conjunction with a French offensive against Vimy farther south. This battle, whose opening stages were attended by a considerable measure of success, did not, in the end, produce the results expected. The fighting had been of the severest character, and the troops engaged, including several New Army divisions, had suffered very heavy losses. At its conclusion some of these divisions were withdrawn for rest and reorganization, and, before they were again put into the line, their weakened brigades were replaced by strong ones from other divisions. The 17th Brigade, being comparatively strong in numbers and very high in morale, was selected for transfer; and so it came about that, on 14th October, the Brigade, after an inspection on the previous day by Lieut.-General Sir John Keir, the Corps Commander, was transferred to the 24th Division (Major-General Sir J. E. Capper). At the same time, Major-General Harper, now promoted to the command of a division, handed over the command of the 17th Brigade to Br.-General J. W. Carrol. After the Brigade's transfer to the 24th Division three of its battalions were put into the line between Ypres and St. Eloi; and the 1/2nd Londons did a short tour of duty on Hill 62, where the opposing

COLONEL J. ATTENBOROUGH, C.M.G., T.D.

LIEUTENANT-COLONEL E. L. MARLER, T.D.

trenches were less than a hundred yards apart and where each side was engaged in very active mining operations.

The 1/2nd Londons held Hill 62 until the 17th October and then went out of the line to Reninghelst, where, or so it was understood, the 17th Brigade was to have its rest-billets throughout the winter. The Battalion's camp was situated on high ground amid beautiful scenery, at no great distance from the little village and out of range of guns of normal calibre. The Battalion was to share the camp with the 1st Royal Fusiliers, and the pioneers of both battalions set to work to make the place as comfortable as possible. In war, however, the best laid schemes are apt to go wrong; and, as it happened, the Battalion was never to return to this camp on which so much care had been lavished.

After the rest at Reninghelst, the 1/2nd Londons, on going back into the line, made their first acquaintance with that notorious rise of ground—it is not worthy of the name of 'hill'—known to fame as The Bluff. The Bluff lay to the south-east of Ypres, and formed the northern bank of a cutting through which passed the Ypres-Comines Canal. The Battalion's defence of this sector of the line deserves a detailed description, because, from a tactical point of view, The Bluff, although of inconsiderable height itself, was of the utmost importance, commanding, as it did, the lower ground between Ypres and St. Eloi. The importance of holding The Bluff and its outer defences to the last had been impressed on every man; and the 1/2nd Londons realized that their selection for this important duty implied a considerable trust in their steadfastness and powers of endurance. Towards the end of the third week, with the unutterable discomfort of body and soul, many of them would doubtless have been perfectly willing to hand over this honour to another battalion, but with no little blasphemy and a really astonishing amount of cheerfulness they kept a precarious hold of their position until relieved.

The Battalion was disposed with two companies in the front line and two in support. It was supported by a Belgian battery, which was very quick at retaliating when asked to do so, but which, being armed with a varied collection of guns and ammunition, fired an inordinate number of 'duds.' The trenches and defences generally were in a very bad condition, and demanded constant attention to keep them even habitable. In the front line, and especially in Angle Trench on the left company's front, the mud was almost solid and everywhere three or four feet deep. This was also the case with the communication trench, running over the top of The Bluff, known as Bluff Wynd; and, as a consequence, men took to leaving the trench in daylight and walking across the open. This practice led to an increase in the enemy's sniping, which at once became very troublesome. In passing along the trenches, men frequently slipped off the duckboards into the mud, and had to be dug out. On several occasions when a man could not be released by other methods it became necessary to untie the fastenings of his gum boots, reaching to his thigh, and pull him out, leaving the boots in the mud.

The weather at this time was incredibly bad, and added to the misery the men had to endure. The effect of three or four hours' rain on the defences was very serious, the mud from the side of The Bluff slipping oozily into the trenches and causing dug-outs to collapse. On one occasion, the collapse of a dug-out had a serious consequence, the roof in its fall injuring C.S.M. Drage, whom, with his familiar 'canary-perches,' the Battalion was truly sorry to lose. Pear Tree Walk, a strongly revetted communication trench, closed in because the mud gave way at the base of the line of stakes, holding the revetment back, although they had been driven in a distance of nearly fifteen feet from its face. By the expenditure of much effort Bluff Wynd was at length completely cleared, and so strongly revetted that the encroachment of the mud was stayed. Materials for improving the trenches were scarce, and could not be procured officially; so, by the aid of the light railway that ran from Brigade Headquarters to the end of Pear Tree Walk, a party of stalwarts, under Capt. Kellett, went out on three successive nights and raided other units' dumps, with such success that the Battalion's dump was increased by fifteen truck loads of timber, corrugated iron, and sand-bags.

The salubrity of The Bluff was not enhanced by the fact that the enemy were mining towards it—indeed, there was a German gallery under the left company's headquarters. To counter this, the Royal Engineers had dug defensive mines at varying depths, and these were apparently most effective. Heavy 'Minnies'[1] were also used largely by the enemy, but bad shooting rendered them quite harmless.

One interesting event occurred during this period: on the 27th October H.M. The King visited Reninghelst, and twenty men of the 1/2nd Londons attended a ceremonial parade in connexion with his visit.

In October no officers joined the Battalion. In the first week of November 2nd Lieuts. A. Whitting, W. Ursell, and H. E. Gretton arrived, bringing with them a draft of sixty-one men. This draft was very welcome to the Battalion, whose numbers were being rapidly depleted by casualties

---

[1] *I.e., Minenwerfer,* or mine-thrower, a type of trench mortar.

and by sickness due to the exceptional exposure. It should be noted that during some part of this period Major Stacey, in the absence of Lieut.-Col. Attenborough in hospital and on leave, commanded the Battalion, and that Capt. Long, whose health had suffered from the effects of the bad weather, exchanged duties with Capt. Kellett and became adjutant, Capt. Kellett assuming command of 'D' Company.

For twenty-six mortal days, from the 26th October to 21st November, the Battalion held The Bluff. It had been officially told by the Brigadier that it would not be relieved until the trenches had been improved, and, despite bodily misery, the natural difficulties, and the lack of adequate material, it faithfully carried out its task. This period, though without all the glamour of the subsequent fighting in which it took part, reflects great credit on the Battalion; and its defence and consolidation of The Bluff are among its most notable achievements.

IV. Last Days with the 17th Brigade

It was with feelings of very real gratitude and relief that on the 21st November the 1/2nd Londons handed over their front line to the 10th Royal Welch Fusiliers and their support trenches to the 4th Gordon Highlanders. The long period on The Bluff, in the defence of which the Battalion had lost 10 killed and 25, including Sergt. R. V. Thomas, wounded, had imposed a great strain on the health and fighting capacity of the men; and proper rest was essential if the Battalion was to be rendered fit to take its place in the line again in the near future. It should be remembered that the Battalion had had no proper 'rest' since it joined the 17th Brigade in the early months of the year and consequently no opportunity for constructive training in the arts of modern warfare that was daily becoming more complicated.

Such a rest as would enable it not only to recoup its strength, but also to increase its efficiency was at last granted to the Battalion and, in fact, to the whole Brigade. On the afternoon of the 22nd November, the 1/2nd Londons joined the rest of the Brigade in column of route and marched to Eecke, through a dense fog and on roads rendered glassy by frost. Owing to the state of the roads, the transport could not keep up, and arrived many hours after the infantry. After a day's rest at Eecke, the Brigade continued its march through Arneke and Eperlecques, spending a night at each, and finally, on the fifth day, reached the scattered village of Recques, where, except the 1/2nd London's Headquarters, who were lucky enough to be allotted the *Chateau de Cossol,* the units were billeted chiefly in barns and stables. These billets contained so much straw that fires had to be prohibited, and considerable hardship thereby imposed on the men in the wet and bitterly cold weather. The local *estaminets* filled the want of warmth and light until their hours of opening were restricted by a Corps order.

A week or so later bales of clean clothing and new uniforms arrived. Hot baths had been provided on arrival; so the men were now able to get rid of the last trace of their long sojourn in the trenches. Representations were made to the authorities that, whereas the New Armies were being granted leave after six months' service overseas, the majority of the 1/2nd Londons had had no leave after sixteen months' service. As a result of these representations, leave was granted forthwith to all who had not been home for a year or more.

Training was at once begun in earnest. Each day was devoted to inspections, drill, musketry, attack practice, or route-marches; and machine gunners, signallers, snipers, and bombers, received special instruction. The men who were such experts with the pick and shovel were not allowed to forget this branch of their work; the trenches over which the attacks were practised had first to be dug, and the opportunity was taken of imparting instructions even in an art in which, it might be imagined, the men were already past-masters.

Christmas Day came and was celebrated in magnificent fashion. Grants were made from regimental funds to enable company commanders to supplement the usual rations. Pork was the special meat selected. One Christmas pudding per man was generously supplied by *The Daily Express;* and so traditional fare was not lacking. The dinner was actually in progress when orders were received for 'A' Company to proceed, before daybreak, to take over various 'H.Q.' duties in the forward areas. After all arrangements had been made for its departure, these orders were fortunately cancelled; and 'A' Company renewed its repast even more vigorously than before.

Officer reinforcements during December included Lieut. T. G. McCarthy and 2nd Lieut. W. J. Keene. During this month the Rev. R. M. B. Morgan was attached for duty as chaplain; he was the first chaplain to be appointed to the Battalion since it left England in 1914. The only casualties were Lieut. L. W. Bindon and one man, who were accidentally wounded on the 31st as the result of the explosion of a detonator during a bombing demonstration.

The period of rest was now drawing to a close; on 1st January 1916,

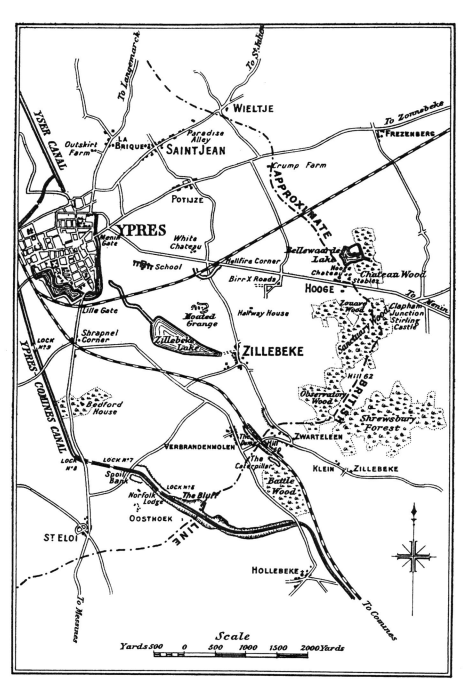

THE YPRES SALIENT, JUNE 1915 TO JANUARY 1916.

'D' Company (Capt. Kellett) proceeded to the big dump at Audruicq to assist in railway construction; and on the 5th a party of 50 men, under 2nd Lieut. H. E. Gretton, was dispatched to Ypres for mining duties in the Salient. This party was detached from the Battalion until the end of the month and was employed most of the time in the Hooge district.

The Battalion left Recques on the 7th January for the Hop Factory at Poperinghe; thence Headquarters, 'B' and 'D' Companies moved into a camp on the Ouderdom-Vlamertinghe road, while 'A' and 'C' Companies proceeded to billets in the cellars of a convent close to the Infantry Barracks at Ypres. The two last-named companies were in brigade reserve, working nightly at Hooge until the 19th, when they were relieved by 'B' and 'D.'

The New Year's Honours List included the following awards to the 2nd London Regiment:

D.S.O.: Major G. A. Stacey.
M.C.: Capt. L. H. R. Inglis.
D.C.M.: C.S.M.'s W. J. Husband, D. Williams, Sergts. A. E. Agutter, F. W. Mould.

Major Stacey was also honoured by the French authorities, who awarded him the Légion d'Honneur.

The following officers joined the Battalion during January:

Lieut. P. C. Taylor, 2nd Lieuts. H. F. Blows, R. L. Hulme, and K. M. A. Fradd.

The 26th January was a red-letter day in the annals of the 1/2nd Londons; thereon was received a secret communication from the V. Corps to the effect that the formation of another London Division[1] in France had been sanctioned, and that the 1/2nd Londons were to be transferred to it forthwith. The first-line battalions of the London Regiment that were still serving in the ranks of Regular brigades felt, not unnaturally, that some such move as this was long overdue. These battalions included in their number some of the first Territorial units to be sent to the front; and it was reasonable to suppose that they had been selected for this service because they were considered fit to take their places alongside Regular units in the field. The need for reinforcing the Regular brigades by attaching Territorial units no longer existed, nor the need for testing Territorial battalions in battle by so attaching them. Moreover, nearly a year had elapsed since the first Territorial division had arrived in France as a complete formation, and even New

---

[1] The 2nd London Division (47th Division) went to France as a unit in March 1915.

Army divisions had come out and been used in battle as complete formations. It will be readily understood, therefore, with what satisfaction this news was received; the 1/2nd Londons, though naturally sorry to leave their old friends of the 17th Brigade, were glad to be restored to a Territorial division. The new division was called the 56th (1st London) Division, and, as will be herein related, was destined to take part in many of the subsequent great battles of the war.

Preparations were made for immediate departure to the place of concentration of the new division, and the two companies in Ypres were relieved on the 26th by the 8th Queen's. In the midst of this activity, Major P. A. E. Wood left on the 7th February to become second-in-command of the 13th Middlesex. Although he had only been with the 1/2nd Londons for about four months, he had, by his straightforward manner, endeared himself to all ranks. It is with regret that his death in England in September 1924 is here recorded.

Having said farewell to the G.O.C. 6th Division, and to the Brigadier, the Battalion entrained at Poperinghe on the 9th February, and left Belgium[1] for Pont Remy.

[1] The Regiment possesses a very interesting souvenir of the long stay that its first-line battalion made at Ypres, in one of the station signboards. This board, having on one side the word 'Ypres' and on the other its Flemish equivalent, 'Yper,' was taken from the station in the autumn of 1915 and was brought to England, not without some difficulty, as may well be imagined, by Major P. A. E. Wood. After the War, in order that the Regiment's possession of this trophy might not be disputed, Major Wood wrote to the Burgomaster of Ypres for permission to retain the board, and he received the following reply :

> STAD YPER,
> VILLE D'YPRES.
> *September 26, 1922.*
>
> DEAR SIR,
> In reference to your letter of 18th of the month, I have the honour to let you know that you may keep as souvenirs of war the objects you have in your possession.
> Cordial thanks for your best wishes expressed in your letter.
> Best regards,
> (*Sd.*) N. COLDEST,
> *Burgomaster of Ypres.*

CHAPTER V

THE 2/2ND LONDONS IN MALTA AND GALLIPOLI

I

ARRIVED at Valletta on 31st December 1914, the 2/2nd Londons did not disembark at once, but remained on board the *Neuralia* for two days, during which they were welcomed by Br.-General the Earl of Lucan and by a number of officers of the 1/2nd Londons who came on board the *Neuralia* for the purpose.

On 2nd January 1915 the Battalion disembarked and marched to St. Andrews Barracks, where it relieved the 1/1st Londons, the latter battalion moving off to new quarters in Floriana Barracks. At St. Andrews, which lies close to the eastern shores of the island some two miles, as the crow flies, north of Valletta, the Battalion was joined by Capt. L. Beck and between 60 and 70 non-commissioned officers and men of the 1/2nd Londons who were not medically fit enough for service in France. This reinforcement brought the strength of the Battalion practically to war establishment.

On the departure from Malta of the 1st London Infantry Brigade on this day, the 2/1st London Infantry Brigade took over its duties, and assumed responsibility for the defence of the Fortress. The latter brigade began its career in the island with one great advantage over its predecessor in that it had not so many guards to find in the initial stages and was thus able to start training at once. One duty of this nature fell to the lot of the 2/2nd Londons, and this, the guard at the Ninth Milestone, was an important one. On the north-east coast of the island lies St. Paul's Bay, which, with its low shores and protected anchorage, offers a very easy landing place for hostile raiding troops. Accordingly, at the Ninth Milestone, four miles from St. Andrews Barracks and about midway between St. Paul's Bay and Salina Bay, a camp was established, and was garrisoned by one company of infantry for the protection of this section of open coast. Except for this duty, the Battalion was free to concentrate on training; and, when spring approached, considerable progress towards efficiency had been made. At a somewhat later date, a system of coastal patrols was introduced as the result of information regarding the activity of enemy submarines; but, although these patrols had to be maintained by the Battalion, they did not largely interfere with its training programme. One other item of interest should be recorded concerning these early days in the island: from the 15th January to 2nd March the whole Battalion was confined to barracks owing to an outbreak of mumps; it is curious how many 2/2nd Londoners, despite this restriction, managed to get to Valletta under one pretext or another.

Hitherto the Battalion had consisted of eight companies, but on 23rd January it was reorganized, in common with all Territorial battalions, into four companies, in order to come into line with the organization of the Regular Army.

This reorganization was accomplished as follows:

> NEW 'A' COMPANY—(Old 'A' and 'H' Companies).
> Capt. M. C. V. Hurst, in command.
> Lieut. O. Shimwell, second-in-command.
> NEW 'B' COMPANY—(Old 'B' and 'G' Companies).
> Major W. Whitaker Thompson, in command.
> Lieut. G. N. Hunter, second-in-command.
> NEW 'C' COMPANY—(Old 'C' and 'F' Companies).
> Capt. J. W. Ginsbury, in command.
> Lieut. P. C. Burnett, second-in-command.
> NEW 'D' COMPANY—(Old 'D' and 'E' Companies).
> Capt. A. E. Rees, in command.
> Lieut. D. Dutfield, second-in-command.

On the day following this reorganization, a machine-gun section was formed under the command of Lieut. H. S. Elton. This section took over the two Vickers-Maxims left behind by the 1/2nd Londons, and began its new training forthwith. During this period the training of the transport section was also taken in hand, the personnel being sent to Musta Fort, where it underwent an advanced course in Army Service Corps duties.

The 10th February was celebrated as a festival on the island, it being the anniversary of St. Paul's shipwreck, and the customary religious processions were held. On the following day, the 2/1st Londons, who, when the rest of the 2/1st London Brigade was sent overseas, had been left in England, arrived to relieve their first-line battalion. The latter had remained in the island on the departure of the 1/1st London Brigade to France, and now sailed for England, whence, after a short period for refitting, it proceeded to France. The 2/1st London Brigade was once more complete with its original units, but was not long to remain so, for on the 8th April the 2/3rd Londons left Malta for Egypt. In the meanwhile the 2/4th Londons, who had been in occupation of St. George's Barracks, succeeded the 1/1st Londons in Floriana, and took over the 'public duties,' including the Main Guard at Valletta.

On 12th February, much to everyone's regret, Sir Leslie Rundle, G.C.B., G.C.V.O., K.C.M.G., D.S.O., having completed his tour of duty as Governor, left for England. He was succeeded by Field-Marshal Lord Methuen, G.C.B., G.C.V.O., C.M.G., who arrived on the 14th. The new Governor at once interested himself in the training of his Territorial garrison; he was a keen critic of the work done, but was unstinted in his praise of the keenness displayed by all ranks and of the progress towards efficiency that was daily being made.

During March the 2/2nd Londons received the following officer reinforcements:

> 2nd Lieuts. D. F. Upton, J. S. Grainger, C. L. Stirling, D. L. Child, H. F. Phillips, A. H. Lewis, and A. M. Thorman.

At this period the position of Malta, in relation to the Great War, underwent a considerable change as the result of two events of first-rate importance. The first of these, the opening on 25th April of the combined naval and military operations against the Dardanelles, made the security of Malta, the base of our Mediterranean Fleet, of vital importance, and this security was practically ensured by the second event, the declaration of war by Italy against Austria on 22nd May. Her entry into the war on the side of the Allies removed the menace of Italy as a possible aggressor against Malta, and the accession to the Allies of her fleet rendered any successful attack on the island by enemy forces highly improbable. Malta, therefore, relieved of all anxiety on the score of security, ceased to be of such primary importance as a fortress, and henceforward became a base for the Gallipoli operations and an evacuating station for casualties. The responsibilities of the garrison were, in a measure, decreased; but the amount of additional work thrown on it was quite extraordinary; and the loading of transport with stores and the unloading of hospital ships became a daily task. The abnormal number of wounded strained the capacity of the island to its utmost. At an early date the regular accommodation proved insufficient; and thus, in order to relieve the congestion, it was necessary for the troops of the garrison to vacate their barracks. The 2/2nd Londons went under canvas in a camp at no great distance from St. Andrews on the road to St. Paul's Bay. Later, when this camp was also wanted by the hospital authorities for convalescents, the Battalion moved to a very unhealthy camp at the Porte des Bombes, situated just outside the fortifications of Valletta and close to Floriana. This move was followed by an increase in the Battalion's duties; for, apart from the various guards, the Battalion had to find a number of military piquets in Valletta and elsewhere for the maintenance of discipline among the large numbers of troops who were now, for various reasons, stationed in the island.

Up to this time the Battalion's experiences in Malta were much the same as those of its predecessor. Elementary training gave place to such field training as the limitations of ground would allow. Trench digging was practised on the Marsa and also on the only other piece of suitable ground, in the neighbourhood of Ghain Tuffieha; and the musketry course was fired on the Pembroke Ranges. Although training and the multifarious garrison duties did not leave much time for anything else, the men's exiguous leisure was occupied in football, swimming, and boating, the two latter being recreations to which the island with its long coast line and excellent harbours admirably lent itself. In April the Malta Garrison played a memorable 'rugger' match against the Fleet, on the Marsa; and of this match, which illustrates the general fitness of the men at this time, Capt. Bateman, M.C., R.A., then serving in the ranks of 'B' Company, writes: 'In the morning the Battalion did a route-march (about five hours) in full kit, and personally I felt pretty tired when we got back. But dinner worked wonders, and we not only played the Navy that same afternoon, but beat them by a dropped goal to a penalty goal. Half the Garrison side came from the 2/2nd Londons and included Sergt. Tombs, Corpl. Calderbank, Sergt. Richardson, Sergt. Lees, Pte. Facer, and myself.' The winning goal was dropped by Sergt. Richardson. It will be noticed that the Marsa loomed as largely on the horizon of the 2/2nd Londons as on that of the 1/2nds, not only as a sports ground, but also as a suitable area on which training could be carried out uninterruptedly.

The exigencies of the service did not permit of the officers entering largely into the social life of the island, such as it was, although several of them had been accompanied by their wives, but they frequented the Club and patronized the occasional performances at the Opera just as their brother-officers of the 1/2nd Londons had done. One social event that occurred during the Battalion's stay in Malta deserves to be chronicled: this was the marriage of 2nd Lieut. A. S. Rawle, whose bride came from England especially for the ceremony.

The Battalion had arrived in Malta in mid-winter, a very pleasant season in the island, when the climate is mild and equable, and when there is plenty of vegetation to please the eye. As summer approached, the heat increased, the green disappeared, and the island began to take on the drab, uniform appearance of barren rock. Khaki 'drill' clothing was issued in the middle of February and was taken into use early in the following month. The summer, indeed, was far from pleasant; the heat was very great; and the scirocco, which had proved somewhat trying to the 1/2nd Londons, now inflicted itself on their successors. The effects of the scirocco, whose enervating tendencies have been referred to in an earlier chapter, on the natives were very noticeable; it is therefore much to the credit of the Londoners that they carried on, and that some of their longest marches and heaviest fatigues were done, while this wind was blowing. Throughout the summer the Battalion continued its training, and, when that was done, spent the rest of the long days on fatigue duties in the docks, loading stores and unloading wounded. The work was arduous and trying, and seemed interminable. Apart from these last few weeks, however, the Battalion had as pleasant and as happy a stay in Malta as the 1/2nd Londons, and it eventually left the island with memories of halcyon days in kindly surroundings.

The following officer reinforcements joined the Battalion:

In April.—Capt. A. P. Stockings.
In May.—Lieut. E. P. Carey, who came to relieve Lieut. E. Coplans as Medical Officer.
In June.—Capt. H. M. Thin.

The following officers were invalided home: In May, Capt. J. W. Ginsbury and 2nd Lieut. C. L. Stirling; and in June, Capt. P. C. Burnett. In addition to these losses, Capt. A. E. Rees proceeded to England on 14th June for special employment on recruiting duties, and his brother transferred to the Army Ordnance Corps. The last named was succeeded as adjutant by Lieut. S. Jones, who was promoted Captain.

The Battalion was sorry to part with Lieut. Coplans, who was a great favourite with all ranks. He was the editor of the Battalion magazine, entitled *The Garrison Goat*. This was a fortnightly production, and proved a great success, its circulation being in the neighbourhood of 5,000. A profit of about £10 was realized on each issue, and was handed to the Red Cross Society. Lieut. Coplans' assistants were Corpl. Leslie Coulson (killed in France in 1917) and Pte. C. B. Pulteney. Corpl. Coulson was assistant editor of *The Morning Post;* and his poems in *The Garrison Goat* attracted considerable attention. After his death they were published in book form, receiving the highest praise from all the leading critics. Pte. C. B. Pulteney, who had never set pen to paper before he wrote for the magazine, became, on his return to England, the creator of ' Mrs. 'Arris,' a popular feature of *The Sunday Herald.*

The early days of August saw an important change in the personnel of the 2/2nd Londons Headquarters, Colonel Carlebach leaving for England to take command of the 100th Provisional Battalion. Colonel Carlebach had worked very hard for the Battalion; he had guided it through its formation and through the difficulties of its early days; and under his command it had attained a high standard of efficiency. It is satisfactory to record that he was subsequently made a C.M.G. He was succeeded in the command of the 2/2nd Londons by Major A. G. Houlder, who was promoted Lieut.-Colonel, Major Whitaker Thompson becoming his second-in-command.

As the summer advanced, the likelihood that the Battalion would be taken for more active service before the expiration of many weeks became a certainty. Indeed, it was a matter of constant speculation why the Battalion had not been relieved earlier in view of the position of affairs on the Gallipoli Peninsula. Towards the middle of August, news of an early move came to hand; and on the 14th H.E. The Governor issued the following farewell Fortress Order :

> It is a pleasure to His Excellency to say with truth that it has been a source of satisfaction to him to have had the four Territorial Battalions of the City of London Regiment under his command. Their conduct has been excellent under trying conditions lately, on account of the heavy and unceasing fatigue work they have had to perform. Their appearance in Valletta, the smart way in which the men salute, the alacrity of the Main Guards in turning out, all show the efficiency of the Battalions. His Excellency wishes Officers, Non-Commissioned Officers and Men ' God speed,' and if from Egypt they go to the front, he looks to them with confidence to uphold the high reputation of the City of London Regiment.

Lord Methuen inspected the 2/2nd Londons on 24th August; and on the night of the 26th the Battalion, embarking on H.T. *Ivernia,* sailed for Egypt. On its departure from Malta, the 2/2nd Londons left a few non-commissioned officers and men behind, and among the number were R.S.M. Pridmore and C.S.M. T. Webley, both of whom had played a notable part in the training of the Battalion. R.S.M. Pridmore was succeeded by R.S.M. Hennessey.

The 2/2nd Londons in Malta and Gallipoli

On proceeding to Egypt, the Headquarters of the Battalion and the Company Commanders were as follows:

> Lieut.-Col. A. G. Houlder, in command.
> Major W. Whitaker Thompson, second-in-command.
> Capt. S. Jones, Adjutant.
> Lieut. W. R. Rawle, Transport Officer.
> Lieut. H. S. Elton, Machine-Gun Officer.
> Lieut. G. J. Bradley, Quartermaster.
> Lieut. E. P. Carey, Medical Officer.
> Capt. O. Shimwell, commanding 'A' Company.
> Capt. H. M. Thin, commanding 'B' Company.
> Capt. G. N. Hunter, commanding 'C' Company.
> Capt. D. Dutfield, commanding 'D' Company.

II

The 2/2nd Londons reached Alexandria late on the 30th August, and, disembarking at 2.45 next morning, proceeded at once by train to Cairo, where they were accommodated in Abbassiah Camp.

The journey to Cairo was a very pleasant experience. After the long summer months in Malta when nothing was to be seen but dusty and barren rock, the refreshing green country through which the Battalion now passed, mile after mile, was a delightful and welcome change. The ground, fertilized by the rich slime brought down by the Nile whenever it overflowed its banks, was highly cultivated; and on every side were crops of maize, cotton, and sugar-cane. Throughout the journey, the Battalion had frequent glimpses of Eastern life and cultivation; the natives in multi-coloured garments, the strings of laden camels, the mud villages, while groups of date-palms completed the picture.

Cairo is a fine city, and the Battalion thoroughly enjoyed its short stay there. The Pyramids lie at no great distance across the Nile, access to them being by a tram-ride of about three-quarters of an hour through delightful avenues of trees, and both officers and men took the opportunity of visiting them. The Battalion remained in Cairo for a month, completing its training and refitting. Service dress was here reissued, and the 'drill' suits returned to store.

On 4th October the 2/2nd Londons were inspected by the Commander-in-Chief, Lieut.-General Sir J. G. Maxwell, G.C.B., K.C.M.G., C.V.O., D.S.O., and on the following day embarked on H.T. *Simla* for the island of Lemnos, *en route* for Gallipoli. Lemnos was reached on the 8th, the *Simla,* without lights, approaching the island in a raging thunderstorm. For four days after its arrival the Battalion remained on board in Mudros harbour, and on the 13th October was transhipped to the H.T. *Sarnia* for the last stage of its journey to the Peninsula, made famous by British heroism and sacrifice. On the voyage from Egypt, the men, who were now in service dress, continued to wear their sun-helmets; on being transhipped to the *Sarnia,* they were ordered to discard them by the simple process of throwing them overboard. This was gleefully done; and the long line of inverted helmets, bobbing up and down in the water and looking like colossal limpet shells, made an amusing spectacle, which every member of the Battalion whom the writer has consulted clearly remembers—an example of the way memory stores up the more useless lumber, and discards pieces of priceless value.

The Battalion landed at Cape Helles at 9 p.m. the same night and bivouacked behind the headquarters of the Royal Naval Division, to which it was now attached. This division, together with the 42nd (South Lancashire) and 52nd (Lowland) Territorial Divisions, formed part of the VIII. Corps (Lieut.-General Sir Francis Davies, K.C.B.) and consisted of the following infantry units:

ROYAL NAVAL DIVISION
Major-General A. Paris, C.B.

1ST BRIGADE—Br.-General David Mercer, C.B.
'Hawke' Battalion.
'Drake' Battalion.
'Hood' Battalion.
'Nelson' Battalion.
2/4th London Regiment.

2ND BRIGADE—Br.-General C. N. Trotman, C.B.
1st Royal Marine Light Infantry.
2nd Royal Marine Light Infantry.
'Anson' Battalion.
'Howe' Battalion.
2/2nd London Regiment.

It is not within the scope of this history to discuss the merits and demerits of the decision to force the Dardanelles. Had the plan succeeded, it is problematical whether the results would have been as far-reaching as its authors hoped; but there is little doubt that, if these results had been achieved, the war would have ended sooner, and the Dardanelles campaign would have been universally acclaimed as a master-stroke of strategy.

The forcing of the Dardanelles was first attempted by naval action alone.

This failed, and thereafter a joint naval and military enterprise was deter-mined upon. A large expeditionary force was assembled; and General Sir Ian Hamilton, G.C.B., was placed in command. A final attack by the war-ships was made on the 18th March, the concluding ſtages of which were viewed by General Sir Ian Hamilton himself on his arrival from England, and, as a result of its failure, the naval attack was abandoned in favour of a general assault by the Army on the Gallipoli Peninsula. The occupation of this Peninsula, which bounds the Dardanelles on the weſtern side, and the capture of the forts commanding the passage would enable the Fleet to pass with little difficulty into the Sea of Marmora.

The Gallipoli Peninsula is a long and narrow tongue of land that ſtretches out in a south-weſterly direction into the Ægean Sea. From the iſthmus of Bulair, where it joins the mainland of Turkey, to Cape Helles, its southernmoſt extremity, the length of the Peninsula is about fifty-two miles, while its width does not at any point exceed twelve miles. The con-figuration of the ground is rugged in the extreme, a mass of hills of varying heights being scored by deep gullies and ravines. In 1915 there was little cultivation except in a few of the valleys, although an occasional olive or cypress grove grew near one of the scattered villages. Roads were few; and water was not very plentiful. The conqueſt of the Peninsula presented a difficult problem for an invading force to solve. The hills and gorges of the interior offered plenty of natural defensive positions, and, if held by a deter-mined enemy, would prove very formidable obſtacles. The problem of gaining a foothold on the Peninsula from the sea was equally difficult. At Bulair the narrow iſthmus was protected by highly fortified lines; and the northern coaſt as far as Cape Suvla was so precipitous as to render a military landing entirely out of the queſtion. The southern part, being more accessible from the sea, alone offered any chance to an invading force; but even at Cape Helles the cliffs rose at once from the sandy beach to a height of 40 feet, and the ground in this area was dominated by several prominent features. The firſt of these was Achi Baba, some four miles from Helles, which rose to a height of 700 feet and completely overlooked the extreme end of the Peninsula. Six miles behind and to the north-eaſt of Achi Baba, lay the Kilid Bahr Plateau, protecting the Narrows from an attack from the northern coaſt, while to the north-weſt of Kilid Bahr and overlooking Suvla Bay, ſtood the broad and precipitous knoll of Sari Bair, close upon 1,000 feet high, cleft by ravines and covered with dense thickets.

Such, briefly, was the unpromising country againſt which a great British Expeditionary Force was to batter itself to pieces, in vain.

The decision to attack Gallipoli having been taken, Sir Ian Hamilton came to the conclusion that a hasty and precipitate descent on the Peninsula would involve too many risks. He therefore decided that the operations must be properly organized, that the southern end of the Peninsula alone was open to attack, and that, in face of the inherent difficulties, success could only be achieved by a tactical surprise, by landing the largest possible force simultaneously at several points.

At daybreak on the 25th April 1915, in face of a galling fire from the Turkish forts and batteries, and despite the almost superhuman difficulties, landings were effected at Cape Helles and at Anzac; and the glorious deeds done that day are now matters of history of which we may well be proud. Thereafter the fighting was fierce and continuous; at first the Allies' hold on the Peninsula was very precarious, but gradually their troops made themselves secure and by the end of the month were definitely established.

Turkish reinforcements were now hurrying to the point of danger; and it was of vital importance that the Allies should exploit their initial success before these reinforcements could arrive; but the enemy's forces already on the scene were so well disposed and his defences so strong that little progress could be made. Nevertheless if the Allies could not themselves advance, they could not be dislodged from the ground they had won, though the fresh Turkish troops, as they came up, made repeated and desperate attempts to drive them into the sea. On the 6th May there was begun another great battle, in which no better success rewarded the efforts of the British and their French allies. At its conclusion, the conditions of trench warfare supervened; and it became obvious that further progress could only be made after elaborate preparation. Accordingly, on 4th June, a general attack was made on the whole of the Helles front in a final attempt to capture the village of Krithia and the slopes of Achi Baba; the battle was costly; and only two or three hundred yards of ground were gained. It was followed by another attack on the left by the French on the 21st June, and by yet another on the right by the British a week later. In each of these, substantial advances were made; but these gains were discounted by the disquieting fact that the fighting in this theatre had now assumed a similar character to that on the Western Front, and that a deadlock appeared inevitable.

It was now decided that additional troops must be allotted to the Gallipoli Army if final success was to be achieved; and, in accordance with this decision, three New Army and three Territorial divisions were concentrated in the area by the beginning of July. As it was quite clear that frontal attacks at Helles were unproductive of any definite result, Sir Ian Hamilton

GALLIPOLI—GULLY RAVINE, CAPE HELLES.

GALLIPOLI—V BEACH, CAPE HELLES.

GALLIPOLI—INNISKILLING INCH, CAPE HELLES.
Overlooking Boyd's Crater.

decided to employ his fresh troops in an endeavour to cut off the main Turkish force by an attack across the Peninsula from Anzac, at the same time supporting this operation by a landing at Suvla Bay and by a vigorous holding attack at Helles.

On the afternoon of the 6th Auguft, the great battle began with the attack at Helles. Simultaneously an attack was made on the right of the Anzac position. This was subsidiary to the main attack, which was launched the same night. The main attack, delivered on the left of Anzac, had for its firft objective the heights of Sari Bair, the key to the Narrows; and such good progress was made that, had the anticipated support been forthcoming from the force landed at Suvla Bay, a decisive success might have been achieved. The landing at Suvla was satisfactorily made on the 8th Auguft and came as a complete surprise to the enemy; but for a variety of reasons the initial success was not immediately followed up; the enemy was reinforced; and the chance of victory was finally snatched from our grasp. With a bitterness, in the circumftances quite comprehensible, the battle is thus summed up by Mr. Winfton Churchill: 'The long and varied annals of the British Army contain no more heart-breaking episode than the Battle of Suvla Bay. The greatness of the prize in view, the narrowness by which it was missed, the extremes of valiant skill and of incompetence, of effort and inertia, which were equally presented, the malevolent fortune which played about the field, are features not easily to be matched in our hiftory.'[1]

After the ill success of this great battle, no further operations were attempted; and the position on the Peninsula became ftabilized. The general situation in the Eaftern theatre, however, was fteadily growing worse; for the defeat of the Russians had released large numbers of the enemy's troops, while the activity of the enemy submarines in the Ægean Sea made the task of supplying our Army one of increasing difficulty. Such, briefly, was the ftate of affairs when the 2/2nd Londons joined the Dardanelles Expedition in October 1915.

For the firft few days after their arrival, the 2/2nd Londons remained bivouacked behind the headquarters of the Royal Naval Division; and during this period parties of officers and non-commissioned officers visited the trenches for inftruction, being attached to units of the 2nd Brigade, which was in the line at the time. While in these bivouacs, the Battalion had its baptism of fire, the enemy sending over a number of shells about breakfaft time on the morning following its arrival; and, as Capt. Bateman

---

[1] *The World Crisis*, 1915. Rt. Hon. Winfton Churchill, C.H.

remarks, 'the souvenir hunters got busy ſtraight away.' Nevertheless the rank and file did not have any experience of the trenches until the 17th October, when two companies went into the Eski Lines, a reserve line about 1,500 yards behind the front trenches.

On the Helles front the Allies had reached a line some 1,000 yards short of Krithia village; and here their trench syſtem, running roughly south-eaſt and north-weſt, ſtretched from the Ægean Sea to the Dardanelles. The road from Krithia to Sedd el Bahr, a village close to Cape Helles, divided this trench syſtem into two practically equal sectors, of which that on the right was held by the French and that on the left by the British VIII. Corps. On the French front there was a feature of considerable importance, a deep gorge, known as Kereves Dere, at the bottom of which a ſtream flowed towards the Dardanelles. This gorge cut deeply into the front on the extreme right, and caused the Allies' right flank to be refused.

The front of the VIII. Corps was divided into three sub-sectors, of which the right was held by the 52nd, the centre by the R.N., and the left by the 42nd Divisions, and it was intersected by two deep ravines, running seaward from the slopes of Achi Baba and parallel to the Krithia road; the one near the Ægean Sea was known as Gully Ravine, and the other, on the immediate left of the Krithia road, as Krithia Nullah. Between these ravines there lay a plateau of high ground covered with scrub and gorse and intersected by small water-courses. On this part of the front the British and Turkish trenches were close together, in some places no more than thirty yards apart. Consequently bombing was continuous, and for this purpose the British had pushed forward sapheads from their main defensive line. In the sub-sector of the Royal Naval Division there were three saps of importance, defended by barricades, two, known as Northern and Southern Barricades, being on the left, and one, Worceſter Barricade (only nineteen yards from the enemy), being in the centre.

Unfortunately for the British, the enemy from his position on the slopes of Achi Baba had direct observation over the whole area. No movement above ground was therefore possible during daylight; and very long communication trenches had to be used by the mules conveying the rations and ſtores. These mule trenches, doubled for up and down traffic, began at the creſt of the plateau above the beaches at Cape Helles and ended only within a hundred yards or so of the front line.

On 20th October the 2nd Brigade was relieved by the 1ſt. The 2/2nd Londons handed over the Eski Lines to the 2/4th Londons and moved back to reſt bivouacs, suffering their firſt casualties during the move.

66

While out of the line the Battalion was employed on the construction of new winter quarters. Apart from the inevitable fatigues, which were the same on either front, to be 'at rest' on Gallipoli was far different from being 'at rest' in France; the area of ground held by us on the Peninsula was so small in extent that troops could not be withdrawn from the range of the enemy's guns, and even the beaches were constantly under the fire of heavy batteries on the Asiatic shore. In this connexion, the names of 'Asiatic Annie,' 'Quick Dick' (a gun of the whizz-bang variety), and 'Lingering Louisa,' will recall unpleasant memories. The last named, a howitzer battery on Achi Baba, did much damage and on one occasion hit the Royal Naval Division's canteen.

The Battalion went back into the line on the 27th October; and on this day General Sir C. C. Monro, K.C.B., succeeded General Sir Ian Hamilton in command of the Dardanelles Army. The new Commander-in-Chief's first duty was to report as to the desirability, on military grounds, of evacuating the Peninsula, or, alternatively, to advise what size force would be required to bring the campaign to a successful conclusion. After a reconnaissance of the position he decided in favour of evacuation, and he telegraphed a report to this effect to England. Thereupon Lord Kitchener determined to go out to the Dardanelles and to see for himself the exact position of affairs. He duly arrived on 15th November, and, after careful deliberation, he agreed to the evacuation.

The 2/2nd Londons spent the early part of November either in the line, where the tours of duty were of seven days' duration, or at rest in the bivouac area. Throughout this period the Turks were quiet except for some activity by their artillery. The following officer reinforcements arrived from England on the 5th of the month:

2nd Lieuts. A. J. Whittle, H. F. James, and G. H. Ticehurst.

On the 15th November, the 52nd Division on the right of the Royal Naval Division carried out a highly successful, though limited, offensive against the enemy's trenches on its front; and as the 2/2nd Londons, who were in the line at the time, took some part in the action, it deserves to be recorded. The operation took the form of two separate attacks from Hope Street by units of the 156th Infantry Brigade, that on the right being directed against the enemy's trenches west of the vineyard bordering the Krithia road, about a mile south-west of the village, and that on the left against the trenches just west of the eastern branch of Krithia Nullah.

Careful preparations were made; and at three o'clock in the afternoon three mines were exploded. The infantry rushed forward at once; and within fifteen minutes all objectives had been gained; the captured trenches were barricaded; and bombing stations established in the communication trenches. The 1st Royal Marine Light Infantry and the 2/2nd Londons, on the left of the 156th Brigade, assisted the operation by rifle fire and by vigorous bombing. Machine guns in Munster Terrace and in Fusilier Street, both points from which enfilade fire could be brought to bear on the objective, did good work in preventing the enemy manning his parapets or massing for a counter-attack; and Turks entering the northern end of the vineyard to support their comrades were caught in the fire from the machine guns and dispersed. The 2/2nd Londons' machine-gun section, now consisting of four guns of the old Vickers-Maxim pattern and two somewhat unreliable Nordenfeldts, took an active part in these operations.

Although the ground had been torn up by the explosion of the mines, the captured position was rapidly consolidated; and at 5 p.m. the attacking troops were relieved. The Turks made no immediate counter-attack—and, when they massed opposite the Royal Naval Division, they were quickly dispersed—; but their artillery put down a very heavy barrage causing considerable loss to our troops. From this shelling the 2/2nd Londons sustained a number of casualties, including Capt. Dutfield, who was wounded. He was succeeded in command of 'D' Company by Capt. A. P. Stockings. The enemy heavily counter-attacked on the night of the 16th, but without success; and subsequent attempts to regain the lost ground were equally futile.

At this period, in addition to the casualties caused by the enemy artillery and snipers, the Battalion began to lose men rapidly through sickness. The weather had now broken; and the summer heat was followed by the autumn rains, which had set in with an almost tropical violence. The first downpour was on the 10th November, the Battalion being in the trenches at the time; and a week later there followed a violent thunderstorm, accompanied by torrential rain that lasted for nearly two hours and flooded trenches and mule tracks. On the day after this second storm the Battalion went back to the rest camp; owing to the flooding of the trenches its progress to the rear was very slow and its arrival in camp much delayed. Worse was to come; no sooner had the Battalion arrived than heavy rain began again and flooded the camp. These storms were followed by several days of rain and high wind, and caused not only discomfort but sickness. Indeed, during the last few months on the Peninsula, sickness accounted for far more casualties in the British ranks than the enemy's fire; for proper billets, hot baths, and dry clothes, which were nearly always available in France for troops returned from the trenches, were quite out of the question on Gallipoli owing to the limitations of space. Consequently the men were in no better plight out of the line than in it; and wet bivouacs and wet clothes soon began to tell their tale of sickness.

The Battalion went back into the line on 24th November, and relieved the Drake and Nelson Battalions in the right sub-sector, two companies taking over a part of the front line from Sap D to the right of Sap 26, known as Rue de Paris, a third company being in support in Worcester Flats, and the fourth in reserve in Munster Terrace. This was the 2/2nd Londons' first tour of duty in the trenches as a battalion and not as component parts attached to other units. After its disagreeable change for the worse, the weather had as suddenly improved, and conditions were ideal; but two days later, on 26th November, a storm of unprecedented violence broke over the Peninsula. Torrential rain rapidly flooded the trenches, converting them into foaming water-courses; and their occupants were obliged to seek safety on the parapets where they clung in imminent danger of being swept away. The floods rapidly overspread the country-side; and, in the rest camps, dug-outs and bivouacs became uninhabitable, the troops being forced to spend the night in the open. An extract from a letter[1] of Pte. T. J. Underwood, of the 2/2nd Londons, gives a picture of the horrors of this night. He writes: ' I was just snatching a sleep on a ledge in the support trenches when it started to rain—rain such as I have never seen before. In a minute I was swept off the ledge and lay in a foot of water, the lightning meanwhile, flashing about incessantly, making the intervals of blackness like ink. I began to think that the Turks were letting a dam loose, as the water was steadily rising.'

This storm was but the prelude to a great blizzard, which swept over the Peninsula and caused untold misery and even loss of life. The great blizzard was, as it were, the last straw laid by Nature on the back of this ill-fated expedition. It has been described by many abler pens than the writer's; and no attempt will be made to describe it here except in so far as it affected the Battalion.

During the afternoon of the 27th the wind shifted suddenly to the north. The rain turned to sleet; and a severe frost set in. The cold was intense; and the water froze round the men's feet as they stood in the trenches. The oil solidified in the bolts of rifles and in the mechanism of machine guns. At one time only about thirty rifles in the Battalion could be used; and

[1] Originally published in the *Drapers' Record*.

Capt. Conybeare, Royal Marines, the Brigade Machine-Gun Officer, found that only one gun, a 2/2nd London gun, in charge of L/Corpl. G. E. Griffiths, would fire on the whole Brigade front. This was due to the initiative of 2nd Lieut. Child, now Battalion Machine-Gun Officer, who, after a search that seemed hopeless, found some glycerine, 'oiled' his gun with that, and kept the water from freezing by continuous bursts of fire. On the 28th snow began to fall; and the blizzard continued throughout this day and the next. The men suffered intensely from the extreme cold, and many were only kept alive at all by continuous work on the defences or by means such as Capt. Bateman describes: 'The men's joints were so stiff from the cold that they had to be lifted on to the fire step and lifted off again when their turn of duty was over. Some were so far gone that in order to keep their blood moving they were pushed about from one man to another like human tennis balls, and it was only the rum served in the mornings that kept them alive at all.' Yet, in spite of the efforts of their comrades, many succumbed to the cold.

This three days' blizzard was, undoubtedly, the outstanding event during the 2/2nd Londons' service on the Gallipoli Peninsula. Many members of the Battalion who subsequently served through the rigours of the winter of 1916-17 in France say that they experienced nothing that could be compared, in the slightest degree, with the great blizzard in Gallipoli. The Battalion was in the line the whole time and had to bear its full force, with little or no protection of any kind; yet the spirit of the men throughout remained magnificent. The blizzard wrought great havoc on Gallipoli, in the defences, in the rest-camps, and on the beaches; it caused much suffering and sickness; and it cost the Dardanelles expedition, in all, 6,000 men. It was thus more deadly in its results than some of the battles.

The 2/2nd Londons were relieved on the 1st December by the Drake Battalion and by the 2/4th Londons, and returned to the rest camp. Fortunately the blizzard was followed by a spell of mild weather; and this improvement was reflected in the general health and spirits of the troops. During this period of rest, 'A' and 'C' Companies occupied the new bivouac that had been recently constructed. On 2nd December, Capt. H. M. Thin, together with two other ranks of the Battalion, was called to Malta to give evidence in an espionage case,[1] and the command of 'B' Company devolved upon Lieut. D. Symes. A change in the command of 'A'

[1] In July 1915 a coastal patrol, under Sergt. J. Bateman, had caught two natives in the act of signalling out to sea.

Company also occurred at this time, Lieut. A. S. Rawle succeeding Capt. Shimwell, who had been taken ill and evacuated from the Peninsula. The reduction in the number of officers was made good by the arrival from England of a second draft, consisting of:

2nd Lieuts. A. S. Gillespie, C. A. Stubbs, W. F. Strange, and A. M. Manson.

At this period the Turkish artillery fire increased in severity as the result of the opening of the Danube route to Germany by the entry of Bulgaria into the war, and the consequent arrival of fresh supplies of ammunition; and both on the 8th and the 10th December the beaches were heavily shelled.

The Battalion went back into the line on the 11th December and for the next eighteen days remained in the forward area, moving from sector to sector. The arrival of the 29th Division from Suvla Bay had led to a readjustment of the Helles front, the Royal Naval Division moving to its right and taking over a sector to the right of Achi Baba Nullah, part of which had hitherto been held by the French. The French native troops could no longer endure the rigours of the winter; and the extent of front hitherto held by the French force had, for this reason, to be reduced. As a result of this readjustment, the 2/2nd Londons took over from a Senegalese regiment part of the Tranchée d'Amade, a continuation of the Eski Lines behind the French front; and it is of interest to note that this was the last occasion on which troops were moved by day. The French were still in occupation of the forward zone, and on the 12th exploded a mine under the enemy's trenches. The 2/2nd Londons duly stood to arms in expectation of some liveliness; but nothing happened except an outburst of hostile fire and some movement in the enemy's lines. On the 16th, the Battalion was joined by a draft from the 2/1st Londons from Suvla Bay, and on the night of the 18th it relieved the 2nd Battalion Royal Marine Light Infantry in the Horseshoe sector of the front line, astride the Achi Baba Nullah, from a small nullah on the west of it to the Eglinton Tunnel on the east.

We are now brought to the first stages of that operation whose successful issue bears almost as much testimony to British skill and daring as the original landing—the evacuation of the Gallipoli Peninsula. As will be remembered, the decision to evacuate Gallipoli was confirmed by Lord Kitchener as the result of his visit to the Peninsula in November, and the actual evacuation was fixed for as early a date as possible in order to minimize the risk of its interruption by the unfavourable weather now likely to set in. The scheme for the evacuation, which had been prepared by

Sir William Birdwood,[1] required the completion of this difficult operation in three distinct stages. During the first stage, the winter stores and miscellaneous supplies not required for a long campaign were removed, and during the second everything but a minimum of food and ammunition for the immediate defence of our positions, together with the first drafts of men. The final stage, which at Suvla only took two nights, involved the embarkation of the rear guards and the destruction of all animals, stores, and equipment, that could not be removed.

The deliberate preparations for the evacuation were conducted with extraordinary skill and stealth. The Turks had not the slightest suspicion of what was in progress and were completely deceived. The final evacuation of Suvla and Anzac took place on the 19th December; and to keep the attention of the enemy fully occupied, the 52nd Division attacked on the Helles front. The 2/2nd Londons, who were on the immediate right of the division, supported the attack by rifle and trench-mortar fire and by a vigorous demonstration, and suffered considerable loss from the reply of the Turkish batteries.

After the evacuation of Suvla and Anzac the troops were informed that the Helles position would be retained, and were urged to exert a continuous pressure on the enemy. Schemes were prepared for building dug-outs and for improving the position generally; and the 9th Corps was reported to be relieving the 8th. Behind this screen of false information the preparations for the evacuation of Helles also went steadily forward.

On 21st December, the 2/2nd Londons were relieved by the Lanark and Ayrshire Yeomanry, and, 'sideslipping' to the right, relieved the Nelson Battalion in the Esplanade sector. Very heavy rain fell during the night; and the parapet of the front-line trench, part of the old Turkish defences that had not been kept in too good a state of repair by the French, started to fall in, and only the energetic measures of the Battalion prevented its complete collapse. The Turks on this part of the front were much more daring, engaging in vigorous sniping and bombing; steps were at once taken by the Battalion to re-establish superiority, and this was soon accomplished, though at the cost of some casualties. A marked increase in the activity of the enemy's artillery was also observable at this time, owing to the release of a large number of batteries from the evacuated areas. Indeed, at noon on Christmas Eve, communication trenches in the Battalion's area

---

[1] Sir William Birdwood was now in command of the Dardanelles Army, Sir C. C. Monro, on the formation of the Salonika Army, having been appointed to the supreme command of all Mediterranean forces.

were subjected to a heavy and concentrated bombardment that lasted one hour and was the heaviest so far experienced. This was followed, at 2 p.m., by a bombardment of the front and support lines, the right of the Battalion's sector being completely smashed up. Movements by the enemy in his trenches were observed; and a serious attack seemed imminent. Lieut.-Col. Houlder immediately notified a French ·75 battery in support of the Battalion, and called for retaliation. This battery opened fire without delay on the front, support, and communication trenches, of the Turks and with such effect that no attack developed.

The Battalion spent Christmas Day in the trenches and made the best of its not very comfortable surroundings.

As there were now unmistakable signs that the weather was breaking up, it was decided to postpone the evacuation no longer; and the 8th January was fixed for the final day. Silent periods during which no firing or bombing was allowed were introduced so as to mislead the enemy when the actual evacuation took place. In fulfilment of this plan, the first silent period occurred between 5 and 9 p.m. on Christmas Day; and at its conclusion there was a brisk interchange of rifle fire, and an artillery duel. The 2/2nd Londons were relieved on 26th December and went back to a new bivouac, called Cæsar's Camp. Of this relief Capt. Bateman writes: 'It was a pitiable sight. Most of the men were suffering agonies from trench feet and the remains of frost-bite, and progress towards Cæsar's Camp was so slow that it took hours to get there, although the distance was certainly not more than three miles.'

The method of evacuating Helles differed slightly from that adopted at Suvla and Anzac, the shipment of troops being spread over a longer period. The French Corps, one of the British Divisions, and the remaining Yeomanry, were embarked under cover of darkness, at the very beginning of January; and by the 4th 10,000 British had gone. Headquarters of the 2/2nd Londons and 313 men left on 1st January, arriving at Mudros next day, where they were accommodated in the Anzac Base Details Camp. A second party left on the 3rd January.

In the afternoon of the 8th January the sea became very rough, and the embarkation on the last night was greatly impeded; indeed, for a time it was very doubtful if it would be possible to get the last troops away. Fortunately these fears proved groundless; and at 3.30 a.m. on the 9th January the ill-omened Peninsula had been completely evacuated by the British. The special Embarkation Staff worked tirelessly and skilfully, with the result that not a man was left behind; and all material was removed except some useless guns and a large quantity of stores that had to be destroyed. This seemingly impracticable operation, organized with great skill and carried out with courage and discipline, will rank for all time as one of the finest achievements in naval and military history.

Two parties of 2/2nd Londoners were amongst the last troops to leave the Peninsula. One of these parties had been attached to the Royal Engineers for fatigue work on W Beach, Corpl. Dickens being one of the non-commissioned officers in charge, and was taken off by H.M.S. *Mars*, the last vessel to leave that beach. The other consisted of 2nd Lieut. W. F. Strange, Corpl. Calderbank, Pte. Facer, and one other man, who had been attached to the Dumezyl Battery,[1] under Commander A. Campbell, R.N.D. 2nd Lieut. Strange and his party, together with others of the battery, were employed up to the last minute in connecting up mines composed of large quantities of explosives that could not be removed. The last of the rear guards left the firing line at 11.30; but this party continued its work until midnight and then made for V Beach, where, passing through the battered hulk of the *River Clyde,* it was taken off in a heavy sea by H.M. Destroyer *Grasshopper,* the last vessel to leave the Peninsula.

So ended the ill-fated Dardanelles campaign, undertaken with high hopes but resulting in heavy losses and bitter disappointment. One is forced to the conclusion that, if at the outset a decision had been made to send an army in support of the Fleet, and if only one quarter of the troops finally sent, could have been landed on Gallipoli in January or February 1915, the objects of the expedition would have been achieved before the enemy could organize an adequate defence. When at last Gallipoli was attacked, and an army landed (to quote Mr. Winston Churchill once more), 'conviction, determination, and the will to win, steadfastly maintained by their High Command, had brought victory to the defence in spite of their inferiority in numbers and in resources of all kinds, and the inherent strategic perils of their position. The lack of these qualities on our side at the summit of power had defrauded the attackers of the reward, pregnant in its consequences to the whole world, to which their overwhelming potential strength and resources, their actual numbers and apparatus, their daring, their devotion, and their fearful sacrifices had given them the right.'[2] But, when all is said, the wonder is that success was so nearly attained. In the face of well-

---

[1] A Dumezyl was a type of trench mortar used by the French. It fired a kind of aerial torpedo. This particular battery had been taken over from the French, and was the first of its kind used by the British Army.

[2] *The World Crisis,* 1915. Rt. Hon. Winston Churchill, C.H.

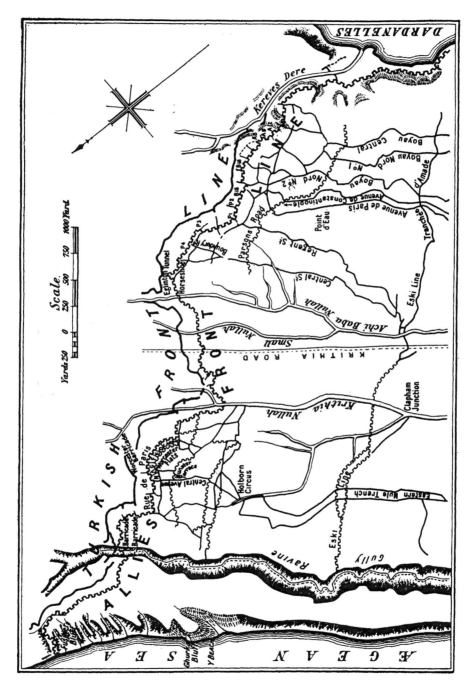

GALLIPOLI—THE HELLES FRONT, OCTOBER 1915 TO JANUARY 1916.

nigh insuperable obstacles, a large force was landed on the Peninsula, was maintained there for close upon nine months, although 800 miles from its base of operations, and finally was brought away with scarcely a casualty, under the eyes of the enemy. Gallipoli will always remain a glorious memory; and the heroism, endurance, and devotion to duty of officers and men, will be written large in the pages of history.

NOTE.—No record was kept of the casualties of the 2/2nd Londons on Gallipoli. As the result of a careful search in Battalion Orders, Part II., it appears that about 50 officers, non-commissioned officers, and men of the Battalion were killed or wounded. In addition to these casualties, a number of men died of exposure or disease; and many more were invalided home from the same causes.

CHAPTER VI

THE 2/2ND LONDONS IN SOUTHERN EGYPT AND FRANCE—DISBANDMENT

I

AFTER the evacuation of Gallipoli the 2/2nd Londons were given a few days' rest in Lemnos to enable them to reorganize. The various parties from the Peninsula had rejoined by the 11th January, when it was found that, as the result of casualties and sickness, the Battalion could muster only 20 officers and 549 other ranks.

The weather was abominable during the Battalion's short stay in the island. Nevertheless, the health of the troops began to improve; all ranks remained cheerful, and contrived to enjoy the hot springs and natural baths that were to be found in the hills at Therma. While in Lemnos the Battalion was temporarily attached to the 29th Division, and its connexion with the Royal Naval Division came to an end. In a letter addressed to Lieut.-Col. Houlder, Major-General Sir Archibald Paris, C.B., G.O.C., Royal Naval Division, expressed his satisfaction with the Battalion's conduct at Gallipoli in the following terms:

> I have been wanting to write you for some days, but have been much occupied, to thank you and your Battalion for all the good work you did when with us on the Peninsula . . . we all much admired the cheerful spirit your men showed under the most trying circumstances.
>
> Wishing you all success and a more prosperous ending to your next campaign.

Embarking on the H.T. *Ionian,* the Battalion left Mudros Harbour on the 18th January, and arrived at Alexandria late on the 21st. It disembarked the following day and entrained for Wardan, a desert camping ground near Cairo. On arrival at this place, it went under canvas in Beni Salama Camp, and was, with the other units of the 1st London Infantry Brigade, temporarily attached to the 53rd Division (Major-General A. G. Dallas, C.B.). At Wardan the time was chiefly spent in company training and daily route-marches into the desert. The Battalion underwent a careful reorganization; and fresh clothing and equipment were issued. Frequent leave to Cairo was granted to all ranks; and in its new and comfortable circumstances the Battalion soon forgot its unpleasant experiences on the Gallipoli Peninsula, while the arrival of large quantities of mails, including Christmas parcels, added to everyone's satisfaction. The strength of the Battalion was still very low; and the arrival on 8th February of a draft, consisting of 2nd Lieuts. J. W. Sanders and L. S. Gray and 42 other ranks, only helped to raise it to just over 600 of all ranks.

This period of rest and reorganization at Wardan came to an end on 16th February, when the Battalion was ordered to join the force formed for the defence of Southern Egypt against the Turks.

The immediate effect of the entry of Turkey into the war on the side of the Central Powers had been to imperil the eastern frontier of Egypt; for the enemy, knowing the importance of the Suez Canal to us, realized that in this direction lay the most profitable line of attack. About a year before the 2/2nd Londons' return to Egypt, a somewhat half-hearted attempt had been made by the Turks against the Canal and had been decisively defeated, while the extensive operations at Gallipoli had had the further effect of drawing off the bulk of the Turkish forces still in this area. As a result of these events, the situation on the eastern frontier once more became normal, and all fear of an invasion from Syria was for the time being allayed. More than six months elapsed before a danger, far more serious than the Turkish attempt to cross the Suez Canal, threatened Egypt. This was the increasingly menacing attitude of the Senussi, a tribe—or rather sect—of warlike Arabs, whose behaviour gave rise to considerable anxiety as to the safety of the western frontier of the country.

After the outbreak of hostilities between Great Britain and Turkey the Senussi had, until 1915, continued their friendly relations with Egypt, and had shown no inclination toward hostile action. But Turkish and German influence was strong; and the advent of Gaafer Pasha, described by Lieut.-General Sir John Maxwell in his dispatches as ' a Germanized Turk of considerable ability,' who brought arms and money, marked a change in their feelings, which became definitely more hostile as the summer of 1915 wore on. Such was the influence of the Senussi, who were the most powerful Mahometan sect in North-East Africa, that a holy war proclaimed by them might have a wide appeal and lead to serious religious and internal disorders in the districts of the Nile Valley and the Delta, where a spirit of unrest was abroad. Care, therefore, was taken by the British to avoid hostilities; but late in the year certain hostile acts on the part of the Senussi led to the withdrawal of some of our frontier posts; and in November the situation became so acute that a final rupture was inevitable.

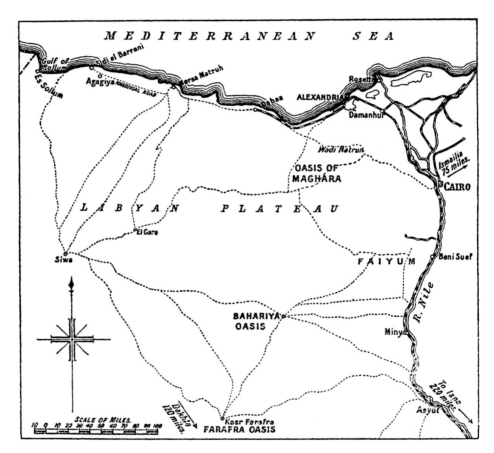

EGYPT—THE WESTERN DESERT.

The long-threatened campaign began; and General Maxwell, determined to show a firm front to the tribesmen, concentrated on 20th November a sufficient force at Mersa Matruh, a town on the shores of the Mediterranean Sea, some 180 miles west of Alexandria, to deal swiftly with the situation,

78

and placed Major-General A. Wallace, C.B., in command. Several vigorous operations on a small scale were successfully undertaken; but the immobility of the force due to lack of camel transport prevented these victories being followed up; and the enemy was encouraged to continue the contest.

On 9th February 1916 information was received that the enemy had concentrated two forces, one at Barrini and the other at Sollum, towns evacuated by the British in the previous November. It was decided that these forces must be attacked forthwith and the towns reoccupied. General Wallace's health having broken down, the chief command in these more ambitious operations was given to Major-General W. E. Peyton, C.B., C.V.O., D.S.O. In the meanwhile, on the 11th February, the enemy occupied Bahariya Oasis—200 miles south-west of Cairo and about 100 miles from the rich and populous districts of Faiyum and Minya—and a fortnight later the more southerly oases of Farafra and Dakhla. To protect the Nile Valley and the southern provinces from this new menace, a force was formed under Major-General J. Adye, C.B., with headquarters at Beni Suef, a small town on the Nile some 175 miles south of Cairo. This force was divided into four groups, the three northern being concentrated at Wadi Natrun, Beni Salama, and Faiyum, under the command of Major-General A. G. Dallas, C.B., and the fourth and southernmost in the provinces of Minya and Asyut, under Br.-General A. Stirling.

'The strategical importance of these oases,' writes Sir John Maxwell in his dispatch, 'is very obvious, but in view of the uncertainty as to what troops would be under my command at any moment, I considered that any enterprise distant from the Nile Valley would be out of place, and I restricted Gen. Adye to purely defensive measures, with, however, instructions to prepare a small mobile column with which he could strike at the enemy, should he approach the cultivation.' In consonance with General Maxwell's instructions, the role of the Southern Force was a purely defensive one, but at the same time of the utmost importance; for the presence of a strong military force was essential to counteract the efforts of the agitators, to quell any disturbances, and to safeguard points of military importance, such as railway bridges and canals; and this was largely the work that fell to its lot.

Such, briefly, was the general situation in Egypt when the 2/2nd Londons joined the Southern Force. Shortly afterwards the outlook materially improved; on the 26th February the enemy was severely defeated by the British under Br.-General H. T. Lukin at the battle of Agagiya; and Gaafer Pasha was captured. The Senussi forces were dispersed, and beat a hasty retreat towards Sollum, which was reoccupied by the British on

14th March. These successes had a marked effect on British prestige throughout Egypt, and a corresponding decline of Turkish influence—a decline that was felt the more because of the repeated failure of the Turks to achieve anything against the defences of the Suez Canal. With the capture of Sollum the campaign virtually came to an end, the small force of Senussi remaining in the field apparently being too disheartened for further offensive action.

On joining the Southern Force, the 2/2nd Londons were split up, Headquarters and 'A' and 'B' Companies going to Beni Suef, and 'C' and 'D' to Beni Mazar, where they became part of the Minya Force. This detachment, under the command of Capt. G. N. Hunter, was temporarily attached to the 2/4th Londons.

At Beni Suef, 'A' and 'B' Companies acted as 'H.Q.' Companies at the headquarters of General Adye, G.O.C. Southern Force, and had a pleasant and comparatively easy time for close upon two months. The work consisted mainly of guards and patrols and the many miscellaneous duties inseparable from the headquarters of a large force. The Sheiks and inhabitants of the neighbouring villages appeared to be very well disposed towards the British, and as a result life was not so complicated as it might have been. 'The Copts,'[1] writes Capt. B. Attenborough, 'welcomed the Tommies at Beni Suef with open arms, and gifts of oranges and cigars were showered on them, as well as of live animals.' In this way the 2/2nd Londons acquired a fine ram which did duty as a mascot during the rest of their stay in Egypt. 'At a Coptic wedding,' continues Capt. Attenborough, 'quite nine-tenths of the guests were supplied by the 2/2nds, one of whom was called on suddenly to take part in the service by reciting a prayer. After the service they were regaled with vast quantities of food and coffee and innumerable cigarettes.' This good feeling between the natives and the British found an outlet in the friendly and frequent rivalry of football matches, in which the former displayed great skill in kicking the ball with their bare toes.

The troops at Beni Mazar, which is on the main railway line 26 miles north of Minya, comprised the following units, at first under the command of Lieut.-Col. V. H. Seyd, of the 2/4th Londons, but later under Colonel Vickers Dunfee, of the same regiment, on his return from England:

2/4th Londons.
Two companies 2/2nd Londons.
One Camel M.G. Section, Lovat's Scouts.

---

[1] Native Egyptian Christians.

GALLIPOLI—FORWARD INCH,
CAPE HELLES.

GALLIPOLI—DUG-OUT AT BARNES,
CAPE HELLES.

GALLIPOLI—FUSILIER BLUFF, CAPE HELLES.

The 2/2nd Londons in Southern Egypt and France

One troop Australian Light Horse.
Detachment of 2/1st Cheshire Field Company, R.E.
No. 2 Armoured Train.

Although no fighting fell to its lot, the duties of the force were highly responsible; for in spite of the defeat of the enemy at Agagiya, the danger was not entirely past; and the continued presence of a large force of Senussi at the Bahariya Oasis constituted a serious menace to the Minya District of the Nile Valley. This district lies on the right bank of the Nile, and is about 65 miles in length, and varies in width from seven to fourteen miles. It is highly cultivated and very fertile, being irrigated by canals from the Nile, and it contains the town of Minya, a place of some size and importance, well worth the attention of bands of marauders.

On 26th February, a detachment of the 2/2nd Londons, consisting of two officers (Lieut. C. R. W. Attenborough and 2nd Lieut. J. S. Grainger) and 54 men, under Capt. G. N. Hunter, left Beni Mazar and proceeded to Nag Hamadi to guard the important bridge over the Nile at that place. This little force was accompanied by an interpreter, and one officer and 10 men of the 2/1st Cheshire Field Company R.E. Capt. Hunter had first to put the place into a state of defence and then to hold it, and he carried out his responsible duty with zeal and efficiency.

At the beginning of March, Sir A. Murray succeeded Sir John Maxwell as Commander-in-Chief in Egypt, and to some extent reorganized the defensive forces in the Nile Valley. As a result of this reorganization the troops at Beni Mazar ceased to belong to the Minya Force, and were transferred to the northern group of the Southern Force (under Major-General Dallas).

As has already been indicated, the troops at Beni Mazar were used for defending and policing the district; and, to fulfil both these duties satisfactorily, it was essential that the force should be always ready to move at a moment's notice. The defensive measures consisted of the detachment at Nag Hamadi, and a guard, of which the infantry, one company strong, was found by the 2/4th Londons, for the bridge at Saqula over one of the irrigation canals, while the policing took the form of demonstration marches through neighbouring villages and runs by the armoured train along the railway. On the 3rd and 8th March experimental mobilizations of the force were carried out. The troops, accompanied by transport, marched to Tambu, where a defensive position was taken up covering the railway crossing; and the experiment provided valuable instruction for all ranks. The detachment of the 2/2nd Londons on these occasions numbered 8 officers and 236 other ranks. The rest of the time was spent in company training and in route-marching, the latter being undertaken to train the men for an advance across the desert to Bahariya, should it be ordered in the near future.

As at Beni Suef, the inhabitants of the neighbourhood of Beni Mazar were very well disposed towards the British troops, and made them frequent presents of eggs, fruit, chickens, turkeys, and other kinds of food, which were very acceptable. Of the attitude of the natives, Lieut. Dearmer wrote at the time:[1]

> At first the 'Gippy' natives watched our movements furtively from behind latticed windows, for they had never seen British soldiers before and trembled at the sight of fixed bayonets. But when they discovered that we were stationed there merely to 'drive away the enemies' they came forth in their thousands and welcomed us as their deliverers.
>
> All this accounts for our present prosperity. Turkeys larger than Cæsar ever knew strut about in our camp waiting for the day of judgment. Chickens in coops (one climbed the Colonel's tent this morning and crowed lustily from the top) and sheep in pens continue to arrive as presents from the admiring populace and from local celebrities. Several hundred eggs arrived yesterday, and to-day an orgy of oranges. The sugar harvest is now in full swing; two or three towering canes may be bought for a penny. The troops buy quite a large quantity of sugar cane, which they chew solemnly or distinguish their tents by making green leafy portals out of the bent cane.
>
> Most of the sugar is packed on camels, and in the evening we often see hundreds of these beasts moving with their long stately strides towards the Nile, to the spot where the sailing boats are laden.

In addition to showing their hospitality and friendliness by gifts of food, the local dignitaries frequently invited the officers to lunch or dine with them; and one such party Lieut. Dearmer describes as follows:[2]

> Our little town boasts two people of supreme importance—the Bey (an Arabic title corresponding to our knighthood) and the

[1] This account appeared in the London Press at the time, and has subsequently been reprinted in the *History of the Old 2/4th (City of London) Battalion, The London Regiment (R.F.)*

[2] *Ibid.*

Mamur, or native government official of the town. The Bey, a rich landowner, entertained a few of us at luncheon recently with true Oriental splendour, for, after devouring an excellent Nile fish, I suddenly noticed the startled face of my Company Commander as he tackled a sheep roasted whole, on a quite colossal dish. A Mahometan strongly dislikes dissecting any animal and prefers to cook it whole. Pigeon came up next—the blue rock pigeon found in upper Egypt—and then we devoured, consecutively, turkey, snipe, and veal. Truly a feast for such Gallipolean appetites as ours. Unfortunately the comfort of the meal was marred by incessant toasts, during nearly every course. During the soup we drank the King's health; the Sultan of Egypt's prosperity was confirmed in a fishy atmosphere; the Prince of Wales, the Colonel, our host and others all had their place; and finally, speeches in English, French, and Arabic completed the experience.

We returned this gargantuan feast a day or two later, and invited the Bey, together with all the local celebrities, to tea and a specially arranged gala football match. They came in their hundreds, and the ground was soon dotted with the local notables in long white garments and scarlet fez. At half-time they began to go away sorrowfully, thinking the game was over, but a police corporal explained the position to them, gesticulating wildly with an enormous piece of sugar cane in his hand.

Naturally at the subsequent tea, social mistakes were made. For instance, an enterprising cab driver, together with a smartly dressed waiter, got placed among the seats of the mighty, and were seen graciously accepting buns from the Colonel's hands. Finally, an interpreter read a patriotic speech expressing satisfaction and pleasure at our presence in Egypt.

This pleasant and interesting period came to an end, so far as 'C' and 'D' Companies were concerned, on 13th March, when the detachment, including the guard at Nag Hamadi, left Beni Mazar for Isna. On the departure of this detachment from Beni Mazar, Colonel Vickers Dunfee, commanding 2/4th Londons, expressed his appreciation of its fine work and good behaviour while under his command. At Isna these two companies were joined by Lieut.-Col. Houlder and Battalion Headquarters from Beni Suef, 'A' and 'B' Companies remaining at the latter town under Capt. H. M. Thin.

The defensive line had now been extended as far as Isna, on the Nile some 300 miles below Minya; and there was much work to be done in making the place secure against the Senussi. At Isna, the Battalion was given about fifty camels, 'on which,' as Capt. Hunter writes, 'we were expected to travel into the desert after the Senussi, though hardly any of us had seen a camel before, except, perhaps, at the Zoo!' The barrage was put into a state of defence; and the desert was constantly watched by camel patrols. The enemy, however, made no move.

II

On 12th April, Headquarters and the two companies of the 2/2nd Londons at Isna were relieved by the 2/5th Devons and moved by train to Alexandria, being joined at Beni Suef by the two companies stationed there. Alexandria was reached on the 14th; and the Battalion went into camp at Sidi Bishr. Here it was joined by the 2/1st, 2/3rd, and 2/4th Londons; and the 2/1st London Infantry Brigade, under the command of Colonel Vickers Dunfee, the senior officer present, now came together for the first time after an interval of nearly a year.

Having handed in the long rifles and drawn those of the short pattern in exchange, the Brigade embarked, on 17th April, on H.T. *Transylvania*. This vessel carried not only the 2/1st London Brigade, but also detachments of other corps; and her complement amounted to 130 officers and 3,000 other ranks. She sailed on the following day, and, after an uneventful voyage, reached Marseilles on the 24th of the month.

The 2/2nd Londons entrained at once for Rouen, arriving there on the 26th, but without their Commanding Officer, Lieut.-Col. Houlder having been admitted to hospital at Marseilles.

On arrival at Rouen, the 2/1st London Infantry Brigade, after being in existence for about nineteen months, was finally broken up, and its units disbanded. The War Office was led to take this disagreeable step by the losses incurred by the first-line battalions of the London Regiment and by the difficulty of keeping one, not to say two, battalions supplied with reinforcements from the reserve units at home. The operations, subsequently famous as the Battle of the Somme, were also at hand, and an increased wastage was thus to be expected. Taking these circumstances into consideration, the War Office decided to make use of this splendid material to fill the gaps that sixteen months of active service had made in the ranks of the first-line London units.

The dispersal of the 2/2nd Londons began on 5th May, when 3 officers and 126 other ranks were sent to the 1/2nd Londons. This party was followed by others to the first-line unit and also by large drafts both to the 1/12th Londons (Rangers) and to the 1/16th Londons (Q.W.R.).[1] By the middle of June the 2/2nd London Regiment, a battalion composed of the finest material, had ceased to exist. It was a sad fate to overtake so splendid a unit; and it is some consolation that its name did not disappear at once, but was transferred to another battalion of 2nd Londoners who worthily upheld it in France at a later stage of the war.

For the work of the original 2/2nd Londons in the Eastern theatre of war the Regiment was awarded two Battle Honours: 'Gallipoli' and 'Egypt,' of which the former is borne on its King's Colour.

[1] Of the draft to the Q.W.R., Major J. Q. Henriques says, in his excellent *War History of the 1st Battalion Queen's Westminster Rifles:* 'On the 24th the Queen's Westminster were reinforced by a draft of 223 other ranks from the 2/2nd London Royal Fusiliers. Many of them had seen service in Gallipoli, and they were an addition of the very highest value to the Battalion. All ranks appreciated the natural feelings of these men, in having their own battalion broken up and being sent to another regiment. The efforts that were made to make them not only welcome but at home in their new unit, were more than fully responded to by them; and, five weeks later, when the Battalion was about to go into action at Gommecourt, these 2nd Londoners, of all ranks and without exception, asked if they might wear the Q.W.R. badge, as they were going to fight with the Regiment.'

CHAPTER VII

THE 3/2ND AND 4/2ND LONDONS AT HOME

I

WHILE the 1/2nd and 2/2nd Londons were actively engaged in the fighting on the Western Front and in the Mediterranean, energetic measures had been taken at home to ensure that these battalions were kept fully supplied with men.

As the normal organization of the Territorial Force did not include any machinery for the maintenance of units in the field, the formation of second-line units was intended to make good the deficiency; and when, as in the case of the 2nd Londons, the second-line units went overseas also, further expansion had to be resorted to. Accordingly on 25th November 1914, shortly before the decision to send the 2/2nd Londons to Malta was promulgated, the formation of a third-line unit was authorized. Hence there came into being the 3/2nd Londons—a battalion that later was to play an important part in the task of stemming the German tide in March 1918 and of completing the overthrow of the enemy in the battles of 'The Hundred Days.'

The 3/2nd Londons began to form at Tattenham Corner, Epsom, in December 1914; and shortly afterwards Lieut.-Col. R. P. Charles arrived to take command. Lieut.-Col. Charles had been in command of the University of London Officers' Training Corps, and he was responsible for introducing to the 2nd Londons a number of officers of that Corps, who served in the Battalion with distinction and of whom the foremost were Lieut.-Col. A. R. Richardson, D.S.O., and Major L. N. G. Filon. The second-in-command of the new unit was Major E. J. Hogan, who had returned from the 1/2nd Londons; and the first adjutant was Lieut. R. Carfax Bailey. Owing to the gradual decline of voluntary recruiting, the task of raising the Battalion was none too easy. Voluntary recruiting was not yet in such desperate straits as it was to be in the summer of 1915, and, although the material was not quite of the same standard as that of the first-line and second-line battalions, the strength of the Battalion eventually reached a respectable figure.

The Battalion remained at Tattenham Corner until 7th May 1915. During this period, its primary duty was the training of drafts for the 1/2nd and

2/2nd Londons, though certain 'service' platoons of trained men were kept in readiness for use for home defence should the necessity arise. The first draft of men actually sent out left for the 1/2nd Londons in France on 16th April 1915, and several other drafts were sent abroad before the duties of draft-finding were taken over by the 4/2nd Londons, formed later for this purpose.

Third-line battalions had been formed by the other regiments of the 1st London Infantry Brigade. These battalions were billeted in various places on the outskirts of London, and hitherto had had no connexion, one with another. At the end of April 1915, it was decided to concentrate them under canvas at Tadworth, as the 3/1st London Infantry Brigade, under the command of Colonel H. C. Cholmondeley, C.B.; and accordingly the 3/2nd Londons left Tattenham Corner on the 7th May to join the new formation. Tattenham Corner was retained for the use of the 3/1st London Infantry Brigade School of Instruction, which had been recently formed; for the training of officers of new units, such as these third-line battalions, was a pressing problem, and the formation of schools of this nature offered the best and quickest solution. Major L. N. G. Filon, of the 3/2nd Londons, was placed in charge of this school, and held the appointment until he was given the command of the 4/2nd Londons on its formation at a later date.

About this time Lieut. Carfax Bailey transferred to the R.A. and was succeeded as adjutant by Lieut. J. A. Miller, a popular and efficient officer, who was later, in France, to command the Battalion for some months.

At the end of May 1915 a general reorganization of reserve units and training cadres at home took place. A number of new battalions was formed consisting largely of men who were medically unfit for service overseas, and the units of the 3/1st London Brigade were ordered to provide the personnel for one such battalion, subsequently known as the 100th Provisional Battalion. This battalion was stationed at Aldeburgh, in Suffolk, and was at a later date commanded by Colonel P. Carlebach, C.M.G., T.D., of the 2nd Londons. At the same time the formation of the fourth-line units of the 1st London Brigade was authorized, and Major L. N. G. Filon left the 3/2nd Londons to take command of the new 4/2nd Londons.

Rumours of a move had been rife for some time, and, although similar rumours in the past had proved without foundation, on this occasion the move actually took place, and the 3/1st London Brigade left Tadworth for billets at Bury St. Edmunds. On the 31st May the 3/2nd Londons moved to this old Suffolk town, where training was continued throughout June, which proved to be the hottest month of the year. At the end of June a further move was made; and, in company with the other units of the

Brigade, the 3/2nd Londons then went to Ipswich, where they were billeted in the eastern part of the town on the Nacton and Felixstowe roads, Battalion Headquarters being established in Hatfield Road. The quarters for all were very good; and a large Recreation Ground in the neighbourhood provided an excellent site for elementary training.

At this period a further reorganization of the various forces in England took place; and towards the end of August all personnel of the Provisional Battalion, except 'home service' men, were returned to their units. The 2/2nd and 2/3rd London Infantry Brigades were also concentrated in the Eastern Counties' area, and these, together with the 3/1st London Brigade, were formed into a new 'Service' division—the 58th (London) Division. Hitherto the 3/2nd Londons had been providing reinforcements for the first-line battalion in France; but, in view of the Battalion's new status of a 'Service' battalion, the duty of draft-finding was taken over entirely by the 4/2nd Londons, and no more personnel, except a few officers, was sent overseas by the 3/2nd. The following officers were sent abroad at various times during the 'draft-finding' period:

To 1/2ND LONDONS:
> Capt. P. A. E. Wood; Lieuts. J. Devane, J. E. Richardson; 2nd Lieuts. G. B. Henderson, F. C. Langley, L. W. Bindon, H. C. B. Way, H. L. Barton, J. H. Clive, J. R. Garland, H. G. Lightbody, F. R. C. Hammond, and T. G. McCarthy.

To 2/2ND LONDONS:
> 2nd Lieuts. C. L. Stirling, C. C. Hirst, and J. G. Garthwaite.

The composition of the 58th Division was as follows:

58TH (LONDON) DIVISION
Br.-General E. J. Cooper, C.B., M.V.O., D.S.O.

DIVISIONAL CAVALRY—
> Hampshire Yeomanry (Carabineers).

ARTILLERY—
> 290th, 291st, 292nd, and 293rd Brigades, R.F.A.
> 58th Divisional Ammunition Column.

ROYAL ENGINEERS—
> 2/1 Wessex Field Company.
> 2/2nd Wessex Field Company.
> 1/5th London Field Company.
> 58th Divisional Signal Company.

173RD INFANTRY BRIGADE—

    3/1st London Regiment (Royal Fusiliers).
    3/2nd London Regiment (Royal Fusiliers).
    3/3rd London Regiment (Royal Fusiliers).
    3/4th London Regiment (Royal Fusiliers).

174TH INFANTRY BRIGADE—

    2/5th London Regiment (London Rifle Brigade).
    2/6th London Regiment (Rifles).
    2/7th London Regiment.
    2/8th London Regiment (Post Office Rifles).

175TH INFANTRY BRIGADE—

    2/9th London Regiment (Queen Victoria Rifles).
    2/10th London Regiment (Hackney).
    2/11th London Regiment (Finsbury Rifles).
    2/12th London Regiment (Rangers).

DIVISIONAL TROOPS—

    1/1st Wessex Divisional Cyclists.
    509th, 510th, 511th, 512th S. and T. Companies, Royal Army
        Service Corps.

The 3/2nd Londons were destined to remain in Ipswich for close upon a year; and, although the life was very pleasant and the inhabitants were very kind, the prolonged period in billets, taken in conjunction with the previous frequent moves to which the Battalion had been subjected, had an adverse effect on the efficiency of the troops. Field training was practically impossible; and route-marches and physical training, though they helped to keep the men fit, were not sufficient to bring the Battalion to a high state of efficiency in the field. As all units were similarly affected, the dispatch of the Division overseas was delayed; and the monotonous routine of training was continued. These very unsatisfactory conditions remained until the spring of 1916, when a move was made from billets to the healthier surroundings of a camp, where *esprit de corps* could be engendered and efficient training carried out.

The 58th Division at this time was included in the Home Defence Forces, and was responsible for defending part of the Eastern Counties. In accordance with a scheme prepared for this purpose, the 3/2nd Londons were detailed to take over the defence of a sector of the coast in the neighbourhood of Ipswich. Trenches were sited, and some were dug; anti-aircraft duties were practised; details for blocking the roads were worked out; and other means of hindering an invader were contrived. This work and the passing excitement of air-raids, of which the Eastern Counties experienced many, were the only enlivening incidents in the deadly monotony of continuous training.

The Battalion, which had never been up to strength, received a welcome addition to its numbers in February 1916, when 230 recruits, called up under the 'Derby' scheme, were posted to it. These men, of course, had had no training, and, in order to bring them quickly to the standard reached by the rest of the Battalion, in view of the possibility of its being sent overseas in 1916, they were temporarily attached, in March, to the 4/2nd Londons for intensive training. After two months with the latter unit, they rejoined the 3/2nd Londons in May. In this month the Battalion was inspected by the Italian Military Attaché, who commented in very favourable terms on its drill and appearance on parade; and, at the end of the month, the move from billets to which reference has been made at last took place, the Battalion going under canvas on Martlesham Heath. An important phase of field training was here begun and was continued henceforward until the Battalion was sent to the front.

The disbanding of the 2/2nd Londons in France, where they had arrived after their service in Gallipoli and Egypt, led to a change in the position of the 3/2nd Londons. The latter, becoming the second-line unit of the Regiment in June 1916, adopted the title 2/2nd Battalion London Regiment; and it was under this name that the Battalion subsequently made history in France.

After remaining in camp outside Ipswich for rather more than a month, the 58th Division moved in the middle of July 1916 to hutted camps at Sutton Veny, near Warminster, and, shortly after its arrival here, the Division came under the command of Major-General H. D. Fanshawe, C.B., who ultimately took it to France.

It was now possible for the Division, concentrated in an area that offered excellent training facilities, to carry out advanced field training. At the same time the opportunity of instilling a 'divisional' spirit into all units was made full use of—an opportunity that was entirely lacking when the Division was scattered in billets over a wide area. Great progress was made; and in a very short time the Division became a homogeneous unit; discipline was tightened; and all ranks rapidly became efficient in the finer points of soldiering. The formation of a Divisional Concert Party, called 'The Goods,'[1] of which Lieut. J. S. Stevens, of the 3/2nd Londons, was

---

[1] 'The Goods' Concert Party consisted of the following:—Bobby Howes (the well-known comedian), Tim O'Connor, Dan Rayner, Charles Marford, Fred Warren (of St. Paul's Cathedral), and Sydney Rosenbloom.

THE OFFICERS, 2/2ND LONDONS, 1914.

BACK ROW: 2nd Lieuts. C. R. W. Attenborough, G. N. Hunter, R. L. Cooper, G. Dearmer, J. W. Ginsbury, J. R. Garland, R. H. Wagner, P. C. Burnett, W. R. Rawle, O. Shimwell, A. S. Rawle, D. Symes, B. Attenborough, H. S. Elton.

FRONT ROW: 2nd Lieut. D. Dutfield, Majors W. Whitaker Thompson, A. G. Houlder, Col. P. Carlebach, T.D., Capts. J. D. Rees, A. E. Rees, Lieut. E. Coplands, R.A.M.C.

THE OFFICERS, 3/2ND LONDONS, 1915.

BACK ROW: 2nd Lieuts. G. B. Henderson, G. D. Porteous, P. A. Tucker, R. Collymore, A. S. Gray, H. R. Barton, H. J. Hawkins, J. S. Stevens, J. A. Miller, P. C. Taylor.

MIDDLE ROW: 2nd Lieut. H. O. Ellis, Lieut. B. Snell, Capts. E. B. Towse, H. M. Thin, Major E. J. Hogan, 2nd Lieut. R. Carfax Bailey, Capt. Yorke, R.A.M.C., Lieut. and Q.M. D. D. Shepherd.

FRONT ROW: 2nd Lieuts. C. C. Hirst, W. Ridgeway.

among the organizers, was typical of this better spirit; as was also the production of a Divisional Magazine. This magazine, called *The Direct Hit,* was very popular; and three numbers were published in England. Although a fourth number appeared after the Division had moved to France, the publication of the magazine then had to be discontinued.

As the winter wore on, signs were not wanting that the 3/2nd Londons would soon go overseas. Drafts of officers, most of whom had already seen service in France, were received from the 1st Reserve Battalion; and the final stages of training were completed. During the final period in England, various changes in the personnel took place, Major A. R. Richardson succeeding Lieut.-Col. R. P. Charles in command, Capt. J. A. Miller becoming second-in-command, and Lieut. H. Leaver adjutant.

Though somewhat anticipating the progress of the general narrative, the history of the 2/2nd Londons has now been brought to the end of 1916, which marks a definite break in its story and forms a convenient point whereat, for a time, to leave it.

II

The formation of a fourth-line battalion of the 2nd Londons has already been briefly referred to in this chapter; and the time has now come for its part in the expansion of the Regiment to be described.

The decision to raise a fourth-line to each of the four battalions of the 1st London Infantry Brigade had been taken early in May 1915; but, so far as the 2nd Londons were concerned, no recruits actually arrived at Tattenham Corner, where the Battalion was ordered to form, until the end of that month. In the meantime, official intimation was received that Major L. N. G. Filon,[1] of the 3/2nd Londons, had been appointed to command the new unit, and accordingly on the 30th May he assumed command at Tattenham Corner, taking over the accommodation that had served for both the 2/2nd and 3/2nd Londons in the early stages of their existence. At the same time, Capt. J. H. Warrener, who had been invalided home from the 1/2nd Londons in France and had now been appointed Quartermaster of the 4/2nd Londons, commenced his duties with the unit.

[1] Before the war, Major L. N. G. Filon was a professor of London University and an officer in the University O.T.C. On the outbreak of war, he went to France on the staff of the B.E.F. He was invalided home in 1915, and on 11th March was gazetted to the 3/2nd London Regiment, with the rank of Major. He was subsequently Commandant of the 3/1st London Infantry Brigade School of Instruction, until his appointment to the command of the 4/2nd Londons.

On 31st May the 3/2nd Londons left Tadworth for Bury St. Edmunds; and Major Filon found himself with an independent command consisting of a Quartermaster and 25 raw recruits. At this time, no other officer or non-commissioned officer had been posted to the Battalion, and the Battalion itself had still to be raised.

It was necessary at once to obtain an adjutant and a sergeant-major. The first was found in Mr. C. G. Langley, a local gentleman who had served in the ranks of the 1/2nd Londons in France and had been invalided home, and the second in Sergt. Parker, of the Grenadier Guards, who had been an instructor at the 3/1st London Infantry Brigade School of Instruction, and for whose attachment to the 4/2nd Londons authority was obtained, though not without difficulty. Sergt. Parker had been through the retreat from Mons and, throughout the whole of the independent existence of the 4/2nd Londons, he proved himself an ideal sergeant-major in whom implicit trust could at all times be placed. 2nd Lieut. Langley reported at once and took up his duties as adjutant on 2nd June, pending gazette.

The raising of the Battalion presented a very difficult problem and called for energetic measures; for by this time all volunteers had been absorbed, and the task of obtaining men was becoming increasingly difficult. Recruiting meetings were held under the auspices of the City of London Territorial Force Association; and an organized scheme was prepared. These efforts met with great encouragement and assistance from Lieut.-Col. Montgomerie Webb, of the 3rd Londons, and from Major Sir Pieter Bam, of the 7th Londons, who did not confine themselves to bringing their own regiments up to strength, but did what they could to help other London units less fortunately placed. Recruiting areas were mapped out and allotted to various units. That allotted to the 2nd Londons included Westminster, south of Victoria Street, to which, by the courtesy of Sir Pieter Bam, were later added Stepney, Wapping, and parts of Aldgate, Bermondsey, and Rotherhithe.

The responsibility for recruiting rested not only upon the unit itself, but also upon the Depot in London. It will be recalled that on the outbreak of war the Depot had been placed under the command of Major E. J. Hogan; for it was essential that, while the 1/2nd Londons were guarding the railway line, there should be a senior officer in London to deal with the multifarious questions likely to arise during the complicated business of mobilization. After the departure of this officer with the 1/2nd Londons for Malta, there followed a short interregnum at the Depot until Capt. C. L. V. Marno, who for a few days had acted as adjutant of the then newly-raised 2/2nd Londons, was appointed to the command. Capt. Marno was still in command in May

1915, and he lent Major Filon invaluable assistance in the task of recruiting his battalion. A staff of non-commissioned officers and men from the 4/2nd Londons was established at Tufton Street to carry on the work; recruiting stations were opened at suitable points in the area; and the streets were actively patrolled by a squad of men, under a non-commissioned officer, who tried to induce men to enlist.

In June Capt. A. E. Rees, who had been invalided home from the 2/2nd Londons, was attached to the Depot Staff for recruiting duties. He was an officer with much originality; and under his ægis recruiting became quite brisk. Open-air meetings were organized; places of amusement, such as cinemas and football grounds, were picketed; and special demonstrations at which well-known people, including Sir Gerald du Maurier and Miss Olga Nethersole, urged men to enlist in the Regiment, were held in Trafalgar Square.

Despite all these efforts, however, the number of men enlisted in 1915 under the voluntary system was very disappointing. The number actually enlisted by the ordinary methods did not exceed four or five hundred; and the proportion that developed unfitness of one kind or another was most discouraging.

It soon appeared that the sources of voluntary recruiting were rapidly drying up; and at the end of August 1915 the individual system was abandoned, the 'Derby' scheme, based on the new National Register, taking its place. Under this scheme the area allotted to the 2nd Londons was restricted to Westminster. The East End area was abandoned, and the recruiting offices closed. The Depot now became merely a registration office; and the men who registered there were not necessarily enlisted for the 2nd Londons. They were sworn-in; and their papers were forwarded to the authorities at the Chief Recruiting Office, by whom they were called up in their various classes. The 4/2nd Londons no longer had any responsibility for the recruiting under this scheme, but continued to assist the O.C. Depot; and Capt. A. E. Rees remained in London for this purpose until the spring of 1916.

The new unit was named the '4/2nd Depot, London Regiment (R.F.),' the word 'Depot' soon giving place to the more appropriate 'Battalion.' Its establishment was at first fixed at two companies, with a third company to be formed later of returned Expeditionary Force men, but was raised in November 1915 to four companies and an Expeditionary Force company, as was the case with all fourth-line units supplying two battalions overseas.

During the first month of its existence the 4/2nd Londons led a practically independent life under the City of London Territorial Force

Association; but at the end of June 1915 Colonel Earl Cairns was appointed O.C. Third Line Depots and Administrative Centres, 1st London Division; and the Battalion then came under his orders. On 11th September the Battalion was transferred to the orders of the 3/1st London Brigade at Tadworth. This brigade was commanded by Br.-General Lord Monk; but the officer who supervised the training was Col. O'Meagher, in command of the infantry at Tadworth camp. On 15th December the Battalion was transferred back to the Third Line Groups (1st London Division), the camp at Tadworth having been broken up. Lord Cairns had just relinquished the command through an illness that eventually proved fatal, and for some weeks Lieut.-Col. Montgomerie Webb acted in his place, until at the end of December Col. S. H. Godman, D.S.O., Scots Guards, took over the command. During the whole of this period the 4/2nd Londons remained at Tattenham Corner.

During its infancy the Battalion was called upon at short notice to supply a large draft of men for the 2/2nd Londons in Malta in circumstances that are of some historical interest.

The draft, consisting of 4 officers and 250 men, was ordered on 21st July. At this time this was practically the whole of the fit men present with the Battalion, and none of these was adequately trained. On enquiry, however, instructions were received that the men were to be sent, irrespective of whether they were trained or not. The draft was duly prepared, and, under the command of 2nd Lieut. A. J. Whittle, it entrained at 11.50 p.m. on 24th July at Epsom Station for St. Budeaux in Cornwall.

On 27th July the draft, having already embarked upon the H.T. *Arcadian,* was as suddenly countermanded, and on 31st July it detrained at Epsom Station at 5 a.m., and marched back to camp. Similar drafts were called for and countermanded from the other units of the 4/1st London Brigade. The reasons that dictated this move and its abandonment have never transpired.

Although the primary reason for the Battalion's existence was the training of recruits, it was instructed to be ready for service in the event of a national emergency, such as an attempted invasion by the enemy, the threat of which was always present. A composite company was specially organized, equipped, and held ready to move at an hour's notice, should the necessity arise; but although several trial mobilizations were made, its services were never actually required.

The training programme, which will later be described in more detail, was so intensive, owing to the short period allowed, that the men did not

94

have very much time for recreation; nevertheless, cricket and football were organized, and matches were regularly played. While the Battalion was at Tattenham Corner, week-end leave was freely granted; and at Christmas 48 hours' leave was granted to all ranks, two leave parties being arranged for the purpose.

Although the Battalion was largely free from the inevitably irksome control of the higher authorities, yet this isolation had its disadvantages, an example of which was the absence, during the whole of its stay at Epsom, of a military Medical Officer. A civilian practitioner, Dr. Peacock, very kindly volunteered his services, and making his headquarters at the Grand Stand Hospital, did a vast amount of very arduous work extremely well. He was very popular with everyone; and the Battalion parted from him with great regret. In like manner, no chaplain was attached. Occasionally the Rev. W. G. Bell, Chaplain of the 1/2nd Londons, came down to conduct a service; but more usually the men were marched to Tadworth or Burgh Heath churches.

In January 1916 orders were received for the Third Line Groups (1st London Division) to move into hutted camps at Fovant and Hurdcott, in Wiltshire. Accordingly, the 4/2nd Londons moved out of Tattenham Corner on 12th January 1916, and, after a very roundabout journey via Chichester and Southampton, reached Wilton the same evening. Thence they marched to Hurdcott, mid-way between Wilton and Shaftesbury, where they took up their quarters in No. 8 Camp.

No. 8 Camp had been recently built; indeed, was hardly completed when the Battalion arrived, and several conveniences, such as electric light, were not available for some days. It was well planned and extremely comfortable; and, although after snow or rain the ground became somewhat muddy and waterlogged, these inconveniences were amply compensated for by the warm, well-ventilated huts, the excellent canteen, and recreation rooms, the electric light, the shower baths, and all the other appurtenances of a really up-to-date military station.

From a purely military point of view the move from the vicinity of London to the Salisbury area was highly beneficial. Discipline could be tightened up, and a proper *esprit de corps* engendered; and the concentration in the area of all third-line and fourth-line groups led to a healthy rivalry between units. Moreover, the facilities for training were excellent and ensured that the best use was made of the very limited amount of time that could be given to each recruit to make himself efficient.

For a variety of reasons the privilege of week-end leave was now curtailed, and only a very small percentage of men was allowed to go on leave at any one time. To keep the men amused in these intervals of training, frequent concerts were organized; and the Y.M.C.A., who had opened a hut on the other side of the Shaftesbury road, did splendid work in helping the men to pass their leisure time profitably.

Soon after its arrival at Hurdcott the Battalion began to suffer from a serious shortage of men. By this time it had supplied several drafts for the two battalions overseas; and this wastage was not being made good by a corresponding influx of recruits. Individual voluntary recruiting having virtually ceased at the end of the previous year, practically no recruits came to the Battalion until the last week in April and the first in May, when 700 men, enlisted under the 'Derby' scheme, arrived. Meanwhile, in the last week of March, 230 men of the 3/2nd Londons joined the Battalion for a course of intensive training to enable them rapidly to reach the standard of the rest of their own battalion. These men were, of course, never available for draft, and in the middle of May were duly returned to the 3/2nd Londons.

No more 'Derby' men were received before the scheme came to an end, and conscription was introduced. Thereafter men were called up under the National Service Act; but no conscripts actually reached the 4/2nd Londons until August 1916, when they were received at the rate of about 20 a day. As the Battalion was amalgamated at the end of that month, this class of recruit never affected the drafts sent abroad during the period of its independent existence.

Early in 1916 the establishment of the Battalion was increased to five companies and an Expeditionary Force company. Owing to small numbers, the 4/2nd Londons retained the original two recruit companies ('A' and 'B') and the Expeditionary Force company ('C') until the arrival of the 700 'Derby' recruits and of the 230 men from the 3/2nd Londons, above referred to, justified the formation of three more companies ('D,' 'E,' and 'F').

On 1st March 1916 the Division was reorganized into two groups, a 'Fusilier' Group at Hurdcott, consisting of 4/1st, 4/2nd, 4/3rd, 4/4th, 3/7th, and 3/11th London Regiments, under Colonel R. B. Williams, C.B., and a 'Rifle' Group, at Fovant, consisting of 3/5th, 3/6th, 3/8th, 3/9th, 3/10th, and 3/12th London Regiments. This 'group' organization, however, does not seem to have been rigidly adhered to; and during June and July Colonel Godman was again acting as sole brigade commander. On 25th July the latter officer left for France to take over the command of a battalion of the Scots Guards, and was succeeded by Colonel Becher, who was still commanding the brigade when the 4/2nd Londons were broken up. Colonel Becher was himself succeeded at a later date (October 1916) by Br.-General Howell.

About May 1916 the name of the Battalion was altered to ' 2nd (Reserve) Battalion London Regiment '; and at the end of the month the establishment was again reduced to three companies and an Expeditionary Force company. This appears to have corresponded to the time when the 2/2nd Londons were brought to France from the Mediterranean and disbanded. The old 3/2nd Londons then became the 2/2nd, and the 4/2nd a third-line unit, supplying only one battalion overseas. At the beginning of July 1916 the establishment was a second time raised to five companies, probably in anticipation of the 2/2nd (old 3/2nd) going overseas. Owing to depleted numbers, the two extra companies were not reformed.

Before turning to a consideration of the methods of training adopted, one event of considerable interest occurred while the 4/2nd Londons were at Hurdcott: this was the inspection of the Brigade by Field-Marshal Lord French on 31st January 1916. The inspection was of a purely formal character, the men being drawn up on a ceremonial parade, and the Field-Marshal going down the line in the usual manner.

The policy initiated for training aimed throughout at keeping the ' training' organization as far as possible in harmony with the 'administrative' organization. For this purpose recruits were posted to a platoon until this platoon was filled up, and they remained with their platoon throughout the whole of their instruction. The drill and tactical instruction was given by the company and platoon officers and non-commissioned officers. Special instruction, *e.g.,* musketry, bombing (which had eventually to be taught to all), physical training, and bayonet fighting, was given by a specialist staff; but platoons were kept together, even for this, each forming a class which the specialist instructor trained at a separate time. The firing of the musketry course completed the training.

By this means platoons were kept homogeneous and were intended to go on draft more or less as a whole. As soon as a platoon had been emptied by a draft, it was available to be refilled by recruits. The Expeditionary Force company (' C' Company) was on an entirely special footing. Permanently unfit men for foreign service were used on regimental employ or as instructors. Those who might become fit again were given graduated exercises with a view to restoring their health.

On 7th February 1916, owing to the depleted condition of the unit, a new training organization was introduced. This aimed at making the company the complete training unit, men being passed from one platoon to another, according to the stage of training reached. The first platoon consisted entirely of trained men ready for draft, the second platoon of men doing a fortnight's preliminary musketry previous to firing, or actually firing their course, the third platoon of recruits, the fourth platoon of unfit men, details, etc. But the large influx of recruits at the end of March 1916 made it impossible to adhere to this new scheme; and there was a more or less complete reversal to the original arrangement.

The policy of the authorities as regards training varied considerably. During 1915, the decision as to whether men were to be regarded as 'trained' was left to the Commanding Officer, who also decided the time necessary for training in each case. When men were reported trained and ordered on draft, the draft was inspected by the Brigadier; but this inspection was of a more or less formal character, and did not include a test of training. After January 1916, a period of fourteen weeks' training was laid down for drafts, which later was cut down effectively to twelve and occasionally to ten; and the inspections by the Brigadier eventually included tests in drill, musketry, bomb-throwing, etc., as well as a formal inspection and examination of kit. After June 1916 it was decided to allow drafts to be sent out as 'partially trained,' on the understanding that they would complete their training in France; and this was the case with the last five drafts that the 4/2nd Londons sent abroad.

Drafts for France and the Mediterranean were not, apart from 'unfit' wastage, the only cause of depletion of the reserve units. Calls of all kinds were constantly made upon their time and personnel. In September 1915 a number of 'skilled investigators' descended upon the Battalion, and took away a number of men who volunteered for munitions work. There were also appeals (February 1916) for men to volunteer for Pioneer Battalions of the Royal Engineers, no engineer qualifications being asked for, and later (July 1916) for the Machine-Gun Corps, and there were continual transfers to various other units.

The two great difficulties with which the Battalion had to contend in its training were, first, the constant demands made for men for regimental employ, for brigade and other fatigues, and, secondly, the sporadic way in which recruits were sent to it. The former was at first a great obstacle to efficiency, until there had accumulated sufficient returned Expeditionary Force men of medical category 'B' to deal with these duties. By the summer of 1916 the organization of these duties had been perfected; and there was little need to interfere with the recruits' training on their account. To assist units to overcome the difficulties of regimental and other employment, instructions were issued that 'training companies' should be formed, as distinct from 'administrative companies'; but, owing to the organization above described, there was no need to adopt this device in the 4/2nd Londons. As regards the second difficulty, the supply of recruits after the first few months was never continuous, so that there were periods when, for training purposes, the Battalion was empty for weeks at a time, and the instructing staff could hardly be kept employed, and other periods (as in April and May 1916) when the Battalion was so full that there were nothing like enough officers and instructors to go round.

For the training of 'specialists' (machine and Lewis gunners, bombers, and signallers) the system adopted was to select promising men and to put them under specialist instruction after they had completed their general training. These men, however, had to be shown on the returns as trained, and they were ordered on draft time after time before their specialist training was completed. Indeed it was not until the spring of 1916 that a distinction was drawn between the specialist and the normally trained man; and so far as the 4/2nd Londons were concerned, only one draft of trained specialists was actually sent out.

Apart from the countermanded draft of which mention has been previously made, sixteen drafts of non-commissioned officers and men were provided by the Battalion during its independent existence.

These drafts aggregated 869 men; and, in addition, six sergeants and six corporals were exchanged with a similar number of sergeants and corporals of the 1/2nd Londons in August 1916. Of these drafts the first nine, numbering in all 451 men, represented the results of voluntary recruiting in 1915, together with a proportion of such returned Expeditionary Force men as had become fit again. The last of these drafts left on 15th April 1916 and entirely emptied the unit of fit men, so that training of men was practically suspended until the 700 'Derby' recruits arrived. The last seven drafts, amounting to 418 men, were derived almost entirely from the 700 'Derby' recruits. Although some of these 'Derby' men still remained to be sent out after the amalgamation of the Battalion, yet the wastage, through medical unfitness, of this class of recruit had been so great that the supply was practically exhausted at the end of August 1916. Owing to the inability of the older men of this class to stand the strain of the intensive physical training insisted upon by the War Office, the wastage among them was far higher than among the 1915 men, who were younger on the average.

The training of young officers was also an important function of the unit. The selection of these officers, with the exception of three or four who were sent down direct by the Territorial Association or by the War Office, rested throughout with the Commanding Officer; and, on the whole, the supply was fairly continuous and well maintained. These officers were drawn principally from two sources: the Officers' Training Corps—more particularly the University of London O.T.C., the Artists' Rifles, and the Inns of Court O.T.C.—, and men of the right standing who had enlisted in the ranks in the earlier part of the war. Many of the latter class had had experience at the front. In the later stages, every candidate for a commission had to undergo preliminary training in an Officer Cadet Battalion.

At first the Commanding Officer was forced by lack of experienced assistants to train all the officers himself; and his aim was to create an effective staff of instructors who should be permanent company and platoon commanders and specialist instructors (machine gun, signalling, bombing, and physical training). Newly-joined officers were then attached to platoons as supernumeraries and were actually trained under the supervision of the permanent instructors. Great difficulty was experienced in keeping up this system, owing to the constant heavy demand for officers. These demands had to be complied with, and often made heavy inroads even upon the staff that should have been kept for instructional purposes. On the other hand, those officers whom the War Office would have allowed the Battalion to retain on account of unfitness were, for this very reason, incapable of standing the severe and continuous physical strain of supervising intensive training.

Towards the end of 1915 Young Officers Companies were formed in various centres, such as Wimbledon; and officers were sent there for a course of instruction after they had joined the unit. These Young Officers' Companies lapsed when the Officer Cadet Battalion system was introduced in 1916.

Every opportunity was taken of sending newly-joined officers to Schools of Instruction, both general and specialist, so as to give them a better chance of learning their work before going to the front; but the demands for drafts of officers were so continuous and insistent that it was often necessary (under instruction from higher authority) to withdraw an officer in the middle of a course in order to send him overseas. In the summer of 1916 cases occurred of officers being sent overseas who had only been three weeks or less with the unit; but it has to be remembered that many of these officers had had considerable preliminary training before joining.

Under these conditions and having regard to the requirements of draft-conducting and special duties, it became impossible to give young officers with the unit anything like a progressive and systematic course; and it was necessary to be content with letting them pick up, by contact with more experienced officers, as much knowledge as possible. Nevertheless, the young officers, as a whole, seemed imbued with the right ideal, and acquitted themselves well at the front.

Altogether about eighty or ninety young officers passed through the 4/2nd Londons, of whom about sixty left for a theatre of war before the Battalion was finally broken up.

The instructional staff, as has already been indicated, consisted almost entirely of officers who had been invalided home from one or other of the Expeditionary Forces. As these officers could not be retained once they were fit again for general service, the staff was constantly being changed; and this fact alone added to the difficulties of organization, and militated against efficiency. Though many of these officers were far from fit, and found the strain of intensive instruction a severe one, nevertheless they did their utmost for the Battalion, and their experience and example were of the greatest value in bringing the recruits to a satisfactory standard of efficiency in a short time.

Mention has already been made of Lieut. (later Capt.) C. G. Langley and Capt. (later Major) J. H. Warrener, O.B.E., and the excellent services that they rendered, the former as Adjutant and the latter as Quartermaster. In February 1916 Lieut. Langley was succeeded by Lieut. A. J. Widdecombe, who acted as adjutant until the breaking-up of the unit, and proved most efficient in this capacity. Major R. I. Marians, of the 1/2nd Londons, acted as second-in-command from 23rd August 1915 to 12th July 1916, being succeeded by Capt. O. S. Sinnatt until 1st September 1916. Both these officers gave assistance of the very highest value in the training and administration of the Battalion.

The following officers commanded companies at various times:

From the 1/2nd Londons: Capts. E. O. Davies, E. E. H. Bate, A. G. L. Jepson, W. E. Grey, J. Devane, Lieut. L. W. Bindon.
From the 2/2nd Londons: Capts. S. Jones, O. Shimwell.
From other Units: Capt. O. S. Sinnatt, Lieuts. P. H. Langley, H. Renwick.

In addition to his duties as a company commander, Capt. Bate contrived, under instructions from higher authorities and with working-parties grudgingly provided by the various battalions, to scarify the beautiful Wiltshire hillside with a rifle-range that it will take Nature many years to efface.

The Specialist Instructors were as follows:

Bombing.—2nd Lieut. J. B. Pittman, Lieut. C. A. L. Pascoe.
Physical Training.—2nd Lieut. C. F. H. Attneave.
Musketry.—2nd Lieut. E. Ford.
Machine-gun.—2nd Lieut. A. Cooper.
Signalling.—2nd Lieut. W. J. Coppen.
Messing Officer.—2nd Lieut. H. F. Phillips (from the 2/2nd Londons).

The first Medical Officer to be attached to the Battalion was Capt. Williamson, who joined on 4th February 1916. He was almost immediately withdrawn for specialist work, and was followed by a succession of Medical Officers, none of whom stayed very long:

Lieut. Dunbar, Capt. Devlin, Lieut. A. B. Thompson, Capt. G. Hackney.

The last-named left the Battalion on 9th August 1916. Thereafter the Battalion had no Medical Officer of its own, Lieut. Pigeon, the Medical Officer of the 4th (Reserve) Battalion London Regiment, looking after both battalions.

On 3rd February 1916 a Chaplain was attached for duty with the four Fusilier battalions. This was the Rev. C. G. Holland, who was quartered in the camp of the 4/2nd Londons. He remained until 20th June, when his place was taken by the Rev. Arnold.

The provision of non-commissioned officers was at first a source of great difficulty. It was quite useless to promote promising recruits when they became sufficiently trained; no sooner had they reached the requisite standard of efficiency than they had to be sent away on draft. The difficulty was eventually overcome by the return of good non-commissioned officers from overseas. Those that were sufficiently fit for the work and were yet not fit enough to be sent back to France were at once made use of; and in course of time a very satisfactory staff of experienced and efficient instructors was collected.

As was the case with the officer staff, these non-commissioned officers, being unfit, found it difficult to stand the severe physical strain imposed upon them by the continuous duty of supervising intensive training. Moreover, the work was, from the nature of the unit, of a peculiarly dull and trying character, lacking in variety and in the stimulus of active service, with very little hope of reward or promotion; yet one and all put their best energies into their tasks, with the result that they were instrumental in making a happy and efficient unit. It may be mentioned, as an example of

A COMPANY OF THE 3/2ND LONDONS OUTSIDE ITS BILLETS ON
TATTENHAM CORNER STATION, 1915.

A GROUP OF OFFICERS OF THE 4/2ND LONDONS AT
HURDCOTT, 1916.

A COMPANY OF THE 4/2ND LONDONS RETURNING TO BILLETS
AT TATTENHAM CORNER STATION, 1915.

the care exercised by the non-commissioned officers in general and by the Quartermaſter's ſtaff in particular, that the claims which the Battalion had to meet, either for loss of equipment or for damages to barracks, etc., on changing ſtation, were always of the lighteſt; and the Battalion finished its independent exiſtence with its Regimental Inſtitutes in a flourishing financial condition.

Among the warrant officers and senior non-commissioned officers the following deserve to be mentioned for their loyal work:

R.Q.M.S. Harrison.
C.S.M.s G. Michaels, R. W. Whitehead (Musketry), Wright, and J. Powell.
C.Q.M.S. Hounson, and L. Smith.
Sergts. W. J. Robinson, A. E. Agutter, D.C.M., Phillipson, L. F. Stone (Bombing), Blackford (Machine-gun), Ayers (Orderly Room), Parrish (Signalling), Price (Sergt.-Dr.), Saunders (Pioneer Sergt.), and Owen (P.T. Inſtructor, attached from Army School of Physical Training).

The officers and non-commissioned officers of the Training Staff had a very hard and somewhat thankless task. To them and to Major Filon, who was very conscientious and untiring in his work and who aimed at a very high ſtandard of efficiency for his unit, is to be attributed, in large measure, the success that attended the efforts of the 4/2nd Battalion London Regiment during the period of its independent exiſtence.

Many amusing incidents of life with the 4/2nd Londons will doubtless remain in the memory of both officers and men; and for obvious reasons the majority of these cannot be recorded here. Few officers, however, will forget the amazing games of piquet between Downey and Phillips, the former's adventure with the Quartermaſter on Chriſtmas Day 1915, or the protracted daily 'C.O.'s Orders' and the arrival of Capt. Bate on such occasions, heralded by a salute which shook the Orderly Room to its very foundations; and all members of the Battalion will recall the discreet, but official, weekly 'hunt for bugs,' the ſtentorian voice of C.S.M. 'Jumbo' Wright, and the inimitable impersonation given by C.S.M. Whitehead in his song *The Fireman*.

With the object of effecting an ultimate economy of ſtaff, a reorganization of considerable importance was carried out on 1ſt September 1916 among the units of the Third Line Groups (1ſt London Division). So far as the Fusilier Brigade was concerned, this took the form of an amalgamation of its four exiſting battalions into two, the 1ſt and 2nd Battalions becoming the 1ſt (Reserve) Battalion London Regiment, and the 3rd and 4th the 3rd (Reserve) Battalion. The command of the 1ſt (Reserve) Battalion was given to Colonel Vickers Dunfee, V.D., of the 4th Londons—an appointment that he was to hold until demobilization in 1918—, and of the 3rd (Reserve) Battalion to Colonel Montgomerie Webb. Each of these new battalions retained a double establishment of officers, non-commissioned officers, and men, and was organized into eight companies, until its numbers were depleted by the dispatch of drafts overseas.

Some loss of *esprit de corps* was the inevitable outcome of this change; and all ranks deplored the extinction of the 4/2nd Londons' individuality. These natural feelings of regret were soon laid aside; and the new unit eventually had a very happy and contented existence, with no sort of distinction between the personnel of its component parts.

On 29th September the 4/2nd Londons marched out of No. 8 Camp, Hurdcott, to the R.E. Camp, Fovant, in preparation for the amalgamation; and its independent existence then came to an end.

CHAPTER VIII

FORMATION OF THE 56TH DIVISION

THE composition of the 56th (1st London) Territorial Division, on its formation, was as follows:

56TH (1ST LONDON) DIVISION
Major-General Sir. C. P. A. Hull, K.C.B.

DIVISIONAL CAVALRY—
 'B' Squadron, King Edward's Horse.

ARTILLERY—
 280th (1/1st London) Brigade, R.F.A.
 281st (1/2nd London) Brigade, R.F.A.
 282nd (1/3rd London) Brigade, R.F.A.
 283rd (1/4th London) Brigade, R.F.A.
 56th Divisional Ammunition Column.

ROYAL ENGINEERS—
 512th (2/1st London) Field Company.
 513th (2/2nd London) Field Company.
 416th (Edinburgh) Field Company.
 56th Divisional Signal Company.

167TH INFANTRY BRIGADE—Br.-General F. H. Nugent, D.S.O.
 1/7th Middlesex Regiment.
 1/8th Middlesex Regiment.
 1/1st London Regiment (Royal Fusiliers).
 1/3rd London Regiment (Royal Fusiliers).

168TH INFANTRY BRIGADE—Br.-General G. G. Loch, C.M.G., D.S.O.
 1/4th London Regiment (Royal Fusiliers).
 1/12th London Regiment (The Rangers).
 1/13th London Regiment (Kensingtons).
 1/14th London Regiment (London Scottish).

169TH INFANTRY BRIGADE—Br.-General E. S. D'E. Coke, C.M.G., D.S.O.
 1/2nd London Regiment (Royal Fusiliers).
 1/5th London Regiment (London Rifle Brigade).[1]
 1/9th London Regiment (Queen Victoria Rifles).[1]
 1/16th London Regiment (Queen's Westminster Rifles).[1]

---

[1] The initials, L.R.B., Q.V.R., and Q.W.R., will be used throughout the rest of this book to designate the 1/5th, 1/9th, and 1/16th Londons respectively.

DIVISIONAL TROOPS—

    1st London Divisional Cyclist Company.
    Pioneer Battalion—1/5th Cheshire Regiment.
    56th Divisional Train.
    2/1st, 2/2nd, and 2/3rd London Field Ambulance.
    56th Divisional Ambulance Workshop.
    1/1st London Sanitary Section.
    1/1st London Mobile Veterinary Section.

The Infantry units posted to the Division were all original first-line Territorial battalions, and were already well seasoned to war; for they had been serving in France with Regular brigades for more than a year. The fact that these units had trained together before the war and had known one another as friends for many years was the foundation of an *esprit de corps* that characterized this London Division throughout the whole of its active service.

The Staff of the 169th Brigade, under Br.-General Coke, consisted of Capt. L. A. Newnham as Brigade Major and Capt. E. R. Broadbent as Staff Captain. Br.-General Coke himself had served continuously since the beginning of the war, fighting at Mons as a regimental officer in the King's Own Scottish Borderers. He was henceforth to command this brigade, with hardly a break, until the conclusion of hostilities. Br.-General Coke was a keen soldier and a strict disciplinarian; he soon gained the confidence of the brigade, and became a great favourite with all ranks. He took a particular interest in the 2nd Londons, which they did their best to repay by carrying out his requirements enthusiastically and without question.

The 56th Division was to concentrate near Pont Remy. At this town, then, in the early hours of the 10th February, the 1/2nd Londons detrained, and marched to the village of Doudelainville (Somme), of which, as the War Diary records, the civil population was 'somewhat unfriendly.'

It will be readily understood that, apart from the actual concentration of the troops, a division is not formed in a few days, or even weeks, however well trained and tried those troops may be. To concentrate a number of heterogeneous units under one staff is but the first step. These units must be welded together, must be trained to act for the common good, must be imbued with a divisional *esprit de corps,* if the best results are to be got out of their joint efforts. And so the formation of the 56th Division was inevitably and properly followed by a long period in the back areas, a period of rest, reorganization, and training, during which infantry, artillery, engineers, and administrative services could get to know one another, and, from the knowledge so gained, could learn to rely implicitly on one another's co-operation and support in battle.

Before passing on to describe this period of unification, a brief reference must be made to the changes in organization that were being made at this time. Various auxiliary services had come into being as the concomitant of trench warfare, and were now being constituted an integral part of every division or brigade. The personnel for some of these services, such as the Brigade Trench Mortar Battery and Machine-Gun Company, had generally to be found by the fighting units, and for this reason their formation was not regarded with particular favour, at the time, by the average battalion and company commanders; but at a later date their value was amply demonstrated.

During February and subsequent months, demands for personnel were made on the 1/2nd Londons by the 169th Trench Mortar Battery, to which they contributed 1 officer (2nd Lieut. J. B. Pittman, newly arrived) and 30 men, and by the 169th Brigade Machine-Gun Company, to whom they contributed 2 officers (2nd Lieuts. Fradd and Hulme) and 35 men. Demands were also made for officer personnel for other duties; and in this way the Battalion lost the services of Capt. Harington, who was appointed Brigade Bombing Officer (an appointment he was to hold for many months), of Lieut. Way, who was appointed A.D.C. to the new G.O.C., and, temporarily at least, of Capt. Taylor, who was appointed Brigade Transport Officer.

This process of reorganization was likewise applied to each individual battalion; and a number of important changes was made. The recently acquired Lewis guns were grouped under the control of a Battalion Lewis Gun Officer (Lieut. Grey). The establishment of bombers was increased, 30 trained bombers, under the Battalion Grenade Officer (2nd Lieut. St. Ledger), being attached to Headquarters—these in addition to one bombing platoon per company—; a Headquarter Company was formed, in which all 'details,' such as Transport Section, Clerks, Band, and the like, were collected. The H.Q. Company had the effect of separating the fighting from the administrative personnel, and made for a considerable simplification of all matters concerning the discipline and administration of the latter.

Nor were the relaxations and amusements of the men forgotten, and the formation, at this time, of two organizations with these ends in view must be chronicled; the Divisional Band, under Bandmaster Tyler, of the 1/2nd Londons, and the 'Bow Bells' Concert Party. Both were to contribute in no small measure to the happiness of the troops, but especially the 'Bow Bells'; and the names of Harry Brandon, Chandler, and Dick

Horn, and others, who at various times assisted the little company, will be remembered with pleasure by all members of the Division.

Training was begun at Doudelainville with as little delay as possible, and suffered no interruption except by the weather, which at times was execrable. The 1/2nd Londons were inspected by their new Brigadier on 15th February; and his comment on the Battalion, as recorded in the 169th Brigade Diary, was ' good all round.' While at Doudelainville the Battalion also made the acquaintance of its new G.O.C., who paid it a visit on the 25th. Major-General (afterwards Sir C. P. Amyatt) Hull was a tall, good-looking man. He had a somewhat abrupt manner, but a singularly charming nature; and it did not take him long to win the affection and complete confidence of his division.

Officer reinforcements during February, in addition to 2nd Lieut. J. B. Pittman, were:

2nd Lieuts. H. Arthur, B. R. Buxton, and R. G. T. Groves.

It should be noted that, as Lieut.-Col. Attenborough was in hospital at this time and Major Stacey on leave, the Battalion came under the temporary command of Capt. Heumann.

Training continued until the 12th March, when the Brigade moved on to Fienvillers, and thence on the 15th to Doullens. The march was continued next day through Bouquemaison and Frévent to Sericourt, where the Battalion was to remain for nearly two months. Sericourt was a pleasant enough French village, but it had recently been in the occupation of French troops, and was in a filthy condition. This latter fact gave rise to the epigram of which Capt. G. Baudains, D.S.O., M.C., R.F.A., then serving in the ranks of the 1/2nd Londons, is reputed to be the author: ' At Armentières we heard of lice, at Ypres we made their acquaintance, but at Sericourt —my God!'

During these two months the Battalion was subjected to intensive training, instruction being received in all the arts of modern war—gas, liquid fire, Lewis guns, trench mortars—nothing was omitted. This programme was varied by cross-country races and by sports, battalion and brigade. In the Brigade Sports, the 1/2nd London's chief success was first place in the Bombing Competition. The weather in the middle of April was atrocious; and for nearly a fortnight training was seriously interrupted by the continuous rain. Except for the arrival of small drafts of non-commissioned officers and men on the 6th April and 1st May, little of interest occurred during this period. The Battalion was, without doubt, grateful to the authorities for its long 'rest' behind the line; but all ranks realized—perhaps not with such gratitude—that they were being trained as 'shock troops,' and that a very grim ordeal lay before them in the near future.

During March and April the following officers joined the Battalion:

Lieut. A. G. L. Jepson and 2nd Lieuts. A. E. Wiggs, W. L. Stone, and H. C. Gosnell.

At length the 56th Division, trained and 'shaken together,' was ordered forward; and on the 4th May the 167th Brigade relieved a brigade of the 48th Division in the Hébuterne sector of the front line. The 169th Brigade did not move forward until the 7th; on that day the 1/2nd Londons left Sericourt, and marched via Ivergny and Lucheux to Halloy, where a stay of ten days was made. The 56th Division was holding the line on a front of one brigade only; and the remaining units were billeted in villages in rear from which they furnished working parties for the forward area. On the 19th the 1/2nd Londons moved up to Souastre. And now we come to the period of preparation for that event with which the 56th Division will ever be especially associated, its first great effort as a unit of the British forces—the holding attack north of the Somme in the famous battle that opened on the 1st July 1916, the attack on the Gommecourt Salient.

CHAPTER IX

THE 1/2ND LONDONS IN THE BATTLES OF THE SOMME, 1916—I

THE ATTACK ON THE GOMMECOURT SALIENT

ALTHOUGH it is not within the scope of this history to discuss the reason that induced the Higher Command to embark on the Somme operations, it will not be out of place to glance at the position of affairs in the early summer of 1916, so that a clearer appreciation may be gained of the fighting in which the 1/2nd Londons took such a useful part.

Plans for a Franco-British offensive had undoubtedly been fully discussed by Sir Douglas Haig and General Joffre; and the two commanders had reached complete agreement. Vast preparations were in progress. The British New Armies were available; and immense quantities of guns and munitions of every description were coming forward. The British Commander-in-Chief naturally desired to postpone the attack as long as possible in order to make the fullest preparations; but by the end of May the general situation had become so serious that further postponement was impossible. The Austrian offensive against Italy had met with considerable success, and the Russian offensive launched for the relief of the Italians had failed. Sir Douglas Haig thus sets forth, briefly but clearly, the objects of the Somme campaign:[1]

> In view, therefore, of the situation in the various theatres of war, it was eventually agreed between General Joffre and myself that the combined French and British offensive should not be postponed beyond the end of June. The object of that offensive was threefold:
>
> 1. To relieve the pressure on Verdun.
> 2. To assist our Allies in the other theatres of war by stopping any further transfer of German troops from the Western front.
> 3. To wear down the strength of the forces opposed to us.

In the plan for the British offensive it was decided that the main attack should be delivered by the Fourth Army, under Sir Henry Rawlinson, on

[1] Sir Douglas Haig's Dispatches.

a front ſtretching from Maricourt on the right to Serre on the left, while farther north the Third Army, under Sir E. H. H. Allenby, should make an attack on both sides of the Gommecourt salient to divert againſt itself enemy infantry and artillery that might otherwise be used againſt the left of the Fourth Army. This subsidiary task fell to the 46th and 56th Divisions of the VII. Corps (Lieut.-General Sir T. D'O. Snow), then holding the front in queſtion.

The 56th Division formed the right wing of the VII. Corps; and its lines were, on an average, 700 yards diſtant from those of the enemy. The task of crossing this wide space without incurring the heavy casualties that muſt have resulted from any attempt to shorten the diſtance by ordinary methods presented a difficult problem. The solution finally adopted by the G.O.C. was of the boldeſt. He decided to trace out a new line about 400 yards in advance of the exiſting one, and then to dig it in the course of a single night.

The task of digging this new line was entruſted to the 167th Brigade; and, although the trench was dug in one night, the whole operation required three nights to complete : the firſt, 25th/26th May, was utilized in marking out the line with ſtring and pegs, the second in digging the trench, and on this night there were 300 men out in No Man's Land. ' By 2.30 a.m.,' says Major Dudley Ward, in his hiſtory of the 56th Division,[1] ' the trench had been made and was held by poſts, found from the covering parties, reinforced with Lewis guns; they had rations, water, and shovels to improve their positions, and were in telephone communication with the old trench, and all the working parties had filed away as silently as they had come. . . . On the night of the 27th/28th May the same number of men were out working again, improving the front line trench, and wire, digging support lines and two other communication trenches. . . . The 56th Division had then ſtarted its career with the aſtounding feat of having in the space of forty-eight hours conſtructed and wired a new syſtem of trenches, comprising 2,900 yards of fire trench and 1,500 yards of communication trenches in No Man's Land and within 250 yards of the enemy. Casualties were 8 killed and 55 wounded. A little luck had waited on audacity, but the success of the whole operation was undoubtedly due to the intelligence and keenness of the men. . . .'

Before proceeding to the details of the actual attack, the part played by the 1/2nd Londons in these preparations must firſt be described. On arrival in Souaſtre on 19th May the Battalion went into billets in huts, and was immediately called upon to find large working parties for the conſtruction

[1] *The 56th Division.* Major C. H. Dudley Ward, D.S.O., M.C.

of roads, light railways, and ammunition dumps, and for burying cables. Although the Battalion took no part in the actual work of making the new front line, it continued to send out large parties daily and nightly to assist in these preparations for the great attack until 29th May, when it moved into the Keep at Hébuterne in tactical reserve. Thence on 3rd June 'C' and 'D' Companies went into the 'Y' sector of the new front line, where Lieut. H. G. Guildford was wounded. No reinforcements of officers had been received in May; but early in June 2nd Lieut. W. H. Sendall arrived from England, and the following officers of the second-line unit, which was at that time being disbanded on its arrival in France from Egypt, joined the Battalion :

Capt. A. G. Houlder, Lieuts. B. Attenborough, G. Dearmer, D. L. Childs, 2nd Lieuts. J. S. Grainger, N. F. Perris, A. M. Thorman, J. G. Garthwaite, L. S. Gray, and J. W. Sanders.

These officers were accompanied by a large number of non-commissioned officers and men from their battalion; and, coming from such a source, this draft was especially welcome to the 1/2 Londons.

The award of the following honours was notified at the beginning of June :

M.C. : Capt. J. P. Kellett.
D.C.M. : Sergts. G. P. Spooner and W. H. Barrett.

'A' and 'B' Companies relieved 'C' and 'D' on the 6th; and there is an interesting note in the War Diary for the 8th : 'The enemy appears to be working very hard on his defences.' The whole Battalion moved back to Bayencourt on the 10th and thence on the 13th to Souastre. Throughout this period it continued night after night, despite appalling weather and constant interruptions by the enemy's artillery, to work at the tasks of improving the front line and of burying cables until the 24th June, the first (or 'U') day of the preliminary bombardment.

The contour of the ground, which falls gently from Hébuterne for a few hundred yards and then rises again in a long slope towards the enemy's position, enabled a panoramic view of the battlefield to be obtained from the British line.

To the right front the white tower of the church of Achiet le Petit was visible in the distance, half hidden among the trees, while in the foreground the ruins of Nameless Farm stood up amid the labyrinth of the enemy's trenches. Further to the right the ground dipped sharply to the valley overlooking Serre, completely cutting off any view in that direction. To the left, standing on slightly higher ground, was Gommecourt, a sinister spot, with a thick wood, now reduced to bare tree-stumps, and with the skeleton of a little village behind it.

The German line at Gommecourt formed a very pronounced salient, of which the south-west corner of Gommecourt Park, the wood mentioned above, was the apex. In order properly to appreciate the task of the 56th Division it will be as well to note briefly how the German defences were organized. They consisted of two trench systems about 400 yards apart. The front system, running in a south-easterly direction from the village, included three lines of trenches roughly parallel; the first and second lines were 100 yards apart, and the second and third about 170 yards apart. Gommecourt Cemetery, which was immediately south of the village, had been converted into a formidable strong point. The second system consisted of two lines of trenches running roughly due east, and was linked to the front system by a series of communication trenches. The most important feature of this second system was a strong point, constructed on a ridge about 250 yards east of the village, and known as the Quadrilateral. The whole defence was liberally provided with dug-outs capable of giving protection from the heaviest shell fire.

The general plan was for the 46th Division to attack the north side of the salient, and the 56th Division the south, the two to meet in the village behind, and to establish a line in the German trenches, cutting off the garrison of Gommecourt Park. The operation was to take place on 29th June, and was to be preceded by five days' bombardment.

The 56th Division was to attack on a frontage of two brigades, the 168th Brigade being on the right and the 169th on the left. The orders of the G.O.C. to the latter were as follows:

> The task of the 169th Brigade will be carried out in three phases. The object of the 169th Brigade in the first phase will be to capture the line of German trenches from the left of the 168th Brigade along Fall, Fellow, the Cemetery, Eck, the Maze, Eel and Fir, and to establish strong points:
>
> 1. From Feud through Ems to the Cemetery (inclusive).
> 2. About the Maze.
> 3. About the south-east corner of Gommecourt Park.
>
> The second phase of the 169th Brigade attack will take place immediately after the first phase.

The objective of the second phase is the Quadrilateral of the trenches in the south-east portion of K.5.a. The artillery lifts will be timed on the assumption that the infantry will reach Ems (between Etch and Fillet) twenty-five minutes after zero time.

The third phase will take place directly after the Quadrilateral is taken and will consist of the securing of the cross-trenches at K.5.a.78 (where Indus crosses Fill and Fillet) and joining hands with the 46th Division along Fill. Fillet will be consolidated facing east.

To carry out these orders, Br.-General Coke decided to attack with two battalions in the front line, the L.R.B. on the left, and the Q.V.R. on the right. Roughly the task of these battalions was to wheel to the left and to hold the line of the edge of Gommecourt Park. The Q.W.R. coming up in rear, were then to push straight on, carrying the attack forward, and capture the Quadrilateral. The 1/2nd Londons, whose labours prior to the attack had been unceasing, were for that reason placed in brigade reserve.

The bombardment continued during 'V,' 'W,' 'X,' and 'Y' days, becoming daily more intense, and was accompanied by occasional discharges of smoke to mislead the enemy as to the actual date and time of the assault. The enemy's reply also grew more vigorous; and the Germans, suspecting what was coming, worked hard, repairing their defences. Early on the 29th ('Y' day) orders were received postponing the attack, owing to the very bad weather, until the 1st July.

In order to give the attacking brigades an opportunity of rest and of preparation, the duty of holding the whole of the divisional front had been taken over on the 24th by the 167th Brigade. This brigade had now been in the line for a considerable number of days without relief and, in view of the postponement of the attack, would have to remain two days longer. It was thought advisable, however, for two of its battalions to be relieved at once; and accordingly, on the 29th, the 1/2nd Londons relieved the 1/7th Middlesex and the 1/3rd Londons in the 'Y' sector and in Hébuterne. The Battalion remained in this position until late on the 30th, when it moved into its assembly trenches behind the 'R' lines (with Headquarters in dugouts in Yiddish Street) in readiness for the part that it was to play on the morrow.

The 1st July dawned bright and clear; and, as a slight north-west breeze sprang up of sufficient strength to drift the smoke across to the German lines, everything promised well for the impending adventure. At 6.25 a.m.

the British guns began their intensive bombardment; and for an hour the enemy was subjected to a rain of shells of all calibres. The rate of fire reached its highest at 7.30, and was maintained at this pitch for ten minutes. At the same time, smoke was discharged from 'Z' hedge, and in five minutes had become dense along the whole front of the Division. At 7.25 the attacking troops rose from their trenches, and, forming up, advanced steadily into the dust and smoke.

The German front line was reached with little loss, in spite of the heavy machine-gun fire from the Park. Although the enemy in some places manned his trenches, his rifle fire was ineffective. 2nd Lieut. J. W. Sanders, who had been detailed with a party of 20 men of 'A' Company to carry trench-mortar ammunition to the German front line, went over with the third wave; although this party had suffered casualties during assembly, and only 2nd Lieut. Sanders and eight men reached the enemy lines, the ammunition was duly delivered.

By 8 o'clock the L.R.B. had gained all their objectives, and were hastily consolidating their position along the edge of Gommecourt Park. The Q.V.R. had gained their first objectives, but, meeting with strong resistance, had not yet reached the cemetery. This check had an unfortunate result; the Q.W.R., closely following the Q.V.R., overtook them at this point, and both battalions became inextricably mixed up. By dint of hard fighting, the cemetery was at last captured; and the attack entered on its second phase, the objective of which was the Quadrilateral. By this time the Q.W.R. were so disorganized and the enemy's resistance so strengthened that operations against the Quadrilateral were inevitably confined to bombing attacks by small parties. These attacks, though most gallantly conducted, were at first unsuccessful; and it was not until nearly 9 o'clock that a party of the Q.W.R., including two non-commissioned officers of the 2/2nd Londons attached, Corpls. F. E. Hayward and W. C. Ide, at last reached the Quadrilateral. In the Q.W.R.'s advance another 2/2nd Londoner, 2nd Lieut. D. F. Upton,[1] played a gallant part; he organized a bombing attack on Fellow, captured it, and from that point reached the cemetery.

While on the left of the divisional front the 169th Brigade was gradually making good its objectives, on the right the 168th Brigade had attacked with equal vigour, and, after some inevitable loss of direction, had likewise gained and held most of its objectives. Up to this point the 56th Division's attack, though slower and more confused than was intended, may be said to have

[1] 2nd Lieut. Upton, who was wounded and captured, was subsequently awarded the M.C. for his gallantry in this battle.

115

made satisfactory progress. This success, however, was but short-lived. The enemy, who had now had time to recover from the first assault, had rallied, and his counter-measures were beginning to take effect. His gunners, who from an early hour had shelled the British assembly positions, switched over first to No Man's Land, and later to their own captured front line. His infantry, emboldened by the loss of power in the British attack, began to counter-attack; and from Gommecourt Park, which was apparently honeycombed with deep dug-outs, crowded with men, strong bombing parties began to work along the captured trenches.

The troops of the 169th Brigade were the first to feel the effects of the enemy's recovery; and the Q.V.R. and the Q.W.R. were both heavily attacked. Finding that they were losing their hold, both battalions called for reinforcements. No reinforcements came in answer to their call, and the reason for this is to be found in the enemy's barrage on No Man's Land, which had increased to such intensity that it prevented any supports getting across, and frustrated an attempt by the 1/3rd Londons (167th Brigade) to dig a communication trench to the enemy's lines.

As the morning wore on, anxiety grew concerning the fate of the leading battalions of the 169th Brigade; and at 12.30 Br.-General Coke called for volunteers from the 1/2nd Londons to carry across a written message. Four men volunteered; and L/Corpl. A. R. Boyce and Corpl. F. Werner were successful in getting across. The message was as follows: ' R.F.C. observers repeatedly report Ems, Etch, and the Quadrilateral empty of Germans— Push on bombing parties at once and occupy Quadrilateral—Barrage on Quadrilateral lifts at 1.30 p.m.' But it arrived too late to be acted upon; the supply of bombs had given out; and the British had already been driven back to the German front line. L/Corpl. Boyce came back with a message that the Q.V.R. were retiring; and Corpl. Werner, after delivering his message to the Q.W.R., volunteered to go back with a request for immediate support. This request never reached its destination, the gallant corporal being killed on his way back.[1]

By this time the enemy was launching concerted counter-attacks from all directions. He was advancing down Epte, Ems, and Etch; he was attacking from Gommecourt Park; he was in Fall on the right; and was slowly forcing the British from his front line.

The situation was desperate, and called for desperate measures. If the hard-pressed troops in the German lines were to be extricated and if our grip

---

[1] Both Corpl. Werner and L/Corpl. Boyce were awarded the M.M. for their gallant conduct on this occasion.

on the ground won was to be maintained, it was essential that further supplies of bombs should somehow be sent forward, and that the flanks of the Brigade should be strengthened by vigorously thrusting back the enemy's gradually enveloping counter-attacks. The Brigadier decided to put his reserve battalion into the fight in a last attempt to retrieve the fortunes of the day.

Between 1.30 and 1.45 p.m., therefore, he issued orders for the 1/2nd Londons to attack Fir and Fen on the left, Ferret in the centre, and Fern and Fever on the right. In its advance the Battalion was to carry as many bombs as possible, so that by this means the pressing need of the forward troops could in part be met. A few minutes later Lieut.-Col. Attenborough gave his orders to his company commanders, and disposed the Battalion as follows:

> RIGHT: 'A' Company (Capt. Garland)—against Fern and Fever, and Female in the second line.
> CENTRE: 'D' Company (Capt Sneath)—against Ferret.
> LEFT: 'C' Company (Capt. Handyside)—against Fir and Fen, and Feast in the second line.
> RESERVE: 'B' Company (Capt. Kellett)—to hold the British front line.

'B' Company, in reserve, moved forward at once, and in due course took up a position to the right of 'Z' hedge, ready for any emergency. At a few minutes before half-past two, 'C' Company moved up the communication trench to the front line at the right end of 'Z' hedge. The men climbed out of the trench, and formed up outside the wire.

The enemy's standing barrage on No Man's Land had reached its greatest intensity. Shells shrieked and whined through the air. The ground rocked under the repeated explosions; and towering columns of earth and greenish smoke sprang skyward. The noise was deafening; and the atmosphere reeked with the acrid fumes of high explosive. From the grim salient of Gommecourt Park on the left machine guns in enfilade swept the slope leading up to the German position, vicious spirts of earth marking where the bullets fell. Into the heart of this inferno 'C' Company slowly moved forward. Great gaps were torn in their ranks; little heaps of dead and wounded marked the company's advance; one by one the officers fell; but no one faltered, and the company pressed steadily on. Capt. Handyside, in the van, fell seriously wounded; he bravely crawled forward, encouraging his men by voice and example, until the burst of a shell killed him outright. Few men could pass through such a galling fire unscathed; those few alone succeeded in reaching the enemy's line. Leaderless, half-stunned by the nerve-shattering experience through which they had passed, they fell into the trench or crouched beneath the parapet, too few in numbers to finish the task so gallantly begun.

Some little time elapsed before 'A' Company was ready to make its attempt. At laſt the men rose from their trenches, and without faltering advanced into the teeth of the barrage. The barrage was ſtill intense on No Man's Land; the company ſtood no better chance than 'C' Company of crossing the shell-torn waſte, and it met the same fate. The ranks slowly melted in the intense fire; and by 3 p.m. all was over. Capt. Garland had been killed; all his officers and moſt of his non-commissioned officers and men had been killed or wounded. Of 5 officers and 97 other ranks of this company, who left the shelter of the British trenches that afternoon, only 10 returned unwounded.

The efforts of these two companies—almoſt foredoomed to failure from the outset—to assiſt their hard-pressed comrades were beyond all praise, and will rank for all time with the fineſt achievements of the Regiment. Speaking, shortly afterwards, of the deeds of the London troops at Gommecourt, the Lord Mayor of London, Sir Charles Wakefield—who, after the war, was to become the Honorary Colonel of the regiment to which he now paid high tribute—compared the heroic attack of the two companies of the 1/2nd Londons with the charge of the Light Brigade at Balaclava. And it is indeed worthy of comparison with this outſtanding example of heroism and devotion to duty; for the 2nd Londons—although there was no queſtion of a miſtaken order—faced the ſtorm of 'shot and shell' as coolly as did the Crimean heroes of old, and, with none of the glamour of a cavalry charge to inspire them and far less chance of survival, by reason of the power of modern weapons, they bravely advanced 'into the jaws of death.' The officers set a gallant example; and the men, nothing daunted by the failure of troops as fine as themselves to cross those dreadful four hundred yards of ground, torn by shells and swept by machine-gun bullets, sacrificed themselves unhesitatingly.

'D' Company was somewhat late in assembly, and for this reason did not reach the British front line until the valiant attack of 'C' Company was in progress. It was preparing to follow the example of this company, when orders were received from the Brigadier that the attack was to be ſtopped. The issue of these very wise orders was obtained by Lieut.-Col. Attenborough, who, from his advanced headquarters, had watched the progress of the battle. His opinion confirmed by Capt. Kellett who had made the laborious journey from the front line with firſt-hand information, Lieut.-

Col. Attenborough represented to the Brigadier that it was merely wasting valuable lives to continue the attempts to reinforce the isolated troops in the enemy's lines. After consulting Divisional Headquarters, Br.-General Coke agreed, and ordered the Battalion to discontinue its attempts, and, instead, to make the 'Y' sector of the British front line secure against possible counter-attacks.

At 4.45 p.m. there followed orders for the Battalion to reorganize and prepare to take over part of the German line at dusk; and 'B' Company was detailed for this task. Long before dusk it became apparent that our hold on the German line was of the slenderest; a party of about seventy men clinging desperately to Ferret was all that could actually be seen in the enemy's trenches. The orders to the 1/2nd Londons were therefore cancelled; and at about 8 p.m. the German line was finally abandoned by the 169th Brigade. On the right, the 168th Brigade, which had likewise suffered heavily from the enemy's bombardment and counter-attacks, and now had an equally slender hold on the German line, was also withdrawn. Less than two hours later the artillery on both sides ceased fire, and the agony of Gommecourt came to an end. When darkness fell, those men of 'A' and 'C' Companies, unwounded or wounded, who had been lying out in No Man's Land or under the shelter of the German parapet, and who could manage to walk or crawl, came back. The two companies could muster between them barely 50 men, most of whom were wounded.

At Gommecourt the 1/2nd Londons failed, but failed gloriously in circumstances that cannot but reflect the highest credit on the Regiment. They were asked to do a desperate thing where troops as fine as themselves had already failed, and they unhesitatingly tried to do it. The men behaving so gallantly as they did, it is not too much to say that their failure proves that the task was utterly impossible. Most regiments of the British Army have cause to remember the First of July; for the 2nd London Regiment, memory, wherein sadness and satisfaction have an equal place, will focus itself on those few minutes of the afternoon when the two companies went forward up the tragic slope before Gommecourt's sinister Wood.

Before we turn to a consideration of the reasons for the apparent failure of the major operations at Gommecourt, it is interesting to note what C.S.M. Macrow says, in a letter concerning 'A' Company's gallant effort:

> At 2 p.m. Capt. Garland received the order to draw three grenades per man and attack a portion of the trench to the right of our position. We proceeded to the communication trench at the rear

of the new front line. We took a long time to get there owing to the number of wounded trying to get back to the dressing ſtation. At the laſt minute Capt. Garland gave me orders to remain in the trench and see that everyone went over. I am very glad to say that not a single man needed any urging on. The men had to dig holes in the sides of the trenches and climb eight feet to get on the top and throw their rifles up before they could get up. No sooner had the men ſtarted than the Germans opened a murderous machine-gun fire and increased the artillery fire which had been going on all the morning. Before all the men had got over, others came tumbling back with two, three, four, and in two cases, five wounds. . . . The number that went over was five officers, six sergeants, and ninety-one other ranks, and the number that reported to me that evening was one sergeant (C. S. Taylor) and six other ranks, and only three reported back while we were there. Our total casualties that day (including the party under Lieut. Sanders, detailed for carrying trench-mortar ammunition) were five officers, six sergeants, and 124 other ranks.

The total casualties of the Battalion were as follows :

KILLED : 4 officers[1] (Capts. P. J. A. Handyside, J. R. Garland, 2nd Lieuts. H. C. Gosnell and B. R. Buxton), and 41 other ranks.
WOUNDED : 6 officers (Lieuts. G. B. Henderson, H. W. Everitt, 2nd Lieuts. N. F. Perris, H. F. Blows, J. W. Sanders, and A. E. Wiggs), and 158 other ranks.
MISSING : 2 officers (Lieuts. J. S. Grainger and A. M. Thorman[2]), and 42 other ranks.

Capt. Percy James Alexander Handyside, the son of Mr. James Handyside, of Petrograd, was born on the 10th December 1878. He was educated abroad, and previous to the war was a merchant in the Brazilian trade. He was commissioned to the 2nd Londons on 7th October 1913, being promoted Captain on 21ſt April 1915. He was a keen soldier, and was dearly loved by all, to whom he was affectionately known as 'Uncle.' Whilſt on leave in England a short time before, he had been married.

Capt. James Richard Garland, B.Sc., A.K.C., aged 23, was the only son

[1] In addition to these, the following 2nd London officers were killed at Gommecourt, while serving in other units of the Division : 2nd Lieuts. F. A. Farley, K. M. A. Fradd, W. F. Strange, and C. A. Stubbs.
[2] Both Lieuts. Grainger and Thorman were subsequently reported killed.

of Mr. and Mrs. R. E. Garland, of Willesden Green. He was a student at London University (King's College), where he gained his degree and where he was a keen member of the O.T.C., in which he had served two years before the war. He was gazetted to the 2nd Londons on the 23rd August 1914, and was promoted Captain on the 14th March 1916. Capt. Garland was well known in the parish of St. Lawrence, Brondesbury, where a memorial service was held for him.

2nd Lieut. Harold Clifford Gosnell was born on the 6th January 1890. He joined the 7th London Regiment on the outbreak of war, and served with this battalion, in the ranks, in France. He was commissioned on the 15th November 1915, and gazetted to the 2nd Londons, but he continued with the 7th Londons in France until 18th December 1915. He then joined the 4/2nd Londons in England, returning to France in March 1916.

2nd Lieut. Bertie Reginald Buxton was born on 1st December 1891. Soon after the outbreak of war he enlisted in the 4th (T.F.) Battalion Seaforth Highlanders, with whom he served for a year in France. He was gazetted to the 2nd Londons on 3rd November 1915.

2nd Lieut. John Scott Grainger was born on 17th November 1889. He enlisted in the 4th (T.F.) Battalion Cameron Highlanders on the outbreak of war, but soon obtained his commission, being gazetted to the 2/2nd Londons on 16th January 1915, with whom he served in Malta, Gallipoli, and Egypt, being transferred to the 1/2nd Londons on the disbanding of the second-line unit.

2nd Lieut. Alan Marshall Thorman, who was born on the 23rd July 1895, was the son of Mr. John Thorman, of Witton Castle, County Durham. He was educated at Charterhouse School, and on the outbreak of war enlisted in the Public Schools Battalion of the Middlesex Regiment. He was gazetted to the 2/2nd Londons on 16th January 1915, and served with them in Malta, Gallipoli, and Egypt, being transferred to the 1/2nd Londons on the disbanding of the second-line unit.

The word 'failure' should perhaps not have been written with regard to Gommecourt. To outward appearances the day had ended in 'failure,' but in reality the attack had achieved its main object, that of diverting the attention of the enemy and of preventing him transferring troops and guns for use against the Fourth Army, where real progress was of vital importance.

The 46th Division, in its attack on the northern face of the salient, met with a series of disasters in the first few minutes, and from these it did not recover. Although a new attack was ordered, postponed, and postponed again, no further help came from this division during the day. Thus within half an hour after the assault was launched the fate of the 56th Division was sealed; the enemy, having this one division alone to deal with, was able to concentrate upon it the large number of guns that he had collected behind Gommecourt and to place an impassable barrage behind the assaulting battalions, so that no further reinforcements nor supplies of ammunition could reach them.

Major-General Hull, in his conclusions on the operation, was of opinion that its lack of complete success was primarily due to a shortage of bombs—a shortage that could not be made good by reason of the enemy's barrage on No Man's Land; that the effect of the British bombardment, moral and actual, was not as great as had been hoped; and that the wisdom of such bombardment which gave the enemy notice of the impending attack was open to question.

To the main attack on the Somme on the 1st July Major-General Hull's conclusions apply with almost equal force. The long bombardment had given the enemy ample warning, and its intensity had not succeeded in subduing his defence. By the magnificent heroism of the assaulting troops, several miles of the enemy's trenches and several thousands of his men had been captured. These results, though not inconsiderable in themselves, can hardly have been all that was hoped for from the enormous preparations, and the enormous efforts on the day itself. Moreover, they had been gained at a great sacrifice; nearly 60,000 British soldiers had been killed, wounded, or taken prisoner. Never before had so great a loss been sustained by the British Army in a single day.

After the battle the following messages were forwarded to the Battalion by Major-General Hull:

> The G.O.C. 56th Division wishes all ranks to know how proud he is of the splendid way in which they captured the German trenches and of the way they held on to them until all their ammunition and grenades were exhausted. He is satisfied that the main task of the Division in containing and killing Germans was most thoroughly accomplished.

Br.-General Coke added the following:

> In forwarding the foregoing congratulatory message the Brigadier wishes to express to all ranks his praise and apprecia-

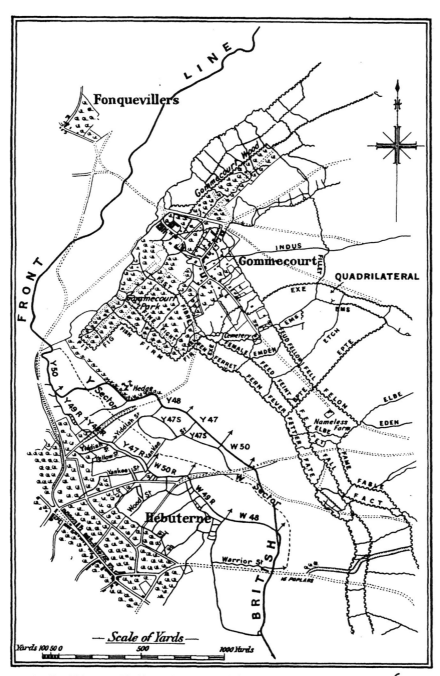

THE ATTACK ON THE GOMMECOURT SALIENT, 1ST JULY 1916.

tion of the excellent work done during the preparations for the attack and of the gallantry displayed during the day's fighting.[1]

For its share in the attack on the Gommecourt salient the 2nd London Regiment was awarded the battle honour, 'Albert, 1916,' this being a subsidiary battle in the operations grouped under the general title of 'The Battles of the Somme, 1916.'

The 2nd July dawned with the guns silent on either side, and thus they remained all day, but for a sharp outburst of shelling against Hébuterne in the morning. About 12.30 p.m. Corpl. A. B. Jones went out to assist a wounded man near the parapet, and was hit by a sniper. But a man who went out to the corporal was not fired on; and shortly afterwards the enemy was seen in Ferret showing a white flag. With Br.-General Coke's permission, Capt. Maxwell Ramsay, the Medical Officer of the 1/2nd Londons, in company with the Medical Officer of the L.R.B., then went down the Gommecourt road with stretchers, and brought in about 45 wounded, the enemy also leaving his trenches for the same purpose. This truce, which lasted about an hour, was honourably kept by the enemy. Many of the wounded lying near the enemy's wire paid a tribute to the Germans, who, they said, had come to them during the night and given them coffee.

The 1/2nd Londons were not relieved until the next day, when they were withdrawn to Souastre. The Corps Commander here reviewed them on parade, and, in a speech that he began, not with the formula usual on such occasions, but with the one simple and expressive word 'Gentlemen,' congratulated all ranks on their splendid work and heroic endeavours.

So severely had the 46th Division been handled by the enemy in its attack on the northern face of the Gommecourt salient that, temporarily at

---

[1] As nearly one-third of the Q.W.R.'s fighting strength was composed of men of the disbanded 2/2nd Londons, it is of interest to record the words with which Major J. Q. Henriques, in his *War History of the 1st Battalion Queen's Westminster Rifles*, 1914-1918, closes his account of the battle :

'So ended a day of supreme endeavour, a day that will ever call forth proud memories of the officers and men who fought and suffered and died, and who have left behind them an example of heroism and sacrifice that can certainly never be excelled.

'Out of 750 officers and men who went into action, 600 were killed, wounded, and missing, and it is believed that not a single unwounded member of the Queen's Westminster Rifles fell into the enemy's hands.'

Some part of the foregoing eulogy can justly be applied to the members of the 2/2nd Londons, and it is therefore reprinted with acknowledgments to its author.

least, it had to be withdrawn from the line. Its place was taken by the shattered units of the 56th Division, which now extended its front to the left. Accordingly the 169th Brigade took over the 'Z' sector of the front line, north of the Gommecourt salient, between Bienvillers and Fonquevillers; and on the afternoon of 4th July the 1/2nd Londons moved to the latter village, in brigade reserve. Owing to the severe losses that they had sustained 'A' and 'C' Companies were amalgamated under the command of Capt. A. G. Houlder; and the combined companies, including the nucleus left out of action, mustered only 3 officers and 100 other ranks.

On the 6th July the Battalion relieved the Kensingtons and the Rangers in the line, the combined 'A' and 'C' Companies taking over from the former and 'B' Company from the latter. 'D' Company went into the reserve line between these two sectors, but moved next day into the front line, it being then decided to hold the latter more strongly. The trenches were in a deplorable condition; parts of the fire trench were nearly three feet deep in water and mud; and in the communication trenches water stood waist-deep, rafts being improvised to enable the men to negotiate them. On one occasion the Lewis-gun team of 'B' Company was isolated in the front line by the water for a day and a night, and the sergeant in charge had to resort to swimming in order to fetch the rations.

Very heavy rain fell throughout the 7th, and the trenches were flooded even worse than before. During the night a patrol reconnoitred the ruins of a sugar refinery standing in No Man's Land, just north of the Gommecourt road. It was believed that the Germans were in the habit of visiting this building; and it was hoped that a capture might here be effected in order to establish the identity of the German regiments occupying the sector. On the next night the Battalion was relieved by the Q.V.R. on the right and by the L.R.B. on the left, and went back to Fonquevillers. Before the Battalion left the line a patrol, under 2nd Lieut. St. J. R. St. Ledger, was sent out to the sugar refinery, but had no better luck than its predecessor.

The weather had now begun to improve, and the opportunity was not lost of putting the trenches into a satisfactory condition; for this purpose the Battalion while in brigade reserve found large working parties every day. On the 11th the depleted ranks of the Battalion received a very welcome draft of 71 non-commissioned officers and men; but it was a great disappointment that the draft included many that were not 2nd Londoners.

The whole system of reinforcing regiments at the front was the cause of considerable heart-burning, and evoked vigorous protests from all sides. Undoubtedly, in times of stress battalions must be filled up as quickly as possible without waiting for reinforcements from their own unit; and admittedly the authorities at the base camps were working under great difficulties. Nevertheless, it was discouraging to see men of a regiment going to other units in the same division. Such a disregard of *esprit de corps* could not but have a bad effect both on the battalion itself and on the reinforcements, who had been imbued with their own regimental tradition. Some improvement was subsequently effected; but, despite strong protests from commanding officers and others, the system of sending officers and men to units other than their own continued during the rest of the war. The opportunity is here taken of paying a grateful tribute to the loyalty to their adopted regiment of the large number of officers and men of different units who served with the 2nd Londons during the war, and of whom the Regiment is justly proud.

The 1/2nd Londons withdrew to St. Amand on the 12th July, and spent the next day in cleaning up. They were back again in the trenches on the 14th, relieving the 8th Lincolns in the line east of Hannescamps, 'B' and 'D' Companies being in front, and 'A' and 'C' in support. During this tour in the trenches a serious attempt to obtain 'identification' of the enemy was made by the Battalion, acting under brigade instructions. For this raid, which was undertaken on the 16th July by a volunteer party, consisting of Capt. Kellett, Lieuts. B. Attenborough and Clive, and 70 other ranks, co-operation was arranged with the Royal Engineers, who were to clear lanes for the attackers by placing bangalore torpedoes under the enemy's wire, and with the artillery, who were to bombard the 'Z' and the enemy's reserve trenches.

The raid, however, did not go quite 'according to plan,' for the Royal Engineer personnel, while going forward to put in the bangalore torpedoes, were discovered by an enemy patrol. Searchlights were turned on them, and machine-gun fire was opened; they were thus obliged to return without accomplishing their mission. Capt. Kellett, who with his party had been lying out in No Man's Land since 11.45 p.m., decided to trust to the barrage to cut the wire. When the guns lifted at 12.10, the raiders moved forward and succeeded in finding a gap in the first line of wire, but they could find no similar gap in the second line. The enemy turned a searchlight on the party, and opened a hot fire, at the same time throwing many bombs, apparently in a state of panic, since many of the fuses had not been lit. At 12.20 a.m. Capt. Kellett gave up all hope of finding a way through the remaining two belts of wire, and accordingly withdrew his party.

On relief by the L.R.B. and Q.W.R. the 1/2nd Londons moved back on the 19th to St. Amand, where they received a draft consisting of 66 non-commissioned officers and men of the 21st Londons (First Surrey Rifles) and 138 of the 22nd Londons (The Queen's). After two days' rest the Battalion, with the exception of a special volunteer raiding party of 50 men, under 2nd Lieut. S. W. Keen, which, by brigade instructions, was left in Bien-villers, returned to the front line, where it remained for the rest of the month. Lieut. J. B. Pittman was wounded on the 29th; otherwise nothing of note occurred.

Among the officer reinforcements who joined during the month—and after the losses at Gommecourt they were badly needed—were the following:

2nd Lieuts. F. C. Langley, W. E. Lockhart, W. C. Cambray, A. E. Elliott, A. J. Sullivan, S. W. Keen, and E. W. Lockey.

The early days of August were spent either in reserve at Bienvillers, whence large working parties were found daily for the Royal Engineers, or in the trenches at Hannescamps. The Battalion was inspected on the 2nd August by Br.-General Coke, who presented cards from the G.O.C., 56th Division, to the non-commissioned officers and men mentioned for gallantry during the attack at Gommecourt. At the same time news was received that Sergts. Aspinall and Brooks and L/Corpl. S. J. Attikin had been awarded the M.M. for their conduct during the same operation. On this day Capt. Houlder left to join the 4th Londons as second-in-command, Capt. J. W. Long succeeding him in command of 'A' Company, and Lieut. T. G. McCarthy becoming Adjutant in succession to Capt. Long.

While the Battalion was in the Hannescamps sector frequent attempts were made to secure the coveted 'identification' of the enemy. Patrols went out every night down the Essarts road or to the Osier Bed, a place that it was believed the enemy also visited. Nothing tangible resulted from these continued efforts, although patrols, under Lieut. Attenborough and 2nd Lieut. Lockey, both encountered the enemy, who did not wait to try conclusions. The enemy attempted one raid himself. His party was discovered lying outside the wire opposite the right ('A') company's front; plans were laid for its reception, and measures concerted with the artillery for making its retreat as unpleasant as possible. Unfortunately the raiders were disturbed by a patrol of 'D' Company, and incontinently withdrew.

The Battalion was finally relieved on 15th, and three days later it marched to Ivergny, via Gaudiempré, Warluzel, and Sus St. Léger. The marching was good, and the twelve miles were covered in five hours. On the next day, the 19th August, the Division ceased to belong to the VII. Corps.

After a stay of three days at Ivergny the Battalion marched, on the 22nd August, via le Souich, Barly, Frohen le Grand, to Maizicourt—a distance of sixteen and a half miles. The country was very hilly, and the day intensely hot; yet despite this and despite the fact that the troops had done little marching for many weeks, the march discipline was very good. On the next day the march was continued via Yvrencheu to Canchy (in the St. Riquier area), the distance of fourteen miles being covered in five hours and a half. Here the Battalion remained for a fortnight, officially 'resting,' but in reality training very hard.

Officer reinforcements during the month included the following:

2nd Lieuts. C. Downey, G. A. Taylor, J. R. Skeet, A. L. B. Sproule, F. C. Baker, J. J. Edmett, and S. H. Stevens.
Casualties were 12 other ranks wounded.

While the 56th Division was in the St. Riquier area there occurred an event, or rather the last of a series of events, fraught with consequences of the highest importance, not only to the course of this war, but to the whole conduct of war in the future. For some time past certain far-sighted persons had been experimenting in England with a new engine of war, one destined ultimately to effect a revolution in mechanical warfare, and to bring to an end the deadlock on the Western Front. This engine, given the purposely misleading name of 'Tank,' had successfully passed its preliminary trials; fifty had been ordered, and were at last coming forward from the manufacturers. They began to arrive in France during the early stages of the Battle of the Somme; and on the 26th August the 56th Division, which had been specially selected to co-operate with the Heavy Section, Machine-Gun Corps, the forerunners of the Tank Corps, assisted in the first demonstration in France of this new weapon. H.R.H. The Prince of Wales, Sir Douglas Haig, and General Joffre were interested spectators of this demonstration, which much impressed everyone, despite the fact that two of the five tanks broke down.

On the 3rd September the Battalion, in company with the rest of the 169th Brigade, entrained at St. Riquier for Corbie, where it arrived the same day. The little town of Corbie, with its quaint tree-lined square and ancient church, is situated at the confluence of the rivers Somme and Ancre, and was, at the time of which we write, full of British wounded and German prisoners, the backwash of the Somme battle. For this reason accommodation was scanty; and after an uncomfortable night the Brigade set out for the Happy Valley, near Bray sur Somme. Up the hill, past the brickworks, between lines of miserable-looking German prisoners engaged in road-making, along the high road overlooking the beautiful valley of the Somme—there is a spot, close to the brow of the hill, where, by turning aside from the road and looking back, one can gain a delightful view of the broad, placid waters of the Somme, with Corbie nestling among the trees at the water's edge, and if at the time the landscape is suffused by the golden light of a setting sun, the scene is of surpassing loveliness—, on through Morlancourt, where the Guards Division was resting, marched the troops, on towards the maelstrom that had already engulfed thousands of men and tons of material—the Battle of the Somme.

The scenes behind the Somme battle-front beggar description; the whole area was packed with troops and pulsating with activity; on every side were camps, transport lines, and dumps; every road was congested with guns and vehicles of all kinds, and the confusion thereon was far worse than any London traffic-block. The road on which the 1/2nd Londons now found themselves was no different from others in this area; its surface was covered with half a foot of mud, and broken every few yards by deep, water-filled holes; and through the masses of guns, lorries, ambulances, waggons, and other vehicles that continually streamed along it the Battalion had to thread its way, often in single file, and with many a halt to enable some particularly confused tangle of traffic to be sorted out. As may well be imagined, the march was very trying; and it was not until 8 p.m., on a miserably cold and wet night, that the Battalion reached its camping ground in the Happy Valley. The tent accommodation was quite inadequate; and half the Battalion was obliged to spend an uncomfortable night in the pouring rain.

The 56th Division now passed into the XIV. Corps (Lieut.-General Lord Cavan), and within a few hours was to be plunged into the desperate fighting that was raging between the Somme and the Ancre.

CHAPTER X

THE 1/2ND LONDONS IN THE BATTLES OF THE SOMME, 1916—II

I. Leuze Wood and the Fighting for Combles

BEFORE proceeding to describe in detail the fighting in which the 2nd Londons next took part it is necessary to trace the course of the British offensive on the Somme since 1st July 1916, in order that a clear appreciation of the operations may be obtained.

The enemy's position that was attacked on the 1st July was situated on the ridge of high, undulating ground between the Somme and the Ancre. It consisted of two main systems, the first well down the southern slope of the ridge, and the second some three to five thousand yards in rear, on or below the southern crest. The German defences were immensely strong, and they cannot be better described than in the words of Sir Douglas Haig himself:[1]

> During nearly two years' preparation he (the enemy) had spared no pains to render these defences impregnable. The first and second systems each consisted of several lines of deep trenches, well provided with bomb-proof shelters and with numerous communication trenches connecting them. The front of the trenches in each system was protected by wire entanglements, many of them in two belts forty yards broad, built of iron stakes interlaced with barbed wire, often almost as thick as a man's finger.
>
> The numerous woods and villages in and between these systems of defence had been turned into veritable fortresses. The deep cellars usually to be found in the villages, and the numerous pits and quarries common to a chalk country, were used to provide cover for machine guns and trench mortars. . . . The salients in the enemy's line, from which he could bring enfilade fire across his front, were made into self-contained forts, and often protected by mine-fields; while strong redoubts and concrete machine-gun emplacements had been constructed in positions from which he could sweep his own trenches should these be taken. . . .

[1] Sir Douglas Haig's Dispatches.

> These various systems of defence . . . formed, in short, not merely a series of successive lines, but one composite system of enormous depth and strength.
>
> Behind his second system of trenches, in addition to woods, villages, and other strong points prepared for defence, the enemy had several other lines already completed.

The attack on this formidable position resolved itself into three more or less distinct phases. The first phase, which opened on the 1st July and closed with the Battle of Bazentin Ridge on the 14th/17th July, gave the Fourth Army possession of the southern crest of the plateau between Delville Wood and Bazentin le Petit. The right of the British line now ran from Maltz Horn Farm, where it joined the French, northwards along the eastern edge of Trônes Wood, to Longueval, while the French line ran southwards from the farm to Hem. The line formed an uncomfortable salient at Delville Wood; and in order to straighten out this salient it was necessary for the British right and the French, in prolongation, to swing up into line with the British centre. The successful accomplishment of this task involved the capture first of Guillemont, Falfemont Farm, and Leuze Wood, then of Ginchy, and Bouleaux Wood, and required the closest co-operation with the French. The operations undertaken with this object formed the second phase, which was practically complete by the end of the first week of September. The fighting was very confused and severe; and it was not until 18th August that the outskirts of Guillemont were reached. A combined British and French offensive was then launched (Battle of Guillemont) on the 3rd September; and by the 5th Falfemont Farm had been captured, and British troops were firmly established in Leuze Wood.

The third phase included the capture of the whole plateau and the extension of the British advance well down the forward slopes of the ridge; but we are not for the moment concerned with this, since the second phase was only drawing to a close when, on the night of the 6th September, the 56th Division relieved the 5th Division on the extreme right of the British line.

On this night the 169th Brigade moved forward from Happy Valley, and the 1/2nd Londons relieved the Royal Irish Fusiliers in the support line at Falfemont Farm and Angle Wood, after a trying march in the dark through the Valley of Death (between Trônes Wood and Favière Wood).

To attempt to describe the battle-fields of the Somme is a work of supererogation; those who have seen them will never forget them, and those who have not can gain from words alone little conception of what they were really like.

The whole countryside had been reduced by shell fire to a wilderness without verdure or growth of any kind. Villages were little more than unrecognizable heaps of rubble; woods looked as if a foreſt-fire had swept over them; the beautiful avenues of trees that had formerly lined the roads had been ſtruck down. On every side the ground itself was pitted with shell-holes; and the soil churned up into an indescribable mass that in wet weather quickly turned to clinging mud; everywhere lay corpses, unburied, or perhaps exhumed by shell fire; and all the debris of war, barbed wire, iron ſtakes, broken rifles, bombs, and ammunition, bits of equipment, petrol tins, battered ſteel helmets, littered the feſtering earth.

Needless to say, no part of Falfemont Farm now remained above ground; and the 1/2nd Londons found that the aid of guides who knew the ground was indispensable. The guides provided by the outgoing brigade proved to have been batmen at brigade headquarters, and they had but the vagueſt ideas as to the whereabouts of Falfemont Farm. They soon loſt the way; and the Battalion was obliged to halt in the middle of the Valley of Death, with shells roaring overhead, until the timely arrival of a party of Royal Engineers, bound for the same deſtination, enabled the march to be continued. There were no dug-outs or trenches at Falfemont Farm; and the Battalion had to spend the reſt of the night in the open. Headquarters were eſtablished in Angle Wood, in a shell-hole with a piece of wood over the top. The night was very cold, but passed uneventfully.

On the following day Lieut.-Col. Attenborough was summoned to a conference at Brigade Headquarters in the Valley of Death, whereat all commanding officers were informed of the impending attack by the 56th Division, and plans were fully discussed. Both on this day and the next the whole area between Falfemont Farm and Leuze Wood was subjeĉted to an intense bombardment by the enemy.

During the 8th the L.R.B. and Q.V.R., who were in the front line at Leuze Wood, made a combined bombing attack with the objeĉt of eſtablishing a line along Loop (or ' V ') Trench (a trench some 300 yards to the eaſt of Leuze Wood and running parallel with its edge), the sunken road from Ginchy to Combles, and the northern edge of Leuze Wood. This attack was made with the intention of getting a better line from which the offensive of the XIV. Corps., in co-operation with the XV. Corps on the left, could be renewed, and was only partially successful.

The ridge of high ground, the objeĉtive of the Allies' present attacks, is

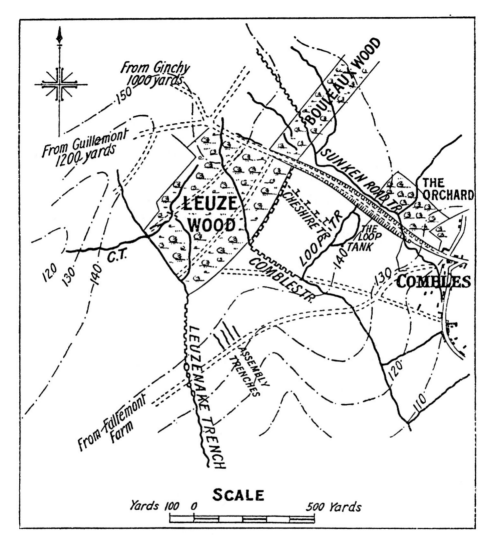

THE FIGHTING FOR COMBLES.

cleft towards its southern end by a broad and comparatively deep valley, known as the Combles Valley from the town of that name situated at its head. Immediately north of the town the valley widens out into a basin and then forks, one branch running north-eastward and skirting the spur whereon stands the village of Morval, the other running back almost due west into the main ridge, forming a short re-entrant. In the angle, made by the junction of this second branch with the main valley, rises the spur, on the summit of which stands Leuze Wood.

Leuze Wood, more generally and picturesquely known to the British Army as 'Lousy Wood,' occupies a commanding position; northwards and eastwards, though the view is somewhat restricted by the Morval Spur in the middle distance, it overlooks the basin and both branches of the Combles Valley, and also the main valley itself, while southwards and westwards it commands all the low ground between Hardecourt and Guillemont. From its southernmost extremity there is a gradual slope towards Falfemont Farm and Angle Wood, while from its eastern edge the ground falls, gently at first, but then more sharply, to the bottom of the Combles Valley, rising beyond to a ridge of equal height whose sides are covered by a wood called Savernake—a name that conjures up visions of the glorious Marlborough downs.

About seven hundred yards long from north to south and four hundred yards wide, Leuze Wood is roughly rectangular in shape, with a long narrow extension to the north-east, under the separate name of Bouleaux Wood. Between the two woods runs the Ginchy road, which, as it leaves the cover of the trees, drops rapidly down the hill to Combles. This sunken road is a very marked feature, and it was to be a source of trouble to the British in their many attacks.

At the time of which we write Leuze Wood, like many another wood on this front, consisted of the bare stumps of trees, whose trunks lay, battered and riven, in the thick undergrowth. The wood was thickly entangled with barbed wire, and its southern face was lined by a number of German concrete gun emplacements. On every side the ground was pitted with shell-holes, the fields scarred with trenches. Combles was little more than piles of brick and masonry; and the narrow-gauge railway in the valley, its track twisted and torn, could hardly be recognized as a railway at all.

Time with its healing hand has effaced the evidences of war. Combles Valley has once again assumed a peaceful and beautiful aspect; green grass covers the shapely downs; the fields over which the 1/2nd Londons struggled so valiantly to gain a footing in Loop Trench are yearly tilled and sown. Combles itself is once again a flourishing little township, with its neat red houses and its strictly utilitarian concrete water-tower that comes first into view as one tops the crest of the road from Ginchy. But high above all stands

Leuze Wood, shattered and still, aloof and forbidding, untouched by the hand of man since the days when it echoed to the reverberations of bomb and shell, a grim reminder of the fighting that raged about it many summers ago.

In the attack of the 9th September (Battle of Ginchy) the 56th Division, which was on the right of the XIV. Corps—the 16th Division being on the left—employed two of its brigades, the 168th and the 169th. The 169th was on the right of the divisional front, and had two battalions in the front line, the L.R.B. on the right and the Q.V.R. on the left. The attack was to be launched at 4.45 p.m.; and at a somewhat earlier hour the 1/2nd Londons moved forward in artillery formation to the Falfemont Farm line—a distance of about a thousand yards—, sustaining only one casualty. Here they took up a defensive position, at the same time remaining ready to reinforce the attacking battalions if required. Battalion Headquarters remained at Angle Wood.

The attack went well at the outset, although the attacking battalions suffered heavy casualties from the stout resistance offered by the enemy, and although an unfortunate shortage of bombs made itself apparent at an early hour. For some unexplained cause all requests by the battalions in the front line for information, ammunition, and the like, were made through the 1/2nd Londons' Headquarters. Needless to say, the latter endeavoured as far as possible to make good these miscellaneous requirements, and its efforts were much appreciated by the battalions concerned.

By 6 p.m. the Q.V.R. had gained their objective outside the north-eastern edge of Leuze Wood; but the L.R.B. had come under fierce artillery and machine-gun fire, and had been driven back into the wood with heavy loss. The Q.V.R., finding their right flank, which was thus exposed by the withdrawal of the L.R.B., threatened by an enemy counter-attack, sent back a runner to the 1/2nd Londons asking for assistance. Lieut.-Col. Attenborough immediately complied; and 'A' Company (Capt. Long) was sent forward. In passing through the barrage 'A' Company suffered some loss, but eventually took up a position at the north-east corner of the wood, where it helped to fill the gap between the two battalions in the front line. It at once came under a heavy artillery fire, and sustained many casualties; nevertheless, its arrival was timely, and made the success of any counter-attack by the enemy highly improbable.

The position had by now become somewhat obscure; so at 7.30 p.m. the Q.W.R., who were in brigade reserve, were ordered up by the Brigadier to clear the wood and to capture Loop Trench. They did not reach the wood until 11 p.m., and consequently the attack on Loop Trench had to be postponed until just before dawn. The brigade clung to its uncomfortable position during the night, although the enemy poured shells into the area about the wood without cessation. Early on the 10th the Q.W.R. assaulted, but, adequate artillery support being lacking, they did not meet with much success.

In the middle of the day Br.-General Coke came up, and, after a personal reconnaissance, ordered a new attack to be made at 3 p.m. from the southeast edge of the wood, and placed one company of the 1/2nd Londons at the disposal of the Q.W.R. for this purpose. The new plan was for 'A' Company of the 1/2nd Londons to bomb up the shallow trench (Combles Trench) that connected Leuze Wood with the southern end of Loop Trench, to its point of junction with the latter. From this point two companies of the Q.W.R. were to carry on and capture Loop Trench, the main objective. The attack was to be purely a bombing attack, supported by Stokes mortars and by an artillery barrage that was arranged to work along the trenches to be captured at the rate of 30 yards a minute. In the event, this barrage was actually to have no effect in keeping down the enemy's rifle fire, and, for all the useful purpose it served, it might just as well have been omitted.

The bombing attack started promptly at 3 p.m.; and 'A' Company nearly succeeded in reaching its objective, but during the advance lost all its officers, Capt. Long and 2nd Lieut. Lockey being killed, and the others wounded. C.S.M. Pellow took command, and handled the remnant of the company in a very commendable manner. He could, however, make no progress, and was eventually forced by the heavy and accurate shelling to retire. The Q.W.R.'s attack also came to nothing; and, although Lieut. Webb, of that regiment, endeavoured to renew the attack, the fire of the enemy's artillery prevented any progress being made. It seems certain that this attack on Loop Trench failed principally by reason of the heavy casualties previously sustained by 'A' Company's bombers, which made a successful bombing attack well-nigh an impossibility; the weak state of the company and the exhaustion of the men also contributed to its failure.

At 6 p.m. the Germans were seen massing for a counter-attack on the right. As a precaution, therefore, 'B' Company of the 1/2nd Londons (Capt. Heumann) was ordered to push forward and occupy Leuzenake (or 'Q') Trench, running almost due south from the corner of Leuze Wood. Before moving, Capt. Heumann held a conference with his officers in the shell-hole forming his headquarters. While the officers were together, a shell burst over the party, killing Capt. Heumann and C.S.M. Mills, and wounding Lieut. Attenborough and 2nd Lieut. Ursell and Childs, of whom the last-named afterwards succumbed to his wounds. 2nd Lieut. W. C. Cambray, the only officer left, took command of the company and succeeded in moving it into 'Q' Trench.

That night the Battalion was relieved by the 13th Composite Brigade of the 5th Division, and moved back to the Citadel (two miles north of Bray).

The Battalion's casualties in these operations were:

KILLED: 4 officers (Capts. R. Heumann, J. W. Long, Lieut. D. L. Childs, and 2nd Lieut. E. W. Lockey), and 23 other ranks (including C.S.M. Mills and Sergt. A. W. Torrance).

WOUNDED: 4 officers (Lieut. B. Attenborough, 2nd Lieuts. W. Ursell, L. S. Gray, and G. A. Taylor), and 91 other ranks.

MISSING: 19 other ranks.

Capt. Richard Heumann was born on the 9th July 1887. He joined the regiment on the 19th August 1908, and was promoted Captain on 1st May 1911. He was in charge of the detachment representing the regiment at the Coronation of H.M. King George V. on the 22nd June 1911; for this he received the Coronation Medal. He served with the 1/2nd Londons throughout the war until his death, being mentioned in dispatches on the 30th April 1916. He was a very popular and capable company commander.

Capt. James William Long was the son of the late Mr. William Long, of Battersea. He was born on the 24th March 1890, and was educated at the Battersea Polytechnic, whence he obtained an appointment in H.M. Office of Woods and Forests. He served in the 2nd Londons before the war, and rose to the rank of Sergeant. He was granted a commission in April 1915 while in France, and was subsequently appointed Adjutant in October 1915—an appointment which he held until he took command of 'A' Company in August 1916. He was married in 1916. He was a gallant and efficient officer, and was a great loss to the Battalion.

2nd Lieut. Ernest William Lockey was born on the 23rd July 1896. On the outbreak of war he joined the 4th Londons, with whom he served until 31st December 1915, when he obtained his commission in the 2nd London Regiment.

Lieut. David Leslie Childs was born on the 21st March 1888. He was gazetted to the 2nd Londons on 4th February 1915, and served with the second-line battalion in Malta, Gallipoli, and Egypt. He was transferred

136

to the first-line battalion in June 1916 on the disbanding of the second-line unit.

Although the operations around Leuze Wood had not resulted in any substantial gain of ground, elsewhere the Battle of Ginchy had been attended with a certain measure of success. The enemy's trenches to the east of the village of Ginchy had been captured, and progress had been made by the British east of Delville Wood, while to the south the French had swung forward in line with the British right wing. The weak salient in the Allied front had been eliminated, and a good position gained from which to launch a further attack.

In this further attack, planned to open on the 15th September, the Fourth Army was directed to make its main effort against the rearmost of the enemy's original systems of defence between Morval and Le Sars, while the French, advancing towards Rancourt and Frigicourt and acting in co-operation with the 56th Division of the British right wing, completed the isolation of Combles by the process known as 'pinching out.' The small town of Combles, though well fortified and strongly held, was now dominated by the British right at Leuze Wood and by the French on the opposite heights, and, by a steady advance along the ridges on either side of the Combles valley, the Allies hoped to make the town untenable by the enemy.

The 1/2nd Londons spent 11th September in the Citadel, resting and reorganizing, amid scenes of intense activity. Throughout the day and night, columns of infantry, guns, horse and motor transport, moved incessantly along all roads near the bivouac of the Battalion. On the next day the Battalion joined the general move forward, reaching Billon Farm, and on the 13th it was back again in Angle Wood, occupying the 'Farm' line. Assembly trenches for the attack were begun the same night in front of the 'Q' Trench and at right angles to the edge of Leuze Wood. One trench was dug that night, during which 2nd Lieut. Downey was wounded, and three more on the following night; but, although the whole Battalion toiled incessantly, the work was not quite complete by zero hour on the 13th; nevertheless, as the Brigade narrative states, the performance was a creditable one.

The attack of the 15th September (Battle of Flers-Courcelette) is particularly notable, for it marks the first occasion on which tanks were used. Three tanks were allotted to the 56th Division, whose main task was to clear Bouleaux Wood and to form a strong protective flank covering all the lines of advance from Combles and the valleys running north-east of the town.

137

One of these three tanks was attached to the 169th Brigade, and was detailed to co-operate with the 1/2nd Londons in another attack on Loop Trench.

The 1/2nd Londons' attack was timed to start at 6.20 a.m., and was to consist of four waves, with two platoons in each. The attacking companies were disposed as follows:

FIRST AND SECOND WAVES: 'D' Company (Capt. A. G. L. Jepson).
THIRD AND FOURTH WAVES: 'C' Company (Lieut. J. H. Clive).
RESERVE: 'A' and 'B' Companies (now amalgamated) in Leuzenake Trench.

Each wave was to move with its right flank directed on the southern end of Loop Trench, and on reaching Combles Trench was to wheel to the right. It was hoped that the configuration of the ground would conceal the advance from the strong German position in the sunken road until the right flank of the attack had gained a footing in Loop Trench. A manoeuvre of this type, involving a change of direction under fire, is always difficult and dangerous, but in this instance was justified by the result.

Punctually at zero hour, 'D' and 'C' Companies assaulted with great dash. The tank—the *Crème de Menthe*—had moved forward at 6 o'clock, and it now travelled successfully as far as Loop Trench, where it broke down. Its crew then had no alternative but to set it on fire, and make their escape, but not before it had served some useful purpose, by assisting the 1/2nd Londons to capture Loop Trench and the end of Combles Trench towards Leuze Wood which had defied their efforts and those of the Q.W.R. on the 10th.

The 1/2nd Londons, having successfully executed the change of direction, and gained a footing in Loop Trench, continued their progress to within a hundred yards of the junction of the sunken road and Loop Trench, where they were held up by trench blocks and much uncut wire. Their important position in the sunken road being threatened by this advance, the Germans at once counter-attacked, and tried by accurate bombing to dislodge the 1/2nd Londons. Against these desperate counter-attacks, 'C' and 'D' Companies, reinforced by 50 men of 'A' and 'B' Companies, sent up at about 7 a.m., held their new line. Blocks were established at the north end of Loop Trench, three sections of Battalion bombers and a trench mortar being sent up to hold them. In this close fighting casualties were very heavy, especially among the officers and the bombers. 'C' Company lost Lieut. Clive and 2nd Lieut. Sproule wounded, and 'D' Company lost Capt. Jepson, Lieut. P. C. Taylor, and 2nd Lieut. Sullivan killed.

So important were bombers in this trench fighting and so reduced in

numbers was the Battalion's bombing personnel that Lieut.-Col. Attenborough was obliged to ask Lieut.-Col. R. R. Husey, M.C., commanding the
L.R.B., for reinforcements. This request was immediately complied with;
and forty-three bombers of the L.R.B. joined the 1/2nd Londons in Loop
Trench. 2nd Lieut. St. J. R. St. Ledger, who had also come up, took command of the line, and, ably assisted by 2nd Lieut. W. E. Lockhart, organized
further bombing attacks to capture the junction of Loop Trench and the
sunken road. These attacks, though supported by two trench mortars sent
forward under 2nd Lieut. A. J. Whittle, made no progress, the resistance of
the enemy, who was holding the line of the road in great strength, being
very determined.

As there was now no senior officer with the attacking companies, Capt.
J. P. Kellett, M.C., who had only rejoined from the 56th Divisional School
of Instruction on the 13th, was sent forward by Lieut.-Col. Attenborough to
take command of the line. On his arrival in the early part of the afternoon,
he found another attack being made on the sunken road. This was followed
by an unsuccessful counter-attack on the part of the enemy to bomb the
1/2nd Londons out of Combles Trench. At 6.50 p.m. Capt. Kellett reported
to Lieut.-Col. Attenborough as follows:

> The Battalion bombers have established a block at junction of
> 'V' Trench (Loop Trench) and Loop. . . . The artillery have
> again shortened their range on sunken road and have wounded two
> more bombers. This line appears to me to be far too thinly held.
> The hostile attack fizzled out.

The trench was in places very narrow and much knocked about, and its
garrison inevitably suffered from the increased activity of the enemy's snipers
and bombers. Capt. Kellett, who had been joined by 2nd Lieuts. F. C. Baker
and S. W. Keen, at once reorganized the defence by allotting a sector to each
company and by strengthening the bombing blocks. By the evening the
trench had been deepened, and fire-steps made. At nightfall, a party came up
from the rear, bringing bags of parcel post, hot food, and fresh supplies of
bombs and ammunition. This party was followed by a detachment of Royal
Engineers and a company of the pioneer battalion (1/5th Cheshires), who
constructed a good strong point around the junction of Loop Trench and
Combles Trench, and partially wired in both sides of Loop Trench. The
position, therefore, could be regarded as far more satisfactory.

At 11 p.m. an attack, in conjunction with the 167th Brigade on the left, was made against the Sunken Road Trench by the L.R.B. bombers; and at the same time another attack was made by the 1/2nd London bombers, under 2nd Lieut. St. Ledger, against the strong point at the junction of Loop Trench and the sunken road. These attacks met with no better success than their predecessors.

In compliance with orders from Br.-General Coke to attack the sunken road at dawn, 2nd Lieut. St. Ledger and his bombers made yet another attack at 5 a.m.; they advanced fifty yards, but, after a stubborn fight, were forced to retire to their original block. 2nd Lieut. St. Ledger, who had bravely led his men in all these attacks, was shot through the head; and at the same time, Sergt. Bullock, the Bombing Sergeant, was killed by a bomb. Mention must here be made of Sergt. Evered, who did splendid work in these repeated attacks on the sunken road; three times he led parties forward to the objective before being severely wounded.

Capt. Kellett, in his diary, stigmatizes this period shortly, as a 'trying night.' On the morning of the 16th, he took stock of his position, and found that the line was held by seven officers (2nd Lieuts. Lockhart, Baker, Keen, Edmett, Whittle, a Brigade Machine-Gun Company Officer, and himself), 13 Battalion bombers, 44 men of 'A' Company, 81 of 'B,' 45 of 'C,' 31 of 'D,' 17 men of the L.R.B., 12 of the Trench Mortar Battery, and 14 of the Brigade Machine-Gun Company. These numbers he considered quite inadequate in view of the bad condition of the trenches; and he was of opinion that a combined bomb attack by the enemy from both flanks, after anything like a bombardment, could only be repulsed with great difficulty.

The physical and mental strain was beginning to tell on the men. Capt. Kellett himself had had no sleep since the morning of the 14th, and most of his officers were in like case. With the enemy in front and on both flanks, the position was always an anxious one. The defenders were constantly worried by snipers from Leuze Wood and the Loop; and the British artillery, though prompt in their response to calls for aid, was short in range, causing many casualties to the troops in front. Indeed, one 8 inch howitzer bombarded part of the trench for some hours, demolishing the Battalion's bombing block in Combles Trench and subjecting the whole garrison to a most demoralizing experience. Repeated attempts by Battalion Headquarters to stop this fire were unavailing; for among the masses of artillery in this area it was difficult to locate the offender. The only consolation was that, while the shelling lasted, the chances of an enemy attack were slight. No stretcher-bearers had been able to get up during the day, and, above all, no rum had arrived. Further improvement of their position was out of the question, the

140

men being too worn out to dig. Fortunately the enemy attempted no serious counter-attack during the day; and at 11 p.m. that night—16th/17th—the remnant of the Battalion, still clinging tenaciously to the position that it had gained, was relieved by the L.R.B., under Capt. Wills.

The casualties of the Battalion in this battle were:

> KILLED: 4 officers (Capt. A. G. L. Jepson, Lieut. P. C. Taylor, 2nd Lieuts. St. J. R. St. Ledger, and A. J. Sullivan), and 10 other ranks (including C.S.M.s H. Wilson and J. Powell, and Sergts. Bullock, Tucker, and Maidiment).
>
> WOUNDED: 3 officers (Lieut. J. H. Clive, and 2nd Lieuts. A. L. B. Sproule and J. R. Skeet), and 19 other ranks.
>
> MISSING: 251 other ranks.

Capt. Arthur George Leslie Jepson was the son of the Rev. Jepson, Rector of Hillingdon, Middlesex. He was born on the 13th December 1894, and was educated at St. Paul's School, where he was a member of the O.T.C. He was gazetted to the 1/2nd Londons on 29th August 1914, and served with it until he was wounded at Hooge on 20th August 1915. He was mentioned in dispatches on 1st January 1916; and was a very capable and popular officer.

Lieut. Philip Churton Taylor, the son of the late Dr. H. Taylor, M.B., of Kennington, was born on 19th May 1895. He was educated at Aldenham, where he obtained a House Scholarship. He was in the Shooting VIII. of 1912 and 1913, was editor of the *Aldenhamian,* and Captain of his House. He was studying for the Indian Police Entrance Examination at the outbreak of war, when he immediately joined the 2nd London Regiment, to which he was gazetted on 29th August 1914. He served with the 1/2nd Londons until he was wounded in March 1915. After a short tour of duty with the 3/2nd Battalion and 4/2nd Battalion, he rejoined the 1/2nd Battalion in January 1916. He was promoted Captain on 1st June 1916; but notification of this was not received until after his death.

2nd Lieut. Arthur John Sullivan was born on 7th March 1891. On the outbreak of war he enlisted in the 5th (T.F.) Battalion Seaforth Highlanders, with whom he served (partly in France) until 9th December 1915, when he was gazetted to the 2nd Londons.

2nd Lieut. St. John Richard St. Ledger was born in May 1885. On the outbreak of war he enlisted in the 5th (T.F.) Battalion Leinster Regiment. He served with it and with the 3rd Battalion Bedford Regiment until he obtained his commission in the 2nd Londons on the 20th July 1915. His was a great loss to the Battalion; his enthusiastic and cheery nature proved a valuable asset in those difficult days; and his heroic efforts to capture the junction of Loop Trench and the sunken road on the 15th/16th September are not likely to be easily forgotten.

On relief, the Battalion moved to Falfemont Farm. Here congratulations on its attack were received from Gen. Guignabaudet, commanding the French left wing, who had watched its progress from Savernake Wood. Lieut.-Col. Attenborough now went on leave, and Major G. A. Stacey assumed command of the Battalion in his absence.

In the evening of the 18th September the 1/2nd Londons (strength 7 officers and 481 other ranks, of which 50 were a new draft) relieved the Q.W.R. in the Combles and Leuzenake trenches, where they remained until 24th, every night being spent in digging the new advanced trenches and improving the position. The Battalion was constantly exposed to heavy shell fire, which included gas shells; and the health of the troops suffered through the long spell in the trenches and the physical exhaustion thereby entailed. During this period further attempts were made on the sunken road by the Q.W.R. on the 18th, and on Combles Trench by the L.R.B. on the same day, and by the Q.V.R. on the 24th. This last was the fifth attack, and, though partly successful, eventually broke down like all its predecessors.

On the 25th September the Fourth Army delivered another general attack in conjunction with the French further south (Battle of Morval). The task of the 56th Division was to form a defensive flank facing south-east, whilst the rest of the XIV. Corps pushed forward. Two tanks were allotted to the Division to clear the Sunken Road Trench, the north end of Loop Trench, the Orchard, and Combles Trench, and to block the north-eastern exits from the town of Combles. Zero hour was 12.35 p.m. The main operation was successful, and in the early morning of the 26th, the enemy evacuated Combles Trench and shortly afterwards Combles itself. At about 8 a.m. a patrol of the 1/2nd Londons, under Corpl. E. Hattemore, was pushed forward by Capt. Kellett, now commanding the combined 'A' and 'C' Companies; this patrol entered Combles, where its arrival coincided with that of the L.R.B. from the left and the French from the right. Capt. Kellett, with the rest of his command, entered the town shortly afterwards, and at 10.10 a.m. reported to Major Stacey as follows:

'A' and 'C' Companies have occupied Tranchée de Combles. 'A' Company is now easing off to its left to get into its proper position. The L.R.B. have searched right through the village and report all clear. They are now moving forward to trench along sunken road, north of village. The French have come in here, and I have given them about 100 yards of trench between railway and track. I have sent out a patrol of eight men and N.C.O. to examine road in front and along street and will send out others. Am converting this trench. Enemy are occasionally crumping Combles with heavy stuff.

A number of wounded prisoners was taken and a large quantity of material. 'A' and 'C' Companies pushed on beyond the village, and established a line in front of the railway, facing north-east. Here the men were in unconnected pits, which they were not able to improve owing to the heavy shelling. They were in touch with the French on the right, and with the 1/1st Londons, of the 167th Brigade, who were about 150 yards to their left front.

That night the Battalion was relieved, and moved back to the Casement Trenches, and on the next day it marched out of the line to Meaulte, a depressing little town near the Ancre. Its casualties in the final stage of the operations against Combles were 7 other ranks killed and 51 wounded.

II. The Battle of the Transloy Ridges

The 56th Division had now been in the line for nearly three weeks. It had taken part in some very severe fighting, and had been exposed to the effects of very bad weather. All its infantry units had sustained heavy losses; and the men were worn out by the arduous tasks they had performed. The left of the British line having now been shortened, and a part handed over to the French, it was reasonable to suppose that the 56th Division on its relief would be granted the long rest that it had so well earned. But the resistance of the enemy was daily weakening; and every available unit was required for maintaining the pressure on his front. Consequently, orders were received on the 29th September for the Division to return to the line on the right flank of the British Army.

The 1/2nd Londons, who had suffered as heavily as any of the battalions, and had, in the two days spent at Meaulte, hardly recovered from the effects of exposure and exhaustion, received this information with some amazement; but in a few moments the men had recovered their cheeriness; and it will ever be memorable how these men, turning from the well-earned rest that they could not be spared to enjoy, marched back to the Somme, with its welter of mud and blood, singing 'Pack up your troubles in your old kit bag.'

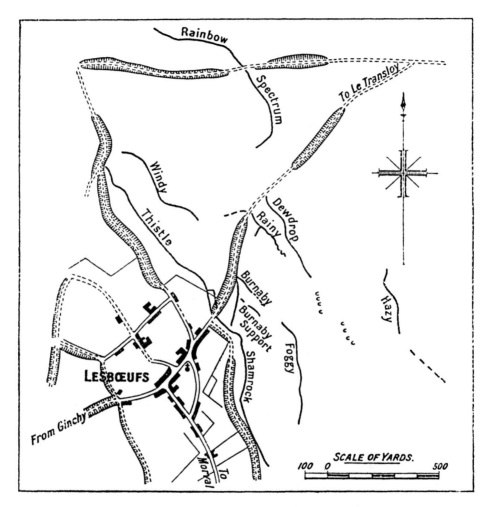

THE BATTLE OF THE TRANSLOY RIDGES.

The same evening, the Battalion went into the reserve line near Carnoy, and, at 5 p.m. on the following day, it relieved the 9th Norfolks in the reserve trenches in the Serpentine-Flers line, midway between Lesboeufs and Ginchy.

144

The casualties among the officers had been very heavy; and, in addition to those killed or wounded of whom special mention has been made, the health of several had given way under the strain, both physical and mental, imposed on them by the continual exposure to shelling and to the appalling weather. The following reinforcement, received during the month or early in October, therefore proved very welcome in filling up the depleted ranks:

> Lieut. C. Gordon, 2nd Lieuts. W. S. Harris, J. W. Sanders, W. A. Francis, H. G. Swaffield, R. Stancliff, J. B. Symes, A. Noel; and attached from the 7th Londons, W. J. Johnstone, G. D. Johnstone, A. G. McLeod, K. G. Anderson, and C. G. Scudamore.[1]

The 1/2nd Londons spent the night of the 1st/2nd October in digging a communication trench forward to the front line, under the direction of the Brigade Major, in an endeavour to improve the position; and on the 2nd they were ordered to relieve the 1/1st Londons in the trenches in front of Lesboeufs, a village that had recently been captured by the Guards Division. The front was a very bad one; and battalions in the line were being relieved every twenty-four hours. The 1/1st Londons had gone in the night before, and during the night and the next morning they had had a bad time. Their commanding officer, Lieut.-Col. ' Biff ' Smith, had been seriously wounded, but had refused to leave his battalion until the relief was completed. Although the relief was supposed to take place as soon after dusk as possible, it was late of accomplishment, because, as a result of the dreadful weather, the ground was well-nigh impassable. Progress was slow and difficult; the narrow lanes were blocked by fallen trees, and their surface was rendered slippery and insecure, while forward of Ginchy the only method of crossing the dreary waste of shell-holes was by duckboard track along which the relieving battalion had to spread itself, snake-like, in single file.

The whole Somme area was now fast becoming a sea of mud. In the early days of the battle, when the weather was still fairly good, the task of crossing the shell-torn, battle-swept ground was by no means easy. But the constant rain of the last weeks had transformed the whole place into a swamp, the shell-holes were full of water, and the new, hastily-made, roads were unable to stand up to the strain imposed upon them; thus progress in the area had become a matter of extreme difficulty, and movement was only accomplished by great physical exertions on the part of the troops.

Eventually the relief was completed, the Battalion being disposed as follows:

[1] The two last-named officers were later transferred to the 2nd London Regiment.

RIGHT : 'A' Company (Lieut. F. C. Baker).
LEFT : 'B' Company (Lieut. H. E. Gretton).
SUPPORT : 'C' Company (Lieut. J. B. Symes).
RESERVE : 'D' Company (Capt. C. Gordon).

Headquarters were established in an orchard, in an old German dug-out that ran under the Ginchy road at the point where it enters the village. The German gunners were suspicious of this place, and frequently subjected it to sustained and accurate shelling.

The fighting strength of the companies at this time was as follows : 'A' 120, 'B' 84, 'C' 95, 'D' 80, and H.Q. 50, giving a total of 429 for the Battalion.

The trenches were in a deplorable condition—not only were they deep in mud, but they were for the most part entirely devoid of any kind of shelter. Three of them (Rainy, Burnaby, and Burnaby Support) were in front of the main line, and were completely cut off from it and from each other, and during the hours of daylight there was absolutely no means of communicating with their garrisons. Thrust forward, as they were, into the open, these three trenches were entirely exposed, and, having been originally constructed by the enemy, they afforded little shelter to their garrisons, the parapets being on the wrong side. The position, therefore, was anything but good, and it was not improved by the extreme difficulty of getting up rations and ammunition. Owing to the appalling state of the ground, this was only effected after many hours of laborious work and at so late an hour that it was impossible to get anything forward to the advanced trenches.

During the 3rd, the enemy shelled Battalion Headquarters and the front line at frequent intervals during the day, making things still more unpleasant for the wretched troops.

The attack of the Fourth Army was shortly to be resumed, and, in order to ensure its success, divisions in the line were ordered to secure, by 5th October, a line of posts in advance of their present positions, and on the forward edge of the ridge, so as to obtain observation of the enemy's main position at le Transloy. The orders for this minor operation were very vague; nevertheless, by a well-planned and neatly-executed enterprise, a post on the front of the 1/2nd Londons was successfully established by Lieut. Symes and 20 men on the night of 3rd October. On the other flank, Capt. Kellett, acting under orders from Brigade Headquarters, took out a patrol, and tried to occupy, as a forward position, what appeared from aeroplane photographs to be a short length of enemy trench on the left of the Lesboeufs-le Transloy road, but, owing to the darkness and the mud, he did not succeed in locating it. After twenty-four hours of extreme discomfort, the Battalion was relieved by the 1/4th Londons. The relief started at 7 p.m., and, owing to the darkness and to the extreme difficulty of movement in the mud, was not complete until 3 o'clock next morning, when the Battalion, less two companies (left behind to dig), eventually reached its destination— the reserve trenches between Trônes and Bernafay Woods. This was the worst relief and march-out that the Battalion had experienced; and everyone was absolutely exhausted.

The attack of the Fourth Army was planned to commence on 5th October; but the weather became steadily worse, and, as no move could be made, the attack was postponed for forty-eight hours until the 7th. For the 56th Division, the operations involved two phases; the first included the capture of Hazy, Dewdrop, Spectrum, and part of Rainbow Trenches, all of which lay somewhat to the north-east of Lesboeufs, and the second the establishment of a line on the forward slope of the ridge. These tasks were entrusted to the 168th Brigade on the right and the 167th on the left, while the 169th was kept in divisional reserve.

Meanwhile the 1/2nd Londons remained near Bernafay Wood, where after almost superhuman efforts shelter of some sort was provided for all ranks. The conditions were appalling; everyone was wet; and even the proverbial cheerfulness of the London men was beginning to fail. During this period, working parties were found day and night for improving the front line and for digging assembly and communication trenches for the forthcoming offensive.

The attack was launched on the 7th October; but owing to the terrible state of the ground and to inadequate artillery support little progress was made. The 1/2nd Londons, whose fighting strength on this day was 14 officers and 354 other ranks, were not called upon, but on the next day stood to arms an hour before the customary time in consequence of a partially successful counter-attack by the enemy on the right of the Division, at its point of junction with the French. The Battalion was placed under the command of the 167th Brigade, and shortly afterwards was ordered forward, reaching the Flers line at 8 a.m., with the 1/3rd Londons on its left and the Rangers on its right. Major Stacey, who had again taken command of the Battalion, Lieut.-Col. Attenborough being granted special leave to visit his brother lying in hospital at Cammiers, established his headquarters in Serpentine Trench.

Nothing further occurred during the day, and at 10 a.m. on the 9th the Battalion was ordered to move back. 'D' Company left the trench first; and

147

when the first two platoons were clear, the enemy started to shell a battery immediately in the rear of the trench. The range of the enemy guns, however, was short, and many shells fell in the trench itself. One of these unfortunately killed Major Stacey. A quarter of an hour later, the orders to move were cancelled, and the Battalion was recalled to the Flers line where it was in position again by 10.40. Meanwhile, Capt. Kellett, as the senior officer present, had assumed command. The Battalion remained in the line until its relief at 4 p.m. by the 12th Brigade; it then moved back to the Citadel.

The casualties of the 1/2nd Londons in the operations about Lesboeufs were as follows:

KILLED: 1 officer (Major G. A. Stacey) and 4 other ranks.
WOUNDED: 11 other ranks.
MISSING: 3 other ranks.

The loss to the 1/2nd Londons of Major Gerald Arthur Stacey, D.S.O., was a very serious one. He was a keen and fearless officer, and he was very popular with all ranks. Major Stacey, who was a cousin of Lieut.-Col. Attenborough, was born on 26th December 1881. He was an accountant by profession, and joined the 2nd London Regiment on 18th November 1902. He was promoted Captain on 25th February 1905, and Major on 21st April 1915. He served with the 1/2nd Londons throughout the war until his unfortunate death, being mentioned in dispatches on the 30th November 1915, awarded the D.S.O. on the 1st January 1916, and the Legion of Honour on 29th February 1916.

On the night of the 9th October, the whole of the 56th Division was relieved by the 4th Division, and the nightmare of the Somme, so far as the Division was concerned, came to an end. Indeed, the Battle of the Somme was now drawing to a close. The opportunity of inflicting a serious defeat on the hard-pressed troops of the enemy had been snatched from our grasp by the very unfavourable weather that had at this time set in; the battle therefore ended with both sides ingloriously stuck in the mud.

The Battle of the Somme represented the chief counter-stroke of the Allies in 1916, and its strategic gain was the relief of Verdun. A considerable force of the enemy was contained at a critical period of the war; and some ground, the possession of which was to have an important bearing on the events of next year, was gained. Moreover, the moral effect of the battle on the German Army was considerable; and the storming of its carefully pre-

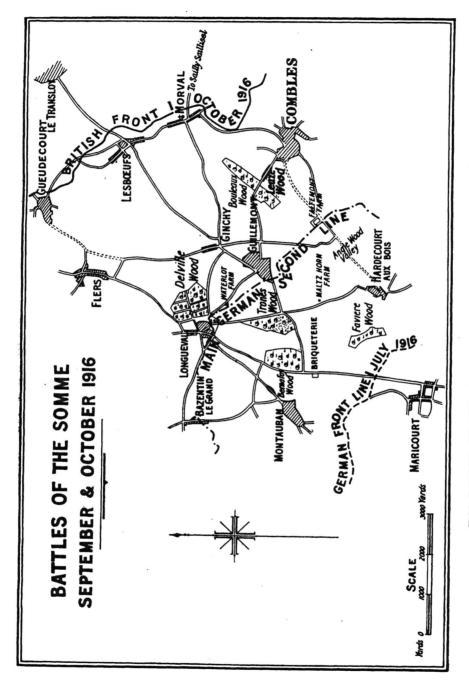

THE BATTLES OF THE SOMME, SEPTEMBER AND OCTOBER 1916.

pared positions, the capture of trench after trench, and the serious losses of the defenders, contributed in a marked degree to the lowering of its morale. On the other hand, severe casualties had been suffered by the Allied armies in achieving these results; a priceless asset of surprise had been sacrificed by the improvident disclosure of the tanks before these weapons were available in sufficiently large numbers or their proper use fully underſtood; and at the close of the operations no decisive victory could fairly be claimed to have been won.

Expert opinion concerning the merits and demerits of the Battle of the Somme has hitherto been sharply divided; and it is not the place of a regimental hiſtorian to contribute to a controversy in which many notable soldiers and ſtatesmen have been engaged; but the present writer ventures to say that, whether the Battle of the Somme be regarded as the turning point of the war or merely as a useless waſte of valuable lives, it at leaſt clearly demonſtrated the indomitable courage and endurance of the British infantry in triumphing over the appalling conditions that at times were well-nigh unbearable, and in overcoming slowly but surely the ſtubborn defence of a redoubtable foe.

The 1/2nd Londons marched from the Citadel on the 10th October to Ville sur Ancre, whence they were conveyed in French motor buses to Breilly, 10 kilometres north-weſt of Amiens. Here they spent the next ten days reſting and reorganizing.

The following awards were made in connexion with the Somme operations:

M.C.: 2nd Lieut. S. W. Keen.
D.C.M.: Sergt. H. F. Hughes.
M.M.: Sergts. T. F. Bisgood, J. H. Cheese, J. Smith, R. Utting, W. Hardy, W. Fittin, Corpl. W. Cheeswright, L/Corpl. H. Berry, H. Carter, Dr. H. May; Ptes. J. S. Parsons, F. G. Howe, G. Grant, G. Morrison, J. Shifford, and D. Williams.

The total casualties[1] of the Battalion during the Somme operations were: 9 officers killed and 8 wounded, and 47 other ranks killed, 291 wounded, and 273 missing.

On the 21ſt October the Battalion moved off at 7 a.m. and marched to Bailleul, about eighteen and a half miles. This was a severe teſt after the recent fighting; notwithſtanding the lack of march training the men

---

[1] Not including those suſtained at Gommecourt.

149

marched splendidly. By a short march on the 23rd the Battalion reached Pont Remy, where it entrained for Berguette, and from the latter place marched to Cornet Malo. On the next day a further march of ten miles brought the Battalion to Fosse, where four days were spent. From 25th October the 169th Brigade was held in Army Reserve, and all battalions received orders to be ready to move at one hour's notice to support either the I. or the IV. Corps at Givenchy or Cuinchy. The Brigade, however, was not called upon for this duty; and on the 29th the 1/2nd Londons proceeded to Croix Barbée, near Neuve Chapelle, their final destination, where the billets, despite the close proximity of the front line (a distance of about a mile and a half), were excellent.

Officer reinforcements during October were:

2nd Lieuts. C. Murray, C. A. Field, and E. D. Holmes.

CHAPTER XI

THE 1/2ND LONDONS DURING THE WINTER OF 1916-17— NEUVE CHAPELLE AND THE LAVENTIE POSTS

THE 1/2nd Londons were destined to remain in the Neuve Chapelle and Laventie sectors from 29th October 1916 until 1st March 1917. The conditions were those of ordinary trench warfare; and, except for about a fortnight in the latter part of January, when an attempt was made by the 56th Division to maintain a series of posts in the German front line, the Battalion found the life very quiet after its strenuous days of fighting on the Somme.

After a few days in Croix Barbée, where 'B,' 'C,' and 'D' Companies found garrisons for a number of defensive posts, the Battalion relieved the L.R.B. on 3rd November in the right (Mauquissart) sub-sector in front of Neuve Chapelle, 'A,' 'B,' and 'C' Companies taking over the front line, and 'D' Company remaining in support. The relief was effected in daylight and without interference from the enemy. It is interesting to note that the principle of defence in depth had been adopted in this sector, and a company had rarely more than two platoons in the front line, a third being in a defended post in rear, with a fourth in support.

The ground in the whole of this area was exceedingly low-lying; and, as the ordinary drainage system of small dykes had been entirely disorganized by the effects of shell fire, it had now become impossible to dig trenches without an immediate inundation of the work by water. The defences, therefore, consisted almost entirely of breastworks—a form of defence with which the Battalion from its previous sojourn in the Armentières area was well acquainted. The Battalion found the breastworks in front of Neuve Chapelle in a condition far from satisfactory; so with its customary enthusiasm it set about remedying the various defects. The necessary work was immediately taken in hand, and considerable improvement was effected.

The Neuve Chapelle sector was one of those luckily few sectors where mining operations by both the British and the Germans were in 'full blast,' in more senses than one. The front line was a mass of craters; and mining was continually in progress by special mining companies, attached to the Corps, who spent all their time, when in the line, underground, and who occasionally succeeded in blowing up the Germans, or in being themselves blown up. Although no mine was exploded on either side during the Battalion's ſtay in this part of the line, there was always the possibility that it might happen; and the presence of the miners, and their attendant blue clay, in the trenches, made trench warfare more fearsome than ever.

During the month of November, the duty of holding this sub-sector of the Brigade front was shared with the L.R.B.; and except for patrolling and trench-mortar aĉtivity little of intereſt occurred. While Br.-General Coke was on leave, Lieut.-Col. Attenborough assumed command of the 169th Brigade from 8th to 19th November, Major Kellett commanding the Battalion in his place.

On the 15th November, while the Battalion was in reſt at Bout de Ville, Lieut.-General Sir Richard Haking, commanding XI. Corps, presented medal ribbons to the recipients of decorations in the Division, and for this ceremony the 1/2nd Londons provided a representative Guard of Honour, under Capt. R. E. F. Sneath.

One notable change in the personnel of the Battalion occurred during November, C.S.M. W. J. Husband, D.C.M., succeeding R.S.M. A. J. Frakes as Regimental Sergeant-Major. The latter had done excellent work during a very trying period, and deserves an honourable mention for his unflagging zeal and enthusiasm. R.S.M. Husband, a popular and efficient warrant officer, was deſtined to hold the appointment from this date until shortly before the end of the war, and throughout this period he carried out his manifold duties with conspicuous ability and success.

The 169th Brigade was withdrawn from the line on the 27th November, for twelve days' reſt and training; and the 1/2nd Londons marched about seven miles to Le Grand Pacant, near Merville. In this village the Battalion occupied comfortable billets until 9th December, when it moved up to Riez Bailleul, and relieved the 1/1ſt Londons in brigade reserve. On the same day Lieut.-Col. Attenborough once more took command of the 169th Brigade, Br.-General Coke being granted sick leave.

Officer reinforcements during November were:

Capts. R. E. F. Sneath and H. Beck, Lieut. H. Renwick, 2nd Lieuts. W. J. Ward, A. S. Jarvis, R. B. Heagerty, and the following from the Royal Welch Fusiliers, H. Rowlands,[1] J. A. Evans, T. P. Albert, A. T. Welsh, R. R. Evans, A. N. B. Clark, V. A. Clappen, C. G. Jones, and D. G. Davies.

On the 15th December the 1/2nd Londons relieved the L.R.B. in the trenches, but this time in the left (Fauquissart) sub-sector of the Neuve

---

[1] 2nd Lieut. H. Rowlands was later transferred to the 2nd London Regiment.

Chapelle front, ' A,' ' B,' and ' D ' Companies going into the front line, and
' C ' Company being in support. Headquarters were established at Winchester House. There was a considerable increase in the enemy's trench-
mortar and artillery activity during this period, and on 17th December ' A '
Company's front was intermittently bombarded all day. The bombardment
increased at dusk, and a raid seemed imminent. Special precautions were
taken in case this anticipation proved correct; the flanks of ' A ' Company's
position were protected by additional machine guns; and strong patrols were
sent out in front. But no raid took place.

The fire of the hostile trench mortars was responsible for numerous
casualties. These included 2nd Lieut. G. D. Johnstone (7th Londons
attached), who was killed on the 19th, and 2nd Lieut. V. A. Clappen
(R.W.F. attached), who was wounded on the same day.

This tour of duty in the front line was marked by one very smart piece
of work. At 6.15 on the morning of 20th December five Germans were seen
outside the Battalion's wire. L/Corpl. D. Miller and L/Corpl. J. Woolley
immediately went over the parapet, and, shooting the leader, captured the
rest of the party. After successfully disposing of their prisoners, these two
non-commissioned officers again went out into No Man's Land, and brought
in the leader's equipment. The four prisoners proved to be Bavarians,
belonging to the 7th Bavarian Regiment, 5th Bavarian Division, III. Bavarian
Corps. The Battalion thus had the satisfaction of securing identification of
the enemy; and for this excellent enterprise L/Corpls. Miller and Woolley
were awarded the M.M.

This effort was typical of the work of the 56th Division throughout the
winter. It was the policy of the Corps Commander to harass the enemy as
much as possible, and to keep him in a state of constant anxiety as to what
was coming next. The 56th Division carried out the Corps Commander's
intentions in an admirable manner, displaying considerable determination
and powers of endurance. The weather was now extremely bad, and No
Man's Land was rapidly becoming flooded; yet, despite this, patrolling was
very active. The enemy's line was entered again and again at night, but on
practically every occasion was found to be empty. The reason for this was
undoubtedly the waterlogged condition of his trenches, which had induced
the enemy temporarily to abandon his front line. It is interesting to note
that the defences occupied by the 56th Division were in as bad a state as
those of the Germans; yet they were held throughout the winter.

The Battalion was out of the line at Riez Bailleul on Christmas Day;
nevertheless it was decided not to hold any celebrations until after the next

tour in the trenches, when the Battalion was due to move back into divisional reserve. The following greeting was received from H.M. The King:

> I send you, my sailors and soldiers, hearty good wishes for Christmas and the New Year and my grateful thoughts are ever with you for victories gained and for your unfailing cheeriness. Another Christmas has come round and we are still at war, but the Empire is confident in you. Remain determined to win. May God bless and protect you.

The only officer reinforcement during December was 2nd Lieut. D. Sloan.

The 1st January found the Battalion once more in the line. The enemy welcomed the advent of the New Year by a persistent bombardment of the front line from noon to nightfall, and he also shelled Laventie and the area of Brigade Headquarters. Considerable damage was done to the trenches; but no casualties resulted. As a retaliation, the British guns and trench mortars carried out, on the following day from 10 a.m. to dusk, an organized shoot against the enemy front and support lines, and thus brought the New Year celebrations of the Germans to a conclusion in a manner highly unsatisfactory to themselves.

The Battalion was relieved on the 3rd January by the 1/12th Londons (The Rangers) and moved back, in divisional reserve, to La Gorgue. It was now at liberty to celebrate Christmas in a fitting manner; and no time was lost in putting the necessary preparations in hand. 'D' Company was first off the mark, and held its dinner on the 5th. 'B' Company followed on the 6th, 'A' Company on the 7th; and the festivities were concluded by 'C' Company on the 8th.

Two days later the Battalion was inspected by Lieut.-General Sir Richard Haking. He expressed himself satisfied with the smart and soldierly appearance of the men, and he presented Meritorious Service Medal ribbons to Sergts. W. Thomas and T. Watson for good and continuous service with the Battalion.

During this period of rest and training there occurred an event of some interest; on the 12th January the 'Marathon' Race—a competition that is still held annually in Camp—took place for the first time. The conditions of this competition require the performance of a march of approximately five miles within one hour, the men wearing fighting order. A handsome silver shield, embodying the grenade and crest of the Regiment, had been provided by the officers, and on this, the first occasion, it was won by 'A' Company (Capt. 'Nap' Baker). Despite the fact that the men had been for many weeks engaged in trench warfare, and had had little time for training, the marching was excellent, and the race was keenly contested.

On the return of Br.-General Coke on the following day, Lieut.-Col. Attenborough handed over command of 169th Brigade, and himself went on leave. Major Kellett, therefore, remained in command of the Battalion.

The Battalion's next period in the trenches was a very strenuous one. During the night of the 10th January the 167th Brigade had established, on a front of about a mile in the Fauquissart sector, four posts (subsequently named Barnet, Flame, Bertha, and Irma) in the German front line, and on the night of the 12th two more posts (Hampstead Heath and Enfield).

These posts were not actually in the waterlogged German trenches, but were constructed in their parapets. At the outset the posts were very small, being hardly large enough to accommodate their night garrisons; in Bertha, for instance, the men had to stand shoulder to shoulder. The enemy had their exact range; and all the advantages for making a surprise raid were in his favour. It is obvious, therefore, that the holding of these posts demanded high courage and endurance on the part of the garrisons. With reference to the occupation of the posts, the following order was issued, on the 11th, by the 169th Brigade:

> The posts will be relieved every 24 hours; the points at which they are established have been selected with a view to watching the western exit of the three main German communication trenches. In the event of heavy shelling, the garrisons of the posts may move to a flank. It is intended that the posts should be stubbornly defended.

On the 13th January the 1/2nd Londons' advance party with Lewis guns was sent up to take over Irma, Bertha, and Flame (on the left of the Fauquissart sector); and on the next day in a thick mist the rest of the Battalion relieved the 1/1st Londons in the line, 'A,' 'B,' and 'C' Companies occupying the front line, and 'D' Company being in support. The relief was not completed until daylight; and it was perhaps unfortunate for the Battalion that it took place when it did; for, in the early morning after its completion, a strong enemy patrol, under cover of the heavy mist, bombed Bertha post, and rushed in upon 'A' Company's garrison. The garrison fought well, but owing to the mist and to the superior numbers of the enemy was not able to beat them off. 2nd Lieut. C. A. Field, three men, and a Lewis gun were captured. The two remaining men of the garrison escaped and returned to our line with information of the raid; whereupon a patrol consisting of Corpl. E. E. Smart, Ptes. A. Prideaux, A. Usher, and H. S. May ('A' Company) went out in broad daylight—for by now the mist had cleared—and re-occupied the post until relieved at night. In the fight a German officer had been killed, and he was identified as belonging to the 19th Bavarian Infantry Regiment.

This untoward incident was a sad blow at the Battalion's prestige; and everyone was very keen to get on terms with the enemy by effecting the capture of one of his patrols.

On the next day orders were received from the Brigade to strengthen and to extend the posts and to protect their flanks from envelopment by wire entanglements in No Man's Land. Major Kellett gave it as his opinion that Lewis guns were useless in the posts, because, in spite of every precaution, they became jammed by the mud. He suggested that the posts should be held by bombers and snipers only, and that the flanks should be protected by Lewis and Vickers guns from the British front line. This suggestion received the approval of the Brigadier, and was adopted. In addition, three rifle-grenade batteries were established in the front line, under Sergt. Fittin, who was in charge of the Battalion Bombers at that time, and one of these was detailed to cover each post.

Despite the dreadful state of the ground, which was everywhere flooded and nearly impassable, patrols visited the enemy trenches on this and subsequent nights. On the night of the 16th a patrol of 'A' Company, consisting of two non-commissioned officers and four men, reconnoitred Bertha Communication Trench as far as the River Layes. In attempting to ascertain the depth of the water, one of the party broke the ice—for the temperature had now fallen considerably—, and the sound evidently reached the ears of the enemy; men were heard approaching; and a bomb was thrown from the other side of the river, but fell harmlessly in the water. Nothing else transpired; so the 'A' Company patrol withdrew.

Except for this incident and for a subsequent encounter on the night of the 17th with a small patrol, the enemy was neither seen nor heard, although attempts were regularly made to ascertain the exact position to which he had withdrawn.

The Battalion was relieved on 20th January—this time by the Q.V.R.—and went back into brigade reserve in Laventie. While the Battalion was at rest, the enemy kept the posts under an almost continual bombardment, and

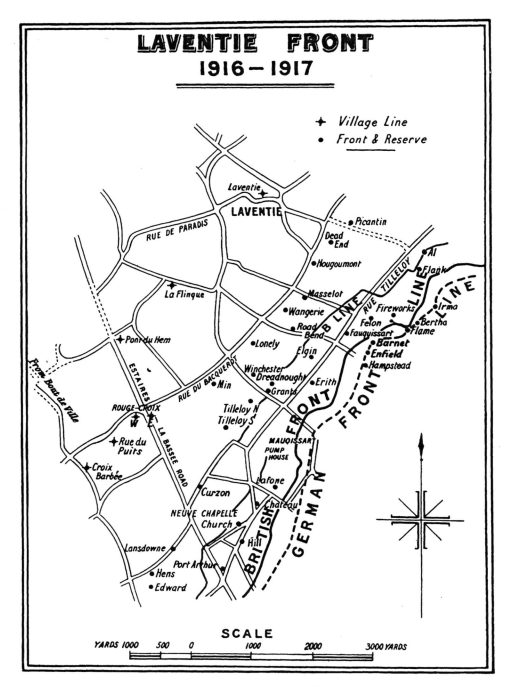

THE LAVENTIE FRONT, NOVEMBER 1916 TO FEBRUARY 1917.

made repeated attacks on them. These attempts, however, were gallantly frustrated by the battalions holding the line; and the only assistance for which the Q.V.R. asked was the loan of the 1/2nd Londons' Medical Officer and stretcher-bearers to help them with their wounded.

On the 26th January the Battalion relieved the Q.V.R. The weather had become exceptionally cold on the 21st, and the ground, which had previously been flooded, was now a sheet of ice. The garrisons of the posts suffered severely from the cold; no fires could be lit, because they attracted the unwelcome attentions of the enemy's artillery, and no warm food could be brought up by day, because the posts were completely isolated.

On this day Irma Post was the target of the enemy's artillery; so on the next day a counter-offensive was undertaken by the British artillery, a cluster of enemy trenches, known as Irma's Elephant, being treated with high explosive. Despite this retaliation Irma Post was again severely bombarded, at 7 p.m., by the enemy with artillery and trench mortars. 2nd Lieut. J. A. Evans (R.W.F. attached) and 2 other ranks were killed, and 8 wounded. As a result, the post was evacuated by the survivors at about 7.30 p.m. Patrols at once went out, but could not approach the post, which had been occupied by the enemy in strength. At 5 a.m. on the next day, after a short, but effective bombardment by the British guns, another strong patrol was sent out; and this time the post was successfully re-occupied. So badly had it been knocked about by the shell fire that it was now found to be quite useless; and a new post had to be established about one hundred yards further to the right.

Later in the day orders were issued by the First Army that the posts, as permanent posts, were to be withdrawn, and that future policy was to aim at making the enemy's front line untenable by him. Before dawn on the following day, the 29th, the first part of these instructions had been carried out; all posts were evacuated; stores were brought in; and the wire anchors holding back the revetments were cut. In accordance with a pre-arranged plan, the posts, together with certain parts of the German front line, communication trenches, houses, and dug-outs, were then very heavily bombarded by the British artillery.

It is not very clear what was the policy of the higher authorities in occupying these posts in the German line. It certainly demonstrated the fact that, despite the enemy, and despite the weather, the 56th Division was quite capable of holding them. Nevertheless it must have afforded the Germans no little satisfaction to see the British in the waterlogged ground— voluntarily abandoned by themselves and of small value to either side—, and to be able to subject the inadequately protected posts to frequent artillery bombardment. On the other hand, the policy of harassing the enemy could have been better carried out by patrolling; this always improved the morale of the troops, whereas the passive occupation of the posts had the opposite effect, the men feeling they were simply in shell-traps with no chance of hitting back.

February was spent either in the line in the Fauquissart sector or at rest in Laventie. While out of the line, the Battalion trained hard, and found innumerable working parties for the front trenches. The weather continued for a time to be very cold, the thermometer sinking to zero on the 3rd; but in the middle of the month the thaw commenced. Needless to say, it caused a wholesale collapse of trenches and breastworks.

The 7th February found the Battalion back in the line for six days, where a week later Lieut.-Col. Attenborough rejoined it from leave. Nothing of much interest occurred during this tour of duty except a small raid undertaken on the 12th. The party consisted of 2nd Lieut. W. A. Francis and 20 other ranks with two Lewis guns; and the following extract from the report of this raid is worthy of note as illustrating the state of the enemy's advanced defences at this time:

> The support trench beyond was practically obliterated. The trenches contained no dug-outs, shafts, or emplacements, and were found to be in a very bad condition everywhere. At 9.30 p.m. the whole party withdrew after having cut many revetment and telephone wires. They brought back three German stick grenades. During the whole of this time, the enemy was neither encountered, heard, nor seen.

The rest of the month passed uneventfully; and on 1st March the 56th Division, as a preface to its move to the Arras front, was relieved by the 49th Division.

CHAPTER XII

THE 2/2ND LONDONS IN FRANCE—THE GERMAN RETIREMENT

AFTER months of training and preparation, the 58th Division at laſt received the orders for which it had long been waiting, and during the laſt few days of January 1917 its units embarked for France. The 2/2nd Londons, with a ſtrength of 27 officers and 966 other ranks, left Sutton Veny on the 21ſt January, and in the afternoon of the same day embarked at Southampton.

The following officers accompanied the Battalion overseas:

Lieut.-Col. A. R. Richardson, in command.
Major J. A. Miller, second-in-command.
Lieut. H. Leaver, Adjutant.
Capt. S. Jones, commanding 'A' Company.
Capt. R. Collymore, commanding 'B' Company.
Capt. H. O. Ellis, commanding 'C' Company.
Capt. H. J. Hawkins, commanding 'D' Company.
Capt. L. S. E. Page, Transport Officer.
Lieut. M. Cooper, Intelligence Officer and Assiſtant Adjutant.
Lieut. J. S. Stevens.
Lieut. J. J. McHardy.
Lieut. H. J. Snell.
Lieut. P. A. Tucker.
Lieut. J. G. W. Wright.
2nd Lieut. F. J. C. Arnott.
2nd Lieut. C. B. Falkner.
2nd Lieut. B. S. Heading.
2nd Lieut. R. W. Bouſtred.
2nd Lieut. P. G. Roberts.
2nd Lieut. A. J. Stevens.
2nd Lieut. L. H. Newton.
2nd Lieut. H. P. Bennett.
2nd Lieut. E. M. S. Wagner.
2nd Lieut. H. E. V. Williams.
2nd Lieut. D. J. Parker (21ſt Londons attached).
2nd Lieut. F. J. D. Goodwin (21ſt Londons attached).
Lieut. E. Miller, Quartermaſter.
Rev. J. P. Stevens, Chaplain.

The Battalion was doomed to a rough passage; and everyone was glad when the ship finally reached the shelter of Havre at the chill hour of 1.30 in the morning. After spending the best part of a day and a night at this port the Battalion took train to Frévent, the concentration area of the Division, arriving there after fifty bitterly cold hours in the usual French troop-train. Thence a tired unit tramped to billets at Bonnières, which Lieut.-Col. Richardson describes as ' poor.'

It was at Bonnières, and before its departure to fresh billets at Ivergny on 29th January, that the Battalion taught itself the art of what the men called ' winning' or ' knocking off.' The Padre, quite unashamed, admitted the attempted annexation of fire-wood from the orchard of the good lady who found herself his temporary hostess. The attempt, however, was a failure; the lady was suspicious, and the Doctor, conspirator with the Padre, was caught in the act. As the Padre tersely sums up, all they could say at the time was ' No compris,' to which the good lady replied, in effect, with ' No fire.'

A further period of four uneventful days in Ivergny was the prelude to the 2/2nd Londons' baptism of fire, the 173rd Brigade being then attached to the 146th Brigade of the West Riding Division for instruction in trench life and routine. The 146th Brigade was at the time holding a very quiet sector of the line south-west of Arras opposite Ransart; and on 3rd February the 2/2nd Londons joined the 1/5th West Yorkshire Regiment at la Cauchie in this sector. ' As the Battalion came within sight of the German lines at the beginning of this instructional tour,' one of the officers records, ' it seemed to me that the eyes of the whole German Army was focussed on the 2/2nd Londons, just arrived to finish the war!'

In the course of this first experience in the front line, which lasted for six days, the Battalion had its first casualties, four men being wounded.

Back to Ivergny by motor lorries for training until 20th February, when the Battalion made the first of a quick succession of those lightning moves that were so much an integral part of war in France and Flanders and, indeed, in other theatres. This time, after an uneventful eleven days of preparation, the Battalion moved to la Souich. Twenty-four hours at la Souich; and then on to Pommera. A brief stay at Pommera; and the Battalion moved to Souastre, in divisional reserve.

' Not long after our tour of instruction with the West Yorks, the 2/2nd Londons,' records the Chaplain, ' were ten minutes late in starting off from billets, and consequently another Battalion was held up . . . to await our passing. Its C.O. told ours in pretty forcible language what he thought of a Territorial Battalion getting in his way, and the words of Colonel Richardson to us afterwards were much to the point! " We are only a battalion, and in a war of this size a battalion was mere dirt." I had this in mind later,' continues the Padre, ' when the Colonel wanted me to take a combatant commission. I thought, however, I should do less harm as a Padre!'

Before leaving Souastre for Bailleulval and Brasseux, again as divisional reserve, the Battalion was engaged in trench repair work at Fonquevillers and near Berles au Bois.

For a proper understanding of the important changes that were to take place in this area during the next few weeks, it is necessary to refer briefly to the operations further south that had followed the close of the Battle of the Somme in November 1916.

The capture by the British of the Thiepval-Morval ridge in the Battle of the Somme had left the enemy in a wide but very pronounced salient between the Ancre on the south, and the Scarpe, near Arras, on the north. This extremely unfavourable situation of the enemy Sir Douglas Haig decided to exploit without delay, before the winter set in and put an end, for a time at least, to active operations. On the 18th November, operations were accordingly re-opened on the left bank of the Ancre, and met with a considerable measure of success. These operations were resumed in January on the other side of the river, and resulted in the enemy's relinquishing Beaumont Hamel and the high ground to the north of it. Continued pressure by the British in this month and in February led successively to the fall of Grandcourt and Serre, and rendered the enemy's tenure of Gommecourt, the apex of the salient, highly dangerous. The early abandonment of this awkward position seemed probable; and on the 27th February the enemy withdrew as expected. Despite a stubborn resistance on the right flank, the enemy was now gradually pressed back to Bapaume, where he had constructed two strong lines of defence and where he might reasonably be expected to make a determined stand. But, after a show of resistance, he abandoned even this line, and continued his withdrawal to the east.

For months the Germans had been working feverishly on a highly fortified defensive line some distance in rear of their present position. This line, the famous Hindenburg Line, sited and constructed with consummate skill, branched off from their original front at Arras and, passing to the west of Cambrai, ran in a south-easterly direction to St. Quentin and beyond. A continuation of their retirement to this line, even though not entirely dictated by necessity, would enable the Germans not only to cut out the dangerous salient, referred to above, but also—and this, at the present juncture, they had good reason for desiring—of avoiding battle altogether; for by systematically laying waste the ground over which they retired they could make it impossible for their pursuers to attack them until after months of valuable time had been spent in preparation. Such, indeed, was the Fabian policy that they now put into practice.

Although no definite news as to the enemy's intentions had so far been obtained, his deliberate withdrawal to the Hindenburg Line was not altogether unexpected by the British G.H.Q. When, therefore, the 2/2nd Londons, on 2nd March, did their second tour of duty in the line, this time in the sector about Grosville (to the left of that previously occupied), the retirement of the enemy on this front, forming the northern face, from Arras to Monchy au Bois, of the salient that he was now gradually abandoning, was daily anticipated.

Information as to his actions and, if possible, his intentions, was eagerly desired; and the five days, or rather nights, from 2nd March that the 2/2nd Londons spent in this sector were busily occupied in active patrolling. The German defensive system hereabouts hinged on two very important points, the Blockhouse, a strongly defended salient in his line, and the Talus, a machine-gun post established in an embankment some 200 yards in front of his line; and, although this system was carefully probed, no sign of weakness could be discovered.

The 2/2nd Londons held their trenches with three companies in the front line and one in support, and, during the period, were subjected to heavy shelling by high explosive and shrapnel. They were relieved on the night of the 7th March by the 2/11th Londons, and moved back to billets in Bailleulval. In this village they stayed, amid intermittent high explosive and gas shelling by the enemy, until 16th March, when they moved into fresh quarters at Bienvillers. The object of this move was to enable them to be in a position to take over next day part of the front line north-east of Monchy.

On the night of the 16th/17th March, the withdrawal of the enemy began on the whole front from Arras to Monchy au Bois, the only part of his original line still in his possession. Reports of patrols seeming to confirm this fact, all forward units made ready for a rapid forward 'bound'; but there was some delay before orders for the pursuit came through from Brigade Headquarters. The anxiously awaited orders for a general advance were at last received; and the 2/2nd Londons had the good fortune to begin the movement of the 173rd Brigade in what became for it an interesting adventure and a most welcome change from trench warfare. Abundant evidence that the enemy's retirement was deliberate was very quickly available; for every conceivable scheme to delay pursuit had been carefully completed. During the night of the 17th, the two leading companies took up a position east of Monchy, 'A' Company (Capt. Jones) having passed round the north of the village and 'C' Company (Capt. Ellis) through it. Connexion was soon established with the 2/4th Londons, who were entering the enemy trenches to the south-east of the village and were reconnoitring towards Adinfer Wood; and at about the same time 'A' Company gained touch with the 2/8th Londons (174th Brigade) on the left. 'D' Company (Capt. Hawkins) moved up in support, while 'B' (Capt. Collymore) remained with Battalion Headquarters at Shell Street in the old British front line. 'A' Company pushed out a patrol, under Lieut. Wright, in the direction of Ransart, but failed to make contact with the enemy. In fact, throughout the 18th no touch was gained; and even from the high ground at Ficheux Mill nothing could be seen of the German troops. By 8.30 a.m. Ransart was reported evacuated.

During the afternoon, orders were received for the Battalion, pivoting on its right flank, to swing round to the east, and at the same time, or as soon as possible afterwards, to extend its left flank as far north as a quarry lying midway between Ransart and Monchy, and just to the west of the road connecting these two villages. 'A' Company successfully carried out this change of front, and, in so doing, covered the right of the 174th Brigade, which was then withdrawn from the line.

The Battalion was ordered to make a further advance at night with the object of taking up an outpost line between the 46th Division on the right and the 175th Brigade on the left. The execution of these orders presented a difficult task, because the exact location of the troops on either flank was not known, and the front given the Battalion to cover was close on 5,000 yards, extending from the south-west corner of Adinfer Wood on the right to the cross-roads midway between Blaireville and Hendecourt lez Ransart on the left. In the intervening hours the 2/4th Londons moved forward to Rabbit Wood, and the 46th Division, on the right, occupied a line from Hameau Farm, through Adinfer, to Windmill Farm. The outpost dispositions had consequently to be altered, the 2/2nd Londons being now given a much shorter front between Hameau Farm on the right to the cross-roads above mentioned on the left. Lieut.-Col. Richardson detailed 'A,' 'B,' and 'C' Companies to hold the line, and kept 'D' Company under his own control.

Night was falling when the companies moved off to take up their position. Touch not being immediately gained with the 46th Division, 'B' Company, on the right, advanced east from Hameau Farm to Adinfer, where patrols in the direction of Windmill Farm finally linked up with the 1/4th Lincolns (46th Division) at Boiry Ste. Rictrude. On the left, 'C' Company pushed into Hendecourt lez Ransart during the night, and meeting with no opposition continued the advance, and rested at dawn on the Boiry Ste. Rictrude road. Owing to the darkness and to some inevitable confusion, 'A' Company lost touch with the rest of the Battalion during the night, but before morning had come into line. Meanwhile Battalion Headquarters, with 'D' Company, remained on the Ransart-Adinfer road. The outpost line was finally established before dawn, on the eastern side of Hendecourt, with patrols pushed out towards Boiry; and Battalion Headquarters were moved up to the former village.

The spirit of the Battalion in face of the trying conditions of time and weather is forcibly portrayed by Lieut.-Col. Richardson when he says : 'The difficulty of moving in the dark and rain across a maze of heavily wired trenches, carrying everything on the person, had exhausted everyone, and it speaks for the keenness of the men that we were able to repair the roads sufficiently to enable the cookers and ammunition carts to be brought up by 6 a.m.'

The continued shortening of the British line, due to the flattening out of the Monchy salient, resulted in the reduction of the front of the 173rd Brigade; and the advance on the 19th was carried on by one battalion only, the 2/1st Londons. After passing through the 2/2nd Londons' outpost line, at 8.30 a.m., the 2/1st Londons pushed on, encountering little opposition, to the vicinity of Boiry Becquerelle.

The advance on this day was carried forward a distance of 10,000 yards; but so elaborately planned was the enemy's withdrawal and so skilfully carried out that practically no fighting occurred; few prisoners and no material worth speaking of fell into our hands. As the Battalion advanced over the area that the Germans were now abandoning, it was able to gain some idea of the thoroughness and ruthlessness with which the enemy had devastated the countryside. He had used the utmost skill and ingenuity to ensure not only that the ground, now voluntarily abandoned, was valueless to his pursuers, but also that considerable exertions and elaborate preparations were necessary before these pursuers could attack him in his new line with any hope of success.

The scene was one of utter desolation. Crops and orchards had been systematically destroyed; the avenues of trees bordering the roads and every insignificant bush had been ruthlessly cut down; flocks and herds had been driven off; and from those places more remote from the original line inhabitants carried away. Every house in the villages had been destroyed by the process of removing the walls, so that the roof fell to the ground; these villages from a distance appeared to be intact, and it was only on a closer inspection that the actual and amazing fact was discovered. Roads had been mined, or blocked with trees felled across them; wells had been poisoned; ingenious traps, disguised in a most innocent and effective manner, had everywhere been set; and everything done to harass and hinder the advancing British.

The discovery of one hundred dynamite sticks on the Ransart-Bellacourt road on the 18th was typical, and was responsible for the issue of a warning to the Battalion to be on the look-out for similar enemy traps elsewhere.

It will be appreciated that during these operations the administrative difficulties were enormous; and it says much for the work of the staff and administrative services generally that the multifarious requirements of the advancing troops were quickly met, and the comfort of the men attended to.

By noon on the 19th, the 2/1st Londons had established themselves on the line between Boiry Becquerelle and Boyelles, and were in touch with the 46th Division on the right in the neighbourhood of Hamelincourt; but no further progress could be made towards St. Léger, the day's objective, because the enemy's resistance had stiffened, and his artillery and machine guns in the area were very active.

The 173rd Brigade was now in charge of the whole of the 58th Division's front, and, as this was too extensive for one battalion to hold, the 2/4th Londons were brought up in the evening to the line of the Boyelles-St. Léger railway, on the right of the 2/1st Londons. In the meanwhile the 2/2nd Londons were sent up in close support to the leading battalions, and at noon marched into Boisleux au Mont, where the remainder of the day was occupied in giving the men a much-needed and well-deserved rest, and in keeping in close touch with the 2/1st and 2/4th Londons in front, who had experienced considerable enemy opposition on the outskirts of Boiry Becquerelle.

' Owing to the failure of the cavalry,' notes Lieut.-Col. Richardson, ' to capture St. Léger, the Brigade did not reach its objective, and took up a poor line, out of touch with the Boche except at Boiry Becquerelle, which formed a very sharp, indefensible salient.'

Whilst at Boisleux, the following officers reinforced the Battalion :

Capt. O. S. Sinnatt, 2nd Lieuts. A. Wright, H. Inwards, A. H. Denly, S. McMurray, G. J. Cooke, H. M. Harris (3rd County of London Yeomanry), C. Smart and R. F. Smith (14th Londons), R. S. Thompson and R. W. T. Chapman (18th Londons), A. J. Evans and M. L. Harper (19th Londons), and A. Denton (20th Londons).

Unable to make any further progress forward, the 173rd Brigade spent the 20th in consolidating its position. The Brigade's line now ran from its point of junction with the 46th Division near St. Léger, in front of Boyelles and Boiry Becquerelle, to the north branch of the Cojeul River south-west of Hénin sur Cojeul, where it joined that of the 30th Division. The enemy who appeared to be in considerable strength was holding the line of the Hénin-Croisilles road, on the other side of a valley running northwards from St. Léger to Hénin sur Cojeul; and it was obvious that he meant to make at least a momentary stand on this advantageous position.

Following a 'rest' that could be counted in hours, the 2/2nd Londons moved forward in the early hours of the 21st March to relieve the 2/1st Londons on the left of the Brigade line between Boiry Becquerelle and Hénin sur Cojeul, with two companies in the line, one in support, and one in reserve at Boisleux St. Marc. The night was foul, the darkness pitch, the rain pitiless and hard, the ground strange to everyone, pitted with shell-holes and mine-craters, and liberally bespattered with mud. It is small wonder that finding one's position became a matter of real difficulty.

The exact dispositions of the enemy were uncertain, though he was known to be in occupation of Hénin, where his working parties had been located, and of the line above mentioned. He was also seen at work on the Hindenburg Line.

Actual contact with the Germans—the first that the Battalion had experienced since leaving England—came on the morning of the 23rd, when an advanced post of a platoon of 'B' Company in Hénin Valley was raided and captured under cover of machine-gun fire. A whole section became casualties, two men being killed, five wounded, and one missing. Withdrawal of the remainder of the garrison was facilitated by covering fire from Lieut. Smith and Sergt. Proctor, who caused considerable loss to the enemy assembled near the post. One badly wounded German was taken prisoner.

It was in the course of the Battalion's tour of duty opposite Hénin that the Germans resorted to a trick that they occasionally practised during the war. An aeroplane, flying low and bearing British identification marks, fired its machine gun on 'B' Company. In all probability it was this machine

166

that was reported by Capt. Collymore to have ' passed, flying very low, along the village street and fired into the billets, and also at Lieut. Stevens's platoon.'

The Battalion remained in the line for three days in most uncomfortable circumstances. Snow had fallen, and was followed by a biting wind. Little cover was available for the troops; and as a result of the severe weather the men suffered from the exposure. On the 24th the Battalion was relieved by the 2/5th Londons, of the 174th Brigade, and returned to Boisleux au Mont, but not before it had suffered five casualties (two dead and three wounded) by shell fire while the relief was being carried out.

The shortening of the British line of which previous mention has been made now enabled a number of divisions, engaged in following up the enemy, to be withdrawn, either for rest in preparation for the spring offensive, or for the task of making good some, at least, of the German devastation. Accordingly the 58th Division was withdrawn; and the 2/2nd Londons, after two days in brigade support at Boisleux au Mont, where conditions were no better than in the front line, were relieved on 26th March by the 13th Northumberland Fusiliers, of the 21st Division, and moved westward to Bienvillers, by way of Adinfer and Monchy au Bois. After a night at Bienvillers and a further march back to Mondicourt and Pommera, between which villages the Battalion was split for billeting purposes, there followed on the 28th March an inspection by the Brigade Commander, Br.-General Hunt, who talked to the officers and men, drawn up in the courtyard of a typical French farm, and praising the men for their excellent work gave them the promise of ' more very soon.'

The 58th Division was now in reserve to the VII. Corps (Lieut.-General Sir T. D'O. Snow); and the Battalion was happy at the prospect of a fortnight's rest at Mondicourt, when, with that scant warning that was the prelude to the sudden end of many a ' rest,' it was pitchforked into action by the order to move to Moyenneville. This was on the 30th, after a bare four days at Mondicourt.

The Battalion proceeded by bus as far as Adinfer, where the state of the roads precluded the further advance of wheeled traffic, thence by route-march to the completely demolished village of Moyenneville, on the Arras-Albert railway. Here in bivouacs, erected in the ruins of the village, and in drained trenches, the Battalion made its quarters as comfortable as existing conditions would permit, though, according to Lieut.-Col. Richardson, ' Men and animals' suffered greatly from the snow and shortage of rations.'

The last two days—nights, rather—of the month were spent working on the railway between Moyenneville and Boisleux au Mont, in preparation for the laying of a new line. On 1st April, 'C' and 'D' Companies were ordered to Agny for further railway construction. Meanwhile, on the 2nd, Battalion Headquarters and 'A' and 'B' Companies marched through a snowstorm to Bienvillers, where they were ordered to bivouac. In this village Lieut.-Col. Richardson took characteristic action, and refused to carry out instructions, with the result that he was successful in getting the half-battalion under shelter, cheered and warmed by fires.

The Battalion was now more greatly segregated than it had been before, or ever was in later months. Not only were 'C' and 'D' Companies at Agny, but rear Battalion Headquarters and Quartermaster's Stores were two miles away, at le Pouchel. The administrative arrangements here did no credit to the VII. Corps, orders being received days after they should have been carried out.

After a period of eight days spent on road work near Monchy, Headquarters and 'A' and 'B' Companies left Bienvillers on the 12th for Bus lez Artois, where, on the succeeding day, 'C' and 'D' Companies rejoined from Agny. Rear Headquarters had already rejoined from le Pouchel. The men were now able to bathe; and clean clothes were issued, and very wonderful they seemed after the long days in the muddied, tattered garments whose place they took. In addition, the shops, canteens, and concerts, brought the Battalion suddenly back to civilization, and served as a useful tonic to all.

The Battalion was seventy-two hours at Bus lez Artois, and then moved eastward to Achiet le Grand, at that time III. Corps rail-head, by way of the old battlefields of the Ancre, where depressing devastation, stinking, clinging, slimy, seas of mud, derelict tanks, staring corpses, and the rest of the inevitable debris and aftermath of war, held grim and soul-destroying sway. In a downpour of rain the march of 20 kilometres was not pleasant. Arrived at their destination the men had to set to and erect their small bivouac tents and get as much comfort as possible from a bare, wet field. Everything and everyone was soaked through; but a rum issue and copious hot tea made the conditions easier to bear.

The Battalion was now in the area of the Fifth Army and was to remain at Achiet le Grand for four weeks. The time was spent in re-fitting, training for attack, and work on the roads, the railways, and the station. Battalion strength at this time was comparatively high—37 officers and 789 other ranks.

Lieut.-Col. Richardson, both in the line and out, always demanded that his battalion should be efficient in the one thing that really mattered more than all else—its ability to attack, and to attack with understanding and success. For even though stalemate loomed largely throughout the war on the Western Front, it was attack that nullified every period of stalemate and brought the war nearer to its end. So it was that, in conformity with his usual programme of training, the Commanding Officer daily had his junior officers at conference, and practised them in field exercises and an 'attack' on the village of Monchy. As Lieut. Harper very dryly remarks, ' the officers were new then, and the C.O. didn't appreciate their efforts.' Those officers who were serving with the 2/2nd Londons at the time will doubtless be able to read a great deal into the Colonel's lack of appreciation! Yet it was all good experience, and was fitting the Battalion for the many fights that lay ahead of it.

Whilst Achiet provided plenty of work, it also gave opportunities for recreation. A cinema was available and the Divisional Concert Party provided entertainment for officers and men.

It was in the course of the weeks at Achiet that Br.-General B. C. Freyberg, V.C., D.S.O., assumed command of the Brigade, taking over from Br.-General Hunt. A fearless soldier, a great leader of men, he was a source of inspiration to the troops whose privilege it was to be under his command; and it was a great loss to the whole of the 173rd Brigade when he returned to the Naval Division at the close of the Third Battle of Ypres in 1917.

CHAPTER XIII

THE 1/2ND LONDONS IN THE BATTLES OF ARRAS, 1917

I. THE CAPTURE OF BEAURAINS

AFTER the winter in the line at Laventie, it was generally expected that the 56th Division would spend some weeks in training, before being called upon to take part in offensive operations. Indeed, instructions to this effect had been received; and the Division actually set out to join the XIX. Corps for training in the Willeman area, but no sooner had it reached the training ground than it was recalled and ordered to join the VII. Corps (Lieut.-General Sir T. D'O. Snow) in front of Arras. Thus in less than a fortnight after leaving the Laventie Sector, it was back again in the line.

The 1/2nd Londons, on relief by the 7th Battalion West Yorkshire Regt. (146th Brigade), began a long trek that finally brought them into the area of the Third Army. For the first eight days of March, in company with the other units of the 169th Brigade, they were continually on the move, and during that time covered close on 100 miles. The weather for the first few days was bright and good for marching, although very cold; but on the 7th and 8th snow fell, and a strong north-east wind made progress very difficult. Nevertheless the marching was excellent despite the inclemency of the weather; and only three men fell out during the whole time the Battalion was on the road. This fact reflects great credit on all ranks, and is the more remarkable when it is remembered that for the past four months the Battalion had been engaged in the static warfare of the trenches, and had had little or no opportunity of practising route-marching.

The daily itinerary of this remarkable march, which in its essentials strongly resembles the famous expedition of a certain Duke of York up a hill and then down again, deserves to be recorded.

1st March.—Laventie to Lestrem (5 miles).
2nd March.—Lestrem to St. Venant via Calonne sur la Lys (8 miles).
3rd March.—St. Venant to Fiefs via Lillers (15 miles).
4th March.—Fiefs to Novelle les Humières via Blancy and Eclimeaux (15 miles).
5th March.—Novelle les Humières to Chérienne via Willeman and Le Quesnoy (12 miles). This was the original destination of the Battalion (Willeman No. 3 area).

6th March.—Chérienne to Fortel (16 miles) in Frohen No. 2 area.
7th March.—Fortel to Ivergny via Bonnières and Bouquemaison (13 miles).
8th March.—Ivergny to Monchiet (near Arras) via Sus St. Léger and Barly (12 miles).

On arrival at its final destination the 169th Brigade was put in Corps reserve, and was notified that it would come under the orders of the 58th Division in the event of a German counter-attack on the line Bellacourt-Wailly, which was at that time very thinly held. The 1/2nd Londons and the Q.W.R. were accordingly placed at the disposal of the 175th Brigade of this division, which, as we know, contained the 2/2nd Londons. In order to be prepared for eventualities, the officers of the battalions in reserve reconnoitred the line at Bretencourt and its approaches from Monchiet, and during this reconnaissance, Lieut.-Col. Attenborough and Major Kellett met Lieut.-Col. Richardson, commanding the 2/2nd Londons.

The next four days were spent in resting and training; and, by way of relaxation, the whole Battalion attended a performance by the 89th Brigade's concert party, 'The Optimists,' which was much appreciated. No officer reinforcements had been received in February; but on the 12th March 2nd Lieut. B. A. Starling, in charge of a draft of 56 men, arrived from the Base.

The Battalion moved to Achicourt on the 13th March, and on the next day relieved the 6th Duke of Cornwall's Light Infantry (21st Brigade) in 'H' Sector opposite Beaurains. The trenches were in a very bad state; and the Battalion spent the next day or two in improving the line. At the same time patrolling was very active; and on the 17th patrols stated that the enemy line appeared to be more lightly held than before and that a retirement by the Germans seemed imminent.

Early in March, instructions had been received by the 56th Division that an offensive, the genesis of which will be discussed later, would shortly be launched by the Third Army on the Arras front with the object of capturing Mercatel and the high ground about Monchy le Preux. In this offensive, the VII. Corps was to operate on the right of the Third Army front, the 30th Division being on the right, the 56th in the centre, and the 14th on the left. Subsequent events, however, were considerably to modify these arrangements; for, as dawn was breaking on the 18th March, scouts of the 1/2nd Londons, lying close to the enemy's wire, came to the conclusion that the enemy's line was not normal, and sent back word accordingly. Immediately on the receipt of their report, Capt. Baker, commanding 'A' Company on the right of the Battalion's front, sent out small patrols to make further investigations. These returned with the information that the enemy's line

171

was empty. Thereupon Capt. Baker, acting with great promptitude, at once pushed forward strong fighting patrols, under 2nd Lieuts. G. C. Scudamore and H. Rowlands, to occupy the German front line, and ordered the remainder of his company to prepare to advance.

As soon as news of these events reached Battalion Headquarters, Lieut.-Col. Attenborough ordered 'B' Company in the centre and 'C' Company on the left to advance. Capt. Symes, commanding the latter company, reported that the line in front of him was still held, and was thereupon ordered to outflank the enemy and to occupy his trenches with as little delay as possible. Advanced Battalion Headquarters were established in the German lines, and arrangements were made for the formation there of dumps of bombs and ammunition.

By 10.40 a.m. 'A' Company had firmly established itself in the German front and support lines immediately south of Beaurains, and had patrols in the village. 'B' Company likewise had patrols in the village; and by noon the whole was in the hands of the 1/2nd Londons. The village of Beaurains, which had been extraordinarily well adapted for defence by the enemy, was found to have been practically destroyed by the Germans before they left it. The roads had been blown up, or obstructed by barbed wire and spikes, and, with the exception of a few bombs, flares, and rockets, all stores had been removed. Four prisoners of the 100th R.G.R. were captured.

The Battalion pushed on through the village, which was being heavily shelled by the enemy; and 'B' Company in the centre occupied Melton Trench (a support trench east of the village), Jäger Weg (a communication trench running east from the village), and Preussen Weg (a long communication trench running parallel with the Beaurains-Neuville Vitasse road, back to the enemy's second line system). 'A' Company was in touch with the battalion on the right, King's Liverpool Regiment, and 'C,' moving up on the left of 'B' to the Brickfields, was endeavouring to get in touch with the battalion on the left. This connexion was eventually established, and the left flank made secure; but by this time the front of the Battalion was so extended that 'A' Company had lost touch with 'B.' Lieut.-Col. Attenborough therefore ordered up one platoon of his reserve company ('D') to fill the gap between the two forward companies.

Shortly after two o'clock orders were received from Brigade Headquarters that the advance was to be continued against the German second-line system on a two-battalion front, with the 1/2nd Londons on the right and the Q.W.R. on the left; and accordingly, at 5 p.m., Lieut.-Col. Shoolbred, commanding the Q.W.R., came up to discuss arrangements for taking over part of the front. In the meanwhile, the 1/2nd Londons continued to push on, and by 6 p.m. had advanced about 2,000 yards in front of the line they had been occupying at dawn. They had occupied the first line of the German second system, and were now holding, with three companies and one platoon, a line of about 4,500 yards in extent from 'A' Company's point of junction with the battalion on the right, along the front line of the enemy's second system, to the point where the communication trench, Preussen Weg, and the Beaurains-Neuville Vitasse road joined this system. Thence the left flank was refused along Preussen Weg to the Brickfields, north-east of Beaurains. The remainder of 'D' Company was still in support in Jäger Weg and Melton Trench, close to the village. To enable the Q.W.R. to take over the left half of this front, 'C' Company was ordered back to the British front line; and two platoons actually withdrew. This move was somewhat premature, because, as it later transpired, the Q.W.R. were not able to take over until early next morning, and the withdrawal of these two platoons left the long defensive left flank dangerously weak. For the better security of his battalion, Lieut.-Col. Attenborough directed the remaining three platoons of 'D' Company, which were still in reserve under his hand, to reinforce along Preussen Weg. The advance had brought the Battalion to the outskirts of Neuville Vitasse; and during the day a patrol, under Sergt. Mann, actually entered the village, which was found still to be held by the enemy in strength.

The total casualties of the Battalion for the day were very slight; among the officers, 2nd Lieut. W. J. Johnstone (7th Londons attached) was wounded.

By 1 a.m. on the 19th the Q.W.R. had taken over the left of the line, and the 1/2nd Londons were redistributed with two companies in the front line, 'A' Company being on the right and 'B' Company on the left, the latter in touch with the Q.W.R. at the point where Preussen Weg joined the German second system. These two companies had posts pushed forward into the support line of the second system, which had been evacuated by the enemy. 'D' Company was in support in the German first system, and 'C' in reserve in the old British front line.

The day passed uneventfully except for a plucky exploit by 2nd Lieut. R. Stancliff, who, single-handed, captured two Germans in the outskirts of Neuville Vitasse after they had fired several times at him. After dusk, although the night turned out very dark, and movement was considerably hindered, 'A' and 'B' Companies pushed forward into the support trenches of the second system, and established posts nearly a quarter of a mile in advance of this line. 'C' and 'D' Companies moved up a corresponding distance in support. To ascertain if the enemy was still holding Neuville Vitasse, 2nd Lieut. Stancliff took out a patrol, which unfortunately ran into a strong party of Germans. In order to escape capture, the patrol had to beat a fighting retreat, and in the course of the fight 2nd Lieut. Stancliff was wounded. This officer, who had displayed considerable initiative and rendered valuable service during the operations of these two days, was subsequently awarded the M.C.

The next day likewise passed without much incident. The men were full of enthusiasm, but had suffered somewhat from the shortage of water that was by this time becoming very serious. Late in the day, orders were received that the Battalion would be relieved by the Q.V.R.; and by 10 p.m. the relief was complete, the Battalion moving back to Achicourt.

On the capture of Beaurains and its subsequent advance, the Battalion received the congratulations of the Corps and Divisional Commanders. For its enterprise on this occasion it justly acquired considerable merit; but the chief praise is due to Capt. Baker, who, grasping at once the full significance of the situation, acted with initiative and determination. Thereafter all ranks displayed great keenness and worked with enthusiasm; and the operations of these three days, during which the losses of the Battalion were only two officers wounded and 20 other ranks killed or wounded, were brought to a satisfactory conclusion in a manner deserving of all praise.

The Battalion spent the next two days in well-deserved rest; but on the night of the 22nd March every available man was sent up to work on the consolidation of the new line. Under the guidance of Major Kellett, who always dropped into the position of Battalion Works Officer when required, the German trenches and communication trenches were cleared and deepened, and fresh trenches were dug. On the 24th the Battalion moved into a support position in the old British front line, from which it continued to work at night on the new advanced trenches until it relieved the L.R.B. two days later in the right sub-sector of the front line. Owing partly to a redistribution, but chiefly to the inclemency of the weather, this relief was not completed until 5.30 on the next morning.

The 1/2nd Londons remained in the line for the rest of the month; and during these five days the position was steadily consolidated and improved. At the same time patrolling was very active, and by this means it was found that the enemy was still holding Neuville Vitasse and, on the left, Telegraph Hill, an important and strongly fortified position.

On the 1st April the Battalion was relieved by the 1/8th Middlesex, and moved out of the line to Beaumetz les Loges.

II. The First Battle of the Scarpe, 1917

The plans for the Allied operations for 1917, as agreed upon by General Joffre and Sir Douglas Haig in November 1916, aimed at a continuation of the Battle of the Somme on a larger scale than before, as soon as the worst of the winter was passed. The extensive salient left in the enemy's line as the result of the Battle of the Somme was to be the object of convergent attacks by the British (to whom was allotted the more important role), between Vimy and Bapaume, and by the French, between the Somme and the Oise. The plan was simple, and the date selected for the opening of the offensive, the 1st February, had the merit of giving the enemy as little respite as possible. Had this plan been carried into execution on the date proposed, it would, without a doubt, have caught the enemy at a moment very unfavourable to himself, and might, conceivably, have had far-reaching results. But Fate decreed otherwise; for at this juncture the French Government decided to make a change in the command of its Army, and on the 12th December the veteran Joffre was succeeded by General Nivelle.

General Nivelle was a comparatively junior officer who had won distinction and, with it, the confidence of his Government, by a brilliant tactical stroke at Verdun. He believed that by applying his successful tactics to an operation on the largest possible scale a breach could be made in the German lines on the Western Front. His ideas, propounded with the great lucidity of which he was the master, won acceptance in the Allied councils; and it was decided to give his plan a trial.

The British were to deliver a preliminary attack in an easterly direction, on a wide front across the face of Arras, and, at the same time, the French Northern Army Group was to attack between the right of the British and the neighbourhood of Rheims. A few days later, the main offensive was to be launched on the Aisne front by two more French army groups, which were to strike in a northerly direction. Such was the essence of the plan; and, broadly speaking, the strategic principle underlying it was the containing of as large an enemy force as possible by the British and the French Northern Army Group, while further to the right a sudden overwhelming blow was struck by the main French forces towards the enemy's flank. Great insistence was placed upon the necessity of this blow being both sudden and overwhelming; for herein lay the novelty of the scheme. This plan, more ambitious than that of General Joffre, required more time for preparation; and the date of the commencement of operations was accordingly delayed from February until April—a delay that was to be attended by the most serious consequences.

So far as the British were concerned, the new plan did not largely affect their preparations; some modifications of detail were required; but in essentials, their tasks, save that they were now relegated to a less important role, remained much the same as for the operations proposed by General Joffre. The Fifth Army was to attack on the Ancre front, and the Third Army from Arras, while the First Army, further north, made a serious bid to capture the commanding Vimy Ridge, an important strategical and tactical feature, with excellent observation over the plains of Douai.

But in the meantime, the enemy, evacuating the whole sector from Arras to Noyon, deliberately withdrew to his carefully prepared positions on the Hindenburg Line.

By the enemy's withdrawal the whole Allied plan was completely upset. The salient in the enemy's line that had hitherto presented such a good object for attack had ceased to exist. Vast tracts of devastated land now separated a large part of the Allied forces from their objective; and only in two places were their troops in contact with the enemy, at Arras, where he had no intention of voluntarily giving up the Vimy Ridge, and on the Aisne. In these two places only could an immediate offensive be staged. Thus the plan had to be recast. But General Nivelle still clung to his original intention of a surprise attack on a huge scale, although by various means the Germans were fully aware of what was afoot, and, as the possible area of attack was now so restricted, were able to make the fullest preparations to meet it.

On the front of the British Fifth Army, where the Hindenburg Line lay a long distance behind the line that the enemy had hitherto occupied, the retirement had been considerable. An attack by the Fifth Army, therefore, was out of the question; and Sir Hubert Gough was ordered to follow up the retiring enemy as closely as possible, while the Third Army, under Sir E. E. H. Allenby, and the First Army, under Sir H. S. Horne, both of which were still in contact with the enemy's main defences, were to carry out their offensives as originally planned, but subject to such modifications as his withdrawal necessitated. These modifications were extensive, and, as will be readily understood, to incorporate them in existing plans demanded much labour and skill; for preparations for the 1917 offensive had now been proceeding steadily for months. It speaks volumes for the work of the British Staff and administrative services that, despite the dislocation caused by the withdrawal of the enemy on the front of attack and the necessity for moving forward the whole of the vast organization into new positions, hurriedly selected and in an area devastated by the enemy with ruthlessness and deliberation, the offensive was opened on the 9th April, and was attended by a most striking success.

The VII. Corps was on the right of the Third Army, and had in the line the 21st, 30th, 56th, and 14th Divisions. The attack was first to be made by the 14th and 56th Divisions on the left, in conjunction with the VI. Corps, since the enemy's withdrawal at this point had been slight; and gradually the 30th and 21st Divisions on the right would be involved, as the enemy's positions were captured. The tasks of the 56th Division were, first, the capture of Neuville Vitasse and, secondly, the occupation of a position just west of Wancourt. The operations, which were to be preceded by four days' bombardment, were originally planned to begin on the 7th April.

The attack, so far as the 56th Division was concerned, presented considerable difficulty. Neuville Vitasse itself was strongly fortified; part of the Hindenburg Line—the Cojeul Switch—ran to the east of the village in a north-westerly direction towards Telegraph Hill, and here it joined a network of trenches known, from its configuration, as The Harp. Another line —the Wancourt Line—ran in a north-easterly direction from Hénin sur Cojeul to Wancourt, and crossed the Cojeul Switch about 2,000 yards southeast of Neuville Vitasse. These lines were very formidable, representing as they did the last word in trench construction.

At the last moment the attack was postponed, owing to bad weather, until the 9th April; and in the meanwhile the 1/2nd Londons remained in Beaumetz les Loges.

At this period platoons were reorganized as self-contained units, and they now consisted of one rifle section, one Lewis-gun section, one bombing section, and one rifle-grenade section. This new organization was a great improvement on anything previously devised; but practice was needed if subordinate leaders were to learn to handle their new commands efficiently. Unfortunately the near approach of active operations demanded that every opportunity should be taken of resting the men; as a consequence all training had to be curtailed, and this essential practice denied to units. Another innovation of importance was the issue of definite instructions as to the number of officers and men to be left out of action—the Battle Surplus. These details were formed into a Divisional Depot Battalion, and thus ensured that a trained cadre was available to build up battalions after an engagement.

For the forthcoming operations, the 169th Brigade was to be in divisional reserve; and on the 8th April—Easter Sunday—it duly moved forward to its battle position. The 1/2nd Londons, leaving Beaumetz at 8.55 a.m., marched towards Achicourt. After marching about two miles, they halted, to prevent congestion in the forward areas, in a field, just east of Bac du Nord on the Arras road, where they remained until 4.30 p.m. The delay had fortunate consequences for them; Achicourt was heavily shelled by the enemy during the day, and—to quote the War Diary—'from the field in which the Battalion was halted, several dumps were seen to explode.' It afterwards transpired that a shell fell upon a lorry, forming part of a convoy, loaded with 9·2 ammunition. In a few moments the ammunition began to explode; the houses in the square were set alight; and a fierce fire was quickly raging. Attempts to extinguish it were of no avail; and in a short time the square was practically destroyed; many billets collapsed; and large quantities of stores were lost. Capt. L. Beck (1/2nd Londons), who was Town Major, did good work in the efforts to fight the fire, and earned the praises of the Divisional Commander.

The Battalion continued its march to Achicourt at 4.30 p.m., and relieved the 1/4th Londons in the railway cutting, east of the village, about six hours later.

At 5.30 a.m. on 9th April the Battle of Arras began. The 56th Division attacked with the 167th Brigade on the right and the 168th on the left, and by the end of the day had made considerable progress. Neuville Vitasse had been captured together with part of the Hindenburg Line. On the left, the 14th Division had been successful in capturing Telegraph Hill; but on the right the 30th Division had not progressed very far, and this partial failure had exposed the right flank of the 56th Division to possible counter-attack from the direction of the Cojeul Switch.

On the next day the attack was continued. The 56th Division captured practically the whole of the Cojeul Switch as far as its junction with the Wancourt Line; and on the left the 14th Division established itself in the Wancourt Line. On the 11th nothing was done on the left; on the right the 167th Brigade made further progress, clearing the Hindenberg Line as far as the Cojeul River and also occupying a long length of Nepal Trench, forming part of the Wancourt Line.

Late in the afternoon of the same day, the 169th Brigade relieved the 167th; and the 1/2nd Londons, who had done nothing during the past few days except to carry up petrol and ammunition for tanks, moved up to Neuville Vitasse in support of the Q.V.R.

The weather conditions on this day were terrible. There was snow, sleet, and a biting wind; and the men had to stand in open derelict trenches with no semblance of protection. The thick mud, too, that made all progress exceedingly laborious did not tend to improve matters.

Late at night, orders were received for an attack by the Brigade on the morrow. Hill 90 (south-west of Wancourt) was to be consolidated, and patrols pushed into Héninel, and later when the 30th Division had occupied the Hindenburg Line the Brigade was to cross the river Cojeul and make good the high ground to the south of the stream.

The attack was launched at 5.15 a.m., with the L.R.B. on the left and the 1/2nd Londons on the right. 'B' Company of the 1/2nd Londons bombed up the Cojeul Switch, and working round the south of Hill 90 joined hands with the L.R.B., who had enveloped the other flank. This successful enterprise resulted in the capture of ten of the enemy and the killing of many others. In order that the converging parties should not bomb each other, a password was necessary; the word chosen was 'Rum-Jar.' As Major Dudley Ward says in his History of the Division, 'The Germans, being bombed from both sides, must have thought it an odd slogan.'[1]

At 5.35 a.m. the enemy were seen to be withdrawing from Héninel; so 'A' Company (2nd Lieut. C. G. Scudamore), the leading company of the 1/2nd Londons, at once pushed on despite heavy machine-gun fire that caused many casualties, and captured the village. As soon as the village was cleared, the advance of the Battalion continued; the high ground east of the village—the Wancourt Tower Ridge—was occupied by 8 a.m.; and connexion gained with the 30th Division on the right.

The attack on Héninel was well arranged and carried through. 2nd Lieut. C. G. Scudamore was wounded soon after the advance commenced, but carried on until he had seen his company enter the village. He then handed over the command to his brother, 2nd Lieut. S. Scudamore. 2nd Lieut. Rowlands did extremely good work in getting his platoon forward, displaying great bravery and initiative. During the day he captured, single-handed, three of the enemy's snipers. Both 2nd Lieuts. C. G. Scudamore and Rowlands were subsequently awarded the M.C. for the services they rendered on this day.

At 9 a.m. L/Corpl. Trowell ('A' Company) and two men entered the outskirts of Wancourt, and captured the sole remaining German. 'A'

[1] *History of the 56th Division.* Major C. H. Dudley Ward, D.S.O., M.C.

Company attempted to push posts further forward on the ridge, but was prevented, as well by the short range of the British guns, as by the enemy machine-gun fire, which was now very heavy. 'B' Company was moved up on the right of 'A' during the afternoon; and at dusk posts were established on the front of both companies.

Meanwhile the Corps Commander had ordered the advance to be continued to the Sensée River. At a later hour these orders were modified; and the 56th Division was ordered to consolidate the position gained and to prepare for a renewal of the attack on the next day.

At midnight, the Brigade orders for the advance were received; no definite zero hour was named, because the launching of the attack depended on the progress of the divisions on each flank, but the Battalion was told to be prepared to move any time after 8 a.m. As an initial step, the forward platoons of 'A' and 'B' Companies occupied a German trench 100 yards in front of their present position; and the support platoons of these two companies moved up into the line just vacated by the forward platoons, thus forming the first two waves for the advance. Battalion Headquarters were pushed forward into the cemetery at Héninel—tactically, perhaps, a sound enough move, as Lieut.-Col. Attenborough says, but hardly tactful. It is worth while recording that now that the Hindenburg and Wancourt Lines had been passed there was no organized trench system between the Brigade and its objective, Chérisy, distant about two miles, and, for the first time in the corporate existence of the 56th Division, the orders issued were those for open warfare.

The night of the 12th/13th April is worthy of note as being the first occasion since the arrival of the 1/2nd Londons in France on which Capt. Taylor and the transport section failed to get the rations up to the troops. Needless to say, it was through no fault of Capt. Taylor, who made untiring efforts to find the Battalion and only gave up the search at dawn. The troops were therefore ordered to eat their 'iron rations.'

During the morning of the 13th, the 21st Division, which had relieved the 30th Division, made no progress on the right; and on the left the 50th Division, which had relieved the 14th, failed in the attack on Guémappe. As the attack of the 56th Division depended on the capture of this village, which was now on its left flank and almost in its rear, no advance on its front was attempted; and orders were received that the operations towards the Sensée were postponed for the time being.

The Battalion was relieved during the night by the Q.V.R., and moved back into support. The enemy blew up the Wancourt Tower, an action that seemed to suggest that he was retiring, and so a general advance towards the Sensée was ordered for the next day. Shortly after midnight, the Brigade orders for the attack were received. Dispositions were as follows:

> RIGHT: Q.V.R.
> LEFT: Q.W.R.
> RIGHT SUPPORT: 1/2nd Londons.
> LEFT SUPPORT: L.R.B.

The attack was to be made in co-operation with the 151st Brigade of the 50th Division on the left; and the plan was apparently to squeeze the enemy out of Guémappe. In preparation, 'C' and 'D' Companies of the 1/2nd Londons moved up to the sunken road in front of Héninel, with their left on the cemetery and their right in touch with the 21st Division on the right, and 'A' and 'B' Companies took up a position in rear along the line of the Cojeul River.

At 5.30 a.m. the attack was launched. By an unfortunate error, Wancourt Tower had been given to the 151st Brigade as the point of direction for its left flank, whereas it was in reality the left point of the 169th Brigade and marked the dividing line between the two brigades. This mistake led to great confusion; and matters were not improved by the disappearance of the tower during the night. Two battalions of the Durham Light Infantry became mixed with the Q.W.R.; the attack on the left never developed; and the leading battalions of the 169th Brigade, inextricably mixed with the two battalions of the Durhams, moving up the hill on a frontage of about half-a-mile—ostensibly in artillery formation, but actually resembling a crowd returning from a race meeting—presented a splendid target to the enemy machine guns in front and in Guémappe on the flank. From the outset the attack was a failure; and the advance was speedily brought to a standstill—unfortunately with very heavy losses to the Q.W.R. and the Q.V.R.

The 1/2nd Londons were not required to move from the position they had at first occupied, and there they remained all day. At nightfall, the 169th Brigade was relieved by the 168th; and the 1/2nd Londons moved back to Neuville Vitasse, arriving there at 5 o'clock next morning. 'C' and 'D' Companies, however, each left one platoon to act as covering parties to the Q.V.R. while the latter brought in their dead and wounded. The Battalion withdrew to Beaurains on the 15th.

Lieut.-Col. Attenborough, in a letter at the time, writes: 'I can only say that Divine Providence has watched over us in a most extraordinary way.' It is certainly a remarkable fact that during the four days of strenuous fighting, in the course of which, despite great opposition, considerable progress was made, the Battalion lost only 1 officer wounded (2nd Lieut. C. G. Scudamore) and 45 other ranks killed or wounded. Lieut.-Col. Attenborough adds:

> The Battalion did as usual extraordinarily well and 'A' Company particularly so in taking Héninel. . . . We've recovered our fatigue a bit and got our five days' beards off. I never lay down for four nights and days, and we were all cooked to the world on arrival here (Beaurains). We captured altogether 14 prisoners and killed a fair amount. I think we must be taken out as a Division soon. I have had Baker and Stevens at H.Q. as I found it impossible to be everywhere at once. The whole show was a perfect nightmare— orders from Brigade at midnight for attacks at dawn, etc.

The Battalion remained at Beaurains for two days, resting and cleaning up, and on the evening of the 18th April was put at the disposal of the 168th Brigade, moving up again to the sunken road in front of Héninel. Its tour in the front line was of short duration; for on the evening of the next day the 56th Division was relieved by the 30th, and the 169th Brigade, handing over to the 21st Brigade, moved back to Beaurains once more.

On relief, the Division moved out of the line to the Souastre area. The 1/2nd Londons embussed on the Arras-Doullens road at 4 p.m. on the 20th April, and by 6 p.m. had reached St. Amand. Here they remained for the next four days, resting and re-fitting.

Training was to recommence on the 24th; but on this day in view of the fresh offensive that had been launched the Brigade was ordered to move at three hours' notice to Wanquetin, in reserve to either VI. or VII. Corps. This move was accomplished with some difficulty owing to the shortness of the notice and to the fact that reinforcements of horses had not arrived. After spending a day at Wanquetin, the 1/2nd Londons moved on to Berneville on the 26th, where they arrived at 4 p.m. and went into comfortable billets.

On the 28th April a change in the Headquarters' personnel of the 1/2nd Londons took place. Lieut. T. G. McCarthy, who had been adjutant of the Battalion since the summer of 1916, joined the staff of the 169th Brigade as 'Q Learner,' and Capt. Sneath took over his duties. Officer reinforcements during April included:

2nd Lieuts. H. C. Carlile, A. W. Dolman, and W. F. White.

While at Berneville, the 1/2nd Londons suſtained a serious loss, Lieut.-Col. Attenborough being obliged to leave them owing to ill-health. Except when on leave or in command of the Brigade, and except for one short absence through illness, Lieut.-Col. Attenborough had served with the Battalion in France since succeeding to its command in December 1914. Through its early days in France, at Gommecourt, on the Somme, and in the opening ſtages of the Battle of Arras, he had been a source of inspiration to the Battalion. By his patience, his good humour, and his power of leadership, he had endeared himself to all ranks; and he is entitled to the greateſt credit for having carried out his difficult task so well.

Major J. P. Kellett, M.C., who was eminently fitted to take over the command, succeeded Lieut.-Col. Attenborough. At this time it was the practice of the higher authorities to appoint Regular officers to the command of Territorial battalions, whenever a vacancy occurred; and it was rarely that the command was given to a Territorial officer, no matter how long he had served nor how efficient he had proved himself. It was therefore a matter for no little satisfaction when, on the 16th May, Major Kellett's appointment was confirmed, and he was promoted to the rank of Lieutenant-Colonel.

III. The Third Battle of the Scarpe, 1917

The Nivelle experiment had failed disaſtrously. The failure was attended by the graveſt consequences to the French Army, whose discipline and morale were seriously affeƈted by its reverse.

The British Army had fulfilled its part in the general plan with vigour and success; not only had the important Vimy Ridge been captured, an operation brilliantly conceived and executed, but also considerable progress had been made at Arras, the enemy had been dislodged from the high ground on a wide front, and a large number of prisoners had been taken, all without undue loss. With the capture of Monchy le Preux, Sir Douglas Haig wished to bring these operations to a conclusion, and to turn his attention to the north, where he hoped, by an offensive at Messines and Ypres, to clear the coaſtal area. But with the French Army in a ſtate of demoralization and with battle ſtill joined in Champagne, he was obliged to renew his efforts on the Arras front, to maintain the pressure on the enemy and so to enable our Allies to extricate themselves from their various difficulties—a course of aƈtion that was rendered the more necessary by the collapse of Russia and the consequent release of large numbers of enemy troops for the Weſtern Front.

The continuance of the British operations was costly, and was unattended by any substantial gain, the resistance of the enemy, who did not intend a further retirement, being very stubborn. On the 23rd April an attack was delivered on a front of about nine miles from Croisilles to Gavrelle. Some

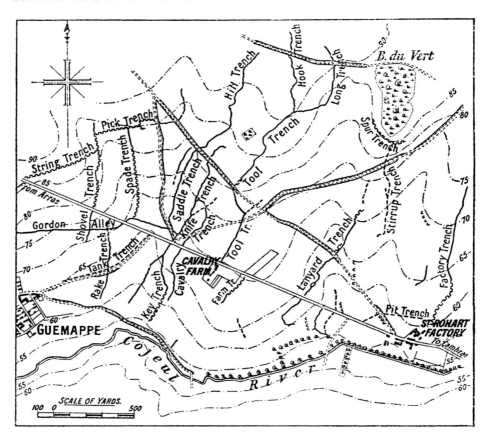

THE THIRD BATTLE OF THE SCARPE, 1917.

progress was made in the sector with which we are at present concerned; and by the evening of the 24th Guémappe had been captured, and the high ground west of Chérisy finally secured. Another attack on an extended front at Arras was planned for the 3rd May. The Third and First Armies were to operate from Fontaine lez Croisilles to Fresnoy, and at the same time the

Fifth Army was to launch a new offensive againſt the Hindenburg Line about Bullecourt. At this juncture the 56th Division returned to the line in the VI. Corps area, between the Scarpe and Cojeul Rivers, taking over the right sector from the 15th Division.

In the projected operations, the immediate objective of the 56th Division's attack was the slight ridge running north from the St. Rohart Factory on the Arras-Cambrai road, weſt of Vis en Artois. On the left, the 3rd Division was to attack the Bois du Vert; and on the right, the 14th Division, of the VII. Corps, was to capture Chérisy.

The attack of the 56th Division was to be delivered on a front of two brigades; accordingly, on the 29th April, the 167th Brigade, which till then had held the whole of the Divisional front, handed over the right, from the Cojeul River to the Arras-Cambrai road, to the 169th Brigade, and the 1/2nd Londons moved up to the trenches in rear of the Wancourt Line in brigade reserve. In the light of their subsequent efforts, the following note in the 169th Brigade Diary is of intereſt: 'The men do not appear reſted yet or ready for a proper offensive.'

During the intervening days the line and the ground over which the attack was to be made were reconnoitred by officers of the 1/2nd Londons. On 1ſt May 'C' Company, with two companies of the Q.V.R., dug three assembly trenches, running due north and south in a slight fold of the ground behind the front line, and 'D' Company, with one company of the Q.V.R., completed these the next night. During this night the 1/2nd Londons relieved the Q.V.R. in the front line, Battalion Headquarters moving up to Tank Trench. The fighting ſtrength of the Battalion was 17 officers and 577 other ranks.

The task of the 169th Brigade was by no means an easy one. The line of its attack was along a slight valley, down which the Cojeul River and the main Arras-Cambrai road converged until they crossed in front of Vis en Artois. On the right rose the northern and eaſtern slopes of the Wancourt Tower Ridge; and on the left was one of a series of spurs projecting southward from the Monchy Ridge towards the Cojeul River. Across this spur ran the main road. Generally speaking, the ground was open and undulating, though the banks of the river were lined with small copses and thick undergrowth. It is manifeſt that the success of the 169th Brigade depended largely on the progress of the troops againſt the higher ground on either flank, since these ridges completely dominated the narrow ſtretch of lowlying country between them. Moreover, the nature of the German defences in this area added to the difficulties of the attack. They no longer consiſted

185

of the heavily fortified and continuous lines of a month earlier; for the Hindenburg Line had been passed, and the Drocourt-Quéant Line still lay far ahead. But, instead, the enemy had everywhere constructed short lines of trench, had converted to his use the many shell-holes with which the area abounded, and had incorporated all into a comprehensive system of defence. By utilizing the ground in his customarily skilful manner and by siting his numerous machine guns so that enfilade or cross fire could be brought to bear on the face of each isolated post, he succeeded in making the task of the attackers no less difficult than when they were confronted with great engineering works like the Hindenburg Line.

At the very early hour of 3.45 a.m. on the 3rd May the attack was launched. The troops of the 169th Brigade were disposed as follows:

> Right: L.R.B.
> Left: 1/2nd Londons.
> Support: Q.V.R.
> Reserve: Q.W.R.

The 1/2nd Londons were disposed in four waves, of which the composition and objectives were as follows:

> First Wave (2nd Lieut. J. W. Sanders): 2 platoons 'A' Company and 2 platoons 'B' Company—Lanyard Trench.
> Second Wave (Capt. F. C. Baker): 2 platoons 'A' Company and 2 platoons 'B' Company—Cavalry Farm, Farm Trench, southern end of Tool Trench, and area up to Lanyard Trench.
> Third Wave (Capt. J. B. Symes): 2 platoons 'C' Company and 2 platoons 'D' Company—Factory Trench and St. Rohart Factory.
> Fourth Wave (Capt. C. Gordon): 2 platoons 'C' Company and 2 platoons 'D' Company—Intermediate ground between Lanyard Trench and St. Rohart Factory.

Two points in this plan call for special notice; first, the mopping-up of the strong point, Cavalry Farm, was not to be undertaken by the first wave, whose orders were to push on as rapidly as possible to Lanyard Trench, and, secondly, the third wave in its progress towards the final objective, the St. Rohart Factory, lying a thousand yards up the valley and just west of the point where the Arras-Cambrai road crosses the Cojeul River, had to 'leap-frog' through the first and second waves—a task easy enough in theory, but always difficult in practice.

It is a curious fact that, unlike most other buildings in this district of Artois, neither Cavalry Farm, an isolated homestead bordering the Cambrai

186

road, nor the St. Rohart Factory, both of which were, of course, utterly destroyed as the tide of battle ebbed and flowed around them, has been rebuilt. Their ruined foundations remain to-day, grass-grown and deserted, and serve to conjure up visions of the fighting that took place on that May morning in 1917.

In planning the attack, the dangerous presence of the Arras-Cambrai road, running obliquely across the front, was not disregarded; for there was every likelihood that the troops, being only human, would align themselves on it, a likelihood liable to be increased by the darkness of zero hour, and by the dust and smoke of the barrage. Accordingly a tape on which the first wave was to form was laid in front of the assembly trenches. In spite of every precaution, one section of the first wave failed to form on the tape, and, pressing forward at a quick pace, came under the British barrage, from which it suffered several casualties. Nevertheless the first wave made good progress. On its left, matters did not go well; and shortly after zero hour the 167th Brigade found itself pinned to the ground by heavy artillery and machine-gun fire; and its attacking troops, unable at first to advance, gradually began to withdraw. The waves of the 1/1st Londons of this brigade retiring in a southerly direction, became mixed with the left of the advancing troops of the 1/2nd Londons, causing considerable confusion, and resulting in the diversion of the greater part of the attack of the 1/2nd Londons to the south of the Cambrai road. The confusion was increased by another, and somewhat unexpected, cause. For some days previously the weather had been quite excellent, and for this reason the advancing troops found the going much better than that to which they had been accustomed in recent offensives. They pressed on therefore at a good pace; but the barrage had been timed to move at 100 yards in three minutes; and the first wave of the attack was, for obvious reasons, bound to conform to this speed. The succeeding waves, free of any such restriction, pushed on as fast as they could, with the result that, on reaching Cavalry Farm, 2nd Lieut. Sanders found that men of each of the other waves were mingled with his own of the first.

As stated above, the first wave was not to attempt the capture of Cavalry Farm, but was to push on to Lanyard Trench, leaving the second wave to make good the intermediate ground. The farm, however, was strongly held by the enemy, and in avoiding it, two platoons of the first wave made so great a detour to the left that they lost touch with their comrades. The remainder pushed on, and finally reached their objective twenty minutes after zero. Lanyard Trench was almost entirely obliterated, but after about an hour's work was restored to a good condition. A German machine gun was captured in the trench; its crew was killed; and the machine gun was then used against the enemy. 2nd Lieut. Sanders' first thought was for his flanks; he established connexion with the L.R.B. on the right, and in the absence of any unit on his left he sent off a party of men to dig themselves in in shell-holes north of the Arras-Cambrai road. During the advance the first wave captured a number of prisoners, and sent them back; but in the darkness many were killed by the succeeding waves, and only 18 reached Battalion Headquarters.

In the meanwhile, the second wave was attempting to capture Cavalry Farm and to complete the clearance of the area in rear of the first wave. The retirement of the units of the 167th Brigade on the left had more seriously disorganized this wave than its predecessor; and a catastrophe was only averted by the courageous energy of Capt. Baker, who, when some of his men showed an inclination to follow the example of these other units, rallied them, and led them forward again. Having thus restored the situation with much pluck, and no little profanity, Capt. Baker then energetically attacked Cavalry Farm. At 4 o'clock he captured Farm Trench, south-east of the farm. Although the farm itself, stubbornly defended by the enemy's machine gunners, still defied his efforts, he did not give up; and his persistence was rewarded an hour later, when the larger part of the farm passed into his hands. Thereafter the enemy clung desperately to the rest of his position in the farm, and was not finally ejected until a much later hour.

At 6.15 a.m. the 1/1st Londons on the left reported that they were back in their original line and were reorganizing. As was learnt afterwards, gallant parties of this battalion and of the 1/7th Middlesex had continued the advance and, overrunning Tool Trench and crossing a sunken road, known as Stirrup Lane, had reached Lanyard Trench; but they were not in sufficient strength to join hands with the 1/2nd Londons on their right, and later in the day they were forced to surrender.

The destination of the 1/2nd Londons' third wave (Capt. Symes) was the ultimate objective of the whole of the attack—the St. Rohart Factory line. The ground up to Lanyard Trench having been secured by the first two waves, it was not anticipated that the third wave would have much difficulty in reaching that point. But for reasons already given its progress in the early stages of the advance was too rapid; and, when Cavalry Farm was reached, the men had become mixed with those of the first two waves. Cavalry Farm was at this time still holding out, and, in attempting to pass beyond it, Capt. Symes and 2nd Lieut. Welsh were killed, and 2nd Lieut.

Davies was severely wounded. 2nd Lieut. Francis, the sole surviving officer of 'C' Company, took command of the company. He collected as many men of 'C' Company as possible, and passing round the right of the farm and keeping to the right of the road, pushed on to Lanyard Trench. He there crossed the road and advanced to within fifty yards of Factory Trench, but, finding both his flanks exposed, he decided that it was wiser to withdraw his party, now consisting of between fifty and sixty men, and to dig in about seventy yards in front of Lanyard Trench, and at no great distance from a line of small pits.

In the meanwhile, the fourth wave (Capt. Gordon) had also reached Cavalry Farm, but at that point, meeting the fate of its predecessors, had disintegrated. Capt. Gordon, collecting as many men of 'C' and 'D' Companies as he could, pushed on to Lanyard Trench, to a point just north of the main road. 'Here,' he says, 'I met 2nd Lieut. Heagerty and a few men digging in. I never saw him again. They were not there later in the day.' This was the last seen of 2nd Lieut. Heagerty, who was subsequently missing and later reported killed. Capt. Gordon then went forward again, and eventually joined 2nd Lieut. Francis and his party. While these two officers were reorganizing their small force, an officer of the L.R.B. came up from the right and informed Capt. Gordon that about fifty men of the L.R.B. were digging in before the St. Rohart Factory, and that, owing to the exceptional machine-gun activity, they could make no further progress forward. It was obvious to Capt. Gordon that the attack on the left had for the moment failed and, apprehensive for the safety of his left flank, he decided to advance no further, but to form a defensive flank along the main road until someone came up on his left, and enabled him to continue the attack. He therefore ordered 2nd Lieut. Francis to cross the road again and dig in on the southern side, roughly in line with the party of L.R.B.

By this time, 2nd Lieut. Sloan, who had been on the left of the fourth wave, had arrived with about 30 men, chiefly of 'D' Company. He attempted to take up a covering position on the left of the Arras-Cambrai road in front of Lanyard Trench and more or less in line with 2nd Lieut. Francis's party. 'At the time, it was getting quite light;' he says in his report, 'we commenced digging in, but the Germans were all round us with machine guns and snipers. I could see large numbers of them in shell holes seemingly prepared to give themselves up, but when they saw the weakness of my party, they took cover and commenced firing. At 4.50 a.m. I received a message from Mr. Sanders, O.C. "B" Company, and thought we could protect our flank to more advantage from Lanyard Trench. We withdrew accordingly. About half an hour later, I took another party across to the left, but it seemed even more hopeless than before, so I again withdrew to Lanyard Trench.' In Lanyard Trench he formed a strong point fifty yards north of and parallel with the main road, and this he held for the rest of the day.

At 5.30 a.m., Capt. Gordon, leaving the advanced troops in charge of 2nd Lieut. Francis and sending 2nd Lieut. Noel to get in touch with the L.R.B. on the right, went back to Lanyard Trench for further information as to the general position of affairs. 2nd Lieut. Noel went over to the L.R.B.'s position, but, in returning, was unfortunately shot through the head and killed. Patrols were sent out to the left and also to the St. Rohart Factory, but saw no sign of any other British troops in the vicinity.

The position of the advanced troops gradually became stabilized; and it appears that at 7.30 a.m. the 1/2nd Londons had between fifty and sixty men, under 2nd Lieut. Francis, in the advanced trench from the right of the Arras-Cambrai road to a point in rear of the left of the L.R.B. The L.R.B. continued the line with forty or fifty men down to the banks of the Cojeul River. In Lanyard Trench were Capt. Gordon, 2nd Lieut. Sanders, and another forty or fifty 1/2nd Londoners, between the main road and the left of the L.R.B.; and on the left of the road 2nd Lieut. Sloan and about twenty men. Owing to heavy machine-gun fire no further advance was possible; and Capt. Gordon decided to hold on to the position he had gained.

We must now go back to Cavalry Farm, and see how the task of clearing this area was proceeding. The failure of the 167th Brigade on the left had enabled the enemy to hold on to Tool Trench on the slope of the hillside just north of Cavalry Farm; and this position was a constant menace to the flank and rear of our troops in and around Lanyard Trench. One platoon of the 1/2nd Londons formed a defensive flank from Cavalry Trench to a point within fifty yards of the southern end of Tool Trench, but could in no wise check the enemy's machine-gun fire from the latter trench. This accurate fire rendered quite abortive every attempt to clear Cavalry Farm itself, where the enemy appeared to be holding the line of the Arras-Cambrai road as a 'T' head to Tool Trench.

At 8.30 a.m. Major Kellett was instructed by the Brigade Commander to take any men of the Q.V.R. (the battalion in support) who were available, to clear the farm, and, if possible, Tool Trench. 'D' Company of the Q.V.R. (Capt. S. Read) was put at his disposal by their commanding officer; and arrangements were immediately made for clearing the farm under cover of fire from the section of the 169th Trench Mortar Battery attached to the

1/2nd Londons, after a short preliminary artillery bombardment of Tool Trench. While the British howitzers were shelling Tool Trench, twenty-two Germans surrendered from Cavalry Farm. Eventually, at about 9.30, supported by hurricane fire from the trench mortars, a strong fighting patrol of the Q.V.R. attacked the farm and the adjacent dug-outs, which they found empty. The 3rd Division on the left had now succeeded in gaining a footing in the northern end of Tool Trench; and it was agreed between it and the 169th Brigade to make a joint attempt to capture the trench by a simultaneous attack from each end. Capt. Read was ordered to bomb up from the southern end, while the troops of the 3rd Division bombed down from the northern end. The two attacks started about 11 a.m., and after heavy fighting were both repulsed. The Q.V.R. tried and failed again during the afternoon; and at 4 p.m. the enemy was still in possession of the greater part of the trench.

All the while, matters were not going well on the right. The 14th Division had made good progress in its first attack, but had been violently counter-attacked and by midday had been driven back to its original line. This unfortunate set-back left the forward troops of the 1/2nd Londons and of the L.R.B. in a very precarious position; for, with the units on either flank back in their original lines, they were holding a narrow wedge of ground, at the bottom of the valley, projecting forward about 1,000 yards and entirely exposed to attack from either flank.

Nothing daunted, these forward troops held on grimly during the day. 'We were greatly worried,' says 2nd Lieut. Francis, 'practically the whole of the day by machine-gun fire, also by the fire of our own artillery, which caused many casualties.' The enemy had two machine guns and a light trench mortar on the near edge of the pit, south of the main road and just in front of the factory. 'The former,' says Capt. Gordon, 'caused a lot of casualties but were eventually silenced by our artillery and one of the guns apparently smashed.'

The concluding stages of this action are somewhat confused. At about 6 p.m. the 169th Brigade issued instructions that the advanced posts near the pits were to be withdrawn, and that the reserve company of the L.R.B., taking up plenty of bombs and ammunition, was at dusk to relieve all men of their own battalion and of the 1/2nd Londons still remaining in Lanyard Trench. The Q.V.R. were ordered to take over Cavalry Farm Trench at the same time, and at 1 a.m. to take over Lanyard Trench as well. No further attempts were to be made to occupy Tool Trench.

The orders for the relief of the forward posts were received by Capt.

Gordon in Lanyard Trench at dusk; and he at once carried out the first part, withdrawing the advanced troops under 2nd Lieut. Francis to Lanyard Trench. The reserve company of the L.R.B. duly arrived at about 9.30, and relieved Capt. Gordon and his 1/2nd Londoners in Lanyard Trench, who then withdrew to the old front line.

In the meantime, at 9 p.m., the enemy opened an intense artillery fire, and though he maintained it for fully an hour and a half, he made no attempt to counter-attack. It appears that a message was sent back to Brigade Headquarters to the effect that the forward troops of the L.R.B. and 1/2nd Londons had evacuated their positions under this bombardment. This information was inaccurate; and there is no doubt that it originated at the time when the forward troops, withdrawing according to orders, passed through the Cavalry Farm line. A subsequent message that Cavalry Farm and Lanyard Trench had been re-occupied is likewise inaccurate, since neither of these points had been abandoned, even temporarily.

At midnight Br.-General Coke issued orders that all troops were to be withdrawn to the original front line, which was to be held by the Q.V.R. and the Q.W.R. On withdrawal, the L.R.B. and the 1/2nd Londons were to go back to the Wancourt Line. When these orders were received, the Commanding Officers of the L.R.B., Q.W.R., and 1/2nd Londons, were all at battle headquarters in Rake Trench. Believing that Br.-General Coke had ordered the withdrawal under a misapprehension that the ground had been lost, they decided to hold on; and at 1 a.m. the 1/2nd Londons were still in Cavalry Farm Trench. As a matter of fact, Br.-General Coke had taken his decision quite independently; for the forward position obviously could not be long maintained, with each flank exposed and the only line of communication along the bottom of a narrow valley. He therefore sent forward his Brigade Intelligence Officer to clear up the situation, and eventually succeeded in withdrawing all the troops of the Brigade before dawn.

In this battle, abortive though it proved to be, the 1/2nd Londons, on the whole, played a gallant part. A battalion cannot do more than capture and hold its objective; and this, save for some yards of ground in the neighbourhood of the St. Rohart Factory, the 1/2nd Londons had done. The critic may object that this attack was hardly carried out in the methodical way envisaged in the Brigadier's plan, nor that the hold on the captured ground was firm enough to resist a really powerful counter-attack. This objection hardly affects the validity of the 1/2nd London's claim that they did their job, and that it was through no fault of theirs that the ground they had won had finally to be given up. The Third of May 1917, therefore, may be written down as one of the days to be remembered by the Regiment with pride, and may take its place in history alongside the Thirtieth of November 1917 and the Twenty-eighth of March 1918. Where many did well, it is perhaps invidious to single out individuals; but mention must be made of Capt. C. Gordon, Capt. F. C. Baker, and 2nd Lieut. W. A. Francis. Nor would any account of the battle be complete without reference to the adventure of Sergt. Klincke. This non-commissioned officer was captured in Tool Trench on the 3rd, and on the next day re-appeared, bringing in his captors—1 officer and 12 other ranks.

In connexion with this battle, the following awards were made:

M.C.: Capt. F. C. Baker, 2nd Lieut. W. A. Francis.
D.C.M.: C.S.M.s E. Dainty, A. E. Easthope.
M.M.: L/Corpl. R. Strode, Ptes. W. Humphrey, C. F. Lane.

Pte. Lane, who was a company runner, made the journey from Lanyard Trench to Battalion Headquarters and back on three occasions during the day, although exposed to observed rifle and machine-gun fire along the whole of his route.

The casualties of the Battalion amounted in all to 192, and were as follows:

KILLED: 3 officers (Capt. J. B. Symes, 2nd Lieut. A. Noel and 2nd Lieut. A. T. Welsh, 3/4th R.W.F. attached), and 16 other ranks.
WOUNDED: 2 officers (2nd Lieut. D. G. Davies, 3/4th R.W.F. attached, and 2nd Lieut. L. F. Giffen, 25th Londons attached), and 114 other ranks.
MISSING: 2 officers (2nd Lieut. R. B. Heagerty, and 2nd Lieut. A. N. B. Clark, 3/4th R.W.F. attached), and 55 other ranks.

Capt. John Bond Symes was born in 1892. He joined the 6th Canadian Infantry on the 1st January 1915, and reached France on 18th September of the same year. He was gazetted to the 2nd London Regiment on 23rd July 1916, and joined the 1/2nd Londons on 21st August, while they were on the Somme.

2nd Lieut. Alfred Noel was the son of Mr. and Mrs. A. Noel of Highbury Hill, and was born on the 26th December 1892. Before the war he was the manager for a firm of jewellers. He was a keen and enthusiastic sportsman. Shortly after the outbreak of war he joined the L.R.B., with whom he served until he was gazetted to the 2nd London Regiment.

The 169th Brigade was relieved on the 4th May; and the 1/2nd Londons moved back to The Harp, south-east of Tilloy. Here they remained for the next fortnight, while the Brigade was in divisional reserve, spending the time in reorganizing and training. Parties were employed on salvage work, and large quantities of copper driving bands were collected from empty shell-cases. At last it was possible to provide some relaxation for the men. Fifty were sent each day to a performance by the 'Bow Bells,' and after the serious work of the past weeks this entertainment was much appreciated. The proximity of Arras, too, presented an opportunity for a proper cleaning-up, and the whole battalion, about 600 strong, bathed in the Schramm Barracks.

The 56th Division remained in the line for the next fortnight. During this time attempts were made by the 167th and the 168th Brigades to capture Tool, Hook, and Long, Trenches. None of these, however, was successful, except a well-planned attack by the latter brigade on the 11th May. This attack was delivered at half-past eight in the evening instead of just before dawn, as was usual, and it was not preceded by an artillery barrage. Thus the garrison, taken completely by surprise, made but a feeble resistance; and the objective, the southern end of Tool Trench, was captured with little loss to the attackers.

The Division was withdrawn from the line on the 20th, the 169th Brigade having already moved off on the previous day. The 1/2nd Londons marched by cross-country tracks to Arras and thence by infantry tracks to Duisans. The Battalion remained in this village until the 24th, and then marched to Agnez lez Duisans, where it was accorded a short period of much needed rest. Training was begun at once, in delightful weather, and was continued till the 9th June.

With the exception of twelve days in June, the Battalion was out of the line until 11th August, and these two months of the summer of 1917 were among the most pleasant that it spent in France during the war. The time was, of course, chiefly occupied in training for the serious fighting to come; but there was no lack of opportunity for sport and recreation; and into both work and play the men, always cheerful, threw themselves with the utmost vigour.

There can be no question that, despite the experience gained in battle, continual training of the British troops in France was essential to their efficiency; for the nature of the warfare on the Western Front was perpetually undergoing change and required changed tactics to cope with it. An example of this, briefly referred to earlier in the chapter, was the new method of defence adopted by the enemy, the cause and effect of which it is now proposed to elaborate.

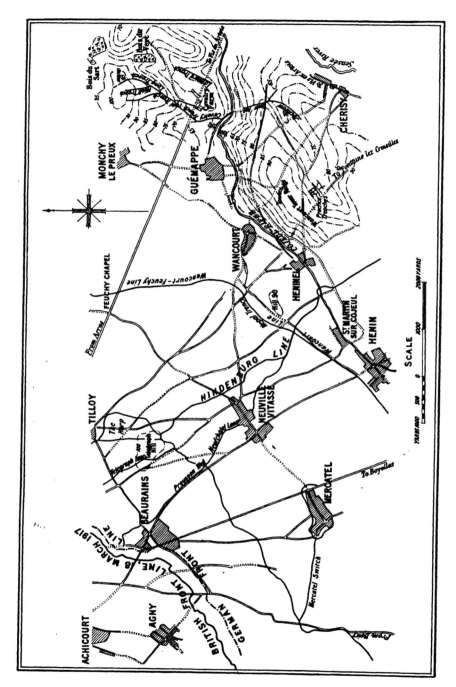

THE BATTLES OF ARRAS, 1917.

The tactics employed by the Germans at the beginning of the war were not based on any consideration for the lives of men. There is little doubt, however, that their experiences at Verdun and on the Somme had shaken their confidence in the fundamental soundness of their methods. They had suffered enormous losses in 1916; and their commanders were certainly anxious as to the conduct of their troops in future engagements. Loss of life and loss of morale, therefore, were responsible for the introduction of a more elastic method of defence—a method that lessened the wastage of men.

. In place of the old system of continuous and rigid lines which clearly marked out the position and which experience showed were always annihilated by artillery fire, the ground to be held was organized as a defensive zone of great depth. A system was developed of converted shell-holes and disconnected strong points, distributed in depth and forming centres of resistance in which were ensconced few men but many machine guns, and from which flanking or enfilade fire could be brought to bear on hostile troops attempting to penetrate the area between them. Some of these strong points, known subsequently as ' pill-boxes,' were made of concrete and were able to withstand a direct hit of all but the heaviest shell. This system of defence enabled the forward positions to be lightly occupied, the troops thus saved being concentrated in reserve, and the principle underlying its employment aimed at disorganization of the attacking troops by these forward posts, and the launching of rapid counter-attacks by the reserves, before the attackers had time to recover.

In making these counter-attacks, the Germans generally had to advance across the open, and, in so doing, provided excellent targets not only for the artillery and the machine guns, but for well-directed rifle fire as well. The spring offensives, however, had shown that the British troops were unable to use their rifles to advantage against targets of this nature. Many are the instances recorded of individuals, as well as of parties of men, missing opportunities for the effective use of the rifle. In extenuation of this failure it must not be forgotten that trench warfare tended to make the troops forget that the rifle was their best weapon. Trench fighting called for a handy weapon that could be used in a trench from fire-bay to fire-bay, and to this fact must be attributed the popularity of the bomb, in the use of which the individual soldier became very proficient. Rapidly trained men cannot be expert with any weapon—certainly not with more than one weapon—; and the rifle, being difficult to use and exposing the firer, was neglected in favour of the bomb, which was easy to use, made a joyful noise, and was effective at a few yards' range. Moreover, there were now in France few officers or men who had had the advantage of an adequate course of musketry. Our armies chiefly consisted of men whose only training was a short intensive recruits' course; and these men, with no previous experience, endeavoured in a limited space of time to become proficient not only in the use of the rifle, but also of the bomb, rifle-grenade, and bayonet. Thus when at a later stage there appeared targets ideal for controlled rifle fire, the necessary skill-at-arms was in many cases lacking.

During these two months, therefore, the 1/2nd Londons underwent a very strenuous course of training. Individual training of the soldier, including instruction in musketry, bomb-throwing, bayonet fighting, and the use of the rifle-grenade, was followed by platoon and company training in which the officers had frequent opportunity of handling their men. Brigade route-marches were included in the programme, and by these the Battalion speedily regained its efficiency in marching.

On the 26th of May, the G.O.C. 56th Division, Major-General Sir C. P. A. Hull, inspected the Battalion and spoke very highly of its conduct in the Battle of Arras. He expressed himself well satisfied with its appearance on parade, and he presented medals and Divisional cards to the officers and men to whom they had been awarded.

The football 'Sixes' competition was held on the 1st June, being won by H.Q. Company; and on the 2nd the Company Sports took place. The afternoon of the 7th was set aside for the Regimental Sports; but heavy rain caused their postponement until the next day. The Boxing Finals, however, were fought; and a concert was held in the evening. The Regimental Sports took place on the 8th and were a great success.

On the 9th June the Battalion left Agnez lez Duisans for the Telegraph Hill area for another spell in the line, and on the following night relieved a composite battalion of the 2/1st Bucks and 2/4th Oxfords (61st Division) in the front trenches north of the Cojeul River.

The trenches were for the most part old German defences, and were in a very bad condition, being both shallow and narrow. On the left flank the front line was, indeed, only waist-deep. During the 11th, 12th, and 13th, steps were taken to improve these defences; and with the assistance of the L.R.B. (the battalion in support) and of the 1/5th Cheshires (the Pioneer Battalion) considerable progress in this direction was made.

Otherwise nothing of interest occurred until 14th June, when at 7.20 a.m. the 3rd Division, on the left, delivered an attack on Hook Trench. In co-operation with this attack, the centre and left companies of the 1/2nd Londons ('C' and 'D') opened heavy rifle and Lewis-gun fire on the system of shell-holes occupied by the Germans, causing many enemy casualties. The attack was a complete success; and Hook and Long Trenches were captured, together with 175 prisoners.

Despite heavy shelling, the 1/2nd Londons only lost 3 other ranks killed, and 12 wounded. On the following night they were relieved by the L.R.B. and moved back, in support, to the Marlière area. While in this area they supplied nightly parties for work on the front trenches until the 20th, when the 169th Brigade was relieved by the 168th and moved out of the line to Achicourt. The total casualties of the 1/2nd Londons for this tour of duty were 2 officers (2nd Lieuts. D. Sloan and C. S. Soloman) wounded, and 8 other ranks killed and 49 wounded.

During May and June, officer reinforcements were:

Capt. J. Devane, 2nd Lieuts. A. J. Widdecombe, W. S. Harris, F. W. E. Spong, and L. Fairney;

and the following were posted from the 7th Londons:

E. E. Brown, A. J. Hasslacher, C. D. Menzies, H. W. Chiazzari, W. E. Polge, R. J. Ross, C. B. Cox, A. J. Williamson, A. Phillips, and C. S. Soloman.

Lieut. S. H. Stevens became adjutant in place of Capt. Sneath, who was now second-in-command of the Battalion and who had been promoted Major.

The following awards were notified:

D.C.M.: R.Q.M.S. J. Lagden.
M.S.M.: C.S.M. L. F. Stone.

On the 1st July, a memorial Church Parade was held for the officers, non-commissioned officers, and men, of the Regiment who fell at Gommecourt on the 1st July of the previous year. In the afternoon, by the courtesy of the Q.W.R., a large number of men attended that battalion's Swimming Sports held at the open-air baths at Arras. Sergt. Hollins ('B' Company) and Sergt. S. B. Taylor ('D' Company) were first and second respectively in the 100 Yards Open.

The 169th Brigade moved to Gouy en Artois on the next day, and thence on the 3rd July to the le Cauroy area. The 1/2nd Londons were billeted in Grand Rullecourt, where they remained for the best part of the next three weeks, spending the time, as usual, in training. On the 8th all arrangements were made for a Brigade Church Parade at which H.M. The King was to be present; but to the disappointment of everyone the bad weather caused its cancellation. The Brigade Horse Show and Sports took place on the

16th and 17th in the *Château* grounds, at Grand Rullecourt, and, in the former, the 1/2nd Londons succeeded in gaining six first prizes and one second—a result for which the Transport Officer (Capt. Taylor) deserves the highest credit. In the Sports, the Battalion was not so successful, the Q.W.R. sweeping the board. The arrangements on the ground were excellent. The Divisional Band was present; and there were numerous side-shows, of which the 'Bow Bells' entertainment was especially popular. At the conclusion of the meeting the prizes were presented by the Comtesse de Kergolay.

The pleasant stay at Grand Rullecourt came to an end on the 22nd, when the Battalion marched to Brevillers, *en route* for Flanders. The march was continued on the next day to Bouquemaison, where the Battalion entrained for Wizernes (3 miles from St. Omer), which was reached after four uncomfortable hours in cattle-trucks. On the 24th the Battalion paraded at 9.30 a.m. and proceeded to Nordausques—a typical Flemish village straggling along either side of the road to Calais—, arriving there at 4.30 p.m. after a hot and dusty march.

The Battalion remained at Nordausques for the rest of the month, entering on a period of more advanced training including field firing and practice in the formations of open warfare. Officer reinforcements during the month were:

Capt. H. W. Everitt, 2nd Lieuts. W. Dyer, W. J. Telford, and H. D. Pratt.

CHAPTER XIV

THE 2/2ND LONDONS IN THE BATTLES OF BULLECOURT, 1917

I

ALTHOUGH the Battle of Arras had died down early in May, operations in the area to the south of it were continued for some weeks longer, and, as they constitute one of the most important phases in the history of the 2/2nd Londons, they must now be described.

As we have seen in the previous chapter, the German withdrawal to the Hindenburg Line had been carried out ' with unhurried deliberation,' and its early stages accompanied by very little fighting of a serious nature. But, once the vicinity of the Hindenburg Line was reached, the enemy's resistance stiffened; and in many places fierce fighting followed the efforts of the British to locate definitely the limits of this new position.

South of the little River Sensée, the area with which we are now concerned, the pursuit of the enemy had been carried out by units of the Fifth Army; and, by the 2nd April, the leading troops had reached the Hindenburg Line in the neighbourhood of Bullecourt, which the enemy was found to be holding in great strength. In this area, the Hindenburg system ran from Héninel to Bullecourt in a generally south-easterly direction; at the latter village it turned sharply to the east to a point some five hundred yards in front of Riencourt, where it turned south-east again, to pass to the westward of Quéant. The system consisted of two lines of massive trenches, some eighty yards apart. Each line was heavily wired and liberally provided with deep dug-outs and concrete strong points; but so rapidly had the British followed up the retreating Germans, that the latter had not had time to complete their defences, and little or no revetting had been done to the trenches.

In conjunction with the operations at Arras, an attack in the neighbourhood of Bullecourt was launched on 11th April by the Australian Corps, of the Fifth Army, but did not meet with marked success, and was followed by heavy counter-attacks on the part of the enemy. As progress in this area was judged to be of special importance—for it was hoped, by breaking this sector of the Hindenburg Line, to cut off the enemy troops driven from the north-west by the Third Army—, preparations were made for an early renewal of the Fifth Army's offensive. This second attack was delivered on the 3rd May, and was attended by varying fortunes. To the right of Bullecourt, the Australians succeeded in penetrating the Hindenburg Line; on their left Bullecourt itself defied the efforts of the 62nd Division, with the result that the Australians found themselves in a marked salient, badly enfiladed from each flank.

The village of Bullecourt, which was to be the scene of fierce fighting for the next thirteen days, consisted of a few dozen houses clustered together between a large brick building at the south-western edge and a refinery at the back. It lay on the flat and almost treeless side of a hill, and overlooked the Hindenburg Line to the south, while, to the north, it was itself protected by rising ground. To an observer the village had the appearance of being ahead of the Hindenburg Line, but actually it lay between the front and support trenches; and its sunken roads, ruined houses, and fences, had the effect of converting the space between these two trenches into a very serious obstacle. Concrete machine-gun emplacements, numerous cellars, and a tunnel through which reserves could be brought up under cover, added to the strength of this veritable fortress.

Such was the importance attached to the possession of this place that attempts at its capture were continuous throughout the early days of May; and at last, by dint of hand-to-hand fighting, the 62nd Division gained a footing in the village. Meanwhile the Australians, to the east of Bullecourt, although subjected to frequent counter-attacks, succeeded in keeping their hold on the Hindenburg front line.

Throughout these operations, the 58th Division, which, it will be recalled, had joined the Fifth Army about the middle of April, was kept in reserve, but at this juncture was given a more important role and ordered to take over a part of the line at present held by the 5th Australian Division. For some days previously the 173rd Brigade, still located at Achiet le Grand, had been under orders to counter-attack in the event of the enemy breaking the line; and, in consequence, the 2/2nd Londons had been standing by in readiness to move at short notice.

With a view to the 173rd Brigade taking over the sector of the line between Bullecourt and the Noreuil-Riencourt road from the 15th Australian Infantry Brigade, advance parties of officers and non-commissioned officers from each of its battalions were sent forward on the 11th May to reconnoitre the ground. The intention being for the 2/2nd Londons to relieve the 59th Australian Battalion in the brigade support position about the line of the

Arras-Cambrai railway, their advance party, consisting of the four company commanders (Capts. Collymore, Ellis, Hawkins, and Lieut. J. G. W. Wright) and a number of non-commissioned officers, went forward to the headquarters of this battalion, which was found to be holding the embankment of the railway itself and a shallow trench some 500 yards in front of it, close to the Bullecourt-Quéant road. Owing to the heavy shelling, the 2/2nd Londons' party had a trying journey forward, but reached its destination safely. The 59th Australian Battalion was very weak in numbers both of officers and men; indeed the remnant of the company holding the railway embankment had only one subaltern left, and Capt. Ellis was asked to take temporary command of it. This he did until its relief on the next night. Throughout the night of the 11th the whole area was subjected to an intense bombardment by the enemy, and, as a result, Lieut. Wright and two non-commissioned officers of the 2/2nd Londons were killed.

The operations against Bullecourt itself had now been taken up by the 7th Division; and in the early hours of the 12th May the village was once more assaulted. Fierce fighting ensued; and, although good progress was made at the eastern end of the village, none was possible at its western end. North of the village, the situation was very obscure; and no part of the Hindenburg support line here remained in our hands. In conjunction with this attack, the 15th Australian Infantry Brigade, to the right of the 7th Division, attacked the Hindenburg support line and succeeded in capturing it. The shelling had been so intense during the fighting in this area that most trenches had been obliterated. The British troops, therefore, were now holding the position by a line of converted shell-holes; and the enemy, ejected from his old lines, had likewise taken up a position in a system of shell-holes on the lower slopes of the spur towards Riencourt.

Throughout the 12th, the Australians were heavily counter-attacked by the 2nd Prussian (Ersatz) Division. They managed to thrust back these attacks and to hold the ground they had gained; but this was only done with the assistance of the 59th Australian Battalion in support, two companies of which went forward to the front line to the aid of their hard-pressed comrades, leaving the shallow trench near the Bullecourt-Quéant road in the sole occupation of the party of 2/2nd Londoners.

On the night of the 12th/13th May, the relief of the 15th Australian Infantry Brigade was duly carried out by units of the 173rd Brigade, the 2/3rd Londons taking over the right sector of the front line and the 2/4th Londons the left, the 2/2nd Londons being in support, and the 2/1st Londons in reserve. The front extended from the sunken cross-roads at the north-east corner of Bullecourt, on the left, to the Noreuil-Riencourt road on the right; on the right of the Brigade was the 2nd Australian Division, and on the left the 2nd Queens of the 7th Division.

The 2/2nd Londons, marching by way of Vaulx Vraucourt, where meals were taken, and passing through a gas barrage at Noreuil, successfully carried out its relief of the 59th Australian Battalion in the support position, 'B' and 'D' Companies taking over the shallow forward trench, 'C' the railway embankment, and 'A' remaining in rear in dug-outs along a road to the north of Noreuil. The railway embankment was a regular target for the German gunners, and any advantages in the way of protection that it afforded were amply discounted by the very heavy shelling to which it was daily subjected. 'The relief was completed,' writes Capt. Collymore, 'without any serious loss, which was remarkable, as the Australians had been badly hammered, had lost most of their effectives, and were consequently unable to hand over in detail, a certain amount of confusion thereby resulting.'

The sole means of communication in this sector, both with the forward line and with the rear, was a single narrow trench, on the right of the Battalion's front, under direct observation by the enemy and in places no more than two feet deep. This lack of adequate communication was obviously a source not only of weakness, but of actual danger; and the B.G.C. decided that steps must be taken to remedy it at the earliest possible moment. He therefore gave instructions that a second trench should be dug, on the left of the Battalion's front, between the railway embankment and the trench held by 'B' Company, with the intention of subsequently enlarging and extending it to form a useful alternative to the existing line of communication. Accordingly, during the night of the 13th, the work was taken in hand; and the trench was dug by 'B' Company working back, and 'C' Company working forward. The enemy's shell fire, which had been heavy all day, now increased to an intense bombardment, and caused the 2/2nd Londons many casualties. 'B' Company, at work on the new trench, suffered especially and lost all its officers, Capt. Collymore, Lieut. Stevens, and 2nd Lieut. Newton being wounded. Lieut. Snell ('D' Company) took temporary command of the depleted company until Lieut. McHardy arrived from the transport lines.

Despite the heavy shelling and the extreme difficulty of communication with the battalions in front, the 2/2nd Londons succeeded in supplying them with water and in evacuating many of their casualties during the night.

The morning of the 14th May passed uneventfully; but at 2 p.m. the enemy subjected the British position to another intense bombardment. This lasted, in all, for close upon fourteen hours, and culminated at 3.30 a.m. on the 15th in the delivery of a fierce attack. At the junction of the 2/3rd Londons with the 14th Australian Infantry Brigade on the right the enemy forced an entry into the trench; but the 2/3rd Londons, to whose support 'A' Company of the 2/2nd was hurriedly sent forward, quickly drove him out and restored the situation. The fact that this was the thirteenth attack in ten days and that the troops employed were of the 3rd Prussian Guard is proof that the enemy was in deadly earnest in his attempts to regain this part of the line.

The strength of the enemy's bombardment can be gauged from the fact that of a platoon of 31 non-commissioned officers and men (2nd Lieut. Harper), which went forward from Battalion Headquarters with bombs for the 2/4th Londons, 21 became casualties. This platoon took an hour and a half to reach the front line; and it speaks volumes for the devotion of the men that, despite these losses, each one of forty boxes of bombs was safely delivered to the 2/4th Londons.

This platoon was ordered to remain, and was temporarily attached to the 2/4th Londons, with whom it had first-hand experience of the enemy's attack. On this flank, the attack did not arrive until 4 a.m. and, although pressed with vigour, was finally repulsed.

During this period the 2/2nd Londons made two interesting captures. The first of these was effected by Ptes. Hewitt and Brown ('A' Company), who, during the attack on the 2/3rd Londons in the early hours of 15th May, succeeded in wounding and bringing in the commanding officer of the 3rd Lehr Regiment of the Prussian Guard. The second was the capture by 'C' Company of two naked prisoners; and the incident is thus described by Capt. Ellis, commanding the company: 'I frequently surveyed the front from a hole in the top of the railway embankment and at daybreak on the 14th believed that I saw a naked man to the left of the company front. A patrol was sent across that night to investigate and brought in two Boches (father and son) who had deserted their unit some days before (probably during the previous push) and had been pinned to the ground effectively by the continuous rifle and machine-gun fire from the Boche line. They were apparently afraid to move at night; they felt secure from observation in their hole and were "de-lousing" at dawn when the one at the farther side of the hole was visible for a moment on account of the height of my position.'

On the night of the 16th/17th May, the 2/2nd Londons relieved the 2/3rd Londons in the right sector of the Brigade front with two companies

('A' and 'C') in the front line, and one company ('D') and one platoon of 'B' Company in support. The remaining three platoons of 'B' Company were sent back to Noreuil. Signs of still further attacks by the enemy were not wanting, and great vigilance was required on the part of our men. Vigorous patrolling, night work to clear the dead, continued strengthening of positions, and improvement of communications, were necessary and made so many demands on the men that fresh labour had to be sought from the transport personnel of the Battalion. Of these days in the line, 2nd Lieut. Harper's diary records the gruesome fact that 'the sun on the dead lying about made the line almost untenable.'

The Battalion experienced further heavy shelling on the 18th and 19th May, during which Lieut. Snell and 2nd Lieut. Williams were wounded, the latter subsequently dying of his wounds, and on the 21st it was relieved by the 2/11th Londons (175th Brigade), and marched to camp on the outskirts of Bihucourt.

Of the engagement through which the Battalion had just come, Lieut.-Col. Richardson, in a rough note made at the time, says: 'All ranks showed magnificent spirit.' The conduct of the Battalion during the actual fighting earned the unqualified praise of the 14th Australian Brigade, and on the Somme, some fifteen months after these events, in the early days of the final advance, the 2/2nd Londons were still remembered by this brigade.

The Battalion's casualties were:

> 3 officers (Lieut. J. G. W. Wright, 2nd Lieut. H. E. V. Williams, and 2nd Lieut. R. F. Smith, 14th Londons attached) killed, and 5 (Capt. R. Collymore, Lieuts. J. S. Stevens, H. J. Snell, 2nd Lieuts. L. Newton and J. D. Goodwin, 21st Londons attached) wounded, and 168 other ranks killed and wounded. The casualties among the senior non-commissioned officers included Sergts. L. Thomas and R. J. McCaul, who were killed.

L/Corpl. W. Brown and Pte. C. Lock were awarded the M.M. for their gallant conduct during this period.

Lieut. John George William Wright was born on 9th September 1886. On the outbreak of the war, he joined the 9th Londons (Q.V.R.), with whom he served until gazetted to the 3/2nd Londons on 4th June 1915.

2nd Lieut. Henry Evan Vincent Williams was the son of Mr. and Mrs. T. Williams, of Colwyn Bay, and was born on 1st February 1897. He was educated at St. George's School, Harpenden, where he was a prominent member of the First Fifteen. He was in the school Cadet Corps, and on leaving school in May 1915, he at once joined the Artists' Rifles. He obtained his commission on 6th December 1915, being gazetted to the 2/2nd Londons. He died, four days after being wounded, on the 22nd May and was buried in the Military Cemetery, Grévillers, near Bapaume.

II

On the road to Bihucourt the fields to right and left were covered with the glory and abundance of the yellow bloom of spring. The few fruit trees that war had not stricken down were in flower. The contrast between this and the field of battle that the Battalion had just left was remarkable, and gave rise to indescribable feelings; here was Nature triumphant, while but a few miles away men were being hurled to destruction or terrible torture.

The 2/2nd Londons seemed well satisfied with the camp at Bihucourt, and a Y.M.C.A. hut added to the comfort. The ensuing few days were occupied in resting, cleaning, and training for attack. On 24th May the Battalion was inspected by the new Brigade Commander, Br.-General Freyberg. A concert at night, two more days of preparation, a Sunday with a largely attended Communion Service, and then back to the line in relief of the 2/5th King's Own Yorkshire Light Infantry (62nd Division) between Croisilles and Bullecourt.

As both the 7th and 62nd Divisions had suffered heavy casualties in the continuous fighting in this area, and badly needed some respite, the 58th Division, during the latter part of May, had extended its front to the left, and had relieved first the one, in and around Bullecourt, and subsequently the other, to the west of the village. By the end of the month, therefore, the 58th Division was holding 4,000 yards of front with two brigades in line. The 173rd Brigade took over the left sub-sector, and was disposed with the 2/1st and 2/2nd Londons in the front line, 2/3rd Londons in support, and 2/4th Londons in reserve.

The dispositions of the 2/2nd Londons are interesting. Two companies held the front line, echeloned in depth to 500 yards on a front of almost a mile, with the remaining half-battalion and Headquarters in a sunken road near Croisilles. The form that the front-line defence took was an outpost one, a series of mutually supporting, self-contained posts, each held by a section or half-platoon. In this we see the development from pure trench warfare that has been discussed somewhat fully in the previous chapter.

After an inter-company relief, the two supporting companies relieving the two outpost companies, the Battalion was relieved on the night of the 3rd/4th June by the 2/4th Londons, and moved back to a camp near the

205

village of Mory. The Battalion's casualties during this tour of duty were 1 officer (2nd Lieut. H. K. McIntosh) wounded, and 1 other rank (Sergt. F. G. Savage) killed, and 11 wounded.

Officer reinforcements in May and in the early days of June were:

> Capt. E. E. H. Bate, Lieuts. W. Ridgeway, G. B. Henderson, 2nd Lieuts. H. K. McIntosh, T. R. Plowman, and A. H. F. Pretty (22nd Londons).

Although to the east of Bullecourt the Hindenburg Line had been successfully captured and held, north-west of the village, on the new front of the 58th Division, it still remained in the enemy's hands. To the left of the 58th Division, the 21st Division had established itself in the Hindenburg front line as far as the Croisilles-Fontaine road, but had not as yet made good the support line. Thus it will be seen that there still remained, in this area, some 2,500 yards of the Hindenburg front line and 3,500 of the support line to be captured by the British in order to bring what are officially designated 'The Flanking Operations round Bullecourt' to a satisfactory conclusion.

It was accordingly decided to make an early attempt to complete the capture of the Hindenburg Line in this area, and preparations with this object in view were begun at once by the 58th Division. Only the wire defending the position, two belts 140 feet in depth and 25 feet apart, could be seen from the British lines, but the position itself had been frequently tested and was known to be very strong. The front line was sited close to the western side of the Héninel-Bullecourt road, and for the most part ran straight, but to the south of the Croisilles-Hendecourt road it contained two small salients, known respectively as the Hump and the Knuckle, that had been converted by the enemy into formidable strong points. A strong support line had been constructed some 200 yards behind the front line.

Owing to the great strength of this enemy line and to repeated failure of attacks upon it, the most careful preparations were made; and day after day the troops selected, including the 2/2nd Londons, practised the attack. Detailed surveys were made of the proposed area of assembly of the attacking troops, so that no hitch might occur during this vital phase; aeroplane photographs of the ground were taken; and maps were prepared for each man taking part, showing his line of advance and his particular task on reaching the objective. The assembly was repeatedly practised—the last few yards had to be taken at a crawl—; and the actual attack rehearsed three or four times each night until every man knew exactly what he had to do. Special arrangements were made to prevent any loss of direction on the left flank, near the Hump, where the maze of trenches and broken wire made such a contingency highly probable.

The attack was originally planned for a date some days earlier than the 15th June, on which date it actually took place, but for a variety of reasons was three times postponed. Although these postponements did not largely affect the general scheme of the operations, the details were constantly undergoing revision during this period; and much of the early training was wasted. Preparations had to be begun all over again, and the attack in its new guise practised afresh. Nevertheless, when the attack was finally ordered, the troops were reasonably prepared, and few hitches occurred, at any rate in the preliminary moves.

The front of attack of the 58th Division extended from the southern angle of the Knuckle on the right to a point about 150 yards north of the Hump on the left; and, as it was intended to attempt the capture of both the front and support lines in the one operation, the operation was divided into two distinct phases, two consecutive days being allotted to the task, one for each phase. By making the capture of the front line one phase and the capture of the support line a second, it was hoped to simplify co-operation with the 21st Division on the left, which, already in the Hindenburg front line, proposed to assault the Hindenburg support line simultaneously with the opening of the second phase of the 58th Division's attack.

The attacking troops of the 173rd Brigade were disposed as follows:

RIGHT: 1 Company 2/3rd Londons.
RIGHT CENTRE: 1½ Companies 2/1st Londons.
LEFT CENTRE: 1½ Companies 2/2nd Londons.
LEFT: 1 Company 2/4th Londons.

For the purpose of this attack, the company of the 2/3rd Londons was placed under the orders of the O.C. 2/1st Londons, and that of the 2/4th under the orders of the O.C. 2/2nd Londons. The attack was to be supported on the left by heavy fire from the 21st Division, while on the right the 174th Brigade was to establish a line of posts in a sunken road in prolongation of the front of attack. An extraordinarily heavy concentration of artillery fire was arranged; the guns of the 7th, 58th, and 62nd Divisions, together with those of the Corps Heavy Artillery and the machine guns of the three Brigade Machine-Gun Companies, were allotted to the task of bombarding the enemy's position and of providing a barrage to cover the assault.

Zero hour was fixed for 2.50 a.m. on the 15th June; and at dusk on the previous day forward tapes to assist the maintenance of direction, and duckboard bridges over Hump Lane, Lone Trench, and Lone Support (communi-

cation trenches), were put down. The task of laying these duckboards fell
to the lot of Capt. Sinnatt, and in his account of the battle he tells how it
was carried out: 'These duckboards had to be placed at a certain angle
(I think it was 105½° whole circle bearing!) so as to be parallel to the line
of advance. . . . I asked for Factory Lane, and, with a corporal and five
men, was wrongly directed, and I, with the others, carried a duckboard half
across France before we discovered we were on the wrong track. I got to
the right place eventually.'

All but he and the corporal were lost; and these two now began laying
duckboards, in a fever to be done before our barrage dropped, and the
advance began. Capt. Sinnatt had to scoop the parapet of the trench with
his hands to get the boards to lie flat and not to rock as the men passed over.
'The hardest work I ever did in my life,' he continues. 'I thought I was
tired and must have a sleep before I could do any good work again. Strange
how civilian habits crept in! I had been used to thinking I must be tired
after being awake for a certain time. But I didn't get any sleep for 72 hours.
. . . I found the rest of the party later, still collecting duckboards.'

A short description of the contour of the ground will enable succeeding
events to be better appraised. From a railway embankment about 1,000
yards to the rear of the forward posts of the British line, the ground rose in
a gradual incline to the crest, a few yards south of which these posts were
situated. The ground then declined eastward to the enemy's position. Thus
any advantage of ground was indisputably ours. On the other hand, the
enemy's position was very strong, and on the front of the 2/2nd Londons
was made still stronger by the existence of four concrete 'pill-boxes' (or
mebus), each a miniature fort. These, for convenience of identification, were
numbered 1 to 4 from left to right of the Battalion's front. Between himself
and the position of the 21st Division in the Hindenburg front line, the
enemy had erected a very strong double barricade; and the task of capturing
this was entrusted to the company of the 2/4th Londons, as was also the
capture of the sunken cross-roads to the left of the Hump and a strong point
about 100 yards to the north of these cross-roads.

'C' Company and two platoons of 'A' Company of the 2/2nd Londons,
and 'A' Company of the 2/4th Londons, were the companies actually
detailed for the attack, and by 2.15 a.m. on the 15th June they had deployed
without a hitch. Lieut.-Col. Richardson established his battle headquarters
in the front line of the 21st Division on the left, and was thus in line with
the objective of his battalion's first attack.

All was now ready. At 2.50 a.m. the British barrage opened; and 'C'

LIEUTENANT-COLONEL J. P. KELLETT, D.S.O., M.C.

LIEUTENANT-COLONEL A. R. RICHARDSON, D.S.O.

Company (Capt. Ellis) on the left and the two platoons of 'A' Company (Lieut. Roberts) on the right advanced to the attack, in company with 'A' Company of the 2/4th Londons. As the ground on the left was much broken by trenches and sunken roads, 'C' Company, with the more difficult task before it, was allotted a frontage of about 180 yards and was disposed in four lines, half of Nos. 10 and 12 Platoons being in the front and the remainder in the second, and half of Nos. 9 and 11 in the third and the remainder in the fourth and laſt, while the two platoons (2nd Lieuts. Harper and Evans) of 'A' Company, on a slightly narrower frontage, were disposed in one line.

The troops keeping close to the barrage reached their objective with little loss. 'Up to the enemy's wire,' says 2nd Lieut. Harper in his report, '"A" Company kept quite a good line, although, through the battalion on our right closing into the left, they were pushed gradually to the left. At the edge of the wire, the line broke up, the men going round the masses of wire.' Hereabouts 2nd Lieut. Evans was seen for the laſt time. As he could not get through the wire to his front, he went off to the right, where he was undoubtedly killed.

Continuing, 2nd Lieut. Harper says, 'I then passed through the wire. A machine gun opened fire from No. 3 *Mebus*. I got round its right and dropped into the trench on to two Germans who were firing flares. These I dealt with.' With the aid of a lance-corporal, he then proceeded to capture the pill-box and, with it, its garrison of seven Germans, whom he sent back in the charge of a wounded man. In the trench itself, 'A' Company also captured a number of prisoners, who were likewise sent back. Lieut. Roberts now arrived and took charge of operations. With the aid of 2nd Lieut. Harper he collected a party of men and tried to clear No. 4 pill-box with the object of eſtablishing connexion with the 2/1ſt Londons on the right. This pill-box, however, resiſted all their efforts; and they were ultimately forced to make a trench block between it and No. 3 pill-box, the next on the left. They then turned their attention to the left, to No. 2 pill-box, from which they were being enfiladed, and between 5.30 and 6 a.m. made three attempts to take it. This pill-box likewise resiſted their efforts.

In the meanwhile, 'C' Company, on the left, had reached the Hindenburg front line, and its two leading platoons (Lieut. Tucker and 2nd Lieut. Heading), in company with personnel of the 2/4th Londons on their left, failing to recognize their objective, went far beyond it. Eventually they reached the enemy's support line, where they captured 17 prisoners, but suffered heavy casualties themselves from the British ſtanding barrage, now concentrated on this spot to prevent the reinforcement of the German front line. Among the casualties were the two platoon commanders, both Lieut. Tucker and 2nd Lieut. Heading being wounded. Ultimately the remnant of this party managed to extricate itself and, with its prisoners, rejoin the remainder of its company. With regard to this incident, Lieut.-Col. Richardson's personal diary records the fact that 'the men were keen and went too far.'

The two support platoons of 'C' Company also made good their objective, although they likewise lost their commanders, 2nd Lieuts. Boustred and Inwards, both of whom were wounded. Thus 'C' Company had completed its allotted task; and when Capt. Sinnatt, sent up by Lieut.-Col. Richardson from his battle headquarters to learn how the attacking companies had fared, arrived and made a complete tour of the line from left to right, he found that the 2/2nd Londons were firmly established on their objective, and, on his return at 6.30 a.m., was able to give a satisfactory report of the general situation.

Consolidation of the position was at once begun and was continued throughout the morning, much hampered, as 2nd Lieut. Harper says, 'by fire from *Mebus* No. 2 and from snipers in front. Parties of enemy were continually seen running from shell-hole to shell-hole in front—these we engaged with rifle and machine gun with good results.'

At this juncture Capt. Ellis, the senior officer present with the attacking companies, was wounded; and therefore Lieut.-Col. Richardson, at 1.30 p.m., sent up Capt. Sinnatt to take command of the captured position. Capt. Sinnatt was accompanied by 2nd Lieut. Martin and 14 bombers, and, working his way to the right of the line, at once decided to attempt the capture of No. 4 pill-box by outflanking it with his bombers. He put his plan into execution forthwith, but owing to the activity of the enemy's snipers and bombers had soon to abandon it until darkness set in. Bombs and ammunition began to run short during the day; and anxiety on this score was only relieved by a party of the 9th Leicesters, of the 21st Division, who providentially arrived, bringing further supplies.

The attack, apart from the failure on the part of some of the leading troops to recognize their objective, was attended by a considerable measure of success. After severe fighting, the Hindenburg front line remained in our hands at the end of the day, and 36 prisoners and one machine gun had been captured. The 2/2nd Londons were still in touch with the 2/4th Londons on the left; the captured trench was divided between them, the latter battalion being responsible for the left half, from the flank of the 21st Division as far as the German communication trench running back from the Hump to the support line, and the 2/2nd Londons for the right half, from their point of junction with the 2/4th to the block mentioned above. One amusing incident of this day deserves recording. Pte. Coles, his head swathed in a blood-stained bandage, was conducting alone 17 prisoners to the rear, when he encountered the G.O.C. 58th Division, Major-General Fanshawe. To the latter's question whether he wasn't afraid to be left in sole charge of so many prisoners he scornfully replied, with a cock of his head in the direction of the prisoners, 'Not that packet.'

The final orders for the second day's attack on the Hindenburg support line were issued late on 15th June. The dispositions of the attacking troops of the 173rd Brigade were the same as for the first attack, save that each battalion's detachment was larger, the 2/3rd and 2/1st Londons supplying three companies each, the 2/2nd Londons two companies and a half, and the 2/4th Londons one company. The dispositions of the 2/2nd Londons were as follows :

RIGHT : 'D' Company (Capt. Hawkins).
CENTRE : 'B' Company (Capt. Bate).
LEFT : 2 platoons 'A' Company (Lieut. Ridgeway).

The formation decided upon was one strong wave, with moppers-up in the rear, in the ratio of three platoons per company in the leading line to one platoon in the second line. Royal Engineer and Light Trench Mortar personnel, with explosives for dealing with the dug-outs in Tunnel Trench, where opposition was anticipated, were to go with each company.

'B' and 'D' Companies were ordered each to push forward one platoon, to be in position on the line of assembly in the Hindenburg front line by 10.30 p.m. on 15th June. These platoons, and two companies of the 2/4th Londons, which for the purposes of the second attack were to be under the orders of the 2/2nd Londons, as had been the case with the one company in the first attack, were to proceed by way of Hump Lane and New Trench and were, if necessary, to drive out any enemy still in the Hindenburg front line—the area of assembly. The remaining platoons were to form up on the assembly ground used for the first attack, and to advance over the open to their assembly positions on the Hindenburg front line.

'B' Company's advance platoon, No. 6 (2nd Lieut. Harris), though leaving camp at Mory by 6 p.m., had not established itself on its assembly lines when the remainder of the company, under Capt. Bate, arrived there several hours later. Fortunately the missing platoon arrived not long afterwards, having been held up by a big block in Factory Avenue. Another misfortune befell 'B' Company's assembly, No. 7 Platoon (Lieut. Henderson) missing its way to the assembly area. At the last minute, therefore, Capt. Bate found it incumbent upon him to redistribute his company and to put No. 6 Platoon in the first wave in the stead of the missing No. 7 Platoon. By 1.30 a.m., however, the wanderers had by good fortune retraced their steps, and were in ample time for the advance at zero hour.

The congestion in rear and the lack of adequate direction marks in front were not the only difficulties with which the Battalion had to contend in its preparations for its second attack. A far more serious matter than these gave rise to considerable anxiety, and led to an interruption in the preparations and very nearly prevented the delivery of the attack altogether; at 10.30 p.m. on the 15th the enemy launched a series of heavy counter-attacks against our new positions, and in the course of the severe fighting that ensued gained a footing in his old front line in the centre and at two other points. In the course of the night he made no less than four such counter-attacks. The first came from the front and was beaten off by rifle fire. The next came from the right, a bombing attack launched from No. 4 pill-box, which was still in the enemy's possession. Like its predecessor, this attack was also beaten off with heavy losses to the attackers. A far more serious attack followed and at an hour most likely to upset the British plans for the second day's battle; at 11 p.m. the enemy forced an entry into No. 2 pill-box, from which he had been driven in the earlier part of the day. Luckily the advance platoons of the two companies detailed for the second attack were now close at hand, and, by immediately joining issue, succeeded in dispossessing him of his gain and in clearing the whole of the front of assembly. The fourth and last attack was, perhaps, most serious of all. By well-directed bombing, the enemy drove back the party of 2/2nd Londons holding the block between Nos. 3 and 4 pill-boxes, on the right of the Battalion's front, and, for the moment, seemed to be in a position to roll up the whole British line. But Capt. Sinnatt by promptly turning a machine gun on to the block checked the attack, and eventually forced the enemy's withdrawal.

The situation remained very critical; and Capt. Sinnatt called upon the men for special efforts to retain the line they had held all day. 'The men responded magnificently,' he says, 'and their behaviour was too splendid for words.' Of the horrors of that night, he gives some vivid impressions :

The solitary candle that burned in the pitch-dark *mebus*—blown out every time the Boche got a direct hit—illuminated fitfully the haggard faces of the wounded . . . the gallant conduct of two stretcher-bearers, one of whom was killed after the most wonderful devotion to duty and outstanding bravery.

That horrible thirst—men begging on their knees for water I hadn't got. Then the arrival of six petrol tins of the warm but precious fluid, and the issue, when every drop was treasured. I can see now the lad with a huge chunk blown out of his neck holding his water-bottle out to catch any drops, as I gave each man his meagre share. Yes; it was a picnic in Hell.

The partial success of these hostile counter-attacks gave rise to another difficulty when 'B' Company was fully assembled on its line of advance, and No. 4 pill-box, hard by on its right flank, expected to be in British hands, was reported to be held by the enemy. A party from the previously missing No. 7 Platoon was sent across to clear it, but, as it happened, found it empty, the Germans having taken fright at the earlier, and unpremeditated, perambulations of this platoon, and retired. Nevertheless it is quite certain that the post for some time after the first advance had been in the hands of the enemy, who was reported to be likewise in possession of part of the assembly positions of the 2/1st and 2/3rd Londons.

At 3.10 a.m. on 16th June, the remaining two companies and a half of the 2/2nd Londons, with the 2/1st on the right and 2/4th on the left, advanced under cover of a barrage from the whole of the Divisional Artillery and Brigade Machine-Gun Companies, and succeeded in establishing themselves in the Hindenburg support line.

Capt. Bate's graphic words, written shortly after the battle, will recall to the minds of all the agonizing moments before the barrage opened, and the strange sensations of 'going over the top.'

It was now about 3.5 a.m. and there was a good deal of gunfire going on from both sides, mostly heavy stuff. It did not seem to strike me at the time as I lay and waited for the barrage to start. I cannot recollect even feeling excited at the moment; I suppose I was too busy thinking out what measures I might have to take in various contingencies.

The noise grew greater gradually and finally reached such a pitch that I did not notice the barrage opening. . . . The walk-over is to my mind a blur of intense noise (so much so that no distinct detonation could be made out), clouds of dust and smoke, and blinding flashes everywhere.

Owing to the shape of the line, the maintenance of direction was a matter of considerable difficulty, some of the men going too far to the right, and Capt. Bate only succeeded in keeping them on the proper course by going close up to them and shouting at them, or, more often, by pushing them to attract their attention; for so great was the din that the human voice had little chance of being heard. 'We had little trouble,' continues Capt. Bate, all of whose men went over wearing sprigs of *Sweet William* in their helmets, because they had seen him wearing it earlier in the day, 'in capturing Tunnel Trench.[1] So far as my immediate neighbourhood was concerned, we encountered no opposition at all on entering the trench.' But on running down it with a few men, he encountered three Germans who at once opened fire on the little party. Capt. Bate emptied his revolver at them, and then closed with his nearest assailant, bringing him to the ground. There was a fierce struggle; Capt. Bate managed to draw a knife that he carried about with him, and by flourishing it before the German's eyes induced him to surrender. Meanwhile, his men had opened fire on the remaining two Germans, who hurriedly made off.

Capt. Bate continued down the trench, posting men at the entrance to each dug-out, and, after passing Fag Alley (a long communication trench running back to the German second system) established connexion with 'A' Company on the left. He then returned, and, with 2nd Lieut. Harris, explored Fag Alley, finally leaving a party of men about fifty yards up it to form a block.

The experiences of 'A' Company, on the left, were, according to Lieut. Ridgeway, much the same, and, keeping direction well, the company succeeded in capturing its objective. 'When we reached the support line,' says Lieut. Ridgeway, 'we bombed three entrances to the tunnel. Only one had any Germans near it—there were three and they were bayoneted.'

On reaching his objective, Lieut. Ridgeway with four of his men went off to the left to get in touch with the 2/4th Londons. 'We found ourselves,' he says, 'being bombed by what I thought was the 4th Battalion. I shouted to them to stop and then discovered they were Boches who were fairly established in one of the concrete emplacements.' This was the first fruits of the loss of direction on the flanks; for here was a strong enemy post established between the left of the 2/2nd Londons and the right of the 2/4th. Lieut. Ridgeway at once attempted to clear this post, but within a few minutes had lost two men, and so was obliged to desist.

[1] Tunnel Trench was the Hindenburg support line, and was so named from a tunnel that ran beneath it for a very considerable distance.

'I think it got light too soon,' he adds, 'and they were able to take careful aim at us. If it had remained dark a bit longer, we could have surrounded the emplacement and taken it by assault, but as soon as we showed ourselves, we got bowled over.'

He then rejoined his company, which was firmly established along the line of its objective; but as his men were being badly sniped and had also run out of bombs, he decided to close to the right and join forces with 'B.' This he accordingly did, and then formed a block across the trench to protect the left flank of the two companies. Hereabouts 2nd. Lieut. Denton ('A' Company) was killed, and Lieut. Pretty ('B' Company) wounded.

With 'D' Company also reaching its objective, it will be seen that the Battalion had successfully carried out its task. The Hindenburg support line was in its hands. As in the attack of the previous day the troops had had the utmost difficulty in recognizing their objectives, obliterated, as they were, by shell fire, while the dust and smoke of the barrage prevented any of the surrounding landmarks being seen. The right platoon of 'D' Company overshot its mark, and left the right flank of the Battalion completely in the air. This platoon carried on its advance for a considerable distance, some men even getting as far as Copse Trench, while on the left the two companies of the 2/4th Londons lost direction and swung away to the left. This loss of direction on each flank was to have serious consequences and was to jeopardize the safety of the attacking companies of the 2/2nd Londons. The enemy was not slow to realize what had happened, and into the gaps now appearing between the flanks and the centre of the attack he quickly began to insert his troops.

The leading platoons of 'B' Company also failed to recognize their objective and went far beyond it. It is to these unfortunate incidents that Capt. Bate refers, when he says: 'At about 4 o'clock (a.m.) half a dozen men came in from the front . . . some of Hawkins' men who had gone on to Hoop or Copse Trench. . . . They said they had been a platoon, but had lost most of their number in coming back through our barrage. They also told me that Henderson was out in front somewhere with a few men. . . . We were not able to send for them. That was all I ever heard of Henderson.'

The Hindenburg support line had been so uprooted by the British barrage that it afforded little or no field of fire for the men now in occupation of it; so, covered by Lewis guns pushed out to the front, the 2/2nd Londons busied themselves, in the light of dawn, in improving the position. The work went on until the advent of broad daylight led to increased activity on the part of German snipers who, working round to the rear, shot the men down as they dug.

Capt. Bate, having set his men to dig in, went off to the right to connect with 'D' Company. He found Capt. Hawkins directing the efforts of his men, who were likewise digging in; and together the two officers concerted the necessary measures of defence.

About 4 a.m. the hostile shelling died away, probably because the enemy was afraid of hitting the many of his men now established in and around the British position; and shortly afterwards, abandoning his attitude of passive occupation of the gaps in the British line, he began his attempts to eject the 2/2nd Londons from their hard-won gains. Parties of Germans appeared on each flank, bombing inwards; and at 7.30 a.m. the block on the left that Lieut. Ridgeway had made some hours earlier was driven in, while 'B' Company's block in Fag Alley was fiercely bombed. The S.O.S. was repeatedly given. No response came in the form of artillery support, although, as Capt. Bate says, 'We had been busy burning red flares and waving our yellow handkerchiefs whenever the contact aeroplanes came over and sounded their horns, and we felt pretty sure that they knew where we were.' As a last resort, the pigeons, which had been carefully saved for such an emergency, were sent back asking for more bombs and for a protective barrage across Fag Alley.

These efforts to obtain artillery support failed for an hour and a quarter after the first request, following the enemy's serious counter-attacks, because the messages did not reach their destination. Nevertheless Lieut.-Col. Richardson was not oblivious of the situation of the men in front, and made frequent attempts to get supports to the leading companies of both the 2/4th Londons and of his own battalion; but every attempt was completely frustrated by the heavy rifle and machine-gun fire with which the enemy swept the intervening ground.

Scattered parties of the enemy had now worked round the flanks of the devoted 2/2nd Londoners in the Hindenburg support line, and before long a machine gun opened fire upon the rear of 'A' and 'B' Companies. In endeavouring to put this machine gun out of action with a Lewis gun, 2nd Lieut. Thompson ('A' Company) was shot through the head by a sniper. 'I saw several Boche,' says Capt. Bate, ' slipping across country to our right, but we could not get the Lewis gun on to them, as they moved singly and only a yard or two at a time. Our riflemen were constantly on the watch for them, to pick them off as they ran.'

The enemy now broke right through the block in Fag Alley, and, as he was likely to cut off the remnants of 'A' and 'B' Companies from 'D,' Lieut. Ridgeway and Capt. Bate withdrew their men along Tunnel Trench past the mouth of Fag Alley, and then rallied them for another effort. At this juncture, Lieut. Ridgeway was wounded, Capt. Bate assuming command of the few men of the 'A' Company still left. That the enemy would make another attack on the left any minute was certain; and Capt. Bate set every man that could be spared to the task of searching for German bombs and bringing them to the left flank, so as to be prepared for the attack when it came.

The expected attack came at last. The survivors of the three companies, now reduced to a mere handful, were heavily bombed and assaulted from each flank. Capt. Hawkins was wounded and made prisoner by the enemy; 2nd Lieut. Harris was seen no more; Capt. Bate was also wounded; and the remnant of this gallant little force wiped out. 'When I last saw Capt. Hawkins unwounded,' writes Lieut. Ridgeway, 'he was endeavouring to rally the men. He was perfectly collected and had his pipe in his mouth and was doing his utmost.'[1]

While these events were happening in front, Lieut.-Col. Richardson, fully realizing the desperate plight of his attacking companies, but unable to help them, had sent Major Miller to Brigade Headquarters to explain the situation; and, as a result of this visit, the B.G.C. came up himself to make a reconnaissance of the position. It was by then quite obvious that although the attacking troops had captured all their objectives, they could not hold their gains, because supports could not reach them. A few survivors, practically all wounded, including Capt. Bate and Lieut. Ridgeway, after amazing adventures, managed to crawl back to the Hindenburg front line during the day and the next night. But with the exception of these and of those men who had been wounded earlier in the action, the whole of the two companies and a half that attacked on 16th June had been killed or made prisoner.

We must now turn to the Hindenburg front line, where we left 'C' Company and the remainder of 'A' at the opening of the second day's battle. These troops, still with Capt. Sinnatt in command, continued to hold the line that they had captured on the 15th June, and to keep it clear throughout the 16th. In the early stages of the second day's battle they had little to do, the attention of the enemy being then focussed on the assaulting

---

[1] As Lieut. Ridgeway, wounded, was making his way to the rear, he caught sight of Capt. Hawkins, apparently wounded, parleying with the Germans. This was the last seen of him; he subsequently died in the hands of the enemy.

troops of the Battalion, successfully established in the Hindenburg support line. But no sooner had the enemy penetrated the gaps in the line of the forward troops than he began to work towards his old front line. At 8 a.m. he was pushing machine gunners and riflemen towards No. 3 pill-box and threatening the right flank. Fortunately these threats did not take on serious proportions; and as the day wore on the enemy seemed less inclined to come to close quarters. As the troops holding the Hindenburg front line were now very weak in numbers, small parties, consisting mainly of slightly wounded men, were sent up, and these, augmented by the survivors of the attacking companies, sufficed to enable Capt. Sinnatt to hold his line intact throughout the day. At dusk the enemy put down a severe bombardment on the Hump, and even made some sort of an attempt to advance, but made no inroads into the British gains of the first day.'

And so ended ' Bloody Bullecourt.'

The second day's fighting had nowhere been attended by success. On the right, the other battalions of the 173rd Brigade had made no progress, while, on the left, the attack of the 21st Division had entirely failed, and the few isolated parties that did succeed in reaching a line of shell-holes in front of Tunnel Trench were ultimately ejected by the enemy. So far as the 173rd Brigade was concerned, the two days' fighting had resulted in the capture and retention of the Hindenburg front line and the sunken road in rear of it, from the point of junction with the 21st Division on the left to the angle of the Hindenburg Line some 1,500 yards north-west of Bullecourt.

At 2.30 a.m. on 17th June, in the midst of a violent bombardment, the gallant remnant of the 2/2nd Londons was relieved by the 2/5th Londons (174th Brigade), and went back to Mory Copse.

The Battalion's casualties were:

KILLED : 2 officers (2nd Lieuts. A. Denton and H. Inwards), and 21 other ranks (including Sergts. C. Elderton and J. L. Hancock).

WOUNDED : 10 officers (Capts. E. E. H. Bate, H. O. Ellis, Lieuts. W. Ridgeway, A. H. Pretty, 2nd Lieuts. P. A. Tucker, A. H. Denly, B. S. Heading, R. W. Boustred, P. G. Roberts, and H. C. Bennett), and 207 other ranks.

MISSING : 5 officers (Capt. H. J. Hawkins, Lieut. G. B. Henderson, 2nd Lieuts. H. M. Harris, A. J. Evans, and R. S. Thompson), and 156 other ranks.

Capt. Harold Ingleby Hawkins was born on 22nd July 1886. Before the war, he served for a number of years in the 16th London Regiment (Q.W.R.). He was gazetted to the 3/2nd Londons on the 4th February 1915.

Lieut. Graeme Bonhôte Henderson was the son of Mr. and Mrs. John

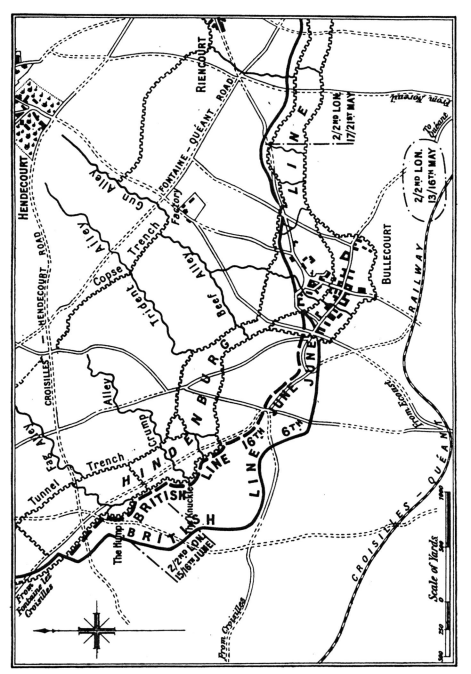

THE BATTLES OF BULLECOURT, 1917.

Henderson of Ealing, and was born on 30th July 1883. He was educated at Winchester, where he was a member of his house football team. Prior to the war, he held an appointment in a well-known commercial house in the City, and also served for some years in the 7th Londons. He was gazetted to the 3/2nd Londons on 16th January 1915.

2nd Lieut. Horatio Inwards was born on 7th January 1879. He served in the South African War in the Imperial Light Horse. Shortly after the outbreak of the Great War, he enlisted in the ranks of the 2/2nd Londons, with whom he served in the Mediterranean, rising to the rank of Sergeant. He was gazetted to the 3/2nd Londons on 19th December 1916.

Bullecourt represents one of the finest achievements of the 2/2nd Londons, not so much from the results gained as from the endurance and self-sacrifice displayed by all ranks; throughout the battle the men behaved with splendid courage and cheerfulness in very trying circumstances. As the result of the heavy casualties sustained, the personnel of the Battalion underwent an extensive change; and, although the Battalion served with distinction throughout the rest of the campaign, Bullecourt was, so far as its original personnel was concerned, its first and last great engagement. For this reason it is especially satisfactory that the battle-honour 'Bullecourt' was selected as one of the ten to be borne on the Regiment's Colours.

After two days of reorganization at Mory Copse, the 2/2nd Londons moved back to Logeast Wood, close by Achiet le Grand, where they stayed until 8th July, receiving drafts, training, and enjoying much-needed rest and recreation.

During the three months that succeeded the Battles of Bullecourt the 2/2nd Londons only once did duty in the line, and that, an eight days' tour, was far from strenuous. The greater part of this period was spent in cheerful, not to say really delightful, surroundings, where rest was enjoyed to the full, while what was virtually a new battalion was being welded together day by day into a cohesive, understanding, fighting unit. To assist in this process there was fortunately a nucleus of experienced officers, non-commissioned officers, and men, available, and under their guidance and with the aid of a systematic course of training, the new elements became quickly absorbed into the Battalion.

On its arrival at Logeast Wood the Battalion was joined by a draft of thirteen officers. With only two company officers remaining (Capt. Sinnatt and 2nd Lieut. Harper) and only five combatant officers in all, this reinforcement was certainly badly needed. It consisted of the following:

2nd Lieuts. M. H. Williams, R. C. Chilvers, O. E. Palin, G. H. Hall, W. Stockins, E. W. Maxwell, G. C. Seers, J. H. J. Dickens, B. J. Barton, H. H. V. Phelps, J. P. Howie, A. V. Hyde, and A. Laithwaite.

After a comparatively uneventful three weeks at Achiet le Grand, the 173rd Brigade moved to Ytres in divisional reserve, the 2/2nd Londons resting on the night of 8th/9th July under canvas at Bancourt.

Ytres provided passably good quarters, though the village in those days was but a ghost of its pre-war self, reduced to a collection of very damaged or completely demolished houses, as a result of the German withdrawal in the earlier part of the year. In its own category of stricken villages, however, it ranked fairly high, and was nothing to many of the villages on other parts of the Arras front and, northwards, in Flanders, through which the Battalion passed or fought.

While the Battalion was at Ytres, notification of the following awards in connexion with the Battle of Bullecourt was received:

D.S.O.: Lieut.-Col. A. R. Richardson.
M.C.: Capt. E. E. H. Bate.
M.M.: L/Corpl. F. Ray, Ptes. H. Green, A. J. Williams, and W. J. Hill.

The 58th Division was now on the point of taking over a sector of the front line opposite Havrincourt; and, accordingly, preliminary reconnaissances of their positions were made by company officers.

Daylight reliefs were rarities in France and Flanders; yet such was the calm that spread itself over this particular piece of front that the Battalion was enabled to take over from the 2/1st Londons at 3 o'clock in the afternoon. This was on 22nd July; and throughout the tour of duty of the Battalion—until the 30th when, in another daylight relief, the 12th Royal Scots (9th Division) took over—a policy of 'live and let live' was continued on both sides. Shelling was infrequent; and even small arms fire was not very troublesome. Certainly, a sniper, who had posted himself in No Man's Land, harried 'D' Company, on the right, but, before the Battalion left this area, he had been faithfully dealt with.

The width of No Man's Land at this point was considerable—at least half-a-mile—; and defensive patrols were the best means of keeping the enemy at a respectful distance and of preventing his possible approach to our line by night. He showed no enterprise, however, in this direction, and 2nd Lieut. Laithwaite even ventured into his front line and found it more or less deserted.

On relief, the Battalion moved by light railway to Ruyaulcourt, where it went under canvas for the night. Here all ranks were glad to dry themselves from the water, through which they had had to wade on leaving the trenches. The following day, the laſt of the month, ſtarted another long reſt, this time at Izel lez Hameau and Ambrines, where, if not out of earshot of the guns, all was peace and quiet.

Casualties during the month were 1 officer (2nd Lieut. R. C. Chilvers) killed, and 9 other ranks wounded. Officer reinforcements were:

> 2nd Lieuts. V. C. Cannan, E. Ford, N. T. Janes, H. L. Browne, B. A. Humphreys, T. H. Gladſtone, and P. D. Gibson.

The ſtrength of the Battalion was now 28 officers and 364 other ranks.

When officers and men were not training for the attack, praƈtising on the miniature range, or engaged in other forms of work, they were enjoying perhaps the beſt billets it had been their good fortune yet to occupy; both at Izel lez Hameau and Ambrines, quiet old-world villages, the billets were extraordinarily good; and the average munificence of the French inhabitants here was much appreciated.

During this long 'reſt,' everything was done to keep the men fit and contented. The Battalion was fortunate in the possession of a clever concert party[1] of its own, which provided lively entertainments, while, occasionally 'The Goods,' the Divisional concert party, paid it a visit. On the 18th Auguſt the 173rd Brigade Sports were held at Ambrines, and included such diverse events as the 100 Yards, Pillow Fighting, and a 'Boat Race.' The Sports were thoroughly enjoyed and greatly welcomed by all ranks, who were not slow to enter for the various events. A race on mules proved a very popular item.

These halcyon days—the happieſt, perhaps, that the Battalion spent in France—passed all too quickly; and on 24th Auguſt, the 58th Division regretfully departed for an 'unknown deſtination,' somewhere in the north. This turned out to be Belgium, where, at Poperinghe, in the chill hours of a late summer morning, the Battalion detrained, and marched to Dirty Bucket Camp, the firſt of many camps to be entered during the course of three diſtinƈt sojourns on this front that covered, from firſt to laſt, the period from 24th Auguſt 1917 to 21ſt January 1918.

---

[1] The exiſtence of this concert party was largely due to the persiſtence of Capt. H. O. Ellis, who formed such a party in the early days of the Battalion, and maintained it, despite official opposition of the 'red-tape' order.

CHAPTER XV

THE BATTLES OF YPRES, 1917—I

THE 1/2ND LONDONS IN THE BATTLE OF LANGEMARCK

THE defence of Ypres brought, perhaps, more fame to the British arms than any other exploit throughout the war. For close upon four years the enemy strove hard to capture the city, but all in vain. Not that it was of much value strategically; but its possession had come to have a great moral significance. Its first defence in October and November 1914 was a glorious feat of arms by the 1st, 2nd, 7th, and Cavalry Divisions, of the old Army; the second battle in April 1915 brought undying fame to the Canadians, to the 4th and 28th Divisions, who clung on in the face of poison-gas, then used for the first time. By most units, however, Ypres will be remembered for the third battle—no defence this time; on the contrary, an offensive operation on a very large scale through whose fire there passed no less than 51 British and Dominion Divisions.

The object of the operations, known as the Third Battle of Ypres, was first to relieve the pressure on the French, whose Army was still seriously demoralized after the failure of General Nivelle's offensive in the earlier part of the year, and, secondly, to secure the Belgian coast in order to prevent, or, at any rate, to curtail, the activities of the German submarines that were using it as a base for their attack on British shipping. But before the main operation could be begun, it was essential for the success of the British plans to capture the Messines Ridge that dominated the southern sector of the Ypres salient, because its continued possession by the enemy would constitute a serious menace to the right flank of an attack further north. To secure this ridge, therefore, the Battle of Messines was fought from the 7th to the 14th July. This preliminary operation, which opened with the explosion of nineteen mines, was a complete success, and at its conclusion the whole of the ridge was in British hands.

Everything was now ready for the launching of the main offensive, and on 31st July the Second and Fifth Armies, with the First French Army on their left, opened the battle. The primary objective was the claw-like ridge on which stand Passchendaele and Broodseinde, and which afforded to the Germans command of all the ground within the Salient. The preparations for the battle had naturally been very thorough, and as the concentration of troops increased, it became impossible to conceal them from the enemy. Attempts at concealment were finally abandoned; and the confined space of the Salient, crammed with men and material, became a target for the German guns. This was not the worst feature; during the afternoon of the first day of the battle the rain began, and continued thereafter without cessation for four days. 'The low-lying clayey soil,' writes Sir Douglas Haig in his Dispatch,[1] ' torn by shells and sodden by rain, turned into a succession of vast muddy pools. The valleys of the choked and overflowing streams were speedily transformed into long stretches of bog, impassable except by a few well-defined tracks, which became marks for the enemy's artillery. To leave these tracks was to risk death by drowning, and in the course of the subsequent fighting, on several occasions, both men and pack animals were lost in this way.' The attack, which at its outset had progressed well, was gradually slowed down; and this delay was of the utmost value to the enemy, who was able to reorganize and bring up reinforcements. The enemy's new method of defence, moreover, proved very successful, and its elasticity and depth further increased the difficulties that the attackers had to face.

On the left, the Fifth Army met with some success, and the crossing of the Steenbeke was secured; but on the right, the II. Corps was only partially successful. After capturing the first of the enemy's defensive systems about Hooge and Sanctuary Wood it was finally checked at Inverness Copse and Glencorse Wood. The first phase of the battle came to an end on the 12th August; and thereafter there was a breathing space of a few days before the fighting was continued.

Such was the position of affairs when the 56th Division reached the Salient and joined the II. Corps. The Division was now under the command of Major-General F. A. Dudgeon, Major-General Hull having been obliged by continued ill-health to return to England. Meanwhile, the 1/2 Londons had remained at Nordausques, where their training was much interfered with by the bad weather at the beginning of the month. At 11.30 p.m. on the 4th August orders were suddenly received for the transport section, with the exception of the cookers, water carts, and Maltese carts, to proceed by road in three hours' time. Despite the late hour and the short notice, it is much to the credit of all concerned that everything was packed and that the transport moved off at 2.30 a.m. as ordered. The rest of the Battalion did not follow until the 6th, when it entrained at Watten for Abeele.

[1] Sir Douglas Haig's Dispatches.

Arriving at the latter place at 10.30 p.m., the Battalion marched to Patricia Camp, a hutted camp, where it remained for four days, the time being spent in a continuation of training.

At this juncture the 56th Division was ordered to take over the sector of the front line from Surbiton Villas to Westhoek, facing Glencorse Wood and Nonne Boschen. On the 11th, therefore, the 1/2nd Londons moved forward to Ouderdom, where they were accommodated in Micmac Camp. In view of the forthcoming important operations, Lieut.-Col. Kellett was recalled from leave, and duly rejoined the Battalion at Ouderdom.

On the 13th August the 1/2nd Londons moved up to New Dickebusch Camp, and on the next day relieved the Q.W.R. on the left of the brigade sector in front of Hooge. 'A' and 'B' Companies took over the front line, each with two platoons in Jargon Trench on the near edge of Glencorse Wood, and two platoons in support in Jargon Switch. 'C' Company was in support in shell-holes in the vicinity of a tunnel under the Menin road. This tunnel was little better than a sewer; but in this unsavoury spot Battalion Headquarters were established. 'D' Company was in reserve at Halfway House. The relief started from Halfway House in daylight, and was very tedious and harassing, heavy enemy shelling and the condition of the ground making progress slow and difficult. On the previous night, the 169th Brigade had undertaken a small operation with a view to improving the position about Glencorse Wood. The Q.W.R. and Q.V.R. attempted to establish a number of posts in advance of their present line—an undertaking that the 18th Division, when holding this sector, had not succeeded in carrying out some days previously. The Q.W.R. and Q.V.R. met with strong opposition, and were likewise ultimately unsuccessful.

The second phase of the great battle was about to open, and the attack of the Fifth Army was to be resumed from the north-west corner of Inverness Copse, on the Menin road, to the point of junction, south of St. Janshoek, with the First French Army, which was to prolong the front of attack on the left. The II. Corps, with two divisions, the 8th and 56th, in the line, was on the right flank of the Fifth Army.

The objective of the 56th Division in this attack was the Green Line, a line running roughly north and south through Polygon Wood some seventeen hundred yards from the Division's original starting line in front of Hooge, and the frontage allotted it was about fifteen hundred yards in extent. Nor was this all. The 56th Division was on the extreme right of the Fifth Army, and was responsible for the safety of its right flank. Not the least important of its tasks, therefore, was the formation of a defensive

GLENCORSE WOOD AND NONNE BOSSCHEN, 16TH AUGUST 1917.
From the air.

flank of about seventeen hundred yards from Black Watch Corner back to the point of juncture with the 24th Division at Stirling Castle. To assist the Division in forming this defensive flank, the 53rd Brigade was attached from the 18th Division, and, as this brigade, owing to heavy casualties, was not alone capable of carrying out so important and extensive an operation, it was strengthened by the addition of the 1/4th Londons (168th Brigade). The formation of this defensive flank required first the capture of an important enemy post at the north-west corner of Inverness Copse, and then the establishment of a number of strong points on the line between Stirling Castle and Black Watch Corner. The success of the whole attack of the 56th Division hinged on this operation, because failure to form the defensive flank must, of necessity, jeopardize the safety of the attacking brigades. The main attack was entrusted to the 169th Brigade on the right, and the 167th on the left, with the 168th, less the 1/4th Londons, in support.

The dispositions of the 169th Brigade were as follows:

RIGHT: L.R.B., with 1 company Q.V.R. for mopping up.
LEFT: 1/2nd Londons, with 1 company Q.W.R. for mopping up.
SUPPORT: 3 companies Q.V.R.—to hold the old front line and to occupy Glencorse Wood, when captured.
RESERVE: 3 companies Q.W.R.—at Halfway House.

It should be noted that the battalions to whom the attack was entrusted had not been in this part of the line before. On the march up to the line, each platoon inspected a model of the battlefield that had been laid out near Poperinghe; but the troops had no actual experience of the ground, particularly of the conditions under foot. The stumps of the trees in Glencorse Wood hid the country from view; and the activity of the enemy prevented any satisfactory reconnaissance. There was no rehearsal of the attack; all the preparations were very hurried; and the whole enterprise lacked the cohesion so necessary to its success.

The line of the 169th Brigade's attack lay obliquely across the north-western slopes of the main Ypres ridge, whose summit is here crowned by Polygon Wood, looking at the time of which we write like a collection of irregular stakes stuck upright in the ground. This ridge, after running roughly south from Passchendaele to a point about half-a-mile from the north-east corner of Polygon Wood, bends south-west, through the wood itself, to cross the Menin road about a mile east of Hooge. At no great distance from this last point a subsidiary ridge, on which stands the village of Westhoek, branches off from the main ridge along the western edge of Glencorse

Wood. Glencorse Wood thus lies on the northern slope of the main ridge and the eastern slope of the Westhoek Ridge, and the ground within it falls toward its northern edge, which roughly marked the boundary between the 167th and 169th Brigades. The low ground in the angle between these two features was water-logged and impassable by troops; and this marsh was continued along the northern edge of Glencorse Wood, and for some distance along the foot of the main ridge. The southern, and higher, part of Glencorse Wood, though not impassable, was very marshy; and its slimy black mud, from which the trunks of stricken trees protruded, like great beasts wallowing in the mire, was pitted with water-filled shell-holes. Nonne Boschen, which lay beyond Glencorse Wood, was drier by comparison, and was passable throughout its length and breadth even by troops in extended order. East of Nonne Boschen the ground rose towards Polygon Wood; and this rise, in conjunction with a stratum of sand in the subsoil, made the going much better.

During the 15th August, the day following their arrival in the line, the 1/2nd Londons were subjected to a continuous and intense bombardment. This fact, together with the appalling state of the ground, made preparation difficult. Nevertheless, Lieut. Francis (Battalion Intelligence Officer) laid out assembly tapes for the two companies leading the attack 150 and 75 yards respectively in front of Jargon Trench; and the companies duly began their assembly on these tapes at about 9 p.m.

The assembly was a nightmare. The ground behind the starting line was for the most part a swamp; the shell-holes, brimful of water, merged into each other; and the troops could only get along by picking their way round the edges. The assembly was finally complete by 2.30 a.m.; and the attacking companies had to lie out in the wet mud until 4.45 a.m.—zero hour. During the night Battalion Headquarters moved forward to a battle position in Jargon Switch.

Although much fatigued by its assembly, and shaken by the constant and heavy shelling to which it had been subjected, the Battalion gamely went forward to the attack on the morning of the 16th August. The hour selected proved a good one; it was still dark enough to conceal the final assembly of the troops, and day broke soon enough to assist the troops to pass the wood. The barrage, which came down at zero hour, was excellent —indeed, it was so terrific that for some moments the enemy held his fire as though in sheer amazement—; but the pace, one hundred yards in five minutes, though suitable while the troops were crossing the marshy ground, proved too slow when they reached the sandy slope east of Nonne Boschen.

The 1/2nd Londons in the Battle of Langemarck, 1917

The 1/2nd Londons were disposed for the attack in four waves as follows:

FIRST WAVE : 2 platoons of 'A' Company (Lieut. S. Scudamore) on the right.
2 platoons of 'B' Company (Capt. H. E. Gretton) on the left.

SECOND WAVE : 2 platoons of 'A' Company on the right.
2 platoons of 'B' Company on the left.

THIRD WAVE : 2 platoons of 'C' Company (2nd Lieut. A. G. McLeod) on the right.
2 platoons of 'D' Company (Capt. C. Gordon) on the left.

FOURTH WAVE : 2 platoons of 'C' Company on the right.
2 platoons of 'D' Company on the left.

The company of the Q.W.R. attached for mopping up followed the second wave of the attack.

The leading platoons of 'A' and 'B' Companies were in extended order, the remainder of the Battalion in small columns, a formation that offered the best chance of successfully crossing the swampy ground. There was to be no 'leap-frogging'; that is to say, the objectives were so allotted that the leading companies had the farthest to go, whilst the supporting companies were given intermediate objectives. This method obviated the confusion that invariably arises when one company has to pass through another. Thus the first wave of 'A' and 'B' Companies was given the Green Line as its objective—or the ultimate line to be reached in Polygon Wood by the attack—; the second wave of these companies was given a line just within the western edge of Polygon Wood; and 'C' and 'D' Companies were given objectives between Polygon Wood and the Nonne Boschen.

At first the attack of 169th Brigade went very well; and the 1/2nd Londons quickly reached the sunken road running through Glencorse Wood. This road was in itself a serious obstacle. It contained four concrete dug-outs, each of which was capable of holding twenty-five men. These dug-outs were mopped up without much difficulty; their garrisons were killed or made prisoner; several machine guns were destroyed; and a gun of small calibre (possibly an anti-tank gun) was captured. Yet more serious was the fact that this road marked the beginning of the marshy ground previously referred to, and could only be crossed—and this with difficulty—at its most southerly point within the Battalion's boundary. This had the effect of diverting the Battalion to the right, and of opening a gap between it and the right battalion of the 167th Brigade, which in its endeavours to avoid the same obstacle had edged away to the left. The gap between the brigades was never filled; and the left flank of the 169th Brigade remained exposed for the rest of the action.

On the right flank of the attack matters went badly from the start; the 53rd Brigade, with the 1/4th Londons attached, failed to capture the German strong point at the north-west corner of Inverness Copse, and was thus unable to form the long defensive flank, so vital to the success of the battle. The effect of this failure was immediately felt by the L.R.B., whose right flank was exposed, and was later felt by all the other attacking troops.

The advance of the 1/2nd Londons continued. All traces of wire or trenches, if they ever existed, had been completely obliterated; and for defence the enemy relied on a large number of machine guns, firing either from behind the trunks of trees, or from emplacements. The crews of these guns, without showing much fight, hastily took refuge in numerous concrete dug-outs and strong points, whose mopping up the leading waves of the 1/2nd Londons then left to the attached company of the Q.W.R.

Having passed through Nonne Boschen without encountering much resistance, the first wave of 'A' and 'B' Companies was crossing the intervening open ground to reach its objective in Polygon Wood, when it bumped into a line of strong points, from which issued a heavy and accurate fire. Nothing daunted, it held its course, and, struggling past this obstacle, at last reached Polygon Wood, and disappeared within. The second wave, consisting of the remainder of 'A' and 'B' Companies, also succeeded in reaching the edge of the wood, though, like its predecessor, losing many men at the line of pill-boxes. These two companies were entirely unsupported; and for this the barrage, whose slowness has already been commented upon, was much to blame. The leading companies, finding that the infantry resistance of the enemy was negligible, and that the condition of the ground underfoot steadily improved as they mounted the slight rise, pushed on at a great speed, and were soon in front of the barrage, which by this time had become a great deal weaker. The supporting companies, on the other hand, endeavoured to keep to their time-table; and at one point, on the right, the advance was temporarily but deliberately checked so that the correct rate of progress should be maintained. Here, then, was an exact reversal of the situation at Cavalry Farm in May, when the leading waves conformed to the barrage, and the rear waves came pressing forward until confusion resulted.

It seems probable that the first wave of the two leading companies reached its objective within Polygon Wood, but, caught by a counter-attack and out of touch with its supports, was wiped out. No survivor returned.

The second wave was checked on the western face of Polygon Wood, just short of its objective, by fire from the front and flanks. The last message from the two leading companies reached Battalion Headquarters at 6.45 a.m., two hours after zero, when a pigeon brought in a message from 2nd Lieut. Ross ('A' Company): 'Have ten men with me in shell-hole before second objective and No. 12 strong point. We are entirely surrounded, and heavy machine-gun fire is being turned on us.' Shortly after sending this message 2nd Lieut. Ross and his party were compelled to surrender. In addition to 2nd Lieut. Ross, 'A' Company lost all its officers; 2nd Lieut. Cox being killed, and Lieut. Scudamore and 2nd Lieut. Menzies wounded; 'B' Company likewise lost all its officers, Capt. Gretton being killed, and 2nd Lieuts. Sanders, Brown, and Polge wounded.

In the meantime, the third and fourth waves, consisting of 'C' and 'D' Companies, pushed on to the above-mentioned line of pill-boxes in front of Polygon Wood, from which point a message, timed 6.30 a.m., was sent back by 2nd Lieut. McLeod to the effect that the fourth wave had reached its objective, and that only a few men of 'A' and 'B' Companies could be seen in front. Up to this point no enemy had been seen; and, as 2nd Lieut. Dyer says, 'We were all merry and bright, and thought the Germans had retired to Berlin.' The pill-box on the right was found by Sergt. Cheese to be empty, and was thereupon occupied by 2nd Lieut. Dyer's platoon; the other pill-boxes were found to be still occupied by the enemy, who opened a brisk fire from them. The mopping up of all ground captured by the first two waves was supposed to be done by the company of the Q.W.R. attached for the purpose. For some reason, probably because the area to be dealt with was far too large, this company did not carry out its task very effectively. Had it done so, this line of pill-boxes would have been in British hands before the third wave reached it. As it was, the pill-boxes delayed the third wave; and the garrisons by brisk sniping and machine-gun fire prevented it from either reaching its objective, which lay between the pill-boxes and Polygon Wood, or consolidating the line gained. The fourth wave, although it had reached its objective, was, for the same reason, prevented from consolidating. Casualties rapidly increased; and the position grew uncomfortably hot. At this moment parties of the L.R.B. were seen falling back on the right; and, though nothing could be seen to substantiate this, it was learnt from them that the enemy had delivered a heavy counter-attack on the exposed right flank. This was naturally discouraging to the 1/2nd Londons, whose left flank was already in the air; and, before anyone realized the thing had started, the now weakened and exhausted 'C' and

'D' Companies began to fall back with the L.R.B. Capt. Gordon was killed rallying his men to ſtand their ground.

Admittedly, the two companies of the 1/2nd Londons, and, for that matter, the reſt of the 169th Brigade, were in an increasingly uncomfortable position; on the right, the vital defensive flank had not been formed, and the lateſt information indicated that the enemy was counter-attacking; on the left, the attack of the 167th Brigade had come to a ſtandſtill, and nothing had been seen of this brigade since the beginning of the action; in front, 'A' and 'B' Companies had disappeared in Polygon Wood, and the enemy was holding no clearly defined position that could be attacked and consolidated; and in rear, parties of German machine gunners, who had remained hidden in shell-holes during the Brigade's advance and had escaped the somewhat perfunctory mopping up, were coming rapidly into action. Nevertheless, there was no juſtification for a retirement at this ſtage; and, when at a later ſtage a retirement was made imperative by the enemy's action on the flanks and in the rear, as undoubtedly would have been the case, it should have been carefully organized and boldly executed. As it was, the retirement, disjointedly begun, disjointedly continued.

Halfway back through Glencorse Wood, one party, consiſting of men of different units, was met by Lieut.-Col. Kellet, who, with Lieut. Francis, had followed the attacking companies in their advance. These two officers had been heavily sniped, but by jumping from shell-hole to shell-hole had escaped the enemy's unwelcome attentions. Lieut.-Col. Kellett rallied the men, and was leading them forward, when he was wounded. Although he carried on for a short time, he was in the end obliged to leave the fight, and hand over the command of the Battalion to Capt. S. H. Stevens, the senior officer left.

The retirement was continued with some loss—as a matter of fact, the 1/2nd Londons were lucky to escape so lightly—to within a hundred yards or so of the original front line, where the troops were rallied on some rising ground, and a number of poſts eſtablished. Except at these poſts the 169th Brigade was back in its original line within four hours of the beginning of the attack.

Lieut. Francis took command of Jargon Trench, which was full of men of the attacking companies, who had returned in small parties. With the help of 2nd Lieut. Dyer and other officers, he succeeded in reorganizing the companies and making Jargon Trench secure. He then went back into Glencorse Wood, where he encountered a party of about thirty Germans, who were gingerly following the retiring British. Though single-handed,

Lieut. Francis made these Germans his prisoners, and escorted them safely back to the British lines. For this remarkable exploit he was awarded a Bar to the M.C.

Glencorse Wood was now clear of the enemy, who made no attempt to counter-attack, and contented himself with putting down a heavy bombardment on the British front line. This bombardment lasted some hours, and added considerably to the strain already imposed on the men. While it lasted C.S.M. Fittin and Sergt. Cheese did good work in going up and down the trench, rallying the men and encouraging them to hold on.

The 1/2nd Londons held Jargon Trench until nightfall, when the exhausted remnant of the Battalion was relieved by the Q.W.R. and withdrew to Halfway House. On the next day the Battalion marched to Château Segard, and from that point was conveyed in lorries to Patricia Camp, near Abeele.

The sad story of this battle must not be concluded without a reference to the equally sad story of the Colonel's breakfast. A day in a sewer, a night in the mud, lack of sleep, and no food for twelve hours, had given the Colonel a healthy appetite. At 6 a.m., therefore, on the morning of the attack, he hailed his servant, Pte. J. Christian, and demanded breakfast. Pte. Christian, being a good servant, had, in view of the importance of the occasion, provided himself with a special breakfast for the Colonel—bread, butter, eggs, and sardines—, and this he had been carrying about in a sand-bag, in addition to all the *impedimenta* that an infantryman was expected to carry. Now in the night, during the Battalion's assembly, Pte. Christian, like the majority of officers and men, had fallen into one of the very numerous water-logged shell-holes that abounded in this area. On hearing the Colonel's hail, therefore, the mud mask that, as the result of his fall, had formed on his face, cracked, as, with a smile, he replied, ' Yes, Sir; ready in a minute, Sir.' He immediately produced a large lump of mud, and untied a piece of string at the top. This was the sand-bag. He inserted a muddy hand, and drew out a smaller lump of mud. This was the bread. After regarding this very dolefully for a moment, he fished out a flat lump of mud. This was the box of sardines. He next looked hopefully for the eggs, but broken eggs mixed with slush are no longer merely eggs, so he turned his whole attention to the sardine tin. The opener, having as usual refused to ' function,' he managed, with the aid of his knife, to harpoon three sardines, which he carefully placed on a spoon. Hot tea was, of course, out of the question, but Christian had overnight carefully filled his waterbottle with cold tea. However, in his dive into the shell-hole, the stopper had come out, and the tea had merely helped to swell the liquid that already covered the ground in every direction. Thus, with a sorry grin, the Colonel's breakfast was announced: bread, black and sodden; butter resembling plasticine; eggs 'na poo,' as Francis remarked, and a few broken sardines on a spoon! The Colonel took the sardines, and was, no doubt, grateful for small mercies; but, as a breakfast, it was a failure.

The second thrust of the Fifth Army met with little success except on the left. The left wing, in conjunction with the French, made some progress and captured Langemarck; but from this point to the Menin road, the day went badly. In this sector the British were strongly opposed, and were subjected to the heaviest shell fire. The German Commander, General Sixt von Armin, finding that he was not being attacked by the British Second Army, was able to concentrate against the British centre and right a large number of extra guns and to employ extra troops in counter-attacks, since the retention of Nonne Boschen, Polygon and Glencorse Woods, and Inverness Copse, was rightly considered by him to be a matter of vital importance. If the British from the Westhoek Ridge should succeed in driving the Germans eastwards through Nonne Boschen and Polygon Wood, they would not only menace Zonnebeke from the south, but would be on the edge of the Passchendaele Ridge. The German Commander, therefore, massed the bulk of his guns and reserves on the line Zonnebeke-Gheluvelt-Zandvoorde, and made sure of retaining the important ground.

The Sixteenth of August must be definitely regarded as one of the Regiment's black days. The 1/2nd Londons lost heavily, and did not particularly distinguish themselves. There are, of course, extenuating circumstances. In the first place, this day's fighting is an apt illustration of the effectiveness of the enemy's new method of defence, to which reference has been made in an earlier chapter. In the earlier stages of the attack the enemy's resistance was negligible; then, as the attackers grew weaker and more disorganized, the resistance they encountered stiffened. 'A' and 'B' Companies, who had gone too fast and lost touch with their supports, were counter-attacked and cut up, 'C' and 'D' Companies were harried by rifle and machine-gun fire, and were forced to fall back with the other units of the Brigade. Other causes contributing to the failure were the inherent weakness of the scheme, with its long defensive flank, the failure of other troops to form this flank, the lack of preparation and the general uncertainty, the loss of touch on the left due largely to the state of the ground, the ineffective mopping up, the lack of experience on the part of the

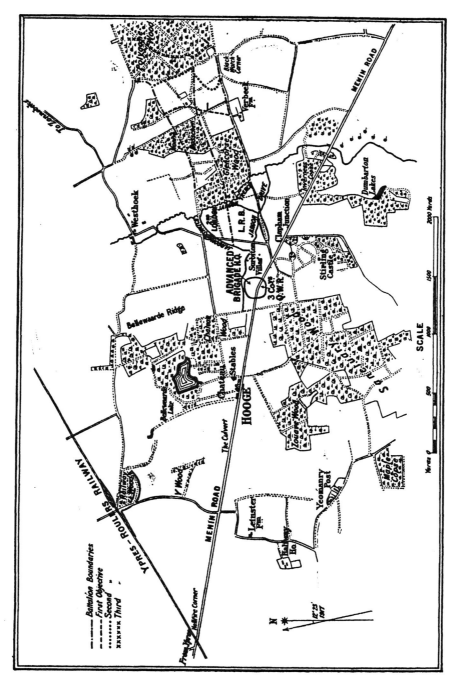

THE BATTLES OF YPRES, 1917—THE BATTLE OF LANGEMARCK.

many junior officers who had recently joined the Battalion, the fatigue of the troops, and their long vigil in the mud, under a heavy bombardment. The foregoing are in no way offered as excuses for the Battalion's failure, but the writer feels justified in quoting them to emphasize the difficulties with which the Battalion had to contend on this occasion.

The casualties of the 1/2nd Londons in this battle were very heavy. The Battalion went into action slightly over 400 strong, and came out with barely 100. The actual losses totalled 329, and were as follows:

KILLED: 4 officers (Capts. C. Gordon, H. E. Gretton, 2nd Lieuts. C. Murray and G. B. Cox, 7th Londons), and 32 other ranks.

WOUNDED: 5 officers (Lieut.-Col. J. P. Kellett, 2nd Lieut. J. W. Sanders, S. Scudamore, A. G. McLeod, and E. E. Brown, the last three of the 7th Londons), and 121 other ranks.

MISSING: 5 officers (2nd Lieuts. W. E. Polge, later reported killed, R. J. Ross, A. Phillips, and C. D. Menzies, all of the 7th Londons, and 2nd Lieut. F. W. E. Spong, later reported killed), and 162 other ranks.

The following awards were made to the 1/2nd Londons in connexion with the fighting of the 16th August:

Bar to M.C.: Lieut. W. A. Francis.
M.C.: Capt. S. H. Stevens.
D.C.M.: C.S.M. Fittin, M.M., and Sergt. J. Cheese, M.M.
Bar to M.M.: Sergt. H. Aspinall.
M.M., Sergts. J. Halbet, C. H. Stump, C. S. Taylor, G. F. Mason, L/Sergt. G. H. Hollings, Corpls. J. Doyle, W. G. Lamerton, J. Regan, C. Wagner, L/Corpls. E. Coventry, W. D. Stewart, A. S. Torrance, Ptes. G. Brooks, J. Cohen, J. Driscoll, A. Harrison, J. Lee, G. T. Preedy, H. Selwood, W. J. Selley, S. Wright and A. J. Watson.

Capt. Colin Gordon was the son of the late W. E. Gordon, Esq., and Mrs. Gordon, of Oakley Street, Chelsea. He was born on the 6th October 1893, and was educated at Winchester, subsequently going to the Agricultural College, Wye, where he tied for the Beadell Agricultural Prize. He joined the 2nd Londons on the outbreak of the war, and was gazetted 2nd Lieutenant on the 29th August 1914. He served with the 1/2nd Londons in Malta and France until April 1916, when he was invalided home with pseudo-enteric fever. He rejoined the 1/2nd Londons in the autumn of the same year, and continued to serve with them until the time of his death. He was mentioned in dispatches in May 1917 in connexion with the Third Battle of the Scarpe.

Capt. Horace Edward Gretton was the son of Mr. and Mrs. E. E.

Gretton, of Goodmayes, Essex, and was born on 7th October 1894. He was educated at the City of London College and King's College, London University. He had passed the Royal Society of Arts Examination and also the examination of the Bankers' Institute, and at the outbreak of war was employed by Messrs. H. S. King and Co., Bankers, of Pall Mall. He joined the Q.V.R. on 31st August 1914, and served with them until he was granted a commission in 1915 in the 2nd Londons.

2nd Lieut. Cyril Murray was born on the 29th March 1897. On the outbreak of war he joined the 12th Londons, with whom he served, partly in France, until he was granted a commission on 8th September 1916 in the 2nd Londons.

2nd Lieut. Frederick William Spong was born in 1892. He joined the 5th (T.F.) Seaforth Highlanders shortly after the outbreak of war, and served with them, partly in France, until gazetted on 3rd February 1916 to the 2nd Londons.

CHAPTER XVI

THE BATTLES OF YPRES, 1917—II

THE 2/2ND LONDONS ON THE NORTHERN RIDGES

I

OWING partly to the bad weather and partly to the new and successful tactics of the enemy, the great battle of the Ypres Ridges had not yielded the results expected by the British G.H.Q. But the reasons for keeping the attention of the enemy fully engaged on this front were still urgent; and it was therefore decided to make a further thrust at the enemy's line in the Salient. Meanwhile, after the limited success of 16th August, there was a general lull in the fighting, although in the northern sector, and in the neighbourhood of St. Julien, minor operations were undertaken to exploit the breach in the German defences. By the success of these operations the British line was advanced east of the St. Julien-Poelcappelle road, and a firm footing gained on the Gheluvelt-Langemarck line on each side of the Ypres-Staden railway.

The heavy fighting attendant on the offensive since its opening at the end of July had caused heavy casualties, and imposed a serious strain on most of the divisions employed. Many had been withdrawn, and among the new divisions substituted for them was the 58th, which, as we have already seen, had recently arrived in Belgium.

The 2/2nd Londons, after a short stay at Dirty Bucket Camp, moved on to Dambre Camp, west of Poperinghe, where, from 1st till 10th September, they were busily engaged in the inevitable training for the attack, now modelled on lines peculiarly adapted to the requirements of the fighting in this area. This and early morning physical and bayonet training, combined with lectures by the Commanding Officer to his officers, and by the latter to their men, made for a full day's work, relieved by the arrival of the mail, by feeding, and by what recreation the neighbourhood afforded.

Officer reinforcements during August were:

2nd Lieuts. A. E. Wiggs, R. Andrews, F. C. Capon, H. M. Cook and H. W. J. Jacobs (16th Londons).

Of all the towns and villages with which the 'back area' of the Salient was liberally besprinkled—Poperinghe, Proven, Houtkerque, Abeele, Elverdinghe, and many others—Poperinghe, simply 'Pop' to the British Army, was best known and most frequented. Here were *Skindle's* and *Cyril's,* restaurants always full of officers of every Corps, enjoying the excellent meals provided. Here, too, was the original 'Toc H,' the seed from which was to spring a now world-wide organization of brotherhood; the Officers' Club, through whose roof the shells of a German long-range gun came one morning in 1917, killing several officers on their way home on leave; the station, within easy range of the bigger guns, whence leave-trains daily departed, and where, despite alterations in the times of departure, the enemy would make direct hits on departing trains with distressing frequency.

Roads in this area were of two classes: the old *pavé* roads along which transport heaved itself over recurrent dips and bumps, and the wooden corderoy roads, constructed by the British labour corps, in many respects preferable to the native product. All day long and right through the night, these roads, vital means of communication, reverberated to the ceaseless rumble of columns of motor lorries, G.S. waggons, field ambulances, cars, and troops on the march. A curious feature, peculiar to Belgium, was the number of wayside shops—mere sheds they were—that lined the length of these roads in the battle area. These shops existed to supply the needs of the British soldier in buttons, badges, clothing, souvenirs, and other articles, and apparently did a very good trade.

On 29th/30th August, the 58th Division relieved the 48th Division in the line north-east of Ypres from the Haanebeek on the right to the neighbourhood of Keerselare on the left. Although two brigades, the 174th and 175th, were in the line, the front was very lightly held, one battalion of each brigade being in the outpost line, one on the canal bank and two in camps west of the canal.

A redistribution of the line occurred on the night 11th/12th September, and the 173rd Brigade took over the whole of the Division's front. The 2/2nd Londons passing round the northern end of Ypres, of which little remained above ground beyond the skeletons of the Cathedral and Cloth Hall, the stout old ramparts, and the piles of masonry and rubble marking the lines of the mediæval streets, moved forward to the Canal Bank Camp, in brigade reserve, whence, after making the unwelcome acquaintance of the enormous rats, gorged with human blood, that infested the dug-outs hereabouts, and particularly those beneath the canal, they moved forward again to the relief of the 2/5th Londons (174th Brigade) in the sector north-east of St. Julien.

Any description of the forward area must necessarily be inadequate, because the conditions are well-nigh indescribable. The ground had been bored by shell fire into thousands of pits and craters, anything from twenty to fifty feet in circumference and three to twenty feet deep, with only a small margin of none too solid earth between the lip of the one and the lip of the next. The continuous rain had filled the craters with water; and these silent pools, ſtretching as far as the eye could see, produced a feeling of the moſt acute depression in the mind of an observer. The passage of this riven feſtering ground was never easy, and in bad weather, which seemed to predominate, actually dangerous. A slip from the seemingly endless duckboard tracks that were provided to carry the troops to their positions was attended by considerable risk; and it was easy enough to sink waiſt-deep in the semi-liquid clinging mud.

Since the Second Battle of Ypres in April and May 1915 the general position in the Salient had not much altered, except in those places where one side or the other had gained a purely local success; and for two years and a half the enemy's line was drawn close about the city. Even the ground won in the operations of July and Auguſt 1917, before either of the 2nd London battalions reached this sector, had not served greatly to lessen the curious impression made on the mind of being isolated and crushed in the narrowness and confinement of the Salient; and it was only necessary to watch the nightly semi-circle of rockets or Very lights, rising noiseless into the air, hovering for one brief moment before sinking in a shower of sparks, to realize how confined the space held by the British eaſt of the canal really was. To defend the Salient in such circumſtances, aggravated by the abnormally bad weather, was a difficult task enough, but to prepare and launch a mighty offensive from so reſtricted an area was an almoſt super-human undertaking; and it says much for the courage and endurance of the British soldier, and more especially of the British infantryman, that, in face of the appalling conditions of ground and weather, and in face of the ſtubborn defence of the enemy, subſtantial gains were made.

The Battalion was disposed in depth with two companies and a half in the front-line poſts, one half-company in close support, and one company in reserve at Alberta Farm, half-a-mile due weſt of St. Julien. A continuous trench syſtem had long since ceased to exiſt in this area, and the syſtem of mutually supporting poſts had been adopted in its ſtead. The many concrete pill-boxes wreſted from the enemy afforded shelter for our troops, but were extraordinarily unhealthy to live in; and, whilſt imparting a pleasant feeling of security to the garrison, they tended to have a bad effect on its morale.

Apart from heavy shelling day and night the Battalion had a quiet tour

237

of duty, although the enemy on the 13th and 18th September made small unsuccessful attacks on Springfield on the right of the Battalion's front. On the night of the 18th/19th the Battalion was relieved by the 2/7th Londons (174th Brigade), and moved back to the Yser Canal. On the following morning, it continued its withdrawal to its old quarters in Dambre Camp. Casualties during this tour of duty amounted to 1 officer (2nd Lieut. E. Ford) wounded, and 47 other ranks killed and wounded.

The third phase of the Battle of Ypres was now about to open; and, in view of the improvement of the weather, the 20th September was fixed as the date for the resumption of the offensive. In these operations practically the whole of the Fifth Army and a large part of the Third were to be employed on a front that extended from the Ypres-Staden railway in the north to the Ypres-Comines Canal in the south, and thus included the front held by the 58th Division.

The attack of the 58th Division was entrusted to the 173rd Brigade on the right and the 174th on the left, on the front immediately north of the Haanebeek, a small stream running almost due east from St. Julien. On the left of the 173rd Brigade was the 164th Brigade (55th Division). The 2/4th Londons formed the attacking force of the 173rd Brigade, with the 2/3rd Londons in close reserve to make a feint attack with dummy figures covering the water-logged and impassable ground to the right of the Brigade's front.

The assembly of the attacking troops on 19th September was extremely trying, owing to the state of the ground, to the darkness of the night, and to a steady downpour of rain, which set in at 9 p.m. and continued for some hours. Six hours were expended in getting the four hundred assaulting troops to their assembly position, each man being tied to the one in front by tape to maintain direction. Although the enemy was within 150 yards of the leading platoon, he apparently remained in complete ignorance of the preparations for the attack.

At 5.40 a.m. on 20th September the troops advanced to the assault; and by the time that the 175th Brigade took over the sector on the night of the 21st, the 173rd Brigade had taken the whole of its objectives despite considerable local opposition, and, although desperately counter-attacked, had kept its new line intact at all points.

Casualties were heavy, among them being the B.G.C., Br.-General Freyberg, V.C., D.S.O., who was seriously wounded. This gallant soldier gave further proof of his courage and devotion to duty in the most difficult and dangerous of situations that had served so materially to inspire his subordinates. 'He continued to command the Brigade,' runs the Secret Order, issued after the battle, 'though wounded in ten places by an H.E. shell, which burst almost at his feet. . . . As our objective had been gained and consolidated, Gen. Freyberg, who had inspired everyone with his own cheerful courage and example, was persuaded to hand over the command (of the Brigade) to Lieut.-Col. Dann, D.S.O., of the 2/4th Battalion.'

Throughout this attack, the 2/2nd Londons, with the exception of one platoon, had remained at Dambre Camp. This platoon (2nd Lieut. A. V. Hyde) was originally intended for the escort of prisoners, but, as no touch with the 174th Brigade on the left had been reported, and as not more than 90 to 100 men of the 2/4th Londons remained effective, it was pushed forward to the relief of a platoon of the 2/3rd Londons east of Winnipeg Cross-Roads, on ground captured in the fighting of preceding hours. It succeeded in establishing contact with the 2/6th Londons (174th Brigade) on the left, and with the 55th Division on the right, and then held an outpost position on this line for a space of thirty hours.

During this period non-commissioned officers and men of this platoon, though exposed to the enemy's artillery and rifle fire, brought in many severely wounded and dying men of other units who had been lying in the open, in agony, parched, and starving, for many hours; and their heroic action is worthy of the highest praise. After being subjected to the most intense bombardment, and after being entirely without food except that taken from dead Germans lying in the vicinity, the platoon was relieved by the 2/11th Londons (175th Brigade) late on the night of the 20th/21st September, and marched back to join the Battalion at Dambre Camp in the early hours of the following morning. It is interesting to note that 2nd Lieut. Hyde's platoon, though exposed to heavy shelling, suffered only two casualties—and those men who were wounded on the way up the day before.

On 22nd September Field-Marshal Sir Douglas Haig, in the course of a personal visit to the headquarters of the XVIII. Corps (Lieut.-General Sir Ivor Maxse), of which the 58th Division formed part, congratulated all ranks on their splendid victory in the battle of the 20th (Battle of the Menin Road Ridge). 'He desired me to convey to you,' runs the Corps Commander's message, 'his high appreciation of the successful attacks of the 51st and 58th Divisions. . . . They were attacked by no less than 10 Prussian battalions . . . between 3 p.m. and 8 p.m. These counter-attacks were all repulsed after fighting at close quarters. . . .'

After two days at Dambre, the 2/2nd Londons moved forward by light railway, and relieved the 2/10th Londons in the line in front of Keerselare, north-east of St. Julien, where they came under the orders of the 175th

Brigade. This brigade was detailed to take part in the next offensive, and its units required an opportunity for rest and preparation. This opportunity was furnished by the 2/2nd Londons, who took over the front hitherto held by two battalions, and thus enabled one-half of the 175th Brigade to be withdrawn from the line for the forthcoming operations.

On the 26th September the 58th Division took part in the next general offensive of the Second and Fifth Armies, officially known as the Battle of Polygon Wood; and its attack, delivered by the 175th Brigade alone, met with considerable success, the high ground about Aviatik Farm being secured. Throughout these operations the 2/2nd Londons held the inactive portion of the 175th Brigade's front, and by occupying the enemy's attention as much as possible rendered the attacking units what help they could. For bravery in daylight patrol work during this period 2nd Lieut. J. E. Sutcliffe was awarded the M.C. The attack was followed next day by the inevitable German counter-attack, which was delivered not only against the new front of the 175th Brigade but also against the 2/2nd Londons. On the front of the 2/2nd Londons the counter-attack developed at 6.45 a.m. on the 27th, and was successfully beaten off by rifle and Lewis-gun fire.

The 58th Division was relieved in the line on 30th September by the 48th Division, and was withdrawn into Corps reserve. It is satisfactory to record that from the opening of the third stage of the Battle of Ypres until the Division's withdrawal its front had been carried forward nearly a mile.

Meanwhile, the 2/2nd Londons had been relieved by two companies of the 4th Oxford and Bucks Light Infantry and two companies of the 5th Gloucesters on the night of the 27th/28th September, and marched back to Reigersberg Camp. On the next morning they moved to Brake Camp, where they remained until the end of the month.

In these operations the Battalion's casualties were:

KILLED: 1 officer (2nd Lieut. F. A. Walton), and 11 other ranks (including C.S.M. W. E. Gardner).

WOUNDED: 3 officers (2nd Lieuts. T. R. Plowman, E. W. Maxwell and H. F. Smith), and 62 other ranks.

Fate plays many a queer and inexplicable trick on mankind. Whilst the Battalion was undergoing terrific ordeal by the most concentrated form of shell fire in the line itself, a cadre of officers, one from each company, left behind in the generally safe seclusion of the transport line in Dambre Camp, was unexpectedly subjected to fire from a German long-range gun, which for a few minutes shelled the back areas known by the enemy to be occupied by our troops. The enemy obtained a direct hit on the tents in which some of the officers and men were resting, and killed 2nd Lieut. M. H. Williams and wounded 2nd Lieut. H. H. V. Phelps and six other ranks. Capt. Harper and 2nd. Lieut. Howie had really miraculous escapes.

2nd Lieut. Frank Arthur Walton was born on 5th April 1888, and was the son of Mr. and Mrs. A. H. Walton, of Walthamstow. He was educated at the Sir George Monoux Grammar School, where he was successful in obtaining a scholarship, and prior to the war he was an accountant by profession. In 1915 he joined the 2/5th London Regiment (L.R.B.), with whom he served until he was commissioned to the 2nd London Regiment in January 1917.

II

By way of Vlamertinghe the 2/2nd Londons travelled by rail to Audruicq in France, marching thence to the village of Louches, where they went into billets and where they were destined to remain, resting and training, for over three weeks. The combatant strength of the Battalion at this time was 22 officers and 798 other ranks.

Officer reinforcements during September and the first week in October were :

Lieuts. L. H. Newton, J. B. K. Preedy, 2nd Lieuts. H. F. Smith, J. E. Sutcliffe, and N. Gardiner.

While the 58th Division was out of the line, the great Ypres offensive was prosecuted with vigour and success. The third stage of the battle was continued until the middle of October, in a series of operations of considerable importance, known respectively as the Battle of Broodseinde (4th October), the Battle of Poelcappelle (9th October), and the First Battle of Passchendaele (12th October). The season was now far advanced, and the weather extremely bad; yet despite the serious obstacle to progress offered by the water-logged ground, important advances were made in the course of these operations, and, as a result, the British line was carried forward to the east of Poelcappelle and to a point a little over a mile from Passchendaele. The conclusion of the third phase of the great offensive was followed by a brief interval for further preparation; and on the 26th October the fourth and last phase was opened with the Second Battle of Passchendaele.

In the meanwhile, the 58th Division, now under the command of Major-General A. B. E. Cator, D.S.O., returned to the line on 23rd October; and the 2/2nd Londons moved by train to Brielen, marching thence to Siege Camp.

The attack of the 26th October was planned to be delivered on a rather narrower front than heretofore, from the Ypres-Roulers railway to north of Poelcappelle; and the portion of this front allotted to the 58th Division extended from the Poelcappelle-Staden road on the north to the Lekker-boterbeek[1] on the south, a distance of some eighteen hundred yards. On its right was the 63rd (Naval) Division and on its left the 57th Division.

The attack of the 58th Division was up the spur, jutting westward from the main Ypres ridge, along which ran the Poelcappelle-Westroosebeeke road, and was mainly directed against the important high ground about Whitechapel and Papa Farm. It was entrusted to the 173rd Brigade, now under the command of Br.-General R. B. Worgan, D.S.O., which was given two definite objectives: the first, a line from Spider Cross-Roads to Moray House, and the final a line astride the Poelcappelle-Westroosebeeke road, some seven hundred yards east of Poelcappelle village. The 2/2nd and 2/3rd Londons were ordered to capture and consolidate the first objective, whereat, after an interval of forty-five minutes, the 2/4th Londons were to 'leap-frog' through them on to the final objective. In brigade reserve were the 2/1st Londons, and two battalions of the 174th Brigade, which had been put at the disposal of the 173rd Brigade and concentrated near St. Julien.

Once again the assembly was beset with extraordinary difficulties. The conditions of the ground underfoot were appalling, and were to be a factor of delay both before the battle and during the battle itself. It seems probable that, had not full plans been made for its continuance, the Passchendaele offensive would have been postponed to coincide with an improvement in the weather conditions. As it was, the troops were to push through the slush and water-logged craters 'according to plan.'

The 2/2nd Londons, with Major Miller in command in the absence of Lieut.-Col. Richardson on leave, were to be in occupation of the front line on the night of the 24th/25th October. Owing to the obliteration of all forward tracks and the failure of guides supplied by the outgoing units in carrying out their functions, only three companies were in position by daybreak of the 25th, the remaining company not reporting until an hour past noon on the same day. The Battalion was disposed with 'D' Company on the right, about Beek Houses, 'C' in the centre, just short of Tracas Farm, 'A' on the left, about Meunier House, and 'B' in support. Battalion Headquarters were established at Gloster House.

[1] *Anglice:* Good-butter-stream.

242

The actual assembly on the night of the 25th/26th October occupied no less than nine precious hours; and it is doubtful if the Battalion would have been on its jumping-off tapes by 1.15 a.m. had it not been for the wonderful degree of tenacity and sense of direction shown by 2nd Lieut. G. C. Seers in laying, almost unaided, and guided only by compass, the tapes along the frontage of the Battalion's advance. Capt. C .B. Falkner (the Adjutant) and 2nd Lieut. Seers were to meet at an agreed spot and work together, with the aid of company officers. The former was killed on the way up; and 2nd Lieut. Seers carried out the work single-handed. Although the hour of attack was so near at hand, the Battalion was not in possession of its assembly tapes until 7.30 p.m. on the 25th, nor of barrage table, zero hour, nor situation maps until 8.30 p.m.

'Assembly,' says Capt. Harper, 'was a terrible job. The proximity of the enemy's forward posts necessitated the strictest silence and vigilance.' But, thanks largely to the magnificent spirit shown by the men, who had to undergo the terrific ordeal of sitting, or lying, in stinking mud-holes for over twenty-four hours before the assault, and to the indispensable work of tape-laying, so ably done by 2nd Lieut. Seers, all was ready for the advance.

In a note made at the time Major Miller records: 'The 2/2nds are ready to kill as many Boche as possible, and we are all happy to think of the possibility of doing a bit of slaughter.'

Up to 3 a.m. the weather was good, and the crater lips of the shell-holes were drying fast; but at that hour the weather broke, and a driving rain, which did not cease until the night of the 26th/27th, set in, making all movement a matter of extreme difficulty. Throughout the 25th and the early morning of the 26th, the enemy shelled the Battalion's front lines and assembly position very heavily, and caused a serious reduction in its strength, before the fight began. '"A" Company especially were sufferers,' says Capt. Harper. 'Before zero 2nd Lieut. Gibson and every N.C.O., except Sergt. Brown, a youngster of nineteen, was either killed or wounded. Owing to casualties already incurred, it was impossible to form up on the formation ordered.' 'A' Company's experience differed but little from that of the other companies; all suffered heavy loss from this preliminary shelling.

The dispositions of the Battalion were as follows:

RIGHT: 'C' Company (Capt. Sinnatt).
RIGHT CENTRE: 'D' Company (2nd Lieut. O. E. Palin).
LEFT CENTRE: 'B' Company (Capt. Stephen).
LEFT: 'A' Company (Capt. Harper).

'A' Company's left, and the junction with the 2/3rd Londons, was the Poelcappelle-Westroosebeeke road; 'C' Company's right, and the southern divisional boundary, a line running from a point a few yards south of Moray House to the Lekkerboterbeek. Within these limits and between the Battalion and its objective lay a number of strong points, whose capture was really the Battalion's most important task this day. These strong points consisted of a group of blockhouses, known as Cameron Houses, on the front of 'A' and 'B' Companies, a blockhouse some two hundred yards east of Tracas Farm, on the front of 'D,' and Moray House on the front of 'C'; and for dealing with them the special formation to which Capt. Harper alludes above was adopted, a leading wave of skirmishers, covering the assault columns of sections in single file, each company being on a two-platoon frontage. Apart from the capture of Moray House, 'C' Company's chief task was the formation of a defensive right flank from Moray House, as far south as the state of the ground would permit. In its attack on the right, the 63rd Division was not passing troops across the Lekkerboterbeek; and a defensive flank was thus essential to ensure that the ground north of the stream be kept under observation and fire. In this defensive right flank we see a strong resemblance to the unfortunate Battle of Langemarck, in which the 1/2nd Londons had recently taken part, the chief difference being that in the present instance the defensive flank was not very long and the front of attack was being extended by another division on the right.

Promptly at 5.30 a.m. a gallant battalion jumped off—waded, rather—from its assembly position. To obviate conspicuousness, the men had been ordered to rub their steel helmets with mud, a task that demanded no special measures and was the simplest that the Battalion had to discharge that day.

To a battalion at zero, disorganized by the casualties of the earlier waiting hours, soaked to the skin, its rifles and Lewis guns fouled with mud, and many rendered useless, has to be added the miserable fact that the creeping protective barrage was such only in name, and only recognizable as a barrage at all owing to its coincidence with the time of our advance. 'Very, very weak,' is Capt. Harper's mild description. Again, its rate of progress from point to point, though allowing the infantry eight minutes in which to cover one hundred yards, did not coincide with the much slower speed that they could actually maintain on the well-nigh totally impassable ground of the advance, with the consequence that the assaulting troops, their movements severely restricted by the nature of the ground, were unable to keep pace with it. 'The shrapnel barrage,' notes the War Diary, 'was hardly perceptible; the heavies were shooting very short.'

On the other hand, as the 2/2nd Londons rose from the mud and began their slow advance, the German machine gunners, secure in their concrete shelters, opened a brisk fire. Quick as lightning news of the advance was signalled back to the German gunners, who at once put down a heavy protective barrage. Within three minutes, the advancing troops were enveloped in a curtain of smoke and flames, as shell after shell burst around them. Gaps appeared in their ranks, and little heaps of dead and wounded marked their progress.

The yielding nature of the ground was all against a straight advance, and made it almost impossible to maintain the correct alignment for two consecutive yards. The men stumbled and slipped in the stinking slime. They crawled and scrambled in and out of enormous craters, and struggled to extricate themselves or their comrades from the embrace of the clinging mud. Many struggled in vain, and were submerged in the mud, from which they could not be rescued for many hours. More than one disappeared into a shell-hole, never to reappear. Out of the reach of their companions, they were gradually sucked down to a death, indescribably horrible.

Although in every part of this area progress was very difficult, in two places it was definitely barred by the condition of the ground. From the spur along which ran the Poelcappelle-Westroosebeeke road the ground sloped southward to the banks of the Lekkerboterbeek; and on the slope, from midway between Cameron Houses and the Tracas Farm-Papa Farm road to the road itself, there lay a wide expanse of marshy water. On optimistic maps this was described as passable by tracks, but actually it was impassable in any way. Between this last-named road and the Lekkerboterbeek there lay another stretch of marsh, which was likewise impassable. These two water-logged areas had an important effect on the Battalion's operations, causing the troops to bunch towards the only passable ground, the area of Cameron Houses and the area of the Tracas Farm-Papa Farm road.

The scheme of operations, wherein attacks by individual companies on definite strong points were given exceptional prominence, taken in conjunction with the bad ground and the enemy's resistance, had the effect of breaking up the unity of the Battalion's attack, and led to a series of isolated efforts on the part of each company, with little or no attempt at co-ordination. From this point, therefore, it will be more satisfactory to follow the fortunes of each company in turn, beginning with that on the right flank.

In view of its special task on this flank, 'C' Company had assembled facing south-east, on a line at an angle to the general assembly line of the Battalion. As the company advanced, it was diverted towards its left by the marsh north of the Lekkerboterbeek, and gradually concentrated on the comparatively dry ground just south of the Tracas Farm-Papa Farm road. At 6.40 a.m. Capt. Sinnatt reported the capture of Moray House with twenty-five prisoners. This was manifestly incorrect, the mistake having arisen through the difficulty of recognizing on the ground a place that could be so easily pointed out on the map. It subsequently transpired that this place was the strong point two hundred yards east of Tracas Farm, whose capture will be described hereafter. Owing chiefly to the state of the ground, 'C' Company made no further progress forward; it remained in this area for the rest of the day, with one platoon pushed southward towards the Lekkerboterbeek, on a patch of slightly drier ground.

'D' Company had an inauspicious start; 2nd Lieut. Palin, commanding the company, was mortally wounded almost at once; and shortly afterwards 2nd Lieut. Laithwaite, who had assumed command, was hit in half-a-dozen places, as he led his men forward. He bravely staggered on, encouraging his men, until a severe lung wound brought him to the ground; even then, though in intense pain, he motioned his men forward.

This company reached the edge of the marsh north of the Tracas Farm-Papa Farm road, where Nos. 13 and 14 Platoons, on the left of the company's front, edged off to the left and encroached on the front of 'B' Company. The remaining two platoons, under 2nd Lieut. Howie, advanced up the road against the strong point two hundred yards east of Tracas Farm. The enemy had sited the machine guns for the defence of this strong point, a concrete pill-box, on its northern side, with the result that the pill-box itself, intervening between these guns and their target, prevented them firing on troops manœuvring from the south. 2nd Lieut. Howie, rapidly grasping the situation, left a dozen men in position on the west and north of the pill-box to engage the guns with covering fire, whilst he himself, with the rest of his small force, worked round its southern side. His plan was completely successful. The strong point was assaulted from the rear and was captured, with its garrison of thirty-two. 2nd Lieut. Howie then established a post on the road, some hundred yards east of the strong point, and reorganized his command. This minor operation was a very successful piece of work, and reflected great credit on 2nd Lieut. Howie, who was awarded the M.C. for the gallantry and power of leadership he displayed on this occasion.

Like 'D' Company, 'B' Company also reached the edge of the marsh between Cameron Houses and the road. In its advance the company captured and demolished a small strong point of a non-concrete type, situated some two hundred yards west of Cameron Houses. On reaching the marsh, it edged off to the left to find a way round, but, with the exception of two sections which became involved in ' A ' Company's operations at Cameron Houses, it made no further progress forward; and the line of the marsh marked the limits of its advance. During the action Capt. Stephen, commanding the Company, was wounded.

Of all the companies, ' A ' had the hardest task to perform, the capture of the group of blockhouses known as Cameron Houses representing a very formidable undertaking. On the other hand, the company was on higher ground, where the going was much better and enabled it to maintain a reasonable formation for its attack. Halfway to its objective, the company found that its left flank was in the air, the right company of the 2/3rd Londons having been held up for some reason some eighty yards to its left rear. Notwithstanding the danger from this exposed flank, Capt. Harper pushed on until his company came under a murderous fire from the machine guns established at Cameron Houses. Getting together in a crater his platoon and section commanders, and handing round a box of cigarettes, Capt. Harper described how he intended to take Cameron Houses; his plan was to cover the front of the position by fire, whilst his assaulting party worked round the northern flank. Including the two sections of ' B ' Company, who had now joined him, Capt. Harper had seventy men available for the task, but only one Lewis gun in fit order to fire; and every rifle in his command was coated with mud, and of doubtful value. Sending No. 2 Platoon off to the left to work round the north of the enemy's position, he arranged for the rest of his company to cover the assault from the west, and for the two sections of ' B ' Company to cover it from the south-west. His tactics were successful; and five out of the six pill-boxes passed into his hands, together with twenty-seven prisoners, including a sergeant-major. ' A ' Company had been brought by this success to within one hundred yards of the Battalion's objective, and thus had the satisfaction of getting farther forward this day than any other troops of the Battalion or, for that matter, of the Brigade. In this operation Capt. Harper displayed a marked power of leadership that was deserving of the highest praise and was later recognized by the award of the M.C.

The enemy delivered his first counter-attack at 7.20 a.m. It developed from the direction of a strong point four hundred yards north of Whitechapel, and from the Whitechapel-Papa Farm road, and was chiefly directed against the front and left flank of the 173rd Brigade. The enemy's counter-attack troops were covered by a cloud of skirmishers, who, from the excellence of their shooting, appeared to be sharpshooters. The 2/3rd Londons, whose left flank was exposed by the failure of the right brigade of the 57th Division to advance, were the first to feel the effects of this counter-attack. They were forced to give ground; their gallant Commanding Officer, Lieut.-Col. Beresford, was mortally wounded; and three companies of the 2/1st Londons had to be hastily sent forward to their support from brigade reserve.

The withdrawal of the 2/3rd Londons exposed 'A' Company's left flank, which the enemy at once vigorously attacked. The single Lewis gun held his troops at bay until its mechanism, as the result of the mud, failed to act. Released from this fire, the enemy then began to work round the company's rear; at the same time, a strong force of Germans debouched from the one pill-box at Cameron Houses that had remained uncaptured, and delivered a fierce frontal counter-attack on the company. An interesting feature of this counter-attack is that the enemy's troops, in spite of the execrable condition of the ground, went into battle free of almost any trace of mud. Apart from a now valueless sacrifice of lives, there was no alternative for 'A' Company but to withdraw; and Capt. Harper, acting with his usual quiet coolness and determination, successfully extricated all that was left of his company. The elements of 'B' and 'D' Companies on his left retired with him, the whole force concentrating about Meunier House, where it took up a defensive position.

'C' Company and the remainder of 'D' at Tracas Farm were not so seriously attacked, and strengthened by 'D' Company of the 2/4th Londons, under Capt. Clarke, they held the ground gained for the rest of the day. 'C' Company lost Capt. Sinnatt, who was badly wounded. At noon Major Miller ordered 2nd Lieut. Howie to establish a post at Beek Houses, lying to the south-west of Tracas Farm, for the better protection of the Battalion's right flank; a small party was detached from 'C' and 'D' Companies for the purpose, and successfully established the post.

The enemy did not follow up his counter-attack, but contented himself with forming a line of posts south of Cameron Houses, and about five hundred yards east of Tracas Farm. Between 4 and 5 p.m. he delivered a second counter-attack; this was not pushed home very strongly, and was easily repulsed by the Battalion, now reinforced by a company of the 2/1st Londons in the area of Meunier House. A second company of the 2/1st Londons was detailed to take over Tracas Farm and Beek Houses; but the orders for this relief were cancelled, and the 2/2nd Londons remained in the line until midnight, when they were relieved by the 2/7th Londons (174th Brigade), and withdrew to Siege Camp.

From the time of leaving this camp on the morning of Tuesday, 23rd October, until it returned thither in the early hours of Saturday, 27th October, the Battalion had had neither hot food nor drink of any sort whatever. This deplorable state of affairs, adding yet another burden to men who were shouldering enough in other directions, was accounted for by the non-arrival of the transport from Louches, from which place the Battalion had set out for Belgium. That water was provided for the Battalion on the eve of the battle was due to the courage and determination shown by Sergt. Thompson, of the transport section. For this work this non-commissioned officer was later awarded the Military Medal.

On account of the operations of 26th October, the following awards were made :

D.S.O. : 2nd Lieut. A. Laithewaite.
M.C. : Capts. O. S. Sinnatt, M. L. Harper, 2nd Lieuts. J. P. Howie, G. C. Seers.
Bar to D.C.M. : C.S.M. R. Blake.
D.C.M. : L/Sergt. J. Fraser.
M.M. : C.S.M. E. J. Phillips, Sergt. W. Thompson, L/Corpl. H. S. Agar, Ptes. W. Bate, J. J. Roberts, and H. A. Wilde.

The casualties of the Battalion were as follows :

KILLED : 3 officers (Capt. C. B. Falkner, Lieut. J. B. K. Preedy, and 2nd Lieut. O. E. Palin), and 36 other ranks.

WOUNDED : 3 officers (Capts. O. S. Sinnatt, A. Stephen, and 2nd Lieut. A. Laithewaite), and 190 other ranks.

MISSING : 2 officers (Lieut. L. H. Newton and 2nd Lieut. H. W. J. Jacobs), and 152 other ranks.

The losses among the senior non-commissioned officers were very heavy, and included C.S.M. H. Beakhouse, Sergts, J. Anthony, A. Hillier, C. Condon, W. Brown, and L. C. Smith, killed.

Of his own losses, Capt. Harper says: 'The total of "A" and "B" Companies which remained to me (at Meunier House) were only thirty-one, eighteen of which were "A." I started with a company over two hundred strong.'

Capt. Clarence Beach Falkner joined the 13th Londons on the outbreak of war, and served with them in France until gazetted to the 3/2nd Londons on 14th October 1915.

Lieut. John Benjamin Knowlton Preedy was born on June 1883. He was educated at Dulwich College and London University, where he took the degree of Master of Arts, obtaining distinction in Classical Archæology. He subsequently joined the Staff of London University, being appointed Secretary of the University Extension Department. On the outbreak of war, he joined the University of London Officers' Training Corps, being granted a commission on 1st November 1914, and promoted Lieutenant on 21st June 1915. He was then posted to the Staff of the O.T.C. and employed in training cadets at Lichfield. He was transferred to the 2/2nd Londons; and went to France on 26th August 1917. He was a very efficient officer and a keen sportsman.

The battle of the 26th October must be looked upon as one of the most unfortunate episodes in the whole history of the 2/2nd Londons. That so little was gained, despite the magnificent bravery of the troops, is attributable largely to the condition of the ground, which made all their efforts of no avail. In the words of the War Diary, 'the great determination and spirit shown by the battalion were worthy of the best traditions of the British Army in the Field.'

The Brigade Commander, in a very interesting report on this engagement, recorded his views of what could be reasonably expected from human beings in the existing conditions of ground and weather in the following terms:

> It is considered that 300 to 400 yards is the limit of advance that can be made by the same troops on the same day—and even this should be carried out under an intense barrage and by troops carrying just the bare necessities for fighting, *i.e.*, water, rifle, bayonet, grenades, and ammunition.
>
> Attacking troops should be bussed or railed up to the farthest possible point—in recent operations the long walk from Canal Bank to the line was a great disadvantage, the majority of the troops being practically exhausted long before zero.

On the 30th October the 175th Brigade made an attempt to carry out the task that had been set the 173rd Brigade four days earlier, but was prevented by the state of the ground from making any better progress.

The Third Battle of Ypres was at last drawing to a close. Despite the appalling conditions of weather and the lateness of the season, the British G.H.Q. for a variety of reasons had been obliged to prolong the course of this costly offensive. The Italian defeat at Caporetto and the situation on the French front seemed to demand a continuance of activity by the British; and as preparations for the offensive at Cambrai were not complete, the attacks at Ypres were continued. By the 6th November the whole of the Passchendaele Ridge was in our hands; and a few days later this stupendous offensive was brought to a close. For a period of nearly four months it had been maintained in conditions of appalling difficulty and at sacrifice of close on 50,000 lives, but in view of the obstacles encountered it was a magnificent achievement by the British troops, and, besides gaining the tactical advantages of the high ground in the Salient, it succeeded in containing a large number of the enemy's divisions at a critical period of the war for both our French and Italian Allies.

III

The few days following the Battalion's withdrawal from the line were spent in the usual routine of reorganization and training, but on 7th November a move was made to F.X. Camp, from which working parties were supplied for Kempton Park. This camp was on the fringe of the forward area, and these working parties resulted in a number of casualties. A week later the 58th Division was concentrated in Corps reserve, and a further move was made, the 2/2nd Londons going this time to Paddington Camp, where three uneventful weeks, marked only by the coming and going of personnel on or from leave to England, were passed.

On the 25th November the Battalion entrained for Wizernes, and thence marched to the pretty and secluded villages of Seninghem and Affringues, where the night was spent. The march was resumed next day to Bournonville, a village not far removed from the sea-shore in the neighbourhood of Boulogne.

Battalion strength was now 24 officers and 530 other ranks. The vacant adjutancy had been filled by the appointment of Capt. G. C. Seers, M.C., to the post. Officer reinforcements during November were as follows:

Lieut. L. W. Bindon, 2nd Lieuts. H. G. Mitchener, E. G. D. Gedge, L. Moutrie, and F. M. Bennett.

Memories of fair fields, and foliage unstunted by the ruthless hand of war, linger of Bournonville; of a huge open field improvised as parade and training ground, of tolerably homely billets, 'square meals,' and a 'one in three' hill which it was the lot of the troops to climb many times daily.

At this time it was rumoured that the 58th Division's next move would be to Italy, and everyone eagerly looked forward to going to a new battle-front; after the experiences of the Ypres Salient, it was felt that any change from France and Flanders must be for the better. These hopes were doomed to disappointment; the Division was wanted again in Belgium, and back to Belgium it went. Once more there was the long march between Bournonville and Wizernes, where the Battalion had detrained a bare fortnight before, broken by another night in Seninghem and Affringues. The Battalion reached Wizernes on 8th December, and on the same day marched via Elverdinghe, with its famous Red Château, to Bridge Camp.

This third move to Belgium was to be confined, so far as trench duties were concerned, to two tours of duty in the line, one immediately preceding Christmas, the other on the turn of the year, at the dawn of a twelvemonth that for the 2/2nd Londons held much in the way of tragedy and loss, glory and honour, good times and bad, until finally they found themselves in the vanguard of the Advance to Victory, and entered Belgium for the fourth and last time shortly before the Armistice.

After six days of training at Bridge Camp, enlivened by visits from 'The Goods,' the Battalion moved forward on 16th December to Kempton Park, in brigade support. On this day the 173rd Brigade became responsible for the whole front of the 58th Division, the 2/1st and 2/3rd Londons being in the line, and the other two battalions in support in captured German trenches about Langemarck and Pilckem.

The front of the Division, which formed the left of the II. Corps, extended from the Lekkerboterbeek on the right to the Broembeek, a small stream not far from the Ypres-Staden railway, on the left, and ran roughly north and south half-a-mile in front of Poelcappelle, practically where the Division had left it a month before.

The 2/2nd Londons were in the right support position, occupying an area 3,000 yards or more in depth, and throughout the five days they spent here they were busily engaged in improving the defensive system, which was in a hopelessly disorganized condition and needed constant attention. On the 20th, the Battalion relieved the 2/1st Londons in the right of the front line, three companies being in front and one in close support for counter-attack purposes. Battalion Headquarters were established at Norfolk House, formerly a German pill-box. The position was held by a series of isolated shell-hole posts, which were being gradually linked up into one comprehensive system.

Little untoward occurred to record of this tour of duty; but it is of

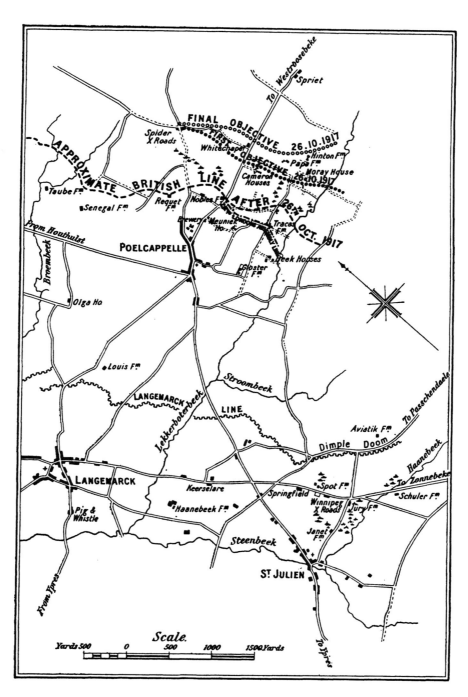

THE BATTLES OF YPRES, SEPTEMBER AND OCTOBER 1917.

interest to note that the hitherto water-logged ground was now frozen hard. A slip in the dark during a journey across country resulted in unwelcome contact with unyielding ice or steel-like soil instead of immersion in the deep mud or slime of the previous month. On the whole the former fate was preferable.

On Christmas Eve, the Battalion moved back to the Canal Bank Camp in reserve, and billeted in the rat-infested subterranean dug-outs that hereabouts formed a veritable network of galleries and cross-galleries. Christmas Day was celebrated with such time-honoured customs as circumstances permitted; and the men settled down to an excellent midday dinner, largely provided by Major Miller, which, if it did not include the seasonable turkey and pudding, was nevertheless fully appreciated. The officers acted as mess-orderlies, and waited on their men. A minimum amount of work was followed in the evening by a concert arranged by 2nd Lieut. Hyde. A convenient Church Army hut was borrowed for the purpose, and, with entirely local talent, the performance contributed largely to the men's enjoyment.

The battalion remained in close divisional reserve until the end of the year. Officer reinforcements during December were as follows:

Lieut. J. L. Harvey, 2nd Lieuts. V. de F. Gillings, H. Godfrey, J. A. Scholfield, W. E. B. Ryder, G. E. Hale, and W. G. Philpott.

Casualties amounted to 1 officer (2nd Lieut. H. Godfrey) wounded, and 2 other ranks killed, 23 wounded, and 2 missing.

On New Year's Day 1918, the Battalion moved up again to Kempton Park, in brigade reserve, two companies and Battalion Headquarters being located here and two companies forward in Pheasant Trench. Improvement of the defences and communications was continued until the 4th January, when the Battalion relieved the 2/1st Londons in the front line and support posts. Trench strength was 26 officers and 370 other ranks.

In the course of a quiet four days' tour of duty, in which the Battalion suffered two casualties, ' A ' Company captured at Helles House Post on its front three prisoners, whose original intention seemed to be to bomb our lines, in the capacity of an offensive or raiding party, and then to get clear. They actually did throw a few bombs, but, on being challenged, lost their nerve, and gladly surrendered. A fourth German escaped back to his own lines.

The ruins of the church in what once had been Poelcappelle, but what was now a mere heap of brick and stone, piled hideously by devastating shell fire, revealed yet another of those extraordinary instances of the Crucifix remaining unscathed through the heaviest fire, when all else was but a mockery of the past. All that remained of the church stood no higher than eight feet from the ground, and that represented the highest point in what only the map told you was Poelcappelle. Lying clear and prominent above the ruins was the figure of Christ, showing not the slightest scratch.

Relief on 8th January in this sector by the 20th Lancashire Fusiliers was the prelude, as events turned out, to the Battalion's departure from the Salient, with which it had by now become all too familiar. The Battalion withdrew first to Bridge Camp for the night, moving thence on the 9th to School Camp, St. Jan ter Biezen. There followed a week or so of rest and training, during which, at a special parade on 12th January, the G.O.C. II. Corps presented ribbons to the officers and men of the Division entitled to them.

The 58th Division, which during this period had been entirely withdrawn from the line, was now transferred to the III. Corps in the Fifth Army, on the extreme right of the British line; and the 2/2nd Londons, in company with the other units of the 173rd Brigade, left the area of Ypres on the 21st January for Fouencamps. But before this date the thaw had set in, and the Salient from a state of ice-bound ground and an unyielding and slippery surface was turned again into a slush of mud and slime. As the 2/2nd Londons found it, so they left it.

With the departure of the 2/2nd Londons in January 1918, we are brought to the close of the Regiment's connexion with the famous Salient. Ypres has become a household word, and it stands more than anything for heroism and self-sacrifice. It is therefore a matter of which the Regiment is justly proud that two of its Battalions took part in the arduous and severe fighting for which the Ypres Salient will ever be remembered.

CHAPTER XVII

THE 1/2ND LONDONS IN THE BATTLE OF CAMBRAI, 1917

I. ON THE CAMBRAI FRONT, SEPTEMBER—NOVEMBER 1917

IN the few days in the line at Ypres and in the attack of the 16th August the 56th Division had been roughly handled. Its losses had been extraordinarily heavy—98 officers and 2,600 other ranks in the three infantry brigades alone—; and Major-General Dudgeon was of opinion that the Division would not be properly fit for further offensive action for at least three weeks. It was accordingly withdrawn from the line on the night of 17th/18th August, the 14th Division taking its place, and was given a much-needed rest after the short but very severe battle in which it had taken part.

The 1/2nd Londons remained at Abeele until the 24th August, and during the intervening days were reorganized under the command of Major Sneath, who was promoted Lieutenant-Colonel. 'A' Company was taken over by Capt. J. Devane, 'B' by Capt. A. J. Widdecombe, and 'D' by Capt. K. Anderson, whilst 'C' Company remained under Capt. W. J. Ward. On the 24th the Battalion moved to Watten by train, and thence marched to le Marais, in the Serques area, where it occupied scattered but comfortable billets. Training was begun at once, and was continued until the 30th, when another move was made—this time for the area of the old Somme battlefields. The Battalion, entraining at Wizernes, reached Miraumont after a long and tedious journey, and thence marched via Achiet le Grand, Achiet le Petit, and Biefvillers, to camp near Bancourt, about a mile to the east of Bapaume, where a draft of 120 men from the 21st Londons joined it.

Not many days elapsed before the 56th Division, which was now in the Third Army (Sir Julian Byng), once more went into the line; and on the 5th September the 169th Brigade took over the Louverval sector astride the Bapaume-Cambrai road. On the same day the 1/2nd Londons moved into divisional reserve close to Lebucquière.

The Battalion was now in the area over which the enemy had withdrawn in the spring of this year, and for the first time had experience of the methodical destruction practised by the enemy in his retreat, which has been described in some detail in an earlier chapter dealing with the advance of the 2/2nd Londons over this ſtricken area. Villages had been deſtroyed, roads blown up, and the rolling downs between Bapaume and Cambrai, once among the moſt fertile in France, had been reduced to a wilderness. The scars of war, as yet unhealed by the lapse of time, made the countryside hideous, though Nature, in a gentle attempt to repair the damage, had covered the earth with a mantle of weeds and rank grass, the habitation of an amazing assortment of inſects and vermin.

Yet despite the difficulties of organizing and maintaining supplies in such a region, the accommodation for the troops out of the line was excellent, and their comfort was in everything considered. During September units were under canvas, but as the autumn merged into winter, huts were put up in the fields, and large 'elephant' shelters were erected in the villages under cover of the ruins. Transport lines were excellent, and, for once, even satisfied the exacting requirements of those critical but very efficient members of the Battalion's ſtaff—the Transport Officer and the Quartermaſter.

The villages were a pathetic sight. The ruins of the houses lay in grotesque heaps. Tattered ſtrips of wallpaper clung to the crazy walls. Pieces of furniture peeped out from the ruins; and a search among the piles of rubbish revealed books, pictures, and other intimate and precious possessions of the original occupants.

While the Battalion was out of the line, plenty of opportunity was given for recreation. Football as usual was very popular, and a number of inter-company matches was played, in the final of which a team from H.Q. Company defeated 'C' Company, and carried off the Challenge Cup. Day excursions to Amiens were arranged, the Headquarters of the Division supplying a lorry, which took a limited number of men to Achiet le Grand, whence they proceeded to Amiens by special train. These excursions proved very popular and were much appreciated. Concerts were given by the Divisional Band in a large hut in Lebucquière; and in Frémicourt the 'Bow Bells' had fitted up a ruined barn as a theatre, where they gave an excellent burlesque of *The Maid of the Mountains*.

On the night of the 13th October the 1/2nd Londons relieved the L.R.B. in the left sub-sector of the Brigade's front. The right of the line, which was over a thousand yards in extent, reſted on the Bapaume-Cambrai road on a high spur from which the clock-tower and the trains running into Cambrai could be easily seen, while nearer at hand were the red roofs of the villages of Moeuvres, Inchy, and Graincourt, which appeared to have been little damaged. The left flank was on the Moeuvres road, also on a spur, whose eastward continuation ran through Tadpole Copse, an important feature in the German position. The ground was undulating, and sloped gently towards the enemy's position. The enemy's defences, a network of trenches along the Canal du Nord and a partly dug outpost line some five or six hundred yards in front of them, were from one to two thousand yards away, and were barely visible owing to the weeds and long grass. The outstanding topographical feature was Bourlon Hill, which dominated the country for miles around, and gave the enemy observation far behind the British lines.

The line was held by two companies, with two in support, in a series of posts, which, when the Battalion first took over, were not connected in any way. These posts, therefore, had to be visited by walking above ground; and full advantage was taken of the opportunity thus presented of training the men in the use of ground and cover. The garrisons varied in strength from a section to a platoon according to the size and importance of the posts. A main system of wire ran along the whole front of the sector; and certain of the posts, constructed for all-round defence, were completely wired in. All the posts were eventually linked up. The trenches were in excellent condition; and dug-out accommodation, although limited, was satisfactory.

Battalion Headquarters were at Louverval near the ruined *château,* at one time the headquarters of the German Crown Prince, and they were accommodated in a well-built dug-out, with bedrooms and a deep emergency dug-out in case of heavy shelling. In the garden in front of these headquarters the 1/2nd Londons, following the precedent of other battalions that had held this part of the line, made a replica of their regimental crest in chipped chalk and brickdust. The details were completed with pieces of blue and green glass; and the whole design was very effective. It is rumoured that its friends, the L.R.B., who alternately with the Battalion occupied these headquarters for many weeks, were of opinion that their own crest was a much finer piece of work, but there can be little doubt that this, if true, is but partisan prejudice.

The Battalion shared the duty of holding the left sub-sector of the line with the L.R.B. throughout September, October, and the greater part of November. The front was a very quiet one, and made a welcome change from the shell-swept battlefields of the Ypres salient.

Little of interest occurred except active patrolling, and the broad extent of No Man's Land particularly lent itself to enterprises of this nature.

In the Battalion's first tour of duty in the front line there occurred one exciting incident. The Battalion, as will be recalled, had only gone into the line on the night of 13th/14th October; and at dawn on the 14th a party of 3 non-commissioned officers and 10 men, under 2nd Lieut. A. F. Williamson, went out to take up its position in an advanced post, only held by day, in the sunken road leading to Tadpole Copse, on the Battalion's left boundary. On arriving at the post, the party was fired on by an enemy patrol already in occupation. Five men were wounded; and the party was obliged to withdraw, leaving on the ground two of the wounded, who were picked up by the enemy. It is interesting to note that, as these were men of the 21st Londons and were still wearing black buttons and badges, the enemy did not secure identification through this unfortunate occurrence. Soon after daylight Capt. H. W. Everitt courageously reconnoitred the approaches to the post, and found them empty. It was thereupon occupied. Apart from this encounter, the enemy was not again found in No Man's Land, although patrols were constantly out.

With the exception of the first and two others, all reliefs of battalions in the line took place by *Decauville* railway—a time-saving innovation that was much appreciated by all ranks. Out of the line the Battalion was either in divisional or brigade reserve. When in brigade reserve, it sent one company in support to each of the battalions holding the Brigade front. These companies were billeted in Doignies for the left and in Sole for the right sub-sector respectively, and were entirely at the disposal of the battalion to which they were attached, either for work on the front line, or for support in the event of an enemy attack. Generally the Battalion had to find a third company at the same time for work for the Royal Engineers. Thus training and adequate rest were only possible when the Battalion was in divisional reserve.

On the 25th September Lieut.-General Sir C. L. Woollcombe, K.C.B., commanding IV. Corps, inspected the Battalion while it was in brigade reserve. Two companies were in the forward area at the time, and one company was working for the Royal Engineers. The remaining companies, 'D' and H.Q., together with the Battalion transport, were formed up at Lebucquière, and were warmly complimented by the Corps Commander, who expressed himself especially pleased with the fine condition of the transport.

Officer reinforcements during August and September were:

Major H. S. Bowen, who came from the Essex Regiment as second-in-command, Lieut. W. L. Stone, 2nd Lieuts. H. F. James, C. A. L. Pascoe, F. H. C. Ludlow, G. G. Shadbolt, J. McNaughton, E. Thurtle, W. Edis, C. P. S. Bradley, H. Tapner, and C. G. Scudamore.

Lieut. T. G. McCarthy, who for some months had been attached to the Brigade Staff, was appointed Staff Captain.

The total casualties during the month amounted to 3 other ranks wounded, and 2 missing.

October opened with some very bad weather, a change from the glorious days at the close of September. Despite the weather and the quietness of the sector generally, aerial activity was very great, and as the result of one combat on the 17th a British machine was brought down about 1,000 yards in front of the Battalion's wire. That night, after several abortive attempts, a party of men, under Lieut. Pascoe and 2nd Lieut. Thurtle, succeeded in extricating the body of the airman and bringing it in.

On 26th October the Battalion was honoured by a visit from the Lord Mayor of London, Sir William Dunn. He was received by Major Bowen, who, in the absence of Lieut.-Col. Sneath on leave, was in command of the Battalion. Apart from this interesting ceremony, the month passed without incident. Casualties were 6 other ranks wounded. Officer reinforcements were:

2nd Lieuts. C. W. Bridgen (20th Londons) and W. E. G. Croselle, W. J. Hewitt, and W. J. Thomas (1/16th Londons).

The bad weather of October continued into November; nevertheless, while the Battalion was in the line, patrolling was carried on as actively as ever. On 4th November one of the Battalion's patrols encountered the enemy in No Man's Land. In the fighting that ensued the patrol lost one man, wounded, but inflicted several casualties on the enemy.

The Battalion went back into divisional reserve on the night of the 8th November, its relief being marred by a most unfortunate accident. C.S.M. E. J. Dainty, a very popular and efficient warrant officer of 'B' Company, was killed in a train collision on the *Decauville* railway. He was buried on the 9th in the presence of the Commanding Officer and a large assembly of officers and men. The response to an appeal for subscriptions towards a wreath was so generous that with the balance of the money collected a memorial tablet was placed in the church with which he had been connected at home. This spell in divisional reserve was conspicuous for a sudden departure from the usual methods of training. New attack formations were tried; the troops were trained especially to co-operate with tanks; attacks with and without artillery barrages, and all the details of open warfare were practised. These facts and the following note in the War Diary are significant:

The increase in the number of dug-outs, the expansion of dumps and the widening of roads in the forward area which were noticed during the recent tour of duty, appears to foreshadow the early resumption of active operations.

The nature of the operations was kept a profound secret; and, except for the above-mentioned indications and a great increase in the number of aircraft, there was little to show that an offensive on a large scale was imminent. Fortunately the weather of late had been misty, and long-distance observation was thus denied to the enemy, who was kept in almost complete ignorance of the surprise attack shortly to be delivered against the Hindenburg Line.

II. The Capture of Tadpole Copse

The original scheme of a surprise attack at Cambrai was conceived by the Tank Corps Staff. The Tank Corps was desirous of proving the value of its weapons on ground suited to their action, as opposed to the shell-swept swamps of Ypres, where they had little chance of successful manœuvre. In the early plans there was no idea of a 'full-dress' battle. The affair was to be in the nature of a surprise raid of twenty-four hours' duration; but circumstances decreed otherwise.

Although the enemy had been largely reinforced by troops released from the Russian front, where the Russian Armies had collapsed as a result of the Revolution, he was effectively pinned down on the French battle-fronts and in Flanders, where the Third Battle of Ypres was drawing to a protracted close. A favourable opportunity was thus presented for striking a sudden blow against a point where it was least expected; and with this the Tank Corps scheme admirably coincided. Thus at last the plan, after many refusals by the Higher Command, was sanctioned; but the limited offensive of the original plan became an attack on a large scale. The Cambrai front, relatively inactive for many months, with its rolling down-lands, lightly shelled, offered facilities for a concealed concentration of tanks, and was therefore selected for the purpose.

The undertaking was distinctly daring; for apart from the lateness of the season, which probably would retard active operations, the position to be attacked formed part of the formidable Hindenburg Line. It had been skilfully sited by the enemy, every advantage which the ground offered being utilized to the full; it had been constructed at leisure over a long period of time; and nothing that unlimited labour or great skill could supply had been omitted.

The main Hindenburg Line here consisted of a front and a support system of trenches. It ran through the village of Havrincourt and then on to Moeuvres, following the west bank of the Canal du Nord, which was itself a serious obstacle, for, although dry, it was of considerable width and in places thirty feet deep. South of Moeuvres the main Hindenburg Line branched, one arm linking up with the Hindenburg reserve system at the point where it crossed the Canal east of the village, and the other running towards the north-west over Tadpole Copse and then turning west to Quéant. Tadpole Copse was of considerable tactical importance, being the key to Bourlon Hill, which was itself the key to the whole position. Five or six hundred yards in front of the main system was an outpost line, and in front of that again immense belts of barbed wire.

About twelve hundred yards in rear of the main system was a reserve system, also of great strength. This consisted of two trenches, likewise protected by wire, which, after crossing the Canal east of Moeuvres, ran through the village and across the lower slopes of Tadpole Copse to Inchy. Behind this line was a third system, the Beaurevoir-Masnières-Bourlon Line, which lay to the west of Bourlon Wood and village.

The essence of an attack on such formidable defences so late in the year was surprise. The usual method of a long preparatory bombardment, by giving the enemy warning, would have enabled him to make such preparations that success could only have been gained at the cost of a tremendous sacrifice of lives. The success of the operations, therefore, depended on the secrecy and speed of the preparations, so that the enemy might have no inkling of what was going on behind an outwardly quiet front. So skilfully were the preliminary work and the massing of troops and guns carried out that this object was achieved; and there is little doubt that the enemy was, very nearly to the last, in ignorance of what was in store for him.

To accomplish this seemingly impossible task the whole of the work was done by night, and no movement of men, of transport, or of guns, was permitted by day. Batteries of artillery were massed and camouflaged; the Cambrai road was widened twelve feet without apparently showing any structural alteration; dumps were formed and concealed; in the front line new trenches were dug and wired, to indicate to the enemy the normal condition of trench warfare; and finally, a day or two before the battle, troops were massed in the existing camps. Every tent and hut was packed to its utmost capacity; nevertheless, every man was kept under cover.

The objects of the operations were, after breaking the enemy's line, first to secure Bourlon and with it a good flank position to the east towards Cambrai, and then, by exploiting the gap thus opened towards the north-east, to roll up the Hindenburg Line. For this attack the III. and IV. Corps and three Brigades of Tanks were to be employed. In the first phase, the IV. Corps, on the left, was to establish a line through Fontaine, Bourlon, and Inchy, back to the old front line held by the 56th Division opposite Tadpole Copse. The main attack of this Corps was to be east of the Canal du Nord, but the 36th (Ulster) Division was to make a subsidiary attack with the object of working its way along the Hindenburg Line west of the Canal. The 56th Division was to join hands with this division at the point reached as a result of the first day's fighting.

On the evening of the 15th November the 1/2nd Londons relieved the L.R.B. once more; and at 6.20 a.m. on the 20th the almost uncanny stillness of the morning was broken by a terrific crash as the British barrage suddenly came down. To occupy the attention of the enemy the 56th Division made a feint attack, and for this purpose a number of full-size dummy tanks and figures had been constructed. At zero hour smoke was discharged all along the divisional front, and behind it the dummy figures and tanks were put out. The 1/2nd Londons had two tanks to put out; one was put into position on the left company's front by Lieut. Francis; the other was completely smashed up. This dummy attack, supported by a heavy machine-gun, rifle, and trench-mortar barrage, was successful in drawing the enemy's fire, the dummy figures looking very realistic in the haze of smoke, discharged from smoke-bombs.

The attack was everywhere a stupendous success; and later in the morning, when the smoke had cleared, it was possible to see large numbers of tanks, followed by small columns of infantry, pushing on far across the plain towards Bourlon. The enemy completely lost his balance; and those Germans who did not fly in panic made haste to surrender. The Hindenburg Line was breached and overrun, and only at points of great tactical importance was any serious resistance encountered. To quote Col. J. C. F. Fuller[1]:

> By 4 p.m. on November 20, one of the most astonishing battles in all history had been won and, as far as the Tank Corps was concerned, tactically finished, for no reserves existing, it was not

[1] *Tanks in the Great War,* 1914-1918. Brevet-Col. J. C. F. Fuller, D.S.O.

possible to do more than rally the now very weary and exhausted crews, select the fittest, and patch up composite companies to continue the attack on the morrow. . . . On November 20, from a base of some 13,000 yards in width, a penetration of no less than 10,000 yards was effected in 12 hours; at the Third Battle of Ypres, a similar penetration took three months.

The 109th Brigade of the 36th Division on the left of the attack, with the aid of an excellent barrage, made good progress, and by the end of the day reached a point about two hundred yards north of the Cambrai-Bapaume road. Here, about midway between the old British front line and the canal, it gained connexion with the Q.V.R., who during the night established a number of posts on either side of the road. On the left of the 169th Brigade's front, the 1/2nd Londons sent forward strong patrols to keep in touch with the enemy, who was expected to evacuate his position. These patrols, having cleared the outpost line, tested the Hindenburg Line, but found the enemy everywhere in great strength.

On the 21st the 109th Brigade continued its progress along the Hindenburg Line. At one time during the day Moeuvres was reported to have fallen. To test the accuracy of this report, three strong patrols were pushed forward by the 1/2nd Londons; on reaching the enemy's wire these patrols were heavily fired on by machine guns, and forced to withdraw. The 1/2nd Londons were later ordered to be prepared to form a defensive flank along the Inchy road; but as the necessity for this did not arise, no action was taken.

It now became apparent that the enemy had recovered somewhat from his surprise, and that more deliberate methods were required to force him from his position in front of the 56th Division. Accordingly the 169th Brigade was ordered to attack Tadpole Copse on the morning of the 22nd November. At 11 a.m. (zero hour) the Q.W.R., the attacking battalion, entered the Hindenburg Line by a communication trench just east of Aldgate, and preceded by a heavy creeping barrage bombed up it. The L.R.B. followed them in support. The attack proceeded satisfactorily despite strong resistance by the enemy machine guns, until shortly after midday, when the supply of bombs began to fail. Requests for more bombs were sent back; and the Q.V.R. and the 1/2nd Londons were ordered to carry up fresh supplies. The latter battalion was engaged for the rest of the day in forming dumps of bombs in rear of the Q.W.R. as they advanced.

The severe trench fighting continued; finally at 5.30 the Q.W.R. captured Tadpole Copse, and began bombing forward to Tadpole Lane.

This successful advance exposed the left flank of the Brigade to possible enemy counter-attacks; so the 168th Brigade was ordered to form a defensive flank from the junction of Barbican and Piccadilly, just behind Tadpole Copse, back to the British front line. This defensive flank was successfully formed by the London Scottish, and the left made secure. During the night the 1/2nd Londons were engaged on work on the roads for the Royal Engineers, who repaired the main road as far as the Canal du Nord, over which a light bridge was thrown.

Though in the end successful, the Q.W.R. had had a very trying time in capturing Tadpole Copse, and in withstanding the frequent counter-attacks that the enemy made during the night in his efforts to regain some of the lost ground. It was therefore decided that they should be relieved, and that the attack should be renewed on the 23rd by the 1/2nd Londons, and by the London Scottish (168th Brigade), while at the same time the 167th Brigade made a demonstration on the left of the divisional front.

In this attack the London Scottish were to work laterally along the Hindenburg front system as far as Adelaide Street, while the 1/2nd Londons endeavoured to gain a footing in the Hindenburg support line between Short Street and Tadpole Lane, and so to isolate the garrison of Moeuvres.

The operation orders from the Brigade were not received until 3.30 a.m., and there was thus no time to issue Battalion Operation Orders, the attack being timed to begin at 6.20 a.m. Lieut.-Col. Sneath, therefore, issued verbal orders to his company commanders. A large part of the Battalion was dispersed at the time in the performance of the many heavy duties imposed on it in the nature of working and carrying parties, and it now had to be reassembled. Although the best endeavours were made, time was so short that the Battalion found it impossible to reach its assembly position in the Hindenburg front line by zero hour. The London Scottish were equally late; and, in fact, both battalions moved across the open at daybreak to get to their positions. On arrival Lieut.-Col. Sneath arranged a new zero hour with Lieut.-Col. Jackson of the London Scottish; and, after a further delay due to the fact that the Q.W.R. had not penetrated so far to the left as reported, with consequent congestion in the assembly area of both the London Scottish and the 1/2nd Londons, the attack was launched.

The dispositions of the 1/2nd Londons were as follows:

RIGHT: 'D' Company (2nd Lieut. H. D. Pratt) in Short Street.
CENTRE: 'B' Company (Capt. Widdecombe).
LEFT: 'C' Company (Capt. Ward).
RESERVE: 'A' Company (Capt. Baker), in the Hindenburg Outpost Line.

Each company had a communication trench, down which it was to operate towards the support line. On reaching the front trench of this support system, 'D' Company was to form a block one hundred yards to the right, while on the left 'C' Company was to get in touch with the London Scottish advancing up Tadpole Lane. The attacking companies were to push on to the second trench, where each flank company was to form a block, while the centre company double-blocked Hobart Street, a communication trench of considerable tactical importance, which the enemy was using for massing counter-attacks.

The Battalion made a gallant attempt to carry out the difficult task set it of attacking frontally up communication trenches that had been thoroughly blocked. Each of the attacking companies worked up the communication trenches; but the enemy had filled them with wire, and beyond these obstacles progress was absolutely impossible owing to the strength of the enemy's bombing blocks. At 3.35 p.m. Lieut.-Col. Sneath reported to Br.-General Coke that slow progress was being made in the centre communication trench, and that his left company was held up. He added that the barrage did not appear to be very effective. Hereabouts 2nd Lieut. F. H. C. Ludlow made a gallant effort to get across the open, and was killed in the attempt. For six hours the Battalion struggled on; it was then realized that the task was beyond achievement without artillery preparation or the aid of tanks, the enemy having now been largely reinforced.

On the left, the London Scottish could likewise make little progress, because, on reaching Tadpole Copse, they found a deep depression not shown on any maps, between themselves and the Inchy Road. Here, on the east side of the road, the enemy had prepared a strong position, and as the London Scottish bombed down the hill, he subjected them to heavy machine-gun and rifle fire. After some severe fighting, his resistance was finally overcome; and the London Scottish reached Adelaide Street, their main objective.

It was not long before the inevitable German counter-attack developed; it was delivered between Adelaide Street and Brisbane Street, and gradually forced the London Scottish back to the Inchy Road. At 7.5 p.m. Capt. Ward, who was in touch with the London Scottish, reported, 'Scottish report falling back on left. Have made block and arranged for Lewis guns, rifles, and bombers. Have sent to "A" Company by 2nd Lieut. Tapner. Will hang on here.' In the meanwhile, however, Lieut.-Col. Sneath, realizing that the London Scottish were hard pressed, had sent his reserve company

('A') to their support; and with the aid of this reinforcement, and by means of supplies of bombs, brought up by the Q.W.R., the enemy was driven off, and the rest of the ground, including the front trench of the Hindenburg Line, was held. For their timely assistance the 1/2nd Londons received the thanks of Br.-General Loch, commanding the 168th Brigade, and of the London Scottish.

Of this day's fighting Capt. S. H. Stevens, who was at the time adjutant of the Battalion, writes:

> On this occasion Battalion Headquarters were in the Hindenburg outpost line at its junction with Houndsditch, a slightly sunken road leading to Moeuvres. Never before or after in the history of the Battalion had so many bombs been used, and on the 23rd the question of the bomb supply was very serious. Headquarters details were busy all day supplying the forward companies with the necessary bombs, when we could get hold of them, but the dumps were very few and far between. It was impossible to attack across the open as the enemy snipers and machine guns were very active, and the slightest appearance above ground was greeted with a rain of bullets. Hence, whichever company you went to, it was the cry of 'more bombs,' and unfortunately until the Q.W.R. brought up a supply in the evening, there wasn't a lot of 'more bombs'!

On the right, Moeuvres was captured by the 36th (Ulster) Division, but was recaptured by the enemy later in the day. Further still to the right, Bourlon was captured by the 40th Division, assisted by thirty-four tanks, but was likewise recaptured by the enemy. There was also a tremendous struggle in Fontaine Nôtre Dame; twenty-three tanks penetrated into this village, which the exhausted infantry of the 51st Division was unable to hold. As previously stated, Tadpole Copse was the key to the Bourlon Wood position, with Moeuvres situated in the intervening valley. Moeuvres, with its cellars and concealed strong points, was never cleared of the enemy, and Tadpole Copse was continually changing hands. 'In the light of subsequent events,' writes Lieut.-Col. Sneath, 'it would appear that the Higher Command erred in leaving the capture of this important flank position out of the main scheme of the attack. Had the 169th Brigade been allotted two or three tanks on the 20th November, there is little doubt but that it would have captured Tadpole Copse and both systems of the Hindenburg Line running south therefrom to Moeuvres, thus isolating that village, of which the defenders, being completely cut off, could have been rounded up without difficulty.'

On the next day the IV. Corps issued orders for the ground gained to be held at all costs, and for the 36th and 56th Divisions to continue the clearance of the Hindenburg Line.

Br.-General Coke ordered a continuation of the operations of the previous day; and directed the 1/2nd Londons, and the L.R.B., acting in co-operation with the 168th Brigade, to attempt to gain a footing in the Hindenburg support line by operating up Short Street and Swan Lane respectively. To clear the wire that had proved so serious an obstacle on the previous day Bangalore torpedoes were to be used. At the last minute this operation was cancelled, and the Division was ordered to consolidate. The work was energetically taken in hand; and the position was appreciably improved. During the morning the boundary between the 168th and 169th Brigades was rearranged; and the London Scottish were ordered to take over part of the front held by the 1/2nd Londons. The former battalion was so weak in numbers that its Commanding Officer, Lieut.-Col. Jackson, arranged that no change be made until reinforcements arrived. Later in the morning two companies of the 1/4th Londons came up, and the rearrangement of the line was then effected.

At 3 p.m. the enemy once more counter-attacked, his bombers coming down all communication trenches, while parties of his snipers advanced from shell-hole to shell-hole across the open. On the front of the 1/2nd Londons he was driven off by rifle and machine-gun fire. On the opposite flank the London Scottish were once more very hard pressed, and finally had to leave go their hold on the Hindenburg support line, and retire across the open to the Hindenburg front line north of Tadpole Copse. The enemy's shelling was very heavy; his attacks persistent; and for a moment the situation was very precarious. Lieut.-Col. Sneath and the Commanding Officer of the L.R.B. each promptly placed a strong platoon at the disposal of the London Scottish, and thus enabled them to hold the Hindenburg front line. The 1/2nd Londons' platoon was intended to regain some of the lost ground; but ultimately it was decided that only a carefully planned operation with far more men had any chance of success, and the idea was abandoned.

On the night of the 24th the 56th Division passed from the IV. to the VI. Corps. The IV. Corps continued its attack on the right; and the 40th Division retook Bourlon, only to be driven out again on the next day.

The morning of the 25th was quiet on the front of the 56th Division.

The Rangers had relieved the London Scottish, and at 12.30 p.m. they delivered an attack to regain the ground lost on the previous day. The enemy immediately put down a heavy barrage, from which the 1/2nd Londons on the right suffered considerably. The attack began well, but ended with only a small gain of ground. During the succeeding night the 1/2nd Londons were relieved by the Q.V.R., and moved back to the right sector of the old British front line.

III. THE GERMAN COUNTER-ATTACK

On the 27th November the first stage of the Battle of Cambrai came to an end. The Third Army resources were almost exhausted, and no fresh divisions were available for carrying on the fight. The tanks had almost all been withdrawn. 'November 21st,' writes Col. J. C. F. Fuller,[1] 'saw, generally speaking, the end of any co-operative action between tanks and infantry; henceforth, new infantry being employed, loss of touch and action between them and the tanks constantly resulted. . . . During the attacks which had taken place since November 21st, tank units had become terribly disorganized and by the 27th had been reduced to such a state of exhaustion that it was determined to withdraw the 1st and 2nd Brigades.' The position in front of Bourlon and Fontaine was most unsatisfactory, and there were indications that the enemy would shortly counter-attack on a large scale.

After its four days' rest, most of which was spent in working on a communication trench across what, formerly, was No Man's Land, the Battalion relieved the Q.V.R. on the evening of the 24th November on the left of the Brigade's front in the Hindenburg Line, 'D' and 'C' Companies taking over the forward trenches, and 'A' and 'B' remaining in support.

The night was a quiet one, and there was little to indicate that the enemy was about to make a desperate attempt to regain the ground that he had lost and to cut off the British forces in the Cambrai Salient.

The day dawned bright with a light mist rising from the ground. At about 6 o'clock the enemy opened a harassing fire on the line held by the 56th Division; but it was not until an hour later that he disclosed his full intentions. At 7.30 the forward companies of the 1/2nd Londons reported that large parties of the enemy could be seen assembling north of Moeuvres and about Quarry Wood. The Battalion was ordered to stand-to-arms at once, since it was evident that the enemy's attack would not be long delayed.

The fighting began at 8 o'clock with an unexpectedly successful attack

[1] *Tanks in the Great War*, 1914-1918. Brevet-Col. J. C. F. Fuller, D.S.O.

on the southern flank of the salient of the British line. The enemy broke through the III. Corps at the junction of the 55th and 12th Division, and penetrated as far as Gouzeaucourt, a village behind the original British front line. The desperate situation then created was saved by the counter-attack of the Guards, and by the gallant defence of the 29th Division, which clung tenaciously to Masnière.

About six German divisions were engaged in this attack, which afterwards proved to be subsidiary to the enemy's main attack. The main attack developed about two hours later on the front between Fontaine Nôtre Dame and Tadpole Copse, held by the 47th (2nd London) Division, the 2nd Division, and the 56th Division. It was preceded by a tremendous barrage of guns of all calibres. The air was rent by the stream of shrieking shells; and the earth reeled under the continuous explosions. It seemed as though only by a miracle could anything continue to live in such an inferno. On every side men were killed, were maimed, were bereft of their senses by this terrible fire. Yet the survivors could not shelter themselves in the dug-outs; they knew that as soon as the pitiless rain of metal ceased the enemy's masses would be upon them.

For close upon an hour the storm of shell relentlessly continued; then at 10.45 a.m. the S.O.S. went up all along the line, and under cover of a heavy trench-mortar barrage the enemy's infantry attacked in enormous strength. 'D' Company on the left of the 1/2nd Londons had suffered severely from the accuracy of the trench-mortar fire, but nevertheless was able to open a very destructive rifle and Lewis-gun fire on the advancing masses. 'C' Company, on the right, did likewise; and the enemy on the front of the Battalion was held up. He had, however, launched his attack down the communication trenches as well as over the open, and in the communication trenches on each flank of the Battalion he was more successful. On the extreme left of the Battalion's line, L/Corpl. F. C. Tyler did splendid work. He was in charge of a Lewis-gun section on the flank of 'D' Company, and, after the enemy's bombardment, he was the sole survivor of his section. Throughout the bombardment he kept his gun going, firing twenty magazines at the advancing enemy, and he did not leave his position until the enemy were in the trench. He then withdrew—the last man of 'D' Company—, taking his gun with him.

At length, after fierce fighting, the enemy worked round the left flank of 'D' Company, and succeeded in cutting it off from the 168th Brigade, through whose line (held by the 8th Middlesex and London Scottish) he had also broken. He then attacked both 'D' and 'C' Companies in the rear, and eventually secured a footing in his old support line. On the left he succeeded even in penetrating to his old front line, and at last forced both the forward companies of the 1/2nd Londons to withdraw down the communication trenches. Things looked very black, when Capt. Baker, commanding the support company ('A'), quickly organized a counter-attack. He was ably supported by Lieut. Rowlands, who, together with all available men from Battalion Headquarters, and with a plentiful supply of bombs, had been sent up by Lieut.-Col. Sneath at the psychological moment; and, after a fierce struggle, the Germans were forced out of their support line, which was recaptured by the 1/2nd Londons and successfully held. Blocks were at once formed in the communication trenches; and the timely arrival of two companies of the Q.V.R., placed at Lieut.-Col. Sneath's disposal, and at once utilized by him in the right place, made the position once more secure. By 1 p.m. touch had been regained with the 168th Brigade on the left.

Fighting of the fiercest character now took place in the communication trenches; and for the next three hours the enemy was unceasing in his efforts to capture the support line. But the resistance of the troops never wavered; by 6.30 p.m. the day had been won, and the enemy's onslaught finally driven off. A third company arrived from the Q.V.R. as a reinforcement for the 1/2nd Londons; and as assistance was really no longer necessary, one of the companies previously sent up was returned.

During this action, a trench running to the Hindenburg front line from the old British outpost line close to the spot where the 1/2nd Londons' Battalion Headquarters had been established in a shell-hole proved of very great value. 'Its junction,' writes Lieut.-Col. Sneath, 'formed a rallying point, and communication from the rear, including supplies of bombs, would otherwise have been almost impossible owing to the intense artillery barrage. The latter was controlled by five enemy aeroplanes, one of which was eventually brought down by Lewis-gun fire. These aeroplanes by the use of coloured flares directed the enemy guns with great precision. For some unknown reason no English planes were seen on the divisional front until late in the evening when all fighting had ceased.'

On the right of the brigade front, the Q.V.R. had been equally heavily attacked. Although their forward troops were pressed back, they had not let the line be broken, and at the end of the day were in touch with the 2nd Division on the right. On the left, the 168th Brigade had also given but little ground. And so after a day of fighting of the severest character, which it is impossible adequately to describe, the 56th Division remained

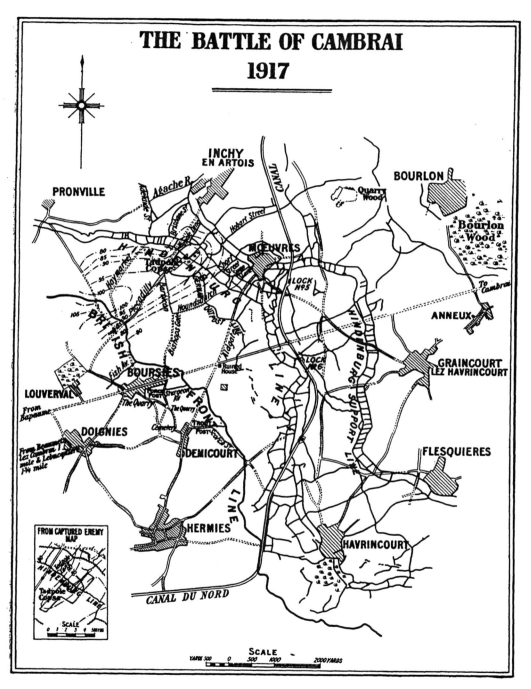

THE BATTLE OF CAMBRAI, 1917.

with its line almost intact. There is little doubt that this stand by the three divisions holding the northern face of the salient saved a very serious debacle; for, had the enemy broken through, the III. and IV. Corps must have inevitably been cut off.

In the 169th Brigade, the Q.W.R. and the 1/2nd Londons had borne the brunt of the fighting, and in the evening of the 30th the remnants of both battalions were relieved, the former by the L.R.B. and the latter by the 1/3rd Londons (167th Brigade). The 1/2nd Londons withdrew to Louverval. During the 1st December the enemy contented himself with heavy shelling, and did not resume his attacks; and on the 2nd the exhausted 56th Division was relieved by the 51st (Highland) Division.

This was, perhaps, the finest and most successful fight in which the 1/2nd Londons took part during the war, and, although it is not possible to chronicle all the heroic deeds that were done, mention must be made of some of the officers who inspired this gallant stand. Lieut.-Col. Sneath handled his battalion throughout the battle with conspicuous ability. He himself attributes his success to the fact that he had established his battle headquarters in a very favourable position. Eschewing the comfortable dug-outs of the Hindenburg Line, he selected a shell-hole whence he could exercise control over his battalion, and could communicate with the rear by visual signalling, for which the nature of the country was eminently suited. In touch with front, both flanks, and with Brigade Headquarters, he was thus able to exercise the proper functions of a battalion commander, and not merely command the handful of men in his immediate neighbourhood, and he was able to make good use of his own reserves and of the two companies of the Q.V.R. that were later placed at his disposal. Capt. Baker, who organized and led the successful counter-attack, Lieut. Rowlands, and Capt. Widdecombe and Capt. Ward, whose companies bore the brunt of the enemy's assault, must also be mentioned.

During the battle the losses of the 1/2nd Londons were as follows:

KILLED : 1 officer (2nd Lieut. F. H. C. Ludlow) and 16 other ranks.

WOUNDED : 3 officers (Lieut. A. J. Whittle, 2nd Lieuts. E. Thurtle and L. Fairney) and 116 other ranks.

MISSING : 1 officer (2nd Lieut. W. E. G. Croselle) and 52 other ranks.

The following honours were awarded in connexion with the battle:

Bar to M.C. : Capt. F. C. Baker and Lieut. H. Rowlands.
M.C. : Capt. W. J. Ward.
Bar to D.C.M. : C.S.M. A. E. Easthope.

The 2nd London Regiment in the Great War

Bar to M.M. : Sergts. R. F. Cowles, J. Halket.
M.M. : Sergts. P. H. Everitt, H. Vincent; L/Sergts. S. England, W. H. French, L/Corpls. F. R. Cross, A. J. Hamshaw, H. Sinfield, F. G. Watkins, M. Winter, A. Haynes, R. S. Ockenden, F. A. Wilson, Ptes. F. Boxall, F. Heffer, R. T. Triance, H. Brewer, E. Townsend, H. C. Winterburn.

It is fitting to close this account of an heroic struggle with an extract from a booklet published some months later by the General Staff, entitled *The Story of a Great Fight: Being an Account of the Operations of the 47th, 2nd, and 56th Divisions in the Neighbourhood of Bourlon Wood and Moeuvres on the 30th November 1917.*

On the morning of November 30th, 1917, the 47th (London) Territorial Division, the 2nd Division, and the right brigade of the 56th (London) Territorial Division were holding a front of about five miles, extending from the eastern ridge of Bourlon Wood to Tadpole Copse, in the Hindenburg Line, west of Moeuvres. From Tadpole Copse, the left brigade of the 56th Division formed a defensive flank across No Man's Land to our old front line.

The 56th Division had been in line before the British attack of November 20th, in which its right brigade (169th) had taken part, and since that date it had captured and held about a mile of the Hindenburg Line, west of Moeuvres, including Tadpole Copse. Almost constant fighting had taken place in this area since our attack, and the Division, which at one time had been holding a front of 11,000 yards, had already been subjected to a very severe strain.

The story of the subsequent fighting on the Bourlon-Moeuvres front is one so brimful of heroism that it deserves to take its place in English history for all time. The most determined attacks of four German divisions, with three other German divisions in support, were utterly crushed by the unconquerable resistance of the three British divisions in the line. November 30th, 1917 will be a proud day in the lives of all those splendid British soldiers who, by their single-hearted devotion to duty, prevented what would have become a serious situation, had they given way. . . . At 9.20 a.m. the enemy had been seen advancing from the north towards the Canal du Nord, and subsequently attack after attack was delivered by him on both sides of the Canal against the 6th and 169th Infantry Brigades. . . . From Moeuvres westward to Tadpole Copse a desperate struggle was taking place for the possession of the Hindenburg Line.

Though much reduced in strength by the fighting of the preceding days, and hard-pressed by superior forces, the troops of the 168th and 169th Infantry Brigades beat off all attacks. Queen's Westminsters, London Scottish, and men of the 1/2nd Battalion London Regiment, and 1/8th Battalion Middlesex Regiment vied with one another in the valour of their resistance.

At the end of this day of high courage and glorious achievement, except a few advanced positions, some of which were afterwards regained, our line had been maintained intact. The men who came triumphantly through this mighty contest felt that they had won a great victory, in which the enemy had come against them in his full strength, and had been defeated with losses at which even the victors stood aghast.

The 169th Brigade was relieved on the 2nd December by the 154th Brigade; and the 1/2nd Londons marched back to Bancourt, where they spent a bitterly cold night in tents. On the next day the whole Brigade moved by train from Frémicourt to the area of Beaumetz les Loges, the 1/2nd Londons being billeted at Berneville. After a day spent in cleaning up—during which the Battalion received the congratulations of Br.-General Coke, in person, on its stand at Moeuvres—, news was received that a fresh move was to be made immediately, since the 56th Division was shortly to relieve the 31st Division in the XIII. Corps area in front of Arras. On the 5th, therefore, the 1/2nd Londons continued their move, marching to Bray. After the long sojourn in the devastated area, the men fully appreciated the excellent accommodation, both at Berneville and Bray, and especially the wire sleeping-bunks that were available for all.

CHAPTER XVIII

THE 1/2ND LONDONS DURING THE WINTER OF 1917-18— ON THE ARTOIS FRONT

WITH the Battle of Cambrai active operations for 1917 came to an end; thereafter the British Army passed definitely to the defensive. Such a complete reversal of policy on the part of the British G.H.Q. needs an explanation, which a brief reference to the outstanding events of the year 1917 will supply. Foremost among these was the political crisis in Russia that had ultimately led to the overthrow of the existing régime and the secession of this great nation from the Allied cause. The removal of so powerful a combatant from the field necessarily had important reactions in every theatre of war. It enabled the enemy to release masses of troops that had hitherto been kept fully occupied on the Eastern Front, to inflict a serious defeat on Italy, and to administer a check to the Allies' efforts in the Balkans and in Palestine. In the West the effect was equally marked. The arrival of large numbers of German troops from the Eastern Front resulted in a complete reversal of numerical superiority in France. The German armies were now being reinforced day by day by divisions that had had no serious fighting for nearly a year, whereas the British and French were hard put to it to find men enough for essential duties, and every one of their fighting units had suffered heavy casualties in 1917. So far as the British were concerned, the continual demands for men from the many fronts on which the Empire was engaged made it difficult to keep their army in France up to strength—a difficulty that was exaggerated by the policy of the Government at home, who, desirous of avoiding a repetition of the costly offensives of 1917, retained as many men as possible in England. It is true that the entry of America into the war on the side of the Allies must eventually redress the balance, but it was now certain that, even using their best endeavours, American troops could not be in the field in sufficient numbers to affect the issue before the summer of 1918.

A grave crisis in the war was thus fast approaching. The probability that the enemy would use his numerical superiority for a large scale offensive in France became a certainty as the winter wore on. There was every reason to believe that the brunt of the fighting in 1918 would fall upon the British

Army; for, although the British held less than one-third of the Western Front, they held nearly all the most active part where the nature of the terrain and good railway communications favoured an enemy concentration and attack. British G.H.Q., therefore, rightly judging that an enemy offensive was imminent and that the British front from Ypres to the Oise would be the chief objective, concentrated on the task of making that front secure. At the close of 1917 and throughout the early months of 1918, every man who could be spared from the actual duties of defence was used for this end; and when the long-expected blow finally fell a large part of the preparation to meet it had been completed.

In the first week of December the 169th Brigade relieved the 92nd Brigade in the Gavrelle sector, north-east of Arras, and the 1/2nd Londons, proceeding on the 7th of the month to a muddy camp at Ecurie Wood, where the accommodation consisted of Nissen huts, came into brigade reserve. On the next day the Battalion moved up into the support position, Headquarters and 'C' and 'D' Companies being accommodated in Round-hay Camp.

Even in the far-off days before the processes of Nature and the workings of man were rudely interrupted by war, the district of Artois in which the 1/2nd Londons now found themselves offered a somewhat uninteresting prospect to the eye. Few woods or trees and fewer villages varied the long stretches of downland, which, though pleasant enough in themselves, were apt to grow monotonous. To the north-west, the verdure-covered slopes of the Vimy ridge added variety to the landscape, but eastward the fertile plains of Douai stretched, unbroken, mile upon mile. The tide of war, ebbing and flowing over the area, had served to accentuate its drab monotony. The devastation of the region was complete, and its desolation struck a chill to the heart of a beholder. To those whose lot it was to campaign in this area the proximity of Arras was the sole alleviation, since at Arras some of the conveniences of civilization were available, and many little things to make life easier and pleasanter could there be purchased.

The front of the XIII. Corps was at this period held by one division in the line; and the sector taken over by the 169th Brigade on the 7th December included the village of Gavrelle and the trenches north and south of it. The Brigade sector of about a mile was divided into two sub-sectors extending to approximately equal distances on either side of the Arras-Douai road, which passed through the village. In the front system there were two defended localities, Towy Post in the right sub-sector, and Mill Post in the left, each garrisoned by a company. The area between these large posts was un-defended, but in order to give warning of any hostile penetration, there were there established two smaller posts, named respectively Gavrelle and Water Posts.

Towy Post was destined to be held by the 1/2nd Londons whenever they were in the front line, and it therefore deserves a brief description. It con-sisted practically of a square of trenches, of which Willie Trench formed the front and Willie Support the rear. Invicta Trench formed the right side, and Colour Trench the left. Each side was roughly fifty yards in length; and through the middle of the post ran a continuation of Towy Alley, the communication trench, five thousand yards long, leading up from the rear.

Gavrelle itself lay in a slight hollow on the left of Towy Post. Little of it remained beyond heaps of rubble; yet the enemy persisted in shelling it daily. On the left of the village was a long flat spur, ending in a round knoll, on which stood a derelict windmill. Here was Mill Post, which was generally held by one of the other brigades of the Division.

A thousand yards behind this front system was a second system—the Naval-Marine Line. This system formed the support to the line of posts at Gavrelle, and the battalion holding the posts was responsible for its security likewise. Behind this again was a third system—the Bailleul-Willerval (or Red) Line—constituting the main support position.

Communications in the area were really remarkably good, when one considers the general desolation. Steam trains ran to a railhead in rear of the line of the Vimy Ridge, and forward of this, but at night only, petrol-electric trains ran to the Red Line. From the Red Line, stores and rations were carried forward by truck.

The 1/2nd Londons were not long in support; on the 11th they relieved the L.R.B. in daylight in the right sub-sector of the Brigade front, being disposed as follows:

> Towy Post: One company.
> Gavrelle and Water Posts: One company.
> Naval-Marine Line: One company.
> Red Line: One company.

The trenches were in a very bad state of repair, and the work of improving them was immediately taken in hand; but the Battalion was so weak in numbers that progress was slow. The wire in front was very thin; in fact, it was so bad that it required the attention of the C.R.E. of the Division, who prepared a comprehensive scheme of wiring for the Brigade front. In the course of the winter a wonderful improvement was made in the defences, so that by the end of March they had become very formidable. The belt of wire had been widened and strengthened; hundreds of 'knife-rests' had been put out; bombing blocks had been constructed; and every convenient point had been converted into a miniature fort.

December passed uneventfully, the 1/2nd Londons sharing the duty of holding the front line with the Q.W.R. Between its tours of duty in front, the Battalion was either in support at Roundhay Camp or in reserve in Ecurie Wood. In the latter, the canteen and cinema and the 'Bow Bells' made things more cheery for the men than would be thought possible in view of the desolation of the area.

On the 16th December orders were issued for the relief of the Division. These orders were almost immediately cancelled; and nearly a month was to elapse before the long-expected rest finally came to pass. There was now little activity on the part of the enemy; and during the month the Battalion had no casualties, although a patrol of 'B' Company that went out on the 23rd to look at the enemy's wire was heavily fired on.

Officer reinforcements during the month were:

2nd Lieuts. D. Sloan and H. E. Coatman.

The Battalion was out of the line on Christmas Day; and the men, aided by a ration of plum pudding, made themselves as happy as possible. As three companies were scattered over the area in various defensive posts, and only Headquarters and one company were in the shelters at Roundhay Camp, it was decided to postpone the Christmas festivities proper until the Division was in rest—an event that was now daily expected. The weather was very seasonable, and snow fell heavily. The Battalion did another tour in the front line before New Year's Day, which was marked by the return of Lieut.-Col. J. P. Kellett, M.C., who had been wounded at Glencorse Wood in the previous August. The New Year opened with some very severe weather, which continued throughout January, the bitter cold being intensified by constant falls of snow.

It should be noted that the New Year's Honours List contained the following award:

M.C.: Capt. T. G. McCarthy.

Early in the month the 56th Division was relieved by the 62nd, and was at last granted the rest that it had certainly earned. For the 1/2nd Londons this period of rest was somewhat delayed; after marching to St. Aubin and spending two days there, the Battalion moved forward again to Trafalgar Camp for work under the C.R.E., XIII. Corps. Two companies were billeted in Roclincourt and two in the Point du Jour-Thélus Ridge Line (Green Line), now constituting the reserve position. Battalion Headquarters were located in Trafalgar Camp itself, which proved an ideal situation. The work was mainly wiring for the 62nd Division and strengthening the defences generally, and the whole Battalion, including the Drums, was employed.

The 1/2nd Londons were ultimately allowed to withdraw on the 16th January, when a move was made to Frévillers. Here the Battalion remained for the rest of the month. Training was energetically proceeded with, but was much interfered with by the inclement weather, the snow continuing throughout the month. The best was made of a bad job; and all ranks were keen and enthusiastic. The growing certainty of an enemy offensive in the near future demanded that all training should be directed towards perfecting the tactics of defence and counter-attack. Special attention was paid to Lewis-gun training, and also to musketry; and once more the principle that the rifle is the soldier's best friend was thoroughly instilled into the men.

A Corps Platoon Competition, with eliminating Divisional and Brigade Competitions, taking the form of a battle practice was held at this time. The Brigade Competition was won by the Q.V.R., the 1/2nd Londons' team, a complete platoon of 'D' Company, under Lieut. J. J. Edmett, being second. At the close of January a Brigade A.R.A. Competition also took place, in which the 1/2nd Londons were represented by No. 5 Platoon ('B' Company), and gained second place.

During this period of rest the opportunity was taken of holding the postponed Christmas festivities. Accordingly each company held a dinner— an example that was followed alike by the Officers' and Sergeants' Messes.

The close of the month was marked by a very sad event, and one that resulted directly from the serious shortage of men in France. The falling-off in the supply of reinforcements, due partly to an actual failing in man-power and partly to the policy of the British Government of which previous mention has been made, of retaining a large force in England, had reduced battalions in France to a very low level, and there now appeared no immediate prospect of the 1917 wastage being made good. Accordingly, under instructions from the Army Council, the establishment of all brigades in France was reduced from four to three battalions. The execution of these orders involved the disbandment of certain battalions; and the G.O.C., 56th Division, ordered to choose one Fusilier and two Rifle battalions, chose in each of his three brigades the highest numbered unit that fulfilled the required conditions. In the 169th Brigade the Q.V.R. was the battalion selected, and everyone in the Brigade was truly sorry to part with this fine unit. Headquarters and a nucleus went to the second-line unit in the 58th Division, and the remainder to the Q.W.R. In the 167th Brigade the 1/3rd Londons, and in the 168th Brigade the 1/12th Londons, were the unlucky battalions. As a result of the disbandment of their battalion on 29th January, 8 officers and 159 other ranks of the 3rd Londons were sent to the 1/2nd Londons, who accorded their new comrades an enthusiastic welcome. These 3rd Londoners, who were, as was only natural, bitterly disappointed at the breaking-up of their own unit, deserve the highest praise not only for the magnificent spirit they displayed at the time, but also for their subsequent loyal services with the 1/2nd Londons.

The officers, who joined the Battalion from the 3rd Londons, were:

Lieuts. H. Lloyd, E. J. Y. Simmonds, H. J. B. Simon, 2nd Lieuts. H. G. Eldon, S. F. Reeves, J. W. T. B. Chambers, H. Dyer, and W. J. Waller.

The period of rest of the 56th Division now drew to a close; and between the 8th and 11th February the Division relieved the 62nd in the same line as before. The 1/2nd Londons had moved forward some days previously, having marched, on the 1st, to Tinques, where they had entrained for Ecurie *en route* for the area of Trafalgar Camp and the Green Line. 'B' and 'D' Companies were billeted in the Green Line itself, and 'A' and 'C' in Roclincourt; and the whole Battalion was engaged during the next week on wiring work for the 513th Field Company, R.E. The normal strength of the Battalion at this period had increased to 48 officers and 1,007 other ranks, and of this the trench strength was 25 officers and 610 other ranks.

The divisional front was at this time reorganized, and was now held by three brigades in the line instead of two. Each brigade was disposed with one battalion in the front system, one in support, and one in reserve. The 169th Brigade still remained on the right flank of the Division, and was responsible for Towy and Gavrelle Posts. The forward battalion was disposed as follows:

Towy and Gavrelle Posts: One company.
Naval Trench and Water Post: One company and two platoons.
Keiller, Pelican, and Halifax Posts: Two platoons.
　　(When these intermediate posts were not manned, their garrisons were located
　　　　in the Red Line.)
Ditch Post: One company.

The support battalion was at Roundhay Camp, with two companies forward in the Red Line, and the reserve battalion was at St. Aubin.

February was spent by the 1/2nd Londons in occupying these positions alternately. The tours of duty in the front line were devoid of incident, and the only casualties sustained were three men wounded. Whenever the Battalion was in reserve during this period heavy demands were made on its personnel for working parties, and never a day passed without two or more companies being so employed. On the other hand, special arrangements were made for the men to attend performances by the 'Bow Bells,' and lorries were provided to take them to the theatre at Arras, which was used for the purpose. This theatre had escaped damage from the German bombardments, and, although somewhat fusty, was quite homelike.

The beginning of March found the Battalion once more in the line; and this tour of duty was remarkable for a number of useful patrols, which made very careful inspection of the enemy's wire. 2nd Lieut. Carlile succeeded in finding a gap in the front belt, and this gap was exploited by subsequent patrols. Another incident of interest was the discovery by 2nd Lieut. Coatman of some very talkative German sentries close to the Gavrelle-Fresnes road. The loud conversations of these men persisted for some nights, and the advisability of bringing up an interpreter to learn what they were saying was even considered.

Two changes in the personnel of Battalion Headquarters that occurred at this time should be noted. Capt. S. H. Stevens, M.C., succeeded Major Sneath as second-in-command, the latter transferring to the Machine-Gun Corps, and Lieut. E. J. Y. Simons succeeded Capt. Stevens as adjutant.

The general situation in the West was daily becoming more anxious; and the tension on the front of the 56th Division was considerably increased by information, received on the 12th March, that an attack that might include the Vimy Ridge was imminent. The 1/2nd Londons, then battalion in divisional reserve, moved up from St. Aubin to Chanticleer, the crossroads south-west of Roclincourt, in close reserve. But the warning was premature, and the rumoured attack did not take place. From that day, however, brigades in the line were ordered to be extremely alert, and the whole division stood to arms from one hour before dawn until half-past eight each morning. The activity of the enemy's artillery and trench mortars steadily increased, and the British trench systems and back areas were subjected to frequent and heavy bombardments.

There were now increasingly ominous signs that the hour of the German onslaught was drawing near. Large concentrations of troops had been observed on various parts of the front; wide areas of ground had been infected by gas to deny their use to either side; and the enemy's aerial activity had shown a marked increase. The British Army, secure behind its defences, awaited with calmness and confidence the bursting of the storm.

CHAPTER XIX

THE 2/2ND LONDONS IN THE FIRST BATTLES OF THE SOMME, 1918

I. Preparations for the German Offensive

THE Twenty-First of March 1918 will remain one of the most memorable days in the annals of the Great War. On that day the enemy launched his hosts in a supreme bid for victory. This proved to be his last effort, but it came very near to success; it was not until the 15th July that, after crossing the Marne, he finally acknowledged that the task of beating the Allies was beyond his powers. How near to disaster we were in those days we now fully realize; and it is therefore right that due appreciation should be given to the courage and steadfastness of the troops that heroically resisted the attacks of an enemy, flushed with success and in far superior numbers, and at the end fought him to a standstill.

Before setting out to describe the parts played by both battalions of the 2nd London Regiment in stemming the German tide, the present writer proposes briefly to examine the reasons that led the Germans to embark on this last offensive and the circumstances that induced them to attack when and where they did.

The transference of large numbers of German divisions from the Eastern Front has already been referred to. This movement continued without cessation until the enemy had a marked numerical preponderance in the West; during the last months of 1917 and the early months of 1918 the number of German divisions in France rose to nearly 200, whereas the French, at this period, had only 95 and the British only 57, and these, too, were sadly depleted in numbers. With this superiority on the main battle-front, with Russia out of the conflict, with Italy defeated, with France and even Great Britain strained to the utmost by the prolonged and costly struggle, the pendulum of fortune seemed to have swung once more in favour of the enemy. On the other hand, there were several factors in the general situation that augured well for the future of the Allied cause. American troops had at last begun to arrive on the Western Front—even now three divisions, the equivalent in numbers of half-a-dozen British or French, were already in the line. The Austrian Army, though it had gained a temporary respite by its victory over the Italians, was growing demoralized and undisciplined. In Germany herself the situation was far from satisfactory; the U-boat campaign had not achieved its object; food was becoming scarce; and revolutionary ideas, inspired by Russia, were undermining the loyalty of an increasing number of the people.

All these facts were undoubtedly in the mind of General Ludendorff, who with his chief, von Hindenburg, virtually controlled the policy of Germany, when he surveyed the situation at the end of 1917. To sue for peace, which might at this juncture have been obtained on favourable terms, was repugnant to his nature; moreover, there was this German superiority on the Western Front for the first time since the early days of the war; and the opportunity of striking what might well prove to be the decisive blow offered itself temptingly. He realized, however, that this superiority was fleeting, that ere long the gigantic forces of America would be thrown into the conflict and would turn the scales definitely in favour of the Allies. If anything was to be done, it must be done without delay.

Accordingly, at a conference held at Mons on 11th November 1917, the German High Command decided that an offensive should be made on the Western Front, that February, or at latest March, should be the date, and that it was the British Army that must be beaten. Broadly, two main alternatives presented themselves: an attack on the Channel Ports with the object of cutting off the British from their bases, or an attack on either side of St. Quentin with the object of cutting off the existing salient in the British line and of rolling up the whole British Army north-westward against the coast. Various plans were prepared on these lines; and in making his final choice Ludendorff was guided by the British dispositions. The British Commander-in-Chief for his part, in making the dispositions on which the safety of the whole British Army and the result of the war was to depend, was influenced by the consideration that he could surrender no ground in the north, where the Channel Ports that must be defended at all costs were at no great distance behind his front line, nor in the centre, behind which lay the collieries of Northern France and important tactical features, covering his lateral communications, but that in the south, in the region of the Somme, where there was a larger area for manœuvre in the event of a considerable break-through by enemy forces, he could, if necessary, do so without serious consequences. A further factor influencing his decision may have been the apparent natural strength of the extreme right of his front between Moy and La Fère, where the Oise Canal and its marshes formed a difficult barrier between the German and British lines. To meet the anticipated offensive, therefore, the British Army was distributed with about one-half of its strength protecting the Channel Ports and the remainder thinly dispersed along the rest of the front, now about one hundred and twenty-five miles in extent. The grouping of the British forces was rendered yet more difficult, because it was quite probable, owing to the strength of his reserves, that the enemy's first attack, although a vigorous one, might be only a feint to be followed by another and heavier blow on a different part of the front—a consideration that could not be overlooked. To meet a second attack of this nature no general reserve was available, and little help could be expected from the French, who were naturally concerned for the safety of Paris.

Ludendorff, realizing the importance to the British of holding the Channel Ports at all costs, was fully alive to the probability of a concentration of their forces in the northern area. He was thus led to adopt the alternative scheme, known by the code name of 'Michael,' of an attack in the St. Quentin area; and he was aided in his decision by his correct assumption of the weakness of the British at the southern end of their line. He therefore decided to deliver his mighty blow at what he conceived to be, and at what actually was, the weakest part of the Allies' line on the Western Front.

To give further relief to the French Army, Sir Douglas Haig, under pressure from both French and British Governments, had somewhat reluctantly agreed to extend his front southwards from the River Omignon to Barisis, a village south of the Oise, in the Forest of St. Gobain; and, as a result of this decision taken in December 1917, the responsibility for the defence of this sector was transferred during the month of January 1918 and the early days of February. The new front was some thirty miles in extent, and its defence, together with twelve miles further north from the Omignon to Gouzeaucourt, hitherto held by the Third Army, was entrusted to General Gough's Fifth Army, which was moved to the southern end of the British line for this purpose.

We left the 58th Division on the point of setting out from Belgium to join the Fifth Army. On its arrival in the area of this Army, the Division was held for a time in reserve and was concentrated near Amiens. The 2/2nd Londons, having entrained at Poperinghe, reached Villers Bretonneux on 21st January and marched thence to Fouencamps, about eight miles south-west of Amiens. Fouencamps was a picturesque little village, picturesquely situated at the junction of the rivers Avre and Noye, and was quite unspoiled by the ravages of war. The Battalion's short stay in this pleasant village, among the kindly peasantry, was a welcome change from the mud and blood of Passchendaele, and remains the source of many happy memories alike to officers and men.

Of Fouencamps one or two recollections stand out clearly: the first is of a disagreement between the officers of Battalion Headquarters and those of 'D' Company on the subject of billets, which, it should be remarked, had been allocated by a 'D' Company officer. The result was a 'stealth raid' one night; no quarter was given; and at the end Capt. Howie, pyjama-clad, had to drop several feet into a kitchen garden to escape a fusillade of brickbats from the Quartermaster. The second concerns 'A' Company, two of whose officers disguised themselves as women with the clothes that they found in their billets, *Numero Trente-trois*. Unfortunately the owners, who had for a time moved further from the fighting, chose this inconvenient moment for their return! The third is the vivid recollection of a gentle old lady pointing to a flag-stone on which the Germans stood in 1870, and wondering if they would ever stand there again. Two months later her home lay in ruins.

The closing days of January were marred by that sad event to which allusion has been made in the previous chapter dealing with the 56th Division, the reduction of infantry brigades from four to three battalions. Once again the 2nd London battalion was spared, the unfortunate battalion to be chosen for disbandment in the 173rd Brigade being the 2/1st Londons. In the 174th Brigade the 2/5th Londons were disbanded, and in the 175th the 2/11th Londons. As a result of the disbandment of the 2/1st Londons, 13 officers and 335 other ranks of that battalion were posted to the 2/2nd Londons on 29th January, the officers being:

> Capts. W. A. Warren, E. B. Ruber, J. A. Houghton, Lieuts. C. M. Roberts, A. Ward, M.C., W. T. James, M.C., 2nd Lieut. G. T. Roberts, M.C., A. W. Green, W. H. Sanders, H. J. Boon, P. R. Taylor, R. J. T. Brown, and A. H. Streets, M.C.

After an uneventful and tranquil fortnight spent in the usual routine of training, this pleasant period of rest drew to a close; but before the Brigade moved forward to more active duties, the Brigadier, on the 5th February, delivered a lecture, bearing on the general situation and the imminence of an enemy offensive, to all officers, warrant officers, and sergeants in the Brigade, and thereat he conveyed to them a stirring message from General Gough, the Commander of the Fifth Army.

The front of the Fifth Army was nearly forty-two miles in extent—about a third part of the whole line occupied by the British forces in France. This wide front was held by four Corps, from left to right, the VII. (Congreve), the XIX. (Watts), the XVIII. (Maxse), and the III. (Butler), with seventeen divisions in the line and three infantry divisions and three cavalry divisions in reserve.[1]

The III. Corps, under Lieut.-Gen. Sir R. H. K. Butler, K.C.M.G., C.B., comprised the 14th, 18th, and 58th Divisions, and the span of its front, running south to Barisis, was thirty thousand yards (only sixteen thousand yards less than that which the whole of the Third Army further north had to protect). The defence of this enormous front, covering, as it did, the very heart of France, was a task far beyond the power of the Corps' twenty-seven battalions, not one of which was up to strength, with a reserve consisting only of two cavalry divisions (the 2nd and 3rd Cavalry Divisions). It is true that one-half of the front was covered by the St. Quentin (Oise-Sambre) Canal, the River Oise and its marshes; and in a wet season the protection offered by these natural obstacles would have been very great. As it happened, very little rain fell between 1st January and 21st March; the marshes dried up; the water channel narrowed and became shallow and fordable; and thus the river line had little defensive value.

Between the 7th and 9th February the 58th Division relieved the 30th on the extreme right of the British line, in the sector extending from just north of Travecy, where it joined the 18th Division on the left, to the point of junction with the French, south of Barisis, on the right. This front of nearly nine miles and a half was held by two brigades in line, the boundary between them being the natural one of the Oise marshes and the St. Quentin Canal, which runs north-west from Chauny to Beautor, close to La Fère, before turning almost due north between the opposing lines. For the defence of so wide a front, even allowing for an assumed inactive sector of about a mile and a half covered by the marsh area about La Fère, by so weak a force of infantry, a continuous line of trenches was out of the question, and the only alternative that offered was a defensive system in depth. Accordingly the position was organized in three deep zones, each of which was designed to play a distinct part in the general defensive scheme. First came a Forward or Outpost Zone, consisting of fortified platoon posts, within company localities, with skilfully disposed machine guns covering the other-

---

[1] The total man-power of the three cavalry divisions was the equivalent of one infantry division.

wise undefended interval between the posts; then fifteen hundred yards behind came the Battle Zone, or main line of resistance, also consisting of fortified posts, co-ordinated with a defensive framework of machine guns; and finally a Rear Zone consisting of a continuous trench system. As the dispositions of the troops holding the Forward and Battle Zones are important to a proper appreciation of subsequent events, they will now be described in some detail. Each zone, as indicated above, was divided into a number of localities, held by one company and comprising a main keep and a number of smaller redoubts, the intervening space being covered by the guns of the Brigade Machine-Gun Company.

In the Forward Zone, the line of the St. Quentin Canal was held by three companies, with the fourth in support to the right flank. The right forward company held the Japy Locality, extending from the road junction opposite the bridge, carrying the main road into La Fère, southward to the banks of the canal, which, as has been indicated above, turned sharply, after passing Beautor, to the north past St. Firmin, a suburb of La Fère. The centre company held the Brickstack Locality, covering the area between the right company and Travecy, a little village on the west bank of the canal. The left company was disposed in and around Travecy in a very isolated position. The support company, together with Battalion Headquarters, was situated partly to the north and partly to the south of the main Chauny-La Fère road, with headquarters in a large quarry immediately to the right of the road, the whole forming the locality known as the Main Keep.

The frontage in all was close upon five thousand yards; and it stands to reason that a force of barely six hundred men cannot adequately protect such a wide expanse of ground. Although Lewis guns and men were sited to the best tactical advantage, few of the small posts that formed the defence were supported by fire from others, and the only posts that could fire directly on the main obstacle—the St. Quentin Canal—were the Railway Post, to the south of the Main Keep, and two others of less importance.

The canal was an important feature of the position. In conjunction with the Oise marshes on the right flank, it alone could justify the policy of spreading a battalion over a frontage of nearly five thousand yards; for the enemy, to attack, must have recourse to rafts or other forms of bridging to effect the passage of his troops. But, as Lieut.-Col. Richardson observes, 'the obstacle of the canal was more apparent than real, as it was not under sufficient fire to prevent bridging.' As for the marsh area, the unusually dry weather had robbed it of its usefulness as a means of defence, and British patrols reported it to be passable by a determined enemy.

In the Battle Zone, Fargniers was defended by one company and a half, disposed in two localities, called Fargniers South (one company) and Fargniers North (two platoons), the line of the Crozat Canal was covered by two more localities, each held by a company, the one (Farm Rouge Locality) being in front of Quessy, and the other (Triangle Locality) on the left flank of the Division about the Travecy-Quessy road. The right flank of the Battle Zone was refused along the Oise and was strengthened by one platoon at the junction of the St. Quentin and Oise Canals and one platoon at Condren. From a glance at the map, the importance of the right flank is at once obvious; here lay the road to Noyon, Compiègne and beyond, and any German attack on the La Fère front would undoubtedly strike in this direction, with the object of widening the breach and severing the British from the French. As will be seen from the foregoing dispositions, the weight of the defence, such as it was, had accordingly been concentrated on the right in order to cover this vitally important flank, now laid open by the rapidly drying marshes.

Early in February the 173rd Brigade moved forward to take over the left brigade sector of the divisional front. The 2/2nd Londons, entraining at Villers Bretonneux on 7th February, reached Appilly the same day, and marched thence to billets for the night in the neighbouring villages of Marest and Dampcourt. On the next day the Battalion continued its forward move, and relieved the 17th King's Regiment in the Battle Zone about Fargniers.

The Battalion was now in a most beautiful part of France. The countryside showed little of the devastations of war; and the villages and woods were largely intact. To the south-east was visible the black mass of the beautiful and densely wooded heights of St. Gobain; and to the front, in a hollow, partly hidden by trees, lay the old fortress of La Fère, with its ancient ramparts and moat. To the north, the ground was open and undulating, and dotted with thickets and woods, some of which, like Frières Wood, were of considerable extent. The quiet and beauty of the countryside formed a marked contrast to the shell-torn swamps of Ypres, and made a great impression on the minds of the men.

Following the Battalion's arrival in this area, there came five weeks idyllically quiet, in the course of which the 2/2nd Londons shared with the other two battalions of the Brigade the task of garrisoning the Battle Zone at Fargniers and the Forward Zone to the east of it. The quietness of the sector was in a great measure to be accounted for by the distance apart of the opposing lines, in places as much as 1,000 yards. The artillery on both sides, of course, had their periods of activity when selected targets were systematically shelled, and herein the enemy had the advantage, because the St. Gobain heights gave him a wide field of observation over the lines and roads of the British position.

These five weeks were spent in an endeavour to make the position as secure as was humanly possible; and with this end in view every man who could be spared was employed, infantry, engineers, and labour battalions alike. That it was necessary for the infantry whose time could have been more profitably spent in practising counter-attacks and the tactics of defence generally to be employed on this work was a great pity; but, faced with such a situation as they found here, the Higher Command had no alternative but to use every available man for making the area as tenable as possible. When this sector of the line was taken over from the French in the early part of the year, very little of the defensive organization above described actually existed. Behind the Outpost Zone practically nothing had been done; the redoubts of the Battle Zone had to be constructed and wired; machine guns had to be sited, and emplacements made; and the trenches of the Rear Zone, which had so far only been marked out, had to be dug. Each day's labour was largely a labour against time; and the men, impressed by the serious need, responded splendidly to the calls made upon them, and, with the knowledge that their safety and that of the whole Army might well depend on the successful result of their labours, worked untiringly to make the position secure.

A fortnight at Fargniers ended on 22nd February with the relief of the 3rd Londons in the Forward Zone. Headquarters, 'B' Company (Capt. Ruber), 'C' Company (Capt. Houghton), and 'D' Company (Capt. Howie) occupied the St. Firmin area, and 'A' Company (Capt. Harper) was detached to hold the Travecy Locality. In the course of this tour of duty a patrol from 'B' Company was ambushed by the enemy, who had crossed the canal close to the St. Firmin bridgehead; Sergt. Roberts and one man were taken prisoners, and a second private was killed in the course of the raid.

The bearing of this incident on subsequent events is contained in the natural desire of the enemy to discover as much as he could concerning the troops immediately facing him. The knowledge that he already had, as revealed to Sergt. Roberts, was positively uncanny in its accuracy. This non-commissioned officer tells how the German officers who interrogated him in La Fère following his capture gave him the name of the commanding officers and other senior officers in the 173rd Brigade, and were only wrong in that they named Br.-General Freyberg as Brigadier, whereas he had left the Brigade when wounded in the fighting of the previous autumn in Belgium. On the point of the completeness of the enemy's knowledge of our positions Lieut.-Col. Richardson also records: 'Maps captured during the fighting in the Main Keep showed that the enemy had got exact knowledge of our dispositions, posts and H.Q.s being clearly marked.' And he adds: 'In the light of events, it would have been better to alter the dispositions on the night of the 20th/21st March as soon as it was certain that an attack would take place.'

On the night of the 5th/6th March the 3rd Londons again assumed command of the Forward Zone, and the 2/2nd Londons, less 'A' and 'B' Companies billeted in Tergniers, moved back to Viry Noureuil (immediately south-west of the former village). The Battalion was now in brigade reserve, supplying working parties in the Battle and Forward Zones.

Officer reinforcements during February and early in March were:

Capt. L. Beck, 2nd Lieuts. R. F. Spencer (12th Londons), S. W. B. Clapham, P. M. With, and L. W. Dixon.

The combatant strength of the Battalion was at this time 22 officers and 585 other ranks.

On the night of the 15th/16th March the 2/2nd Londons relieved the 3rd Londons in the Forward Zone for the last time. For this, the fateful tour of duty, the companies were disposed as follows:

'A' Company (Capt. Harper)—Travecy Locality.
'B' Company (Capt. Bindon)—Brickstack Locality.
'C' Company (Capt. Houghton)—Main Keep.
'D' Company (Capt. Howie)—Japy Locality.

Lieut.-Col. Richardson, with Battalion Headquarters, was as usual in the Main Keep. Of the other units of the Brigade, the 2/4th Londons held the Battle Zone, which they had occupied continuously from the beginning of the month, and the 3rd Londons were in brigade reserve at Viry Noureuil. Brigade Headquarters were established at Quessy Château, near the Crozat Canal.

The Germans conducted their preparations for the great offensive with their usual thoroughness and skill, and the greatest secrecy was preserved throughout. The divisions selected for the attack had been gradually withdrawn from the line over a wide area, and had been concentrated at a considerable distance behind the battle-front; and so skilfully was this withdrawal and concentration effected that they had attracted no special attention. After a systematic course of training, in which nothing was left to chance, this enormous force began to move forward about the middle of March, and, marching by night and remaining closely concealed by day, was in position by the 20th March. The enemy now had an overwhelming concentration of troops opposed to the devoted Fifth Army. On the front of the right Corps alone, the XVIII. and III., consisting of 9 weak divisions, there were 21 divisions of von Hutier's Eighteenth German Army and 6 divisions of the Second German Army.

Throughout these long weeks the British were kept in anxious suspense. That the Germans would shortly attack no one could doubt; when and where no one could tell. For the forward troops especially this was a time of tension and anxiety. An ominous quietness brooded over the front; the hushed atmosphere was charged with foreboding; yet day succeeded day, and nothing happened. The waiting and uncertainty began to prey on men's nerves. And then, in the afternoon of the 20th March, there came the long-expected warning—long-expected, yet, when it came, startling in its suddenness: 'Prepare for attack.'

II. THE TWENTY-FIRST OF MARCH

The evening of the 20th of March was strangely still and peaceful; few of war's usual discordant sounds disturbed the last quiet hours of the departing day. The whole countryside was instinct with the sweetness and vigour of approaching spring; woodland scents filled the keen, crisp air; a gentle breeze played among the yet leafless branches of the trees; and, away from the line, only the Very lights, waxing and waning noiselessly above the tree-tops, served to dispel the illusion, bred of the enshrouding darkness, that peace had returned to this beautiful land. Yet over all there was a presage of impending disaster.

On the front of the 58th Division, all remained quiet, save for the *staccato* crack of a rifle, or the stutter of a machine gun, that at intervals awoke the echoes of the night; and, although the canal patrols of the 2/2nd Londons were trebled, they found nothing unusual to report. But northward in the direction of St. Quentin heavy firing broke out during the evening—the accompaniment of a raid by troops of the 18th Division.

The raid was successful; the enemy's trenches were entered; and before midnight the important warning that in a few hours the German attack would be launched was passed along the British line.

When the growl of this gun-fire had died away, a deathly hush settled over the countryside, and scarcely a sound broke the eerie stillness of the night. As the hours slowly lengthened towards day, a thick ground mist began to arise, wreathing both British and German positions in its clammy folds; and gradually friend and foe alike faded from the defenders' sight. The sense of loneliness and isolation was acute; few who passed the early hours of the 21st March on duty in either the Forward or Battle Zones will ever forget that tense and nerve-racking experience.

At 4.50 the German guns rent the air, and shattered the stillness of the dawn. The long-threatened attack had come at last. The bombardment was stupendous; great columns of flying earth shot skyward as the shells burst in sheets of orange flame; the ground shook with the continuous explosions; the noise rose in volume until it became deafening, and the opening of the British guns in reply passed almost unnoticed. One hundred guns were brought to bear on each one thousand yards of the Fifth Army's front, and the effect of their carefully controlled fire was instantaneous and overwhelming. To this tremendous concentration of artillery were added innumerable trench mortars, which, placed well forward, brought their fire to bear on the British positions in the Forward Zone. In the area of Travecy, on the 2/2nd Londons' left flank, the enemy sent over a large number of gas shells, which caused many casualties, and added to the troubles of the garrison of that locality.

The bombardment lasted until 7 p.m., and under the cover it afforded the enemy crossed the canal at many places by means of floating bridges, and at St. Firmin by long planks thrown over the broken arch of the road bridge. The enemy employed his tactics of 'infiltration,' which he had adopted so successfully in his counter-attack at Cambrai in the previous November, and in the execution of his plan he was at this stage much helped by the mist. The British defence, with its wide gaps between the fortified posts, depended on good observation for the machine guns, and, in a lesser degree, for the artillery; with this observation denied to the defenders, the enemy was able to penetrate the gaps in the line and to establish his machine guns and trench mortars on either flank and in rear of the posts.

One by one the posts in the Japy and Brickstack localities passed into the enemy's hands. All communication was cut at an early hour; and each garrison was left to fight its fight against odds entirely unsupported. It is established beyond any question that the defences of all posts in this area, save Railway Post alone, were destroyed by the fierce preliminary bombardment, and that those garrisons, who had no shelter to go to, were either wiped out to a man or rendered quite incapable of serious resistance. Their trenches blown in, the wire in front torn and twisted into uselessness, their leaders and comrades killed or wounded, the few survivors, blinded by the mist, stunned by the tremendous explosions, were suddenly confronted by lines of grey-clad figures, as the creeping barrage lifted from their post, and after a varying degree of resistance were overwhelmed. On the other hand, the garrisons of such posts as were furnished with dug-outs found themselves in an unhappy dilemma: if they manned their trenches they would certainly be annihilated by the heavy and accurate shell fire; if they took shelter in the dug-outs, they would run the risk of being caught like rats in a trap by the waves of the enemy's infantry. Of the posts whose garrisons, either by luck or by taking cover, escaped annihilation some were immediately captured by the enemy, others managed to put up a spirited fight. Of the latter, the shining examples were the Railway Post, mentioned above, and the Brickstack Keep. Railway Post, south of the Main Keep, covered one of the canal crossings, and, under the command of L/Corpl. Errington, engaged the enemy for over two hours, until every man of its garrison was wounded. The Brickstack Keep, which was under the command of Capt. Bindon in person, put up an equally splendid defence, and held out until 2 o'clock in the afternoon, causing considerable loss and confusion in the ranks of the enemy.

Of 'D' Company's fate we can learn something from Capt. Howie's diary, which throws a vivid light on the events in Japy Keep. The garrison of this keep had taken refuge from the preliminary bombardment in the solitary dug-out; no one can impugn Capt. Howie's gallantry, and the decision to keep his men under cover during the bombardment was undoubtedly reached after carefully weighing up all the circumstances. As it happened, his decision did not serve to save the keep; the enemy's troops, closely following their barrage, were too quick for him, and rushed in before any but a few of his men could man the defences. A handful of the defenders, under Capt. Howie himself, erupted from the dug-out in time to see a large party of the enemy in a quarry in front of the post. Before fire could be brought to bear, the enemy rushed in; Capt. Howie was severely wounded, and his little band overcome. The men in the dug-outs fought to escape; C.S.M. Phillip, S.O.S. in hand, led two attempts; Sergt.

Parkinson led a third; the latter had nearly succeeded in forcing his way out, when he was wounded and thrust violently back. The enemy thus swiftly overcame all resistance and took possession of the keep.

After the fall of the majority of the posts in the Japy and Brickstack localities, the fighting was transferred to the Main Keep, held by 'C' Company. Capt. Houghton had been killed early in the battle, and Capt. Barton was now in command. The last seen of this company was by the Adjutant, Capt. Seers, who, in the course of a graphic narrative, says:

> At 9 a.m. the C.O. sent me to get in touch with 'C' Company (Capt. Barton). Found him and men safe and cheery. No casualties. Boches cutting through their wire, but being shot down as they did so.
>
> Returning to H.Q., encountered several Boche round old Quarry. Missed them with revolver, but, with aid of Mills bombs, got back to B.H.Q. Shortly afterwards went out looking for them again, but could not see any, though I heard their voices. Mist very heavy. Slight enemy rifle fire. Heard them cutting through wire.

Shortly after Capt. Seers's visit, fighting broke out on all sides of the Main Keep, where, overcoming a stubborn resistance, the enemy gained an entrance on the south-eastern, north-eastern, and western boundaries. He was promptly counter-attacked by the garrison. The counter-attack was partially successful; the western edge of the keep was cleared; and a number of prisoners was taken from the 7th Jägers. But the infiltration of the enemy continued; and parties of his troops gradually established themselves in the ruins inside the keep, from which they could not be ejected.

All the while the mist clung. Although it had been disastrous to the defence, it undoubtedly proved to be a hindrance to the attackers, who at this stage could hardly have been fully aware of their position. They had broken through in many places, but merely formed elements of a force fighting in scattered units, few knowing how far their comrades had advanced, all looming out of the mist like grey-clad ghosts. This gives point to the quaintly worded sentence in the War Diary: 'The enemy appeared lost in small parties.'

During the morning Lieut.-Col. Richardson sent back a message asking for counter-attack troops to be sent up to clear the Forward Zone. His request was refused by Divisional Headquarters on the ground that the troops allotted for the defence of the Battle Zone were not to be weakened.

Towards noon, Lieut.-Col. Richardson, realizing that nothing more could be done to save the Forward Zone, ordered the remains of Headquarters' personnel, under the adjutant, to withdraw to Fargniers and to join the 2/4th Londons in the Battle Zone. To carry out this withdrawal, this small party had to fight its way through the girdle of the enemy's forces, and, in so doing, encountered no little resistance. Germans would loom up out of the fog, to be picked off 'or otherwise dealt with,' as Capt. Seers dryly remarks, before the party could proceed. At other moments voices would echo through the fog—German voices. It was all very uncanny.

Shortly after noon the mist began to clear, and the enemy renewed his attack. 'C' Company was at last driven out of the Main Keep; and Lieut.-Col. Richardson, collecting the survivors, took up a position about 500 yards to the west for a final stand. At 2 p.m. fighting in the St. Firmin area came to an end with the capture of the few remaining elements of the Battalion. In consonance with his proved courage and steadfastness, Lieut.-Col. Richardson fought on until he was grievously wounded, and was one of the last 2/2nd Londoners to be taken by the enemy on this ill-fated day. With the exception of Capt. Seers, 2nd Lieuts. Capon, and H. L. Browne, of whom the two last were wounded and evacuated, all Headquarters and company officers in the southern area of the Forward Zone were either killed or captured. In addition to Capt. Houghton, the killed included Lieut. H. P. Bennett (Signalling Officer) and 2nd Lieut. H. M. Cook, the latter by a British shell shortly after capture. The missing, most of whom were wounded, numbered 11, making a total of officer casualties in the St. Firmin sector of 16.

That the Forward Zone should be overrun by the enemy was inevitable and had been foreseen. The 2/2nd Londons, by holding out until midday and after, had undoubtedly fulfilled their part in the general scheme of defence, and had seriously delayed an overwhelming force of the enemy. Great heroism and devotion to duty were required from the men who had to hold the small posts of which the defence consisted, in many cases beyond the eyes and ears of their nearest comrades, and completely cut off from all communication with the rear at an early stage of the battle. It was by the astute practice of delaying actions such as this along the whole of the enemy's front that he was prevented from the full realization of his designs. Gough's woeful lack of numbers was in great measure counterbalanced by the extraordinary heroism and doggedness of the men whom he commanded; and the Empire should be proud of the glorious deeds that lie to the credit of the Fifth Army.

The 2nd London Regiment in the Great War

The story of 'A' Company of the 2/2nd Londons has been left to the last. The epic of its defence of isolated Travecy against overwhelming odds is now a matter of history, and has been told again and again in the many narratives of the battle. In one and all, it is used as an historic example of the heroism and endurance of the British regimental officer and man; and the measure of its fame may be gathered from the fact that it is told by Mr. Winston Churchill in what is, perhaps, the greatest of all contributions to the literature of the war, *The World Crisis.*

At least eight determined assaults beaten off with heavy losses to the enemy, a German aeroplane disabled by Lewis-gun fire, German staff officers rendered casualties, German transport, artillery, and working parties on the roads behind their front line, continually under effective fire, a three-hour opening bombardment of high explosive and gas shells withstood, 18,000 rounds of small arms' ammunition, 400 Mills grenades, and 200 trench-mortar shells expended—such are the bare facts of 'A' Company's gallant stand. But the most serious loss to the enemy was that of time. It was not until 1 a.m. on 23rd March, when every round of ammunition was exhausted, when the garrison, reduced to a mere handful, was completely cut off from the rest of the British forces, when 'our further resistance could in no way help our Army'—to use his own words—, that Capt. Harper capitulated.

The last message received by Battalion Headquarters from Capt. Harper before communications were cut between the two headquarters was timed 6.30 a.m., 21st March, and read 'Being heavily gassed.' Meanwhile the thick mist had enveloped Travecy from dusk of the 20th, causing Capt. Harper to double his frontal and flanking patrols. The enemy's bombardment, which in this area did not lift until 8 a.m., severed all means of communication, while the dense and all-encircling mist rendered the use of visual signalling abortive. Thus the company was early debarred from any retaliatory fire from our own artillery. It was now entirely without support. To fire the S.O.S. was so much wasted effort. No S.O.S. would have been seen in that atmosphere fifty yards off.

To neutralize the loss of its right-hand post on the canal bank by the battalion on his left flank, Capt. Harper moved half of his left platoon (2nd Lieut. Roberts) and two sections of his centre platoon (2nd Lieut. Dixon), to cover this flank, simultaneously shifting 2nd Lieut. Gibson's platoon to other and pre-arranged positions for the protection of his right flank. He then moved his headquarters to the keep, which was under the command of 2nd Lieut Clapham.

With the lifting of his barrage, the enemy advanced in mass formation, captured several forward posts, and penetrated 'A' Company's defences to the north and south. Sharp fighting continued on Lieut. Gibson's front until 10 a.m., when the whole of his platoon, except himself and one man, had been killed or wounded. Lieut. Gibson, who had fought with the greatest determination, now fell back to the keep. He reported the enemy to be in possession of the southern and eastern edges of Travecy village, and that vast numbers of the enemy were concentrated in the area of 2nd Lieut. Dixon's platoon on the left.

At 11 a.m. a renewed attack, assisted by aeroplane, developed from the north; and 2nd Lieut. Roberts and his two sections were forced to fall back on the keep. The keep was now under continuous fire by machine gun and rifle grenade.

The enemy was obviously unaware of the advanced position of two sections of Capt. Harper's central platoon; and during the morning several of his parties in close order loomed up out of the mist and were mown down by Lewis-gun fire at twenty yards' range. At noon, as the mist was clearing, a party of about 50 of the enemy was seen digging in behind these two sections, and was promptly driven off by a heavy and accurate fire. Eventually, after doing yeoman service, these advanced sections were overwhelmed by superior numbers, and wiped out. Coincident with the lifting of the mist at noon, the enemy under cover of heavy fire attempted to rush the keep, but was repulsed. As the day wore on, several similar attacks were made, in each case with similar results.

At 5 p.m. Capt. Harper called for volunteers to acquaint Brigade Headquarters with the situation. These (Ptes. Banks and Ancliffe) returned after two hours with the information that Quessy, Fort Liez, and Fort Vendeuil, were in enemy hands. This meant that the enemy had penetrated two miles to the north-west of Travecy and from two to three miles to the west and south-west. With its flanks driven in and with the enemy now in its rear, the stubborn garrison of Travecy was completely surrounded.

Capt. Harper's force now comprised 3 officers—of 2nd. Lieut. Dixon nothing had been heard—and approximately 60 non-commissioned officers and men, including 10 Trench Mortar Battery personnel attached.

Immediately before dusk, at 7.15 p.m., the enemy once more renewed his attacks, advancing on the keep from all sides, and for an hour he strove in vain to enter. In the course of close fighting he suffered terrific losses. Once again was he beaten off and denied the passage that his hordes had made elsewhere. To this attack he summoned the aid of all his available weapons—machine guns, trench mortars, rifle grenades, hand bombs, and rifle fire.

And so the night fell. Under cover of the darkness, continuous efforts were made by the enemy to bomb the garrison out. Private Lax, single-handed, repulsed one dangerous attack of this nature.

Dense mist was again the prevailing feature of dawn of the 22nd. Under its cover the enemy continued his now desperate attacks. He did gain a fleeting footing in the southern edge of the keep, but was driven out by the efforts of C.S.M. Pascal and a handful of men—men who were fast becoming exhausted. Between the furious German attacks, the men would crawl out amidst the ruins of the village and engage with fire the enemy's machine-gun teams and infantry lurking near. Conspicuous in this work were Corpls. Ansell and Shilton, L/Corpl. Long, and Ptes. Smith and Ancliffe.

Midday came, and with it the lifting of the blinding mist. A column of enemy transport on the St. Quentin-La Fère road beyond the canal marshes was engaged by Lewis-gun fire and dispersed. A British aeroplane flew over, acknowledged our signals, and flew back. Later, another aeroplane, bearing British markings, dropped two bombs on Capt. Harper's position. Whether this was actually a German aeroplane and a further example of a trick that the enemy had seen fit to practise on other occasions, it is hard to say. Despite the fact that the earlier air patrol had seen and answered our signals and therefore presumably reported them, few would give thought to the possibility that, twenty-four hours after the beginning of the advance that elsewhere had penetrated to the Battle Zone and beyond, a beleaguered garrison was still holding its own in the Forward Zone, and on its original defensive position. It may well have been, therefore, a British aeroplane bombing what it took to be German troops.

Actual enemy aeroplanes, on the other hand, were extremely active, and continually fired on the company. Excellent retaliatory work was accomplished by Lewis-gun fire, and L/Corpl. Long succeeded in disabling one of these aeroplanes.

The rest of the story cannot be better told than in Capt. Harper's own words :

> Ammunition by this time had been almost exhausted, and after repulsing an attack at dusk, I found that the last box had been used. At 7.30 p.m. on 22nd March, I had a Council of War with my officers and C.S.M.

We summed up the situation as follows:

(i.) Our ammunition was exhausted.

(ii.) We were entirely cut off from the rest of the Army, and there was no prospect of a counter-attack reaching us.

(iii.) The men were so exhausted that they could hardly stand.

(iv.) We were outnumbered by at least fifty to one.

(v.) Our casualties were exposed to the enemy's fire.

(vi.) Our further resistance could in no way help our Army.

In consideration of these points, I decided, when next the enemy attacked, to hand over the position rather than attempt to resist them with the bayonet, which would only have meant the needless sacrifice not only of the garrison, but probably of the casualties also. I consequently gave orders to destroy all maps and plans, the remaining two Lewis guns, and the trench mortars.

The enemy later attacked, and I went out to meet them and capitulated.

During these two days, the enemy suffered extremely heavy casualties to parties other than the attacking force; on both days the Travecy-Achery road across the marshes was being repaired by a battalion who were continually dispersed by our Lewis-gun fire at 1,500 yard range. Enemy transport and artillery, using the St. Quentin-La Fère road, were under our fire, and several groups of staff officers became casualties. The crew of an observation balloon were forced to pass through our fire to and from their balloon.

Apart from Capt. Harper himself, whose heroism, determination, and dauntless and unflagging energy against overwhelming odds, were at once a source of the greatest inspiration to the rest of his officers, non-commissioned officers, and men, others who conspicuously distinguished themselves were 2nd Lieut. P. D. Gibson, C.S.M. Pascall, Corpls. Ansell and Shilton, L/Corpl. Long, and Ptes. Gibson, Ancliffe, Jones, Smith, and Lax.

The capture of all that remained of 'A' Company put the total losses of the battalion since the opening of the offensive at 21 officers and 550 other ranks, out of a trench strength on 20th March of 22 officers and 585 other ranks. Only Capt. Seers and his small party, Major J. A. Miller, Capt. A. Wright, Lieut. J. L. Harvey, 2nd Lieuts. A. H. Streets, A. V. Hyde, and leave personnel, remained as a cadre; and of this cadre none was engaged in the fighting except Capt. Seers, C.S.M. Boag, and the 34 other ranks who accompanied them back to the Battle Zone on the morning of the 21st.

III. THE RETREAT

The capture of all the Forward Zone positions completes the first phase of the attack; and the progress of the fighting in the Battle Zone must now be briefly described in order to preserve the continuity of the story.

Immediately the enemy's bombardment opened on 21st March, the troops of the 2/4th Londons moved forward to take up their positions in the Battle Zone; but owing to the intensity and accuracy of the enemy's artillery fire the various companies were not reported in position until 7.30 a.m. This delay, however, had no serious consequences, the troops being in position long before the enemy reached them.

Owing to the mist nothing could be seen of the progress of events in the Forward Zone; and it was not until a message came in from Lieut.-Col. Richardson at 7.10 a.m. that anything definite was learnt of the German movements. At 9 a.m. a further message was received in the Battle Zone to the effect that the enemy was in possession of the Main Keep Locality. This statement was not true; for, as we have seen, the Main Keep did not fall until nearly three hours later. But, in that it indicated heavy enemy pressure on the vital right flank, the message was correct enough. Prompt action was taken, a company of the battalion in brigade reserve (3rd Londons) being sent up to Fargniers, and artillery and machine-gun barrages put down on the canal crossings at St. Firmin and Beautor.

The lifting of the mist and the fall of the Forward Zone coincided about noon, and shortly afterwards the enemy began his attacks on the Battle Zone. These at first met with little success, except on the extreme right near the canal and in the Farm Rouge Locality, where he succeeded in penetrating the British line. By the judicious employment of another company of the 3rd Londons and some platoons of the 1/4th Suffolks (Pioneer Battalion) his progress was for a time stayed; and in the evening the Battle Zone, except at the two points above mentioned, was still intact. Capt. Seers and his small party of 2/2nd Londoners, who had reached Fargniers shortly after noon, did duty with a company of the 2/4th Londons in this area for the rest of the day.

To the left of the 58th Division, the 18th Division was holding firmly to its Battle Zone; to the left of the 18th, the 14th Division had been dealt a heavy blow and forced to give some miles of ground. By the enemy's successful penetration in this area the whole front of the III. Corps was endangered; and, to prevent the front being broken, as must otherwise inevitably happen, a general withdrawal was ordered. To conform with this movement the 173rd Brigade was ordered to fall back to the line of the Crozat Canal. After a stubborn rear-guard action this withdrawal was effected before nightfall, when the now very mixed force under the command of Lieut.-Col. W. R. H. Dann, of the 2/4th Londons, crossed to the west bank of the canal.

Early on the 22nd March this force, consisting of the remnants of the 2/2nd, 3rd, and 2/4th Londons, the 1/4th Suffolks, and elements of the 503rd Field Company, R.E., and the 182nd Tunnelling Company, who had been hurriedly thrown into the fight, was relieved by the 8th Londons. The relief was complete by 6 a.m.; and Lieut.-Col. Dann's little force marched back to the Butte de Rouy, west of Vouel, where, after a hurried reorganization, it took up a defensive position.

When at last night closed over the battle-field, the situation from the British point of view seemed black enough. It is true that in the north the German right wing had not gained the success anticipated by Ludendorff, and had not seriously penetrated the Battle Zone of the Third Army. But on the other flank, by dint of surprise and the lavish use of gas, the enemy had achieved considerable success against the Fifth Army; and at Essigny, and Ronssy, and, as we have seen, on his extreme left at La Fère, his hordes had penetrated the defence. At La Fère, by employing no less than four divisions, he had overwhelmed two weak battalions deployed over a front of 5,000 yards, and by these tremendous odds had succeeded in capturing both the Forward and Battle Zones, and with them almost all the defensive works existing in the area.

The position at Vouel to which Lieut.-Col. Dann's composite force had fallen back consisted of an unfinished work, in places no more than a foot deep, extending from the twin hills of the Butte de Rouy to the Chauny-Tergniers road. The nucleus of the 2/2nd Londons did not remain long on this line, being ordered to leave Lieut.-Col. Dann's force and to continue their withdrawal to Viry Noureuil. After joining the Battalion's battle surplus and other details at this town, the party moved on to Ognes, three-quarters of a mile west of Chauny, where it spent the night of the 22nd/23rd March.

Although the 2/2nd Londons took no part in the fighting of the 22nd and 23rd, the course of the battle on these two days must be briefly described.

301

During the 22nd March the enemy made further progress. Early in the afternoon he attacked the line of the Crozat Canal, and, aided by a little luck, succeeded in forcing it. Although all the bridges had been prepared for demolition, the charges, in every case, did not explode; and this unfortunate circumstance materially aided the enemy in the actual crossing of the canal. Once over the canal, the enemy extended the gap northward, and by continued pressure forced the 8th Londons, late in the afternoon, to abandon the canal line and to fall back on the Vouel line.

The 23rd March marked an important change in the general situation. On this day Ludendorff made the vital decision to abandon his original plan, and to exploit the unexpected success of his left wing. In the original plan, the 'Michael' offensive was to be followed on 23rd March by the 'Mars' offensive, to be delivered by the German Sixth Army and the right of the Seventeenth against Arras and the Vimy Ridge. The opening of this attack, however, had been anticipated by General Byng, commanding the Third Army, who made a short but effective withdrawal on this front, and unexpectedly placed four miles between his forces and those of the enemy. The British withdrawal and the slow progress of his Seventeenth Army forced Ludendorff to abandon his main strategic intention of pushing the British back to the coast, and, to substitute for it, that of capturing Amiens and of severing the British forces from the French.

On the 23rd March the break of day was again heralded by a heavy mist, which served effectually to cloak the movements of the enemy. To aid the hard-pressed 58th Division in its task of covering the gap on the right of the British line, some French troops had been rushed up during the night of the 22nd/23rd. These arrived in the early hours of the 23rd without guns or administrative equipment, and were at once hurled into the fight. At 8 a.m., without any reconnaissance, two battalions of the 125th French Infantry delivered an attack with the object of retaking the line of the Crozat Canal. Owing to the mist, to ignorance of the ground, and to lack of essential equipment, as mentioned above, the attack was unsuccessful; and the French were forced to fall back to the Vouel line, wherein they caused considerable overcrowding and confusion.

During the morning the 18th Division, on the left of the 58th, was forced back towards Villequier Aumont. Its withdrawal exposed the left flank of the Vouel line; and at noon this line had to be abandoned, the 173rd Brigade falling back to the Green Line, a partly-dug line running east of Noureuil and Viry Noureuil. The continued retirement of the 18th Division opened a gap in the British line in the vicinity of Frières Wood,

302

and into this gap the enemy quickly penetrated, and by the infiltration of his troops round its left flank not only endangered the position of the 173rd Brigade on the Green Line, but threatened to roll it up against the St. Quentin Canal. To guard against such a contingency, a further withdrawal was decided upon; and the Green Line and Viry Noureuil were then abandoned.

The British retirement was now approaching Chauny; and the threat to this town was fast becoming serious. With a view to saving the town, the Brigadier early in the afternoon ordered Major A. Grover (2/4th Londons), who was in the town with the battle surplus of his battalion, to collect and organize what troops he could for its defence, and 'with remarkable skill and despatch,' writes Capt. Grimwade in his history of the 4th London Regiment,[1] 'Major Grover collected a heterogeneous force of clerks, cooks, officers' servants, transport drivers—anyone who could hold a rifle—and by dusk reported himself in position on the eastern outskirts of Chauny with a force of 10 officers and 270 other ranks at his command. This little force included all that was left of the 2/2nd Londons, except Capt. Seers and the transport section, who had gone back to Appilly.

'Saturday, 23rd March,' writes the Chaplain, 'was an exciting day. The road behind Chauny was "chock-a-block" with civilians, British transport and other evidences of war. I met Garraway, our Brigade Staff Captain, and asked him what the orders were. He said, "We go back to Noyon, but the Germans have broken through on our left, and their cavalry will be in Noyon before us." We both agreed it looked as though we were caught, but we crossed the Oise and did not see Noyon.'

Grover's Force took up a position covering the eastern exits of Chauny from the St. Quentin Canal to north of the Chauny-Viry Noureuil road. On its right was the 18th Entrenching Battalion astride the canal, and on its left the 6th Dismounted Cavalry Brigade. To the left again, were details of the 2/4th and 8th Londons. These units now comprised the 173rd Brigade Group, the Headquarters of which had withdrawn to Abbécourt. On the left of the Brigade Group, the 18th and 14th Divisions, and various French units, continued the line to the north.

As on the three preceding days, dawn of the 24th March was accompanied by a thick mist. This mist began to clear at 11 a.m., and at about the same time the enemy, after a heavy bombardment, violently attacked Grover's Force, making a serious attempt to work round its right flank by

---

[1] *The War History of the 4th Battalion, The London Regiment (Royal Fusiliers),* 1914-1919. Capt. F. Clive Grimwade.

the canal. To frustrate the enemy's efforts in this direction, where his success would have serious consequences by endangering the whole Oise line, now of primary importance to the defence, the Brigadier ordered a further withdrawal of the Brigade Group. After maintaining its position for several hours, the Brigade Group began its withdrawal in the afternoon, and fell back, fighting a skilful rear-guard action, to a prepared position about 1,000 yards east of Abbécourt. At 4.30 this position was likewise abandoned; and the Brigade Group crossed the Oise to Manicamp, blowing up behind it all bridges except a few that were to be kept open to the last moment. During this day's fighting the party of the 2/2nd Londoners did useful work, Lieut. Harvey especially distinguishing himself.

With the retirement of the 173rd Brigade Group behind the Oise, the whole of the 58th Division was concentrated south of the river, and was disposed on a front of some thirteen miles, the original front of the 174th Brigade from the river to Barisis accounting for four of these, and the river lines from Quierzy to Servais for the remaining nine. The units of the 173rd Brigade Group were reorganized during the early hours of the 25th March; and a battalion was formed under Lieut.-Col. Dann (2/4th Londons) comprising one company from each of the following units, 2/2nd, 3rd, 2/4th, and 8th Londons.

After this reorganization, the 2/2nd Londons' company, reinforced by some dismounted cavalry and by 114 other ranks from England, took up a position covering the Quierzy bridgeheads, which it held all day. During the day the three remaining bridges at Quierzy were blown up in expectation of the enemy's attack. This attack duly followed at night, but was successfully driven off, no German troops crossing the river.

On the night of the 25th/26th March Lieut.-Col. Dann's battalion was relieved by the 246th French Infantry Regiment, and marched back to Besmé (four miles south-west of Abbécourt), where, on the 27th, a Fusilier Battalion was formed from what remained of the three battalions of the 173rd Brigade. Lieut.-Col. W. R. H. Dann, D.S.O. (2/4th Londons) was placed in command; Major J. A. Miller (2/2nd Londons) became second-in-command; Lieut. F. W. Walker, D.S.O. (2/4th Londons) Adjutant; Capt. L. S. E. Page (2/2nd Londons) Transport Officer; C.S.M. Boag (2/2nd Londons) R.S.M.; and the four companies were organized as follows:

No. 1 Company—117 other ranks, 2/4th Londons, under Capt. S. G. Askam.
No. 2 Company—88 other ranks, 2/4th Londons, under 2nd Lieut. W. Blair.
No. 3 Company—179 other ranks, 2/2nd Londons, under Capt. A. Wright.
No. 4 Company—189 other ranks, 3rd Londons, under 2nd Lieut. Curtis.

In addition to the Fusilier Battalion, the 173rd Brigade included the 12th Londons and the 18th Entrenching Battalion.

The III. Corps was now wholly withdrawn south of the Oise, and in consequence passed under the command of the French, who had large forces in the area.[1]

On the night of the 29th March the 173rd Brigade relieved the 175th in the left (Manicamp) sector of the Division's front, the 12th Londons being on the right, and the Fusilier Battalion on the left, in the neighbourhood of Manicamp village. During the past few days the River Oise had shown a continuous rise and, breaking its low banks, had overflowed the flat meadows that bordered its channel. The ground once more became marshy; and the task of patrolling the Division's front was made one of real difficulty. Yet a most active system of patrols was maintained.

A great quiet had suddenly fallen on the Oise front. The enemy's masses had now passed far to the west, and were pressing on towards Amiens; and up till the time of the Brigade's relief on the night of the 2nd/3rd April no operations beyond a temporary and localized advance by the enemy on another part of the Division's front was carried out by either side. The enemy's artillery and machine guns were inactive; and little was seen of his infantry. It is interesting to note that prisoners captured on the Division's front on 30th March declared that, in one German division at least, much dissatisfaction existed among the troops.

After relief on 3rd April by the 246th French Infantry Regiment, the Battalion marched by way of Blérancourt to Audignicourt, where it passed the night in a vast cave. On the afternoon of the 4th the march was continued, across the River Aisne, to Ambleny, where the Fusilier Battalion was broken up, and the 2/2nd Londons regained their identity. At the same time the 12th Londons left the 173rd Brigade, and were replaced by the 16th Entrenching Battalion.

The 2/2nd Londons moved to Dommiers on the 5th April, and to Longport on the 6th. At Longport they entrained with the remainder of

[1] On the vexed question of putting British troops under French commanders, Mr. Shaw Sparrow, in his story, *The Fifth Army in March,* 1918, comments as follows: 'Perhaps nothing in this battle is more distressing or more controversial than the act of putting British officers and men under French commanders, before the French troops were *à pied d'œuvre,* on a complete war footing, with all necessary equipments, both military and administrative.' And elsewhere: 'Both cavalry and infantry were doing all that was possible under their own officers, and how is anyone to believe that these British officers did not know more about current events and needs, both local and general, than the French officers who arrived in great haste?'

the Division for Longeau, on the south-western outskirts of Amiens, to which area the III. Corps had now been transferred.

The total casualties of the Battalion from the 21st March to the 3rd April were 22 officers and 618 other ranks. Those of the Division for the same period amounted to 2,204.

The officer casualties of the Battalion were as follows:

KILLED: Capt. J. R. Houghton, Lieut. H. P. Bennett, and 2nd Lieut. H. M. Cook.

WOUNDED: 2nd Lieuts. F. C. Capon, H. L. Browne, and E. G. D. Gedge.

MISSING: Lieut-Col. A. R. Richardson, D.S.O.,* Capts. M. L. Harper, M.C.,* L. W. Bindon,* B. J. Barton,* J. P. Howie, M.C.,* 2nd Lieuts. H. E. Boon,* P. D. Gibson,* G. T. Roberts, M.C., L. W. Dixon, S. W. B. Clapham, T. H. Gladstone, W. G. Philpotts, R. J. H. Brown,* V. de F. Gillings,* L. Moutrie, and P. M. With.

Those marked * were also wounded.

Lieut. Harold Percy Bennett was the son of Mr. and Mrs. Bennett, of Streatham, and was born on 8th January 1893. He was educated at King's College, whence he passed into the Civil Service, being given an appointment in the Board of Education. On the outbreak of war he joined the 15th Londons (Civil Service Rifles), with whom he served until gazetted to the 2nd Londons on 24th December 1915. He was recommended for the M.C. for his gallant conduct on the day of his death.

In connexion with the battle, the following honours were subsequently awarded:

Bar to M.C.: Capts. M. L. Harper, and G. C. Seers.
M.C.: Capt. J. R. Houghton, Lieut. J. L. Harvey, and 2nd Lieut. P. D. Gibson.
D.C.M.: R.Q.M.S. C. Wren, C.S.M. H. Boag, L/Corpl. R. Skews.
Second Bar to M.M.: Corpl. E. Cousins.
Bar to M.M.: L/Corpl. F. Fulbrook.
M.M.: Corpl. F. Dowle, L/Corpls. A. Tucker, C. J. Hamilton, Ptes. A. Kemp, C. Rivers, W. E. Clarke, and A. Bryant.

IV. THE ACTION OF VILLERS BRETONNEUX

Circumstances, as we have seen, had induced or compelled Ludendorff to abandon his original strategical intention of forcing the British back against the coast, and, instead, to exploit the tactical success of his left wing and to endeavour to separate the British from the French. The result of this change of plan was to direct the main German thrust towards Amiens

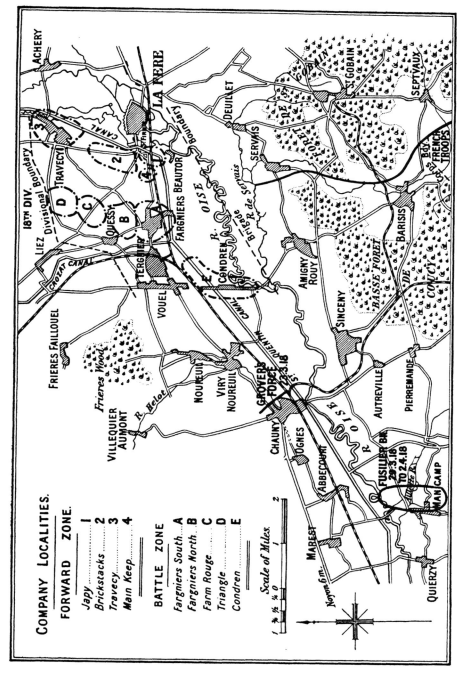

THE FIRST BATTLES OF THE SOMME, 1918—THE BATTLE OF ST. QUENTIN AND THE RETREAT FROM LA FÈRE.

and the lateral railway, so vital to the Allies, of which that city was an important centre.

At first the great offensive met with conspicuous success. In the earlier part of this chapter we have followed the course of the offensive on the extreme left during 21st March and succeeding days, and have seen how rapid was its progress. Further to the north the progress was equally rapid; and the British Fifth Army was forced to retire hurriedly on the whole of its front, across the desolation of the old Somme battle-fields. By the 30th March, the enemy was a bare ten miles from Amiens. But his attack was perceptibly losing its impetus; his troops were becoming exhausted; and the difficulty of keeping them fully supplied in so rapid and deep an advance was beginning to have its inevitable effect. Moreover, the Allied line was daily becoming denser, as more and more troops were thrown into the fight. By 4th April the crisis had definitely passed, and, for the time at least, Amiens was safe.

Ludendorff had failed in his strategic aim. His stupendous offensive had achieved no decisive results. It is certainly true that the German gains were vast as compared with those of any previous offensive on the Western Front, but they were, in the main, illusory.

> No fertile province, no wealthy cities, no river or mountain barrier, no new untapped sources were their reward. Only the crater fields extending abominably wherever the eye could turn, the old trenches, the vast graveyards, the skeletons, the blasted trees, and the pulverized villages—these, from Arras to Montdidier, and from St. Quentin to Villers Bretonneux, were the Dead Sea fruits of the mightiest military conception and the most terrific onslaught which the annals of war records.[1]

The limit of the enemy's advance on Amiens was marked by a line running north-east and south-west across the face of the city. It ran from Albert in the north (now in German hands) across the Ancre marshes, through the outskirts of Villers Bretonneux, to the River Avre and Montdidier. Some indication of the depth of the enemy's advances lies in the statement that the 2/2nd Londons were now to defend the ground whereon had stood their peaceful back-area billets of two months ago. Villers Bretonneux was about ten miles south-east of Amiens, and Fouencamps, in which the Battalion had passed several happy weeks in January,

[1] *The World Crisis*, 1916-1918. Right Hon. Winston S. Churchill, C.H., M.P.

was five miles and a half south-west of Villers Bretonneux. The Battalion was actually fighting over the identical ground on which it had been practising a few weeks earlier.

Detraining at Longeau on 6th April, the 2/2nd Londons marched to Gentelles Wood, midway between Fouencamps and Villers Bretonneux, and on the main Amiens-Noyon road. Immediately after their arrival at Gentelles they were joined by large drafts of men from the 20th Londons and the 1st Devons, and on the next day by nearly 500 of all ranks of the 12th Battalion Middlesex Regiment.[1] This welcome addition brought the Battalion once more up to effective fighting strength; but it should be noted that these reinforcements included many boys under nineteen years of age, who had been sent out to France before their time to make good the heavy losses caused in the British ranks by the enemy's offensive. All that remained of the personnel of the old 2/2nd Londons was grouped together in 'D' Company.

The officers of the 12th Middlesex who joined the 2/2nd Londons were as follows:

> Capts. B. J. Alexander, R. Charlesworth, J. L. Garstin, V. D. Corbett, Lieuts. B. Simpson, S. Fores, 2nd Lieuts. A. H. Chipperfield, F. G. Hayes, J. R. Mundy, W. E. May, M.M., J. H. Clarke, W. H. S. Cheavin, H. Poole, C. W. Tucker, C. L. Prebble, H. Seaward, V. A. Vasey, H. S. Baines, S. Bandy, and T. D. Stringer.

Major R. D. Sutcliffe, D.S.O., of the 3rd Londons, also joined the Battalion, and took over the duties of second-in-command.

Battalion Headquarters and the Company Commanders of the reorganized Battalion were as follows:

> Lieut.-Col. J. A. Miller, in command.
> Major R. D. Sutcliffe, D.S.O., second-in-command.
> Capt. G. C. Seers, M.C., adjutant.
> Capt. L. S. E. Page, Transport Officer.
> 2nd Lieut. C. W. Tucker, Signalling Officer.
> Lieut. E. Miller, Quartermaster.
> Capt. C. C. Austin, Medical Officer.
> Capt. V. C. Corbett, commanding 'A' Company.
> Capt. J. L. Garstin, commanding 'B' Company.
> Capt. R. Charlesworth, commanding 'C' Company.
> 2nd Lieut. A. H. Streets, M.C., commanding 'D' Company.

---

[1] This battalion had more recently been one of the Entrenching Battalions, formed from units left supernumerary to establishment as a result of the reorganization of divisions in January, 1918.

The firſt task of the reconſtructed Battalion on the Villers Bretonneux front was the consolidation of a reserve line eaſt of Gentelles Wood. This work was rapidly pushed forward, but under conditions made difficult by the enemy's conſtant and heavy bombardment. These bombardments were not confined to the forward areas alone, and Amiens itself was at this time being made very unpleasant and unsafe. It was gradually being converted from a fine city and an important military centre into a shell-torn waſte, deserted by all except troops and transport that were compelled to pass through it.

From these conſtant bombardments the 2/2nd Londons suffered many casualties. Capts. Seers and Page were wounded on the 8th April; and Capt. R. Charlesworth was killed on the 10th. The burſt of firing that killed the laſt-named officer also accounted for one of the two V.C.s whom the 12th Middlesex had brought to the Battalion. Capt. B. J. Alexander succeeded Capt. Seers as adjutant, and 2nd Lieut. J. H. Clarke succeeded Capt. Charlesworth in command of 'C' Company.

On the 17th April the 58th Division relieved the 5th Auſtralian Brigade in the sector of the front line eaſt of Cachy. The line taken over by the Division ran from the Villers Bretonneux-Demuin road, through the middle of Hangard Wood, to the outskirts of Hangard, a little village lying close to the marshes of the River Luce, and was held by one brigade (the 173rd). On the day of the relief the 2/2nd Londons were given the same role as that of the Auſtralian battalion they relieved, counter-attack battalion to the brigade, but on the next day were ordered forward to take over the centre position of a three-battalion front. On the Battalion's right were the 3rd Londons, and on the left the 2/4th Londons. To the right of the 3rd Londons was the 41ſt French Division; to the left of the 2/4th Londons the 54th Brigade of the 18th Division. To the left of the 54th Brigade was the Anzac Corps, in occupation of the village of Villers Bretonneux. The 2/2nd Londons were disposed as follows:

> RIGHT: 'A' Company (Capt. Corbett).
> CENTRE: 'B' Company (Capt. Garſtin).
> LEFT: 'D' Company (2nd Lieut. Streets).
> SUPPORT: 'C' Company (2nd Lieut. Clarke).

The laſt-named company was to be used for counter-attack purposes, in the event of the enemy penetrating the front line, and was placed about 700 yards weſt of the front line and midway between it and Battalion Headquarters. The front line in this area had originally consiſted of a line of isolated posts; these were in process of being linked up, but much work yet remained to be done to convert them into a complete system. It should be noted that in Hangard Wood the line ran through the clearing that separated the western and smaller part from the eastern. This clearing was some two or three hundred yards in extent, and the ground here was mainly flat and offered little concealment to advancing troops.

So far as the 2/2nd Londons were concerned, the first few days in the new sector were comparatively uneventful. Capt. Garstin was wounded on the 18th, and was succeeded by Lieut. B. Simpson in the command of 'B' Company.

With the greatest of good fortune, as events were to prove, a German deserter was shot and captured on 'A' Company's front on the evening of the 23rd, and, before he died, he gave Battalion Headquarters the fullest details regarding an attack planned to take place at dawn next day. The barrage, he said, was due to open at 3.40 a.m., and the infantry to advance exactly three hours later; the objective was the Cachy Switch Line; and the advance was to be driven to a depth of three kilometres. This was good luck indeed. There was ample time to warn all companies and other units; and everyone was thus put on the alert and fully prepared for any emergency.

The importance to the enemy of capturing the Villers Bretonneux position cannot be overstated. From Hill 104, to the north of the village, the ground falls in a long sweep towards the city of Amiens, and in the distance the grey mass of the Cathedral, with its slender tapering spire, is clearly visible. If the enemy could gain this vantage point, as well as the high ground about Cachy, to the south of the village, he could by means of his artillery, dominate the city, and the vital railway system of which it is the centre.

As had been the case a month earlier the enemy's attack was favoured by the weather. Once again the break of day was accompanied by a thick mist that limited observation to less than two hundred yards and added greatly to the troubles of the defenders. On the front of the 173rd Brigade, the enemy's barrage opened shortly before 4 a.m. Heavy and accurate, and including a large proportion of gas shells, it inflicted serious losses on the defenders.

From the various accounts of the battle, it appears that the enemy's attack developed at different times on different parts of the front. At Hangard Wood it was about 6 a.m. when his troops loomed like grey ghosts out of the mist and attacked the 2/2nd Londons. The S.O.S. was fired, but was effectively blotted out by the mist, and no acknowledgment was made by the British artillery in the shape of retaliatory fire. All wires had been cut long before; so a message calling for immediate artillery support was hurriedly sent back by runner. When at last the British guns opened, their range was very short, and, far from being any help to the front-line troops, they were a source of acute discomfort.

The three companies of the 2/2nd Londons holding the front line successfully beat off the enemy's first attack. 'D' Company, by well-directed rifle and Lewis-gun fire, mowed down the German masses as they assembled in front of their own wire, and continued to inflict heavy casualties on them as they advanced. In the centre and on the right, the fire of 'B' and 'A' Companies was equally effective. Everywhere the Battalion's front was maintained intact, and the enemy drew off his shattered forces to reform them for a second attempt.

Unfortunately, on the left matters had not gone so well for the British. On this flank, the enemy's attack against the 2/4th Londons was preceded by a number of his huge unwieldy tanks, and these, although not very skilfully handled, succeeded in surprising the defence. As the History of the 4th Londons records,[1] 'the sudden appearance of these monsters shook our defence for a moment, and the men fell back a short distance.' Having thus succeeded in piercing the British line, the German tanks, some six in number, turned south in rear of the 2/2nd Londons' left company ('D') and narrowly missing this company's posts began to work rapidly to the right of the British line. But retribution was fast approaching. Three heavy British tanks came hurrying up out of the mist and, catching three of the German tanks in the open, engaged and routed them in what is the first recorded tank duel of the war. Shortly after this episode, seven British whippet tanks attacked obliquely from between l'Abbé Wood and Cachy and, catching the enemy's infantry in massed formation, did great execution to his serried ranks. The partial retirement of the 2/4th Londons uncovered the flank of the 2/2nd Londons; and into the gap that rapidly appeared between the two battalions the enemy at once flung his infantry. Although suffering heavy casualties from the small-arms' fire, the Germans pressed on to the British support line north-west of Hangard Wood.

Owing to the bad visibility, none of these events could be seen at the 2/2nd Londons' Headquarters; and it was not until runners arrived that it was learned that the Battalion's line was still intact, that a serious shortage

[1] *The War History of the 4th Battalion The London Regiment (Royal Fusiliers), 1914-1919.* Capt. F. Clive Grimwade.

311

of ammunition had manifested itself, and that the point of danger was the left flank, where, as we have seen, the enemy had broken through. On receipt of this information at about 7 a.m., Lieut.-Col. Miller ordered 'C' Company, carrying as much ammunition as possible, to reinforce the left and centre of the line, and at the same time forwarded a report of the situation to Brigade Headquarters.

The enemy's infiltration continued; and at 7.30 his troops were not only well beyond the Battalion's left flank, but also 300 yards in the Battalion's rear. 'D' Company was truly in perilous plight, and, although it had beaten off every frontal attack, now found itself almost surrounded. The measure of the danger that so suddenly threatened can be gauged by the fact that 2nd Lieut. Streets, carried wounded on a stretcher by men of his own company, was captured on his way to Battalion Head-quarters.

An hour passed. As yet no connexion had been established with the 2/4th Londons on the left; and at 8.30 Lieut.-Col. Miller, fully alive to the peril that threatened his battalion from the unfilled gap, directed 'C' Company to form a defensive flank to protect the left and rear of 'D' Company. The situation on the front of the other two companies remained the same; and he was able to report to Brigade Headquarters: 'Three companies are intact in front system. They have been hard pressed, but so far have killed many Boche.' At this critical juncture, a company of 2/10th Londons, sent forward by the Brigadier as soon as he learned the dangerous nature of the threat to the left flank, arrived, and with 'C' Company succeeded in form-ing a defensive flank. Connexion was speedily established with the 2/4th Londons, the remnants of whom, under Capt. Morton, the senior officer left, had rallied, and were occupying a line of shell-holes in the neighbour-hood of the Cachy Switch.

On the front of the 2/2nd Londons, the enemy had employed his tactics of infiltration with considerable success, and had surrounded several of the smaller posts and killed or captured their garrisons. Notwithstanding the enemy's penetration, the three companies of the front line had hitherto successfully maintained their positions against every attack. But now a new and serious danger threatened. By his capture of the ground north and north-east of Hangard Wood, the enemy had gained an excellent vantage point from which to observe and enfilade the 2/2nd Londons' original front line; and, as soon as the mist began to clear, a brisk rifle and machine-gun fire was opened from this direction. For a time the situation remained un-changed; but so hot grew the fire that the 2/2nd Londons could no longer maintain themselves in this exposed position. At 9 a.m., therefore, the remnants of 'A,' 'B,' and 'D' Companies began slowly to fall back, and at 9.30 were established on the line of the Hangard road.

Although his battalion had thus been forced to withdraw, Lieut.-Col. Miller did not despair of recovering his old line, and, in sending a message of praise and encouragement to Capt. Corbett, who was now virtually in control of all that was left of these three companies, he urged him to try to regain the lost ground. Capt. Corbett, however, found the task beyond the power of his small and exhausted force, and was obliged to content himself with making his new position secure.

During the morning the British line was gradually stabilized. It now ran from the Cachy Switch, immediately to the east of Cachy village, along the Hangard road, to the 3rd Londons' position about Hangard village. On this part of the front the Germans seemed content with the capture of Hangard Wood, and made no further move. To the north, they had succeeded in capturing Villers Bretonneux; and it is somewhat of a mystery why they wasted their efforts on its gas-filled ruins instead of capturing the vital high ground on its flanks.

At 11.30 a.m. 'A' Company, together with troops of the 2/10th Londons, led by their commanding officer (Lieut.-Col. Symons) in person, made a spirited attempt to regain a footing in Hangard Wood. Some progress was made at first; the enemy began to give ground; and then at the critical moment, Lieut.-Col. Symons fell mortally wounded, and the counter-attack lost its impetus. The enemy rapidly recovered, seized his opportunity, and repelled the attackers with heavy loss.

The day wore on; and throughout a relatively quiet afternoon and evening the situation remained unchanged. Although they had suffered heavy losses and could now muster barely 150 effectives, the 2/2nd Londons were firmly established on their new line. Their flank was in touch with the company of the 2/10th Londons, and their right rested on the support line of the 3rd Londons.

Late in the afternoon the enemy's troops were observed to be massing in Hangard Wood, and a number of his tanks was seen in the vicinity. Capt. Corbett, in calling for artillery fire on this concentration, described the enemy's presence 'in hundreds.' Nothing came of this threat; the troops were dispersed by artillery fire; and the tanks disappeared from view. In the evening the enemy vigorously bombarded the new British line, but again made no attempt to attack.

In view of the importance of the Villers Bretonneux position in the scheme for the defence of Amiens, General Rawlinson, commanding the Fourth Army, insisted on a counter-attack on the whole of the front the same night. This counter-attack was delivered at 10 o'clock by the 9th Londons, the 54th Brigade (attached to the 58th Division for the purpose), and the Australians, on either side of Villers Bretonneux, with the object of pinching out the village and re-establishing the line beyond it by the junction of the wings of the attacking force.

The task of the 9th Londons was the recapture of Hangard Wood and the restoration of the original line in that area. The remnants of the 2/2nd Londons were attached to the 9th Londons for the attack; 'A,' 'B,' and 'D' Companies, now under Lieut. Simpson, were to follow the second wave on the right flank, to fill any gaps between the 9th and 3rd Londons on the line of the objective, 'C' Company (2nd Lieut. Clarke) was to act as liaison behind the left flank. In support to the 9th Londons were the 2/10th Londons.

The counter-attack was successful beyond all expectations. Villers Bretonneux was regained, and a large number of prisoners captured. On the front of the 58th Division, the counter-attack troops won their way through Hangard Wood, and finally re-established the line about halfway between the Cachy Switch and the original position.

Thus ended a day of bitter strife, with the advantage first to the enemy, and at the end to the British. The part played by the 58th Division at Hangard Wood cannot be too highly extolled. Once again had the men of London stood, and stood well, between the enemy and his objective. Had the enemy succeeded in capturing the Cachy Line, he would have been in possession of the southern ridge of high ground commanding the approaches to Amiens, and an important step towards the fulfilment of his main object would have been gained. That the 58th Division gave so little ground is really remarkable, and an interesting comment on the fact is furnished by General Rawlinson himself in his diary[1]:

> The 8th and 58th Divisions have been fighting more or less continuously since March 21st, and the reinforcements which they have received are mainly composed of young boys who were under fire for the first time. I fear that the heavy bombardment which the Germans put on before the attack must have shaken these children a good deal, hence the success of their second effort.

[1] *Life of Lord Rawlinson.* Major-Gen. Sir F. Maurice.

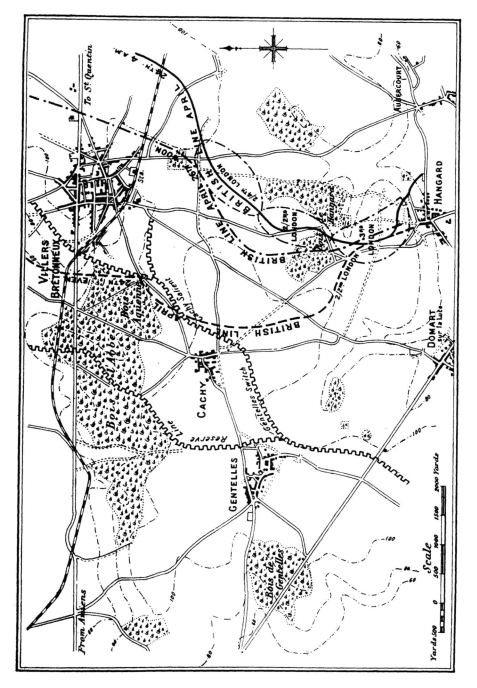

THE ACTION OF VILLERS BRETONNEUX.

In this action the losses of the 2/2nd Londons were very heavy. 'D' Company, for all practical purposes, was wiped out, its personnel captured or slain, and with it disappeared the majority of the personnel of the old battalion who had survived the 21st March and the retreat. Practically no fighting personnel of the original 2/2nd Londons now remained save the transport section and sundry Headquarters' details.

The Battalion's casualties were as follows:

KILLED: 1 officer (2nd Lieut. A. H. Chipperfield) and 29 other ranks.

WOUNDED: 3 officers (Lieut. B. Simpson, 2nd Lieuts. W. E. B. Ryder and J. H. Clarke), and 127 other ranks.

MISSING: 8 officers (2nd Lieuts. A. H. Streets, M.C.,* W. E. May, M.M.,* F. G. Hayes, J. R. Mundy,* N. Gardiner,* H. G. Mitchener,* J. A. Scholfield, and P. R. Taylor) and 301 other ranks.

Those marked * were also wounded.

The following honours were awarded in connexion with this action:

D.S.O.: Lieut.-Col. J. A. Miller.
M.C.: Capt. V. D. Corbett.

The Battalion remained in the line during the 25th April, but was not engaged. The enemy's artillery put down a heavy barrage at 7 p.m.; and the S.O.S. was fired by units on either flank. The British artillery replied; and an artillery duel, which lasted for some hours, followed. The Battalion was relieved the same night by the 2/8th Londons (174th Brigade), and moved back to a camp near Boves.

During the 26th the counter-attack was continued by the French Moroccan Division, which had relieved the 58th Division. At its conclusion the line prior to the German attack had been restored; and with this last desperate thrust the German attempt to gain Amiens came definitely to an end.

315

CHAPTER XX

THE 1/2ND LONDONS IN THE FIRST BATTLE OF ARRAS, 1918

ON the 21st March, the opening day of the great German offensive, no attack developed upon the front of the 56th Division in Artois. The day was marked by an increase in the activity of the enemy's artillery; the Bailleul-Willerval Line was subjected to a gas bombardment; Arras was heavily shelled, and all civilians were evacuated. At the same time the enemy's aircraft became increasingly active, and his low-flying aeroplanes were constantly over the British lines.

On this day the 1/2nd Londons were holding the line in the Gavrelle Sector, and took every precaution against an immediate attack; but, so far as they were concerned, the day passed uneventfully enough.

The disposal of the troops to the best advantage for the defence of this area had long been an anxious and seemingly insoluble problem for Corps Headquarters. The method of holding the line had been changed on more than one occasion, and now came orders for yet another change. This was effected on the night of the 21st/22nd March, and resulted in each division holding its sector with two brigades in the line and one in support. In the 56th Division, the 167th Brigade was consequently withdrawn; and the Division's front divided between the 168th and 169th Brigades.

The next four days passed uneventfully, save for a clear indication of the enemy's intentions, given on the 23rd March, when he exploded a land-mine under the wire of Towy Post. There was indeed an accumulation of evidence that the enemy's offensive, now apparently making good progress on the front of the British Fifth Army in the south, would be extended by an attack on Arras. As we have seen, this extension of the area of active operations had been delayed by the strategic withdrawal of a part of the Third Army holding the front south of the Scarpe; but the enemy had followed up the retiring British troops, and was even now pressing them hard in the area south of Arras. A further extension of the battle-front with the object of enveloping Arras from the north of the Scarpe by the capture of the Vimy Ridge could be logically anticipated. In view of the certainty of an early attack by the enemy on this front, the relief of the 56th Division by the 62nd was cancelled; and subsequent orders for its relief by the 2nd Canadian Division were likewise cancelled.

Meanwhile, on the 25th March, the 1/2nd Londons were relieved in the front line by the Q.W.R., and the growing activity of the enemy was then demonstrated in a dramatic manner; for when the relieving party of the Q.W.R. reached Gavrelle Post after dark, it found that the 1/2nd Londons' garrison had disappeared. This little post, consisting merely of a dug-out and a short length of trench, blocked at each end with wire, was maintained for the purpose of giving warning of any attempt by the enemy to enter the undefended locality between the larger posts. Owing to the presence of ruins on one side and hedges on the other, the post was difficult to defend against a raid, and during the hours of daylight the garrison was completely isolated. On the present occasion the garrison consisted of 15 men, under Sergt. J. Carr, who had relieved 2nd Lieut. Shadbolt at 8 p.m. on the evening of the 24th. During the night the post was visited three times, and on the last occasion, at 4 a.m., everything was found to be in order.

On entering the empty post, the Q.W.R. found on every side abundant evidence of a struggle. The dug-out was immediately searched, and two bodies were found; both had been bayoneted. This left no doubt that the post had been successfully rushed by the enemy, and that the garrison had not been overcome without a fight. In view of the fact that no warning had been given, it was more than likely that a large body of the enemy had penetrated into Gavrelle village behind the post. With as little delay as possible, therefore, a cordon was formed round the village, and patrols sent to search the ruins; but the area was found to be quite clear of the enemy.

The 1/2nd Londons moved back to Roundhay Camp, and during the afternoon of the 26th received orders that, in response to an urgent appeal from the Corps for identification, they were to carry out a raid the same night on Chaff Trench, simultaneously with raids by the L.R.B. and the Q.W.R. on adjacent parts of the enemy's line.

After three practices during the afternoon, the raiding party, consisting of a platoon (Lieut. Sloan), assembled at Gavrelle Cemetery, and at 10.45 p.m. took up a position about 200 yards in front of the line, ready to advance as soon as the Royal Engineer personnel, attached for the purpose, had fired a Bangalore torpedo into the enemy's wire. Unfortunately, there was a bright moon, and, despite blackened faces and bayonets, the party was discovered; bombs were thrown, and rifle fire was opened by the enemy. Heavy machine-gun fire prevented the firing of the torpedo; and, as the preliminary artillery bombardment had not succeeded in cutting the enemy's wire, Lieut.

Sloan, after trying vainly for an hour to get through, was obliged to withdraw his party. The withdrawal was successfully effected, all material, including the torpedo, being brought back; and no casualties resulted. The enemy fired a large number of rockets; and the raiders were able to discover by this means that his trenches were crowded with men.

On the night of the 27th the 56th Division was ordered to extend its left flank and to take over 1,500 yards of front hitherto held by the 3rd Canadian Division. This entailed an extension of the front of the right (169th) brigade to include Bradford and Bird Posts, and of the left (168th) brigade to include Tommy and Arleux Posts. The Division was also ordered to hold the Bailleul-Willerval (Red) Line as the line of resistance, and the line of posts at Gavrelle as an outpost line. Very shortly after the issue of this order, the second part was cancelled; and the Division was ordered to hold the line of posts at all costs, so as to conform to the front of the 4th Division on the right. The reasons for this redistribution have not transpired, but obviously they must have been sufficient and urgent enough to justify the dislocation of the whole defensive scheme on what was known to be the eve of a great attack.

As a result of the redistribution, the dispositions of units of the Division were given as follows:

RIGHT—169TH BRIGADE:
    Front Line System (posts and Naval-Marine Line): Q.W.R. on the right, L.R.B. on the left.
    Bailleul-Willerval (Red) Line: 1/2nd Londons from right boundary of the Division to Bailleul East Post (inclusive).
    Farbus-Vimy (Brown) Line: 1 company 1/5th Cheshires.
    Thélus-Point du Jour (Green) Line: 2 companies 1/1st Londons, attached from 167th Brigade.
LEFT—168TH BRIGADE:
    Front Line System: 1/4th Londons on the right, 1/13th Londons on the left.
    Red Line: 1/14th Londons.
    Brown Line: 2 platoons 1/5th Cheshires.
    Green Line: 2 companies 1/1st Londons; 1½ companies 1/5th Cheshires.
DIVISIONAL RESERVE:
    167th Brigade (less 1/1st Londons); 3 Field Companies, R.E.

The verbal orders for the redistribution were received by the 1/2nd Londons at 4.30 p.m. The Battalion moved off at once and relieved those companies of the Q.W.R., L.R.B., and the Kensingtons that were holding the Red Line in support to the remainder of their battalions. Although the

1/2nd Londons were in position shortly after 11 p.m., on the rest of the Division's front the relief resultant on the redistribution had not been completed by 3 o'clock next day. Indeed, one company of the 1st Canadian Mounted Rifles remained in Sugar Post throughout the battle, and coming under the 168th Brigade fought with the greatest gallantry.

The dispositions of the 1/2nd Londons were as follows:

RIGHT: 'C' Company (Capt. Ward) from the Divisional boundary to Ditch Post. The right flank of this sector, which included the Arras-Douai road, was separated from the left flank of the 4th Division by a gap of 400 yards.

RIGHT CENTRE: 'A' Company (Capt. Scudamore), with one platoon and a half in Ditch Post, half-a-platoon in Dummy Trench in rear, and two platoons in the Red Line to the left of the Post.

LEFT CENTRE: 'B' Company, with two platoons in Bailleul Post, and two platoons in the Red Line, one on either side of the Post.

LEFT: 'D' Company (Capt. Anderson), with two platoons in Bailleul East Post, and two platoons in the Red Line to the right of the Post.

BATTALION HEADQUARTERS (Lieut.-Col. Kellett) in Bailleul Post.

At 3 a.m. the enemy opened an intense bombardment of gas shells on the Red Line, and followed it with a bombardment of high explosives. The 1/2nd Londons, standing to arms at once, manned the fire-bays for three hours, the men wearing their respirators until the affected area was finally cleared of gas by a favourable breeze. The bombardment lasted in all for seven hours before lifting to the rear lines of defence, and the Battalion suffered heavily from its effects. At about 5 a.m., a very heavy artillery and trench-mortar bombardment was opened on the front-line system; and it then became evident that the enemy's infantry attack was about to be launched. The reserve brigade (167th) and all the reserve machine guns of the Division were ordered up; and the British guns opened fire on the enemy's trenches.

A few minutes after 7 o'clock, the S.O.S. went up from Towy Post, and was immediately followed by the signal all along the line. At last the enemy's attack had come; and, under cover of a creeping barrage, his men were swarming round the flanks of Towy Post and were pressing forward to the Naval-Marine Line. All the forward posts on the front of the Division, except Towy and Wood, were obliterated by the bombardment. The garrisons of these two posts put up a gallant stand; indeed, the former was held by the Q.W.R. until nearly half-past eight, when it was finally evacuated by the few survivors, who fought their way back through the enemy to the Naval Line.

Having overwhelmed the forward posts, the enemy rapidly pressed on, through gaps in the wire and down old communication trenches, towards the Naval-Marine Line. Both the Q.W.R., on the right, and the L.R.B., on the left, the latter under their very gallant commanding officer, Lieut.-Col. R. Husey, fought magnificently, and held the Naval Line until the increasing pressure of the enemy on either flank and in their rear made the position untenable. They were then ordered to withdraw to the Red Line, and extricating themselves with some difficulty from their isolated position they slowly fought their way back through the enemy's hordes. The losses of the L.R.B. and Q.W.R. were appalling; yet their sacrifices were not in vain, for, although the Germans still pressed on, the impetus of their attack had clearly been checked.

The front-line system having fallen, the enemy's attention became focussed on the Red Line, in which the gallant remnants of the L.R.B. and of the Q.W.R. had joined the 1/2nd Londons. Information had come to hand that Orange Hill, south of the Scarpe, had fallen; and the Divisional Commander made it known that it was imperative the Red Line be held at all costs. One battalion of the 167th Brigade was placed under the orders of Br.-General Coke; six machine guns were sent forward to Point du Jour to strengthen the right flank of the Division and its point of junction with the 4th Division; and two Field Companies, R.E., were also ordered up to strengthen this flank by holding Tongue and Blanche Posts. One company of the Middlesex was sent up to the 1/2nd Londons during the day; but its help was not needed.

In response to the request of Br.-General Coke, who wished to be kept fully informed of the progress of events, Lieut.-Col. Kellett moved his headquarters from the centrally situated Bailleul Post to Ditch Post, which was connected with Brigade Headquarters by a buried telephone. From Ditch Post Lieut.-Col. Kellett watched the progress of the enemy's assault on the front-line defences, and at 8.45 a.m., observing that the German troops had penetrated the Naval Line in front of 'B' Company, issued a warning to that company to be prepared to meet an immediate attack.

Ditch Post itself was very thinly held, and the enemy's barrage on it now increased to great intensity. The post and the line between it and the Arras-Douai road suffered severely from the bombardment; and in this area it soon became difficult to locate even traces of the original line.

The enemy's first attack on the Red Line does not appear to have been co-ordinated in any way, and developed at different times on the company fronts. It was about 9 a.m. when, after the penetration of the Naval-Marine

Line, he advanced towards Ditch Poſt. He was received by very heavy fire from the only two Lewis guns left, and his attack was brought to a ſtandſtill. After an anxious quarter of an hour Lieut. Dyer, who was here in charge of the defence and who was subsequently awarded the M.C. for his work on this day, was able to report that the garrison of the front line, ſtrengthened by a number of men of the L.R.B. and Q.W.R. who had come in, though much shaken, was equal to any emergency.

On the front of 'B' Company, in the left centre, the attack developed about 9 a.m., and for a time the situation caused considerable anxiety, the line, especially between Ditch and Bailleul Poſts, being but thinly held. Lieut.-Col. Kellett had sent Major Stevens to assiſt in maintaining the defence of this seſtor; and the latter officer, with the splendid backing of all ranks of 'B' Company, quickly succeeded in making the line secure. In this area, Capt. Whittle, of the Q.W.R., with a party of men of his battalion, ſtill held out in Caſtleford Poſt in Thames Alley; and Lieut.-Col. Kellett, by sending up a reinforcement of men with a supply of bombs, did what he could to help him in his gallant defence.

On the left, opposite Bailleul Eaſt Poſt, where 'D' Company was holding the line, the enemy entered North Tyne Alley at about 9.30 a.m. Capt. Anderson immediately had wire pulled across the Gavrelle-Bailleul road, and by forming a block in North Tyne Alley in conjunſtion with the L.R.B. and the London Scottish on the left, he succeeded in delaying the enemy's attack. The attack aſtually developed at about 10 a.m., when lines of skirmishers advanced; German officers were seen urging on their men to the cover of the railway embankment; and fully 150 Germans rushed from the Gavrelle-Bailleul road into North Tyne Alley. On these parties heavy Lewis-gun and rifle fire was opened with such success that the attack was repulsed.

A few of the enemy had been seen by 'C' Company on the right of the line as early as 9 a.m., but it was not until 10.15 that this company was aſtually attacked. Despite desperate efforts on the part of the enemy and an alarming shortage of bombs, the company managed to hold a forward block in Towy Alley and to maintain for some time connexion with the 4th Division on the right. Ultimately the enemy by putting in more and more troops succeeded during the afternoon in penetrating between the two divisions, and thereby created a very grave situation, which was only reſtored some hours later by the efforts of Lieut. Sloan.

Throughout the enemy's attack, his aircraft was very aſtive along the whole front. His aeroplanes were conſtantly signalling to his artillery with flares; and his low-flying aeroplanes caused many casualties to the defenders by the fire of their machine guns.

The force of the enemy's first attack had by now been broken; but during the morning he made two more attempts to secure the Red Line.

On each occasion his troops attacked across the open; and, in many cases, the men first throwing forward their rifles, advanced themselves, with their hands up, to the spot where the rifles had fallen. This method of progression was speedily stopped by rifle fire. The German troops were in full marching order, and appeared to be well-trained physically, but seemed to lack leadership and enthusiasm. Both attacks were repulsed; and at 2 p.m. small parties of the enemy were seen retiring.

At this hour a second intense bombardment was opened on the Red Line, and was continued until 6 p.m. The wire in front was completely destroyed, and the defenders anxiously awaited another serious attack; but apparently the enemy's infantry had no stomach for further fighting, and no attack developed. At 4.45 four field guns were brought into the open by the Germans. They were dragged out of Gavrelle by horses, and were then bravely manhandled into action south of Towy Post, near Naval Trench. Here they were observed by Lieut.-Col. Kellett, who warned the British artillery, and they were quickly and effectively silenced. About a quarter of an hour later a heavy attack developed on Bailleul East Post on the left, but within a few minutes it had crumpled up before the concentrated fire of the defenders, and Capt. Anderson was able to report that, despite a shortage of bombs, the situation in this area and in North Tyne Alley was unchanged.

Early in the afternoon Major-General Dudgeon circulated the following message: 'Corps Commander has informed First Army, 56th Division fighting splendidly. Stick to it.' By 6 p.m. the work of the 56th Division was done; the enemy had acknowledged his defeat; and the Division's line was still unbroken. Half-an-hour later the front was comparatively quiet; and a reorganization of the 169th Brigade was effected; the Q.W.R. took over the sector south of the Arras-Douai road, relieving 'C' Company of the 1/2nd Londons, who joined the rest of the Battalion north of the road.

Early in the morning of the 29th, the 169th Brigade was relieved; and the 1/2nd Londons, handing over to the 7th and 8th Middlesex, moved back, Headquarters, 'A,' and 'C' Companies withdrawing to Briley Hill, where they came under the 168th Brigade, and 'B' and 'D' Companies to the railway cutting on the left of the Thélus-Point du Jour (Green) Line, coming under the 167th Brigade. Later in the day the Battalion concentrated at Roundhay Camp, and on the 30th it went into billets at St. Aubin.

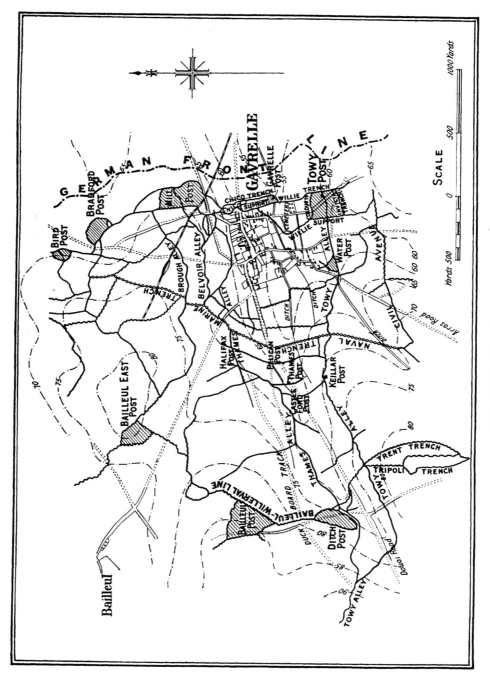

THE FIRST BATTLE OF ARRAS, 1918.

The Battalion's casualties were as follows:

KILLED: 1 officer (2nd Lieut. B. A. Starling), and 23 other ranks.
WOUNDED: 2 officers (2nd Lieuts. G. P. S. Bradley and W. Eddis) and 69 other ranks.
MISSING: 15 other ranks.

2nd Lieut. Benjamin Alfred Starling was the son of Mr. and Mrs. J. H. Starling, and was born in Victoria, Australia, on the 6th September, 1878. He was educated at Hawthorn College and Melbourne University, where he gained the degree of B.C.E. He was a civil engineer by profession. He joined the 3rd Londons on 4th April 1916, and was gazetted to the 2nd Londons on 26th January 1917. He was buried in the Military Cemetery at Roclincourt.

Although the casualties of the 1/2nd Londons do not compare with those of the Q.W.R., who lost 214 men, or of the L.R.B., who lost 476, nevertheless the Battalion carried out its allotted task efficiently and well. Its firmness under the very heavy bombardment to which it was subjected was highly creditable and made the repulse of the enemy's attack on the Red Line a comparatively easy matter; there was no need for the warning from the Division: 'In no case must any portion of the Red Line be given up.'

The Division had done its work better than it knew. One of the bloodiest defeats of the whole war had been inflicted on the enemy; and its effects were far-reaching. When the war was over Ludendorff made it known that the failure of this attack, in which eleven divisions were employed, was an important factor in the breakdown of the German offensive, and he expressed the opinion that if the two British divisions (4th and 56th) had not stood firm north of the Scarpe, and the two (3rd and 15th) on the south Vimy and Arras would have fallen, and that in all probability this would have been the beginning of the end of the Allies' cause. He writes:[1]

The 17th Army had already attacked, in the last days of March, in the direction of Arras, making its principal effort on the north bank of the Scarpe. It was to capture the decisive heights east and north of Arras; the next day the 6th Army was to prolong the attack from Lens and carry the high ground in the area. I attached the greatest importance to both these attacks. To have the high ground in our possession was bound to be decisive in any fighting in the

[1] *My War Memories,* 1914-1918. Field-Marshal von Ludendorff.

plain of the Lys. In spite of employing extraordinary masses of artillery and ammunition, the attack of the 17th Army on both banks of the Scarpe was a failure.

Apart from the heroic defence of the British infantry, the failure of this attack must be attributed largely to the almost complete absence of the element of surprise. Von Below, the German commander on this front, clung to the old-fashioned artillery methods; and the preliminary ranging of his batteries disclosed his intention. Thus his attack when it came caused no surprise; whereas the success of von Hutier on the front of the Fifth Army on 21st March had been attained because the opening of his bombardment was the first indication to the British that there was any large concentration of guns on that part of the front.

The following honours were awarded to the 1/2nd Londons in connexion with this engagement:

M.C.: Capt. K. Anderson, Lieut. W. Dyer.
D.C.M.: Sergt. P. M. Money.
M.M.: Ptes. W. Cook, R. L. Knuckey, C. R. Treadgold, F. H. Cooke, and W. J. Swift.

Among many congratulatory messages received by the Battalion the following is especially interesting:

April 1st, 1918.

The Army Commander personally expressed to the G.O.C. Division his appreciation of the good work done by the Division and of its tenacious defence during the enemy attack on March 28th. The G.O.C. Division also had the honour of being received by H.M. The King, who was graciously pleased to express his approval of the gallantry displayed by all ranks of the 56th Division.

CHAPTER XXI

THE 1/2ND AND 2/2ND LONDONS DURING THE SUMMER MONTHS OF 1918—THE RESERVE BATTALION AND THE DEPOT

I

ALTHOUGH his main scheme had miscarried and his forces had been definitely checked before Amiens and Arras, Ludendorff's resources were by no means exhausted. In addition to the Somme offensive, his plans included an attack in Flanders, called by the code-name 'St. George,' the preparations for which were to be completed early in April; and on the 9th April this, his third battle-effort against the British, was duly set in motion.

To oppose the thrust to Amiens, Sir Douglas Haig had been compelled to weaken other parts of his front. Inevitably he had to take risks; but the weighty reasons that governed his original dispositions still held good, and he felt that it was not possible to draw the reinforcements for his southern wing from his centre, which covered the Lens coalfields and included the commanding ground of the Vimy Ridge. He was therefore compelled to denude the relatively quiet sector to the north of his centre between the La Bassée Canal and the Lys; and it was on a front of eleven miles in this area that 'St. George' finally fell.

A Portuguese division holding a front of 10,000 yards was overwhelmed by the first onset; and a situation of extreme gravity was created. On the next day the Germans delivered another attack on a front of four miles north of Armentières; and thereafter until the 29th April the fighting raged with unprecedented fury. The crisis of the battle was reached on the 12th; and on this day Sir Douglas Haig felt constrained to issue his now famous Special Order of the Day to all ranks of the British Army in France and Flanders, which ranks with Nelson's signal at Trafalgar, and, like it, will ring gloriously in the ears of future generations of our race:

There is no other course open to us but to fight it out. Every position must be held to the last man; there must be no retirement.

325

With our backs to the wall, and believing in the justice of our cause, each one of us must fight on to the end.

The Battle of the Lys, in which neither battalion of the 2nd Londons took part, continued throughout April. The British line bent, but did not break. The fighting was very bitter, the losses very heavy; but in the end the enemy, after capturing the Passchendaele Ridge and Kemmel Hill, and penetrating beyond Bailleul, was brought to a standstill in front of Hazebrouck.

By the end of April the German offensives on the British front had spent themselves; and thereafter followed a period of comparative quiet, lasting throughout May, June, and July. As practically every division of the British Army had taken some part or other in the task of stemming the German tide, and as losses of men and material had been exceedingly heavy, this quiet period was welcomed by the British, and was used by them mainly in filling up their depleted units, in training the reinforcements that were daily arriving, and in making good the losses of guns and material.

To this general rule of preparation, the life of each battalion of the 2nd Londons was no exception; and only the salient points of this period of their history need be touched upon.

On the last day of March the 1/2nd Londons left St. Aubin, and marched to Fraser Camp, Mont St. Eloy. After a day devoted to cleaning up and to welcome baths at Ecurie, training was begun, but was interrupted on 3rd April, when a large working party consisting of 17 officers and nearly 600 other ranks, under Capt. Ward, was supplied for work on the Haute Avesnes Switch, one of the numerous switch lines that were being hastily constructed to maintain an unbroken front. In the midst of this activity, with the enemy, as it were, still knocking at the gates, it was found possible to hold on the 6th April a Corps Band Competition, in which the 1/2nd Londons' Band gave a very creditable account of itself.

Owing to the heavy fighting still in progress the 56th Division could not be given a long rest. During the first week of April it was transferred to the XVII. Corps (Lieut.-General Sir C. Fergusson), and immediately relieved the 4th Canadian Division in front of Arras, the 1/2nd Londons moving to Dainville, where they occupied scattered billets. The 169th Brigade was at the time in divisional reserve, and, in view of the very critical military situation, had to be ready to move at five minutes' notice at any time of the day or night.

The 1/2nd Londons during the Summer of 1918

The 1/2nd Londons remained at Dainville until the middle of April, training, and working hard on the rear defences. The strength of the Battalion at this time was 41 officers and 931 other ranks. On the 14th, in company with the other units of the Brigade, which was still in support to the Division, the Battalion moved to Ronville, on the southern outskirts of Arras, where it was billeted in the famous caves.

The Ronville and St. Sauveur Caves were a remarkable feature of the defences of Arras; they were of considerable extent, and were of great antiquity, having been excavated from the chalk—or such is the theory—to provide material for the construction of the original Cathedral, the *Hôtel de Ville,* and other of the older buildings in the city. They consisted of a maze of passages from which large caves opened out, and to which access was gained by some forty entrances, one of these being through the main sewer of Arras. The British had installed electric light throughout and provided a light railway which ran down the main thoroughfare. The accommodation was good; and wire beds were available for the men. Water was obtainable from a main supply; and cooking was possible in the vicinity of the air shafts.

These subterranean billets were never very popular with the men, because they were damp, dark, and dirty. No one was allowed to go outside during the day; and the life underground was depressing and unhealthy. Nevertheless, from a military point of view, the caves were of the utmost value; and a division could be assembled therein in complete safety.

The 1/2nd Londons remained in the caves until the 20th April, providing working parties at night on the Blangy Reserve System. They then moved into the line in the sector in front of Arras. This sector consisted of two main systems, each with front, support, and reserve lines, known as the Tilloy and Blangy Systems. The latter lay in rear of the long rise, called Observation Ridge, and the former about the crest of the ridge, its front line being on the forward slope. The two systems were connected by numerous communication trenches, of which two ran back to Arras. To the north of Observation Ridge the line was carried forward in a north-easterly direction by a series of switches to the banks of the Scarpe, and to the south, it bent back westward of Neuville Vitasse.

Tilloy Trench, the front line referred to above, was held as the line of resistance, with posts pushed out in front. On the front of the 1/2nd Londons there were four posts, either shell-holes or old trenches; and it is interesting to note that No. 2 Post was in an old trench that, strangely enough, had been occupied by Battalion Headquarters after the battle at

Cavalry Farm on 3rd May 1917. The trenches in this sector were very bad, and much time and labour were expended in putting them right.

The Battalion remained in the line until the 28th, and during this tour, besides working on the defences, actively patrolled its front. Identification was secured on the 23rd, when a patrol succeeded in capturing a prisoner of the 161st I.R. This patrolling activity culminated in a more ambitious effort on the 24th, when a 'cutting-out' raid was attempted on a length of trench only recently occupied by the enemy.

Special preparations were made for this raid, which was under the command of 2nd Lieut. Shadbolt. The party consisted of 39 men of 'A' Company and 2 men of the 169th Trench Mortar Battery, and was divided into four groups. The men wore no equipment except their box-respirators, ammunition and bombs being carried in their pockets; and their faces, hands, and bayonets were blackened. Wire-cutting was carried out by the British howitzers during the preceding afternoon, but, as subsequently transpired, was not wholly successful.

Punctually at zero (9.15 p.m.) an intense barrage was opened by three British field batteries, and under its cover the raiding party advanced. A German machine gun at once opened fire; nevertheless, the party pushed on, and was soon within striking-distance of its objective. The two groups on the right, meeting with little opposition, rushed forward, and gained the German trench. Keeping the enemy at bay by rifle grenades, they proceeded down the trench, bombing all shafts that they could find, and about half an hour later they safely withdrew to their own lines. With the two groups on the left, however, things did not go so well. They suffered eight casualties during the advance, and on reaching the enemy's wire found it still intact, and were compelled to halt. After several vain attempts 2nd Lieut. Shadbolt decided that it was impossible for these two groups, now reduced to six men, to reach their objective through the wire and heavy machine-gun fire. He accordingly ordered them to withdraw, and then went off himself to the right to see how matters were faring on that flank. While making his way in that direction, 2nd Lieut. Shadbolt was severely wounded in the thigh, and lay unconscious where he fell, until picked up by the enemy some hours later. In addition to 2nd Lieut. Shadbolt, the casualties were 1 non-commissioned officer killed and 11 other ranks wounded.

Shortly before the end of the month the 56th Division became responsible for the whole front of the XVII. Corps. Hitherto it had been disposed with one brigade in line, but now extending its left flank and taking over the sector north of the Arras-Cambrai road it was disposed with two brigades in line. The 169th Brigade was relieved on the 28th and moved into divisional reserve. The 1/2nd Londons, on relief by the 1/4th Londons, withdrew to Dainville, where they remained until 4th May. This period of rest was marked by the formation of an education class for non-commissioned officers and men under the Chaplain (Rev. R. F. Diggle) and Lieut. W. T. B. Chambers.

Casualties during April, in addition to those mentioned above, were:

> KILLED: 1 other rank.
> WOUNDED: 9 other ranks.
> MISSING: 1 other rank.

The following reinforcements of officers were received:

Lieut. J. W. Sanders, 2nd Lieuts. A. Willson, B. S. Freestone, and P. Hollman.

Lieut. E. J. Y. Simmonds took command of 'B' Company in succession to Capt. Widdecombe, and 2nd Lieut. H. D. Pratt was appointed adjutant in succession to Lieut. Simmonds. On 21st April Capt. T. G. McCarthy, M.C., who had served on the Brigade Staff for some months and had acted for a time as Brigade Major in November and December 1917, was appointed Brigade Major of the 169th Brigade.

During May, which was marked by the return of Major-General Hull to the command of the Division, the 1/2nd Londons had one long spell of seventeen days (from the 5th to the 21st) in the line in the Observation Ridge Sector. The rest of the month they spent in divisional reserve at Dainville, with the exception of a few days at the end when they moved into comfortable billets in Arras. During its tour in the front line, notable for increased artillery activity on the part of the enemy, the Battalion sent out a great many patrols, an aggregate of 22 officers and 381 other ranks being employed on this duty. Besides patrolling, much work was done on the trenches; and large quantities of salvaged material were collected and sent back. On the 9th a fighting patrol, under 2nd Lieut. J. L. Hewitt, encountered a German patrol in No Man's Land. A brisk fight ensued, in which 2nd Lieut. Hewitt was wounded and one man captured by the enemy.

The total casualties for the month were:

KILLED: 3 other ranks.
WOUNDED: 3 officers (Capts. C. G. Scudamore, M.C., E. J. Y. Simmonds, and 2nd Lieut. J. L. Hewitt) and 32 other ranks.
MISSING: One other rank.

Capt. Scudamore was succeeded in the command of 'A' Company by Capt. E. J. Harington, and Capt. Simmonds in the command of 'B' Company by Capt. C. R. W. Attenborough.

Officer reinforcements during the month were:

> Capts. E. J. Harington,[1] C. R. W. Attenborough, 2nd Lieuts. A. F. Sterckx, H. R. Davis, A. E. Kimber, D. H. Marshall, F. P. Deere, E. M. D. Mackie, and G. H. Merrikin.

The Battalion spent the first half of June in the Blangy Reserve System in support to the 169th Brigade, now holding the right of the divisional front, and provided large working and salvage parties daily. The salvage work was under the general direction of 2nd Lieut. Telford; and large quantities of stores and ammunition were collected. At this period the influenza epidemic made its first appearance. No man was allowed to rejoin a unit in the line from the back area; yet despite this precaution the 1/2nd Londons did not wholly escape the disease's ravages, and suffered a consequent reduction of fighting strength and efficiency.

The Battalion was relieved on the night of the 17th/18th, and moved back to Dainville, leaving 'A' and 'C' Companies behind in Arras for work under the C.R.E. These two companies rejoined the Battalion on the 21st. While the Battalion was at Dainville, a reorganization consequent upon a reduction of establishment took place. Companies, which since March had consisted of three platoons, now consisted of four, the number of sections per platoon being reduced to three—one Lewis-gun and two rifle sections.

The 1/2nd Londons were inspected by Br.-General Coke on the 25th June; and in the afternoon of the same day the Battalion Sports were held. The weather was glorious, and the meeting, at which Br.-General Coke was present, proved a great success. The outstanding items were the Blindfold Drill Competition and the Regimental Transport Gymkhana, both of which caused much amusement. No. 13 Platoon of 'D' Company was the most successful platoon, winning three events and gaining second place in one and third place in two. The Football Final was played, 'C' Company winning the cup amid scenes of great enthusiasm. The Sports were followed by an excellent concert given in the Y.M.C.A. hut at Dainville.

The end of the month found the 1/2nd Londons once more in the line, as right battalion of the left brigade, on Observation Ridge. In this sector the normal defensive disposition provided for advanced observation posts in and in front of Tilloy Trench, while the battle stations, to be occupied in the

---

[1] Capt. Harington had been Brigade Bombing Officer since the formation of the Brigade in 1916.

event of a hostile attack, included Pelves, 'F' and 'G' Posts, and Pelves and Wilderness Alleys. During this tour of duty, which lasted until 9th July, patrols were out every night, generally towards Battery Trench, but did not encounter the enemy except on the night of the 3rd, when a patrol of 'D' Company, under 2nd Lieut. Mackie, met a German patrol. There ensued a sharp fight, in which the Battalion lost one man wounded; no identification of the enemy was secured by the 1/2nd Londons, but a wounded German from this patrol was captured by the battalion on their left.

On relief by the Q.W.R., the 1/2nd Londons moved into brigade support in the Blangy system, until the 13th, when the 56th Division was relieved by the 2nd Canadian Division. The 1/2nd Londons then marched back to the Schramm Barracks at Arras, arriving at 2 a.m. on the 14th. On the next day they moved to Dainville, where they entrained for Diéval. A period of rest and training that lasted until the end of the month now began. The training was very intensive and of an advanced nature; and on the 24th all stages of the attack were practised in the presence of the Corps Commander. On the 30th, the Battalion left Diéval and marched to Bethonsart.

Casualties during June were 30 other ranks killed and 15 wounded, and during July 1 other rank killed and 10 wounded. Officer reinforcements were:

> Capt. W. R. Rawle, 2nd Lieuts. F. G. Garside (6th Londons), J. F. Pulford (7th Londons), A. C. Wilding, G. T. Gill, and L. May (20th Londons).

Notification of the following awards was received at this period:

> D.S.O.: Lieut.-Col. J. P. Kellett.
> M.S.M.: Sergt. G. E. Attwood.

In the absence of Major Stevens at the Senior Officers' Course at Aldershot, Capt. Anderson acted as second-in-command of the Battalion, being promoted Major, and Capt. Sloan succeeded Capt. Anderson in command of 'D' Company.

Leaving Bethonsart on the 1st August, the 1/2nd Londons marched to Mingoval, where they entrained for Dainville Wood. After a short halt to enable the men to obtain a meal, the march was continued; and in the evening the Battalion relieved the 13th Royal Canadian Highlanders in the Telegraph Hill area, taking over the left of the Brigade sector, 'A' and 'D' Companies being in the line, 'B' in support, and 'C' in reserve. This tour in the front line was comparatively quiet, but was marred by one unfortunate episode. An enemy airman was in the habit of flying daily above part of the line held by 'D' Company, and of subjecting the trench to a hail of machine-gun bullets as he passed along. On the 7th he succeeded in wounding Capt. Rawle, who died next day from the effect of his wounds. The only other casualty during this tour of duty was 2nd Lieut. Mackie, who was wounded.

Capt. William Richard Rawle was born on 19th June 1893. Immediately on the outbreak of war, he applied for a commission and was gazetted to the 2/2nd Londons on the 6th October. He served with that battalion in Malta and Gallipoli, and was then invalided home. He did not join the 1/2nd Londons until early in July, and he was doing his first tour in the trenches with this battalion when he met his death.

The 56th Division was relieved on the 17th August; and the 1/2nd Londons, who a few days earlier had moved back into brigade support at Beaurains, now withdrew to Grand Rullecourt.

II

By the 2/2nd Londons the summer of 1918 was passed in much the same way as by the 1/2nd Londons. It was inevitably a time of recuperation, of rebuilding a battalion that had been twice decimated since the 21st March. On withdrawal from the line at Hangard Wood, the 2/2nd Londons spent the night of the 25th/26th April at Boves. Next day, by means of 'Generals,' whose pristine glory of red paint had departed and given place to sombre grey, the Battalion proceeded by way of Amiens to the peaceful little village of Neuilly l'Hôpital, seven miles distant from Abbeville. The 56th Division was now in Corps reserve, and was given a short but much-needed rest.

Neuilly was essentially a charming spot, and the Battalion enjoyed every moment of its short stay of ten days there far from war's alarms. Abbeville was within easy reach of the village; and the frequent opportunities of visiting this quaint old town, with its beautiful Gothic church, were not missed. It was a strange sensation to tread once again the well-ordered streets of a town, to gaze at shop windows and to enjoy a properly served dinner, such as was provided at the old-fashioned *Tête du Bœuf,* an hotel justly famed in the British Army for its cleanliness and excellent cooking.

At the end of April the following officer reinforcements joined the Battalion at Neuilly:

> Lieuts. H. G. Hopper, W. Gray, 2nd Lieuts. C. F. Hyde, P. J. Grundlingh, M. E. C. Gilsenan, W. Urquart, G. F. Prior, H. G. Howard, W. Reynolds, A. Gimson, D. V. Druery, H. W. O. Smith, and R. A. Bradford (7th Londons).

The 2/2nd Londons during the Summer of 1918

Little need be said of this uneventful period. Sunny days came and went; training followed reorganization; and then, like all other good things, the rest came to an end; and on 7th May the Battalion 'embussed' for Molliens au Bois, seven miles north-east of Amiens, and ten miles distant from the line. The depth of the German penetration on the Somme front had thrown out of gear the whole 'back area' organization of the British in this area; billets were very scarce, and, when available, were generally bad; and units in brigade or divisional reserve had usually to bivouac in the shelter of the numerous woods. Molliens au Bois was no exception; and here the 2/2nd Londons encamped in the wood from which the place took its name.

The III. Corps, consisting of the 18th, 47th, and 58th Divisions, was now responsible for the defence of Amiens in the area west of Albert from the Ancre to Aveluy Wood; and the move of the 58th Division from Corps reserve into the line had been the cause of the 2/2nd Londons' forward move on 7th May. Thereafter the 58th Division remained in the Amiens defences until the opening of the decisive British offensive on 8th August.

On the 9th May the 2/2nd Londons made yet another move, this time to Béhencourt, five miles east of Molliens au Bois, where, as before, they were billeted in a wood on the outskirts of the village. From Béhencourt they worked on a new trench system flanking Baizieux on its western face— one of many similar defensive systems in course of construction in front of Amiens. These, under various names, stretched down over the Ancre, over the Somme, and across the face of the city of Amiens, through the Bois de Gentilles and Boves, behind Hangard and the Battalion's position of 24th April. It must be remembered that the enemy's advance of March and April had penetrated even beyond the old Somme defences, and that practically nothing in the nature of a defensive organization existed in what was formerly a lines of communication area. A defensive system had to be created in entirety from the line of converted shell-holes at which the enemy's advance was finally checked. The forward posts had now to be linked up; strong points and dug-outs constructed; rear lines and communication trenches dug; machine-gun positions sited; barbed wire put out; and the whole gamut of constructional engineering by which the old line had been built had to be run up and down again.

The Battalion moved into brigade reserve on 16th May and took over a trench position between Hénencourt and Senlis, less than three miles west of Albert, and not far removed from the famous Aveluy Wood. This move was but a prelude to its relief on 22nd May of the 12th Londons in the right sector of the left brigade's front, two companies being in the line, one in support, and the fourth in reserve, with Battalion Headquarters in Melbourne Trench. This sector was within a few hundred yards of Albert, and the opposing lines were here very close together, in places within easy bombing distance.

In an otherwise featureless stay in this sector there remains the vivid recollection of the dawn of glorious summer days over the ruins of Albert.

It seems something of a paradox to suggest that beauty may be found in war and in the dreary waste and soul-destroying ugliness that war creates. Yet sometimes amidst war's worst manifestations beauty would flash out most unexpectedly; perhaps in the silhouette of a tree standing on the sky-line of a parapet in the half-light of a summer evening; perhaps in a wood transformed by the white glare of a curving Very light into fairyland; perhaps in the broad and placid waters of a river like the Somme winding untroubled towards the sea.

The dawn of a fine day over Albert, as viewed from the British positions on the high ground westward, was a wonderful sight. Of the once-prosperous town little had escaped destruction; churches and houses, factories and shops lay in ruins, brick piled grotesquely on brick; and in the full light of day the skeleton of Albert presented a truly pathetic appearance to the beholder. Yet, suffused by the red-gold glow of the rising sun, the grim grey ruins became instinct with a strange beauty, impossible to describe. From their midst rose the shell-scarred mass of the youthful cathedral, its graceful spire now fallen in the dust, and with it the tragic figure of the Mother and Child, which had so long defied its inevitable fate, and clung precariously to the spire's summit, leaning forward as though bowed down with grief at the sorrow and suffering around it.

The 2/2nd Londons spent seven days in the front line before Albert, seven days wherein nothing but shelling, and very little of that, disturbed the quiet of the sector.

On relief by the 3rd Londons, the 2/2nd Londons moved back into brigade reserve immediately in rear of the line they had recently occupied, in a network of trenches, known from its configuration as The Maze. Here the Battalion remained until 1st June, when it was relieved by the 8th Berkshires (18th Division) and marched to a camp in a wood near Warloy.

Casualties during May were: 1 officer (2nd Lieut. E. F. Hyde) wounded, and 1 other rank killed and 14 wounded.

Officer reinforcements were:

Capts. W. A. B. Conran (A.S.C.) and D. Dutfield.

The 2/2nd Londons during the Summer of 1918

After five days at Warloy the Battalion moved back on 6th June to Daily Mail Wood, east of Mirvaux. At Mirvaux attempts were made to carry out some training, but were not very successful owing to the existence of standing crops, which were on no account to be damaged. An event of interest occurred on the 9th, when the Corps Commander, Lieut.-General Sir R. H. K. Butler, presented medal ribbons to officers and men of the Division at a special parade held for the purpose.

To understand the reasons for the next move of the 2/2nd Londons we must follow the progress of events on the French front. On 27th May Ludendorff struck his fourth great blow, and on the Chemin-des-Dames front 18 German divisions attacked 4 French divisions and 3 weak British divisions, sent to a supposedly quiet sector to recover from the severe handling of the earlier German offensives. Few reserves were immediately available; and, despite a most gallant resistance by both British and French, the enemy succeeded in reaching the Marne at Château Thierry. The exploitation of this success by a further blow at the junction of the British and French Armies seemed a logical course for the enemy to pursue; and, in order to be prepared for such an eventuality, the XXII. Corps was reformed under Sir A. J. Godley in G.H.Q. reserve, and the 12th, 37th, and 58th Divisions were posted to the new formation. The 173rd Brigade was accordingly moved to the neighbourhood of Amiens, the 2/2nd Londons being billeted at Ferrières, six miles on the ' safe' side of the city.

At Ferrières, as at Neuilly a month before, the Battalion was able to enjoy the advantages of a village that had escaped the ravages of war— indeed, the fighting had not been within a dozen miles, and that as late as March and April of this year—, and to indulge in those little luxuries that so rarely came within its reach. There followed days of training in pleasant surroundings, social intercourse with other units, and a general relaxing from the mental and physical strain of the forward areas.

On 9th June the expected German blow fell between Montdidier and Noyon; and one British division (the 13th) was moved south. The danger passed, however, without the 58th Division being called upon; and at the end of the week, the Division, now under the command of Major-General F. W. Ramsay, returned to the III. Corps and to its old line before Albert.

The 2/2nd Londons' pleasant stay at Ferrières was abruptly cut short on 17th June by orders to ' embus' for Molliens au Bois. After a night at Molliens au Bois in the same billets as before, they moved forward, first, to a position east of Laviéville, two miles and a half south-west of Albert, where they were in brigade support, and then on the night of the 19th/20th to the right sector of the left brigade, where they relieved the 23rd Londons (47th Division) on a line flanking the main Amiens-Albert road. In this sector they remained four days, during which nothing but the usual artillery and machine-gun activity broke the quietness of the front. After a short rest and another short spell in the line, they were relieved on the night of 1st/2nd July and went back to Laviéville. Casualties during June were 1 other rank killed and 9 other ranks wounded.

The whole of July was spent by the Battalion either in the line or in brigade support; and during this period the 58th Division steadily 'side-slipped' to its right until by the first week in August it was actually on the banks of the Somme.

The Battalion's next tour of duty in the front line began on the 10th July, when it relieved the 3rd Londons in the right sector of the right brigade front, Headquarters being established in a quarry north of Buire sur Ancre. This represented another definite drift to the south.

One incident of this tour in the front line may be recorded. This was a raid on a particularly awkward angle in the German front line north-west of Dernancourt, where the enemy occupied a strongly defended position athwart an embankment between the respective front lines. The object of the raid was to obtain identification, and the raiding party consisted of Capt. Grey, 2nd Lieuts. Gilsenan and Grundlingh, and 28 other ranks. Co-operation was arranged with the trench mortars and artillery to cut the enemy's wire and to prevent reinforcement of his front line during the raid.

Owing to a misunderstanding that occurred when 2nd Lieut. Grundlingh was wounded, the raiding party withdrew before its object was achieved; but the operation served to demonstrate to the enemy that we were not content with pursuing a totally inactive policy on this front. Casualties were 2nd Lieut. Grundlingh and 2 other ranks wounded.

On relief on the night of the 17th/18th July by the 6th Londons, the 2/2nd Londons went back to the St. Lawrence Valley, south-east of Baizieux, moving thence on the 20th to Round Wood, east of Béhencourt. At this period 2nd Lieut. A. V. Hyde assumed the duties of adjutant in place of Capt. Alexander, who had been taken ill. It should also be noted that at this period Br.-General C. B. Corkran succeeded Br.-General R. B. Worgan, D.S.O., in command of the 173rd Brigade.

On its next visit to the front line, the Battalion relieved the 31st Battalion A.I.F. in the trenches east of Buire sur Ancre, and found itself yet further to the south. This tour of duty was marked by an important move on the part of the enemy. On the 2nd August he evacuated his front-line

LIEUTENANT-COLONEL A. G. HOULDER.

MAJOR L. N. G. FILON.

LIEUTENANT-COLONEL J. A. MILLER, D.S.O.

CAPTAIN M. L. HARPER, M.C.

trenches in the low-lying ground east of Dernancourt and Ville sur Ancre, and withdrew to the higher ground in rear. The 2/2nd Londons immediately followed him, and made good the line he had evacuated, Battalion Headquarters being established in Ville sur Ancre, one mile east-south-east of Buire sur Ancre. This move on the enemy's part was undoubtedly dictated by the swampy nature of the ground in the valley of the River Ancre; and the enemy took the wise course of yielding an insignificant amount of ground to gain a drier and more easily defensible position for his troops.

The 2/2nd Londons were relieved on the 3rd August by the 9th Essex (12th Division), and 'embussed' for St. Léger les Domart. A long rest seemed in prospect, but once more the Battalion was to be summoned back to the fighting, and this time to take part in the decisive battle of the Great War.

Casualties during July were: 1 officer (2nd Lieut P. J. Grundlingh) wounded, and 4 other ranks killed and 16 wounded.

III

The lull in the fighting on the British front in France and the comparatively quiet time experienced by the two battalions of the 2nd London Regiment during the summer of 1918 present a suitable opportunity for a brief reference to the activities in England of the Reserve Battalion and of the Depot.

It will be remembered that the amalgamation of the 4/2nd Londons with the 4/1st Londons was effected on 1st September 1916, and thereafter the amalgamated unit adopted the title of 1st (Reserve) Battalion London Regiment. This Battalion, though no longer bearing the name of the 2nd London Regiment, deserves a short notice in this history, because it continued to supply the two remaining service battalions of the 2nd Londons with reinforcements, and, for a time at least, to receive those of their officers or men who had returned from the front either sick or wounded.

Shortly after the reconstruction of its component units, the 1st London (Reserve) Brigade was moved from its camps at Hurdcott and Fovant to various towns on the coast of South Devon. For the 1st (Reserve) Battalion this move resulted in a considerable change for the better, so far as its surroundings were concerned, the Battalion going into comfortable billets in Torquay in December 1916. After the discomforts of the hutted camps, and the bleakness of the Salisbury Plain area, the change was a very pleasant one, although from a military point of view the quartering of the troops in scattered billets, and the lack of adequate training grounds, were unsatisfactory features of the new ftation.

The routine of the Battalion's training at Torquay was at firft much the same as that at Salisbury, but was shortly modified to a considerable extent by the introduction of the syftem of Command Depots, which relieved the Reserve battalions of much of the irksome medical and convalescent work in connexion with returned Expeditionary Force men for which they were ill-equipped. The new Command Depots received on their discharge from hospital all officers and men returned from overseas who were not fit enough to resume their full duties, and retained them until their recovery was complete. Under this syftem convalescent men were able to regain their health and ftrength in more suitable surroundings, were given such light exercise as their condition permitted, or received whatever special treatment the needs of their particular cases required. After complete recovery at the Command Depot, the men were pofted to their respective Reserve battalions for a short 'refresher' course before being once again sent overseas. The Command Depot of all London Regiments, and of the Guards Brigade, was eftablished at Shoreham by Sea, Sussex.

The winter of 1916-17 passed pleasantly enough for the 1ft (Reserve) Battalion at Torquay; and it was with regret that all ranks received the orders in April 1917 for another move, which they realized could not lead to any improvement in the surroundings of their ftation or the comfort of their quarters. The short ftay of the Brigade at Torquay is commemorated by the exiftence of ' The Torquay Football Cup,' which is ftill competed for annually by teams from the four battalions of the 1ft London Brigade.

The new deftination of the Brigade was Blackdown, in the Aldershot Command, a pine-clad hill some seven miles north of Aldershot itself. Here, accommodated in hutted camps, moft of the units were to remain until the end of the war.

From a military point of view, the return of the 1ft (Reserve) Battalion to a military ftation was entirely satisfactory. The concentration of the Battalion resulted in a tightening of discipline; and the unrivalled training areas of the Aldershot Command enabled a high ftandard of efficiency to be reached. At the same time the recreation of the men received due consideration; a sports ground was placed at the disposal of each unit of the Brigade; the usual excellent inftitutes of the Y.M.C.A. and the Church Army were available; and the Blackdown Garrison Theatre received weekly visits from very good touring companies.

The training routine requires no detailed description; but it should be noted that a special organization had to be evolved to deal with lads under nineteen years, who, by the terms of the Military Service Act, could not be sent overseas until they had reached that age.

Little occurred during the remaining months of 1917 and the first months of 1918 to disturb the even tenor of the Battalion's ways, until the opening of the great German offensive in March. Its effects were magical. The losses inflicted on the fighting units of the British Army in France had to be made good without delay. Training staffs of the Reserve battalions were cut down to a minimum; every fit officer and man, and every recruit who had had a bare minimum of training, was at once sent overseas. The order with regard to boys of under nineteen was rescinded; and an appeal, to which a splendid response was given, was made for volunteers from this class. By these urgent calls for men the Battalion was speedily emptied of its personnel.

This state of affairs continued until August, when the order permitting boys under nineteen to volunteer for active service was revoked; training was then resumed on the same lines as before, and was continued until the Armistice, when the need for the Battalion's existence practically ceased. Immediately after the Armistice, the 1st and 3rd (Reserve) Battalions were amalgamated under the command of Colonel Vickers Dunfee; and thereafter upon this one unit devolved the duty of meeting the now small requirements of each of the five Territorial Fusilier battalions still in existence.

Early in December Lieut.-Col. A. Mather (Leinster Regiment) succeeded Colonel Vickers Dunfee in command; and in January 1919 the demobilization of the Battalion began. Most of the boys under nineteen were transferred to Young Soldiers' Battalions, with a view to their subsequent dispatch to join the Army of the Rhine; and in February the Battalion was moved to Shoreham by Sea, where at the end of the month it was finally disbanded.

IV

No history of the Regiment would be complete without some reference to the work of the Depot in the later stages of the Great War. The part taken by the Depot in the task of raising and equipping the four battalions of the Regiment has been touched upon in the earlier chapters of this book, and it is not proposed to enlarge further upon this period of its activities.

So far as recruiting duties were concerned, the Depot's share in the work under the voluntary system and the 'Derby' scheme has been described. The

'Derby' scheme came to an end in 1916, when conscription was introduced. Thereafter men were called up under the National Service Act. This much simplified the work of the Depot, which became merely an agent for demanding and collecting from the Chief Recruiting Office such men as were required from time to time by the Reserve Battalion.

The title of the Depot was changed twice during the course of the war, first to 'Administrative Centre, 2nd London Regiment,' and later to 'No. 32 T.F. Depot.' The scope of its duties was widened at the end of 1916, when it became the depot of eight 'Service' battalions of the Rifle Brigade (18th to 25th inclusive). The first seven battalions were serving overseas, and the eighth was a reserve battalion, stationed at Falmouth.

In addition to the whole routine of receiving, clothing, and fitting out recruits, the Depot staff had to deal with all men returned from abroad. The 'casualties' had to be posted to the Reserve Battalion or to the Command Depot, on their discharge from hospital or on their arrival in England from overseas. A large number of records of various kinds had to be kept, and a vast amount of clerical work disposed of. It must be remembered, too, that this applied not only to the 2nd London battalions but also to the Rifle Brigade battalions for which the Depot was acting.

At a later date, owing to its central position, the Depot was also used for the issue of such clothing and necessaries as were required by any soldier arriving in England on short leave. This, of course, entailed the maintenance of large stocks of clothing; and the arrival of the 'leave' trains in the evening was generally followed by a most extraordinary parade in Tufton Street, at which men from all arms of the service attended with their clothing in various states of disrepair.

Before this brief account is closed, one other—and important—function of the Depot must be mentioned. Early in the war it became the head-quarters of an association that had for its object the relief of the wives and families of the men of the Regiment and of prisoners of war. An influential committee of ladies and gentlemen was formed to administer the regimental funds collected for this purpose. Colonel Carlebach, Lieut.-Col. Marler, and Stanley Attenborough, Esq., the father of Lieut.-Col. Attenborough, acted as trustees of the fund, of which the balance remaining at the end of the war formed the nucleus of the present Regimental Association Benevolent Fund.

Another organization that gave great help to the 2nd London prisoners was Lady Victoria Herbert's Scheme for Prisoners of War, which had its headquarters at 60, Curzon Street. Lady Victoria Herbert and her voluntary assistants packed the clothing that the Regiment was able to send out to its men, and also sent six parcels every month to each soldier in captivity. At one time, after March 1918, as many as 700 2nd Londoners benefited by her care and attention to their welfare. After the war, Lady Victoria Herbert continued her good work by helping repatriated prisoners, invalided, and demobilized men, to find work, and she was instrumental in obtaining employment for a number of 2nd Londoners.

Shortly after the Armistice Capt. Marno was demobilized. He had conducted the multifarious business of the Depot very efficiently, and had helped the various battalions, both at home and abroad, in every possible way. His mention in War Office Letters for his services was very well earned. He was succeeded by Capt. E. J. Harington, who in turn was succeeded by Lieut. W. A. Francis, M.C. in December 1918. The last-named officer remained in command until July 1920, when, on the reconstruction of the unit, the functions of the Depot, as apart from the Regiment, came to an end.

CHAPTER XXII

THE 2/2ND LONDONS IN THE BATTLE OF AMIENS AND THE SECOND BATTLES OF THE SOMME, 1918

I

THE four months of ceaseless fighting that had succeeded the opening of the enemy's offensive on 21st March had witnessed a complete change in the strategic situation of the opposing forces. The main German Armies were now deeply committed; they no longer had the great factor of surprise on their side. One after another the vast offensives had been launched, first against the British, then against the French; and, as a result, the possible courses of future action open to the enemy were now restricted, and, to some extent, defined. The German reserve of man-power had inevitably become exhausted by these tremendous efforts, whereas, on the Allies' side, the American Army was rapidly arriving in France, and the great losses of the French and British were thus being made good.

By stubborn defence the enemy was held in check throughout June, while the process of recovery from his earlier blows was taking effect in the ranks of the Allies. A last effort was made by Ludendorff to gain a decision, when, on 15th July, he delivered another mighty blow against the Allies' quivering line, this time east and west of Rheims. Marshal Foch, now the Allied Generalissimo, foreseeing this last great stroke, had gathered his reserves to meet it; and the attack, when it came, was successfully held. The Marshal realized that the Germans had shot their bolt, and seizing the fleeting opportunity he launched his carefully husbanded reserves in a great counter-attack on the Château Thierry-Soissons front three days later. The strength and direction of this attack was entirely unexpected by the enemy, many of whom were peacefully harvesting the abundant crops behind the threatened front, and its success was everywhere immediate and complete. Not only were heavy losses inflicted on the enemy, but a complete change was effected in the whole military situation; and, although the decisive battle had yet to be fought, the initiative now passed definitely to the Allies.

The next step was to free Amiens and the Paris-Amiens railway, and with this end in view it was arranged that the British Fourth Army should take the offensive, in conjunction with the French, from Morlancourt to Moreuil, with the object of regaining the old Amiens Defence Line. The battle was to be a tank battle on the Cambrai model, and the main attack was to be delivered south of the Somme by the Australian and Canadian Corps, while to the north the III. Corps, with the 18th and 58th Divisions in line, covered the left flank of the attack by occupying strong defensive positions towards the north-east in the neighbourhood of Gressaire Wood, and by forming a defensive flank along the heights overlooking Morlancourt from the south.

The importance of the task of the 58th Division in this operation will be better appreciated if the nature of the terrain is first briefly described.

The Somme is a typical canalized river of Northern France, winding through a marshy, and in places very beautiful, valley. The reaches of the river with which we are immediately concerned are bordered on the south by undulating and generally featureless meadowland, but the north bank is formed by the plateau of high ground lying between the Somme and its tributary, the Ancre. The southern edge of this high ground is divided by numerous steep gullies, running north from the Somme, into a succession of spurs, many of which meet the river in the form of abrupt chalk cliffs. These cliffs rise in places to a considerable height and completely dominate the southern bank, so that a resolute enemy, occupying trenches on these heights, would be able to enfilade with deadly effect troops crossing the plain south of the river. Of these spurs the most marked is the long, bare Chipilly Ridge, lying east of the little village of that name, which, jutting out nearly a mile south of the general line of the high ground into the plain beneath, causes the river to make a long but narrow sweep round its base.

The capture of this important tactical feature, commanding a wide expanse of country south of the Somme and lying athwart the line of advance of troops in that area, was entrusted to the 58th Division, while the 18th Division formed the defensive flank from the northern end of the ridge about Gressaire Wood to Morlancourt.

Between the 58th Division and its objective lay two miles and a half of difficult country, bristling with obstacles, both natural and artificial. Immediately in front of the Division's starting line lay Sailly Laurette, a village on the banks of the Somme, whose continued occupation by the enemy would constitute a serious menace to the flanks of attacking troops. A mile and a half east of Sailly Laurette and on either slope of one of the

343

gullies above-mentioned lay Malard Wood; and halfway between Malard Wood and Chipilly Ridge lay a second deep gully, completely overlooked from the ridge itself.

A frontal attack against this naturally strong position developed over such difficult ground as above described was a formidable undertaking for the attackers, and, in order to facilitate the task of the 58th Division, it was decided to threaten the flank of the Chipilly position by an earlier advance on the part of the Australians south of the Somme, and by their capture of the high ground about Méricourt simultaneously with the opening of the attack of the 58th Division on its final objective. Such a threat, it was hoped, would render the enemy's position at Chipilly untenable, and lead him to beat an early retreat.

The attack was ordered for the 8th August—now a very famous date in the annals of the Great War—; and during the first six days of the month the attacking troops were concentrated. The utmost secrecy was enjoined during the preparations, and the concentration of men and guns was carefully concealed.

We left the 2/2nd Londons at St. Léger les Domarts, where they had arrived on the 3rd August with the prospect of a long rest before them. On the next morning—Sunday—the Battalion received sudden orders recalling it to the line, and the same night it 'embussed' for la Houssoye on the Amiens-Albert road, whence it marched to billets in le Bois Escardonneux.

So as to be in the proper position for its attack, the 58th Division was ordered to take over part of the front held by the 18th Division on its left; and accordingly, on the night of the 5th/6th August, the brigade in the line, the 174th, relieved part of the right front of the 18th Division. In the early hours of the 6th, while the relief was still in progress, the enemy delivered a heavy attack on the 18th Division, in which the relieving troops of the 174th Brigade were slightly involved. The enemy captured some trenches, together with a number of prisoners, and penetrated as far as the newly-constructed gun-positions, and the dumps of ammunition and material, that had been made ready for the coming offensive. He was immediately counter-attacked; and by the 7th the line had been restored. Although it seemed inevitable that the enemy must become aware of the great attack in preparation, the significance of dumps and gun-positions so far forward apparently escaped him; and it subsequently transpired from prisoners' statements that the British offensive, when it came on the 8th August, was a complete surprise to the German High Command. Apart

344

from the casualties caused, this attack had other serious consequences: a new starting line 300 yards further west had to be made, a new artillery programme had to be drawn up, and, above all, officers of the attacking battalions were prevented from reconnoitring the assembly area.

The first objective of the 58th Division was a line just east of Malard Wood (the Green Line), whose capture was entrusted to the brigade in the line, the 174th, assisted by the pioneer Battalion (1/4th Suffolks). This first phase involved the capture of Sailly Laurette; and in order that a subsidiary operation of this nature should not delay the whole advance, the task of capturing and mopping up this village was given to the 2/10th Londons, attached from the 175th Brigade for the purpose. The 173rd Brigade was ordered to follow the 174th in close support, and one hour after the first objective had been made good to pass through the leading brigade, and to carry the attack to the final objective on Chipilly Ridge (the Red Line). A Tank Company was attached to the Division, and, with the exception of two tanks specially detailed to assist in the capture of Sailly Laurette, was ordered to work with the 174th Brigade in the first phase and with the 173rd Brigade in the second.

For the attack of Chipilly, the dispositions of the 173rd Brigade were as follows:

RIGHT: 3rd Londons.
LEFT: 2/4th Londons.
SUPPORT: 2/2nd Londons.

Two platoons of the last-named battalion were especially detailed to mop up Chipilly village on the right flank, for which purpose close co-operation with the tanks was arranged.

On the night of the 7th August the 173rd Brigade moved forward to its starting line; and the 2/2nd Londons eventually took up a position in a valley running north of Sailly le Sec. The march of about two miles in the dark was exceedingly trying; gas-masks had to be worn some part of the way; and intermittent shelling and the inevitable confusion attendant upon the concentration of large masses of troops led to frequent delays. The assembly of the large number of tanks to be employed presented a problem in concealment that was solved by the use of smoke and by the employment of low-flying aeroplanes, which drowned the noise of the tanks' engines by their own.

At 4.20 a.m. on the 8th August the British tanks surged forward, and simultaneously the British guns rent the air. Everything had been subordinated to the tank attack, and, although 120 brigades of artillery were

345

employed, no registration or preliminary bombardment was permitted. Thus the surprise of the enemy was complete.

Under cover of a terrific barrage and preceded by the company of tanks, the units of the 174th Brigade advanced. A thick ground mist accompanied the dawn of day, and, although it facilitated the final assembly of the tanks and the troops and served to cover their advance, it was to have other and less happy effects, and by limiting visibility to some twenty yards was to make the task of maintaining direction one of the utmost difficulty. To the 174th Brigade, whose units had had the advantage of being in the line some days previously, this mist was at first no disadvantage, but it was to have a very marked effect on the advance of the 173rd Brigade, whose officers had been prevented by the German attack of the 5th/6th August from reconnoitring the proposed line of advance, and whose units had never been on the ground before.

Mist or no mist, however, the 173rd Brigade had to advance, and at the appointed interval of time it followed the 174th in the direction of the enemy's position. The advance of the troops of the latter brigade had been the signal for the opening of a heavy barrage by the enemy; and the 173rd Brigade, closely following the wake of the 174th, was caught in a curtain of fire, and immediately suffered serious losses, among the casualties being Lieut.-Col. Grover, commanding the 2/4th Londons. Much about the same time the effect of the mist first began to be felt, and its presence caused confusion and loss of direction. It was originally intended that the 173rd Brigade should reach its assembly position on the first objective by following the attacking troops round the north edge of Malard Wood; but, owing to the mist and to the presence of small pockets of the enemy that had to be mopped up as the troops advanced, the 3rd Londons and part of the 2/4th Londons drifted off some 500 yards to the left into the area of the 18th Division, where they were followed by the 2/2nd Londons, who eventually encroached upon what should have been the front of the right company of the 2/4th Londons.

Referring to the loss of direction on the part of his battalion, the author of the History of the 4th Londons comments as follows: [1]

> This is regrettable, but comprehensible if a close study be made of the contoured map. The gullies which had to be crossed ran obliquely across the line of advance. If anyone cares to try hill

[1] *The War History of the 4th Battalion The London Regiment (Royal Fusiliers), 1914-1918.* Capt. F. Clive Grimwade.

climbing in a fog he will realize the extreme difficulty of maintaining a sidelong direction.

The mist began to clear at 8.30, when it appeared that the 3rd Londons and a part of the 2/4th Londons were in Malard Wood, mixed up with troops of the 174th Brigade, which had not yet secured the Green Line east of the wood, and that the remainder of the 2/4th Londons had reached the north-western edge of the wood, and were in touch with the 18th Division on the left. As soon as these two units debouched from the cover of the trees, they came under such an intense machine-gun fire from the direction of Gressaire Wood that only a few isolated parties succeeded in reaching their assembly position on the Green Line, and were thus ready to follow the creeping barrage when it moved forward to the final objective.

At about 10 a.m. the 2/2nd Londons arrived on the scene; and Lieut.-Col. Miller, as the senior officer present, began immediately to reorganize the now hopelessly mixed-up units of the 173rd Brigade. That done, Malard Wood was completely cleared of the enemy. Egress from the wood, however, was still quite impossible for the infantry without the support of the artillery or tanks, and, as none of the latter had arrived in the vicinity of the Green Line, the 173rd Brigade had to be content with holding the forward edge of the wood.

While this was happening, the British barrage had moved forward at the scheduled hour on to the final objective, Chipilly Ridge, but, for reasons explained above, only elements of the two attacking battalions were available to follow it, and of these probably none actually reached the ridge.

As the continued occupation of Chipilly by the enemy was seriously delaying the left of the Australian Corps south of the Somme, the attempt to capture it was renewed. The attack took place during the afternoon, and was delivered by the 2/2nd Londons. Owing to the reported presence of some British troops on the final objective, a barrage was out of the question, and the 2/2nd Londons' attack, which was launched at 3 p.m., had to be delivered without artillery support. With great gallantry the Battalion advanced under a storm of machine-gun and rifle fire and pressed forward to Chipilly Ridge. It reached the western slopes, but was there held up by the intense machine-gun fire from the village of Chipilly on the right and from Gressaire Wood on the left. In the teeth of this leaden hail, the continued occupation of so exposed a position was impossible; and the Battalion, unable to advance without support, was forced to fall back to

347

the cover of Malard Wood. The two platoons that had been detailed before the battle to deal with Chipilly itself had an unfortunate experience. Their attack, it will be recalled, was to be made in co-operation with two tanks, and a rendezvous was arranged with the tanks just east of Malard Wood. The platoons duly reached the rendezvous, and, while awaiting the arrival of the tanks, were heavily shelled and suffered a number of casualties, each losing its commander. In the end the attack was never delivered, because the tanks, for some reason that has never been explained, failed to put in an appearance.

The Battalion's casualties in this very gallant attack were extremely heavy, and many of these must be laid at the door of the inaccurate, but persistent, aerial reports that the ridge was in our hands, when nothing of the sort could have actually been the case. Had it not been for these reports, a barrage might have been arranged, and the Battalion might well have met with success; at least it would have stood a better chance in its attack on what was virtually an ideal machine-gun position.

This attack was typical of the many instances furnished by the Great War of the powers of the machine gun in defence. Carefully sited and with a strip of open ground in front of them, these weapons, unless blinded by smoke or crushed by an intense barrage, absolutely controlled the situation, and made the advance of the boldest infantry impossible. Even the heaviest bombardments did not always succeed in putting them out of action; and the only effective counter to them was the tank, which, impervious to small-arms' fire, could convey men across the otherwise impassable ground and crush the machine guns in their positions.

In view of the importance of securing Chipilly, another attempt was made in the evening, the 2/10th Londons being attached for the purpose to the 173rd Brigade, now much reduced in numbers. At 7.30 p.m., the 2/10th Londons advanced to the attack, under a heavy barrage, and, although they succeeded in penetrating the village, they could not hold the position gained, and were forced to withdraw.

No further advance was attempted that day; and the 173rd Brigade consolidated the position gained. In addition to the heavy casualties among the officers, the 2/2nd Londons lost Major Sutcliffe, who went to take command of the leaderless 2/4th Londons.

So the day ended. Although, on the left of the 58th Division, the 18th Division had been able to make no progress beyond its first objective, south of the Somme a stupendous success had been gained. Over 400 fighting tanks had been employed, and the enemy, surprised and demoralized, had been

348

unable to hold his ground. An advance of about seven miles had been made; the main thrust of the Fourth Army had achieved all its objects; and the crushing defeat of the enemy was at last in sight.

The following morning found the enemy still in occupation of Chipilly Ridge. Patrols, pushed out by the 173rd Brigade to substantiate certain aerial reports that the enemy was beginning to thin his line, could make little headway; and Malard Wood was heavily shelled.

A continuation of operations was ordered for this day with the object of gaining the general line Bray sur Somme-Dernancourt. It was decided, in view of its heavy losses in the previous day's fighting, to strengthen the 58th division by the addition of the 133rd American Regiment (Colonel Samborn), then in Army reserve. This decision had the effect of delaying the attack until late in the day, because the Americans had first to be brought forward from a position some miles in rear. The main attack was to be made by the 175th Brigade on the left and by the Americans in the centre, while the 173rd and 174th Brigades were given the task of capturing Chipilly and Chipilly Ridge.

The orders for the attack were received by 173rd Brigade Headquarters at about 1 p.m., but owing to lack of telephone communication it was not until nearly two hours later that they reached Lieut.-Col. Miller, commanding all the advanced troops of the Brigade. Lieut.-Col. Miller at once summoned the officers commanding the advanced troops of the 3rd Londons and 2/4th Londons to his headquarters, and informed them what their tasks in the forthcoming action would be. The story of the meeting of Lieut.-Col. Miller and Capt. Croll of the 2/4th Londons is told by Capt. Grimwade, and is worth repeating here.[1] 'The grim humour of the situation was succinctly summed up in Lieut.-Col. Miller's greeting: "Hullo, Croll, aren't you dead yet?" "No, Sir!" replied Croll. "Then you damned soon will be." And orders for the attack were issued.'

The dispositions of the battalions of the 173rd Brigade were as follows:

RIGHT: 3rd Londons.
CENTRE: 2/4th Londons.
LEFT: 2/2nd Londons.
RESERVE: 2/10th Londons (attached).

The assembly position of the Brigade for this attack extended from the quarry just east of Malard Wood down to the banks of the Somme, and

[1] *The War History of the 4th Battalion The London Regiment (Royal Fusiliers), 1914-1918.* Capt. F. Clive Grimwade.

its battalions, being still in Malard Wood and thus too far to the left, had now to 'side-slip' some distance to the right. This somewhat difficult manœuvre was successfully carried out under heavy machine-gun fire from the enemy. At the same time the fighting patrols that had been sent out earlier to ascertain if Gressaire Wood was still occupied by the enemy were hurriedly recalled in order that their continued presence in front should not prevent the barrage from opening.

By this time the fighting strength of the 2/2nd Londons had been reduced to between 150 and 200 men; and this small force was under the immediate command of Capt. Wright, the senior officer left in the front line. The message summoning Capt. Wright to Battalion Headquarters for his orders for the attack apparently did not reach him; and Lieut.-Col. Miller was eventually constrained to send up his adjutant, Lieut. Hyde, to the forward troops. The attack was to be delivered at 5.30; time was getting short. Lieut. Hyde hurried forward, found Capt. Wright at last, and delivered the orders shortly before the barrage was due to open. Although the 2/2nd Londons were at a less distance from their assembly position than the other battalions of the Brigade, there was no time to lose, and Lieut. Hyde stayed to help Capt. Wright to assemble his small command. This done, Lieut. Hyde conversed for a few moments with some of the men, as they awaited the opening of the barrage, and then, turning to begin his journey back to Battalion Headquarters, was badly wounded.

Although the Americans had been rushed up from the rear in motor-buses and had doubled the last mile to their starting line, they had had so far to come that they were not quite in position when the creeping barrage opened at 5.30. The delay was but momentary, and within a few minutes of zero the attack was launched. The barrage, though heavy, was inaccurate, and the shells fell harmlessly in the Chipilly valley, allowing the enemy on the spur itself to keep his machine guns in action against the advancing troops. The 2/2nd Londons cleared the northern end of les Celestins Wood, and, despite heavy frontal fire and equally heavy enfilade fire from Chipilly village on the right and Gressaire Wood on the left, pushed on until they reached the sunken road on the slopes of Chipilly Ridge. Beyond this point further advance was impossible; the Americans were not yet up on the left; the enemy's fire was devastating; and movements indicating an imminent counter-attack were descried in the enemy's position. There seemed to be no alternative but to dig in on the line reached.

Then, in a flash, the situation suddenly changed. The 2/10th Londons, who had been sent from brigade reserve to work round south and east of

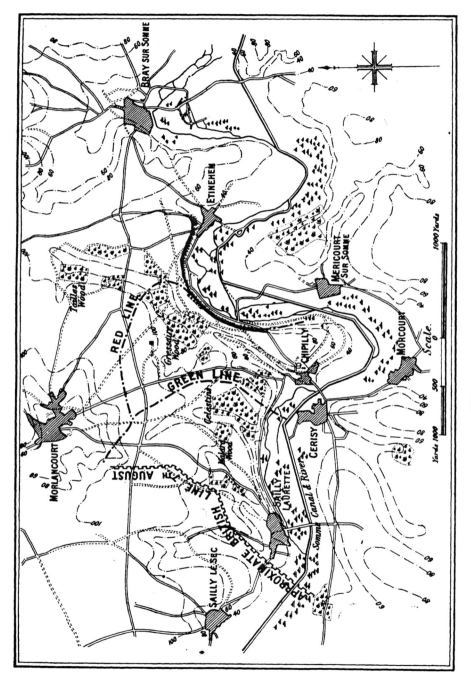

THE BATTLE OF AMIENS.

Chipilly itself, succeeded in clearing the village. Having gained a footing on the southern end of the spur, they began to clear out the machine-gun nests on the terraces that had so long delayed the advance of the Brigade. At the same time the comparatively fresh Americans came up on the left, and delivered a vigorous attack in the direction of Gressaire Wood.

The threat to his flanks made the position of the enemy on Chipilly Ridge highly dangerous, and, when the troops of the 173rd Brigade rushed forward with great enthusiasm, he beat a hasty retreat, narrowly escaping being caught by the converging wings of the British forces. By 11 p.m. the ridge was ours, and all resistance on the part of the enemy had been overcome.

The casualties of the 2/2nd Londons during the battle were 7 officers and 272 other ranks. The casualties among the officers were as follows:

KILLED: 2nd Lieuts. C. L. Prebble and H. R. Howard.
WOUNDED: Capt. P. Fores, Lieut. A. V. Hyde, 2nd Lieuts. A. N. Cunningham, M. E. C. Gilsenan, and G. E. Hale.

The following honours were subsequently awarded in connexion with the battle:

M.C.: Capts. A. Wright, W. Gray, Lieuts. A. V. Hyde, W. Urquart, 2nd Lieut. C. L. Prebble.

During the morning of the 10th August the Battalion consolidated the ground gained, and later in the day it was relieved and moved back to a valley about a mile south of Heilly. The relief of the whole of the 173rd Brigade was effected at about the same time as the result of a redistribution of the Fourth Army front. The two days' fighting had proved that the River Somme was an unsatisfactory boundary between the III. and Australian Corps, by reason of its irregular course and the inter-supporting nature of the hills on either bank. It was therefore deemed advisable to bring both banks into the area of one command; and accordingly the Australian Corps took over a short sector of the III. Corps' front north of the Somme, and henceforward became responsible for clearing both banks of the river. This redistribution had the effect of shortening the front of the 58th Division, the 173rd Brigade on the right being withdrawn and the 175th on the left remaining in the line.

The 58th Division continued its advance with the 175th Brigade on the 10th, and, having captured Tailles Wood, occupied the old Amiens Defence Line. The Division was relieved on the 12th August, and concentrated in the Querrieu area.

This virtually concluded the Battle of Amiens. The battle was decisive in its results; Amiens itself, so long threatened by the enemy, had been freed; an advance of twelve miles had been made; huge numbers of prisoners and vast quantities of material had fallen into our hands; the German communications were threatened; and the enemy was forced to begin an extensive withdrawal on the Montdidier front. Not the least satisfactory result was an intangible gain to the British, as evidenced by the morale of the opposing forces. On the British side, it was satisfactory to note that the losses of the early part of the year and the long months of recuperation, had in no way impaired the spirit of the troops, whereas the Germans fought with far less enthusiasm than heretofore, and gave ample proof that their morale had been adversely affected.

The lack of success on the first day of the battle on the part of the III. Corps, and particularly the 58th Division, has been the subject of much unfavourable criticism. The failure to capture the Chipilly Ridge on that day, though it in no way affected the ultimate issue of the battle, delayed the Australians on the right and caused them serious losses that might otherwise have been avoided. In judging the Division's performance, however, there are several circumstances that should not be overlooked: the enemy's counter-attack against the 18th Division on the 6th August, which disorganized all preparations and completely prevented all reconnaissances; the mist of the 8th August, which seriously hindered troops new to the ground; and the failure of the tanks to put in an appearance on the Green Line, or, in fact, to take any part in the attack on the final objective. On the other hand, the operations of the Division during these four days met with a large measure of success, as a glance at its tangible gains will show: an advance of 6,000 yards, and the capture of 1,925 prisoners, 68 guns, 190 machine guns, and 36 trench mortars. That the Division is far from ashamed of the part it played in one of the most important battles of the war is evidenced by the fact that Chipilly was selected as the site of its memorial in France.

II

On the relief of the 58th Division, the 2/2nd Londons left Heilly on the 13th August, and marched to Pont Noyelles, where a very welcome draft of 314 non-commissioned officers and men was received. After a day spent in cleaning up, the march was resumed to Querrieu—the area in which the Division was to rest.

There now followed a lull in the fighting on the British front while guns

THE 58TH DIVISION'S MEMORIAL AT CHIPILLY SUR SOMME.

ALBERT CATHEDRAL, 1918.

ARRAS CATHEDRAL, 1918.

CHIPILLY CHURCH, 1918.

and material were moved forward in preparation for the opening of the next phase. The consequence of this, so far as the 2/2nd Londons were concerned, was a week's rest, which was spent in reorganizing and training. While the Battalion was at Querrieu, it was visited by the Commander-in-Chief, Sir Douglas Haig, who watched the whole of the 173rd Brigade at its training, and expressed himself well satisfied with what he saw. On 17th August a Brigade Church Parade took place, at which Lieut.-General Sir Alexander Godley, now commanding the III. Corps, was present. At its conclusion, the Corps Commander inspected the Brigade; and the units then marched past, headed by the bands of the 2/2nd and 3rd Londons. Another event of interest during this period was the Battalion Sports Meeting, which took place on the 22nd in the grounds of the *château*, and proved very successful and enjoyable.

Officer reinforcements received between the 10th and 22nd August were as follows:

> Lieut.-Col. J. Walsh, D.S.O., Northumberland Fusiliers, who succeeded Lieut.-Col. Miller in command of the battalion.
> Major S. J. M. Sampson, M.C., who came from the 4th Londons as second-in-command.
> 2nd Lieuts. R. W. T. Chapman, H. H. Graham, G. N. Glanfield, F. Emerson, C. E. Green, R. F. Larcombe, L. G. West, J. H. J. Dewey, A. R. Fox, E. M. Tatlow, F. S. Wallis, L. Cantrell, F. L. Howells, and E. G. Evans.

The strength of the Battalion at this time was 26 officers and 931 other ranks.

After the Battle of Amiens, the fighting spread to the north between the Somme and the Scarpe. For several reasons, foremost of which was the increasing resistance of the enemy in this area, the British G.H.Q. decided to break off the offensive south of the Somme, and to make the next attack in a new direction. Although this plan was not at first approved by Marshal Foch, who desired a continuation of the advance south of the Somme, Sir Douglas Haig remained firm in his intention, and the wisdom of his policy was fully proved by subsequent events. In giving the reasons for his decision, we cannot do better than quote his own words: [1]

> In deciding to extend the attack northwards to the area between the Rivers Somme and Scarpe, I was influenced by the following considerations.

[1] Sir Douglas Haig's Dispatches.

2 A

The enemy did not seem prepared to meet an attack in this direction, and, owing to the success of the Fourth Army, he occupied a salient the left flank of which was already threatened from the south. A further reason for my decision was that the ground north of the Ancre River was not greatly damaged by shell-fire, and was suitable for the use of tanks. A successful attack between Albert and Arras in a south-easterly direction would turn the line of the Somme south of Peronne, and give every promise of producing far-reaching results. It would be a step towards the strategic objective, St. Quentin-Cambrai. . . .

It was arranged that on the morning of the 21st August a limited attack should be launched north of the Ancre to gain the general line of the Arras-Albert railway, on which it was correctly assumed that the enemy's main line of resistance was sited. The day of the 22nd would then be used to get troops and guns into position on this front, and to bring forward the left of the Fourth Army between the Somme and the Ancre. The principal attack would be delivered on the 23rd August by the Third Army and the divisions of the Fourth Army north of the Somme, the remainder of the Fourth Army assisting by pushing forward south of the river to cover the flank of the main operation.

On the 21st August the offensive was resumed by the British; and the Third Army, reinforced by 100 tanks, and striking south-east over country not unsuited to the employment of these weapons, broke through the enemy's defences. On 22nd August the Fourth Army, on the right of the Third, was involved; and the III. Corps, with the 47th, 12th, and 18th Divisions in line, attacked in the general direction of the Albert-Bray road with the object of freeing Albert. The attack was everywhere successful; the passage of the Ancre was forced; Albert was regained; and the 47th Division, on the right, reached the high ground east of Happy Valley. On this day the 58th Division was in Corps reserve, and was not actively engaged.

A general advance on a front of thirty-three miles had been ordered for the 23rd when the situation was to some extent modified by the action of the enemy. The enemy, whose main forces were disposed three miles behind a false front, counter-attacked late on the 22nd along the whole line. Although in most sectors this counter-attack was repulsed, on the right the 142nd Brigade (47th Division) was driven back almost to its start-line, and its retirement had the effect of leaving in an uncomfortable salient the left flank of the Australian Corps, which, still farther to the right, had succeeded in occupying the high ground north of Bray.

During the night of the 22nd August and the early morning of the 23rd the 58th Division moved forward. The 175th Brigade was put at the disposal of the 47th Division, and relieved the 142nd Brigade in the line; the 174th Brigade was put at the disposal of the 18th Division; and the 173rd Brigade, moving up to the old Amiens Defence Line, remained in divisional reserve. The 2/2nd Londons left Querrieu at 4.30 a.m., and marched *via* the main Amiens-Albert road to a valley south of Méricourt l'Abbé, where they spent the remaining hours of daylight. At 11 p.m. the forward move was continued; and the Battalion eventually took up a position in a trench system two miles east of Morlancourt.

On 23rd August the great attack was launched, and was attended with considerable success. On the front of the III. Corps, the 18th Division made good progress in the neighbourhood of Albert. The 47th Division took no part in this day's attack, but spent the day reorganizing and preparing for a resumption of the attack on the morrow.

At 1 a.m. on the 24th, the 12th and 47th Divisions of the III. Corps continued the attack in conjunction with the 3rd Australian Division on the right. The attack of the 47th Division, which was carried out by the 140th Brigade and the 175th Brigade (attached), with the 173rd Brigade in support to the latter, was entirely successful; and Happy Valley once again passed into our hands. On the right the Australians captured Bray, and on the left the 12th Division advanced towards Fricourt. A notable feature of this day's fighting was the increasing demoralization of the enemy, which was manifest in the lessened resistance of his infantry.

During the morning the command of the right sector of the III. Corps' front passed from the 47th to the 58th Division; and the 174th Brigade was moved up into the line on the right of the 175th. Intelligence reports seeming to indicate that the enemy was only fighting a delaying action preparatory to a retirement on a large scale, orders were issued for a resumption of the attack at 4 p.m., and Lieut.-Col. Walsh was summoned to a conference of commanding officers of the 173rd Brigade, whereat all arrangements were made. Subsequently these orders were amended, the attack being postponed until 2.30 on the following morning. On the 24th the 2/2nd Londons remained near Morlancourt in reserve to the 173rd Brigade.

In the early hours of the 25th August the attack of the 58th Division was launched, the 175th Brigade being on the right and the 140th Brigade (47th

Division), attached for this operation, on the left. The 173rd Brigade was in close support, and was disposed with the 2/2nd Londons on the right, the 3rd Londons on the left, and the 2/4th Londons in brigade reserve. The 2/2nd Londons had moved up to a trench system west of Happy Valley during the night, and now advanced in the wake of the 175th Brigade.

A very thick mist prevailed, and, although each of the leading brigades gained its objective with little difficulty, touch with the enemy was lost. At 7.30 a.m. the 173rd Brigade was therefore ordered to pass through, and to regain contact with the enemy with as little delay as possible. An advanced guard, consisting of the 2/4th Londons, who had not yet deployed and were for that reason more easily accessible, a troop of Northumberland Hussars, a section of the 86th Brigade R.F.A., and a section M.G.C., was hastily formed; and, in conjunction with the 3rd Australian Division on the right and the 12th Division on the left, the advance was continued in the general direction of Bronfay Farm and Maricourt.

For some time the friendly mist persisted, and under the cover it afforded the advance rapidly continued. But as the advanced guard approached Bronfay Farm, the mist began to disperse, and the troops came under a brisk machine-gun fire from Billon Wood and the high ground to the north of it. The leading company of the 2/4th Londons, having succeeded in clearing Bronfay Farm, were soon heavily engaged about the south-western edge of Billon Wood. The remaining companies of this battalion were rapidly thrown in on the left of the leading company, but owing to the heavy fire from the high ground to the north could not immediately effect the clearance of the wood. The 2/2nd Londons, with the 3rd Londons in support, were ordered to make good this high ground with as little delay as possible, and to capture Billon Avenue, a long trench running east of the wood.

The attack was delivered at 4.30 p.m., and met with a considerable measure of success. Although the resistance of the enemy's infantry was not very serious, the attacking troops were subjected to an intense artillery bombardment, and to heavy machine-gun fire from Maricourt and Billon Avenue, and from Billon Wood itself. Notwithstanding this heavy fire, good progress up the long spur leading to Maricourt was made by the 2/2nd and 3rd Londons; a part of Billon Avenue was captured; and Billon Wood was finally cleared by the 2/4th Londons.

At the conclusion of the operation the 2/2nd Londons, with two companies on the final objective, were astride the Péronne road in a chain of small copses in front of Maricourt. As no connexion had been established on the left with the 12th Division, which was held up before Carnoy, the

Battalion's left flank was refused, one company being established in Laprée Wood, south-east of Carnoy. Further progress was quite out of the question with the enemy in strength in Carnoy on the flank and in the western outskirts of Maricourt in front. At dusk the 2/2nd Londons were reinforced by two companies of the 3rd Londons, and the 2/4th Londons were relieved by units of the 174th Brigade, which 'side-slipped' to the left for this purpose.

In co-operation with the 12th Division on the left, the attack was continued on the 26th; but the operations on this day were not so successful as heretofore. At 4.30 a.m. the 3rd Londons, who led the attack, with the 2/2nd Londons in support and 2/4th Londons in reserve, advanced on Maricourt, covered by a heavy barrage. Although the troops penetrated the village in the face of desperate opposition from the enemy in Crest Avenue, they could not maintain their hold, being unsupported by the flanking brigades, which were still held up. The safety of the left flank was further threatened by the massing of enemy troops at this point, apparently with the object of counter-attacking, and, although this counter-attack did not actually develop, the threat made it advisable for the three battalions to fall back. The rest of the day was passed in consolidating a position about 500 yards west of Maricourt.

At 4.55 a.m. on the following day the 173rd Brigade resumed its attack on Maricourt. The leading battalion, the 3rd Londons, captured the village, and, aided by the 2/4th Londons, pushed the enemy back to the old British front line of 1916 on the eastern fringe of Marrières Wood. The Germans, whose resistance was very stubborn, were in great strength, three fresh divisions being identified on the front of the 58th Division. The 2/2nd Londons dropped back into brigade reserve, and held a trench system running north and south through 'U' Works. Later in the day they were ordered to mop up Maricourt; and one company raked the town from front to rear. Although all cellars and dug-outs were carefully searched, few prisoners were taken.

The troops on either flank of the Brigade were equally successful, Vaux being captured by the Australians on the right, and the high ground about Maltz Horn Farm by the 12th Division on the left. The total advance by the British on this day covered about a mile.

Although the troops were fast becoming exhausted by this continuous fighting, the pressure on the enemy could not be relaxed for a moment; and the 58th Division was ordered to continue the advance on the 28th August. The 173rd Brigade was still in the line, and its attack was entrusted to the 2/2nd Londons, who were brought up from brigade reserve for the purpose.

The orders for the attack did not reach Lieut.-Col. Walsh until 1 a.m.; nevertheless the Battalion assembled successfully on the eastern edge of Maricourt Wood, and at 4.55 a.m. advanced under a creeping barrage, with the 3rd Londons in support. The objective of the Battalion was a line from Support Copse to the Bois d'en Haut, and required only a short advance. Although the hostile shelling was heavy, the resistance of the enemy's infantry was not very pronounced, with the result that 'A' Company on the right was soon in Support Copse; and by 8 a.m. the whole objective, except its northern end in the Bois d'en Haut, was in the hands of the 2/2nd Londons. Attempts were at once made to secure the wood; and a series of patrol encounters resulted. At 10.15 a.m. Clapham Farm was reported to be occupied; but it was not until shortly after noon that the whole of the wood was cleared, and Clapham Farm finally made good. During the morning the Battalion's right flank was pushed forward for half-a-mile in front of Support Copse; and during the afternoon the line gained was consolidated. In the evening the 173rd Brigade was relieved by the 175th, which, reinforced by the Pioneer Battalion (1/4th Suffolks), took over the whole of the divisional front. The 2/2nd Londons withdrew to Death Valley, and marched by companies to Hem Wood next day.

The Battalion's casualties during this fighting were:

KILLED : 2 officers (2nd Lieuts. C. E. Green and J. Emerson) and 53 other ranks.
WOUNDED : 6 officers (Lieut. H. Gimson, 2nd Lieuts. E. M. Tatlow, J. Cantrell, F. S. Wallis, H. Seaward, R. W. T. Chapman), and 252 other ranks.
MISSING : 59 other ranks.

During the few days in divisional reserve that were now accorded to the 2/2nd Londons, the attack of the 58th Division was taken up first by the 175th and later by the 174th Brigade; and on the 29th August the former carried the line forward to the east of Maurepas. On the next day the 47th Division relieved the 12th Division on the left; and the two London divisions found themselves once again advancing shoulder to shoulder.

The Fourth Army was now approaching Péronne; and the Australians had reached the west bank of the Somme. Although the river offered a naturally strong line of defence to the enemy, it was not allowed to delay the British advance. On the night of the 30th/31st August the Australian Corps crossed the river, and by a remarkable feat of arms stormed Mont St. Quentin, a conspicuous landmark, and a position from which observation could be obtained over large areas of the surrounding country. This place was the key to Péronne, and its capture compromised the whole German line on the Somme. This success was immediately exploited by the III. Corps on the left of the Australians; and during the 31st August the 174th Brigade attacked and captured Marrières Wood and the high ground overlooking Bouchavesnes.

On this day unexpected orders were received for the 173rd Brigade to return to the line, and to deliver an attack on the morrow on Bouchavesnes and the high ground beyond it. 'Embussing' at 2 p.m., the 173rd Brigade eventually relieved the 175th Brigade on the line of the Bapaume-Cambrai road. Although the march from the point at which the units left the buses to their assembly positions was much delayed by the congestion of traffic, the attacking troops were assembled by 3 a.m.

Zero hour was 5.30 a.m.; and on a cold clear morning the 2/4th Londons on the right and the 3rd Londons on the left, with the 2/2nd Londons in support, attacked under a creeping barrage. The village of Bouchavesnes was captured, and the old British line east of it was made good. The Brigade's advance was then checked by the stubborn resistance of the enemy and by the loss of connexion with the flanking units, whose progress had been slower than its own. This connexion was eventually re-established; and the Brigade made good its final objective on the high ground overlooking the River Tortille and the Canal du Nord.

The position gained was made secure, and at dusk was handed over to units of the 74th Division, which then relieved the 58th Division in the line. The 58th Division now passed into Corps reserve; and the 2/2nd Londons spent the opening days of September in rest and training.

The casualties of the 2/2nd Londons on the 1st September were:

> KILLED: 5 other ranks.
> WOUNDED: 1 officer and 24 other ranks.
> MISSING: 2 other ranks.

The following officer reinforcements were received at the end of August or during the first week of September:

2nd Lieuts. J. Carter, H. Dowsett, A. H. Edge, and P. C. H. Grist.

It is interesting to note that the advance of the 2/2nd Londons since the 23rd August had passed close to the scenes of the 1/2nd Londons' fighting in the historic Battle of the Somme almost exactly two years before. But how vastly different were the experiences of the two battalions! In 1916 progress was very slow, and every advance was carried out over water-logged crater fields at a great sacrifice of life and with a great expenditure of energy.

A gain of a few hundred yards was hailed as a victory. And so indeed it was, a victory over a redoubtable foe, as well as over the inexorable forces of Nature. In 1918, although the fighting was often heavy, the conditions were far different, and the advance was rapid. Since the opening of the battle the line had been carried forward more than ten miles, and the devastation of the old Somme battlefields had been left behind.

Without belittling in any way the magnificent prowess of the British troops of 1918, it is but fair to observe that their more rapid progress was in part attributable to the demoralization that was now becoming manifest in the ranks of the enemy. Although in certain instances they made a gallant resistance to the British advance, generally speaking the German infantry displayed little of that stubbornness that had so characterized their defence in previous British offensives. It was left to the German machine gunners and artillery seriously to delay the British during the operations of August and September, and very well they discharged their task. The artillery personnel, especially, displayed great skill in fighting a succession of rear-guard actions. Field guns were bravely and skilfully handled, being kept in action in the little copses with which the countryside abounds, and firing over open sights until the last possible moment. When at last these field guns were forced to withdraw, the fire was taken up by high velocity guns, firing at extreme ranges in rear. The plucky action of the gunners occasionally ended in disaster; and more than one gun could not be removed owing to the rapidity of our advance, and fell into our hands.

The operations in which the Battalion had taken an important share are officially known as the Second Battles of the Somme, 1918,[1] of which the first phase, 21st-23rd August, constitutes the Battle of Albert, and the second phase until the 2nd September, the Second Battle of Bapaume. These operations had important and far-reaching results, the bearing of which on the general situation will be discussed later.

---

[1] The British Commander-in-Chief designated the whole of the fighting from the 21st to the 31st August and on subsequent days the Battle of Bapaume, and he has been followed by Mr. Winston Churchill and others.

The author, however, has thought it best, in describing the final British advance, to adhere to the official nomenclature of the Battle Honours Committee in order to identify the honours awarded to the Regiment with the actual fighting in which one or other of its battalions took part.

Wherever a divergence between the name given to a battle by the Commander-in-Chief and that finally adopted by the Battle Honours Committee occurs it will be duly noted in the text.

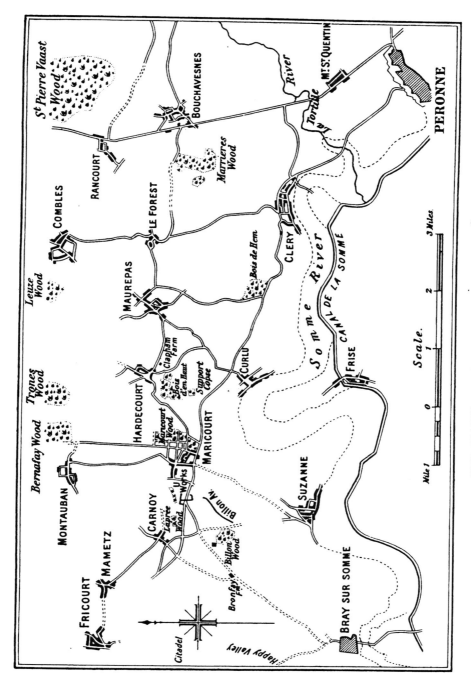

THE SECOND BATTLES OF THE SOMME, 1918.

CHAPTER XXIII

THE 1/2ND LONDONS IN THE SECOND BATTLES OF ARRAS, 1918[1]

IN the previous chapter the reasons that led Sir Douglas Haig to extend the British offensive northward between the Somme and the Scarpe have been set forth, and the general course of the resulting battle, so far as it affected the Fourth Army, has been described. It now remains to describe the course of the battle on the front of the Third Army, which had become involved by the northward extension of the fighting.

It will be recalled that the object of the Third Army, comprising, from right to left, the V., IV., VI., and XVII. Corps, was first to make good the line of the Arras-Albert railway, and then to threaten by a vast enveloping movement the flank of the German line on the Somme and to open a way to the main strategic objective, Cambrai-St. Quentin. Formidable as this task appeared to be, there were certain factors in the situation favourable to its success.

The British troops now held the commanding ridge of high ground south of Arras about Bucquoy and Ablainzeville, giving observation over a wide area, and at the same time were either astride or east of the intricate trench system that in the days of the old Somme battle had proved such a formidable obstacle. Moreover, the successful British advance south of the Somme on the 8th August and subsequent days had had the effect of making the enemy very nervous as to the safety of his troops in the salient between the Somme and the Scarpe, and had even induced him to withdraw from his most advanced positions about Serre.

On the other hand, if the British aims were to be fully realized, it was desirable to avoid a repetition of the skilful German retreat of 1917. It was therefore essential that the British offensive be opened without undue delay, and prosecuted with the utmost vigour. As we have seen, the 21st August was chosen for the opening day of the attack, after a minimum of time had been spent in essential preparation.

---

[1] The fighting in which the 1/2nd Londons took part between the 27th and 31st August conforms to the limits laid down by the Battle Honours Committee for the Second Battle of the Scarpe, 1918, which constitutes the first phase of the Second Battles of Arras, 1918. The whole of the operations of the Third Army between these dates are included by Sir Douglas Haig in his Battle of Bapaume.

We left the 1/2nd Londons at Grand Rullecourt, whither they had gone for a reſt on the withdrawal of the 56th Division into Corps reserve. A long reſt, however, was not given them; for on the 19th Auguſt orders were received for the 56th Division to take part in an attack on the front of the XVII. Corps againſt Orange and Chapel Hills, south of the Scarpe; and, although these orders were almoſt immediately cancelled, the Division was transferred on the 21ſt to the VI. Corps (Lieut.-General Sir J. A. L. Haldane) for the purpose of taking part in the attack of the Third Army.

On the 19th Auguſt the 1/2nd Londons moved by buses to Berneville, marching thence to Dainville for the night. In the evening of the next day they marched to Fosseux, where they were rejoined by Lieut.-Col. Kellett, recalled from leave, and on the 21ſt their march continued to Saulty. After reſting at Saulty during the 22nd, whereon Lieut.-Col. Kellett attended a conference at Brigade Headquarters to discuss the plans for the forth-coming operations, they moved forward to Basseaux on the 23rd. This day's march was very trying; the road was congeſted with advancing cavalry and artillery; and progress was slow and difficult. Nevertheless, the men were in splendid spirits and ready for the now imminent battle.

Officer reinforcements received during the month to date were:

Lieut. A. S. Jarvis, 2nd Lieuts. S. H. Clifford, J. H. T. Andrews, J. Line, L. Fairney, and J. C. Summers.

Only two divisions of the VI. Corps (2nd and Guards) were actively engaged in the preliminary fighting of the 21ſt Auguſt, resulting in the recovery of Albert on the 22nd, but in the main operations opened on the 23rd the 56th Division was also engaged.[1]

On this day the 168th Brigade attacked and captured Boyelles and Boiry Becquerelle, and subsequently advanced about 1,000 yards to Boyelles Reserve Trench. On the next day the attack was taken up by the 167th Brigade with the object of enveloping Croisilles from the north, while the Guards Division carried out a similar operation from the south. The 167th Brigade succeeded in securing its firſt objective, Summit Trench, which lay about 800 yards weſt of the village, but failed in its attack on Croisilles itself owing to the ſtrength of the enemy's machine-gun defences. Renewed attempts on the next day proved equally abortive.

On the 26th Auguſt the 52nd and 56th Divisions were transferred to the XVII. Corps (Lieut.-General Sir C. Fergusson), and continued the

---

[1] The 56th Division was thus present at the Battle of Albert, 1918, which con-ſtitutes the firſt of the Second Battles of the Somme, 1918.

attack. The 52nd Division cleared the line from the Cojeul River to Hénin Hill, while the 167th Brigade made another unsuccessful attack on Croisilles. At 6 p.m. the 167th Brigade was relieved by the 169th with all three battalions in line, the Q.W.R. on the right, the L.R.B. in the centre, and the 1/2nd Londons on the left; and orders were issued for the next day's attack to be pressed round the north of Croisilles to the Hindenburg Line.

The progress of the 1/2nd Londons to the front line had been gradual. After spending the night of the 23rd/24th in the fields between Basseux and Bailleulval, they marched through Blaireville to Mercatel Switch, where a halt of a few hours was made. In the afternoon the march was continued to Boiry Reserve Trench and Boiry Work. The Battalion remained in this position during the whole of the 25th and the greater part of the 26th, whereon orders for the relief of the 167th Brigade were received. At 5 p.m. the Battalion moved forward in artillery formation, and eventually relieved the 1/1st Londons in Summit Trench.

Immediately after the relief was complete, the 1/2nd Londons were ordered to establish posts in Fooley Trench opposite their front. With this object two platoons each from 'A,' 'C,' and 'D' Companies formed up outside the uncut and very thick wire of Summit Trench, and at 2.45 a.m. on the 27th made a stealth attack on Fooley Trench. The trench was still occupied by the enemy in strength; and heavy machine-gun fire from it, as well as from the Hindenburg Line and from the direction of Croisilles, held up the attackers. A section of 'A' Company, under Sergt. Ayton, succeeded in getting within measurable distance of its objective, but in its gallant effort was wiped out to a man. Although the line of Fooley Trench was not made good, a number of posts was firmly established in advance of Summit Trench.

The Battalion suffered in all 43 casualties; and many of the wounded were lying in No Man's Land. 2nd Lieut. Merrikin at once volunteered to take out a party to bring them in, and, while gallantly carrying out this task, was killed by machine-gun fire.

In the area with which we are now concerned, the main system of the Hindenburg Line, after coming in a south-easterly direction from Héninel, ran almost due east for a distance of about 2,000 yards to the outskirts of Fontaine lez Croisilles before bending again south-east towards Bullecourt. The 52nd Division, on the left of the 56th, was now advancing along the Hindenburg Line eastwards towards Fontaine lez Croisilles; and the task of the 169th Brigade was to keep in touch with this division by sweeping round the north of Croisilles. Accordingly, while the Q.W.R. on the right made a frontal attack on Croisilles, the L.R.B. in the centre and the 1/2nd Londons on the left were ordered to gain the Hindenburg Line on their front and then to face half-right with the object of pushing down the Hindenburg Line and enveloping the village from the north-east.

The dispositions of the 1/2nd Londons were as follows:

RIGHT: 'A' Company (Capt. Harington).
LEFT: 'C' Company (2nd Lieut. Coatman).
SUPPORT: 'D' Company (2nd Lieut. Thomas).
RESERVE: 'B' Company (Capt. Attenborough).

At 9.36 a.m. on the 27th August the attack was launched. The weather was fine, and the ground dry, circumstances favourable to the attackers; but the barrage, moving one hundred yards in four minutes, was very weak and afforded little protection. Fooley Trench was cleared, a number of prisoners and 12 machine guns being captured; and despite heavy enfilade fire from Croisilles the advance was continued as far as Farmer's Trench.

Lieut.-Col. Kellett went forward with the Battalion; he had not gone far before he was overtaken by a perspiring orderly with a message that the Brigadier wished to speak to him on the telephone. Handing over the command of advanced Battalion Headquarters to Capt. Ward, he returned to Summit Trench. While stationed in Summit Trench, he observed that the right flank of the Battalion had become uncovered in its advance, and was exposed to attack from Croisilles. Collecting all the men who were in Summit Trench, chiefly Headquarters' personnel, he immediately sent them forward, with such machine guns as were available, to protect the right flank, and at the same time warned Capt. Ward to take similar precautions. Fortunately for the attackers, the opportunity of administering a serious check to their progress was let slip by the enemy, and the danger passed.

The Battalion's advance had been very creditably carried out, and represented the nearest approach to open warfare that had hitherto been attempted. Further progress over the open being impossible owing to the steady increase in the enfilade machine-gun fire from Croisilles, the Battalion remained deployed in Farmer's Trench for the rest of the morning. Shortly after midday, Lieut. Telford, the Battalion Intelligence Officer, showing commendable initiative, found that Sensée Avenue, a covered approach to the Hindenburg Line, was clear of the enemy, and reported this fact to Lieut.-Col. Kellett, who, grasping its full significance, ordered him to lead the Battalion along it with as little delay as possible. 'B' Company having been left at the junction of Farmer's Trench and Sensée Avenue to form a defensive flank facing Croisilles, the rest of the Battalion moved forward along Sensée Avenue at 3 p.m., and, being now under cover from the enemy's machine guns, ultimately reached without much difficulty the line of Nellie Avenue and Sensée Reserve in the Hindenburg Line. It was at this point that Lieut.-Col. Kellett rejoined the Battalion after an exciting journey, of which the story is best told in his own words:

> Christian[1] and I carried out a masterly advance on our own by short rushes, in accordance with the teaching in the manuals. The grass was long, and the day was very hot. After each rush we got down and then crept forward. We thus got up in advance of the last spot in which we had been sited. Hence by the time the machine gun could lay on us and open fire, we had again disappeared. In this way we defeated the machine gun, which could not observe 'strike' in the long grass although many bursts passed perilously near. However, the alternatives for us were to remain *in situ* until about 8 p.m., creep forward for over 1,000 yards in daylight, or do as we did.
>
> During one of the rushes my revolver and I parted company; we had seen nothing of the Battalion all this time, but I decided to do the last rush to the Hindenburg Line without it. I was armed only with a malacca cane, and Christian with his rifle. When I explained the situation to him, he said: 'That's all right, sir, I'll give 'em hell if they are there!' You can judge my delight when leaping in and turning a corner we met a London soldier with a typical battle-grin on his face.

The Battalion had made good its objective in the Hindenburg Line, and was now facing south-east in readiness for an advance along its length. Its left flank was in touch with the 52nd Division, but its right flank was still in the air owing to the continued occupation of Croisilles by the enemy. Of Sensée Avenue and its important contribution to the Battalion's success on this day Lieut.-Col. Kellett writes:

> Looking at the map, it is the obvious way to the Hindenburg Line from Farmer's Trench. Prior to the show, a solemn procession along the trench was not judged to be the best way to the

---

[1] Lieut.-Col. Kellett's servant.

objective. However, the event proved this was the only possible way, and as such, it was used by the whole Battalion. I cannot think why the enemy was not holding it.

During the day's fighting, besides gaining its objective, the Battalion captured 4 prisoners, 15 machine guns, and 1 anti-tank gun; on the other hand it had not achieved these results without considerable loss, and its casualties amounted to more than 200, in which number were included all the officers of 'A' Company. The Medical Officer (Capt. Bowden) was among the wounded, but remained at duty.

Croisilles was the obstacle that stood in the way of the British advance. The Guards Division had attacked to the right of the village, but after an initial success, had been counter-attacked severely and forced to fall back. Although Croisilles was still holding out, orders were issued to the 56th Division to attack the Bullecourt area the next day.

During the night the dispositions of the Division were changed. The 167th Brigade took over the right of the divisional front; and the 168th Brigade moved into position to support the 169th in the attack along the Hindenburg Line. The objectives of the last-named were, first, Queen's Lane-Jove Lane (communication trenches within the Hindenburg Line system), and, secondly, the trenches south-east of Bullecourt. The attack was to be delivered by the Q.W.R., with both the L.R.B. and the 1/2nd Londons in support.

The difficulties inherent in any assembly for an attack were increased in the case of the 1/2nd Londons on this occasion by the abnormal congestion in the trenches resulting from the assembly of units of the 52nd Division in the same area for a continuation of their attack. Notwithstanding these difficulties, the assembly was completed in King's Avenue by 11.45 a.m., and the Battalion was disposed as follows:

RIGHT: 'D' Company (2 officers and 48 other ranks).
LEFT: 'B' Company (2 officers and 51 other ranks).
SUPPORT: 'A' and 'C' Companies (3 officers and 59 other ranks).
    The fighting strength of the Battalion, including the 4 officers and 35 other ranks of Battalion Headquarters, was thus 11 officers and 193 other ranks.

The barrage opened at 12.20 p.m., and at zero, ten minutes later, the attacking troops went forward. The action that followed is one of the utmost confusion. The left company of the Q.W.R., which had assembled in Nellie Avenue (North) at right angles to its line of advance, had to effect a change of front before advancing. In executing this manœuvre— always a difficult one in the face of an enemy—, this company lost direction and went off to the left, followed by the reserve company of the same battalion. At the same time, the right company of this battalion, on emerging from its assembly position, found the space between the enemy's trenches completely filled with uncut wire. Progress down this was obviously impossible; and, as a result, this company likewise edged off to the left. In the case of this company the drift to the left instead of to the right resulted from the natural tendency to follow the line of least resistance. The weight of the attack was on the left flank, where the 52nd Division was making good progress, whereas, on the right flank, the advance was still held up in front of Croisilles. These three companies of the Q.W.R. were followed by 'A' and 'B' Companies, the two left companies of the 1/2nd Londons; and all became inextricably mixed with units of the 52nd Division.

Meanwhile, on the right front of the 1/2nd Londons, 'C' and 'D' Companies, following the barrage, which, though stronger than on the previous day, did not succeed in keeping down the enemy's machine-gun fire, worked along Tunnel Trench—the identical Tunnel Trench that had defied the efforts of the 2/2nd Londons in the Battle of Bullecourt in June 1917. Lewis guns were brought into action in shell-holes, and materially assisted the advance. Three German machine guns were rushed, and some prisoners taken.

The 1/2nd London Headquarters' details were in Burg Support, where they had joined the Headquarters of the Q.W.R. and of the L.R.B. The situation at this time was very confused, and, with the object of producing some kind of order out of the general chaos, Lieut.-Col. Kellett proposed to the commanding officers of these battalions that his battalion should deal with Tunnel Trench, while they made themselves responsible for all the trenches between it and Croisilles. This suggestion was approved, and forth-with put into practice. The Headquarters' parties of the three battalions continued their own advance along Burg Support, and after progressing for about 500 yards came in contact with strong enemy forces. Believing that his companies were still ahead of him and that they had not properly mopped up the trench, Lieut.-Col. S. A. Savill, commanding the Q.W.R., sent back word for reinforcements. These reinforcements were inevitably a long time in coming up, and in the interval the Headquarters' parties, by strenuous and gallant fighting, reached the junction of Hump Lane and Burg Support. Eventually a company of the 1/4th Londons arrived, one platoon of which was put at Lieut.-Col. Savill's disposal to help to clear the trench.

In Tunnel Trench, despite a serious shortage of rifle-grenades and Lewis-gun ammunition, 'C' and 'D' Companies, supported by two companies of the 1/4th Londons that had been sent up to their assistance, continued to make good progress. At 5.30, Lieut.-Col. Kellett was able to report:

> My men and 4th Londons in Tunnel Trench have cleared the numerous machine guns which have been holding them up. They are now advancing along Tunnel rapidly.

And about two hours later he reported:

> My men have reached U.14.c.95.65, and are dealing with a machine-gun nest near Knuckle Avenue. I have only 45 men in this trench (Tunnel) but two companies of 4th Londons are supporting, and in view of the extreme fatigue of my men and their shortage of munitions, Col. Marchment is undertaking operations to clear out the still numerous machine guns which are active on the ridge. My men are helping him. Have had four officer casualties (including my Adjutant).

At 8.30 Lieut.-Col. Kellett established his headquarters at the junction of Bow Lane and Tunnel Trench, and at this point reorganized the remnant of his battalion, which, excluding Headquarters' personnel, was now reduced to 3 officers and 80 men.

Nothing had been heard of 'A' and 'B' Companies throughout the day. It subsequently transpired that they had followed the straying companies of the Q.W.R., and had eventually reached Cemetery Avenue in front of Hendecourt lez Cagnicourt instead of a point in front of Bullecourt. In extenuation of this loss of direction it must be remembered that the ground had been reduced by the ebb and flow of battle to a featureless waste, covered with weeds and long grass; villages and other landmarks shown on the maps had long ceased to exist; and these facts largely discounted the possible advantages accruing from a daylight advance.

During its misdirected advance on Hendecourt, 'A' Company attacked a German post, and succeeded in killing many of its occupants and in capturing 11 prisoners. On reaching the neighbourhood of the village, the two companies, in conjunction with the Q.W.R., took up a position alongside the 172nd Brigade (52nd Division), where they remained until the following day.

The casualties of the Battalion on this day included Capt. Pratt, the Adjutant, whose duties were taken over by Capt. Dyer.

Early on the 29th orders were received that the attack was to be continued by the 56th Division, whose objective was the trench system lying east of Bullecourt and south of Riencourt. The 168th Brigade was on the right, the 169th on the left, and the 167th in support. The 169th Brigade assembled in the trenches north-west of Pelican Lane, which was still held by small parties of the enemy. The L.R.B. led the attack with two companies, 40 men of the Q.W.R—all that could be found—being in close support, and the 1/2nd Londons, with a total strength of 7 officers and 95 other ranks, being in reserve for mopping up. It should be noted that the 1/2nd Londons' numbers included the errant 'A' and 'B' Companies, which had been collected and had rejoined the Battalion at daybreak.

By 11.45 a.m. the 1/2nd Londons had assembled, the 50 men of 'A' and 'B' Companies being on the left, and the 45 men of 'C' and 'D' Companies and Battalion Headquarters on the right, and at zero (1 p.m.) moved forward in the teeth of intense machine-gun fire from the front and both flanks. The whole brigade gradually fought its way forward, and by 6.30 p.m. reached Saddler Lane and the sunken road on the left of the village of Bullecourt. During the advance, the 1/2nd Londons, who ultimately reached the sunken road, put out of action 8 machine guns and captured a number of prisoners.

The position at the end of the day was somewhat obscure, but was eventually cleared up by 2nd Lieut. Coatman, who, in full view of the enemy and in face of heavy machine-gun fire, made a daylight reconnaissance of the line of isolated positions that the Brigade had reached. He then succeeded in fighting his way back to Battalion Headquarters, where he made his report, and, as the result of his information, new dispositions for some of the posts were made by Br.-General Coke. 2nd Lieut. Coatman was again sent forward, and, after disposing of several snipers on his way up from Battalion Headquarters, was successful in manning and establishing the posts for the night. For his courage and initiative on this occasion he was subsequently awarded the M.C. The 169th Brigade was relieved on the evening of the 29th August by the 167th Brigade; and the 1/2nd Londons moved back to Tunnel Trench.

The casualties of the 1/2nd Londons on the 29th included Lieut.-Col. Kellett, who was slightly wounded in the arm.

Throughout these operations, the British artillery could find no positions from which to bombard the Hindenburg Line except at long range; hence the stubbornness of the enemy in Croisilles, and the intensive activity of his machine-gun defence. The heavy machine-gun fire made the attacking troops keep to the trenches, and much delayed the assembly on the night of the 27th/28th and the attack next day. As no other means proved effective, it became necessary on the 28th to carry up trench mortars— 'more agony,' is Lieut.-Col. Kellett's comment—to break the resistance of the German machine gunners. Most of these were young men, who fought stubbornly, and were dislodged only with the greatest difficulty. In these trying circumstances the Battalion had fought very well, its advance on the 27th being especially commendable.

The total casualties of the Battalion during these operations were:

KILLED: 1 officer (2nd Lieut. G. H. Merrikin) and 39 other ranks.

WOUNDED: 13 officers (Lieut.-Col. J. P. Kellett, D.S.O., M.C., Capts. E. J. Harington, H. D. Pratt, E. C. Bowden, Lieut. A. S. Jarvis, 2nd Lieuts. C. W. Conolley, L. Fairney, F. P. Deere, L. May, W. J. Thomas, A. C. Wilding, J. McNaughton, and A. J. Hasslacher) and 220 other ranks.

MISSING: 1 officer (Lieut. F. G. Garside). This officer was subsequently reported as killed.

The following honours were awarded in connexion with these operations:

M.C.: Capt. E. C. Bowden, Rev. R. F. Diggle, 2nd Lieuts. H. E. Coatman and W. J. Telford.

The Division was relieved on the 31st August, and marched out of the line. The 1/2nd Londons, on relief, withdrew from Tunnel Trench, and, after a march of three hours, reached a trench system near Boisleux au Mont.

The 56th Division had played a distinguished part in the great battle now drawing to a close. In the course of nine days it had met and defeated three German divisions; it had advanced six miles over very strongly fortified country; it had captured 1,076 prisoners, 3 guns, 210 machine guns, and more than 50 trench mortars. Its achievement in this successful battle was the subject of an article published in *The Times* early in September, 1918, of which we may be pardoned for reprinting the following extract:

This year it was one of the divisions which beat off the German attack towards Arras on March 28th when the enemy suffered one of

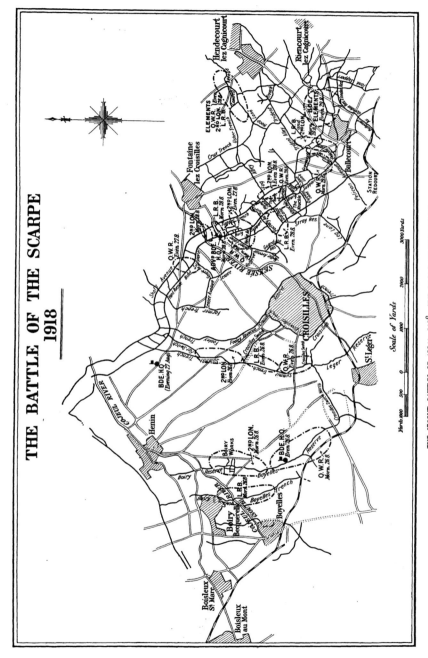

THE SECOND BATTLES OF ARRAS, 1918—THE BATTLE OF THE SCARPE.

the bloodiest defeats of the whole war; so that with this fighting
and that at Cambrai to its credit it has probably killed as many
Germans as any division in the British Army. Now to this proud
record is to be added the splendid advance of which the Commander-in-Chief has told. The 56th Division has proved itself a
great fighting division.

The great Battles of Bapaume and Arras ultimately achieved all their
objects. Bapaume was regained on the 29th August, and Péronne on the
1st September. On the 2nd September the left of the First Army joined in
the advance; and the Canadian Corps and the 4th Division assaulted and
captured the powerful Drocourt-Quéant Switch Line. Whereupon, the
enemy abandoned the whole line of the Somme, and from the River Oise
to the Sensée began a general retirement to the Hindenburg Line.

In these successful operations, which, in the words of Marshal Foch,
will 'serve as a model for all time,' the three British armies had advanced,
on an average, to a depth of 20 miles, and had captured 53,000 prisoners
and 470 guns. But of far more importance to the Allies' cause even than
these substantial material gains was the evidence of the continued loss of
morale on the part of the enemy and of the rapid consumption of his
reserves.

CHAPTER XXIV

THE 2/2ND LONDONS IN THE BATTLE OF EPÉHY

WHEN the 58th Division came back to the battle-zone on the 6th September, it found the enemy in full retreat to the Hindenburg Line. Evidence of this was not wanting; the air was filled with the reverberations of exploding dumps; and near and far the night sky was illumined by the glow of burning villages. Nevertheless, the Germans were contesting the ground every inch of the way; and strong rear guards barred the progress of the attacking troops as long as possible.

The 58th Division relieved the 47th Division in the centre of the Corps front on a line running from a point a quarter of a mile east of Aizecourt to the eastern edge of Lièramont. The 12th Division was on the left, and the 74th on the right. On the 7th September the advance was continued, the 58th Division capturing Saulcourt and assisting the 12th Division in the capture of Guyencourt. On this day the 173rd Brigade was brought up by buses into divisional reserve.

The Corps front was now reduced to two divisions; and the 58th Division, handing over the southern portion of the centre sector to the 74th, took over the left sector from the 12th Division. The 174th Brigade was in the line, and on the 8th attacked the villages of Epéhy and Peizière. Little progress was made, the enemy resisting stoutly and by means of counter-attacks maintaining his hold on the villages. The 2/2nd Londons, acting as advanced guard to the 173rd Brigade, moved on this day into Lièramont, where they were heavily shelled. After the unsuccessful attempt of the 174th Brigade to force the enemy from his position, there was a breathing space of a day while arrangements were made for the renewal of the attack, this time by the 173rd Brigade, on the 10th September.

The villages of Epéhy and Peizière, which topographically are really one, stand on the last ridge on the western side of the Canal du Nord, in a position that nature and the hand of man had combined to make strong for defence. They formed part of the outpost system of the Hindenburg Line, and constituted a very formidable position to be attacked without considerable artillery preparation or without the assistance of a large force of tanks. Nevertheless, the stiffening of the enemy's defence made it essential for Fourth Army Headquarters to learn whether its leading divisions were still only opposed by rear guards or had now 'bumped' into a position on which the enemy intended to make a determined stand; to obtain this information an attack by the III. Corps was ordered for the 10th September, the 58th Division being given Epéhy and Peizière as its objective, and the 74th Division Ronssoy Wood.

The 173rd Brigade was detailed for the attack, of which the plan was as follows: The 2/2nd Londons, with the 2/4th in close support, were to attack Peizière from the west through Wood Farm; at the same time the 3rd Londons were to attack Epéhy from the south-west, directing their advance along the spur running north-east and south-west. The final objective of both battalions was Prince Reserve Trench, lying just east of the villages. The 2/4th Londons were to follow the 2/2nd in the initial stages, and were then to turn south in order to mop up the area between the two leading battalions. Flank protection was to be furnished by the 2/7th Londons (174th Brigade) and by one company of the 2/8th on the right, and by the 21st Division on the left. Immediately the villages were captured, the 21st Division was to attack the ridge running north and south beyond them.

Although time for reconnaissance had been short, and although the darkness and heavy rain made conditions very difficult, the approach march of the attacking troops was very good. The battalions formed up in their assembly positions, and at 5.15 a.m. they moved forward under a creeping barrage. The bad weather persisted; and the enemy's resistance, especially on each flank, was very stubborn. Nevertheless, the British troops struggled through the villages. No news of their progress came back until 8 o'clock, when it appeared that the 2/2nd Londons had passed through Peizière, and that elements of the Battalion under Capt. Wright had reached their objective in Prince Reserve Trench. The 3rd Londons passed through Epéhy in like manner and reached the line of the railway to the east of it. Enemy machine-gun nests abounded in each village, and these held out stubbornly; the artillery did not deal with them effectively, and the 173rd Brigade, whose strength was now reduced to about 900, could not mop them up unaided. The 2/2nd Londons found themselves surrounded, and, their position rapidly becoming untenable, they had to fight their way back. In this they were successful, and withdrew eventually to the trenches just west of Peizière, retaining hold on Tottenham Post in advance of the left of the line.

The task had proved too much for the Brigade. The frontage of the attack was 2,000 yards, and as battalions were very weak, all three had to be employed in the front line; and although one company of the 8th Londons was placed at the disposal of the Brigadier for defensive purposes, the lack of sufficient troops prevented adequate mopping-up of the captured posts and trenches. Moreover, the 21st Division, on the left flank, did not capture its objectives, which included Chapel Hill and the ridge running south of it; and from these points the enemy effectively enfiladed the approaches to Peizière and Epéhy.

At 1.30 p.m. the 173rd Brigade was ordered to make an attempt to establish a line from McPhee Post, in Peizière, through Morgan Post to the eastern outskirts of Epéhy, since the enemy was believed to be very disorganized and in no condition to continue an effective defence. A battalion of the 175th Brigade was attached to the 173rd Brigade for this purpose; and, as no deliberate attack was possible, infiltration tactics were adopted to establish the line. No better success rewarded this further effort; and in the evening the 173rd Brigade was relieved by the 175th, the 2/2nd Londons withdrawing to Guyencourt.

The Battalion's casualties in this day's fighting amounted to 9 officers and 164 other ranks. The officers were as follows:

KILLED: 2nd Lieut. J. S. Lamb.
WOUNDED: 2nd Lieuts. E. G. Evans and W. Reynolds.
MISSING: 2nd Lieuts. F. M. Bennett, A. R. Fox, A. H. Edge, J. H. J. Dewey, H. A. Graham,* and R. F. Larcombe.*
Those marked * were later reported wounded.

The ill-success of this somewhat unprepared attack on the Hindenburg outpost line clearly demonstrated that the enemy was making a determined stand on this line. It was wisely decided to make no further attempt until adequate preparations could be made, and a deliberate assault carried out in all its details. For the next week, therefore, no further advance was made on the front of the 58th Division, touch being maintained with the enemy by active patrolling.

Both battalions being much reduced in numbers, the 2/4th Londons were amalgamated with the 2/2nd Londons on the day after the attack on Peizière. The latter battalion was allowed to retain its identity, and, as a consequence of the amalgamation, received the welcome addition to its strength of the following nineteen officers:

Major F. G. Tollworthy, M.C. (who became second-in-command), Capt. G. H. Hetley, M.C., Lieut. A. B. Carpenter, 2nd Lieuts. W. H. G. Newman, J. T. Spencer, A. W. Tucker, J. Blair, E. V. Grimsdell, M.C., F. P. Johnson,

The 2/2nd Londons in the Battle of Epéhy

A. R. Armfield, J. Slattery, L. A. Still, W. J. Till, C. C. Gibbs, D. A. S. Manning, G. C. Ewing, W. A. Davies, T. R. A. Maynard, and W. C. B. Hall.

The two last-named officers were 2nd London officers who had been attached to the 2/4th Londons.

Other officer reinforcements received early in September were:

2nd Lieuts. A. K. Chesterton and A. McLaren.

The establishment of the 173rd Brigade was maintained at three battalions by the posting to it of the 2/24th Londons, who had recently joined the Division.

On the same day, 11th September, the 2/2nd Londons left Guyencourt, and marched back to Lièramont, where the next five days were spent in reorganization and training.

The first stage of the great advance may be said to have ended on the 3rd September, and, as a result of the successful issue of the battle, the Allies now found themselves in a position to strike towards the enemy's communications. The nearest point at which a deadly blow could be delivered was the railway junction at Aulnoye near Mauberge; and a British advance on the front Cambrai-St. Quentin in the direction of Mauberge would compel an early withdrawal of all the enemy's forces deployed between that town and Verdun. With this object in view, Marshal Foch issued instructions for the British Army, in conjunction with the left of the French, who had now reached La Fère and the line of the Crozat Canal, to continue the attack in the direction of Cambrai-St. Quentin, while the centre of the French Army pressed the enemy beyond the Aisne and the Ailette, and in the south the American Army attacked towards Mezières. At the same time a northern group, consisting of the Belgian Army, the British Second Army, and a French contingent—the whole under the command of the King of the Belgians—, pivoting on the Lys near Armentières, was to take the offensive in Flanders, where, constrained by the turn of events further south, the enemy had already begun, on the 18th August, a preliminary withdrawal from the Lys salient.

The opening of this ambitious plan was fixed for the end of September; and the interval was used for moving forward the Allied armies to the new front of attack. This involved a number of preliminary battles, the most important of which were the capture of the St. Mihiel Salient by the Americans and the Battle of Epéhy on the front of the British Third and Fourth Armies. The latter, in which the 58th Division was engaged, was fought with the object of capturing by deliberate methods the outpost system of the Hindenburg Line and of bringing the main British forces within striking distance of the Hindenburg Line itself.

The task of the 58th Division, in the centre of the III. Corps front, was to attack and capture Peizière and to make good the Green Line beyond, the 12th Division co-operating on the right and the 21st on the left. Once the Green Line was secured, the 58th Division was to be pinched out by the two others, who were then to attack the Red Line. The divisional front having been reduced to 1,200 yards, for which one brigade in the line was deemed sufficient, the 173rd alone was detailed to make the attack.

The first objective of the 173rd Brigade was the railway embankment just east of Peizière, and its final objective was Fir Support and Poplar Trench—the Green Line—some 1,500 yards further east. On the right flank the 35th Brigade was to attack Épéhy, and on the left the 62nd Brigade was to make good the ridge running north from Peizière. As neither the extent of front nor the limit of advance was unreasonable, the task of capturing both objectives was entrusted to one battalion, the 2/2nd Londons. The 2/24th Londons were placed in close support for mopping-up, while the 3rd Londons were given the duty of attacking a small area of ground between the right of the 2/2nd Londons and the left of the 35th Brigade, of dealing with Fisher's Keep, a strongly fortified work, and of garrisoning the three strong points in the village after their capture— McPhee Post, Morgan Post, and Proctor Post. Two tanks were allotted to the Brigade; both were to follow the 2/2nd Londons in the initial stages; one was then to clear Peizière, the other to go as far as the first objective and then, turning south along the railway, to mop up Épéhy.

The attack was originally ordered for the 16th September, but was postponed until the 18th. On the evening of the 16th the 2/2nd Londons moved up to Guyencourt, where orders for the operations were issued, and at 1 a.m. on the 18th assembled west of Peizière as follows:

RIGHT: ' C ' Company and 1 company of the 3rd Londons.
CENTRE: ' A ' Company.
LEFT: ' B ' Company.
SUPPORT: D. Company.

The three companies of the front line only were to be used to make good the first objective; but the whole battalion was to be used in the attack on the second objective. In this second phase three companies were to secure Fir Support, while the remaining company went forward to capture Poplar Trench beyond. Despite heavy gas-shelling, the assembly was carried out successfully. A steady drizzle began at 1.30 a.m. and lasted for some hours, adding considerably to the discomfort of the waiting troops.

At 5.30 a.m., in the darkness of a dawn delayed by clouds and rain, the attack was launched. There was no preliminary bombardment; but a creeping barrage came down for three minutes on the start-line and then lifted one hundred yards every four minutes. The attack went well; and within an hour the Battalion, though stubbornly opposed by units of the Alpine Corps, had captured Peizière, and had made good the railway embankment to the east of it.

At 7 o'clock the rain ceased; and, although the resulting mist did not clear for another hour, the conditions improved considerably. The whole battalion at once moved forward against its second objective; and at 9.10 a.m. Lieut.-Col. Walsh was able to report: 'We hold Fir Trench, but no news has been received concerning Poplar Trench. Boche are still in Morgan Post, Fisher's Keep, and McLean Post, and are stubbornly opposing the advance of the 2/24th Battalion.' Two companies of the 2/2nd Londons reached the railway, and, in conjunction with the 3rd Londons, speedily dealt with all the enemy posts in the village, except Fisher's Keep and Proctor Post. With the troops on either flank the day, thus far, had gone equally well; on the right, the 35th Brigade had captured Epéhy; and on the left, the 62nd had cleared the Peizière ridge.

'B' Company (Capt. Hetley) had been detailed for the attack on Poplar Trench, which lay beyond and somewhat to the right of Fir Support, and was the farthest point at which the attack aimed. The company successfully reached its objective, where it lost Capt. Hetley, who was wounded, but was so reduced in numbers that it could not hold the position gained, and was at last forced to fall back.

Early in the afternoon, the enemy was found to be still holding Poplar Trench and Chestnut Avenue with a strong block in Fir Support; and at 2 p.m. Lieut.-Col. Walsh received orders to make another attack on this line. A conference was held at Battalion Headquarters, which were now established in the railway cutting east of Peizière; and it was decided that the attack should be made at 9 p.m. by a force composed of elements of the Battalion, under Capt. Wright. In the meantime, Fisher's Keep and Proctor Post were reduced by the 3rd Londons at 7.30 p.m.; and at 8.15 the 37th Brigade, which had taken over from the 35th on the right, successfully attacked Chestnut Avenue, and eventually reached Tetard Wood. At 9 p.m. Capt. Wright's small force attacked Poplar Trench, but was checked by the enemy, who was in great strength, and only found it possible to establish three small posts close to the road in front of its objective.

At dawn on the 19th and again at 6 a.m. Poplar Trench was attacked, but with little better success. The situation was now as follows: The 2/2nd Londons held Fir Support and had established a block in Poplar Trench; the 37th Brigade on the right had a post in Chestnut Avenue and held the trench running through Tetard Wood. At 11 a.m. the 37th Brigade continued the attack, under a creeping barrage, with the object of securing Room Trench, which was in line with Poplar Trench on the right; and in co-operation with this attack, the 2/2nd Londons, after a barrage by the trench mortars, once again tried to clear Poplar Trench and the remaining portion of Fir Support. The trench not having been bombarded by artillery, an attack across the open was rendered impracticable, and it thus resolved itself into a bombing operation. Progress was very slow; the enemy, aided by numerous machine guns, resisted stubbornly; and the Battalion's left flank was in the air, although 'D' Company of the 2/24th Londons, from the north end of Fir Support, made a spirited but unsuccessful effort to get in touch with it.

The troops of the leading companies of the 2/2nd Londons were getting steadily weaker in numbers; so 'D' Company was ordered to send a platoon (2nd Lieut. Chesterton) to reinforce Capt. Wright's small party. 2nd Lieut. Chesterton and this platoon came speedily into action, and did splendid work. Gradually the 2/2nd Londons gained the upper hand; and at 7 p.m., after eight hours' strenuous fighting during which every inch of the ground had been bitterly contested, Lieut.-Col. Walsh was able to report that the whole of Poplar Trench had been cleared, and that the Battalion was in touch, by patrols, with the unit on the right, which had captured Room Trench.

At 10.50 p.m. the Battalion was relieved by the 2/24th Londons; two companies withdrew to the railway cutting east of Peizière, and two to Prince Reserve Trench.

The 173rd Brigade was withdrawn from the line on the 20th, the 2/2nd Londons marching to Guyencourt, where they reorganized.

The total casualties of the battalion amounted to 7 officers and 176 other ranks. The officer casualties were as follows:

KILLED : Lieut. P. C. H. Grist and 2nd Lieut. A. McLaren.
WOUNDED : Capt. G. H. Hetley, M.C., Lieut. A. B. Carpenter, 2nd Lieuts. C. C. Gibbs, J. T. Spencer, and G. C. Ewing, M.C.

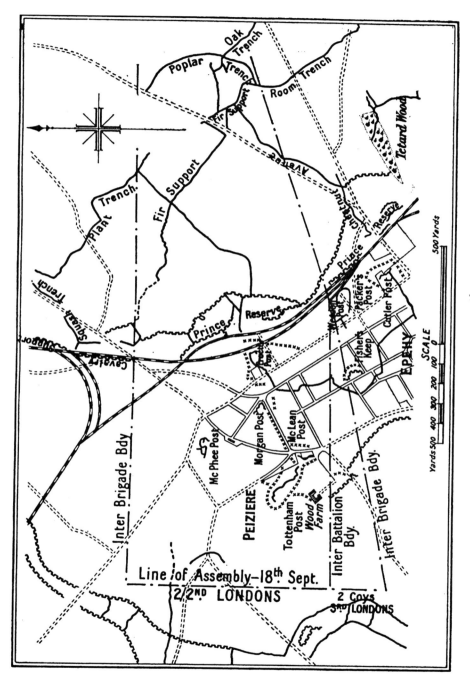

THE BATTLE OF EPÉHY.

The 2/2nd Londons in the Battle of Epéhy

The following honours were awarded in connexion with the battle:

D.S.O.: Capt. A. Wright, M.C.
M.C.: 2nd Lieuts. D. A. S. Manning and A. K. Chesterton.

In continuation of the operations of the 18th and 19th September, the 58th Division successfully attacked Lark Spur during the 21st and 22nd. Having thus helped to open the way to the Hindenburg Line, the Division was finally relieved on the 23rd, the 12th Division taking its place in the line. The Battle of Epéhy had been fought on a front of seventeen miles, and along its whole length the fighting had been most severe. The British advanced about three miles, capturing 12,000 prisoners and 100 guns, and achieved their main object, but only at a heavy cost to themselves.

The story of the 2/2nd Londons has now been brought to a point where it may be conveniently broken off, while we return to the 1/2nd Londons and follow their fortunes in the main operations that resulted in the ultimate breaking of the Hindenburg Line.

CHAPTER XXV

THE 1/2ND LONDONS IN THE BATTLE OF THE CANAL DU NORD—THE ACTION OF AUBIGNY AU BAC

I

WHEN the 1/2nd Londons returned to the neighbourhood of Boyelles on the 31st August after four days of severe fighting in the Hindenburg Line, they saw an amazing change. Boyelles itself, which a week before had been in German hands, was now our railhead. The lines were laid, and trains were coming through. The roads were crammed with lorries; and on every side huge dumps of material of every kind were being formed. This was the first example the 1/2nd Londons had of the manner in which the administrative services endeavoured to keep pace with the fighting troops during the great advance; their success added materially to the efficiency and comfort of the troops, and was a remarkable tribute to the British powers of organization.

After the continuous and heavy fighting of the preceding week, the 1/2nd Londons welcomed a respite from active operations in the early days of September, with its chance of a short rest and opportunity for reorganization. The men were utterly worn out; casualties had been heavy; yet everyone was entirely satisfied with the results of his strenuous labours. Both the G.O.C. and Br.-General Coke took an early opportunity of visiting the Battalion and of proffering their congratulations in person on its good work in the Hindenburg Line.

At this period the Battalion lost the services of R.S.M. W. J. Husband, D.C.M., who went to England on a tour of duty. His place was taken by C.S.M. A. E. Easthope, D.C.M., M.M.

The rest was not destined to be of long duration, the 169th Brigade being ordered to move to the Quéant-Pronville area on 5th September in preparation for the relief of the 63rd Division by the 56th. The 1/2nd Londons moved forward at 9.45 a.m. in the direction of Bullecourt, but, shortly after passing Croisilles, were informed that the relief had been cancelled, and they were ordered to return to Boisleux au Mont. They forthwith turned about, and after a long march in the heat of the afternoon, rendered the more trying by the congested and dusty state of the roads, reached Boisleux au Mont at 5.30 p.m.

The 1/2nd Londons in the Battle of the Canal du Nord

The 56th Division was now transferred to the XXII. Corps (Lieut.-Gen. Sir A. J. Godley) in the First Army, and relieved the 1st Division in the line due east of Arras. The 1/2nd Londons, after being inspected in the morning of the 6th by Lieut.-General Sir C. Fergusson, commanding the XVII. Corps, who said good-bye to them, moved later in the day from Boisleux au Mont to Vis en Artois, where they occupied trenches in divisional reserve.

The front taken over by the 56th Division lay due north of Cambrai, where there is a very marshy tract of country, fed by the Sensée and Cojeul Rivers. The Canal du Nord, after passing Moeuvres and Marquion, cuts across this marsh from the village of Palluel to join the Schelde and Sensée Canals. The water covers a wide stretch of ground, running to the west towards the Scarpe and tailing off near the village of Etaing. At this period the British front line ran quite close to the edge of the marsh.

After two days at Vis en Artois, the 1/2nd Londons moved into the main defence line, between Dury and Récourt, where the accommodation was very limited and where, in consequence, the men suffered much from the very stormy weather that now set in. There followed a short spell in the outpost line in the area of Lécluse, and then a further period in brigade reserve; and on the 19th the Battalion was once more back in the neighbourhood of Vis en Artois in divisional reserve.

The great triple offensive of the Allies, of which the general scheme has been outlined in the previous chapter, was punctually launched on the 26th September. On the front of the British, it chiefly resolved itself into a series of struggles for the Hindenburg Line, with Cambrai-St. Quentin as the strategic objective. At their conclusion the enemy's long-prepared defensive positions were in our hands, and there remained only the open-warfare pursuit of his forces, who endeavoured to postpone the inevitable by holding natural defensive positions on the line of retreat. These battles have been grouped under the general title of 'Battles of the Hindenburg Line,'[1] and they included the Battle of the Canal du Nord, in which the 1/2nd Londons took part.

The main battle opened with an attack by the Third and First Armies in the direction of Cambrai. This attack, which met with the fiercest opposition, since, as has been previously explained, it was of vital importance

---

[1] Sir Douglas Haig designates these operations 'Cambrai-St. Quentin,' and divides them into three phases, the operations of 27th-30th September constituting the first and second phases, and those of the 8th-10th October the third.

to the enemy to maintain his front opposite St. Quentin and Cambrai in order to protect his lateral communications, had a superficial resemblance to the Battle of Cambrai, 1917; it was over the same ground, but was simplified in its most important phase, the attack on Bourlon Wood, by the capture of the Drocourt-Quéant Line earlier in the month. It was followed two days later by another, further south, on the front of the Fourth Army; the result of these two blows was a brilliant and decisive victory.

This narrative is concerned with the left of the attack on the 27th September. In this sector the northern part of the Canal du Nord constituted a formidable obstacle to be crossed in the face of the enemy. It was therefore decided first to force a passage on a narrow front about Moeuvres, and then to turn the line of the canal further north by an attack developed fan-wise from the point of crossing. The task of forcing the crossing was entrusted to the Canadian Corps; the Canadians were to cross the canal on a front of about two miles near Marquion and were to make good the eastern bank, where the 11th and 56th Divisions were to relieve their left flank units and carry the attack north along the canal towards the marshes of the Sensée. In this operation the 56th Division was on the extreme left, and its line of advance was actually along the canal. Its task was to capture Sauchy Lestrée and Sauchy Cauchy, two villages on the east of the canal, and then to make good the line of a sunken road running north-east, about 1,500 yards beyond the latter village. One brigade—the 169th—was detailed to cross the canal and to capture these objectives, while another—the 168th—pushing forward in co-operation, cleared the western bank.

The general plan for the 169th Brigade required the delivery of two simultaneous but distinct attacks, for which purpose its units were to be disposed as follows:

RIGHT: 1/2nd Londons, with their left flank on the east bank of the little Agache River, which ran parallel with the Canal du Nord.
LEFT: Q.W.R., from the point where the railway crossed the west branch of the river to the canal.
SUPPORT: L.R.B. 1 company to cover the bridging of the Canal du Nord.
1 company to clear the ground between the two branches of the Agache River as far as their junction south-east of Sauchy Cauchy.
2 companies—in close support to the 1/2nd Londons.

The immediate object of the right attack (1/2nd Londons) was the capture of Sauchy Lestrée and the eastern end of Sauchy Cauchy (including Cemetery Wood), and of the left attack (Q.W.R.) the capture of the main part of the latter village. This achieved, the Brigade was then to press on to the final objective. Both attacks were to be launched from the railway line just south of Sauchy Lestrée (the Blue Line), on which the 169th Brigade was to relieve the Canadians. An interesting point in connexion with the battle was the very complete series of air photographs prepared by the Royal Air Force. These photographs had been taken a few days previously; and copies of many of them were supplied to all officers on the morning of the attack.

The dispositions and tasks of the 1/2nd Londons' companies in the first phase (the capture of Sauchy Lestrée and Sauchy Cauchy) were as follows:

RIGHT: 'A' Company (Capt. Sterckx)—
    2 platoons, working along the easternmost trench of the Marquion Line, to clear Kamwezi Copse, Kiduna Copse and the continuation of the trench to its point of junction with the sunken road running east and west through Cemetery Wood.
    2 platoons in Marquion Trench to clear Cemetery Wood and to establish a post about the centre of its northern face.

CENTRE: 'B' Company (Capt. Telford)—
    To capture the south-eastern part of Sauchy Lestrée, and then to clear the area to Chib Wood and to come into line on the road running east and west through the northern end of Sauchy Cauchy, between 'A' and 'C' Companies.

LEFT: 'D' Company (Capt. Sloan)—
    To capture the western and main part of Sauchy Lestrée, and then, clearing the area between 'B' Company and the Agache River, to capture the eastern end of Sauchy Cauchy.

RESERVE: 'C' Company (Lieut. Kimber)—
    2 platoons to follow 'D' Company to the centre of Sauchy Lestrée, and then to clear the road running north-east from the village.
    2 platoons to clear the trench-system lying east of this road. This company was to reform in readiness for the second phase, and was to push on to the road running east and west through the northern end of Sauchy Cauchy, coming into line between 'B' and 'D' Companies.

In the second phase (to begin immediately after the capture of Sauchy Cauchy), the tasks of the companies were as follows:

'C' Company to advance and occupy the line of the final objective with posts pushed forward to gain observation towards Palluel and the Bois de Quesnoy.
'B' and 'D' Companies to reform, and the former to consolidate the broad curve of the railway north of Sauchy Cauchy, while the latter held the line of the road from that village to Oisy le Verger.
'A' Company to remain in the vicinity of Cemetery Wood, with posts pushed out 1,000 yards to the north-east to gain connexion with the 34th Brigade.

The 1/2nd Londons, with a strength of 20 officers and 481 men, moved forward from Vis en Artois at 7.30 p.m. on the evening of the 26th to their assembly positions in the area between Villers lez Cagnicourt and Baralle, south of the Arras-Cambrai road. The night was one of heavy rain; and the Battalion had a most uncomfortable time, all the men being soaked to the skin.

The morning of the 27th broke wet and misty. The Canadian attack was launched at 5.20 a.m., and was timed to reach the line of the railway immediately south of Sauchy Lestrée at noon. At this point the 169th Brigade was to relieve the Canadian left flank and carry on the attack at 2.48 p.m. It was intended that the Canadians in their advance should clear the area north of the village of Marquion and so enable the 512th and 513th Companies, R.E., to bridge the canal in two places, one north and the other south of the Arras-Cambrai road, for the crossing of the 56th Division. At the outset the Canadians made good progress, but during the morning it became obvious that they were meeting considerable opposition on the extreme left and had been unable to clear the village. The stand made by the enemy at Marquion inevitably delayed the bridging operations; for on their arrival in the neighbourhood of the canal the bridging parties and their covering party from the L.R.B. were heavily fired on, and were for some time prevented from setting to work.

Meanwhile, the 1/2nd Londons moved off at 9.20 a.m., and, keeping about three hundred yards south of the Arras-Cambrai road, advanced to the vicinity of the lock north-west of Marquion, where they were obliged to halt and wait while the Canadians completed the clearance of the village. This was finally effected at noon; and the Battalion, headed by 'D' Company, crossed by an assault bridge immediately south of the lock and entered the village. The enemy's resistance in Marquion had by this time been practically overcome; and the few machine guns and snipers still holding out were speedily disposed of by the Canadian Royal Highlanders.

So far as the 1/2nd Londons were concerned, the approach to the start-line was by no means a simple matter. On the extreme left 'D' Company, moving up the Canal du Nord Line, found the area of the Blue Line had not been cleared. Capt. Sloan was therefore obliged to make an attack to reach his assembly position; in this he was successful, capturing 35 prisoners. Further to the right, 'B' Company in the Canal du Nord Support Line also had to fight its way forward, and finally reached the Blue Line by clearing out a party of about 50 Germans, who made hastily

384

for Sauchy Leſtrée. On the right 'A' Company passed through Marquion, and turned north along the road leading to the eaſtern end of Sauchy Leſtrée. No sooner had the company begun to descend the slight hill than it came under fire from a machine gun on the cross-roads south-eaſt of the latter village, and actually located on the Blue Line. The company moved to the left of the road, and, with the assiſtance of a Canadian gun that had somehow crossed the canal, eventually overcame the enemy's opposition and reached the Blue Line with only one casualty.

The 1/2nd Londons had reached their ſtart-line by about 2.30 p.m., and at zero (2.48 p.m.) were ready to go forward. As a result of the obſtinacy of the enemy in Marquion earlier in the day, it had been decided to poſtpone zero hour for forty minutes. Information to this effect reached Lieut.-Col. Kellett only fourteen minutes before the original zero hour, and, although he dispatched runners immediately to his company commanders, the runner entruſted with the message for 'A' Company could not reach the right flank in the time. Actually, it was not until 2.52 p.m., by which time his company had already been advancing for four minutes, that Capt. Sterckx received the news of the alteration. He at once halted his men, and, to avoid the barrage that was due to come down at the new zero hour, reformed them on the Blue Line.

By 3 p.m. the whole of the 169th Brigade was in position on the Blue Line, and at 3.28 p.m. advanced to the attack, the troops moving forward under an excellent barrage from artillery and trench mortars. On the right flank very little resiſtance was encountered at the outset by 'A' Company, which went ſteadily forward as though on a training area. It is of intereſt to note that the firſt 34 prisoners captured by this company were a German medical officer and the whole of his aid poſt ſtaff. Kamwesi Copse presented little difficulty, and by 4 p.m. had been cleared. In Kiduna Copse the enemy made some show of resiſtance; the two platoons of 'A' Company detailed to clear this area attacked in great ſtyle; and half-an-hour later this copse, too, had been captured, and connexion had been eſtablished with the 34th Brigade on the right.

In the centre, the capture of Sauchy Leſtrée was effected according to plan. Here, as on the right, the enemy did not make the moſt of his opportunities, and his resiſtance was not very ſtrong. Prisoners ſtated afterwards that this attack on their flank had completely disorganized them, since they were under the impression that, with the canal in front of them, they were entirely secure. Whatever the cause, it was patent that the German morale had deteriorated; on the other hand, the attacking troops were in splendid spirits, and everywhere went forward with great determination.

Leaving the second company of the L.R.B. to complete the clearance of the village, the 1/2nd Londons continued their advance, 'D' Company moving due north for its attack on Sauchy Cauchy and 'B' Company towards Chib Wood. 'C' Company cleared the road leading north-east from Sauchy Lestrée and the trenches lying to the east of it, and then rapidly reforming wheeled to the left to reach its position between 'B' and 'D' Companies on the Sauchy Cauchy line.

During their advance both 'B' and 'C' Companies came under fire from Cemetery Wood, which the enemy was still holding, but were not seriously delayed. 'C' Company cleared the houses at the eastern end of the village, 'D' Company came in from the south; and the two companies were soon in touch with the Q.W.R., who, after advancing steadily along the bank of the canal, had attacked and captured the main part of the village. After its fall the village was subjected to heavy shell fire by the enemy.

In the meantime, 'A' Company had attacked Cemetery Wood, and was finding the task of clearing it one of some difficulty. The wood was full of snipers, and the northern corner was held by several machine-gun posts. 'A' Company's efforts, however, were finally rewarded; by 5.45 p.m. the wood was cleared, and the company was occupying the trench that skirted the wood to the north-east. Posts were immediately pushed forward towards the north-east in the direction of Oisy le Verger, where a considerable number of the enemy was found in the dug-outs and trenches between the wood and this village.

Slowly but surely all opposition was overcome, except in the case of a machine-gun nest, which, situated in a trench some 300 yards from the northern point of Cemetery Wood, put up a splendid resistance. This gun covered the whole of the northern face of the wood by its fire; and No. 2 Platoon, in attempting to push out a post along a trench running north-east from the wood, sustained several casualties. The post was later established under cover of darkness by Corpl. Higgins, who captured 30 prisoners and 4 machine guns in the trench in question. Nos. 1 and 3 Platoons (2nd Lieut. Davis) made four unsuccessful attempts to capture the enemy's machine gun, and in their endeavours lost Sergts. Stevens and Cann and Corpl. Brazier. A fifth attack was delivered in the gathering dusk and was rewarded with ultimate success. One German gallantly fought the gun to the last and was captured with it. Of the remaining members of the crew, some

386

SAUCHY LESTRÉE AND THE CANAL DU NORD, SEPTEMBER 1918.

From the air.

were killed, and the others fled, only to be taken prisoners a few yards further up the trench by No. 2 Platoon's post.

The rest of the Battalion had been held up on the line of the road running east and west through the northern end of Sauchy Cauchy by fire from machine guns in the marshy ground due north of the village, and, in a lesser degree, by the machine gun that had been the object of 'A' Company's operations. The Q.W.R., on the left, eventually accounted for the machine guns in the marsh; and, released from their pressing attentions, 'C' Company pushed on to the final objective, the sunken road just north of the railway, while 'B' Company made good the railway itself. The night was now far advanced; and it was not until 3 o'clock on the following morning that the final objective was reached. 'A' and 'D' Companies remained in the area between the railway line and the north-east side of Cemetery Wood, in touch with the 34th Brigade on the right.

During the night orders had been received that a further attack was to be made by the 56th Division with the object of clearing the enemy out of the ground as far as the Sensée Canal, now about a mile ahead.

At 10.30 a.m. 'C' Company of the 1/2nd Londons, with 'B' Company of the Q.W.R. in close support, advanced along the east side of the Canal du Nord under a creeping barrage. Little opposition was encountered; and by 1.30 p.m. a line of posts had been established from north of the Bois du Quesnoy to Palluel, covering the line of the Sensée, the left post being on the Palluel-Oisy le Verger road, where connexion was made with the 8th Middlesex Regt. In its advance 'C' Company captured 5 prisoners and 2 trench mortars. The other companies of the 1/2nd Londons remained in the area they had reached in the early hours of the morning.

On the night of the 28th September the Battalion was relieved by the L.R.B., and moved back to Sauchy Lestrée.

Thus was concluded one of the most successful operations in which the Battalion took part during the war. In addition to crossing the canal and capturing all objectives—a task that entailed an advance of close upon 5,000 yards—the Battalion took many prisoners and a great quantity of material, and at the same time inflicted heavy losses in killed and wounded upon the enemy. The total captures were 6 officers and 454 non-commissioned officers and men, 19 heavy and 8 light machine guns, 4 anti-tank rifles, and 4 trench mortars. Of the individual companies, 'A' had the best 'bag,' its captures amounting to 1 officer and 147 other ranks, 10 heavy and 8 light machine guns, and 2 anti-tank rifles.

In view of the results obtained, the Battalion's casualties were very light. They were as follows:

KILLED: 6 other ranks.
WOUNDED: 4 officers (Lieuts. A. J. Whittle, J. C. Summers, 2nd Lieuts. S. H. Clifford and A. E. Kimber), and 61 other ranks.

In connexion with the battle the following honours were subsequently awarded:

Bar to D.S.O.: Lieut.-Col. J. P. Kellett, D.S.O., M.C.
M.C.: 2nd Lieut. H. R. Davis.

II

After their successful advance of the 27th and 28th September, the 1/2nd Londons were given two days' rest in brigade reserve, and on the night of the 30th were back in the area between Palluel and Arleux, where they took over the left of the Brigade front from the L.R.B. The latter extended their right flank as far as the bend of the Sensée Canal north of Oisy le Verger. Palluel was held in a series of posts established at the lock on the canal and at other points of tactical importance. The sector was very quiet, and movement in the open was possible at all hours.

Officer reinforcements received during September were 2nd Lieuts. J. H. Stotesbury and J. F. Mason.

On the 1st October the enemy surprised a post of the L.R.B., causing its evacuation by the garrison. The post was re-established the same night; and in order to be prepared for possible developments, 'A' Company, on the right of the 1/2nd Londons, took special precautions for defence, and a platoon of 'D' Company—the support company—was sent forward to strengthen the flank along the Canal du Nord. The enemy gave no further sign of activity; and the situation on the following morning was quite normal.

All the while attempts were being made to 'feel' the enemy; and patrols were pushed out to ascertain if his withdrawal was being continued on any part of the front. On the 3rd October one such patrol of 'C' Company, under 2nd Lieut. Marshall, had an exciting encounter. The patrol had gone out at 7.10 p.m. to reconnoitre the Arleux road and to obtain identification of the enemy. On the road stood a house, believed to be occupied by the enemy, which 2nd Lieut. Marshall thought would repay a visit. Having disposed his Lewis gun to give covering fire, should the necessity for this arise, 2nd Lieut. Marshall, with the rest of his small force, stealthily

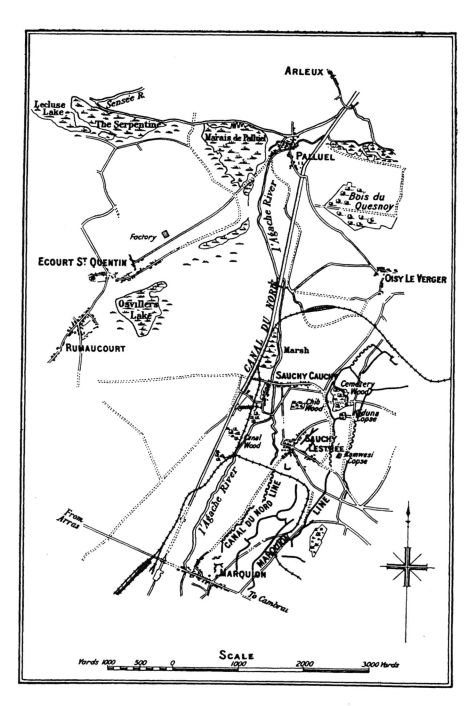

THE BATTLE OF THE CANAL DU NORD.

approached the house. The ground was so littered with debris that an absolutely silent approach was out of the question; the garrison of the house heard sounds of the advancing patrol, and, sending up a flare, opened a brisk machine-gun fire. The patrol at once returned the fire, and, despite several casualties, gave a good account of itself. Unfortunately, the Lewis gun jammed, and, realizing that without it he could not silence the enemy's machine gun which, from behind cover, commanded the approaches of the house, 2nd Lieut. Marshall withdrew his patrol. His total casualties were 8 wounded, one of whom was missing.

The activity of the enemy now became very marked. He had posts in the neighbourhood of the Arleux road; and his patrols, crossing the Palluel marshes in boats, gave frequent evidence of their presence and watchfulness. To locate accurately one of these posts with a view to its bombardment by our artillery, a patrol, under 2nd Lieut. Missen, went out on the 4th. The patrol was suddenly fired on at close range by a German machine gun; and 2nd Lieut. Missen and 1 man were killed, and 8 men were wounded. The patrol succeeded in its object, and from the information obtained the British artillery was able to deal effectively with the enemy's post.

The Battalion was relieved on the 5th October by the 1/1st Londons, and withdrew to Rumaucourt, a village comparatively intact and well furnished, where they remained until the 11th.

2nd Lieut. Edward Roland Cecil Missen was the son of Mr. and Mrs. Missen, of Cambridge, in which town he was born on the 5th December 1898. Before the war, he was a clerk in the Bishops Stortford branch of Barclays Bank, Ltd. He only left England on the 19th September, and had been at the front barely three weeks before he met his death. He was buried at Cagnicourt on the Arras-Cambrai road.

The great British thrust towards the line Cambrai-St. Quentin had been completely successful. In the battle that had raged between the 27th September and the 9th October, the First, Third, and Fourth Armies had pierced and broken the enemy's last prepared line of defence; over 30,000 prisoners and 300 guns had been captured; and the whole of the Hindenburg Line had at last passed into our hands. On the 9th October Cambrai fell; and on the same day the pursuit of the enemy to the line of the River Selle began. Of this great victory Sir Douglas Haig writes:[1]

[1] Sir Douglas Haig's Dispatches.

389

The effect of the victory on the subsequent course of the campaign was decisive. The threat to the enemy's communications was now direct and instant, for nothing but the natural obstacle of a wooded and well-watered country lay between our Armies and Mauberge.

In the north the Northern Army Group had struck on the 28th September, and in one day gained more ground than had been won in the whole of the Passchendaele offensive of 1917. By reason of the tremendous centre thrust and of this northern battle, the enemy in the Lys salient, facing the Fifth Army, found his position untenable, and, as will hereafter be described, was compelled to begin his withdrawal from this area on the 2nd October.

The 56th Division, holding a position along the Sensée Canal, covered the left flank of the Canadian Corps during the advance on Cambrai. On the 9th October the Division, extending its right flank as far as Fressies, relieved the 11th Division, thereby enabling the latter to follow the enemy, who was now evacuating the area between the Sensée and Schelde Canals as a result of the fall of Cambrai. On the 11th the 168th Brigade successfully attacked and captured Fressies; and on the evening of the same day, the Division was transferred to the Canadian Corps. The 169th Brigade took over the right sector of the Division's front along the Sensée Canal; and the 1/2nd Londons moved up in brigade reserve to Epinoy.

In the meantime, north of the Sensée River, the VIII. Corps had taken up the advance, and was pushing forward in the general direction of Douai. To assist this new movement by exerting pressure on the left flank of the retiring enemy, units of the 56th Division were ordered to establish themselves on the north bank of the Sensée Canal. Accordingly, on the 12th October, the 167th Brigade completed the clearance of Arleux; and on the next day the 169th Brigade made a daring attempt to capture Aubigny au Bac.

At this time the 169th Brigade was holding the line with the L.R.B. and the Q.W.R., these two battalions being widely extended over a considerable front. For this reason the 1/2nd Londons, who were in brigade reserve, were employed by Br.-General Coke to carry out the attack. To effect the capture of Aubigny au Bac it was necessary to pass troops across a canal 70 feet wide, the bridges of which had been destroyed. The enemy was holding the further bank in some strength, and had posts at two points where bridges formerly stood. The ruins of these bridges were about 1,250 yards apart, and it was decided to attempt the crossing in the area between them.

The task of bridging the canal for the assaulting troops was entrusted to a detachment of Royal Engineers from the 416th Field Company, under Lieut. A. E. Arnold. It was originally intended that, before the bridge was begun, a patrol of the Q.W.R. should be conveyed across on rafts to find out if the ground on the further bank was suitable for the assembly of at least one company, and then, if their view were favourable to a continuation of the enterprise, to act as a covering party for the bridging operations. Silence and speed, however, were the essence of the whole operation; time for reconnaissance and for carrying up material was short. In view of these considerations, Lieut. Arnold decided to dispense with the rafts and to proceed at once with the foot-bridge. Even so, the task of bringing up material for the bridge alone took carrying parties (which had to be found by the attacking company of the 1/2nd Londons) close upon two hours; the distance to be covered was nearly half-a-mile; the ground was marshy; and throughout the greater part of the work, the rain came down incessantly. The wisdom of Lieut. Arnold's decision can hardly be disputed; and, although no covering party was in position on the further bank of the canal, the bridge was completed by 3 a.m. on the 13th October without any molestation by the enemy. Lieut. Arnold himself did most of the dangerous work, and was the first man to cross the bridge. Unfortunately, he was killed later in the day.

As soon as the foot-bridge was finished, the patrol of the Q.W.R. was passed across, but could not proceed far, because there were several German posts close to the bridge-head, and it was essential to the success of the operation that the alarm should not be given at this stage. Meanwhile, 'D' Company of the 1/2nd Londons (Capt. Sloan), detailed for the attack, had moved up at dusk from Epinoy to Aubencheul au Bac, a village on the south side of the canal immediately opposite Aubigny, where one platoon was employed in carrying up material for the Royal Engineers, while the remainder awaited the completion of the bridge. As soon as the Q.W.R. patrol was in position on the far side, a platoon of 'D' Company crossed the bridge as carefully and as silently as possible, and, passing through the Q.W.R., searched a line of corrugated-iron shelters standing about twenty yards north-east of the bridge-head. Two Germans, the only enemy to be found, were quickly overpowered without the alarm being raised.

The night was very dark, and the heavy rain persisted. The task of crossing the narrow bridge with no hand-rails was very difficult, and inevitably a few men fell into the water, but by 4.50 a.m. the whole of 'D' Company was across. The assembly area on the far side of the canal was very bad, the ground being intersected by two streams, la Navie and la

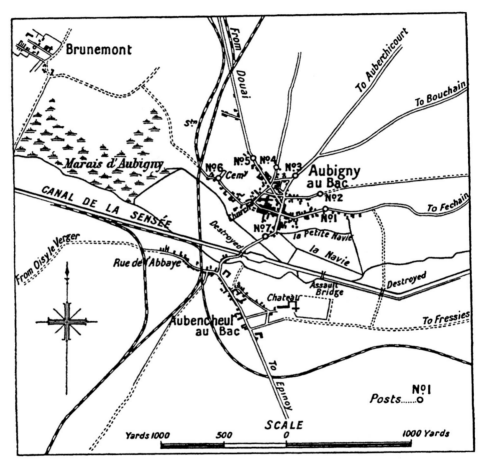

THE ACTION OF AUBIGNY AU BAC.

Petite Navie. Little or nothing was known beforehand of these streams, of which the former was found to be 20 feet wide and quite unfordable. After a search, a suitable spot for a crossing was found; an improvised bridge

392

of two fallen trees was thrown across; and the company passed over in single file.

The attack was to be covered by an artillery barrage, moving in a north-westerly direction. Capt. Sloan soon saw that the nature of the ground, intersected by hedges and ditches, would prevent the attacking troops from following a barrage in the ordinary way, and, having assembled his company as well as possible in early dawn, ordered each platoon to go straight for its objective as soon as the barrage opened. Zero was timed for 5.15 a.m.; in silence the attacking troops waited for the guns to open fire.

The surprise was complete. 'D' Company attacked the village from east to west—from the flank, indeed, whence such an attack was least expected by the enemy. The leading platoon made for the Aubigny-Féchain road, and with little difficulty cleared the houses in its vicinity. One of these contained a number of Germans with a machine gun, who, on being attacked from the rear, incontinently surrendered. The remaining platoons, entering by way of the Auberchicourt road, speedily cleared the village. Two machine guns and 160 prisoners were captured; and by 6.30 a.m. a number of pre-arranged posts had been established on three sides of the village at points of tactical importance.

In the meantime, 'C' Company (Lieut. Kimber) arrived at advanced Battalion Headquarters in the *château* at Aubencheul au Bac at 4.30 a.m. By 5.35, two of its platoons had crossed the canal in support of 'D' Company. These reported to Capt. Sloan at 6 a.m., and were used by him to reinforce such of his posts as had suffered casualties from sniping and machine-gun fire. Capt. Sloan's report, timed 8.55, reads as follows:

> Casualties, 15; number of rifles, 70. Enemy are shelling village with 77 m/m rather heavily. All of two platoons of 'C' Company have been utilized to reinforce 'D' Company. Our position is now quite secure. All posts are established and in touch with each other. Trench mortars arrived, and have been sent up to right posts to deal with machine-gun fire.

The last sentence refers to one of four light trench mortars attached to the Battalion for the operation. This was sent across the canal by Lieut.-Col. Kellett at 7.30 a.m. The others remained on the south bank, and engaged the enemy's machine-gun posts as opportunity offered.

In order to maintain a local reserve, Lieut.-Col. Kellett, at 6 a.m., ordered forward a third company—'A' Company (Capt. Sterckx). This company moved from its trenches near Epinoy, and advanced in artillery formation towards Aubencheul. During its advance it was seen by the enemy, whose artillery at once opened a heavy fire. Notwithstanding this fire, the company kept its formation excellently, and was brought by Capt. Sterckx safely through the barrage to the railway-cutting due south of the *château* at Aubencheul. The rear section of the company was just disappearing into the safety of the cutting when the barrage caught it and caused several casualties, including Lieut. James, who was severely wounded.

On his arrival at the *château,* Capt. Sterckx found the Colonel, despite the obscurity of the situation and the heavy shelling, in the best of spirits, as was evidenced by his turning to a piano that stood in a corner, and playing a few bars from *The Mikado.* The calm and natural spontaneity of this action impressed Capt. Sterckx, as it would any beholder, and the incident is recounted as exemplifying Lieut.-Col. Kellett's coolness and courage in the face of a trying situation.

'A' Company was immediately made use of, one platoon (2nd Lieut. Watson) being sent across the canal to reconnoitre towards Brunemont, and a second being detailed for carrying up material—a matter of vital importance, if the bridge was to be maintained.

Orders had been received from Brigade Headquarters that three new posts were to be established near the railway station, which lay nearly half-a-mile north-west of the centre of Aubigny au Bac. For this purpose Lieut. Kimber and the two remaining platoons of 'C' Company were hurried across the canal to Aubigny, where they arrived at 9.30 a.m. Prevented by heavy machine-gun fire from reaching the station by the shortest route, the Douai road, the two platoons were led by Lieut. Kimber past Aubigny church to No. 6 Post on the Brunemont road, where they fell in with 2nd Lieut. Watson and 'A' Company's patrol. As neither 2nd Lieut. Watson nor himself could carry out his allotted task owing to the activity of the enemy's machine-gun posts near the railway station, Lieut. Kimber decided to attack and capture these posts without delay. While he was making his reconnaissance, Aubigny came under a very heavy barrage from the enemy's guns, and immediately afterwards a German 77 m/m gun opened fire on No. 6 Post at a range of barely 1,000 yards. Lieut. Kimber's party moved forward to the attack under heavy fire, and simultaneously the enemy debouched in considerable strength from the station. The barrage on Aubigny increased in intensity; Lieut. Kimber's advance was checked; and the enemy, with a force that was later identified as a complete reserve

394

battalion, delivered a violent attack on the front and flanks of the garrison of the village. The time was then about 10.30 a.m.

Overcoming an heroic resistance, the enemy forced his way into the village, and, one by one, outflanked the posts, all of which had been badly damaged by the bombardment. The brunt of the enemy's attack fell on the north and west of the village, where the fighting was particularly severe. In the former quarter, No. 4 Post especially distinguished itself by its gallant resistance, and the survivors of its garrison could be heard firing their Lewis gun long after the post had been surrounded. The parties under Lieut. Kimber and 2nd Lieut. Watson, having hurriedly taken up a defensive position, likewise gave a good account of themselves, and stoutly resisted the enemy's repeated attacks.

Weight of numbers at last had its inevitable effect, and left Capt. Sloan with no other choice but to order a withdrawal. The remnants of his force extricated themselves as best they could, and fought their way back to his headquarters in the centre of the village; and from this point an organized retirement was carried out to la Petite Navie. A stand was made on the banks of the stream; and the enemy was prevented by rifle fire from debouching from the village. Throughout the withdrawal, Sergt. May was conspicuous for his good work, and set an inspiring example to the men under his command. He twice charged the enemy with his small party, and held him at bay, inflicting heavy casualties.

The British artillery now came into action again, and kept the village under fire for three-quarters of an hour. Under cover of this bombardment, Capt. Sloan and his small force, now reduced to about 20 men, made a gallant but ineffectual attempt to recapture Aubigny. Finding the enemy too strong for him, Capt. Sloan decided to hold on to the south bank of la Petite Navie as long as he could; and for upwards of an hour he contrived to remain in this position until the enemy began to work round his flanks in considerable numbers. Forced by this threat to his communications to abandon the line of la Petite Navie, he next took up a position 100 yards further back, and at last, when it became evident that the enemy was making frantic attempts to cut off his whole party, he conducted an orderly withdrawal to the bridge-head. Thence all that was left of the attacking force crossed safely to the south bank, a few of the men swimming the canal; all the wounded were brought back; and Capt. Sloan himself was the last man to cross into safety.

As soon as the enemy's counter-attack, in which he employed upwards of 500 men, began to develop, Lieut.-Col. Kellett ordered Capt. Sterckx to move 'A' Company, now reduced to the strength of little more than a platoon, to the support of the troops in Aubigny. On the arrival of 'A' Company at the bridge, it was found that the enemy was drawing near the bridge-head, and that the bridge itself was under observed machine-gun fire. Capt. Sterckx, realizing that the village was lost, hurried a party across the bridge to maintain the northern bridge-head, and disposed the rest of his men to support Capt. Sloan's party with fire from the south of the canal. Having disposed his small force in a position on the bank, Capt. Sterckx, aided by 2nd Lieut. Stotesbury, rallied the men of 'C' and 'D' Companies on this line as they came back across the canal, and soon had a respectable number of rifles covering the bridge. The bridge-head on the north bank was with difficulty maintained until 5 p.m., when the party holding it was withdrawn under orders from Brigade Headquarters.

The night passed uneventfully except for some heavy shelling. During the hours of darkness 'B' Company, which hitherto had not been employed, was brought up, and next morning took part in an incident which, in that it earned a V.C. for the Division, deserves a brief description.

In the early dawn a patrol of the company was sent across the canal to find out if Aubigny were still occupied by the enemy. Heavy fire was opened on the patrol as it began to cross the bridge, and the men bunched, breaking the frail bridge by the excessive pressure in one spot. With the aid of Corpl. McPhie (416th Field Company, R.E.) and another member of the Royal Engineers maintenance party, who jumped into the water and held the broken bridge together, the patrol scrambled across to the farther bank.

Obviously the safety of the whole patrol now depended on the speedy repair of the bridge. Corpl. McPhie, realizing this, at once set about collecting the necessary material. Undeterred by the heavy fire he began the repairs, and bravely carried on until he was mortally wounded at the moment when his task was completed. By his courageous action Corpl. McPhie enabled the patrol to return to safety, and he was posthumously awarded the V.C.

The 1/2nd Londons, having successfully completed the repair of the bridge, thus gallantly begun, were relieved on the night of the 14th October by the 46th Canadian Battalion, and marched to Sauchy Lestrée.

In this very dashing enterprise a total of 6 officers and 165 other ranks crossed the canal, and these captured 4 officers and 203 other ranks (from the 58th and 234th German Divisions) and 10 machine guns. That the expectations of the higher command—namely, the attainment of a firm footing on the north bank of the canal—were not fulfilled was no fault of the 1/2nd Londons, but was due rather to the entire absence of reserves to follow up and exploit the initial success. The Battalion rightly received very high praise for this exploit; and, in forwarding a report of this action to the Corps Commander, Major-General Hull made the following comment:

> The O.C. 2nd London Regiment, who personally supervised the operations, is worthy of much praise, and the Battalion has added another success to its many achievements.

The Battalion's casualties were:

KILLED: 8 other ranks.
WOUNDED: 1 officer (Lieut. H. F. James), and 51 other ranks.
MISSING: 1 officer (2nd Lieut. T. N. W. Watson), and 56 other ranks. 2nd Lieut. Watson was subsequently reported as wounded.

The following honours were awarded in connexion with this action:

M.C.: Capt. D. Sloan, Lieut. A. E. Kimber, 2nd Lieuts. C. W. Bridgen and J. F. Mason.
M.M.: Sergts. Hay, Atkins, May, Corpl. Vale, L/Corpl. Bryant, Ptes. East, Schnabel, Quinn, Humphrey, Pearman, Sage, and Daley.

CHAPTER XXVI

THE FINAL ADVANCE—I

THE 1/2ND LONDONS IN THE BATTLES OF VALENCIENNES AND THE SAMBRE

THE 56th Division was now withdrawn into Army reserve, and by the 16th October all its units had concentrated in the outskirts of Arras. The 1/2nd Londons marched from Sauchy Lestrée on the morning of the 15th to Marquion, where they entrained, and by the evening of the same day reached Haute Avesnes, six miles north-west of Arras.

At Haute Avesnes, the Battalion was established in very comfortable quarters, with recreation rooms and canteens for the men, and messes for the officers and sergeants. Training was begun at once, and was carried on energetically; at the same time the men were given plenty of opportunity for sport and recreation, and the 'Bow Bells' helped to while away the evenings.

Lieut.-Col. J. P. Kellett, D.S.O., M.C., whose second tenure of the command of the Battalion had begun on 1st January 1918, left for England on the 18th October for a three months' tour of duty at home. Although Lieut.-Col. Kellett fully deserved this rest, it was a matter of regret to all ranks that he was not actually with the Battalion when its fighting days came to an end. He rejoined in January 1919, and had the satisfaction of commanding the Battalion during its last few months overseas. Major S. H. Stevens, M.C., assumed command of the Battalion in his absence, and was promoted Lieutenant-Colonel.

During October the following officer reinforcements were received:

2nd Lieuts. H. L. C. Hosegood, W. Townsend, F. E. Powell, A. Tillett, and F. W. Charles.

During the latter part of October events on the British front had moved with startling rapidity; the final stage of the war had in truth begun. The capture of the Hindenburg Line in the early days of the month had been followed by open warfare, and the pursuit of the enemy to the line of the River Selle, initiated on the 12th October, had been entirely successful. The success of this advance enabled British G.H.Q. to open the next stage of its operations against the new strategic objective, Mauberge.

This battle (the Battle of the Selle) opened on the 17th October, the

Fourth, Third, and First British Armies being involved in succession; and by the 20th the enemy had been driven across the Sambre, and le Cateau had been occupied. The main attack was delivered on the 23rd, and, when the battle closed on the 25th, the British forces had reached the western edge of the Forest of Mormal and the outskirts of le Quesnoy, and had crossed the le Quesnoy-Valenciennes railway on the front of the XXII. and Canadian Corps of the First Army.

In Flanders the Northern Army Group was advancing through Belgium. Menin, Thorout, and Ostend were occupied in succession; the coast was rapidly cleared; and shortly after the middle of the month the Dutch frontier was reached. This advance had the effect of turning the defences of Lille, and on the 18th October the city was occupied by the British.

Elsewhere equally striking successes had been gained. The French and American Armies were pressing steadily forward in the south. In Italy the Allied forces had hurled themselves across the Piave. The Serbians had reached the Danube. On the 30th September Bulgaria had capitulated; on the 27th October Austria-Hungary sued for peace; on the 30th October Turkey was granted an armistice. The plight of Germany herself was desperate.

Sir Douglas Haig reviews the existing military situation in the following words:[1]

> By this time the rapid succession of heavy blows dealt by the British forces had had a cumulative effect, both moral and material, upon the German Armies. . . . His reserves of men were exhausted. . . . The capitulation of Turkey and Bulgaria and the imminent collapse of Austria—consequent upon Allied successes which the desperate position of her own armies in the western front had rendered her powerless to prevent—had made Germany's military situation impossible. If her armies were now to be allowed to withdraw undisturbed to shorter lines, the struggle might still be protracted over the winter. The British Armies, however, were now in a position to prevent this by a direct attack upon a vital centre which should anticipate the enemy withdrawal, and force an immediate conclusion.

The capture of Valenciennes itself was regarded as essential to the furtherance of the British plans; and accordingly, on the 1st November,

[1] Sir Douglas Haig's Dispatches.

an attack was launched on a front of six miles south of Valenciennes by the XVII. Corps of the Third Army, and by the XXII. Corps and the Canadian Corps of the First Army. By the evening of the 2nd November the Rhonelle River had been crossed, and on the right the high ground east of Préseau had been occupied, while on the left the Canadians had entered Valenciennes and had passed some way beyond it.

On the 31st October the 56th Division had been transferred back to the XXII. Corps, and had relieved the 49th Division in the forward area. The 1/2nd Londons left Haute Avesnes early on this day, and proceeded by bus, in company with the other units of the 169th Brigade, to Lieu St. Amand, about nine miles south-west of Valenciennes.

The 169th Brigade, after remaining for twenty-four hours at Lieu St. Amand, moved forward on the 2nd November, and, having made a short halt south of Maing, completed the relief of the 147th Brigade of the 49th Division in the line on a ridge immediately to the west of the Préseau-Valenciennes road. The right of the Brigade was at a point a few hundred yards north-west of the *château de Préseau,* where connexion with the 11th Division was established, whilst its left, in touch with the 168th Brigade, rested on the cross-roads a mile east of Aulnoy. The 1/2nd Londons, relieving the 7th West Ridings, were on the right of the Brigade front, the Q.W.R. on the left, and the L.R.B. in reserve. Battalion Headquarters were established in an old mill on the Rhonelle River, where the staff shared three mattresses in a tiny cellar with the headquarters' personnel of the Q.W.R., two artillery officers, and four civilians (one man, two boys, and a girl).

The relief proved very trying; the guides were even less reliable than was usually the case with their kind, since the troops about to be relieved had just advanced over this stretch of country, and this single journey in the ranks of their battalion was the sole qualification which these men had to act as guides at all. There was a considerable amount of shelling; and, to add to the difficulties, the rain fell in torrents. All these factors delayed the relief so much that it was not complete until dawn on the 3rd November.

The attack was to be resumed on the 4th, and orders had been issued to this effect. The 56th Division was to attack in the centre with the 11th Division on its right and the 4th Canadian Division on its left, the final objective being l'Aunelle River and the high ground beyond it. This attack, however, was anticipated by the events of the early hours of the 3rd November.

At 9 a.m. a sentry of the 1/2nd Londons observed a German ride up to a hedge and hand a message to someone on the ground. The German then rode off, and a few moments later a party, carrying a machine gun, left the hedge. Patrols were sent out at once, when it was found that a general withdrawal by the enemy was taking place on the Brigade's front.

In the meantime, the G.O.C. 56th Division, having learnt that the enemy had retired on the front of the Canadians, ordered the 168th and 169th Brigades first to make good by strong patrols the ridge between Curgies and Estreux and then to push on to the Red Line, the high ground extending north-east from Curgies. The advance of the 169th Brigade began; and at 11 a.m. a patrol of the Q.W.R. entered Saultain. At noon the 1/2nd Londons were ordered to take over the whole of the Brigade's front and to continue the advance, the Q.W.R. dropping back into support. The 1/2nd Londons moved up to Saultain, passed through the village, and pushed forward with the companies disposed as follows:

RIGHT: 'A' Company (2nd Lieut. Willson).
LEFT: 'B' Company (Capt. Rowlands).
SUPPORT: 'C' Company (Capt. Ward).
RESERVE: 'D' Company (Capt. Sloan).

The line of the ridge between Curgies and Estreux was made good by 2 p.m., and the Red Line by 4 p.m., there being little opposition on the part of the enemy. On the Red Line a patrol of cavalry was passed through the Battalion with instructions to take Sebourg and to force the crossing of l'Aunelle River. 'C' Company of the 1/2nd Londons was ordered to follow the patrol as closely as possible, and to establish a bridge-head on the further side of this river. As the enemy was found to be holding Sebourg in some strength, these orders were subsequently cancelled; the Red Line was consolidated for the night; and connexion was made with the units on either flank. Battalion Headquarters were established in the railway cutting close to the cemetery at Curgies.

At dawn on the 4th November the Q.W.R. and the L.R.B. passed through the 1/2nd Londons, and the advance was continued by the battalions in that order, the Q.W.R. being preceded by a cavalry patrol. Sebourg was occupied, and l'Aunelle River was crossed by 8 o'clock, but serious opposition was encountered on the high ground east of the river, and the Q.W.R., who had suffered heavy casualties from artillery and machine-gun fire, although reinforced by the L.R.B., were unable to advance further.

At noon the 1/2nd Londons were ordered to move up into close support. Thereafter no progress was possible that day; and the night was spent in the positions reached. The enemy put down a heavy barrage on Sebourg, opening with a direct hit on the church, and subjected the Battalion throughout the night to spasmodic bursts of heavy shelling, one man being killed and three wounded.

No respite was allowed to the enemy; and on the 5th the 56th Division continued to press back his rear guards. The immediate object of the 169th Brigade was the capture of the high ground between Sebourg and Angreau, and the occupation of an outpost line along the sunken road west of the latter village. The attack was entrusted to the L.R.B., with the Q.W.R. in close support, the 1/2nd Londons remaining in reserve. The L.R.B. advanced at dawn, covered by a creeping barrage, and found that the enemy had retired during the night. They were ordered to push on to the line of the railway east of the Bois de Beaufort; and by 7.30 a.m. they were across the Angreau River, and had established a bridge-head on the further side. The enemy's resistance now stiffened up, and his active machine-gun fire and sniping delayed the advance. On the left flank, the London Scottish (168th Brigade), being unable to make much progress owing to their weakness in numbers, were fully a mile in rear, while on the right the village of Roisin remained in the enemy's hands until late in the afternoon. In view of the position on either flank, the L.R.B. were ordered to make no further advance, but to consolidate a position on a line just east of Angreau.

Shortly after the opening of the attack, the 1/2nd Londons were ordered up to the area of Nouveau Monde. The Battalion moved off by companies at 8.30, and by 11.30 was in its new position, having crossed the Belgian frontier on its way. Battalion Headquarters were established in the cellar of a farmhouse, shared also by the Q.W.R. and the L.R.B. The old farmer, his wife, and family were overjoyed at the arrival of the British, and gave a practical demonstration of their pleasure by brewing coffee all day and pressing it upon all and sundry.

At 7 p.m. the Battalion received a warning order to take over the right of the Brigade front and to be prepared to continue the attack on the next day in conjunction with the L.R.B. Orders for the attack were not received until 11.30 p.m. After a hurried conference with his company commanders, Lieut.-Col. Stevens disposed the Battalion as follows:

RIGHT: 'C' Company.
LEFT: 'D' Company.
RIGHT SUPPORT: 'B' Company.
LEFT SUPPORT: 'A' Company.

The 1/2nd Londons in the Battle of the Sambre

The companies moved off to their assembly positions at midnight. The night was dark, and rain was falling heavily; consequently, the relief proved very difficult, and the assembly, which was not finally complete until 4 a.m. on the 6th November, in the end went wrong. 'C' and 'D' Companies had been ordered to take over part of the front hitherto held by the L.R.B., and this they eventually did. It appears that the actual position of the L.R.B. was not accurately known when the plan of attack was drawn up, and the right half of their front proved to be further to the right than was contemplated by Brigade Headquarters. On the other hand, the support companies of the 1/2nd Londons, who had no relief to carry out and had merely to form up in second line, assembled in the position outlined in the orders for the attack, and, instead of being immediately behind the companies of the front line, were actually to their left rear. This mistake later gave rise to considerable confusion.

During the assembly the hostile shelling was very heavy, and caused the Battalion many casualties, 'D' Company losing over half its effectives. Among the casualties was C.S.M. J. A. Reynolds, D.C.M., who was killed just as he was leaving the farmhouse in which his company's headquarters had been established, by a direct hit on the building. This was a very sad occurrence. C.S.M. Reynolds had served in France during much of the war, and had taken part in most of the battles in which the Battalion had been engaged.

Throughout the rest of the day the enemy kept up a continuous and heavy fire of high explosives and inflammatory shells on Angreau, and the village, which contained many civilians, was badly knocked about.

At 5.30 a.m., under cover of a barrage from a brigade of artillery, which had been put at the disposal of the 169th Brigade for the operation, the L.R.B. and the 1/2nd Londons moved forward. It should be observed that just before zero the enemy had put down a heavy concentration of gas shells, which compelled the attacking troops to wear their gas-masks, and materially added to their difficulties.

The country over which the attack was made abounded in natural obstacles. First came a deep ravine, whose slopes were covered with trees and thick undergrowth. Behind this was the River Honnelle, swollen with recent rains, and bordered on either side by steep banks. On the far side of the river was the Bois de Beaufort—a steep, well-wooded slope—, where in the thick undergrowth the enemy had taken up a strong position, with the intention of contesting the passage of the river. As was the case in most of this rear-guard fighting, the enemy's machine-guns formed the backbone of his resistance, and the nature of the country was entirely suitable for their successful employment.

'C' and 'D' Companies of the 1/2nd Londons succeeded in reaching and crossing the river in the teeth of a determined opposition, though suffering many casualties from the heavy and accurate machine-gun fire. These two companies then pressed on to the Bois de Beaufort, where they found themselves out of touch with the flanking units and completely isolated. On their right the 11th Division had been checked on the river line; on their left the L.R.B., with easier country to negotiate, had rapidly gone ahead.

The impetuosity of the L.R.B. later cost them dear; they were heavily counter-attacked by the enemy, and, already weak in numbers, were unable to hold their ground, and were ultimately thrust back across the river. 'C' and 'D' Companies of the 1/2nd Londons were involved in this counter-attack, and were also forced by the pressure of superior numbers to withdraw to the west bank.

We must now revert to 'A' and 'B' Companies, which had assembled, as has already been described, to the left rear of the leading companies. The result of this mistake, if mistake it can be called, made itself apparent as soon as these two companies advanced, when, instead of finding themselves in support to 'C' and 'D' Companies, they came up on their left.

As they approached the river, they immediately attracted the attention of the enemy's machine guns, and lost many men from the heavy fire that was at once opened on them. On reaching the near bank of the river, they were completely held up for fully twenty minutes, and were unable to cross until some Lewis gunners forced their way over. These gunners worked away to a flank, and, finding a suitable position, brought their guns into action. Under cover of a brisk fire from these guns, the two companies crossed the river and fought their way gallantly up the opposite slope, through the thick wood and undergrowth, being subjected the while to heavy gas shelling and machine-gun fire. At last a force of about 30, the remnants of the two companies, with Capt. Rowlands, Lieut. Willson, and 2nd Lieut. Tillett, succeeded in reaching the railway line at the edge of the wood, about 500 yards short of the first objective. Further advance was found to be impossible, because the open country beyond was swept by a hail of machine-gun bullets.

The little force found itself completely isolated, every attempt to connect with the units on the flanks proving unsuccessful. No sooner had the

British advance come to a standstill than the Germans began a series of counter-attacks; first they delivered a heavy frontal attack across the open, which was repulsed by Lewis-gun fire; next they tried to approach by the left flank. The first party that appeared in this direction was threatened with the bayonet, and did not stay to try conclusions. A second party succeeded in working its way round the left flank through the undergrowth, and at length appeared in the 1/2nd Londons' rear. The officer in command called upon the 1/2nd Londons to surrender. Capt. Rowlands' reply to this was delivered at the point of the bayonet; and by his gallant action he routed the Germans and put them to flight. But his position was fast becoming desperate; the enemy was working round the flanks in ever-increasing numbers; and the machine-gun fire was growing in volume. Capt. Rowlands had no alternative but to withdraw. This difficult task was successfully accomplished; the river was recrossed; and all wounded brought in.

Capt. Rowlands acted with conspicuous gallantry during this engagement, and it was largely due to his personal efforts and leadership that the remnants of 'A' and 'B' Companies were successfully extricated, after inflicting very heavy losses on the enemy. Capt. Rowlands was subsequently awarded the D.S.O. He was ably backed up by Lieut. Willson and C.S.M. R. F. Cowles, M.M.

This day's fighting proved to be the last in which the 1/2nd Londons took part during the Great War. They were reorganized in their assembly positions of the morning, and on the relief of the 169th Brigade by the 167th, they handed over their position to the 8th Middlesex, and withdrew to Sebourg.

The casualties of the 1/2nd Londons during these four days of active operations, in the course of which the 56th Division had advanced nearly seven miles, were:

KILLED: 8 other ranks.

WOUNDED: 4 officers (2nd Lieuts. G. T. Gill, W. Townsend, F. E. Powell and D. H. Marshall), and 79 other ranks.

MISSING: 1 officer (2nd Lieut. J. H. Stotesbury), and 20 other ranks. 2nd Lieut. Stotesbury was subsequently reported as wounded.

On the night of the 6th November the 63rd Division was put into the line in front of the 168th Brigade. Thus the 56th Division was now on a one-brigade front, with the 11th Division on the right and the 63rd on the left. The line of the Division's advance, which lay almost due east, and roughly parallel to the Canal de Condé (connecting the Schelde with Mons), was crossed by innumerable small streams, draining northward into the marshy ground that bordered the canal. All bridges having been systematically destroyed by the enemy, these streams, with their steep banks, afforded naturally strong positions for the German rear guards to defend, and might well have caused a serious delay to the advancing British. But the enemy's resistance was broken; and the opposition offered to the troops of the 56th Division in their advance was negligible.

On the 7th November the Honnelle was crossed, and Montignies sur Roc was occupied. The advance was continued on the 8th; and on this day the 169th Brigade moved up from Sebourg to Angreau. The weather had now broken, and the rain was continuous; yet nothing could damp the ardour of the troops, whose enthusiasm in this last advance knew no bounds.

The enemy was in full retreat on the whole of the British front. The Guards Division had entered Mauberge; the Canadians were drawing near to Mons. The 56th Division pushed forward, its leading brigade, the 167th, occupying the villages of Rieu-de-Bury and Quévy in succession, and by the night of the 10th had reached a line just east of the Harmignies.

The entry of the British into every village in this area was the occasion of an extraordinary demonstration of gratitude on the part of the inhabitants, who greeted the relieving troops with fervour, and showered flowers upon them as they marched through the streets. The plight of these unfortunate inhabitants was really deplorable. In their retreat the Germans had driven off all live stock, and had removed all food and utensils of every description. In many cases the inhabitants of these villages were on the verge of starvation, having nothing left to live on; and at this period the Division was feeding about 16,000 civilians on an allowance of one 'iron ration' to four persons.

At Harmignies orders were received for the 63rd Division to carry on as advanced guard to the XXII. Corps; and the 56th Division was relieved.

On the 11th November the Armistice was signed, and the Great War came to an end.

The rest of the story is soon told. The 56th Division did not go to the Rhine, as was at first anticipated, but remained in the area it had reached at the end of its final advance.

The 1/2nd Londons reached Athis on the 10th November, and remained in this village until the 26th. Shortly after the Armistice the Regiment's Colours arrived, having been brought to Flanders from the sanctuary in

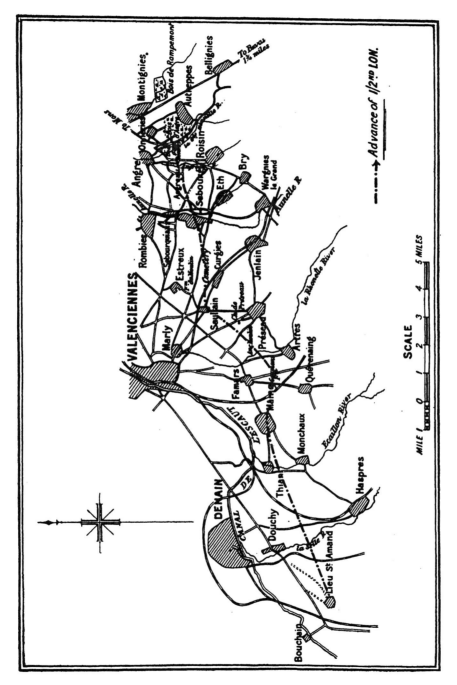

THE FINAL ADVANCE—THE BATTLES OF VALENCIENNES AND THE SAMBRE.

which they had been preserved throughout the war,[1] to share in the Regiment's final triumph. On the 15th November General Sir H. S. Horne, commanding the First Army, made his official entry into Mons. For this historic ceremony detachments of troops were supplied by the various Allied formations in the vicinity. The detachment from the 169th Brigade, which included 3 officers and 77 other ranks from the 1/2nd Londons, was under the command of Lieut.-Col. Stevens.

On the 26th November the 1/2nd Londons moved to Harmignies, where the Headquarters of the Battalion were to remain until the following March. Of their pleasant stay in this quiet Belgian village the personnel of the 1/2nd Londons retain the liveliest recollections, although the general state of flux in which the British Army found itself at this time caused uncertainty concerning the Battalion's immediate future and ultimate fate.

None but the briefest reference to this period is necessary. Demobilization began at an early date; and the Battalion's personnel was rapidly reduced by the departure of 'pivotal' men. Work consisted largely of educational training, so long as instructors were available; and organized games occupied much of the men's spare time. The Brigade Football Cup was won by the 1/2nd Londons; and the Battalion Football Cup by 'B' Company. Christmas was celebrated with special enthusiasm; and January was marked by the return of Lieut.-Col. J. P. Kellett, D.S.O., M.C., who resumed command of the Battalion on the 20th.

The New Year's Honours List contained the following well-deserved awards:

> O.B.E.: Capt. and Quartermaster A. G. Shackleton.
> M.C.: Capt. A. T. Taylor.

The simultaneous recognition of those staunch allies, the Quartermaster and the Transport Officer, was peculiarly appropriate. From almost the day the Battalion landed in France these two officers had been associated in providing for the comfort of the troops. In this they had been singularly successful; and in view of the truth of Napoleon's oft-quoted dictum: 'An army marches on its stomach,' some part of the Battalion's success during the long and arduous campaign must be attributed to their unremitting zeal.

Towards the end of March the Division—or what was left of it—was concentrated in the area of Jemappes, and on the 24th the 1/2nd Londons left Harmignies for Quarignon. Although demobilization and the departure of volunteers for the Armies of Occupation had by now reduced its personnel

---

[1] Christchurch, Streatham Hill, *vide* p. 7.

to a cadre, the Battalion remained abroad during April and the first half of May.

On the 18th May the Cadre, under the command of Major Stevens, left Quarignon for Antwerp, and on the 23rd sailed for England. It disembarked next day at Gravesend, and, after handing in all stores and transport at Newhaven, reached London a week later. With the return of the Colours and Cadre to the Headquarters of the Regiment the service of the 1/2nd Londons in the Great War came to an end.

THE OFFICERS, 1/2ND LONDONS, 1919.

BACK ROW: Lieut. B. S. Heading, 2nd Lieuts. D. H. Marshall, J. F. Mason, M.C., F. J. Machon, H. L. C. Hosegood, J. H. T. Andrews.

MIDDLE ROW: Capt. and Q.M. A. G. Shackleton, O.B.E., Rev. R. F. Diggle, M.C., 2nd Lieuts. C. W. Bridgen, M.C., F. E. Powell, G. T. Gill, Capt. H. Rowlands, D.S.O., M.C., 2nd Lieut. H. R. Davis, M.C., Lieut. A. E. Kimber, M.C.

FRONT ROW: Capts. D. Anderson, M.C., A. T. Taylor, M.C., Major S. H. Stevens, M.C., Lieut.-Col. J. P. Kellett, D.S.O, M.C., Capts. W. Dyer, M.C., W. J. Ward, M.C., A. F. Sterckx, E. C. Bowden, M.C., R.A.M.C.

CHAPTER XXVII

THE FINAL ADVANCE—II

THE 2/2ND LONDONS IN THE PURSUIT TO THE SCHELDE

AFTER the Battle of Epéhy the 58th Division was withdrawn from the III. Corps, with which it had served almost continuously for over six months. During this period the Corps had seen some of the severest fighting that had taken place in the course of the whole war, notably on the Oise in March, before Amiens in April, and on the banks of the Somme in August and September. In all this fighting the 58th Division had played a conspicuous part; it had bravely faced annihilation on the 21st March, and had well begun the Advance to Victory on the 8th August. And now, after six weeks of continuous and progressive fighting, the Division was moved to a quieter part of the front, and was transferred to the VIII. Corps of the First Army in the area of Lens.

We left the 2/2nd Londons at Guyencourt, whence, after a short rest, they moved by buses on the 24th September to Mametz Wood. On the 26th the northward move was begun, the Battalion entraining at Méricourt l'Abbé for Mont St. Eloy, where it arrived the same day. After two days in camp at Mont St. Eloy the Battalion was carried in buses to the twin villages of Bully and Grenay on the Béthune-Lens railway.

Officer reinforcements during September and the first week of October were:

Major E. A. Bye, Capt. H. S. Daw, and 2nd Lieut. A. Irvine.

During the last days of September the 58th Division relieved the 24th Division in the line between Lens and Loos on a front of 5,000 yards, all three brigades being in the line, the 175th on the right, the 173rd in the centre, and the 174th on the left. The dispositions of the 173rd Brigade were as follows:

RIGHT: 2/2nd Londons.
LEFT: 2/24th Londons.
SUPPORT: 3rd Londons.

The 2/2nd Londons moved forward on the 29th September, and relieved the 1st North Staffords (17th Brigade) in the area of the Black Line north of the Lens-Béthune road, companies being disposed as follows:

The 2nd London Regiment in the Great War

FRONT LINE: 'A' and 'D' Companies.
SUPPORT LINE: 'B' and 'C' Companies.

During the operations that have been described in the foregoing chapters, the enemy's position in the Lys salient had not been attacked by the British. It was obvious that any considerable success further south would render this advanced position quite untenable by the Germans, and G.H.Q. was therefore content to await the natural development of the situation in this area. The immediate effect of the successful battle on the Cambrai-St. Quentin front had been as anticipated, and in the north the enemy fell back to a line between Armentières and Lens.

The situation underwent a further important change on the 28th September, when the Allies' Northern Army Group, under the King of the Belgians, opened its offensive in the neighbourhood of Ypres. The immediate success of this offensive, taken in conjunction with the continued advance of the British in the south, made the enemy's position in the Lys salient one of extreme peril, and, if his troops were not to be caught between the converging forces of the Allies, a speedy withdrawal was essential.

This withdrawal the enemy duly began on the 2nd October. The first intimation of the movement to reach the 58th Division came from its neighbour on the left, the 15th Division, which reported that the enemy on its front had retired east of the Haute Deule Canal. Each brigade of the 58th Division was ordered to exploit the situation without delay by pushing forward the units holding the line. On the front of the 173rd Brigade, the advance began at about 10 a.m.; and 'A' and 'D' Companies of the 2/2nd Londons pushed forward without encountering any opposition. When they were east of Cité St. Laurent, a suburb of Lens, a German officer of the 29th I.R. (16th Division) surrendered to them. His reasons for his surrender were war-weariness and a belief that Germany was beaten, and they are interesting as illustrative of the feelings that now permeated the whole German Army.

By 4 p.m. the 173rd Brigade had occupied Cité St. Auguste, a mining village north of Lens, and had cleared the road running thence to Lens. The line of the Lens-Pont à Vendin railway, which lay a short distance east of this road, was next made good; and patrols were pushed forward towards the Blue Line (the Oppy-Méricourt-Vendin Line). The enemy's opposition was practically negligible; and 2 officers and 33 other ranks were captured. Equally satisfactory progress was made by the 15th Division on the left, but not by the 20th Division on the right, which still found the enemy in considerable strength on its front.

410

The advance was continued at dawn on the 3rd; and by noon the 173rd and 174th Brigades were on the line of the Annay-Loison railway, just east of the Blue Line. 'A' and 'D' Companies of the 2/2nd Londons were established in Nymph and Lottie Trenches (the front trenches of the Oppy-Vendin Line, mentioned above), and had outposts on the railway, while 'B' and 'C' Companies remained in support. By 6 p.m. the leading troops of the 173rd Brigade had firmly established themselves on the line of the railway. During the day the 175th Brigade reported Lens to be clear of the enemy, and the 15th Division that the line of the Vendin-La Bassée railway was in our hands.

The evening was marked by heavy gas-shelling on the part of the enemy; yet his resistance was still weak along the whole front of the 58th Division. By 10 p.m. the 174th Brigade had occupied Annay, and the 173rd had patrols on a line south of that village down to the north bank of the Souchez Canal. During the night the 175th Brigade was pinched out, and withdrawn into divisional reserve. Connexion between the 173rd Brigade and the 20th Division, now the next formation on its right, was made by the 2/2nd Londons along the bank of the Souchez Canal.

A continuance of the advance was ordered for the next day, the objective of the 2/2nd Londons being the western outskirts of Harnes. The advance was timed to begin at 3 a.m., but the enemy's resistance had now stiffened so considerably that no progress was made, and the Division remained in the area of the Blue Line throughout the day. During the night the 3rd Londons relieved both the 2/2nd Londons and the 2/24th Londons in the outpost line of the 173rd Brigade. 'A' and 'D' Companies of the 2/2nd Londons were withdrawn to the line held by the Battalion before the advance of the 2nd October, and 'B' and 'C' to the Lens-Pont à Vendin railway.

No substantial progress was made during the next five days, although on the evening of the 9th the 3rd Londons pushed patrols into Loison, and succeeded in establishing a line of posts east of the village. During the night of the 8th/9th the 175th Brigade had relieved the 174th on the right; and during the night of the 10th/11th the 2/24th Londons took over the 173rd Brigade's outpost line from the 3rd Londons. The 2/2nd Londons, who had been in brigade reserve throughout this period and done nothing, moved up into brigade support, 'A,' 'B,' and 'D' Companies being established in the area of the Blue Line, and 'C' Company (in reserve) in Nudge Trench (a German trench on the Cité St. Auguste-Lens road). During the 10th Noyelles, south of the Souchez Canal, was cleared by troops of the 12th Division, which had relieved the 20th Division.

Early on the 11th October patrols found that the enemy's withdrawal was being continued. By noon the leading battalion of the 173rd Brigade (2/24th Londons) had occupied Harnes Fosse, a mine-shaft west of Harnes, and was pressing the enemy's rear guards back to the Harnes-Montigny Switch. The line of the branch railway from Harnes Fosse to the canal was reached; and patrols were pushed forward to test the strength of the Harnes-Montigny Switch. During this day 'B' Company of the 2/2nd Londons moved into the Canal Maze, a group of trenches on the bank of the Souchez Canal to the south of Harnes Fosse.

At dawn on the 12th October the 2/24th Londons occupied the front line of the Harnes-Montigny Switch, and at 9 a.m. cleared Harnes village. During the day the advance was carried to within 1,000 yards of Courrières, and the 2/2nd Londons moved up to the Harnes-Montigny Switch. The progress of the 58th Division had been very satisfactory, except on the left, where the 175th Brigade had encountered a stubborn resistance about Annay.

As the British line of advance was now in a generally north-westward direction, the 58th Division, to preserve its relative position in the Corps front, 'sideslipped' to the right during the night of the 11th/12th; the 174th Brigade came into the line on the right of the 173rd Brigade, taking over the left sector of the 12th Division; and the 175th Brigade dropped back into divisional reserve. The Souchez Canal formed the boundary between the two leading brigades.

In the evening of the 13th the 2/2nd Londons relieved the 2/24th Londons in the front line about the North Annay road, east of Harnes, and their fighting patrols gained immediate contact with the enemy on the south of the Haute Deule Canal, which joins the Souchez Canal close to the Carvin-Courrières road. The enemy was holding the buildings of a distillery and chemical works on the banks of the canal close to the spot where this road crosses it, with a line of advanced posts in front, and it seemed probable that he would try to make a determined stand on this naturally strong line. For the furtherance of the British plans, however, it was imperative to give his rear guards no opportunity of making such a stand; and the 2/2nd Londons were ordered immediately to make good the line of the canal by means of fighting patrols. The battalion was disposed as follows:

RIGHT : 'B' Company.
CENTRE : 'C' Company.
LEFT : 'D' Company.
SUPPORT : 'A' Company.

The fighting patrols sent out by the leading companies met with varying success. 'D' Company's patrol encountered marked opposition at the outset, and could make little progress towards the canal; 'B' Company's patrol, on the right, came under heavy fire from the distillery and chemical works and from the little hamlet of Vert Gazon, on the north-east outskirts of Courrières, and was forced to withdraw. 'C' Company's patrol alone was successful in reaching the canal bank, but, later, being entirely unsupported, had likewise to withdraw.

At midnight Lieut.-Col. Walsh received orders that the 2/2nd Londons would take part in a general advance by the 58th Division at dawn next day to secure the line of the canal. The task of the 2/2nd Londons was the capture of the distillery and other buildings about the bridge on the Carvin-Courrières road, and the clearance of the wooded country on the south bank of the canal. 'B' Company was detailed for the attack on the distillery, while 'C' and 'D' Companies cleared the south bank of the canal.

The enemy's position having first been subjected to a heavy bombardment, the attack was opened at 5.30 a.m. The troops of the 173rd and 174th Brigades, advancing under a creeping barrage, speedily found that the enemy was prepared to offer a stubborn resistance, and they could not definitely make good the canal line. 'B' Company of the 2/2nd Londons gained part of its objective and captured a number of prisoners, but, after a plucky fight, was later forced to withdraw. 'C' and 'D' Companies made some progress towards the canal, and succeeded in maintaining the line they had reached. The attack then relapsed into a series of patrol encounters, which continued all day. The casualties of the 2/2nd Londons included 2nd Lieut. C. C. Gibbs, who was wounded.

At dawn on the 15th October, patrols reported that the enemy's withdrawal had apparently been resumed. On the front of the 2/2nd Londons a general advance immediately took place; and the buildings on the south bank of the Haute Deule Canal were speedily occupied. As the bridge carrying the Carvin-Courrières road was found to be destroyed, foot-bridges were hastily put together; and 'B,' 'C,' and 'D' Companies, crossing the canal, established themselves on a line in advance of it.

At the conclusion of this move, the 173rd Brigade was withdrawn into divisional reserve; and the 2/2nd Londons moved back to Harnes, where the other units of this Brigade were concentrated. The 58th Division was now transferred from the First to the Fifth Army and joined the I. Corps, its southern boundary becoming the southern boundary of this corps.

The enemy was now rapidly retiring. On the 17th October the 58th Division occupied Oignies, Ostricourt, and Thumeries, on the 18th Bersée, and on the 19th Wattines and Nomain.

In the meanwhile, the 173rd Brigade, still in divisional reserve, had been following the advancing troops. On the 17th the 2/2nd Londons moved to Courrières, and on the 18th reached la Petrie. In the latter village they were received with scenes of wild enthusiasm by the inhabitants, who were now liberated from a captivity that had lasted four years, and Lieut.-Col. Walsh and many of the officers were the recipients of bouquets of flowers. After passing through numerous small hamlets, where the enthusiastic welcome of la Petrie was repeated, the Battalion reached Nomain at 4 p.m. on the 19th. The inhabitants of this place, which had only been evacuated by the enemy at noon, were very cowed, and appeared to expect that the Germans would shortly return. There was, however, no lack of evidence of the reality of the German retirement, houses and stacks of straw being everywhere on fire.

During the night of the 19th October the 173rd Brigade passed through the 174th, and on the morning of the 20th continued the advance in conjunction with the 175th Brigade on the right, the 3rd Londons acting as advanced guard. On this day Lannay and Planard were occupied. On the 21st the 2/24th Londons took over the advanced-guard duties, and, although vigorously opposed, occupied Rongy, Lesdains, and Bleharies, and finally reached the line of the Schelde before nightfall. At 10 a.m. on this day the 2/2nd Londons crossed the frontier, and entered Belgium near Hovardries. After a short rest in the village, the personnel of the Battalion was employed for the rest of the day in repairing the roads that had been mined or damaged by the enemy in their retreat.

The River Schelde is a canalized river about 40 yards wide and 18 feet deep, and presents a formidable obstacle to a force advancing in an easterly direction. The ground on its eastern bank is flat and low, and is intersected by innumerable small dykes. It is usually inundated and marshy, and quite unsuitable as a place of assembly for troops who had effected a successful crossing. The road to the east is carried across this inundated area on a causeway, raised about 12 feet above the level of the surrounding country. The west bank is generally featureless, except for some high ground about Maulde, but Espain and Bleharies, standing more or less intact, afforded plenty of cover to advancing troops from view and small-arms fire.

The enemy was holding the line of the river in considerable strength. He had an advanced bridge-head on the west bank in an old fort on the high ground near Maulde, and on the east bank he was occupying in strength the copses and houses of the little village of Cin, which commanded the river line and the whole of the inundated area. He had demolished two culverts in the causeway, above mentioned, thus making the passage of the water-logged ground yet more difficult.

Late on the 21st October orders were received from the I. Corps that the 173rd Brigade was to force the crossing of the river, and to make good the line Flines-Roeux-Sart Colin. In view of the lack of bridges, which precluded the use of a wide front, Br.-General Corkran detailed one battalion, the 2/2nd Londons, for the task. Early on the 22nd the Battalion moved up from Rongy, where it had been billeted, and assembled in Bleharies. The enemy proved to be very alert along the whole front, the slightest movement on the part of the British provoking a heavy fire; nevertheless, the Royal Engineers completed and launched a foot-bridge opposite Espain, and at dawn ' B ' and ' D ' Companies made a plucky effort to cross the river in the teeth of heavy machine-gun fire. One platoon actually succeeded in gaining a footing on the further bank, but, in so isolated and exposed a position, could not long retain its hold. The Battalion was then ordered to discontinue its attempts, and was withdrawn to Rongy, where it remained during the 23rd.

On the following day it relieved the 2/24th Londons in the outpost line at Bleharies, 2nd Lieut. L. G. West being killed during the relief. The next two days passed without incident; but on the 26th another attempt was made to force the crossing. Unfortunately the German bridge-head in Maulde, unsuccessfully attacked by the 175th Brigade on the 22nd, still held out, and from it enfilade fire was brought to bear on the river line to the north. For this reason the 2/2nd Londons' effort on the 26th proved no more successful than its predecessor, although once again the crossing of the river was effected by a small party. The enemy's machine guns and trench mortars were capably handled by the personnel of his rear guards, and their fire was very accurate and heavy. Later in the day the enemy, having first blown up the church and many of the houses in the main street, evacuated Maulde, which was immediately occupied by patrols of the 175th Brigade. The 2/2nd Londons, whose casualties in this action included 2nd Lieut. V. A. Vasey, wounded, were relieved on the 28th by the 3rd Londons, and moved into billets in Lesdains.

To enable as many troops as possible to be withdrawn for training, the G.O.C. decided that the outpost line of the 58th Division should be held by four battalions. Accordingly on the night of the 27th/28th October the

174th Brigade relieved the 175th, and on the night of the 30th/31st relieved the 173rd, less the 2/24th Londons, who remained in the line under the orders of the B.G.C., 174th Brigade. The remaining units of the 173rd Brigade were withdrawn into divisional reserve; and the 2/2nd Londons moved back to Nomain, where four days were spent in rest and training.

On the 5th November the Battalion again moved forward to Rongy, and on the next day took over the left sector of the outpost line in and about Espain, coming under the orders of B.G.C., 174th Brigade, who was still in command of the outpost line of the whole Division. The Battalion was disposed as follows:

RIGHT: 'A' Company.
LEFT: 'C' Company.
RIGHT SUPPORT: 'B' Company.
LEFT SUPPORT: 'D' Company.

Battalion Headquarters were established in a brewery in the outskirts of Bleharies on the Espain road.

In the early hours of the 7th October the enemy concentrated a heavy bombardment of gas shells on Bleharies. 'B' and 'D' Companies, whose positions were on the eastern edge of the village, suffered many casualties, and the area occupied by the latter company had to be temporarily evacuated, the company being ordered to withdraw to Rongy.

There were now definite indications that the enemy, as the result of the Battle of Mauberge, was about to resume his retirement; and orders for the pursuit were issued. At 9.30 a.m. on the 8th November information was received from the Mayor of la Plaigne, a little village on the eastern bank of the river, that the enemy was retiring, and that la Plaigne and Cin had been evacuated by him. The outpost troops were ordered to cross the river and make good the line Flines-Roeux-Sart Colin, the objective of the operations of some days earlier. The crossing of the river was to be effected with the aid of rafts and assault bridges opposite Espain on the front of the 2/2nd Londons and opposite Montagne du Nord on the front of the 174th Brigade. 'B' Company of the 2/2nd Londons was detailed to assist the Royal Engineers in bringing up materials for the rafts and bridges.

By 11.30 the leading companies of the 2/2nd Londons had crossed the river; 'A' Company on the right had established a bridge-head at Cin, and had occupied la Plaigne; and 'C' Company on the left was advancing towards Belloy and l'Homois. On the Battalion's left flank the 44th Brigade (15th Division) had pushed patrols over the river in the neighbourhood of Hollain; and on the right the 174th Brigade had reached the outskirts of

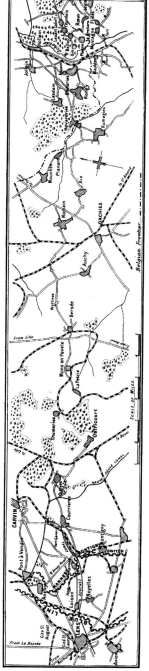

THE FINAL ADVANCE—THE PURSUIT TO THE SCHELDE.

Montagne, where it was held up. 'A' Company, having sent out a patrol to clear up the situation on that flank, eventually gained touch with the 174th Brigade at la Brelière. By 3 o'clock in the afternoon, the 2/2nd Londons had reached their objective, and were occupying the line Roeux-Sart Colin, Battalion Headquarters being established in Cin.

At 10 o'clock next morning the 2/2nd Londons were relieved by the 6th Londons of the 174th Brigade, and concentrated in Sart Colin, where they were rejoined by 'D' Company from Rongy. The advance was continued on this day by the 174th and 175th Brigades, the line Rivage-Wiers-Calenelle being reached, and on the 10th the line Neufmaison-Belœil. On the 11th November the Armistice was signed, and hostilities came to an end.

The casualties of the 2/2nd Londons during the operations of October and November were as follows:[1]

> KILLED: 1 officer (2nd Lieut. L. G. West) and 14 other ranks.
> WOUNDED: 4 officers (Capt. W. Urquart, M.C., Lieut. A. B. Carpenter, 2nd Lieuts. C. C. Gibbs and V. A. Vasey) and 62 other ranks.
> MISSING: 3 other ranks.

The 2/2nd Londons remained at Sart Colin on the 10th, and on the 11th marched forward to Basecles, where they were destined to spend the next four months. During the march, the Battalion passed through the villages of Roeux, Legis, Rouillon, Wiers, and Peruwelz, and in each village the scenes of enthusiasm surpassed description. The population was overjoyed at the arrival of the British troops; and the 2/2nd Londoners were hailed as liberators, and welcomed with emotion and gratitude.

At the conclusion of hostilities, the G.O.C., 58th Division, Major-General Ramsay, issued to all units of the Division a congratulatory message, of which the following is an extract:

> From the 8th August to 29th September, the Division delivered twenty-two attacks, each carried out with the greatest gallantry and success. From the commencement of the enemy's withdrawal in October, the Division continued to press back his rear guards with the same spirit and determination as was shown on the battlefield of the Somme.

---

[1] No separate record was kept of casualties during this period, and these figures have been compiled from entries in Battalion Orders, Part II. They must therefore be taken as approximate only.

The existence of the 2/2nd Londons was now nearing its end. The Battalion remained at Basecles until within a fortnight of its final disbandment. The time was spent in training and recreation. At an early date education classes were formed under Lieut. S. H. Stedman, and the men took full advantage of the opportunity of fitting themselves for their return to civilian life.

December was marked by two notable events. On the 2nd, the 58th Division, having been again transferred to the First Army, was reviewed by the Army Commander, General Sir H. S. Horne, who expressed his appreciation to all ranks by a Special Order of the Day; and on the 5th, H.M. The King, accompanied by the Prince of Wales and Prince Albert, during a tour of this area, visited Basecles. On this occasion there was no formal inspection; the troops collected at the cross-roads and other points of vantage; and the Royal Party passed through the crowd amid scenes of great enthusiasm.

Christmas Day came, and was celebrated with special enthusiasm.

Among the New Year's Honours were the following awards:

Promotion to Brevet-Major : A/Lieut.-Col. J. Walsh, D.S.O.
D.C.M. : Sergt. W. Beavington.
Bar to M.M. : Pte. D. Dorrington.

The award of the following foreign decorations was also notified:

Croix de Guerre : Capt. V. D. Corbett, M.C., C.S.M. J. Burroughs, D.C.M.

January and the first days of February passed without incident of note. On the 11th February a ceremonial parade of the 58th Division took place at Peruwelz, at which the Corps Commander presented King's Colours to each of the battalions in the Division.[1]

On the following day the Battalion moved to Stambruges, and in this village on the 26th February it was disbanded.

[1] In the case of the 2/2nd Londons this Colour now hangs in the Guildhall of the City of London.

EPILOGUE

THE story told in the foregoing pages differs but little from the story of many another British regiment in the Great War. Although nothing particularly sensational marks—or, for that matter, mars—its service, the 2nd London Regiment did its job in the war, generally speaking, with efficiency and a commendable absence of self-advertisement. In this regimental record no attempt has been made to gloss over the Regiment's failures, which have been recounted as faithfully as its successes; its several battalions had many difficult, and, not infrequently, impossible, tasks set them to perform, and that they sometimes failed is not very remarkable; what is perhaps remarkable, in the light of subsequent knowledge, is that they often succeeded so well. Suffice it to say that its battalions, composed largely of typical Londoners, with the cheerfulness, good humour, and adaptability, of their kind, gained universal approbation and popularity wherever they went, as is proved by the pleasure with which every higher commander found them under his command, and the unfeigned regret with which every formation wherein one or other of them served saw them depart. On the march, in camp or billets, in the arduous labours of trench-digging, in attack or defence, they could always be relied upon to do their best; and from their efforts the Regiment can justly lay claim to an honoured place among the units of the British Army.

As has been herein recorded, the Regiment was present with one or more battalions at the campaigns of Gallipoli and Egypt, and at no less than eleven of the major operations on the Western Front; and the writer feels that there can be no better epitome of its war effort than the Battle Honours that it has been awarded:

SOMME, 1916-18.
ALBERT, 1916-18.
Guillemont.
Ginchy.
Flers-Courcelette.
Morval.
Le Transloy.
ARRAS, 1917-18.
Scarpe, 1917-18.
BULLECOURT.

419

YPRES, 1917.
Langemarck, 1917.
Menin Road.
Polygon Wood.
Passchendaele.
CAMBRAI, 1917.
St. Quentin.
Villers Bretonneux.
AMIENS.
Bapaume, 1918.
HINDENBURG LINE.
Epéhy.
Canal du Nord.
Valenciennes.
Sambre.
FRANCE AND FLANDERS, 1915-18.
GALLIPOLI, 1915-16.
Egypt, 1915-16.

The ten battle honours printed in capitals are emblazoned on the King's Colour of the Regiment.

Here, then, we take leave of the 2nd Londons; but before we do so, it will be fitting to add, by way of conclusion, a few words concerning the Regiment's fortunes after the war.

So far as the Territorial Force was concerned the year 1919 was one of uncertainty. No immediate decision was taken as to the Territorial Force's place in the British post-war army, and its units remained throughout the year in a state of suspended animation. From the final disembodiment of its first-line battalion in May 1919 until the middle of the following year the 2nd Londons, with the exception of a small staff at Headquarters, which had the duty of settling the many matters of administration inevitably arising at the end of so extensive a campaign, existed only in name.

During this period, the Regiment shared in the various Peace Celebrations with which the year 1919 was associated. Its Colours were present at the parades held in London and Paris; and a large contingent, representative of all its battalions, took part in the march of the London Troops through London on the 5th July 1919. This year was also notable for the formation of an association of Old Comrades, of which Colonel J. Attenborough, C.M.G., T.D., was appointed first President. This association, under the guidance of its president and of two successive, and enthusiastic, honorary secretaries in the persons of Lieut. G. G. Shadbolt and Lieut. W. A. Francis, M.C., has done excellent work in keeping past members of the Regiment together and in administering the Regimental Benevolent Fund, the genesis of which has been referred to in an earlier chapter.[1] At a later date the Old Comrades' Association was merged into a Regimental Association, membership of which is open not only to past but also to serving members of the Regiment.

The auxiliary military forces of the Crown were reconstituted in 1920 under the title of the Territorial Army; and in the summer of that year the 2nd Londons were reformed under the command of Lieut.-Colonel M. F. Scott, T.D. Major J. Walsh, D.S.O., Northumberland Fusiliers, who had commanded the 2/2nd Londons from August 1918 to February 1919, was appointed the first adjutant of the reconstituted battalion. In August the battalion went into camp at Shoreham by Sea to undergo its annual training, but apart from this training wherein the soldiering was of a not very serious character, it passed the year inevitably in an attempt to lay afresh those foundations on which an efficient Territorial unit is built up.

The first ceremonial parade the reconstituted battalion was called upon to attend took place at the Horseguards on the 26th February 1921, when H.R.H. Princess Mary presented King's Colours to all second-line and third-line[2] battalions of the London Regiment. The new colours were trooped with due ceremony, and those of the 2/2nd and 3/2nd Londons were then deposited in the Guildhall of the City of London, where they hang at the present day.

In the same year Colonel Sir Charles Wakefield, Bart., C.B.E., who had been Lord Mayor of London in the dark days of 1915 and 1916, accepted the Honorary Colonelcy of the Regiment, left vacant by the retirement of Colonel P. Carlebach, C.M.G., T.D., and immediately signalized his appointment by saving the Regiment from extinction, or, at best, amalgamation— a fate that threatened to overtake it in common with many distinguished units of the British Army, then undergoing reduction for reasons of economy.

The next year, 1922, was marked by several events of interest. On the 24th June the Regiment's War Memorial was unveiled in the Drill Hall at Headquarters by Lieut.-General Sir G. Montague Harper, K.C.B., D.S.O., and was dedicated by the Chaplain-General of the Forces (Bishop J. Taylor Smith, C.V.O., D.D.) in the presence of a large and distinguished company.

---

[1] *Vide*, p. 340.
[2] The King's Colour of the third-line battalion of the 2nd Londons had been handed over to it in France by Major-General F. W. Ramsey, commanding the 58th Division—*vide*, p. 418. It was now formally presented to the Regiment.

The memorial, which was erected by subscriptions from members of the Regiment and from the relations and friends of its dead, took the form of a brass tablet and a Roll of Honour. The brass tablet is of similar design to the South African War Memorial, beneath which it has been placed, the two being enclosed in an ebony panel. The Roll of Honour, written on parchment by Mr. M. C. Oliver and suitably bound, is kept in the Officers' Mess. The other events of the year were a Review of the 56th and 47th (London) Divisions by H.M. The King in Hyde Park on the 22nd July and the unveiling of the Royal Fusiliers' War Memorial at Holborn Bars on the 4th November. For this ceremony, in the absence of both Regular battalions of the Royal Fusiliers abroad, the four Territorial battalions supplied a composite Guard of Honour, the Regimental Colour being found by the 2nd Londons.

In 1923 the unit was raised to the status of a Regiment, with a peace establishment of one battalion, and its sonorous, but somewhat cumbersome, title, which had been ruthlessly, and inevitably, abbreviated during the War, gave place to one of a simpler and more concise form : ' The 2nd City of London Regiment (Royal Fusiliers).' This title has continued in use until the present day.

Since the war the usual changes in the active command of the Regiment have taken place : in 1922 Colonel H. M. Pryce-Jones, D.S.O., M.V.O., M.C., succeeded Lieut.-Col. Scott, and in 1926 Lieut.-Col. P. R. Whalley, D.S.O., succeeded Colonel Pryce-Jones.

Throughout these post-war years the Regiment has had somewhat of a chequered career. The war weariness that not unnaturally permeated all classes of the Nation at the conclusion of its exhausting life-and-death struggle, the industrial and economic conditions that then supervened, the inadequacy of the existing Headquarters, and the steadily declining value of its neighbourhood for recruiting purposes, have all contributed in varying degree to the manifold difficulties that have had to be faced in building up a battalion afresh. Nevertheless, under the politic command of successive commanding officers, the Regiment has contrived to weather every storm, and has yet before it a career of usefulness to the Nation, in which, let us hope, it will maintain the honourable name won by it on the battlefields of the Great War.

THE REGIMENT'S WAR MEMORIAL IN THE DRILL HALL,
9, TUFTON STREET, S.W. I.

ROLL OF HONOUR

THE SOUTH AFRICAN WAR, 1899-1902

Adams, W. J.	Private	Marsh C. P.	Private
Dexter, J.	Private	Norris, A. E.	Private
Forſter, T.	Private	Tucker, W.	Private
Freeman, W. E.	Private	Walters, T. E.	Lance Corporal
Lane, A. H.	Corporal		

THE GREAT WAR, 1914-1919

Stacey, G. A., D.S.O.	Major	Gosnell, H. C.	2nd Lieutenant
Falkner, C. B.	Captain	Grainger, S. J.	2nd Lieutenant
Garland, J. R.	Captain	Hammond, F. R. C.	2nd Lieutenant
Gordon, C.	Captain	Heagerty, R. B.	2nd Lieutenant
Gretton, H. E.	Captain	Howard, H. Q.	2nd Lieutenant
Handyside, P. J. A.	Captain	Inwards, H.	2nd Lieutenant
Heumann, R.	Captain	Lockey, E. W.	2nd Lieutenant
Jepson, A. G. L.	Captain	McMurray, S.	2nd Lieutenant
Long, J. W.	Captain	Martin, S., M.M.	2nd Lieutenant
Rawle, W. R.	Captain	Merrikin, G. H.	2nd Lieutenant
Symes, J. B.	Captain	Missen, E. R. C.	2nd Lieutenant
Winterbourne, F. T.	Captain	Murray, C.	2nd Lieutenant
Bennett, H. P.	Lieutenant	Noel, A.	2nd Lieutenant
Child, D. L.	Lieutenant	Perris, N. F.	2nd Lieutenant
Coppen, W. J.	Lieutenant	Prince, F. G.	2nd Lieutenant
Henderson, G. V. H.	Lieutenant	Rolleston, F. L.	2nd Lieutenant
Keen, S. W., M.C.	Lieutenant	Royce, P. F.	2nd Lieutenant
Preedy, J. B. K.	Lieutenant	St. Leger, St. J. R.	2nd Lieutenant
Richardson, J. E.	Lieutenant	Smoothy, A. V.	2nd Lieutenant
Skeet, J. R.	Lieutenant	Solley, B. J.	2nd Lieutenant
Taylor, P. C.	Lieutenant	Spong, F. W. E.	2nd Lieutenant
Williams, H. E. V.	Lieutenant	Starling, B. A.	2nd Lieutenant
Buxton, B. R.	2nd Lieutenant	Strange, W. F.	2nd Lieutenant
Clayton, A. J., M.C.	2nd Lieutenant	Stubbs, C. A.	2nd Lieutenant
Cooke, G. J.	2nd Lieutenant	Sullivan, A. J.	2nd Lieutenant
Farley, F. A.	2nd Lieutenant	Thorman, A. M.	2nd Lieutenant
Fradd, K. M. C.	2nd Lieutenant	Walton, F. A.	2nd Lieutenant
Gant, H. H.	2nd Lieutenant	Wright, J. G. W.	2nd Lieutenant

Aarons, J.	Private		Baker, W. C. L.	Private
Abel, J.	Private		Baldock, R. H.	Private
Ablewhite, S.	Sergeant		Baldwin, J. H.	Private
Abrey, J. W.	Private		Balfour, W.	Private
Adams, A.	Private		Ball, A.	Private
Adams, A.	Private		Ball, A. E.	Private
Adams, D.	Lance Corporal		Ballantine, C. H. W.	Private
Ainger, W.	Sergeant		Balls, W. H.	Private
Aldersley, A. E.	Private		Bareham, W.	Private
Alford, J. C.	Acting Sergeant		Barnes, A. H.	Private
Allen, J. C.	Private		Barnes, C.	Corporal
Allen, A. G.	Private		Barnes, L.	Private
Allen, H.	Lance Corporal		Barnes, S. C.	Private
Allen, T.	Sergeant		Barnett, H. W. N.	Private
Allport, W.	Private		Barr, J. W.	Private
Alway, S. J. C.	Private		Barrett, C.	Private
Ambrose, J.	Private		Barrett, E.	Private
Anderson, C.	Private		Barry, S. E.	Private
Annall, J. H. C.	Private		Bartlett, F. B.	Private
Anthony, J. J.	Lance Sergeant		Bartlett, J.	Private
Appleby, J. E.	Private		Bartlett, W. R.	Private
Appleyard, L. F.	Private		Barton, C. J.	Private
Archer, E. C.	Private		Barwick, J.	Private
Archer, J.	Private		Baskett, G. O.	Private
Archibald, J.	Private		Bates, F. E.	Private
Arding, P. J.	Sergeant		Bates, J.	Private
Arnall, C.	Private		Bavington, J. G.	Private
Arnold, J. W.	Private		Baxter, P.	Private
Ashley, S. J.	Private		Bayliss, H. E.	Private
Aspinall, H., M.M. and Bar	Sergeant		Bayly, H. H.	Private
Atkins, A. J.	Acting Corporal		Bayman, S. J.	Private
Atkins, H. L.	Corporal		Bayston, J. W.	Private
Atlee, F. A.	Private		Bazely, J. A.	Private
Attikin, S. J., M.M.	Corporal		Beadle, L.	Private
Austin, R.	Private		Beakhouse, H.	
Austin, W. A.	Private			Company Sergeant-Major
Avery, J.	Private		Beale, H. G.	Lance Corporal
Avis, W. A.	Private		Beale, T.	Private
Axford, R. H. B.	Private		Beams, A. H.	Lance Corporal
Ayton, V. J.	Lance Sergeant		Bean, W. J.	Private
Bacon, J. H.	Private		Beanland, H.	Corporal
Bagnell, A.	Private		Beard, A. E.	Private
Bagwell, P. W.	Lance Corporal		Beavan, C. T.	Private
Bailey, H. M.	Private		Beckett, C. F.	Private
Bainbridge, W.	Private		Beckett, S. W.	Private
Baker, E. J.	Private		Bedwell, W.	Private
Baker, J. H.	Private		Beeching, W.	Sergeant
Baker, J. J.	Private		Beer, H. J.	Corporal
Baker, W. J.	Private		Benjamin, J.	Private

Bennett, C. W.	Private		Brown, A. W.	Private
Bennett, W. A. C.	Private		Brown, A. G.	Private
Bentall, A. E.	Private		Brown, A. F.	Private
Benzing, A. C.	Corporal		Brown, H.	Private
Bernstein, B.	Private		Brown, J.	Private
Berry, H. A., M.M.	Sergeant		Brown, J.	Private
Bevan, J. A. G.	Private		Brown, W., M.M.	Sergeant
Bew, S. J.	Corporal		Brown, W. C.	Private
Biddle, J.	Private		Broxholm, A. L.	Private
Bignell, A.	Private		Brumpton, G. A.	Private
Billing, S. M.	Lance Corporal		Brush, A. J.	Lance Corporal
Billington, J. G.	Corporal		Bryant, A. J.	Private
Black, H. S.	Private		Bryant, E.	Private
Blackburn, A.	Private		Bryant, F.	Private
Bobey, S.	Private		Bryant, J.	Private
Boggis, J. J.	Private		Bryant, R., M.M.	Private
Boggis, R. G.	Private		Buckingham, L. C.	Private
Bonnamy, H. C.	Private		Buckley, E.	Private
Bonner, G.	Private		Bucknell, A. E.	Private
Booker, G. J.	Sergeant		Bucknell, E.	Private
Booker, H. C.	Private		Bull, A.	Private
Borrie, A. L.	Private		Bull, W. R.	Private
Bow, P.	Private		Bullock, A. E. A.	Sergeant
Bowditch, C. F.	Private		Bunnett, E.	Corporal
Bower, G. W. A.	Private		Bunting, J.	Private
Bowyer, R.	Private		Burden, E. C.	Lance Corporal
Box, J.	Private		Burfitt, T. H.	Corporal
Boxall, F.	Private		Burgess, J. A.	Private
Boxall, L. C.	Private		Burgess, F. W.	Private
Boyce, H.	Lance Corporal		Burke, E. J.	Private
Boyce, H.	Private		Burnell, S.	Private
Bradbury, C. R.	Private		Burrows, A.	Private
Bradley, G. W.	Private		Burrows, R. W.	Private
Brasier, F. W.	Private		Burton, C. A.	Private
Braybrooke, J.	Private		Burton, F. C., M.M.	Sergeant
Bremer, H. J.	Private		Butler, F. H. W.	Private
Brett, G. H.	Private		Butler, W. J.	Corporal
Brett, J. D.	Private		Bye, W. H.	Private
Brettell, J. T.	Private		Byford, C.	Private
Brewer, A.	Private		Cable, C. H.	Private
Brewer, R. L.	Corporal		Cahill, E. C.	Private
Bridger, E.	Private		Calder, J.	Private
Brier, E. C.	Private		Caley, J. C.	Private
Briggs, H.	Sergeant		Callaby, W. S.	Lance Corporal
Brodie, R. C.	Corporal		Campbell, W. A.	Sergeant
Brooks, A.	Lance Corporal		Campbell, P. W. C.	Private
Brooks, G. W.	Private		Cannon, E. H.	Private
Brown, A.	Lance Corporal		Cannon, H. H.	Private
Brown, A.	Private		Cannon, J. B.	Private

Card, J. W.	Corporal	Cohen, J.	Corporal
Carnell, F. W.	Private	Cohen, L.	Private
Carpenter, E. J.	Private	Cohen, M.	Private
Carson, W. W.	Private	Cohen, S.	Private
Carter, A. G.	Private	Cole, F.	Corporal
Carter, F. F.	Private	Cole, G. W.	Lance Corporal
Carter, H. J.	Private	Cole, W. J.	Private
Carter, S. W.	Lance Corporal	Cole, S. E.	Private
Carter, W.	Private	Cole, W. A.	Lance Corporal
Case, E.	Private	Coleman, H. J.	Private
Case, W.	Private	Colgrove, F. L.	Private
Castle, A. V.	Lance Corporal	Collins, E.	Private
Catling, W. G.	Private	Collins, F.	Private
Champion, A. T.	Private	Collins, G. W.	Lance Corporal
Chapman, A. J.	Private	Collins, J.	Private
Chapman, C.	Private	Collins, T.	Private
Chapman, G.	Private	Colwill, R. R.	Private
Chatterway, R.	Private	Compton, J.	Corporal
Cheeseman, G.	Private	Conn, F.	Sergeant
Chiddy, A.	Private	Connell, J.	Private
Child, J.	Corporal	Constable, H. R.	Private
Ching, W.	Private	Constant, W.	Private
Chinnery, A. J.	Private	Conway, G. A.	Private
Christie, T.	Private	Conway, A. C.	Private
Church, A.	Private	Cook, F. P.	Private
Churchward, B. F.	Private	Cook, W. E.	Private
Clark, A. S.	Private	Coomber, W. P.	Private
Clark, C. C. G.		Coombs, E. R.	Private
	Company Sergeant-Major	Cooper, A.	Private
Clark, E. J.	Private	Cooper, B. C.	Private
Clark, E.	Private	Cooper, J.	Private
Clark, F.	Private	Cooper, R. J.	Private
Clark, G.	Private	Coote, C.	Private
Clark, H. A.	Private	Coote, S. C.	Lance Corporal
Clark, J. V.	Private	Cope, R. F.	Corporal
Clark, J.	Private	Copeland, J.	Private
Clark, L. D.	Private	Coppin, G. F.	Private
Clark, R. S.	Private	Copsey, A. C.	Private
Clark, V.	Private	Corker, J. A. F.	Lance Corporal
Clark, W.	Private	Cormack, H.	Private
Clark, W. H.	Private	Corrall, G.	Lance Corporal
Cleaver, E.	Private	Cosgrove, L. P.	Corporal
Clifford, E. R.	Private	Cotton, W. G.	Private
Coakley, J.	Private	Coult, F. W.	Private
Cobbold, G. C.	Private	Coutts, R. E.	Private
Cockram, F. W.	Private	Cox, T.	Private
Cocks, E. A.	Private	Cracknell, H. T.	Private
Coffey, W. M.	Private	Craft, J. J.	Private
Cohen, H.	Private	Craft, H .A.	Lance Corporal

426

Cranstone, J. J.	Private	Doel, G.	Private
Creasy, H. B.	Private	Doel, J.	Sergeant
Creed, E. J.	Private	Donhue, J. K.	Private
Cridland, G.	Private	Dopson, F. E.	Private
Crocker, H. H.	Private	Dormer, E. C.	Private
Croker, W. C.	Private	Dowden, C.	Private
Crook, A. H.	Private	Downing, T. J.	Lance Corporal
Crook, H. W.	Private	Drake, F.	Private
Crowhurst, J.	Private	Drennan, A. E.	Private
Culf, B.	Private	Drew, F. L.	Corporal
Culling, T.	Private	Driscoll, D.	Private
Culpitt, J.	Private	Duck, A. J.	Private
Culver, C. F.	Private	Duggan, W.	Private
Curran, T.	Private	Dunford, C.	Private
Curtis, S. W.	Private	Dunkley, J.	Private
Cutbush, F.	Private	Durden, L. S.	Private
Cutler, F.	Private	Durrant, P. C.	Private
Dack, H.	Private	Eady, A.	Private
Dainty, E. J. P.		Eastwell, J. M.	Private
	Company Sergeant-Major	Eastland, W. J.	Lance Corporal
Daley, C.	Private	Eaton, W.	Private
Daniels, H. E.	Private	Eddy, P.	Drummer
Dare, C. W.	Private	Edmonds, J.	Private
Davenport, F. J.	Private	Edmunds, A. J.	Private
Davey, R. J.	Private	Edser, E. G.	Private
Davies, C. C.	Private	Edwards, A. F.	Sergeant
Davis, C. H.	Private	Edwards, R. T.	Private
Davis, E. J.	Private	Egan, P. E.	Private
Davis, P. J.	Private	Elderton, C.	Sergeant
Dawe, W. C.	Corporal	Ellington, W.	Private
Dawson, E. J.	Acting Sergeant	Elliott, E. W.	Private
Dawson, F. H.	Sergeant	Elson, A.	Private
Dawson, H. E.	Private	Emerson, A. E.	Sergeant
Dawson, W.	Private	Empson, J. J.	Private
Day, A. J.	Private	English, H. J.	Private
Dean, W. G.	Private	Evans, J. R. H.	Private
Deane, H. R.	Private	Eyres, J.	Private
Debenham, J. B.	Private	Fabes, E. W.	Private
Delaney, W.	Sergeant	Fage, H.	Private
Dennis, R. C.	Private	Faichnie, W.	Private
Devenish, T. W.	Private	Fair, A.	Private
Dewar, F. A.	Private	Fairbank, R. J.	Private
Dewell, R. H.	Private	Fairweather, H. W.	Private
Dexter, A. G.	Lance Corporal	Farmer, H.	Private
Dicker, F. A. G.	Private	Farmer, H. W.	Private
Dine, G. R.	Private	Farmer, W.	Private
Disney, A. B. C.	Lance Corporal	Farrell, T. W.	Private
Dixon, L. F.	Corporal	Faucherre, C. W.	Lance Corporal
Dixon, W. H.	Acting Sergeant	Faulkner, J.	Private

427

Fellerman, C.	Private	Fuller, H.	Private
Fenner, A.	Private	Gale, M.	Private
Ferdinand, W.	Private	Gammons, S.	Private
Ferguson, A. G.	Private	Gannaway, H.	Private
Ferguson, T., M.M.	Private	Gant, H.	Lance Sergeant
Few, A. W.	Lance Corporal	Gardener, G.	Private
Fickling, A. S.	Private	Gardner, J. F.	Lance Corporal
Field, E.	Private	Gardner, P.	Private
Field, J. H.	Corporal	Gardner, W. E.	
Finch, A. V. J.	Private		Company Sergeant-Major
Finch, C. J.	Private	Garwood, W. G.	Private
Finnigan, C.	Private	Gates, E.	Private
Fisher, E. A.	Private	Gavin, J.	Private
Fisher, F.	Private	George, A. H.	Private
Fisher, H.	Private	Gibson, A. B.	Private
Fisher, J.	Private	Gidley, J. G.	Lance Corporal
Fisher, L.	Private	Gifford, E. A.	Private
Fisher, W.	Private	Gilbert, E.	Private
Fisher, W.	Private	Gilbert, S.	Lance Corporal
Fittin, J.	Corporal	Gilley, J. F.	Private
Fitzgerald, G. A.	Sergeant	Gillson, E.	Private
Fitzgerald, W. H. M.	Private	Glennie, W.	Private
Flatt, A. J.	Private	Goddard, R. H. M.	Private
Fletcher, G.	Private	Godwin, A. E.	Private
Flemming, H.	Lance Corporal	Godwin, J.	Private
Flynn, W.	Private	Good, F. T.	Private
Foakes, A. W.	Private	Goodall, S. P.	Private
Fogerty, J. F.	Private	Goodbody, W. P.	Private
Folkard, P. C.	Private	Goodbun, W.	Private
Ford, A. E.	Private	Gooding, A. E.	Private
Ford, A. H.	Private	Goodwin, A. J.	Private
Ford, G.	Private	Goodwin, W. G.	Private
Fordy, F. P.	Private	Goodyear, F.	Private
Forse, A. W.	Private	Gold, F. T.	Private
Fosbrooke, J. L.	Private	Golding, W. S.	Private
Foster, F. C.	Private	Goldstein, A.	Private
Foster, G. J.	Private	Goldston, M.	Private
Foster, H.	Private	Gornall, W.	Private
Foster, W. H.	Private	Gowans, M. H.	Private
Fowler, M. H.	Private	Grace, W. G.	Private
Fowler, G. E.	Private	Grainger, F. W.	Private
Fox, C. A.	Lance Corporal	Granby, F. J.	Private
Fraser, A.	Private	Gransee, E. C.	Private
Fraser, J., D.C.M.	Lance Sergeant	Grant, R. W.	Private
French, W. H., M.M.	Lance Sergeant	Grant, W. R.	Private
Freshwater, R. J.	Private	Graves, A. F.	Private
Fringe, C. J.	Private	Graydon, H. C.	Private
Frogley, R. W.	Private	Green, A. J. M.	Private
Fuller, D. W. J.	Private	Green, C.	Private

Green, H.	Private		Hearne, W. J.	Private
Green, H. W.	Private		Heath, W. G.	Lance Corporal
Greensdale, A. J.	Private		Hedley, C. W.	Private
Gregory, F. C.	Private		Henderson, R. F.	Private
Grierson, G. E.	Private		Hendy, C. J.	Private
Griffin, A.	Private		Hesson, J.	Private
Griffin, G.	Private		Hewitt, H.	Private
Griffiths, E.	Private		Hewlett, H. G.	Private
Grigg, W.	Lance Corporal		Hickman, A. J.	Private
Groom, A. J.	Private		Hickman, J.	Sergeant
Groves, W. E.	Private		Hicks, F. W.	Private
Gudmundson, G. F.	Private		Hidden, F. A.	Lance Sergeant
Gusterson, E. R.	Private		Higgins, E. C.	Private
Hainzinger, A.	Private		High, J.	Private
Haitsch, C.	Sergeant		Hill, C.	Private
Hale, G.	Private		Hill, J. E. W.	Private
Hales, T. W.	Private		Hill, R. S.	Corporal
Hall, A. R.	Private		Hill, R. W.	Private
Hall, B.	Private		Hill, S. C.	Private
Hall, P.	Private		Hill, W. B.	Private
Hall, W.	Private		Hilliker, C.	Private
Hammond, H. H.	Private		Hills, G.	Private
Hancock, J. L.	Sergeant		Hitchcock, G. W.	Private
Handley, A.	Lance Corporal		Hoare, R. A.	Private
Hannell, A.	Private		Hoare, W. S.	Sergeant
Harding, F. H.	Corporal		Hobbs, H.	Corporal
Harding, W. J.	Private		Hobbs, T. W.	Private
Harris, D. B.	Private		Hodgson, L. W.	Private
Harris, G. R.	Private		Hogg, F. R.	Private
Harris, J. G.	Private		Hogwood, P. T. S.	Private
Harris, R. W.	Private		Holden, H.	Private
Harris, R.	Private		Hole, J. L. N.	Lance Corporal
Harris, R. T.	Private		Hollamby, E. H.	Private
Harris, W. S.	Lance Corporal		Holland, J.	Private
Harrison, S. D., M.M.	Private		Holloway, C. V.	Private
Harrold, E. J.	Private		Holman, W. E.	Private
Hart, A. F.	Private		Holmes, G.	Private
Hart, C.	Private		Holt, J. D.	Lance Corporal
Hartless, G.	Private		Honey, G.	Corporal
Harvey, H. S.	Private		Hood, P. L.	Private
Harvey, H. S.	Private		Hooper, J.	Lance Corporal
Haseldine, A.	Private		Horley, A. H. W.	Private
Hastings, A.	Private		Hornsby, J. B.	Lance Corporal
Hatchard, G. W.	Private		Horton, R. A.	Private
Hawkins, H.	Private		Howard, C. J.	Private
Haynes, R. H. G.	Private		Howell, A. J.	Private
Hazell, H. T.	Private		Howell, H. F.	Lance Corporal
Head, A. G.	Private		Hoyle, F. F.	Private
Heard, F. J.	Private		Huckle, S. C.	Private

Hull, H. B.	Acting Corporal	Jones, W. F.	Private
Hull, J.	Lance Corporal	Jones, W. W.	Private
Humphreys, B. W.	Private	Jopling, A. E.	Lance Corporal
Humphries, W.	Private	Juniper, R. H.	Private
Hunt, B. P.	Private	Kay, S.	Private
Hunt, F. W.	Private	Keeble, G.	Private
Hunt, H. E.	Private	Keene, E. V.	Private
Hutchins, P. E.	Private	Keep, J. A.	Private
Hyde, E. H.	Private	Kelley, J. E.	Sergeant
Ibbotson, A. H.	Lance Corporal	Kelly, J. H.	Private
Ilsley, C. V.	Lance Corporal	Kelly, J. R.	Private
Inglefield, F. L.	Private	Kempson, E. R.	Private
Ings, W.	Private	Kenny, A.	Private
Ivers, E.	Private	Kent, C.	Private
Jackson, B.	Private	Kent, J. E.	Private
Jackson, W.	Private	Kerry, C. B.	Private
Jacobs, E.	Lance Corporal	Kerton, B.	Private
Jacobs, J.	Private	Kilby, R.	Private
James, J.	Private	Kilty, H.	Lance Corporal
James, L. J.	Private	Kimpton, C.	Lance Corporal
James, W. G.	Lance Corporal	Kimpton, C. W. H.	Private
Jeffries, F. W.	Private	Kind, W. E.	Lance Corporal
Jenkins, A. H.	Private	King, C. R.	Corporal
Jenkins, A. R.	Private	King, F. T.	Private
Jessop, A.	Private	King, J. F.	Private
Jessop, J.	Private	King, W. T.	Private
Jezzard, B.	Private	Kingsford, W. T.	Private
Johnes, F. J.	Private	Kipps, J. W.	Private
Johns, A. F.	Private	Kirby, J.	Private
Johnson, C. E.	Sergeant	Klimcke, C. T.	Private
Johnson, F.	Lance Corporal	Klyen, E.	Private
Johnson, F.	Private	Knibbs, W.	Private
Johnson, G. B.	Sergeant	Knight, E. C. F.	Private
Johnson, H.	Private	Knight, W. H.	Private
Johnson, J.	Lance Corporal	Kosman, G. E.	Private
Johnson, W. E.	Private	Kyte, F. J.	Private
Jolly, A. A.	Private	Lacey, A. W.	Private
Jolley, G.	Private	Lacey, G. J.	Private
Jones, A. E.	Private	Laker, A.	Private
Jones, A. E.	Private	Lamb, A. A.	Private
Jones, A. L.	Private	Lambert, A.	Private
Jones, A. W.	Lance Corporal	Lambert, L.	Private
Jones, H.	Private	Lambourn, E.	Private
Jones, H. B.	Private	Lambourne, L.	Private
Jones, H. W.	Private	Lancaster, H.	Private
Jones, J.	Private	Lane, A. J. R.	Private
Jones, P. J.	Private	Lane, B.	Sergeant
Jones, R. J.	Private	Lane, C. F.	Private
Jones, S. J.	Corporal	Lane, G. A.	Private

Langan, T. R.	Private	Macdonald, E. F.	Private
Langham, A.	Private	Mack, J.	Private
Lankford, W.	Private	Mackerness, A.	Private
Larue, E.	Private	Macknish, C.	Private
Lattimore, C.	Private	Maddox, A. H.	Private
Lauer, A. C.	Lance Corporal	Magee, T. H.	Private
Laurens, W.	Private	Maginn, H. J.	Private
Lawford, C. J.	Private	Magrath, J.	Private
Lawrence, B.	Private	Maidment, H. G.	Sergeant
Lean, F.	Sergeant	Malinsky, S.	Private
Lear, A.	Private	Manwaring, C. A.	Private
Le Bas, A.	Private	Mann, C.	Private
Leclair, S. A.	Private	Manning, J. D.	Corporal
Lee, H. A.	Lance Corporal	March, H. S.	Private
Lee, J. N.	Private	Marchant, C.	Lance Corporal
Lewis, D. H.	Private	Marjeram, A.	Private
Lipsham, A. F.	Private	Markham, C. T.	Private
Llewellyn, F. W.	Lance Corporal	Markworth, A.	Private
Lloyd, C.	Private	Marney, A.	Private
Loates, J.	Company Sergeant-Major	Marshall, A. E.	Private
Lock, C.	Private	Marshall, A. E.	Private
Lock, W.	Private	Marshall, H. W.	Private
Logan, J.	Private	Marshall, J. C.	Private
Loker, B. H. A.	Corporal	Marshall, W. H.	Private
Lomas, C.	Drummer	Martin, A. E.	Private
Long, H. T.	Private	Martin, E.	Private
Loring, H. T.	Private	Martin, J. J.	Private
Louis, P.	Private	Martin, J.	Private
Love, G. E.	Private	Martin, L. A.	Private
Lovely, J. W.	Lance Corporal	Maskell, G.	Private
Lowe, J. W.	Private	Maslen, W. J.	Private
Lowe, S. S.	Private	Mason, R. S.	Private
Lucas, H. J.	Sergeant	Massey, S. J.	Private
Lucas, R.	Corporal	Mathews, G. W.	Private
Lucking, H. C.	Private	Matthews, W. A.	Private
Lumley, D. C.	Private	Maulkerson, J. T.	Private
Lungley, A. F.	Private	Maxsted, G.	Private
Lunn, F.	Private	May, G.	Private
Lunn, S. J.	Private	May, W.	Private
Lush, A. H.	Private	Meadows, S. C.	Private
Lyddon, G.	Private	Meagan, C.	Private
Lyon, E. F.	Lance Corporal	Meeres, H. W. H.	Lance Corporal
McGowan, R.	Private	Mellish, W.	Private
McInnes, R.	Corporal	Meredith, W. H.	Private
McKay, C.	Private	Merrit, H.	Private
McKenzi, A. V.	Private	Meyer, G. L.	Private
McMillan, F. J.	Private	Middlebrook, J.	Private
Mabey, A.	Private	Millan, C. S.	Private
Mabey, G.	Private	Miller, D.	Corporal

431

Miller, R.	Private		Northfield, R.	Private
Miller, R.	Private		Norton, C. J. T.	Private
Miller, W. H.	Lance Corporal		Norton, W. G.	Private
Mills, A. E.	Private		Nottingham, A.	Lance Corporal
Mills, B.	Company Sergeant-Major		Nutt, R. H.	Private
Mills, H. L.	Private		Ockenden, G. D.	Private
Milsom, T.	Private		Odell, A.	Private
Mobbs, C. A.	Private		O'Neill, J. E.	Private
Mogg, W.	Private		Osborne, W. G.	Private
Money, V. E.	Private		Owen, T.	Private
Monypenny, A.	Private		Paddon, F. O.	Lance Corporal
Moody, W. F.	Private		Padley, R. A.	Private
Mooney, J. E.	Private		Paine, C. D.	Private
Moore, C. J.	Private		Palmer, E.	Corporal
Moore, F. W.	Lance Corporal		Palmer, F.	Drummer
More, W. M.	Private		Palmer, J. J.	Private
Morgan, F. H.	Corporal		Palmer, S. E.	Corporal
Morgan, G. D.	Private		Palmer, W.	Private
Morgan, R. C.	Private		Parker, H. T.	Private
Morris, A. J.	Lance Corporal		Parkes, A. G.	Private
Morton, J. W.	Private		Parry, F.	Private
Mulford, W.	Acting Corporal		Parslow, C. F.	Private
Mullender, H.	Private		Parsons, A. J.	Acting Sergeant
Mundy, R. E.	Private		Parsons, G. C.	Private
Murcutt, E. H.	Private		Pask, H. F.	Private
Murphy, F.	Acting Corporal		Patience, F. W.	Private
Murphy, W. G.	Private		Patrick, A.	Private
Murray, R. L.	Private		Payne, F.	Private
Murray, R. M.	Private		Peacefull, H. J. P.	Private
Musk, J. A. G. S.	Private		Peacock, A. W.	Private
Myers, J. F.	Lance Corporal		Pearman, W. C.	Private
Myers, S.	Private		Peggs, E.	Sergeant
Napp, J.	Private		Peneyead, W.	Private
Narraway, S. C.	Lance Corporal		Penson, R.	Private
Nash, P. H.	Private		Percival, W. J.	Private
Nelson, H. W.	Lance Corporal		Perrin, H.	Private
Nelson, W.	Private		Pestell, S. J.	Private
Newbold, R. H.	Acting Sergeant		Peterken, H.	Private
Newell, R. A.	Private		Phillips, A.	Private
Newlands, T. W.	Corporal		Phillips, V.	Private
Newman, A. G.	Private		Phillips, W. W. J.	Private
Newman, A. J.	Corporal		Philpot, E. T.	Private
Newman, J. C.	Private		Pidgeon, A. A.	Private
Nicholson, A. E.	Private		Pilgrim, G.	Lance Corporal
Noller, C.	Private		Pink, F. H.	Private
Noon, R.	Private		Pinkstone, A.	Private
Norman, A.	Private		Platt, H.	Lance Corporal
Norris, R. F.	Private		Pollock, J. T.	Private
North, J., jun.	Private		Poole, E. J.	Private

Poole, H. H.	Private		Robinson, H.	Acting Lance Sergeant
Portch, T.	Private		Robotham, F.	Corporal
Porter, B.	Private		Robus, F.	Private
Potter, W. G.	Private		Roe, J. W.	Private
Powell, A. R.	Private		Roe, S.	Lance Corporal
Powell, C. E. R.	Private		Roffey, F.	Private
Powell, J.	Company Sergeant-Major		Rogers, A.	Private
Preece, P. G.	Private		Rogers, F.	Private
Price, B.	Private		Rolph, E. J.	Private
Price, C.	Private		Rose, W.	Private
Price, R. J.	Private		Rosenberg, L.	Lance Corporal
Priest, H. F.	Lance Corporal		Ross, J.	Private
Priestley, A. P.	Corporal		Rowan, T.	Private
Proctor, R.	Private		Rowe, A.	Private
Proctor, T. W.	Private		Rowe, L. E.	Corporal
Proctor, W. J.	Private		Rowlatt, W. H.	Private
Pugh, H.	Private		Rudston, E.	Private
Puleston, H.	Private		Rumsby, C.	Private
Quarterman, L.	Private		Rumsey, C. W.	Private
Radford, W. J.	Sergeant		Rumsey, G. R.	Private
Radley, A. G.	Private		Rush, S.	Private
Radley, H.	Private		Russell, E. G.	Private
Randall, S.	Lance Corporal		Ryall, W.	Private
Ratcliffe, G. T.	Sergeant		Ryan, P. J.	Private
Ray, A. E.	Private		Ryder, T. J.	Private
Rayner, G.	Private		Sales, W. R.	Private
Read, A. G.	Lance Corporal		Salisbury, P. H.	Private
Reading, A. V.	Lance Corporal		Salmon, C. J.	Private
Redd, H.	Private		Sampford, F. M.	Lance Corporal
Reddin, W. H.	Corporal		Sanckson, A. H.	Private
Redward, F. J.	Private		Sancto, F. E. W.	Private
Reeves, E. F.	Private		Sanders, G.	Private
Reeves, W.	Acting Lance Sergeant		Sanders, W. A.	Private
Reid, A. M.	Corporal		Sanderson, W.	Private
Reitz, H. J.	Private		Sandford, S.	Private
Remon, W. T.	Private		Sandle, C. W.	Private
Reynolds, J.	Private		Sandwell, W. J.	Private
Rhodes, J. W. J.	Private		Sare, E. J. W.	Private
Richardson, A.	Private		Saunders, H. T.	Private
Ricketts, H.	Private		Saunders, J. J.	Private
Riddle, R. W.	Private		Saunders, R.	Private
Ridley, F. W.	Private		Savill, F. W.	Private
Riley, A. C.	Private		Say, T. C.	Private
Ringrose, W. W.	Private		Scase, W. R.	Sergeant
Riva, N. V.	Private		Schildt, B.	Private
Robbins, W. B.	Private		Schofield, F.	Private
Roberts, A. E.	Private		Schofield, H.	Corporal
Roberts, G. H.	Private		Scholey, C. W.	Private
Roberts, W. C.	Private		Scott, A. W.	Private

Scott, B. J.	Private	Smith, J. E.	Corporal
Scott, E. S.	Sergeant	Smith, L.	Sergeant
Scrivener, B. E.	Private	Smith, M. R.	Private
Seabrook, F. J.	Private	Smith, M. W.	Corporal
Sears, F.	Private	Smith, T. S.	Private
Seth, T.	Private	Smith, W. G. N.	Private
Shaw, A. E.	Lance Corporal	Smith, W.	Private
Shedd, P.	Private	Smith, W.	Private
Shedrick, J.	Private	Smith, W.	Private
Sheehan, R.	Private	Smitheringale, J. H.	Private
Sheehy, J.	Private	Snocken, J. A.	Corporal
Shelley, W. G.	Private	Snoxell, P. E.	Private
Shepherd, F. W.	Private	Soper, C. E.	Lance Corporal
Sheppard, T.	Sergeant	Soundy, A. H.	Sergeant
Sheridan, W.	Private	Sparrow, H.	Corporal
Sherrell, F.	Private	Spearing, H.	Corporal
Shields, A.	Private	Spencley, F.	Private
Shon, R.	Private	Spenn, A. J.	Lance Corporal
Short, W.	Private	Spooner, A. T.	Private
Sibley, G.	Private	Stacey, P. C.	Private
Sidney, W. H.	Private	Stacey, T.	Private
Sim, J.	Private	Stacey, W.	Private
Simmons, W. J.	Private	Stacey, W. T.	Private
Simpson, A. C.	Private	Stagg A. W. R.	Private
Simpson, P.	Private	Stanton, W.	Private
Sinclair, P. C.	Lance Corporal	Stanynaught, V.	Private
Skinner, L. G.	Private	Stapleton, C.	Private
Skinner, T. W.	Private	Starling, G.	Private
Slack, C. K.	Private	Starling, H. F.	Private
Slade, T. H.	Private	Starling, N.	Private
Slater, W. G.	Sergeant	Stenner, R. F.	Private
Small, H. E.	Private	Stephens, J. E.	Private
Small, W. L.	Private	Stephens, R.	Private
Smart, E. F.	Private	Stevens, A.	Corporal
Smith, A. St. C.	Private	Stevens, W. P.	Private
Smith, A. S.	Lance Corporal	Stevenson, P. G.	Private
Smith, C. A.	Private	Stevenson, J.	Private
Smith, C. H.	Lance Corporal	Stewart, C. H.	Private
Smith, E.	Private	Stewart, K. A.	Private
Smith, E.	Private	Stone, A. G.	Private
Smith, F.	Private	Stopford, C. J.	Private
Smith, F.	Private	Storey, A. A.	Private
Smith, F. E.	Private	Storey, T. B.	Lance Corporal
Smith, F. G.	Private	Stratford, F. E.	Private
Smith, G.	Lance Sergeant	Strauss, R. S.	Private
Smith, H.	Lance Corporal	Street, F. J.	Private
Smith, H.	Private	Strickland, A.	Private
Smith, J.	Private	Strike, P. H.	Private
Smith, J. H.	Private	Strivens, L.	Private

Strows, W. H.	Private		Thorp, R. E.	Private
Stuckey, J.	Private		Thraves, A. H.	Private
Sudwell, W. J.	Private		Thurgood, F. G.	Private
Summers, G.	Private		Thurley, G. F.	Private
Summers, T.	Private		Tinsley, J.	Private
Sumner, O.	Sergeant		Tinsley, S.	Lance Corporal
Surridge, F. G.	Private		Tinworth, H.	Private
Swan, E.	Private		Toft, C.	Private
Swiss, P. A.	Private		Tombs, W. J.	Sergeant
Sycamore, F.	Private		Tomes, J. W.	Private
Sykes, R.	Private		Tomkies, G.	Private
Syrett, A. E.	Private		Tomson, W.	Private
Tanner, W. J.	Private		Torrence, A. W.	Sergeant
Tarbox, R.	Private		Townsend, H. H.	Private
Taylor, A.	Private		Townsend, W.	Private
Taylor, A. L.	Private		Trenchard, J.	Private
Taylor, B. A.	Private		Trodd, R. E. G.	Private
Taylor, C. S.	Company Sergeant-Major		Trott, W. A.	Private
Taylor, G. W. H.	Drummer		Trueman, W. A.	Private
Taylor, P. J.	Private		Tucker, P.	Sergeant
Taylor, T. H.	Private		Tull, R. G.	Private
Taylor, W.	Lance Sergeant		Tuney, W.	Private
Taylor, W.	Private		Turner, A.	Private
Teader, E. J.	Private		Turner, C. J.	Lance Corporal
Tedder, T.	Private		Turner, E. V.	Private
Tennenbaum, J.	Private		Turpin, G. H.	Private
Terry, C. A.	Private		Twyford, C.	Private
Tester, A. E.	Private		Twyman, T.	Private
Tester, F. C.	Lance Corporal		Underwood, T.	Private
Thatcher, H. G.	Lance Sergeant		Underwood, T.	Private
Thatcher, W.	Private		Ullinger, J.	Lance Corporal
Thearle, W. N.	Private		Upton, J.	Sergeant
Thirkell, J. C. W.	Private		Urry, L.	Lance Corporal
Thomas, A. G.	Private		Vass, S. O.	Lance Corporal
Thomas, D.	Private		Veal, W. R.	Private
Thomas, E. J. A.	Private		Venables, E.	Corporal
Thomas, F. S.	Private		Vickery, G. W.	Private
Thomas, F. R.	Lance Corporal		Vidler, L.	Private
Thomas, G.	Private		Vincent, F. J.	Private
Thomas, H. J.	Corporal		Vines, E. H.	Private
Thomas, H. R.	Private		Voisey, F.	Private
Thomas, R. F.	Private		Voller, W. H.	
Thomas, W. J.	Private		Regimental Quartermaster-Sergeant	
Thompson, E. C.	Sergeant		Voysey, A. V.	Private
Thompson, E.	Corporal		Wadhams, J.	Private
Thompson, G. F.	Private		Waldock, A.	Private
Thompson, W. L. B.	Acting Sergeant		Wales, W. J. J. D.	Private
Thorn, A.	Private		Walker, A. E.	Private
Thorne, R. W.	Private		Walker, C. A.	Corporal

Walker, E. A.	Private		White, J.	Private
Walkling, H.	Private		White, P. C.	Private
Wall, E. H.	Private		Whitehead, P.	Private
Wallis, J.	Private		Whitehorn, W. J.	Private
Wallis, R. W.	Private		Whittingham, E. A.	Private
Wallis, T.	Private		Wiggins, C.	Private
Walsh, M. J.	Acting Sergeant		Wilden, G. H.	Private
Walter, A. C.	Private		Wilder, G. C.	Private
Walter, W. H.	Sergeant		Wiley, W.	Private
Walton, J.	Corporal		Wilkin, F.	Private
Ward, A.	Corporal		Wilkins, S. F. B.	Private
Ward, A. R.	Private		Wilkinson, J.	Private
Ware, W. G.	Private		Wilkinson, T.	Private
Warner, F.	Private		Wilks, A.	Private
Warner, G. A.	Private		Williams, F.	Private
Warren, A.	Lance Corporal		Williams, F. J.	Private
Warren, A.	Sergeant		Willis, A. C.	Private
Warren, E. C.	Private		Wills, W. G.	Sergeant
Warren, S.	Private		Wilshire, E. C.	Private
Waters, S. E.	Private		Wilson, A. E.	Private
Waters, T.	Lance Corporal		Wilson, F.	Private
Watling, W. J.	Corporal		Wilson, H.	Company Sergeant-Major
Watson, A. G.	Private		Wilson, J.	Private
Watson, C. H.	Private		Wilson, L. E.	Private
Watson, F. E.	Corporal		Wilson, R. C.	Private
Watson, F., M.M.	Private		Wilson, W.	Corporal
Watt, H. C.	Private		Wilton, S.	Private
Watts, E.	Private		Winfield, G.	Private
Watts, S. F.	Private		Winter, C. R.	Private
Weaver, E. J.	Acting Corporal		Wise, A.	Private
Webb, A. E.	Private		Withers, G.	Private
Webber, H.	Lance Corporal		Withey, J.	Private
Webster, V.	Private		Wood, E.	Private
Weeden, W. B.	Private		Wood, E.	Lance Corporal
Wells, S.	Private		Wood, G.	Private
Welsh, J.	Private		Wood, H. R.	Private
Werner, F. S., M.M.	Corporal		Wood, R. A.	Private
West, A.	Private		Wooder, A.	Private
West, C. F.	Private		Woodfield, H.	Lance Corporal
Western, J. T.	Private		Woodham, A. E.	Private
Weston, W. W. E.	Private		Woodnutt, J. W.	Private
Whalley, S. J.	Private		Woodward, H. E.	Corporal
Wharam, R. W.	Sergeant		Woolven, H. E.	Private
Whiskard, G. W.	Private		Wooton, A. B.	Lance Corporal
Whitaker, E. S.	Private		Worley, C.	Private
White, C. W.	Private		Worster, A. A.	Private
White, G. F.	Corporal		Wright, A. G.	Private
White, G. H.	Private		Wright, C.	Private
White, J.	Private		Wright, D.	Private

436

Wright, F. L.	Private	Wyatt, P.	Private
Wright, H. T.	Private	Wynne, T. F.	Private
Wright, R.	Private	Yeo, A. T.	Private
Wright, R. J. D.	Private	Young, A. V.	Private
Wyatt, J.	Private	Young, C.	Private

SUMMARY OF DECORATIONS AWARDED TO OFFICERS

BRITISH

Companion of the Order of St. Michael and St. George ...	2
Companion of the Distinguished Service Order with Bar ...	1
Companion of the Distinguished Service Order	7
Officer of the Order of the British Empire	3
Bar to the Military Cross	6
Military Cross	46
Mentioned in Despatches	42
Mentioned in War Office Communiques	9

FRENCH

Croix de Guerre	1
Croix de Légion d'Honneur	1

PORTUGUESE

Military Order of Avis	1

SUMMARY OF DECORATIONS AWARDED TO WARRANT OFFICERS, NON-COMMISSIONED OFFICERS, AND MEN

BRITISH

Bar to the Distinguished Conduct Medal	1
Distinguished Conduct Medal	36
Bar to the Military Medal	8
Military Medal	162
Meritorious Service Medal	16
Mentioned in Despatches	23

FRENCH

Medaille Militaire	1
Croix de Guerre	4

RUSSIAN

Order of St. George	3

ITALIAN

Medal for Military Valour	1

ROUMANIAN

Medaille Barbatie si Credintia	1

SERBIAN

Serbian Silver Medal	1

INDEX

INDEX OF ARMS, FORMATIONS, UNITS, ETC.

Index of Arms, Formations, Units, Etc.

INFANTRY (*continued*):

Machine-Gun Companies—
169th, 107, 140
173rd, 287

ROYAL ARMY MEDICAL CORPS:

Field Ambulances—
2/1st, 106
2/2nd, 106
2/3rd, 106

Ambulance Workshops—
56th Divl., 106

Sanitary Sections—
1/1st London, 106

ROYAL ARMY SERVICE CORPS:

Divisional Trains—
56th, 106

S. and T. Coys—
509th, 89
510th, 89
511th, 89
512th, 89

ROYAL ARMY VETERINARY CORPS:

Mobile Section—
1/1st London, 106

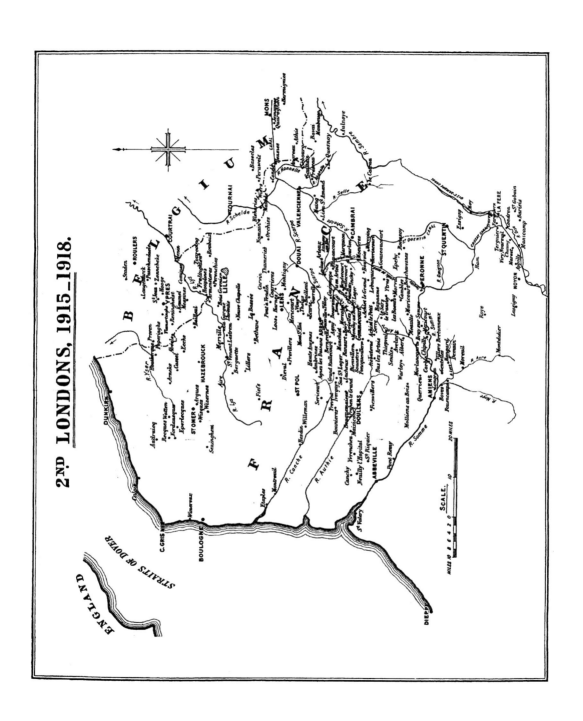

Printed in the United Kingdom
by Lightning Source UK Ltd.
131891UK00001B/70/A

9 781843 423690